Criminal Law

12th EDITION

THOMAS J. GARDNER

Attorney at Law

TERRY M. ANDERSON

Creighton University School of Law

CENGAGE
Learning·

Australia · Brazil · Mexico · Singapore · United Kingdom · United States

Criminal Law, Twelfth Edition
Thomas J. Gardner and Terry M. Anderson

General Manager: Erin Joyner

Senior Product Manager:
Carolyn Henderson Meier

Content Coordinator: Casey Lozier

Product Assistant: Audrey Espey

Media Developer: Ting Jian Yap

Senior Marketing Manager: Kara Kindstrom

Senior Content Project Manager:
Christy A. Frame

Art Director: Brenda Carmichael, PMG

Senior Manufacturing Planner: Judy Inouye

Rights Acquisitions Specialist:
Don Schlotman

Production and Composition:
Lynn Lustberg, MPS

Text and Photo Researchers: PMG

Copy Editor: Laurene Sorensen

Text and Cover Designer:
Brenda Carmichael, PMG

Cover Image: Tim Pannell/Corbis

For product information and technology assistance, contact us at
Cengage Learning Customer & Sales Support, 1-800-354-9706.

For permission to use material from this text or product,
submit all requests online at **www.cengage.com/permissions.**
Further permissions questions can be e-mailed to
permissionrequest@cengage.com.

Library of Congress Control Number: 2013947068

Student Edition:

ISBN-13: 978-1-285-45841-0

ISBN-10: 1-285-45841-9

Cengage Learning
200 First Stamford Place, 4th Floor
Stamford, CT 06902
USA

Cengage Learning is a leading provider of customized learning solutions with office locations around the globe, including Singapore, the United Kingdom, Australia, Mexico, Brazil, and Japan. Locate your local office at **www.cengage.com/global.**

Cengage Learning products are represented in Canada by Nelson Education, Ltd.

To learn more about Cengage Learning Solutions, visit **www.cengage.com.**

Purchase any of our products at your local college store or at our preferred online store **www.cengagebrain.com.**

Printed in the United States of America
2 3 4 5 6 7 17 16 15 14

Dedicated to Eileen Gardner
January 25, 1925–September 26, 2005

THOMAS J. GARDNER, after earning a Bachelor of Science degree in economics, served three years as a naval officer in the South Pacific during and immediately after World War II. He then attended and graduated from Marquette Law School with a Juris Doctor degree in 1949. During the Korean War he worked in procurement for the Air Materiel Command. He also earned a Master of Arts degree in political science. His long association with the criminal justice system began as a criminal defense lawyer. He then worked as a prosecutor, as a police legal adviser, and in police in-service legal training. He was a member and president of a police and fire commission. For 28 years, he taught courses in Criminal Law, Criminal Evidence, and Arrest, Search, and Seizure at the Milwaukee Area Technical College complex of campuses. He lives in Milwaukee, Wisconsin.

TERRY M. ANDERSON is a Professor of Law at Creighton University School of Law in Omaha, Nebraska. He was a Visiting Professor at Denver College of Law for the 2002–2003 academic year, and at the University of New Mexico during the 1980–1981 academic year. He received his Bachelor of Arts degree in 1968 and Juris Doctor degree in 1971 from the University of North Dakota, where he was a member of the Order of the Coif and the Case Editor of the *North Dakota Law Review*. After earning a Master of Laws degree from Harvard Law School in 1972, he joined the Creighton Law School faculty. He teaches Contracts, Criminal Law, Insurance, and Commercial Law. E-mail: tanderson @creighton.edu

Contents in Brief

Contents

CHAPTER 12

Sexual Assault, Rape, Prostitution, and
Related Sex Crimes   322

PART THREE
CRIMES AGAINST PROPERTY

CHAPTER 13

Theft   358

CHAPTER 17

Terrorism   472

CHAPTER 18

Organized Crime and Gangs   494

CHAPTER 19

Immigration Crimes, Contempt, and Other Crimes Against Government   520

Boxed Features

CHAPTER 15

White-Collar Crime, Cybercrime, and Commercial Crime

CHAPTER 16

Drug Abuse and Alcohol-Related Crimes

CHAPTER 17

Terrorism

CHAPTER 18

Organized Crime and Gangs

CHAPTER 19

Immigration Crimes, Contempt, and Other Crimes Against Government

Preface

Goals

The first edition of this text was published more than 30 years ago. Its goal was to introduce law enforcement personnel and others in the criminal justice field to the main principles of American criminal law. In the subsequent editions, including this, the twelfth edition, we have tried to adhere to that goal and at the same time broaden the scope of the text while also keeping it current. As in past editions, we have included recent court opinions and legislative acts that illustrate the current status of those principles of American criminal law. We have also tried to include information we believe to be helpful to the study of criminal law, taken from governmental reports, empirical studies, and news accounts of current criminal cases and developments. We hope these additions and changes in the twelfth edition serve to advance our goal for this text.

We make extensive use of court opinions, especially U.S. Supreme Court opinions, and case citations in the text. We use these opinions and case citations primarily to illustrate how the majority of courts interpreted and applied criminal statutes within their jurisdiction. We also identify and cite decisions on key points of criminal law so that teachers and students will have a sound basis for doing more extensive research into such points. It has always been our plan to create a text that would prove useful as both a classroom learning tool and a reference book for post-classroom use. We are gratified that users of our text have found that it met that plan in previous editions, and we hope they will conclude the same about this edition.

Features

In this edition we continue to use more detailed case excerpts called Case Close-Ups to examine courts' analyses of difficult or emerging criminal law issues, sometimes including our observations about the possible effect of a court's decision on a particular issue. These case excerpts generally include a more detailed factual statement, and a more complete discussion of the court's reasoning, than in the other case excerpts found in the text. Also, in some chapters we examine an important U.S. Supreme Court case or cases, and then discuss lower court cases that apply the rules announced by the Supreme Court. As an example, in Chapter 8 we include an extensive analysis of the two recent U.S. Supreme Court cases involving juvenile life sentences, *Graham v. Florida*, and *Miller v. Alabama*, together with important lower court decisions decided subsequently.

Where possible, we chose U.S. Supreme Court cases for the Case Close-Up features. In subject areas where the Supreme Court does not ordinarily issue opinions, we chose opinions of the federal circuit courts or the highest state courts. Cases were usually selected because their topics were of current interest, but not necessarily because the opinion represented the majority view on the topic. We hope these closer looks at important cases will add substance to our coverage of the issues framed in those cases.

We continue to make references to specific state and federal criminal statutes, as well as illustrations from the Model Penal Code, which we have expanded in this edition. For example, in Chapter 6, we include excerpts from the Florida "Stand Your Ground" statute, which has been a model for similar legislation in twenty-nine other states.

In this edition we have retained the chapter-opening vignettes, with new vignettes for most chapters. We also retained the chapter-ending "Case Analysis and Writing Exercises" feature. Most of the cases highlighted in the exercises are new to this edition, though we did retain a small number from the previous edition. In this edition we also continue to use charts, boxes, and lists as supplements to text and case summaries. We intend the textual materials and case summaries to serve as the main exposition of criminal law principles, with the boxes and other tools helping to illustrate specific applications or examples of those principles.

New to This Edition

In addition to the features just discussed, we have made other changes and additions to this edition. While we have always striven to incorporate new cases and statutes into each new edition, in the twelfth edition we did this on a very broad scale. We not only added many cases decided since the eleventh edition was published; we also replaced a substantial number of older cases that illustrated legal principles with more recent cases that accomplish the same result, but in a more current setting. There are hundreds of cases cited or discussed in our book; in this edition over **250** court decisions will have come from cases decided in the years 2010–2013. With this effort we believe we have made the twelfth edition as up to date and complete as possible, while at the same time maintaining the clarity and ease of understanding that we hope are the hallmarks of our Criminal Law textbook.

Finally, we have added the most recent reports available in the many places in the book where we include statistical information. There is commonly a lag between when statistics are gathered and reports are published, and we tried our best to minimize that lag time.

We have always been appreciative of the efforts of those who review our book before we begin work on a new edition. In this edition, as in the past, we have made it a point to incorporate specific suggestions made by our reviewers and others who have taken the time to communicate with us. We thank them and invite all our readers to share their thoughts on the book with us at Terry Anderson's e-mail address, which is listed in the brief biography that appears in the front pages of this edition.

New Content

In addition to the changes discussed above, in the twelfth edition we have made many substantive additions as well. They include the following:

- **Chapter 1, Criminal Law: Purposes, Scope, and Sources:** We made one organizational change: we moved the box on "omission crimes" to Chapter 3. The box on SORNA cases was updated, since courts continue to struggle with the scope of that legislation and its relation to the Ex Post Facto Clause. In that regard, we included a brief discussion of the 2013 U.S. Supreme Court decision in *Peugh v. United States* on when changes in minimum sentences trigger the Ex Post Facto Clause. In the Case Analysis section we included the California Proposition 8 case, *Hollingsworth v. Perry*. Though not a criminal law case, it does have an interesting discussion of equal protection in the lower court decision, and introduces the concept of standing and how the Supreme Court applies that doctrine.

- **Chapter 2, Jurisdiction:** We updated facts and cases in the various jurisdictions, including jurisdiction of the sea and Indian tribal jurisdiction, focusing on the Tribal Law and Order Act of 2010. We condensed the section on military jurisdiction and martial law.

- **Chapter 3, Essential Elements of a Crime:** We added materials, a new box and new cases, on general intent, specific intent, and scienter as elements of crimes. We also expanded our discussion of the various causation issues that may arise in criminal prosecutions. We added two new boxes on causation: one that distinguishes "but for" from "proximate" cause, and one that looks at multiple causes in homicides. We also added new cases on the effect of a substantial time gap between injury and death in homicide crimes.

- **Chapter 4, Criminal Liability:** We added new cases on solicitation to illustrate both attempts to persuade another to commit a crime, and attempts aimed at victims of crimes. The distinction between "bilateral" and "unilateral" approaches to conspiracy convictions has been expanded and, we hope, clarified. We used current cases to illustrate the difference between those approaches. We added several recent cases, including a U.S. Supreme Court decision, on abandonment of and withdrawal from a conspiracy. The attempt section was rewritten with subheadings to direct attention to the classic elements of crimes, *actus reus* and *mens rea*, as they apply to attempt crimes. We updated the accomplice liability and *Pinkerton* rule sections with new cases, as well as a new box distinguishing accomplice liability from liability under rules like the *Pinkerton* rule.

- **Chapter 5, Criminal Responsibility and the Capacity to Commit a Crime:** In the capacity materials, we expanded the box on juvenile courts to include several recent cases and statutes that highlight changes making transfer from juvenile to adult courts more common. We added a new box on corporate liability for environmental crimes to illustrate both how corporations are treated as criminal defendants and how environmental laws are applied to corporate activities. We updated the diminished capacity, competency, and involuntary medication to restore competency sections with recent cases and statutes.

- **Chapter 6, The Law Governing the Use of Force:** In this chapter we added many new cases, examples, and boxed material to illustrate the use of force in self-defense. This includes updating cases under the "stand your ground" laws, with a new box on the meaning of "unlawful" activity under those laws, as well as a new box tracing the evolution of use-of-force rules. In the use of force by police materials we added a new (and relatively rare) case on the right to resist an unlawful arrest. We also discuss the 2013 U.S. Supreme Court case of *Missouri v. McNeeley*, in which the Court discussed the requirements for police to use force to obtain a blood sample from a DUI suspect.

- **Chapter 7, Other Criminal Defenses:** We added a 2011 case on legislative immunity under the Speech and Debate Clause of the Constitution. We have not previously included a case under this clause. We rewrote the section on the mistake defense, using several recent cases to illustrate when a mistake defense is permitted and when it is not allowed. We also added a 2012 case illustrating the limited rules on when the defense of coercion can be used in murder trials. We added new recent case examples on use of the necessity defense. Finally, we expanded the Double Jeopardy materials, adding a box on the meaning of "acquittal" after the 2013 U.S. Supreme Court's decision in *Michigan v. Evans*. We also discuss the Supreme Court's 2012 decision in *Blueford v. Arkansas* on mistrials and the Double Jeopardy Clause and include a new box that summarizes the various outcomes in a criminal trial and their effect on retrials and the Double Jeopardy Clause. To make room to do all of this we deleted the material on *res judicata* and collateral estoppel that appeared in the eleventh edition.
- **Chapter 8, Criminal Punishment:** We added the 2013 U.S. Supreme Court case of *Alleyne v. United States* on the distinction between elements of an offense and sentencing facts for *Apprendi* purposes, a continuing problem in the courts. We added a box that discusses both of the U.S. Supreme Court's decisions on life sentences for juvenile defendants, *Graham v. Florida* (2010) and *Miller v. Alabama* (2012). We updated prison statistics, and discussed the U.S. Supreme Court's 2012 decision in *Brown v. Plata*, which likely has significant consequences for California prisons in 2013. We also included in a new box the 2012 U.S. Supreme Court case of *Southern Union Co. v. United States* on the constitutionality of fines against corporations for violation of environmental criminal laws.
- **Chapter 9, Free Speech, Public Order Crimes, and the Bill of Rights:** The title of this chapter was changed, thanks to a helpful suggestion from a reviewer, to substitute "Public Order" for "Street Crimes." We think the change more accurately expresses the content of the chapter. We highlight the 2012 U.S. Supreme Court "Stolen Valor" case, *United States v. Alvarez*, by using the case both in the chapter-opening vignette and as a Case Close-Up. We made room for this by deleting the campaign finance box, and greatly shortening the box on obeying police orders. We extensively updated with recent cases the sections on abusive language toward police officers and threats using the U.S. mail, telephones, and the Internet. Finally, we deleted the long box on state gun control laws, and substituted a new section, "Regulating Guns After *Heller*," with seven 2011–2013 cases that considered the constitutionality of state gun regulations after the *Heller* decision. The law on gun regulation is evolving.
- **Chapter 10, Homicide:** This chapter has been substantially changed. Many reviewers suggested we give more attention to the corpus delicti requirement, so we expanded our discussion in that section, including adding a 2013 Colorado case that illustrates how a court-created *corpus delicti* rule can also be abrogated by a court. We substituted two 2012 cases on "no body" *corpus delicti* problems for the older case in the eleventh edition, and a 2011 case on proving *corpus delicti* in "no proof of death" cases. We deleted the Case Close-Up of *United States v. Begay*, because in 2011 the Ninth Circuit Court *en banc* reversed the panel decision. We discuss the reasons for that reversal. We rewrote part of the transferred intent section, substituting a 2011 Maryland Supreme Court case

for the older Maryland case used in previous editions. We also added several 2012 state cases illustrating how states that use the "intent-to-do-serious-bodily-harm" and "depraved-heart" forms of murder construe their statutes. We extensively rewrote the felony murder section. We introduce the "continuous transaction" doctrine to illustrate how states using that doctrine apply the felony murder rule to deaths that occur after the felony has been committed, such as during an escape. We also added several recent cases that address the issue of the application of the felony murder rule to the death of a co-felon. We made room for all of this by deleting the felony murder box used in previous editions. Finally, we greatly expanded the imperfect self-defense/manslaughter section by using examples of the defense, and several recent cases applying the defense.

- **Chapter 11, Assault, Battery, and Other Crimes Against the Person:** We clarified the elements under the federal assault statutes by deleting the "simple assault" box (which some thought too complicated) and added three recent cases that do a better job of illustrating assault, both under the federal statutes and the common law. We updated and expanded the discussion of hate crimes with recent cases. The "faith healing" case in Wisconsin went to the Wisconsin Supreme Court in 2013 on the meaning of the "religious healing" exception to child neglect. Other states have similar exceptions, and the decision might have ramifications outside Wisconsin. We updated the kidnapping cases, with emphasis on the "moving" requirement when another felony, like robbery, is being committed. This is an evolving issue, so we also used a case on the moving requirement in the case analysis exercises. We substantially rewrote the domestic violence section, noting the status of the Violence Against Women Act in Congress. We deleted two sections (court order violations and duty to report laws).

- **Chapter 12, Sexual Assault, Rape, Prostitution, and Related Sex Crimes:** We substantially rewrote the forcible rape section, with new titles and subsections. We replaced older cases with new ones. We deleted the lengthy Case Close-Up box on consent, force and resistance, and instead cover this important topic in the text, with new cases. We rewrote and expanded the report of rape section. We added several new cases under various rape shield laws, including a controversial 2012 Michigan Supreme Court decision. We discuss statutes and cases on the mistake of age defense in statutory rape, expanding the discussion of this issue found in Chapter 7. We also add a 2013 case of first impression under the federal sex trafficking statute. We added national statistics and a 2013 report that cast doubt on (1) the need for civil commitment of sexual offenders, and (2) the wisdom of child pornography prosecutions based on Internet use. We deleted the section on sexual harassment, which is mainly civil in nature.

- **Chapter 13, Theft:** We updated cases that illustrate the classic elements of theft, such as property of another, lost property, and abandoned property. We also added new cases on shoplifting to replace older cases. To illustrate the perils of merchants confronting suspected shoplifters, we included a Case Close-Up that involves an action by a supposed shoplifter against the merchant who confronted her.

- **Chapter 14, Robbery, Burglary, and Related Crimes:** The chapter-opening vignette is taken from a 2012 case from New Jersey that in 2013 will be reviewed by the New Jersey Supreme Court. We think it is interesting to see how our readers believe that review will (or should) turn out. In this chapter we substantially deleted older cases (and an older box) on the elements of the crimes covered in this chapter, and added new cases and statutes. Those include bank robbery, carjacking, and extortion. We rewrote the robbery–theft distinction section, adding new cases of what force is required, when force must be used, and the lack of the necessity of a completed robbery. In burglary we added new cases on "dwelling of another" and "intent to commit a crime therein," including a 2012 case that ties in with the Double Jeopardy materials in Chapter 7. Finally, in the Case Analysis exercises we look at two federal cases under the Hobbs Act, where courts found violations under doubtful circumstances. In 2013 the U.S. Supreme Court agreed to review one of these cases, perhaps to consider how federal prosecutors are using the Hobbs Act.

- **Chapter 15, White-Collar Crime, Cybercrime, and Commercial Crime:** In one organizational change, we moved the materials on receiving stolen property and possession of burglary tools to Chapter 14, where they seem to fit better. We did substantial updating in the identity theft section, and the discussion of computer access crimes. This includes a new box on the criminal liability of employees who use employer computers for illegal purposes. We also updated the product tampering section. We added a new box on environmental crimes and corporate responsibility for those crimes, keeping with our goal (based in part on reviewers' requests) for more cases on environmental crimes.

- **Chapter 16, Drug Abuse and Alcohol-Related Crimes:** We continue to update the statistics on the international drug war/gun sales/border problems. We also updated the news on medical marijuana and recreational use of marijuana. We rewrote the drunk driving section, adding recent cases on how courts are handling the issues in such prosecutions, including a Case Close-Up case from Illinois that illustrates how presence of a controlled substance in a driver's system relates to aggravated drunk driving. We include in that Case Close-Up discussion of a 2013 Michigan case that struggles with a similar issue: a driver who has marijuana in his system, but is a registered medical marijuana user.

- **Chapter 17, Terrorism:** Once again, the various tables and boxes with statistical information have been updated. We added a new Case Close-Up on the meaning of "material support of terrorism" under federal law. We believe it is likely the U.S. Supreme Court will grant review in one of these cases very soon to address that issue.

- **Chapter 18, Organized Crime and Gangs:** We substituted newer cases for older cases where we could, including those on money laundering, and Congressional legislation designed to overturn some controversial decisions. We note the passage of the sports betting statute in New Jersey, but include reference to the federal district court decision that recently struck down that statute. We added more material on RICO prosecutions, a subject some of our reviewers asked us to expand.

- **Chapter 19, Immigration Crimes, Contempt, and Other Crimes Against Government:** Immigration cases and statutes are the news in this edition. The U.S. Supreme Court decision in the Arizona immigration statute litigation leads off our discussion of immigration crimes. We also discuss lower court decisions and the impact of the Arizona decision on those decisions. We discuss in detail the "fraudulent marriage" scheme to illegally gain entry to the United States, and in a new box focus on the *mens rea* needed for violation of immigration laws. We list the highlights of proposed Congressional legislation on immigration reform. We include a U.S. Supreme Court case that has important implications in civil contempt cases, where it is now the law that in some circumstances a defendant in a civil contempt hearing must have appointed counsel. Finally, we deleted the environmental crimes section; as reviewers suggested, crimes against the environment are not crimes against government. As we noted earlier, we have tried wherever possible to integrate prosecutions for environmental crimes into other chapters.

Supplements

A number of supplements are provided by Cengage Learning to help instructors use *Criminal Law*, Twelfth Edition, in their courses and to aid students in preparing for exams. Supplements are available to qualified adopters. Please consult your local sales representative for details.

For the Instructor

Instructor's Manual Updated by Valerie Bell of Loras College, the manual includes learning objectives, key terms, a detailed chapter outline correlated to each chapter's PowerPoint slides, a chapter summary, lesson plans, discussion topics, student activities, "What If" scenarios, media tools, a sample syllabus, and an expanded test bank with 30 percent more questions than the prior edition. The learning objectives are correlated with the discussion topics, student activities, and media tools. Each chapter's test bank contains questions in multiple-choice, true false, completion, essay, and new critical thinking formats, with a full answer key. The test bank, revised by Scott Rudeen of Globe University, is correlated to the chapter objectives that appear in the main text as well as to Bloom's taxonomy levels and includes the sections in the main text where the answers can be found. Finally, each question in the test bank has been carefully reviewed by experienced criminal justice instructors for quality, accuracy, and content coverage—so you can be assured that you are working with an assessment resource of the highest caliber.

PowerPoint Slides Helping you make your lectures more engaging while effectively reaching your visually oriented students, these handy Microsoft PowerPoint® slides outline the chapters of the main text in a classroom-ready presentation. The PowerPoint® slides, updated by Lisa Briggs of Western Carolina University, reflect the content and organization of the new edition of the text and feature some additional examples and real-world cases for application and discussion. Available for download on the password-protected instructor book companion website, the presentations can also be obtained by e-mailing your local Cengage Learning representative.

Cengage Learning Testing Powered by Cognero The accompanying assessment tool is a flexible, online system that allows you to

- Import, edit, and manipulate test bank content from the Gardner/Anderson test bank or elsewhere, including your own favorite test questions.

- Create ideal assessments with your choice of fifteen question types (including true/false, multiple choice, opinion scale/likert, and essay).
- Create multiple test versions in an instant using drop-down menus and familiar, intuitive tools that take you through content creation and management with ease.
- Deliver tests from your LMS, your classroom, or wherever you want—plus import and export content from and into other systems as needed.

Cengage Learning Video Program (Courtesy BBC, CNN and more) CNN videos feature short, high-interest clips from current news events as well as historic raw footage going back 30 years. CBS and BBC clips feature footage from nightly news broadcasts and specials to *CBS News Special Reports, CBS Sunday Morning, 60 Minutes*, and more. Taken together, the brief videos offer the perfect discussion-starters for your classes, enriching lectures and providing students with a new lens through which to view the past and present, one that will greatly enhance their knowledge and understanding of significant events and open up to them new dimensions in learning.

For the Student

CourseMate Companion Website Cengage Learning's Criminal Justice CourseMate brings course concepts to life with interactive learning, study, and exam preparation tools that support the printed textbook. CourseMate includes an integrated eBook as well as critical chapter review tools, including pre-tests students can use to quiz themselves in advance of reading the assignment so they are focused on issues that present a particular challenge to them personally. Also included are quizzes mapped to chapter learning objectives, flashcards, and videos, plus EngagementTracker, a first-of-its-kind tool that monitors student engagement in the course. The accompanying instructor website offers access to password-protected resources such as an electronic version of the instructor's manual and PowerPoint® slides. The web quizzes were developed by Cornel Plebani of Husson College.

Careers in Criminal Justice Website This unique website gives students information on a wide variety of career paths, including requirements, salaries, training, contact information for key agencies, and employment outlooks. Several important tools help students investigate the criminal justice career choices that are right for them.

- *Career Profiles:* Video testimonials from a variety of practicing professionals in the field as well as information on many criminal justice careers, including job descriptions, requirements, training, salary and benefits, and the application process.
- *Interest Assessment:* Self-assessment tool to help students decide which careers suit their personalities and interests.
- *Career Planner:* Resume-writing tips and worksheets, interviewing techniques, and successful job search strategies.
- *Links for Reference:* Direct links to federal, state, and local agencies where students can get contact information and learn more about current job opportunities.

Current Perspectives: Readings from InfoTrac College Edition These readers, designed to give students a closer look at special topics in criminal justice, include free access to InfoTrac College Edition. The timely articles are selected by experts in each topic from within InfoTrac College Edition. They are available free when bundled with the text and include the following titles:

- *Cyber Crime*
- *Victimology*
- *Juvenile Justice*
- *Racial Profiling*
- *White-Collar Crime*
- *Terrorism and Homeland Security*
- *Public Policy and Criminal Justice*
- *Technology and Criminal Justice*
- *Ethics in Criminal Justice*
- *Forensics and Criminal Investigation*
- *Corrections*
- *Law and Courts*
- *Policy in Criminal Justice*

Acknowledgments

We would like to thank our reviewers for their helpful comments as we prepared this twelfth edition:

Yury Cheryachukin, California State University, Stanislaus

Megan Cole, Brown College

Howard Jordan, Hostos Community College

Thomas McAninch, Scott Community College

Amy Pinero, Baton Rouge Community College

Robert Simpson, Champlain College

M. Lisa W. Clayton, College of Southern Nevada, Cheyenne Campus

Diane K. Sjuts, Metro Community College

Lisa A. Hoston, Allegany College of Maryland

John C. Kunich, University of North Carolina at Charlotte

Lizbeth P. McManus, Prince George Community College

Peter J. Puleo, William Rainey Harper College

Thomas J. Gardner

Terry M. Anderson

Criminal Law: Purposes, Scope, and Sources

The United States Supreme Court building in Washington, D.C.

OUTLINE

Important Concepts in Criminal Law

Substantive Criminal Law

Criminal Law and Moral Law

Goals and Purposes of Criminal Law

The Permissible Scope of Criminal Laws in the United States

The Use and Limitations of the Police Power to Maintain Public Order

The Principle of "No Punishment Without a Law for It"

Classifications of Crimes

Felony and Misdemeanor

General Constitutional Limitations on Criminal Laws

Ex Post Facto Laws

Bills of Attainder

The Second Amendment and Gun Control

Due Process, "Void for Vagueness," and the "Overbreadth" Doctrine

Status Crimes

Equal Protection of the Laws

Sources of Criminal Law

Common Law Crimes

Statutory and Administrative Crimes

LEARNING OBJECTIVES

In this chapter we introduce criminal law and the role it plays in the American legal system. The learning objectives for this chapter are the following:

- Identify the branches of government, and their relationship to the criminal law.

- Describe the difference between public law and private law, including the difference between criminal law and tort law.

- List the reasons people commit crimes, and why they do not.

- Understand the four generally recognized goals of the criminal justice system.

- Know the meaning of police power.

- Identify the general limitations on the exercise of the police power by government.

- Know the meaning of the phrase *nulla poena sine lege.*

- List and describe five specific constitutional limitations on the power to create a criminal law.

- Define circumstances that would make a criminal law a status crime.

- Trace the origin of the common law to its place in criminal law today.

The city of Chicago passed a municipal ordinance, § 8-4-010 (d), which made it a crime for a person to refuse to disperse after a police officer so ordered, whenever a nearby group was causing "serious inconvenience, annoyance, or alarm." Three men observing a group protesting the war in Iraq were arrested and charged under this ordinance when they refused to disperse after police ordered them to do so. The police had arrested one member of the group of protesters for disorderly conduct, and this was the basis for the police order to the three men to disperse under the ordinance.

3

In a 2012 decision the Seventh Circuit Court of Appeals held the statute unconstitutional under the First and Fourteenth Amendments to the U.S. Constitution.[1] The court stated that the ordinance was "overbroad" because it infringed on the rights of free speech and assembly. It stated the ordinance was unconstitutionally "vague" because it failed adequately to give citizens notice of what kind of conduct was prohibited, and made possible arbitrary and discriminatory enforcement of the ordinance, in violation of the Due Process Clause of the Fourteenth Amendment.

In this chapter we examine the basis for the power of states and the federal government to pass criminal laws, and the constitutional limitations on that power.

Important Concepts in Criminal Law

Crime has been part of the human condition since people began to live in groups. Ancient documents indicate that conduct we now call murder, theft, or robbery was identified as criminal by civilizations that existed thousands of years ago. Criminal laws regulate human conduct and tell people what they cannot do and, in some instances, what they must do under certain circumstances. Though their content may have differed, all societies have had criminal codes regulating conduct.

Democracies have always sought to translate their basic principles and ideals into achievable goals through a system of laws that balance the rights of individuals with the compelling needs of society as a whole. These goals include public order, domestic tranquility, and protection of the basic rights of individuals.

Because governments in democracies are the servants and not the masters of the people, laws are seen as the product of the will of the people. Criminal justice systems in democracies operate most successfully when the majority of the people believe that laws are fair and that the system can operate efficiently and effectively.[2]

The issue of what laws should be enacted often causes intense public debate. Laws are enacted by elected representatives of the people. They are enforced, administered, and interpreted by civil servants and elected officials in other branches of government.

In the United States, those branches are as follows:

1. *The legislative branch:* Laws (including criminal laws) are enacted by the legislative branch. The chief executive officer participates in the legislative process by signing or vetoing proposed laws. State governors and the U.S. president provide leadership on many proposed laws by either supporting or opposing them and by providing information about proposed laws.
2. *The executive branch:* Agencies within the executive branch of government administer and enforce laws. Law enforcement agencies are found within the executive branch of government and are charged with the enforcement of criminal laws, in addition to the performance of other duties.
3. *The judicial branch:* People who are charged with crimes have a right to be tried before a judge or a jury in a court in the judicial branch of government. Fact finders (jury or judge) determine the issues in cases presented to them, including the issue of guilt or innocence. Judges in the United States have the power of judicial review in determining the constitutionality of laws or ordinances.

certiorari A form of review of lower court decisions by the U.S. Supreme Court. Certiorari is discretionary with the Court, and most petitions requesting it are denied. Traditional legal doctrine is that no conclusion can be drawn from a denial of certiorari.

habeas corpus A writ that compels the authority holding a person in confinement to explain the basis for that confinement. Used frequently as a method for state and federal prisoners to attack the constitutionality of their imprisonment. Both the federal government and states have some form of habeas corpus laws, often called post-conviction relief laws.

public law Laws or statutes that apply to all people within a state or nation. Criminal laws in England and the United States are examples of public law.

Tort A noncontractual civil wrong.

In the United States each state and the federal government has its own judicial system. These systems are generally independent of one another. Each state has a tier of trial courts, where jury trials take place. After a defendant has been convicted of a crime, the conviction may be appealed to the state's appellate courts. Many states have a two-tiered appellate court plan: a first tier, generally called the court of appeals, and a top tier, generally called the supreme court. Appeals of convictions for violation of criminal law proceed first in the state's appellate court system.

Once a conviction has been affirmed by the highest state court, it is usually final. However, if the defendant raises an issue about the constitutionality of the conviction, under the U.S. Constitution he or she is entitled to ask the U.S. Supreme Court to review that issue. The defendant would do so by asking the Supreme Court to issue a writ of **certiorari**, a discretionary writ issued by the Court to review the decision of a lower court. Writs of certiorari are infrequently granted. If the writ is denied, the conviction is final. Limited post-conviction review is possible under state post-conviction review laws, and through use of the writ of **habeas corpus**, discussed later in this chapter.

In the federal system, federal district courts serve as trial courts. The United States is divided into eleven judicial circuits, plus the District of Columbia Circuit and the Federal Circuit (which handles special areas such as patent law). The judicial circuits each have a court of appeals, which hears appeals from the federal district courts located in the circuit. Decisions of the circuit courts may be reviewed by the Supreme Court through the certiorari process, though here also such review occurs infrequently.

As discussed more fully later in this chapter, criminal law in the United States traces its beginnings to the criminal law and its development in England. In early England, actions we now define as crimes, such as robbery, murder, or theft, were classified as private matters. As a result, victims were responsible for remedying their own problems. Victims and their families usually responded with violence if they knew or suspected the identity of the offender. They also had the option of bringing the matter before a civil court, but such courts were few and the chances of success minimal. During the reign of Henry II (1154–1189), English law began to recognize that crime was more than a personal affair between the victim and the perpetrator and that punishment should not be left to individuals.

Today, criminal law in England and the United States is part of each nation's **public law**. The criminal law applies to all persons within each country, and it is enforced by public officials rather than by the victims of criminal conduct. Apprehension and prosecution of criminals are public matters. Public law enforcement agencies, public prosecutors, courts, jails, and correctional institutions make up the criminal justice systems in both countries.

Because the same action can be a violation of the criminal law and a civil wrong known as a **tort**, victims of a crime may bring civil actions in civil courts to seek compensation from the offender. The crimes of sexual assault, battery, theft, and criminal libel are examples of actions that may be prosecuted as crimes under public law, and also serve as a basis for a civil action. If the victim obtains a judgment in the civil action, the victim is responsible for collecting that judgment from the offender. The tort laws governing such a civil action are examples of private law. Private law deals with relationships between individuals in matters such as divorce, contractual issues, real estate law, and private inheritance.

Criminal law in the broadest sense refers to the many laws and statutes that define and regulate prohibited, criminal conduct. These laws and statutes are called substantive criminal law. In addition, criminal law in this sense includes many rules and statutes designed to set out and regulate the steps that are followed from the criminal incident through punishment and release of the offender. This part of criminal law is called criminal procedure. Many of the rights guaranteed by the U.S. Constitution in criminal investigations and prosecutions serve as limitations on the process used by the government in those investigations and prosecutions. For example, the well-known *Miranda* rule requiring police to inform a suspect of his rights at the time of arrest stems from the Fifth Amendment. The requirement that police obtain a search warrant based on probable cause is found in the Fourth Amendment; the rights to have the assistance of counsel and confront witnesses against an accused are contained in the Sixth Amendment. There are also many statutory rules in both the federal and state criminal codes regulating the procedures that must be followed in criminal investigations and prosecutions. Because of the immense scope and complexity of criminal procedure rules and principles, it is generally treated as a subject distinct from substantive criminal law. *See* Gardner & Anderson, *Criminal Evidence* (8th edition, Cengage Learning, 2013). Thus, while this chapter discusses many of the constitutional limitations on the power of governments to define and punish conduct, such as the Ex Post Facto Clause and the "overbreadth" doctrine, it should be remembered that a significant part of the constitutional and statutory limitations on the investigation and prosecution of criminal conduct must be learned by studying criminal procedure.

criminology The sociological and psychological study of the causes, development, and control of crime, as well as the conditions under which criminal law developed.

forensic science scientific principles and tests used in courts of law.

Criminology and criminalistics are fields that are separate from but related to substantive criminal law. **Criminology** is the sociological and psychological study of the causes of crime, the control of crime, and the conditions under which criminal law developed. Criminalistics, often called **forensic science**, is the professional and scientific discipline directed to the recognition, identification, individualization, and evaluation of physical evidence by application of the natural sciences. Criminology is a branch of sociology; criminalistics is the application of science to criminal investigation, and encompasses forensic science.

Substantive Criminal Law

Substantive criminal law is an important branch of public law. It defines the standards of conduct that the society and the community require for the protection of the community as a whole. It establishes the standards necessary to preserve public order and to protect property rights. It seeks to protect the right of individual privacy and the right to move about freely without fear of molestation. It does this primarily by defining conduct that is unacceptable and punishable.

In earlier times in our history people "took the law in their own hands" to punish criminals. With the establishment of a system of laws and the growth of public confidence in the ability of the criminal justice system to preserve ordered liberty, people have generally ceased taking the law into their own hands. Public confidence that the government, as an agent of the people, has the ability and the desire to maintain public order is an indispensable ingredient of a successful criminal justice system.[3]

Not all legal wrongs come under substantive criminal law. Some legal wrongs are only civil violations. A *civil wrong* is a private wrong, such as a tort or a contract violation, done to a person or property, and involves only the private individuals affected by the wrong. A *criminal wrong* is one in which the state and the public have declared an interest. Ordinarily, when a private wrong occurs, only the injured party or the party's representative may seek civil redress in a civil court of law. Nearly every large American community has three or four times as many civil courts, which hear civil cases of alleged private wrongs, as criminal courts, which hear criminal cases involving public wrongs. In cases of public wrong, the state may file a criminal action in a criminal court, seek relief for the alleged public wrong in a civil court, or do both concurrently, as is done occasionally in obscenity, antitrust, or consumer fraud cases.

Criminal Law and Moral Law

Criminal laws are strongest when they reflect the moral and ethical beliefs of the society. Murder, for example, is considered morally wrong, and most people would not murder another person even if it were not a crime. Murder is forbidden not only by the criminal law but also by the moral law. This moral or ethical commitment to the law is important because it compels most people to conform to standards necessary for public order regardless of whether a police officer is watching them. Public order is not possible without that commitment,

WHY SOME CONDUCT MAY OR MAY NOT BE DESIGNATED AS CRIMINAL

Reasons a Legislative Body Might Designate Specific Conduct as Criminal

- The conduct may be designated as criminal to protect the public from violent or dangerous conduct.
- The conduct may be designated as criminal to protect public health.
- The conduct may be designated as criminal to maintain public order.
- The conduct may be designated as criminal to protect the right of privacy of individuals.
- The conduct may be designated as criminal to protect public morality.
- No other apparent way to promote a desired public policy is available.

Reasons a Legislative Body Might Not Designate Specific Conduct as Criminal

- The government does not have constitutional power to prohibit such conduct.
- The conduct in question is constitutionally protected.
- No influential public or private groups or individuals have demanded the regulation of such conduct.
- Enforcing a law criminalizing such conduct would not be economically feasible.
- Passing a law criminalizing such conduct would not be politically popular.

RIGHTS OF CRIME VICTIMS

A majority of states have amended their state constitutions to include a guarantee of rights for crime victims. This guarantee, which is often posted on courtroom doors, generally includes provisions such as the following:

- The right to notification of all court proceedings related to the offense
- The right to be reasonably protected from the accused offender
- The right to have input at sentencing, such as by offering a victim impact statement
- The right to information about the conviction, sentencing, imprisonment, and release of the offender
- The right to an order of restitution from the offender
- The right to notice of these rights
- The right to enforce these rights

Source: See FS 00301, United States Office for Victims of Crime, April 2002.

because not enough police officers are available to enforce criminal law without this moral and ethical backing.

The standards set by moral laws are often higher than those set by criminal laws. Moral law attempts to perfect personal character, whereas criminal law, in general, is aimed at misbehavior that falls substantially below the norms of the community. Criminal conduct is ordinarily unjustifiable and inexcusable.

Criminal law alone cannot bring all conduct into conformity with the standards expected by the community. Society uses many sanctions besides criminal law to encourage people to behave properly. Civil law judgments, licensing regulations and revocations, loss of employment, and simple peer pressure are examples of the ways a society can use sanctions other than the criminal law to control offensive conduct.

DISTINGUISHING CRIME, TORT, AND MORAL WRONG

Type of Wrong		Court Determining Wrong
Crime	A public wrong against society	Criminal court
Tort	A private wrong against an individual	Civil court or individuals
Moral wrong	Violation of a moral or religious code	No punishment unless the moral wrong is also a crime or tort

A crime may also be a tort and a moral wrong. For example, murder is a crime, a tort, and also a moral wrong.

FACTORS INFLUENCING WHETHER TO COMMIT A CRIME

Why a Person Would Not Commit a Crime	Why a Person Would Commit a Crime
Moral or ethical commitment to obey the law	Insufficient moral or ethical commitment to obey the law
Fear of arrest and punishment	Belief in ability to get away without detection, arrest, and punishment
Social and peer pressures of friends, associates, family, and community	Peer pressure
Fear of embarrassment to self, family, and friends	Belief that detection and associated embarrassment can be avoided
Lack of motive or compelling drive to commit crime (no compelling desire to steal, murder, assault, rape, and so on)	Compelling desire or motive to achieve illegal objective (narcotic addiction, for example, provides motive for a person who would probably not otherwise commit a crime)
Lack of opportunity, or lack of capacity or skill, to commit crime	Opportunity combined with capacity and skill
Fear of economic sanction, such as loss of job or promotion, lawsuit and damages, or loss of license (driver's license, liquor license, credentials for lawyer, doctor, nurse, and so on)	Sees crime as a quick, easy way of obtaining money, drugs, power, or other objectives. (Even if caught, the odds are good that the person will not go to prison. Few persons convicted of nonviolent felonies go to prison.)

Goals and Purposes of Criminal Law

People in all societies have the inherent right to protect their society and those living in that society from acts that threaten either the society or the people. Societies throughout history have exercised this inherent right, through laws either written or unwritten forbidding and punishing acts or omissions considered detrimental to the group or the individual.

From colonial days through World War I, the criminal codes of the various American states were generally limited to those crimes that were considered serious wrongs against the society. Moreover, because criminal laws were used to define and enforce public morality, the traditional attitude of lawyers and judges was that a crime was essentially a moral wrong and should primarily be enforced through family, religious, and social pressures.

The first decades of the twentieth century saw the rapid change of the United States from an agricultural society to an industrial one. This transformation, plus the unbelievable array of economic, social, and political changes that accompanied it, hastened the arrival of the mass industrial society. These changes reduced the influence of American religious institutions, the community, and the home in molding and shaping behavior (particularly of the young) to the standards expected by society. To compensate for this change, many new criminal laws were enacted. The burden of maintaining public order and public safety gradually shifted to local, state, and federal governments, so that today the U.S. criminal justice system is both large and complex and assumes a greater role in shaping conduct than ever before.

The U.S. Constitution is the supreme law of the United States. Its preamble states that the purposes of the U.S. Constitution are to "establish Justice, insure domestic Tranquility, . . . promote the general Welfare, and secure the Blessings of Liberty to ourselves and our Posterity." As the U.S. Supreme Court stated in the famous *Miranda* case, the "most basic function of any government is to provide for the security of the individual and his property." *Miranda v. Arizona,* 384 U.S. 436, 539 (1966).

The generally recognized goals and purposes of the criminal justice system are to

- Discourage and deter people from committing crimes.
- Protect society from dangerous and harmful people.
- Punish people who have committed crimes.
- Rehabilitate and reform people who have committed crimes.

The U.S. District Court for the District of Columbia expressed the objective and purpose of criminal law in these terms in the first-degree murder case of *United States v. Watson:*

> The object of the criminal law is to protect the public against depredations of a criminal. On the other hand, its purpose is also to prevent the conviction of the innocent, or the conviction of a person whose guilt is not established beyond a reasonable doubt. The Court must balance all these aims of the trial. This view was eloquently stated by Mr. Justice Cardozo in *Snyder v. Commonwealth of Massachusetts,* 291 U.S. 97, 122, 54 S. Ct. 330, 338, 78 L. Ed. 674: ". . . [J]ustice, though due to the accused, is due to the accuser also. The concept of fairness must not be strained till it is narrowed to a filament. We are to keep the balance true."[4]

In forbidding burglary, assault, rape, robbery, and other crimes, criminal laws protect the right of privacy of individuals. The U.S. Supreme Court recognized this important function in the case of *Katz v. United States,* when the Court wrote,

> The protection of a person's general right of privacy—his right to be left alone by other people—is, like the protection of his property and his very life, left largely to the laws of the individual States.[5]

Many factors contribute to the causes and prevention of crimes. The criminal laws passed by the state and federal governments are intended to affect, and do affect, decisions by citizens to commit crimes. Other factors are also present. Statistics collected by the U.S. Bureau of Justice Statistics (BJS) show that the number of violent crimes and major property crimes committed in the United States decreased by over 30% between the years 1994 and 2004. In the FBI Uniform Crime Reports, Violent Crimes Report, released in 2012, the FBI stated that violent crimes declined from 1,251,248 in 2010 to 1,203,564 in 2011. The drop in violent crime since 1994 is likely due not only to more and harsher criminal laws, but also to factors such as the aging of the population and falling unemployment rates during much of that period. Declines in drug and alcohol use also played important roles in lowering the crime rates.

Architect of the Capitol

The signing of the U.S. Constitution, the supreme law of the United States.

The Permissible Scope of Criminal Laws in the United States

Criminal laws have been used by totalitarian governments, from Hitler's Nazi Germany to the rule of the Taliban in Afghanistan, as a means to control their citizens by brute force and terror. In a government like that of the United States, criminal laws and the criminal justice system are essential parts of the democratic system, serving to strike a balance between maintaining public order and preserving basic freedoms. To prevent misuses of the criminal justice system, in the United States constitutional limits are placed on the power of government to regulate the conduct and lives of its citizens through the use of criminal laws. Some of these constitutional limitations are presented in this chapter. Other limitations are presented in Chapters 5, 6, 7, and 8 of this book.

The Use and Limitations of the Police Power to Maintain Public Order

Each state is responsible for the maintenance of public order and public safety within that state. To do this, states enact criminal laws and establish a criminal justice system under the police power of that state. The **police power** is an inherent power vested in each state. The Tenth Amendment of the U.S. Constitution provides that "[t]he powers not delegated to the United States by the Constitution, nor prohibited by it to the States, are reserved to the States respectively, or to the people."

The term *police power* refers to the broad legislative power of a state to pass laws that promote the public health, safety, and welfare. The U.S. Supreme Court has stated:

police power The inherent power of every state and local government, subject to constitutional limits, to enact criminal laws.

The police power of a state extends beyond health, morals and safety, and comprehends the duty, within constitutional limitations, to protect the well-being and tranquility of a community. A state or city may prohibit acts or things reasonably thought to bring evil or harm to its people.[6]

Following this reasoning in *Village of Belle Terre v. Boraas,* the U.S. Supreme Court sustained a zoning ordinance restricting land use to single-family dwellings:

The police power is not confined to elimination of filth, stench, and unhealthy places. It is ample to lay out zones where family values, youth values and the blessing of quiet seclusion, and clean air make the area a sanctuary for people.[7]

In enacting criminal laws through the use of the police power, the state is regulating the conduct of citizens within the state by telling them what they may not do or what they must do. However, the police power is not absolute. In addition to limitations placed on the police power by the U.S. Constitution or state constitutions, the state may not regulate conduct capriciously or arbitrarily.

In enacting criminal law, the state must be able to show

- A compelling public need to regulate the conduct the state seeks to regulate, and that the power to regulate is within the police power of the state. The U.S. Supreme Court held in *Lawton v. Steele* that "it must appear, first, that the interests of the public generally. . . . require such interference; and, that the means . . . are not unduly oppressive upon individuals."[8]
- That the law does not contravene the U.S. Constitution or infringe on any of the rights granted or secured by the U.S. Constitution or the constitution of that state.
- That the language of the statute or ordinance clearly tells people what they are not to do (or what they must do) and that the law prohibits only the conduct that may be forbidden.

To understand these limitations, suppose some of the states create the following offenses as misdemeanors:

- State A enacts a law requiring that all people in the state go to a church of a specific religion every Sunday.
- State B enacts a law forbidding skateboarding.
- State C enacts a law forbidding the sale, use, or possession of any tobacco product.
- State D enacts a law requiring operators of motorcycles and their passengers to wear protective headgear.[9]

State A would violate First Amendment rights to the freedom of religion by passing a law of this nature; furthermore, the statute would not be within the police power of a state because it serves no valid function of government.

Regulation of skateboarding in State B could be done by governmental units, such as cities and school districts, for public safety reasons and to minimize interference with pedestrian and motor vehicle traffic. But no compelling public need exists to completely forbid such conduct because of public health, safety, or morals; therefore, such regulations could hardly stand under attack. The right to be free from interference by government has been described as follows:

No right is more sacred, or is more carefully guarded, by the liberty assurance of the due process clause than the right of every citizen to the possession and control of his own person, free from restraint or interference by the state. The makers of our Constitution conferred, as against the government, the right to be let alone—the most comprehensive of rights and the right most valued by civilized man.

* * *

However, personal freedoms are not absolute, and the liberty guaranteed by the due process clause implies absence of arbitrary interferences but not immunity from reasonable regulations.[10]

State C could show that its regulation is within the police power of the state because medical studies show that the use of tobacco products does affect people's health. As of October 2012, 36 states had adopted some type of ban on smoking that includes public buildings, government buildings, private workplaces, child-care centers, and food service centers. The other states do not have statewide bans, but many cities in those states have prohibited smoking in some but not all these locations. Enforcement of a complete ban on smoking in public and private spaces has not been advocated by any group because it would be difficult if not impossible to enforce. A total ban on smoking could lead to the kind of lawlessness associated with attempts to outlaw alcohol in the 1920s.

The Principle of "No Punishment Without a Law for It"

nulla poena sine lege The principle of legality; no act should be made criminal or punished without advance warning in the form of legislative act.

A basic principle of both English and American law is that no one can be lawfully punished for his or her conduct or omission unless that conduct or omission has been clearly made a crime by statutory or common law of that jurisdiction. The Latin maxim **nulla poena sine lege** ("no punishment without law") long ago established this principle.

This principle, generally known as the *principle of legality,* was made part of American law in 1791 by the enactment of the Fifth Amendment of the U.S. Constitution, which provides that "No person shall be . . . deprived of life, liberty, or property without due process of law."[11]

In American jurisprudence the principle of legality has two main tenets: one, it prohibits retroactive definition of criminal behavior by judicial decision, and two, it requires statutory definitions of crimes to be sufficiently clear and precise so as to enable reasonable people to understand what conduct is prohibited. By the end of the nineteenth century, it was generally accepted in this country that courts lacked the power to "create" crimes that had not previously existed under statute or common law (see later in this chapter). Most states have passed statutes similar to section 720 ILCS 5/1-3 of the Illinois Criminal Code, which states:

Applicability of Common Law. No conduct constitutes an offense unless it is described as an offense in this Code or in another statute of this State.

The second tenet of the principle of legality requires that a statute must define criminal conduct clearly enough that people affected by the statute will receive adequate notice of the behavior prohibited. If the statute is too vague, courts might construe the statute to include conduct not reasonably understood to be prohibited, thus effectively creating a new crime. The "void for vagueness" doctrine is discussed in more detail later in this chapter.

Although the "prior notice" doctrine requires that fair warning be given in language that the ordinary person will understand, it does not require that the statute list in detail the many ways in which a forbidden wrong may be committed. The following example illustrates this:

EXAMPLE

Criminal homicide can be committed by many different unlawful acts such as using a gun, knife, poison, a crowbar, a truck, or another vehicle; pushing the victim off a cliff or a bridge or down stairs; or strangulation. Murder statutes do not have to list the hundred or more ways of committing murder. Such statutes forbid the defined evil and clearly provide notice as to the act or acts forbidden.[12]

Therefore, in view of the principle of "no punishment without a law for it," the following questions must be asked before any person is arrested, charged with a crime, or convicted: What has the person done that violates the statutes of the state? Was the person legally (not just morally) obligated to act, and then failed to perform this legal (not moral) duty?

Classifications of Crimes

Many acts have been designated as criminal offenses in the United States. In 1790, only 20 federal criminal statutes existed. Today, the federal government alone has designated more than 4,500 offenses; 42 of the 51 titles in the federal statutes include listed crimes. A much larger number of state and local offenses exist.[13]

The large number of crimes in the United States may be classified as follows:

- According to their sources, as statutory, common law, administrative, or constitutional crimes (see later in this chapter).
- As felonies or misdemeanors; this determines how the crimes are tried and, in many states, affects the law of arrest for such crimes. Many states classify felonies and misdemeanors as class A, class B, and so forth. In this way, punishment can be standardized, though it is common for each classification to have punishment ranges. As an example, Section 28-105 of the Nebraska Statutes lists a class IA felony as life imprisonment without parole, a class IB felony as 20 years to life, and a class IC felony as 5 to 50 years.

Felony and Misdemeanor

The felony/misdemeanor classification is the most common and most important classification of crime. A **felony** is the most serious type of crime and generally is punished by one year or more in prison or a penitentiary. As of 2012, thirty-seven states and the federal government had laws providing for the death penalty for a few very serious felonies.

A **misdemeanor** is a less serious offense and usually carries a sentence of imprisonment for no more than a year, though some states may provide for longer sentences (Figure 1.1). An offense that does not provide for possible jailing or imprisonment is generally not classified as a crime but rather as a civil offense. For example, ordinary speeding is punished by a fine and imposition of points but is not a crime.

felony The most serious grade of crime; usually includes possibility of prison sentence.

misdemeanor Offenses that carry punishment of a degree less than felonies. Usually misdemeanor crimes do not involve prison sentences.

QUALITY-OF-LIFE CRIMES AND THE BROKEN WINDOW THEORY

Many veteran law enforcement officers subscribe to the broken window or quality-of-life theory of crime. This theory holds that small quality-of-life crimes will eventually encourage greater lawlessness. For example, if graffiti and broken windows are tolerated, more serious property damage and other crimes will follow. If prostitution is tolerated, other crimes will follow, since prostitution often fuels illegal drug activity. With prostitution and illegal drug activity come purse snatchings, robbery, theft, burglary, and other felonies.

Law enforcement officers believe a community should be concerned and take action when the first signs of a breakdown in the quality of life appear, such as the abandoned building with broken windows, loud drunken bar patrons out on the street after closing hours, or the presence of street gangs.

FIGURE 1.1 Government May Regulate Conduct by Making the Conduct Either a Criminal or a Civil Offense

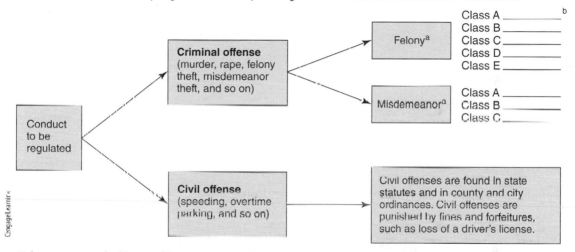

[a]Felonies are punished by possible imprisonment for one year or more in state prison. Misdemeanors are usually punished by possible imprisonment for up to one year in a jail or a detention center. Both felonies and misdemeanors may also be punished by fines and forfeitures. Capital felonies can be punished by death in states.
[b]Fill in maximum imprisonment in your state.

Whether a crime is a felony or a misdemeanor is important for the following reasons:

1. Conviction of a felony would, in most states, stand in the way of some types of employment, affect a person's credit rating or ability to adopt a child, and prevent a person from entering the armed forces, becoming a law enforcement officer, or obtaining a license as a nurse, doctor, lawyer, and so on, unless a pardon is obtained.[14] A misdemeanor conviction would not ordinarily have these effects.
2. People charged with felonies have the right to a preliminary hearing or a "presentation or indictment of a grand jury."[15]
3. The law governing making an arrest for a felony differs from the law governing making an arrest for a misdemeanor in the following ways:

VICTIMLESS CRIMES

The term *victimless crimes* is used to designate crimes that do not directly inflict personal or property harm on another person in the sense that murder, robbery, rape, and theft do. The term is controversial when applied to crimes such as drug violations because the deadly drug trade in the United States results in many victims.

Examples of Victimless Crimes[a]	Examples of Victimless Crimes that Have Been Abolished by Many States	Examples of Crimes that Have Been Declared Unconstitutional
Possession or use of a small amount of a drug such as marijuana	Fornication	Use of contraceptives (even by married couples)—*Griswold v. Connecticut,* 381 U.S. 479 (1965)
Public drunkenness (decriminalized by many states)	Adultery	Drug addiction as a crime in and of itself—*Robinson v. California,* 370 U.S. 660 (1962)
Prostitution	Cohabitation	Possession of or reading obscene material in privacy of one's home—*Stanley v. Georgia,* 394 U.S. 557 (1969)
Gambling (many forms of gambling are now legal)		Homosexual relations between consenting adults in privacy of one's home—*Lawrence v. Texas,* 123 S. Ct.2472 (2003)
Obscenity offenses involving consenting adults		

[a]Some people take the position that society is the victim of many of these offenses.

a. There is broad authority for law enforcement officers to make a felony arrest; however, law enforcement officers in states using the "in presence" requirement cannot arrest for misdemeanors unless the misdemeanor is committed in their presence or unless other statutory or common law authority exists.

b. "Citizen's arrest" is generally limited to felonies committed in the presence of the citizen unless the statutes or common law of a state provide additional authority.[16]

General Constitutional Limitations on Criminal Laws

The U.S. Supreme Court has stated that "[b]roadly speaking, crimes in the United States are what the law of the individual States make them, subject to (constitutional) limitations."[17] States, therefore, have broad authority to create criminal laws.

The authority to enact criminal laws cannot be exercised in a manner that violates the rights of persons guaranteed by the U.S. Constitution or the constitution of a state.

In succeeding chapters we discuss some of these rights in detail: States cannot criminalize conduct protected by the First Amendment, including freedom of speech, freedom of religion, and freedom to move about freely (see Chapter 9). Nor may states impose a punishment that violates the Eighth Amendment prohibition against "cruel and unusual punishment" (see Chapter 8). Chapters 6 and 7 on defenses also present other constitutional limitations. The following materials present some of the general, constitutional limitations on criminal laws and the exercise of the police power.

Ex Post Facto Laws

ex post facto Criminal law made retroactive to punish prior conduct not criminal when done. Prohibited by Article I, Sections 9 and 10, of the Constitution.

Sections 9 and 10 of Article I of the U.S. Constitution forbid the U.S. Congress and all states from enacting **ex post facto** (after the fact) laws. Therefore, no state or the U.S. Congress can create a new crime in November and make the law retroactive so as to punish conduct that was lawful prior to November of that year. Most state constitutions also forbid ex post facto laws. Ex post facto restrictions apply only to criminal laws, and not to civil laws such as tax laws. The ex post facto restriction also only limits the power of state and federal legislative bodies; it does not apply to the judicial branch of government. See the U.S. Supreme Court case of *Rogers v. Tennessee*, 532 U.S. 451 (2001). The Ex Post Facto Clause forbids the following:

1. Laws made retroactive so as to make conduct before the enactment of the law a criminal violation.
2. Laws that aggravate a crime retroactively (e.g., making a misdemeanor a felony as of a date six months before the enactment of the legislation).
3. Laws that increase the punishment for a crime retroactively.
4. Laws that alter the legal rules of evidence and permit conviction on less or different evidence than the law required at the time of the commission of the offense.[18]

In 2013 the U.S. Supreme Court discussed the retroactive increased punishment prohibition under the Ex Post Facto Clause as applied to the Federal Sentencing Guidelines. In *Peugh v. United States*, 133 S. Ct. 2072 (2013), the Court held that use of Federal Sentencing Guidelines amended after the defendants committed the crimes charged violated the Clause. Under the amended guidelines, the range of possible sentences for those crimes was increased substantially over the earlier range for the same crimes. Although the guidelines are not mandatory, the Court held that the higher range of possible sentences created a high risk of increased punishment for the crime, which violates the Ex Post Facto Clause.

The Ex Post Facto Clause does not necessarily apply every time a statute incorporates past behavior into a new designation of criminal conduct. For example, in 1996 Congress enacted the Domestic Violence Offender Gun Act, which amended the 1968 Federal Gun Control Act, 18 U.S.C. § 921. The 1968 Act prohibited convicted felons from owning or possessing firearms. The 1996 amendment made it a violation of the Act for any person convicted of a "misdemeanor crime involving domestic violence" to own or possess a firearm. A person convicted of a domestic violence misdemeanor in 1990, for example, could lawfully possess a firearm prior to the 1996 amendment. After 1996, however, that same person could be convicted under the amended Act. This is not an Ex Post Facto Clause problem because the amendment did not make past conduct criminal; rather, it provides that the future action of possessing a firearm after the amendment's effective date, 1996, by persons convicted of misdemeanor domestic violence crimes would be a crime. Since people are presumed to know the law, those affected by the amendment were under a duty to avoid ownership or possession of firearms after the Act became applicable to them. The U.S. Supreme Court considered the meaning and applicability of the Domestic Violence Offender Gun Ban in *United States v. Hayes,* 129 S. Ct. 1079 (2009), discussed in Chapter 11.

The applicability of the Ex Post Facto Clause to statutes of limitation was discussed by the U.S. Supreme Court in the 2003 case of *Stogner v. California,* 123 S. Ct. 2446. Most crimes, except murder and some other violent crimes, have limitation periods for prosecution. If prosecution does not occur during the statutory period, it is barred. Courts have often held that the Ex Post Facto Clause does not prevent a state from increasing the limitation period for future offenses, or offenses that were not time-barred when the increased limitation period became law. Thus, an offender who committed a crime that had a 5-year limitation period when committed cannot raise an ex post facto objection if the legislature increases the limitations period to 10 years during the initial 5 years after the crime was committed. In *Stogner,* the California legislature increased the limitation period for sexual crimes committed against children and expressly made the increased period applicable to offenses that had become time barred under existing limitation periods prior to the time the statute increasing the limitation was adopted. The Supreme Court held the statute unconstitutional under the second part of the test, concluding the statute aggravated the crime of sexual assault retroactively.

In order to run afoul of the Ex Post Facto Clause a statute must have the effect of retroactively "punishing" an offender. When is a law "penal" and subject to the Ex Post Facto Clause? In the 2003 case of *Smith v. Doe,* 538 U.S. 84, the U.S. Supreme Court held that the Alaska Sex Offender Registration Act (so-called Megan's Law, see Chapter 12) was not punitive in nature, and thus the ex post facto limitations did not apply. The defendants contended that because they committed their crimes before the act was passed, its registration requirements could not be applied to them. The Supreme Court disagreed. Because the act was intended by the Alaska legislature to set up an administrative system to track sex offenders, the Court held it was civil and non-punitive in nature. Though the act did contain information about sex offenders that might "taint" those forced to register, the Court held such forced registration was not a penal law because the information was already a matter of public record.

Bills of Attainder

FIRST

Article I, Sections 9 and 10, of the U.S. Constitution also forbids Congress and the states from enacting any bill of attainder. A **bill of attainder** is a legislative act that inflicts punishment without the person (defendant) already having had a trial in a court before a judge. In 1965, the U.S. Supreme Court stated the history of the bill of attainder in *United States v. Brown,* 381 U.S. 437:

> The bill of attainder, a parliamentary act sentencing to death one or more specific persons, was a device often resorted to in sixteenth-, seventeenth-, and eighteenth-century England for dealing with persons who had attempted, or threatened to attempt,

bill of attainder
Legislative act that inflicts punishment without trial; prohibited by Article I, Sections 9 and 10, of the Constitution.

to overthrow the government. In addition to the death sentence, attainder generally carried with it a "corruption of blood," which meant that the attained party's heirs could not inherit his property. The "bill of pains and penalties" was identical to the bill of attainder, except that it prescribed a penalty short of death, e.g., banishment, deprivation of the right to vote, or exclusion of the designated party's sons from Parliament. Most bills of attainder and bills of pains and penalties named the parties to whom they were to apply; a few, however, simply described them.

SORNA AND EX POST FACTO CLAIMS

After Congress passed the Sexual Offender Registration and Notification Act, 42 U.S.C. §16901 (SORNA) in 2006, adults and young persons over the age of 14 charged with sexual offenses or adjudicated delinquents under the Federal Juvenile Delinquency Act, 18 U.S.C. §5031, were required to register as sex offenders. The federal statute delegated to the U.S. Attorney General the decision whether to apply the registration requirement to persons who committed sexual offenses before SORNA became effective. The Attorney General promulgated such a rule in February 2007.

Adults

All federal courts of appeals that have considered ex post facto claims by persons who were adults when they committed sexual offenses before SORNA was enacted have rejected that claim.[19] The U.S. Supreme Court has not reached a decision on this issue, though in the 2012 case of *Reynolds v. United States,* 132 S. Ct. 975, it concluded that SORNA did not apply to adults whose offenses occurred before the time the Attorney General determined SORNA was retroactive.

Juveniles

In 2010 the Ninth Circuit Court of Appeals held that the Ex Post Facto Clause prohibited application of SORNA to persons who were juveniles when they committed the sexual offenses that triggered registration under SORNA. The Court concluded the registration burden for juveniles, held not to be punishment in *Smith v. Doe* when applied to adults, was punishment for juveniles and thus retroactive.[20] However, in 2011 the U.S. Supreme Court vacated the Ninth Circuit's decision, holding that because the juvenile had been ordered to register only until he was 21, after he turned 21 the case became "moot".[21]

In a related case under SORNA, the U.S. Supreme Court in 2010 held that a defendant who was convicted of a criminal sexual offense and who traveled in interstate commerce, both of which occurred before SORNA was passed, could not be convicted of failing to register as a sex offender. SORNA states that any convicted sex offender who travels in interstate commerce must register under applicable state sex offender laws. Failure to do so is a federal offense. The defendant traveled to a new state without registering, but did so before SORNA was passed. The Court found the Act inapplicable and reversed the conviction because SORNA by its terms only applied to sex offenders who traveled in interstate commerce after the Act was passed. The Court therefore did not resolve any ex post facto issues raised by a conviction under SORNA for failure to register based on a pre-2006 sex offender conviction. See *Carr v. United States,* 130 S. Ct. 2229 (2010).

In forbidding bills of attainder, the U.S. Constitution and state constitutions limit legislatures to the task of writing laws (making rules). Persons charged with a crime must be brought before a court to determine guilt or innocence.

The Second Amendment and Gun Control

Before 2008 it was unclear whether the Second Amendment to the U.S. Constitution created an individual right to "bear arms," or only a "public" right to keep an armed militia. However, in *District of Columbia v. Heller,* 128 S. Ct. 2783 (2008) the Supreme Court held that the Second Amendment protected an individual's right to own and possess firearms, at least under federal criminal laws. As a result, the Court held that the District of Columbia's prohibition on gun ownership must comply with the Second Amendment's right to bear arms. The *Heller* case and the limits placed on federal gun control laws are discussed in more detail in Chapter 9, as is the opinion of the U.S. Supreme Court in the case of *McDonald v. City of Chicago,* 130 S. Ct. 3020 (2010), on the applicability of the Second Amendment to state laws.

Due Process, "Void for Vagueness," and the "Overbreadth" Doctrine

The Due Process Clause of the Fourteenth Amendment prohibits a state from depriving a person of life, liberty, or property without **due process** of law. In some situations, the Due Process Clause works to prohibit a state from making protected conduct criminal.

due process The constitutional guarantee that criminal arrests and trials must meet certain minimum standards of fairness (procedural due process) and that laws not violate constitutional rights (substantive due process).

For example, it is clear a state could not make it a crime for a person to leave the state, because the right to travel is a protected right. A state could make leaving the state an offense if it aggravated some other crime, such as abandonment of a child. See *Jones v. Helms,* 452 U.S. 412 (1981). In 2003 the U.S. Supreme Court applied the Due Process Clause to invalidate a Texas sodomy statute. In *Lawrence v. Texas,* 123 S. Ct. 2472, two adult men were convicted of engaging in homosexual conduct in the privacy of their home. The Texas statute provided: "A person commits an offense if he engages in deviate sexual intercourse with another individual of the same sex." The statute defined "deviate" sexual intercourse as including contact between the genitals of one person and the mouth or anus of another. The Court held the statute violated the Due Process Clause because it deprived the defendants of their liberty interest under the Fourteenth Amendment: "The State cannot demean their existence or control their destiny by making their private sexual conduct a crime. Their right to Liberty under the Due Process Clause gives them the full right to engage in their conduct without intervention of the government." In doing so, the Court reversed the decision reached in *Bowers v. Hardwick,* 478 U.S. 186 (1986), which upheld a Georgia sodomy statute.

"void for vagueness" doctrine The constitutional law doctrine that invalidates criminal laws written in such a manner as to make it unreasonably difficult for a defendant to know whether or not conduct is prohibited by the law.

The Due Process Clause of the U.S. Constitution also requires that a legislative body, when writing a criminal statute or ordinance, must use clear and precise language that gives fair and adequate notice of the conduct that is forbidden or required. If the language of a statute or ordinance is vague, it may be held unconstitutional under the **"void for vagueness" doctrine**.

The "void for vagueness" test asks whether a statute or ordinance on its face or as applied to a particular defendant "is so vague that men of common intelligence must guess at its meaning and differ as to its application."[22] A vague criminal statute or ordinance creates uncertainty as to what the law requires and may have some or all of the following results:

1. It may trap those who desire to be law abiding by not providing fair notice of what is prohibited.[23]
2. It may cause arbitrary and discriminatory enforcement because those who enforce and apply the law have no clear and explicit standards to guide them.[24]
3. When a vague statute "abut(s) upon sensitive areas of First Amendment freedoms, it operates to inhibit the exercise of (those) freedoms. Uncertain meaning inevitably leads citizens to steer far wider of the unlawful zone . . . than if the boundaries of the forbidden areas were clearly marked."[25]

"overbreadth" doctrine The constitutional law doctrine that invalidates laws that regulate conduct so broadly that they interfere with individual freedoms.

Criminal statutes and ordinances may also be held to be unconstitutional if the manner in which they are written violates the **"overbreadth" doctrine.** The U.S. Supreme Court has stated that overbreadth "offends [when the words of a statute or ordinance] . . . sweep unnecessarily broadly and thereby invade the area of protected freedoms."[27] A vague statute or ordinance may be overbroad if its uncertain boundaries leave open the possibility of punishment for protected conduct and thus lead people to avoid such protected activity in order to steer clear of violating the uncertain law.[28] However, a clear and precise statute may also be overbroad if it prohibits constitutionally protected conduct.

DROWSEY DRIVING: CAN STATES MAKE IT A CRIME?

The American Automobile Association (AAA) calls drowsy driving "one of the significant unrecognized safety problems" on American roads. Signs like "Drive Alert, Arrive Alive" have not resulted in significant reductions of deaths and injuries caused by drowsy drivers.

Could a new criminal law be written that clearly states the required objective standards needed to identify what conduct the law prohibits as "drowsy driving"? How would such a law be drafted to avoid being so unclear that people "of common intelligence must guess at its meaning"? How can arbitrary enforcement be avoided? Unlike drunk driving, where objective measurements of blood alcohol can be used to determine if a driver is drunk, how "tired" is "too tired"?

Would a statute that defines "drowsy driving" in any of the following ways run afoul of the "void for vagueness" or "overbreadth" doctrines: "sleepy driving," "driving while tired," "driving while fatigued," "driving under conditions of sleep deprivation," or "driving while suffering sleep disorders"? Could a reasonable person look at these definitions and know when driving would be a crime? Or is it better to let existing laws handle the problem?

Laws that are now used by law enforcement officers and prosecutors to deal with the problem include laws prohibiting "inattentive driving" or "driving too fast for the conditions" existing at the time. In some northern snow-belt states, state troopers routinely give out traffic tickets for "driving too fast under road or visibility conditions" to persons who spin out on icy roads.

These laws also can be used as a way of assigning criminal blame for a highway accident or injury based on the actual driving that occurred. If a highway death occurred, the driver could be charged with involuntary manslaughter or vehicular manslaughter. (See Chapter 10, "Manslaughter.") For example, in 2012 a bus driver in Virginia who fell asleep while driving a bus and caused the death of four passengers and injuries to many others was convicted of involuntary manslaughter.[26]

The "void for vagueness" test and the "overbreadth" test are separate and distinct. However, when First Amendment rights are at issue, the U.S. Supreme Court uses the two tests in a manner that makes them virtually one doctrine. From the cases, it can be stated that statutes and ordinances that regulate conduct must comply with the following requirements:[29]

- Fair and adequate notice must be given of the conduct that is forbidden or required.
- A precise standard of conduct must be specified in terms of results that can reasonably be expected.
- The statute or ordinance cannot permit or encourage arbitrary and discriminatory law enforcement that may result in erratic and arbitrary arrests and convictions.
- The statute or ordinance cannot violate or infringe on rights that are secured or granted by the U.S. Constitution.

Status Crimes

A state may regulate and control the use of such drugs as heroin, cocaine, and crack in a number of ways. The government may and does forbid the importing or manufacturing of the drugs; the law forbids possession and transportation of the forbidden drugs; the sale, use, or possession of such drugs is also forbidden. All of these specific acts (conduct) have been determined to be harmful to others or to the society as a whole. But can a state make addiction to heroin, cocaine, or crack, by itself, a crime?

To do something about its increasing heroin problem in the late 1950s, California passed a law making heroin addiction, by itself, a crime. The issue before the U.S. Supreme Court in the case of *Robinson v. California* was whether a person could be arrested and convicted for what he or she is or was.[30] The U.S. Supreme Court considered the question of whether a state could make a status or a "chronic condition" a crime in itself. This type of crime is referred to as a **status crime**.

status crime Criminal laws that punish a status, such as drug addiction, with no act requirement.

The Court held that a state law that made the "status" of narcotic addiction a criminal offense for which an offender might be prosecuted and imprisoned at any time inflicted a "cruel and unusual punishment" in violation of the Eighth and Fourteenth Amendments to the U.S. Constitution. The Court stated that "even one day in prison would be a cruel and unusual punishment for the 'crime' of having a common cold." In the case of *Powell v. Texas,* the defendant was an alcoholic with approximately 100 arrests for acts of public intoxication.[31] In this case, the defendant argued that because he was compelled to drink and because he could not control his "status," the state did not have the power to punish him for his acts of public intoxication.

The U.S. Supreme Court, however, affirmed Powell's conviction, holding that he was arrested and convicted for what he did (being drunk in a public place) and that Powell was not convicted for what he was (status). In refusing to extend the rule of law that had been established in the case of *Robinson v. California,* the Supreme Court held:

> Traditional common-law concepts of personal accountability and essential considerations of federalism lead us to disagree with appellant. We are unable to conclude, on the state of this record or on the current state of medical knowledge, that chronic alcoholics in general, and Leroy Powell in particular, suffer

"VOID FOR VAGUENESS" AND "OVERBREADTH" DOCTRINES

The Due Process Clause of the U.S. Constitution, made binding on states by the Fourteenth Amendment, requires that criminal legislation clearly identify prohibited conduct so as to give a reasonable person fair notice of that conduct. A criminal statute written so broadly as to invade the area of constitutionally protected rights such as free speech is unconstitutional under the "overbreadth" doctrine. This table shows representative cases applying the "void for vagueness" and "overbreadth" doctrines.

Vagueness

Coates v. City of Cincinnati Supreme Court of the United States 402 U.S. 611 (1971)	Ordinance made it illegal for three or more people gathered on a sidewalk to "annoy" passersby. Because what annoys one person may not annoy another, the Court held that "[t]hus the ordinance is vague . . . in the sense that no conduct is specified at all."
Papachristou v. City of Jacksonville Supreme Court of the United States 405 U.S. 156 (1972)	Ordinance making being a "vagrant" a crime and defining vagrants as "rogues and vagabonds," "dissolute persons," or "common night walkers" held unconstitutional. The ordinance did not give fair notice of prohibited conduct.
Warren v. State Florida Supreme Court 572 So.2d 1376 (1991)	Statute making it a crime to keep a "house of ill fame" held unconstitutionally vague.
State v. Lara Kansas Court of Appeals 853 P.2d 1168 (1993)	Statute making criminal "excessive and unusual" motor vehicle noises held not void for vagueness.
State v. Bohannon Washington Court of Appeals 814 P.2d 694 (1991)	Statute making it a crime for causing a minor to engage in "sexually explicit conduct" held not void for vagueness.

Overbreadth

City of Houston v. Hill Supreme Court of the United States 482 U.S. 451 (1987)	Ordinance making it unlawful to "interrupt policeman in execution of his duty" held overbroad, because it made otherwise protected speech a violation of the ordinance. (A citizen who interrupted a police officer to tell the officer of a bank robbery could lawfully be arrested under this ordinance.)

from such an irresistible compulsion to drink and to get drunk in public that they are utterly unable to control their performance of either or both of these acts and thus cannot be deterred at all from public intoxication.

The *Robinson* status/*Powell* acts distinction is illustrated by two examples. A law making it a crime for a homeless person to sleep on the sidewalk is a status crime, if the act of sleeping on the sidewalk occurred because there was no other shelter available.[32] A law making it a crime for a felon to possess a weapon is not a status crime, because the act of possessing the weapon constitutes the crime, not the status of being a felon.[33]

Equal Protection of the Laws

If a state made the crime of burglary in that state applicable only to males, the first man charged with burglary in that state would challenge the statute, arguing that it violated the Fourteenth Amendment requirement of "equal protection of the laws." Women could commit burglary in that state, but for the same conduct a man could be convicted and sent to jail.

The Equal Protection Clause of the Fourteenth Amendment requires that states must treat all people alike, not only in enacting criminal and civil laws but also in enforcing rules. For example, all states have consanguinity laws forbidding marriages between brothers and sisters; most also prohibit marriage between other close relatives, such as first cousins. Consanguinity laws apply to all persons, regardless of status, race, or religion.[34] They represent a valid exercise of the police power of a state because children born to closely related parents are more apt to have abnormalities.

However, a state may not make it a crime (under so-called "miscegenation laws") for a black person to marry a white person (or vice versa), as in the past some states did.[35] Such a prohibition would violate the Equal Protection Clause because a black person marrying a white person would be guilty of a crime, whereas a white person marrying another white person would not. Since all persons, black or white, are of the same class when it comes to marrying another person, the law would operate unequally as to some members of the class.

Sources of Criminal Law

Substantive criminal law can be found in the following sources, each of which is discussed in the next sections:

- Criminal law, on rare occasions, can be found today in the common law of some states.
- Most criminal law is found in the statutes of each state and in the statutes of the federal government.
- Criminal law can also be found in commercial, sanitation, health, financial, and tax administrative regulations that have criminal sanctions. These regulations are enacted by state and federal administrative and regulatory agencies.
- A few sections of state constitutions and one section of the U.S. Constitution contain criminal law. Treason is the only crime defined by the U.S. Constitution. For material on treason, see Chapter 17 on terrorism.

Common Law Crimes

common law The earliest type of law. Common law was created by judges based on custom, usages, and moral concepts of the people. Most law today is statutory law enacted by legislative bodies.

Because the **common law** was the first and earliest source of criminal law, it is presented first here. And because the historic source of U.S. criminal law lies in the common law of England, a review of the development of criminal law in England and in the American colonies is necessary.

When the English kings gained control of the whole of England in the Middle Ages, royal judges began deciding civil and criminal cases throughout all of England, thus supporting the Crown by preserving the peace and dispensing justice. Few people in those days could read or write, and England was not a democracy. The king, the judges, and the ecclesiastical authorities played important roles not only in creating (sometimes inventing) criminal laws but also in defining the elements and the scope of the criminal offenses. Judges became familiar with the general customs, usages, and moral concepts of the people and based judgments on them. In doing so, the judges determined which customs and moral concepts should prevail as law.

By the early 1600s, the criminal law of England was composed primarily of the mandatory rules of conduct laid down by the English judges, with only a few criminal statutes. In formulating the **common law crimes** of England, the royal judges believed that their decisions represented the best interests of the king and of the country as a whole. These decisions became the common law of England. As authoritative precedents, they were followed and applied in future cases wherever English common law was used and followed.

common law crimes
Crimes created by judges.

During this period of development of the criminal law in England, the English Parliament enacted a few criminal statutes, such as embezzlement, false pretense, and incest. The English ecclesiastical courts (religious courts) both defined and punished offenses, such as private acts of fornication, adultery, and seduction, that were held to be violations of the moral code, but were not public offenses. The English settlers who began colonizing North America in the early 1600s brought with them the English common law. This formed the basis of the law in each of the individual colonies. Modifications and adjustments were made to meet the needs of each colony. A great deal of discretion was vested in colonial governors, councils, and judges with respect to the enforcement and scope of offenses and with respect to the creation of new laws. However, for the most part, English common law crimes continued as the common law crimes in each of the American colonies.

During the American Revolution and for some time after it, a great deal of hostility was directed toward the English in America; this hostility extended to the common law. Justice Hugo L. Black of the U.S. Supreme Court referred to this situation in his 1958 dissenting opinion in *Green v. United States*, in which he stated:

> Those who formed the Constitution struck out anew free of previous shackles in an effort to obtain a better order of government more congenial to human liberty and welfare. It cannot be seriously claimed that they intended to adopt the common law wholesale. They accepted those portions of it which were adapted to this country and conformed to the ideals of its citizens and rejected the remainder. In truth, there was widespread hostility to the common law in general and profound opposition to its adoption into our jurisdiction from the commencement of the Revolutionary War until long after the Constitution was ratified.[36]

American lawyers and judges knew the value of many of the English common law principles, which at that point had been developing for more than 200 years. But the public wanted American law for Americans, and many changes were thus made by the new state legislative bodies, which transformed English common law into statutory law.

IMPORTANT DOCUMENTS OF THE ENGLISH-SPEAKING WORLD

Magna Carta, 1215. A civil war in England forced King John to sign the **Magna Carta** ("great document"), which provided:

- There will be no criminal "trial upon . . . simple accusation without producing credible witnesses to the truth therein."
- "No freeman shall be taken, imprisoned . . . except by lawful judgment of his peers or the law of the land."

The signing of Magna Carta in 1215 was the first step toward democracy in England, because it was the first time that a king relinquished some of his power to the people. Until Magna Carta, English kings ruled with almost absolute power under the concept of "divine right of kings," and the people had only the little freedom the kings chose to give them.

The writ of habeas corpus developed in English common law to protect the new rights of English people under Magna Carta. In 1679, the English Parliament enacted the first habeas corpus statute. The U.S. Constitution of 1788 guarantees and protects the writ of habeas corpus in Article I, Section 9. All of the original thirteen states guaranteed the writ in their original constitutions. Today, people who believe they are being illegally detained can use the writ of habeas corpus to challenge their imprisonment.

Mayflower Compact, 1620. As the *Mayflower* rode at anchor off Cape Cod, some of the passengers threatened to go out on their own, without any framework of government. To avoid this threat of anarchy, the Mayflower Compact agreed that "We . . . doe . . . solemnly and mutually . . . covenant and combine our selves together into a civil body politike for our better ordering and preservation . . . and by vertue hereof to enact . . . such just and equal laws . . . unto which we promise all due submission and obedience."

English Bill of Rights, 1689. Because of numerous attacks on personal liberty, the English Parliament forced King James II to abdicate, and Parliament produced a Bill of Rights. This document served as a guide for Americans and provided:

Magna Carta The document signed by King John in 1215 giving certain rights to his nobles. Successive kings affirmed this charter before Parliament.

Common Law Crimes in the U.S. Federal Courts. In 1812, the case of *United States v. Hudson and Goodwin* came before the U.S. Supreme Court.[37] The defendants were charged with the common law crime of criminal libel because they wrote in a newspaper that the president of the United States and the Congress had secretly voted to give $2 million as a present to Napoleon Bonaparte. No federal statute made libel a crime, but criminal libel was a common law crime.

The Supreme Court pointed out that state courts could punish a person for a violation of the common law crime of libel under their police power if they chose to adopt and incorporate the offense as part of the crimes of that state. But the Supreme Court held that federal courts had only that power and jurisdiction given to them by the U.S. Constitution and the Congress, and had no power to adopt

- "Suspending laws . . . without consent of Parliament is illegal"
- "Keeping a Standing Army within the Kingdom in Time of Peace unless it be with Consent of Parliament is against the law"
- "Election of Members of Parliament ought to be free"
- "Freedom of Speech . . . ought not to be impeached or questioned."

Declaration of Independence, July 4, 1776. After King George declared the American colonies to be in a state of rebellion and the English Parliament forbade all trade with the colonies, an eloquent statement of the American democratic creed was made in the Declaration of Independence:

> We hold these truths to be self-evident, that all men are created equal, that they are endowed by their Creator with certain unalienable Rights, that among these are Life, Liberty and the pursuit of Happiness.—That to secure these rights, Governments are instituted among Men, deriving their just powers from the consent of the governed,—That whenever any Form of Government becomes destructive of these ends, it is the Right of the People to alter or to abolish it, and to institute new Government, laying its foundation on such principles and organizing its powers in such form, as to them shall seem most likely to effect their Safety and Happiness.

U.S. Constitution, ratified 1788. Because of the failure to achieve a workable government under the Articles of Confederation, delegates from the American states met in Philadelphia in 1787. George Washington presided for months over the debates and arguments that led to the adoption and ratification of the Constitution that has been used by the United States since that time.

The Bill of Rights. The first ten amendments were made part of the U.S. Constitution in 1791. See the appendix of this book for applicable sections of the U.S. Constitution.

common law crimes. The rule that there are no federal common law crimes has since been affirmed many times over the years. In 1949, Justice Robert H. Jackson wrote that "it is well and wisely settled that there can be no judge-made offenses against the United States and that every federal prosecution must be sustained by statutory authority."[38]

Common Law Crimes in State Courts. Most states have abolished criminal common law crimes, but many states continue to use common law rules of criminal procedure. Some states, however, have not abolished common law crimes and continue to allow prosecution for common law crimes. In those states, prosecution is rare and not often successful.

For example, Dr. Jack Kevorkian, the medical doctor who championed assisted suicides, was charged in Michigan with the common law crime of assisting two suicides. Angry over being charged with an "unwritten" law, Dr. Kevorkian shouted a number of times in court during his trial, "This is not a trial! This is a lynching! There is no law! No law!" The jury acquitted Dr. Kevorkian of the common law charges. (Later, using the Michigan criminal code, Dr. Kevorkian was charged and convicted of murder in 1999 and sentenced to 10 to 25 years in prison. He was paroled in 2007.)

Because of the difficulties and limited success of prosecuting for common law crimes, prosecutors use the modern statutory crimes that are available in the criminal codes of their state.

Statutory and Administrative Crimes

After the American Revolution, the new state legislatures began converting common law crimes to statutory form. Through the police power of the state, they had the power to amend, affirm, change, extend, abolish, modify, or alter any common law crime or rule.

In many instances, state legislatures kept the common law crime intact by merely restating the law in statutory form. In other instances, legislatures created new crimes by forbidding and punishing conduct that was not a crime in common law. In still other instances, they redefined the common law crime by changing elements of the crime or removing common law limitations and extending the crime to cover conduct not included in the common law crime. If the common law punishment was considered too severe, changes were made in the degree or form of punishment. Attempts were made to clarify areas of doubt or uncertainty in common law crimes.

Practically all criminal laws that are enforced today are statutory laws enacted by legislative bodies. Many of today's statutory crimes were unknown in common law. Most of these criminal laws were enacted to meet the problems of a mass industrial society.

In the early twentieth century Congress began passing laws creating administrative agencies whose responsibility was to adopt and enforce regulations to further the purposes of federal laws. As some of the regulations adopted could be enforced by the imposition of criminal penalties, the question of the authority of administrative agencies to make criminal laws was raised. In 1911, that issue came before the U.S. Supreme Court in the case of *United States v. Grimaud*.[39] Congress had passed a statute authorizing the secretary of agriculture to make regulations to preserve and maintain government forests as forest reserves. Congress made violation of these regulations a criminal offense. The defendant (Grimaud) had continued to graze his sheep on U.S. forest lands without obtaining permits as required under the new regulations. Because the federal courts were divided on the question of whether a violation of such regulations constituted a crime, the government appealed the case to the U.S. Supreme Court.

The Supreme Court held that Congress may constitutionally delegate to an administrative agency the power to make regulations that are enforced by criminal penalties established by that legislative body. The Court stated that the secretary of agriculture does not exercise the legislative power of declaring the penalty or fixing the punishment for grazing sheep without a permit; the punishment is imposed by the act itself. The offense is not against the secretary but, as the indictment properly concludes, is "contrary to the laws of the United States and the peace and dignity thereof."

Today, established practice allows Congress and most state legislatures to delegate to an administrative agency the power to make rules, and the legislature may provide by statute that such rules may be enforced by criminal penalties. In a few states, this procedure has been held to be unconstitutional. But in the majority of states, criminal laws may be created by the legislature establishing the framework and by the administrative agency providing the specific regulation or rule within that framework. The delegation of such authority is constitutional in the majority of the states if

administrative crime Crime created by government administrative agencies under specific authority and guidelines granted to the regulatory or administrative agency by law of that state or the federal government.

- The legislative act sets forth sufficient standards to guide the administrative agency, and the act provides for criminal penalties for the violation of the administrative regulations created within the guidelines, and
- The administrative agency stays within the guidelines established by the legislative body in creating rules enforced by the criminal penalties, but
- The rules of the administrative agency "must be explicit and unambiguous in order to sustain a criminal prosecution; they must adequately inform those who are subject to their terms what conduct will be considered evasive so as to bring the criminal penalties of the Act into operation,"[40] and
- The determination (adjudication) of whether a violation of the **administrative crime** has occurred is made by a court with proper jurisdiction and is not made by the administrative agency

COMMON LAW, STATUTORY, AND ADMINISTRATIVE CRIMES

Common Law Crimes (used in the early days of the United States)	Custom, usage, or moral values, and concepts of a community built up over a period of many years	Plus	Adoption by judges of these customs or concepts in court decisions as crimes
Statutory Crimes (make up the vast majority of crimes today)	Enactment of bills by a legislative body	Plus	Signing of the bills by the chief executive officer (governor or president)
Administrative Crimes (used in the fields of health, drugs, stock market, taxation, and other areas the government must regulate)	Enactment of sufficient guidelines by a legislative body that are signed into law by the governor or president	Plus	Authorized regulatory agencies that create rules within the guidelines established by law

WHO WILL POLICE THE POLICE WHEN POLICE COMMIT CRIMES?

The criminal laws, goals, and protections discussed in this chapter depend on many societal elements for success, such as a concerned citizenry and a fair court system. One of the most important elements of the criminal law system is a professional, honest, corruption-free law enforcement body.

As a whole, police departments in the United States meet this standard. While citizens may file complaints about police misconduct with oversight bodies, such as police commissioners or inspectors general, statistics show that a large percentage of these complaints are without merit. When problems arise, most states and cities have internal accountability systems to review police misconduct. Los Angeles uses an "inspector general" office to oversee the police department. The FBI and the CIA use a similar system to monitor federal law enforcement agents. These inspector general offices have broad powers to review the practices and policies of the police department in the interest of the general public. Other cities and towns use civilian police and fire commissions to respond to citizen complaints and oversee hiring and firing of police officers.

However, there are times when the system of overseeing police conduct breaks down for one reason or another. When that happens, others are called in to "police the police," as happened in the cases discussed here.

Some cities, such as Los Angeles and Pittsburgh in recent times, have invited the U.S. Department of Justice to participate in resolving problems the city was having with the local police department. Likewise, the people of New Orleans experienced extensive police corruption, in particular when and after Hurricane Katrina struck the city. There were many troubling incidents during this period, including one incident where police fired into a crowd crossing a New Orleans bridge during the flooding after Katrina struck, killing two people and wounding four others.

In response to these problems, in 2010 the people of New Orleans, through their newly elected mayor, invited the Justice Department to come to the city and help clean up the 1,300-member police department. At the time Mayor Landrieu stated, "We have a systemic failure."

After hundreds of interviews and ten months of investigation the City and the Justice Department negotiated a far-reaching agreement to overhaul the New Orleans police department so as to

Summary

- In American jurisprudence, legislatures make criminal law, and the judicial branch determines when the criminal law has been violated.
- Criminal laws, which are public laws, are applicable generally to every person within the jurisdiction of the law. Private law, such as tort and contract law, applies only to the individuals affected by conduct of other individuals.
- The reasons for making conduct criminal are closely tied to the goals of the criminal law, which are to deter prohibited behavior, protect

society from dangerous individuals, and both punish and reform those convicted of a crime.
- The police power of a state can be broadly used to define criminal conduct, but it is subject to many constitutional limitations. Among these limitations are the principle of legality (*nulla poena sine lege*), the Ex Post Facto Clause, the bill of attainder clause, the "void for vagueness" and "overbreadth" doctrines, and the Due Process and Equal Protection Clauses.
- A "status" crime is one that makes a condition or character trait a crime without any requirement

improve safety in the city of New Orleans. The investigation showed that corruption and dysfunction existed throughout the NOPD. Evidence showed that police used excessive force on civilians, and that police failed to investigate serious crimes involving sexual assaults on women. The investigation also discovered serious problems of discrimination and lack of accountability for unlawful actions of police officers.

In July 2012 the city and the Justice Department signed a 122-page agreement (known as a "consent decree"). At the time, U.S. Attorney General Eric Holder stated,

> "[T]he ability of a police department to protect the community it serves is only as strong as the relationship it has with the community … Effective policing and constitutional policing go hand in hand."

On January 11, 2013, a federal court approved the consent decree and provided for immediate implementation of its recommendations. *See* Department of Justice, *Justice News*, January 11, 2012.

The New York Police Department (NYPD) is the largest police department in the United States, with 34,500 sworn officers. It also has one of the largest intelligence-gathering operations in the world, and has broad powers that extend into neighboring states. It has functioned very well since the 9/11 terrorist attacks devastated lower Manhattan.

However, late in 2012 the New York City Council concluded that the NYPD oversight review boards were too weak to deal with police misconduct. It urged the creation of an inspector general office, similar to that used by Los Angeles and the FBI, to serve as an additional overseer of the NYPD. New York City mayor Michael Bloomberg publicly opposed this effort, saying it was unnecessary because crime in New York was at an all-time low, and that current police leadership was working well. The issue will probably be decided in 2013, the year Mayor Bloomberg leaves office under term limits.

For more on the subject of police corruption see the May 2012 *FBI Bulletin* entitled "Police Corruption: An Analytical Look into Police Ethics," which can be found at http://www.fbi.gov.

of a criminal act. Such a crime inflicts a cruel and unusual punishment in violation of the Constitution.

- Common law crimes—those without a specific statute defining the criminal conduct—were at one time the predominant source of criminal law.

By the twentieth century virtually all criminal law was statutory, and under federal law no conduct may be adjudged criminal without a specific statutory authority.

Key Terms

Case Analysis and Writing Exercises

1. In Illinois, a 32-year-old man had consensual sex with a 17-year-old girl. He filmed the sexual encounter. Under Illinois law, a 17-year-old girl can give consent to having sex, so the man did not violate the statutory rape law. However, he was charged with possession of child pornography, because the Illinois statute defines child pornography as sexually explicit depictions of a child under 18. Does the man have any due process or equal protection arguments? How do you evaluate those arguments? See *People v. Hollins*, 971 N.E.2d 504 (Ill. 2012).

2. St. Louis, Missouri, enacted a municipal ordinance making it a crime for a person to engage in conduct on a public street so as to "impede either pedestrian or vehicular traffic." A person holding a sign that said "911 was an inside job" during rush hour traffic was prosecuted under this ordinance. Does the person have a good due process argument? See *Stahl v. St. Louis*, 687 F.3d 1038 (8th Cir. 2012).

3. In *Perry v. Brown*, 671 F.3d 1052 (9th Cir. 2012), *cert granted,* 133 S. Ct. 786 (2012), the Ninth Circuit Court of Appeals declared Proposition 8, adopted by the people of California, unconstitutional. Under Proposition 8, only persons of the opposite sex can be legally married in California. Assuming the Equal Protection Clause requires that the people of California must have a "rational basis" for limiting the marriage right to persons of the opposite sex, what do you think arguments for that rational basis would be? Why did they fail? What did the U.S. Supreme Court decide? See *Hollingsworth v. Perry,* 133 S. Ct. 2652 (2013).

4. Under the reasoning of *Robinson v. California* and *Jones v. City of Los Angeles,* discussed in this chapter, may the city of Chicago pass an ordinance that permits the police to order a homeless person found sleeping in an airport seating area to leave, and if that person does not, to arrest the homeless person? Is this ordinance the same or different from the ordinance declared unconstitutional in *Jones?* In what way or ways? See *Benson v. City of Chicago,* 2006 WL 2949521.

Endnotes

1. *Bell v. Keating,* 697 F.3d 445 (7th Cir. 2012).
2. Polls taken in recent years report that Americans have less confidence in the criminal justice system than they do in other institutions, such as public schools, the medical system, big business, news services, and organized labor. Only 23 percent of white and 25 percent of black respondents expressed confidence in the criminal justice system. By contrast, 61 percent of those polled expressed confidence in the police, and 52 percent felt confident in the Supreme Court. See Pew Research Center Report, May 1, 2012. A 2009 report by the Pew Institute indicated that only 48% of Hispanics and 36% of blacks believed the police would not unfairly use force in confrontations with members of these minorities.
3. Failure to protect citizens breeds crime. When the government fails to protect citizens, some persons are likely to take the law into their own hands. An example of private justice (vigilantism) may have occurred in a New York City subway in December 1984. Bernhard Goetz told New York police that he believed he was about to be robbed and that he produced a gun, shot his presumed assailants, and then left the scene. A New York grand jury would not indict Goetz for the shooting but did indict him for the illegal possession of a handgun. He was convicted and punished for that offense.

4. *United States v. Watson,* 146 F. Supp. 258, 262 (D.D.C. 1956), *judgment reversed,* 249 F.2d 106 (C.A.D.C. 1957).

5. 389 U.S. 347, 350 (1967).

6. *Kovacs v. Cooper,* 336 U.S. 77, 69 S. Ct. 448 (1949).

7. *Village of Belle Terre v. Boraas,* 416 U.S. 1, 94 S. Ct. 1536 (1974).

8. *Lawton v. Steele,* 152 U.S. 133 (1894).

9. State laws that require motorcycle operators and passengers to wear protective headgear have generally been upheld by state and federal courts as being a valid use of the police power of the state. The Supreme Court of Nebraska reviewed these cases in *Robotham v. State,* 488 NW.2d 533 (1992), in which the Nebraska motorcycle helmet law was upheld. However, some motorcycle groups have mounted considerable political opposition to state helmet laws. As a result, though in the 1970s 47 states had mandatory helmet laws, as of April 2012, when Michigan repealed its helmet law for adult riders, only nineteen states had mandatory helmet laws for all riders. The remaining states, except for Iowa, Illinois and New Hampshire, which do not have helmet laws, require helmets for young riders.

10. *Bykofsky et al. v. Borough of Middletown,* 401 F. Supp. 1242, *affirmed* 535 F.2d 1245 (3rd Cir. 1976) *rev. denied* 97 S. Ct. 394 (1976).

11. See the appendix of this text for applicable sections of the U.S. Constitution.

12. See the case of *United States v. Bass,* 404 U.S. 336, 92 S. Ct. 515 (1971), in which the U.S. Supreme Court held that "a fair warning should be given . . . in language that the common world will understand."

13. *Wall Street Journal,* September 27, 2011. "As Federal Crime List Grows, Threshold of Guilt Declines."

14. When good reasons are given, state governors are likely to grant a pardon for a felony or misdemeanor conviction. The pardon will wipe the slate clean for the person. Depending on the law of the state, governors have the authority and power to grant clemency in different ways. They may grant a pardon, or commute or modify a sentence. Such clemency may be conditional if authorized by state law.

15. Fifth Amendment to the U.S. Constitution.

16. Some states authorize store employees to arrest persons for shoplifting, which in most cases is a misdemeanor or is charged as an ordinance violation. The shoplifting statutes of other states authorize the store employees to detain the suspect until the police or sheriff arrives.

17. *Rochin v. California,* 342 U.S. 165, 168, 72 S. Ct. 205, 207 (1952).

18. See the May 2000 U.S. Supreme Court decision in *Carnell v. Texas,* 529 U.S. 513, where the sexual assault conviction of the defendant was reversed because a Texas law retroactively reduced the amount of proof necessary to support the sexual assault conviction in violation of the Ex Post Facto Clause.

19. See *United States v. Leach,* 639 F.3d 769 (7th Cir. 2011). Ten of the eleven federal circuit courts have heard and rejected ex post facto claims by adults.

20. *United States v. Juvenile Male,* 590 F.3d 924 (2010).

21. *United States v. Juvenile Male,* 131 S. Ct. 2860 (2011).

22. *Connolly v. General Construction Co.,* 269 U.S. 385, 46 S. Ct. 126 (1926).

23. See *Papachristou v. City of Jacksonville,* 405 U.S. 156, 162, 92 S. Ct. 839, 843 (1972) and *United States v. Harris,* 347 U.S. 612, 617, 74 S. Ct. 808, 811 (1954).

24. See *Coates v. City of Cincinnati,* 402 U.S. 611, 614, 91 S. Ct. 1686, 1688 (1971); and *Shuttlesworth v. City of Birmingham,* 382 U.S. 87, 90-91, 86 S. Ct. 211, 213-214 (1965).

25. *Grayned v. City of Rockford,* 408 U.S. 104, 109, 92 S. Ct. 2294, 2299 (1972).

26. See the December 1, 2012 *New York Times* article entitled "Push to Prosecute Drowsy Driving May Hinge on its Definition."

27. *Zwickler v. Koota,* 389 U.S. 241, 250, 88 S. Ct. 2294, 2299 (1972).

28. See *Grayned v. City of Rockford,* 408 U.S. 104, 109, S. Ct. 2294, 2299 (1972); *Dombrowski v. Pfister,* 380 U.S. 479, 486, 85 S. Ct. 1116, 1120 (1965).

29. See 119 S. Ct. 1849 (1999).

30. 370 U.S. 660, 82 S. Ct. 1417 (1962).

31. 392 U.S. 514, 88 S. Ct. 2145 (1968).

32. *Jones v. City of Los Angeles,* 444 F.3d 1118 (9th Cir.2006), *vacated* by settlement agreement, 505 F.3d 1006 (9th Cir. 2007). The city's agreement not to enforce a similar ordinance unless public shelter was available saved the ordinance in *Bell v. City of Boise,* 834 F. Supp.2d 1103 (D. Idaho 2011).

33. *Shivers v. State,* 688 S.E.2d 622 (Ga. 2010).

34. State statutes also often provide that marriage licenses may be issued to women beyond childbearing age who wish to marry a close relative. Under such statutes, two first cousins could marry if the woman met the requirements of the state statute. The results of six major medical studies reported in 2002 concluded that only small medical risks are seen in children born to first cousins who marry. The report recommended that the term *incest* should not apply to sexual relations between cousins—only to sexual relations between siblings and between parents and children. (See the *New York Times* article "Few Risks Seen to the Children of First Cousins," April 4, 2002.)

35. *Loving v. Virginia,* 388 U.S. 1 (1967). It is reported that there are now more than 1 million married interracial couples living in the United States. For example, U.S. Supreme Court Justice Clarence Thomas is a black man and is married to a white woman.

36. *Green v. U.S.,* 356 U.S. 165, 78 S. Ct. 632 (1958).

37. *U.S. v. Hudson and Goodwin,* 11 U.S. (7 Cranch) 32, 3 L. Ed. 259 (1812).

38. *Krulewitch v. U.S.,* 336 U.S. 440, 69 S. Ct. 716 (1949).

39. *U.S. v. Grimaud,* 220 U.S. 506, 31 S. Ct. 480 (1911).

40. *M. Kraus & Bros., Inc. v. U.S.,* 327 U.S. 614, 66 S. Ct. 705 (1946).

Jurisdiction

Rapport Press/Newscom

Detainees at the Guantanamo Naval Base detention center, Guantanamo Bay, Cuba. As of March 2013, 166 enemy combatants or suspected terrorists remain at "Gitmo". Attempts to close the detention center have stalled, and the U.S. Supreme Court has declined to take review of cases brought by inmates challenging the legality of the detention center.

OUTLINE

LEARNING OBJECTIVES

In this chapter we discuss the basis of the power of a court to try a defendant charged with a crime. The learning objectives for this chapter are as follows:

- Explain why a state has general power to make criminal laws and to prosecute those who violate the law.

- List the specific powers granted to the federal government to make criminal laws.

- Draw the boundaries of congressional power under the Commerce Clause to regulate actions through criminal laws.

- Explain the basis for an international court to claim jurisdiction over a person charged with a violation of international law.

- Describe the "Federal Domain."

- Identify the jurisdiction of military courts.

- Describe the jurisdiction of Indian tribal courts.

O n April 1, 2010, in the Indian Ocean just off Somalia, a small skiff carrying Somali pirates attacked the U. S. Navy frigate *U.S.S. Nicholas*. The frigate was disguised to resemble a vulnerable merchant ship as part of the Navy's efforts to combat piracy attacks in that part of the high seas. The Navy crew repulsed the attack, chased down the attackers, and captured them. They were transported to Virginia and charged in federal court with piracy under 18 U.S.C. § 1651. The defendants sought to have the charges dismissed, claiming U.S. federal courts lacked jurisdiction over their crimes.

The U.S. Constitution, article I, section 8, clause 10, gives Congress power "to define and punish Piracies and Felonies committed on the high Seas, and Offenses against the Law of Nations." Section 1651 states: "Whoever, on the high seas, commits the crime of piracy as defined by the laws of nations, and is afterwards brought into or found in the United States, shall be imprisoned for life." In 1820 the U.S. Supreme Court interpreted "piracy" under this statute as meaning "robbery or forcible depredations. . . . upon the sea." Based on this definition the defendants claimed the federal courts lacked jurisdiction because they did not complete the planned robbery of the *U.S.S. Nicholas*. The U.S. district court disagreed, and after the jury convicted the defendants of piracy the court sentenced them to life imprisonment. On appeal, the federal appeals court affirmed the convictions, stating that Congress intended in section 1651 to define "piracy" according to prevailing definitions in the "law of nations," which currently includes any violent attacks on a vessel at sea with the intent to rob or unlawfully detain passengers or crews for private gain.[1]

In this chapter we discuss the various jurisdictions in the United States with the power to make criminal laws and apply them to persons who act in violation of those laws. In some situations, like the *Key* case, one jurisdiction may "assimilate" criminal laws passed by another jurisdiction.

Jurisdiction of the Federal Government to Enact Criminal Laws

The American criminal justice system is a huge, complex system serving over 300 million people living in thousands of cities, counties, and parishes in the fifty states and in U.S. territories. As we saw in Chapter 1, under the American system of federalism, states have, through the exercise of the "police power," the primary responsibility for maintaining public order and safety within each state, including passing criminal laws.

The states' power to pass criminal laws is extremely broad. The U.S. Supreme Court has stated, ". . . crimes in the United States are what the law of the individual state makes them, subject to (constitutional) limitations".[2] The federal government, however, does not have an inherent "police power"[3] and is thus limited to enacting criminal laws pursuant to the powers granted to the federal government in the U.S. Constitution. Every federal criminal statute must trace its jurisdictional origin to one of those powers.

The power to regulate "Commerce . . . among the several states," found in Article I of the U.S. Constitution, is the basis of a great part of the authority the federal government has to enact criminal laws. If an activity (e.g., legal or illegal drug trade) involves more than a single state, Congress may regulate it by either criminal or civil laws.

On the other hand, an activity that is solely within a single state (e.g., maintenance of local public schoolyards) can be regulated by the state or local communities, but not by the federal government.

Jurisdiction Power to create and enforce laws. The federal government has power to create laws under the U.S. Constitution; each state has the legislative power to create laws effective within the state; city and village police departments have the power to enforce the laws; and local and state courts have power to sit in judgment of those accused of violating the laws.

EXAMPLE

The conviction under a federal statute of a Texas schoolboy for carrying a gun in a Texas schoolyard was held invalid by the U.S. Supreme Court in the case of *United States v. Lopez*.[4] Schoolyards are not ordinarily part of interstate commerce, and thus the U.S. Congress may not enact criminal laws regulating them. Texas and the school may punish Lopez for carrying a gun in a schoolyard, but the federal government may not. Most states make this conduct a specific crime.

Federal crimes fall into the following three classes, which reflect the power of the federal government under the Constitution to pass criminal laws:[5]

1. Crimes that affect interstate or international travel or communication, such as the Travel Act (interstate travel or use of U.S. mail, telephone, and so on to facilitate a crime); the Wire Fraud Act (interstate transfer of stolen or illegal funds); the National Stolen Property Act (interstate transfer or possession of stolen property); the Fugitive Felon Act (fleeing across state lines to avoid prosecution); the Mann Act (interstate prostitution); the Hobbs Act (extortion); and the Lindbergh Act (interstate kidnapping).
2. Crimes committed in places beyond the jurisdiction of any state. These include crimes committed in the District of Columbia and crimes committed overseas by the military or on U.S.-controlled ships or aircraft.
3. Crimes that interfere with the activities of the federal government.[6] Because the federal government's scope of activities is broad, this category of federal crimes is broad. It includes fraud by use of the U.S. mails, robbery of federally insured banks or savings and loan associations, violation of the federal income tax laws, and attempted overthrow of the U.S. government.

Situations in which the federal government has jurisdiction over a criminal homicide include the following:[7]

- Within the special maritime and territorial jurisdiction
- When death results from terrorism, sabotage, or certain cases of reckless or negligent destruction of federal transportation facilities
- When the victim is the president of the United States, the vice president, or successors to the office of the president
- When the victim is engaged in performing federal functions
- When the victim is killed "on account of the performance of his official duties"
- When death occurs in connection with a federally punishable bank robbery
- When the homicide occurs during an offense defined by the Civil Rights Act of 1968 (18 U.S.C.A. § 245)
- When an American citizen is killed anywhere in the world under the Comprehensive Crime Control Act of 1984

Federal Crimes Frequently Used to Support State and Local Enforcement

The power of state and local law officers generally can be exercised only within their borders. Federal law officers, however, are not limited to the borders of a state. For example, a child is missing and may have been kidnapped. If the child is not recovered after a few days, the FBI will presume that the child has been transported to another state, which will give the FBI jurisdiction to become involved in the case. In such cases, federal laws and agencies serve as important forces in complementing state and local law enforcement.

The following are some of the many federal crimes that are of particular and frequent interest to state law enforcement officers.

Unlawful Flight Statute (Fugitive Felon Act)   (18 U.S.C.A. § 1073): This law permits federal agencies to assist in locating state fugitives who may have fled from one state to another. The fugitive may be seeking to avoid prosecution for a felony or may be a potential witness in a felony case. If apprehended by a federal agency, the person will be returned to the state from which he (or she) fled. There is seldom federal prosecution under this law.

Federal Kidnapping   (18 U.S.C.A. § 1201): Kidnapping or abduction of any person for reward or ransom when interstate transportation or use of special maritime or territorial jurisdiction of the United States is involved.

Interstate Transportation of Stolen Motor Vehicles   (18 U.S.C.A. §§ 2312, 2313); **Interstate Transportation of Stolen Property** (18 U.S.C.A. § 2314): These are large areas of criminal activity. More than 1 million vehicles are stolen every year in the United States and more than 3 million vehicles are entered by individuals seeking valuables or accessories. Proof of interstate transportation is needed, as is proof that $5,000 or more of goods, wares, merchandise, security, or money were known to be stolen, converted, or taken by fraud. See Chapters 13 and 14 for further material on theft offenses.

Mail Thefts and Forging and Uttering of U.S. Treasury Checks   (18 U.S.C.A. §§ 1708 and 495): Every month millions of Social Security, pension, and other checks are sent through the mails, as well as packages and other materials. Many of these items are stolen, often coupled with the crimes of forging and uttering of regular checks and U.S. Treasury checks. See Chapter 12 for further material.

Federal Conspiracy   (18 U.S.C.A. § 371): The federal crime of conspiracy makes it illegal for two or more persons to "combine or conspire" either to commit any offense against the laws of the United States or to defraud the government of the United States. As there are a vast number of "laws of the United States" on the books, this covers a vast amount of territory. See Chapter 4 for material on the law of conspiracy.

RICO (Racketeer Influenced and Corrupt Organizations)   (18 U.S.C.A. §§ 1963 and 1964): See Chapter 18 for the history and wide use of this federal statute. State RICO statutes are commonly called "Little RICOs."

Mail Fraud   (18 U.S.C.A. § 1341): This crime prohibits the use of the mail as part of a scheme to defraud. Traditionally, the mail fraud statute has been aimed at con men, dummy corporations, fraudulent franchise schemes, and other frauds. It is sometimes used against corrupt public officials. Sending a letter proposing extortion, bribery, or blackmail, or a demand for ransom in a kidnapping case through the mail would ordinarily be held to justify federal jurisdiction. The mail fraud statute has been extended not only to mail but also to any facility in interstate or foreign commerce.

The Travel Act   (18 U.S.C.A. § 1952): This statute provides that "Whoever travels in interstate . . . commerce or uses any facility in interstate . . . commerce including the mail, with intent to. . . . (3) . . . promote, manage, . . . carry on . . . any unlawful activity. . . . shall be fined not more than $10,000 . . . or imprisoned for not more than five years, or both." (b) . . . "unlawful activity means (1) any business activity . . . (involving and including) prostitution offenses in violation of the laws of the State in which they are committed . . ." See Chapter 18 for further material on the Travel Act.

The Federal Domain—One-Third of America

The federal government owns and controls up to one-third of all of the land in the United States in the form of territories and federal enclaves.[8] The U.S. Constitution (Art. IV, Sec. 3) states that "In the Territories of the United States, Congress has the entire dominion and sovereignty . . . and has full legislative power over all subjects. . . ."

For example, the District of Columbia (Washington, D.C.) is one of the territories of the United States, and Congress thus has full police power to enact a full criminal code necessary to maintain public order and security in this large American city.

Federal Enclaves, Territories, and the Assimilative Crimes Act

federal enclaves
Federally owned and controlled lands.

Federal enclaves are federally owned and controlled lands. They can be found in all states. Military installations—such as Army posts, Navy yards, Air Force bases, Coast Guard stations, and Marine bases—are enclaves if they are within the borders of states. National parks and forests and federal buildings, such as post offices, federal court buildings, and federal office buildings, can under certain circumstances also be enclaves.

Before 1948, some of the enclaves had a degree of autonomy, which created some problems throughout the United States. In 1948, Congress passed the Assimilative Crimes Act (ACA) (18 U.S.C.A. § 13), which incorporates by reference the state criminal law of the surrounding state in force at the time of the defendant's conduct. In the case of *United States v. Sharpnack,* the U.S. Supreme Court held that the ACA was constitutional.[9] In that case, the defendant, who was a civilian, was convicted of committing sex crimes involving two boys at the Randolph Air Force Base, a federal enclave in Texas. In affirming the conviction, the Court stated:

> There is no doubt that Congress may validly adopt a criminal code for each federal enclave. It certainly may do so by drafting new laws or by copying laws defining the criminal offenses in force throughout the State in which the enclave is situated. As a practical matter, it has to proceed largely on a wholesale basis. Its reason for adopting local laws is not so much because Congress has examined them individually as it is because the laws are already in force throughout the State in which the enclave is situated. The basic legislative decision made by Congress is its decision to conform the laws in the enclave to the local laws as to all offenses not punishable by any enactment of Congress. Whether Congress sets forth the assimilated laws in full or assimilates them by reference, the result is as definite and as ascertainable as are the state laws themselves.

The ACA will generally not operate to incorporate a state law making conduct a crime if the federal government has already passed a statute or regulation that makes the same conduct a federal crime. For example, in *Lewis v. United States,*[10]

USE OF EXTRADITION AND FORCIBLE ABDUCTION TO BRING FUGITIVES BEFORE COURTS

Extradition

Extradition is the removal of a person from one jurisdiction to another so that he or she can face charges in the requesting jurisdiction.

International Extradition

The United States has more than eighty treaties in force with foreign countries that allow for extradition of fugitives between sovereign nations. A compilation of these treaties can be found in the notes following 18 U.S.C.A. Section 3181. There are many interesting and newsworthy international extradition cases, including the following:

General Manuel Noriega (former dictator of Panama)

Because Panama was the center of illegal drug and money laundering activities, the United States invaded Panama in 1990 in what was called the "biggest drug bust in history." More than 200 people were killed and $1 billion in property damage occurred. With the consent of the new Panamanian government, General Noriega was taken to Miami, Florida, and was convicted in a U.S. federal court of drug charges as a prisoner of war (746 F. Supp. 1506). After completing his sentence in Florida, Noriega was extradited to France in 2010, where he had been convicted *in absentia* of money laundering. Panama is also seeking extradition. The U.S. Supreme Court turned down Noriega's appeal in 2010 (*Noriega v. Pastrana*, No. 09-35).

Rendition and the War on Terror

"Extraordinary rendition" is the practice of seizing foreign nationals (mainly suspected terrorists) in one country and transporting them to another country for questioning or prosecution. The C.I.A. has been authorized to use this tactic by Presidents Clinton, Bush, and Obama, though President Obama has authorized this practice only for transportation to a jurisdiction that has authority to prosecute the person rendered. At least twenty-eight countries have served as hosts for suspected terrorists who have been transported under this practice.

Roman Polanski (Hollywood film director)

In 1977 Polanski was charged with drugging and raping a 13-year-old girl. He pleaded guilty to lesser charges but fled to France prior to his sentencing. After being a fugitive for years, he was taken into custody in 2010 by Swiss authorities on an international arrest warrant, pending extradition requested by Los Angeles prosecutors. After holding Polanski for several months of house arrest, the Swiss authorities refused to extradite Polanski, and declared him a free man. Polanski returned to his native France, a country that refuses to extradite its citizens. The arrest warrant on Polanski still exists, which effectively prevents him from travelling to the United States. The

the Supreme Court reversed a conviction of defendants for first-degree murder of a child under Louisiana law, which the federal district court held was applicable under ACA. Because Congress had passed a second-degree murder statute that would apply to the murder of a child on an Army base in Louisiana, the Supreme Court said that law should have been the basis for the defendants' conviction and sentencing.

victim of Polanski's crime, Samantha Geimer, has publicly stated that she wants the case dropped (*Los Angeles Times*, July 13, 2010). Polanski, famous for directing the Oscar-winning movie "The Pianist" in 2002, released the film "Carnage," starring Jodie Foster and Kate Winslet, in 2011.

Interstate Extradition. Article IV, Section 2 of the Constitution, as well as 18 U.S.C.A. Section 3182 and the Uniform Criminal Extradition Act,[a] provide that fugitives who flee to another U.S. state can also be extradited to the original state for trial.

Forcible Abductions. Two significant United States Supreme Court cases on forced abduction of criminal defendants are described in this table.

Case	Year	Facts	Holding
Ker v. Illinois, **119 U.S. 43**	1886	The defendant was forcibly abducted from Peru in South America to face trial for robbery in Illinois.	The U.S. Supreme Court affirmed the robbery conviction, holding that the forcible abduction was "no sufficient reason why the defendant should not answer" for the robbery charges.
Kasi v. Angelone, 300 F.3d 487	2002	The defendant was abducted in Pakistan and returned to Virginia to face charges he murdered two CIA agents outside CIA headquarters. He was convicted and sentenced to death. He appealed, claiming his abduction violated a treaty with Pakistan that deprived the Virginia courts of jurisdiction.	The Court of Appeals, relying on the U.S. Supreme Court's decision in *United States v. Alverez-Machain*, 112 S. Ct. 2188 (1992), held that the abduction did not violate the treaty with Pakistan and therefore under the rule in *Ker* the Virginia courts had jurisdiction to try Kasi for murder. Kasi was executed by lethal injection in 2002.

[a]Courts in the United States have held that the Uniform Criminal Extradition Act (adopted in many states) has changed the common law. Bail bond agents and law enforcement officers can be sued civilly for violations in failing to comply with the Uniform Criminal Extradition Act in forcing a person to return to another state without that person's consent. For cases involving bail bond agents, see *State v. Lopez,* 105 N.M. 538, 734 P.2d 778 (App. 1986), *review denied* 107 S. Ct. 1305 (1987), and *Loftice v. Colorado,* (Colo. Ct. App. 1988), *review denied* 490 U.S. 1047, 109 S. Ct. 1957 (1989). However, in many states bail bond agents continue to have greater arrest power than private citizens. See *Shiffiett v. State,* 319 Md. 275, 572 A.2d 167 (1990).

In a 1998 unanimous decision, the U.S. Supreme Court held that states have essentially no discretion and must extradite as long as proper procedures are followed and the wanted person's identity and fugitive status are confirmed. See *New Mexico v. Reed,* 118 S. Ct. 1860 (1998).

extradition The surrender of an accused criminal under the provisions of a treaty or statute by one authority to another having jurisdiction.

A federal statute must be of "general applicability" to prevent assimilation of a state criminal law. Thus, in the 2010 case of *United States v. Dotson*[11] the court upheld the conviction of civilians working on a military base for selling liquor to minors in violation of a state statute. While military regulations prohibited the same conduct, these regulations were not applicable to civilians working on the military base, and thus the state statute could be assimilated.

Nation-to-Nation Jurisdiction

Nations long ago realized that the world could not afford criminal jurisdictional gaps between nations. An alarming situation would exist, for example, if a person could commit a murder in the middle of the Atlantic or Pacific Ocean, with no nation having criminal jurisdiction. Because of this, the jurisdiction of each nation was extended to follow its ships over the high seas. The English common law gave jurisdiction to English courts over crimes committed on British ships and over crimes committed by British subjects on foreign ships.

United Nations Convention An agreement between nations on a specific subject, such as piracy at sea.

Today, statutes in both the United Kingdom and the United States give each country jurisdiction over crimes committed not only on ships but also on aircraft controlled by each country. By virtue of the international convention ratified by the Tokyo Convention Act of 1967, the courts of any country in the world may try individuals accused of piracy (armed violence at sea committed on a surface ship or an aircraft), even though the piracy was not committed within that country's territorial waters.[12] In addition to piracy, international conventions of nations have sought the elimination of slave trading, war crimes, hijacking and sabotage of civil aircraft, genocide, and terrorism.

Because of the statutes giving many nations jurisdictions over crimes, situations could exist in which a number of nations had concurrent jurisdiction (that is, the same crime could be tried in the courts of multiple nations).

EXAMPLE

A Romanian man was on an American airliner flying from Europe to New York City. While in the air, the man placed his hand on the genitals of a 9-year-old Norwegian girl. It was held that jurisdiction existed to try the man for sexual assault in a New York federal court under the federal "special aircraft jurisdiction."[13]

International Criminal Law

Article I, Section 8 of the U.S. Constitution provides that "The Congress shall have Power . . . to define and punish Piracies and Felonies committed on the high Seas, and Offenses against the Law of Nations." Over the years, the United States has participated with the other nations of the world to define international criminal law—*offenses against the law of nations*—by international treaties and international conventions. In 1928, sixty-three nations, including Germany and Japan, outlawed aggressive warfare by signing and agreeing to the Kellogg-Briand Pact. The brutalization of civilians and the deportation of people from their homelands to slave labor camps were defined and forbidden by the Geneva Convention of 1897.

After the end of World War II, the Allied nations tried some of the Nazi and Japanese military and civilian leaders for war crimes in trials held at Nuremberg, Germany,[14] and Tokyo, Japan. Special temporary criminal courts were created to try these leaders for crimes like ethnic cleansing, deportation of thousands of people to slave labor camps, use of slave labor in German and Japanese war factories, and killing millions of people.

Other temporary criminal courts were established in 1993 to sit at The Hague, Netherlands, to try persons charged with crimes committed during the civil war in the former Yugoslavia (Bosnia).[15] A similar court was established in Africa in 1994 after the slaughter of half a million Tutsi and Hutu people.[16]

CRIMES AGAINST SHIPS AND AIRCRAFT

Piracy or Hijacking	The seizure of a ship or aircraft while it is underway. This is a federal crime and also a crime against the law of nations.
Mutiny	When the crew (or some of the crew) seizes an aircraft or ship and revolt against lawful authority, the crime of mutiny is committed. In military law, the crime also includes an insurrection of soldiers against lawful authority.
Barratry or Barretry	Unlawful acts committed by the captain or officers of a ship that are contrary to their duties. The term is also used for the offense of frequently exciting and stirring up quarrels or lawsuits.

The Treaty of Rome, which was ratified in July 2002, created the world's first permanent war crimes court, the International Criminal Court (ICC), which sits at The Hague. This court has the power to investigate and prosecute people accused of genocide, war crimes, and crimes against humanity. The court's jurisdiction extends to all countries that ratified the treaty and to crimes committed in countries that ratified the treaty. The United States did not ratify the treaty and is currently negotiating for immunity from prosecution by the ICC for the U.S. military.

The ICC has issued only two verdicts in its 10-year history, both in 2012. In December of 2012 the court acquitted Mathieu Ngudjolo of charges he led a Congolese militia that raped and killed 200 people in a Congo village in 2003. Earlier in 2012 the ICC convicted Thomas Lubango of using children as soldiers in Congo battles. He was sentenced to 14 years in prison.

Jurisdiction of the Sea Approaches to the Continental United States

Each nation has established territorial jurisdiction in the waters and airspace around it. In 1983, the United States claimed sovereignty over waters extending 200 nautical miles from the United States and its possessions.[17] Vessels within these waters or on the high seas may be stopped under any of the following circumstances:

1. When there is reasonable suspicion or probable cause to believe that contraband such as illegal drugs exists or other criminal activity is occurring,[18] or
2. If a ship or vessel is without nationality (stateless) or "a vessel on the high seas whose nationality (is) unclear,"[19] or
3. With consent or a statement of no objection from the foreign nation where the vessel is registered, *United States v. Bustos-Useche,* 273 F.3d 622 (5th Cir. 2001), or if the ship meets the statutory definition of a "hovering vessel," *United States v. Gil-Carmona,* 497 F.3d 52 (1st Cir. 2007).

Maritime jurisdiction
Jurisdiction of the United States over actions within territorial waters of the United States on U.S. ships, or stateless vessels on the high seas.

Under maritime jurisdiction, criminal laws can be created to govern the conduct of persons (either Americans or aliens) aboard American ships or aircraft in the territorial waters, on the high seas, or elsewhere. The United States has jurisdiction of crimes committed on aircraft or vessels of whatever nationality in its internal waters and territorial seas and waters, including "stateless vessels," that is, vessels not operating under the authority of any nation.

The Crimes of Piracy, Felonies Committed on the High Seas, and Offenses Against the Law of Nations

When the U.S. Constitution was written, the Barbary Pirates were a problem that led the United States government to send the U.S. Marines to " . . . the shores of Tripoli" (memorialized in the Marine Hymn). The authority for this action is found in Article I, Section 8 of the U.S. Constitution, which provides, "The Congress shall have Power . . . to define and punish Piracies and Felonies committed on the high Seas, and Offenses against the Law of Nations."

Since around 2003, pirates operating off the coast of Somalia have plagued international shipping by seizing ships and holding their crews and passengers for ransom. At the height of these piracy attacks in 2008, hundreds of millions of dollars in ransom had been paid to the pirates. However, starting in 2009 many countries, including the NATO members, begin policing the seas near Somalia. While pirates took forty-six ships in 2009, and forty-seven in 2010, in 2011 only twenty-five were successfully attacked by the pirates. NATO reported in December 2012 that only five successful pirate attacks occurred in 2012, and none in the second half of the year. At that time, 140 persons were still being held hostage by pirates.

The Military, Martial, and War Powers Jurisdiction of the Federal Government

The constitution and Congressional acts give the federal government the power to raise and maintain a military force, to declare and conduct war, and in certain circumstances to use military forces within the several states. Incident to this power is the need for federal laws and courts to oversee the military forces and those associated with the military forces.

Jurisdiction of Military Courts[20]

A person who enters U.S. military service becomes subject to the Uniform Code of Military Justice.[21] Over the years, hundreds of thousands of military personnel have been tried for many offenses, ranging from "military" crimes such as desertion, unauthorized absences, willful disobedience of orders, and drunkenness on duty, to "civilian" crimes such as rape, murder, and drug violations that took place on leave.

Article I, sec. 8, cl. 14 of the U.S. Constitution gives Congress the power to "make Rules for the Government and Regulation of the land and naval Forces." From 1866 to 1960 the only requirement for military court jurisdiction over a defendant charged with a crime was the military status of the accused. The U.S. Supreme Court in 1969 held as an additional requirement that the offense charged must be "service connected" before a military court had jurisdiction; however, this limitation was eliminated by the Court in the 1987 case of *Solorio v. United States.*[22] It is now the law that the military justice system has jurisdiction to try a member of the armed service for *any* crimes committed (on- or off-base) as long as the accused was a member of the military service at the time of the alleged offense.

Civilians working with military units can also be subject to the Code of Military Justice. In 2011 the Army Court of Criminal Appeals upheld the court-martial of a civilian interpreter assigned to a combat unit engaged in "Operation Iraqi Freedom."[23]

When U.S. Citizens or Military Are in a Foreign Country

Americans who commit crimes in foreign countries, whether they are military personnel or tourists, are subject to prosecution before foreign courts. U.S. civilians have been sentenced to serve long prison terms in Turkey, Mexico, and other countries for narcotics violations—a grim reminder that sentences in some countries are quite severe.

U.S. military personnel are stationed in many countries throughout the world. A service person who commits a crime while off base, while off duty, and in a foreign country is subject to the jurisdiction of the laws of that country. Under a status of forces agreement (SOFA), or visiting forces agreement, which many countries have with the United States, the military person could be tried by the courts in the host country.[24] However, in many instances the prosecutor in the foreign country waives jurisdiction and turns the offender over to the U.S. military authorities for trial before a military court.

Examples of crimes that American service personnel have been charged with are murder of a West German taxi driver and desertion *(Plaster v. United States),*[25] rape of a South Korean girl,[26] and rape of a German woman *(Bell v. Clark).*[27]

Because foreign countries in the past generally wanted a continued U.S. military presence, they often waived criminal prosecution. However, in November 1995, Japan did not waive jurisdiction to try three U.S. servicemen for the rape of a 12-year-old schoolgirl on the island of Okinawa. Before a Japanese court, one serviceman pleaded guilty, and the other two admitted assisting in the rape. Thousands of Okinawans demonstrated to demand the removal of U.S. military bases from Okinawa and removal of the 47,000 U.S. troops from Japan.[28] In 2006, the governments of the Philippines and Italy asserted their right to try American military personnel for crimes committed in their countries.

The Use of National Guard Troops and Curfews to Assist Police with Riots and Disorders

Military forces have been used many times in the history of our country to maintain public order and enforce laws. In 1787, the year when the Constitution was formulated, the governor of Massachusetts used the militia to cope with Shays' Rebellion. President Washington sent federal troops into Pennsylvania to suppress the Whiskey Rebellion of 1794. Federal troops were used by President Lincoln to prevent the withdrawal of the southern states from the Union and to maintain public order. Federal troops remained in the South until the 1880s. During some of this time, **martial law** was in effect in the southern states where federal troops remained.

martial law
A state of military control over civilian populations as declared by state or federal government.

GENERAL JURISDICTION REQUIREMENTS

To charge a person with a crime, the state or federal government must

- Charge under a statute or ordinance that is constitutional on its face.
- Charge in the county or place in which the crime is alleged to have occurred.
- Produce the person to be charged before the court that will try him or her.

Indians who commit crimes while not within their reservation or Indian country are subject to the jurisdiction of the state or government, just as non-Indians who commit crimes while on a reservation or within Indian country can be tried (1) by the tribal court and punished by not more than 1 year of imprisonment and/or a $5,000 fine (25 U.S.C.A. § 1302(7)) or (2) before a U.S. federal court for the fourteen serious crimes under the federal Major Crimes Act (18 U.S.C.A. §§ 1153 and 3242).

U.S. military personnel may be tried by a military court for any crime they commit while they are in the military service, whether the offense was committed on or off a military base, ship, aircraft, and so on.

People who commit crimes on federal enclaves can be tried before

- A federal court, using the criminal code of the surrounding state under the Assimilative Crimes Act (18 U.S.C.A. § 13)
- A military court, if the person was a member of the U.S. armed services

Federal troops were used by President Eisenhower to secure compliance with Supreme Court school desegregation orders in Arkansas in 1957 and by President Kennedy in Mississippi in 1962 and in Alabama in 1963. In the 29-month period between January 1968 and the end of May 1970, National Guard troops were called upon 324 times to cope with urban riots and disorders and unrest on college campuses. In all the incidents in the 1950s, 1960s, and 1970s, troops and National Guard units provided assistance to civilian law enforcement agencies that had the primary responsibility for preserving public order. People arrested or taken into custody were brought before federal and state courts, where they were advised of their constitutional rights.

The Crime of the Improper Use of National or State Guard Troops

Posse Comitatus
Latin, meaning "power of the country." In the United States, it traditionally has referred to the military forces.

National Guard troops can lawfully be used in disaster assistance, search and rescue missions, domestic terrorist events, civil disturbances, and other specific circumstances when they are needed to protect constitutional rights, to support a request from a state, or to enforce federal authority. However, the 1878 Posse Comitatus Act makes it a federal offense to use military forces to execute the law without specific congressional authorization.[29]

The December 2001 *FBI Law Enforcement Bulletin* article "Military Support of Domestic Law Enforcement: Working Within Posse Comitatus" (http://www.fbi.gov) lists specific circumstances where U.S. military forces may be called upon to directly perform domestic law enforcement duties.

FIGURE 2.1 Who Backs Up the Police Officer on the Street?

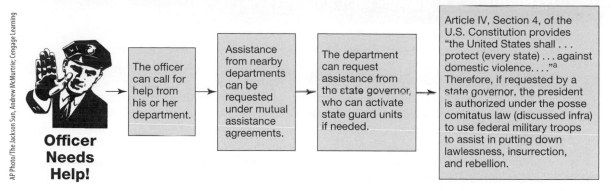

Officer Needs Help!

The officer can call for help from his or her department.

Assistance from nearby departments can be requested under mutual assistance agreements.

The department can request assistance from the state governor, who can activate state guard units if needed.

Article IV, Section 4, of the U.S. Constitution provides "the United States shall . . . protect (every state) . . . against domestic violence. . . ."[a] Therefore, if requested by a state governor, the president is authorized under the posse comitatus law (discussed infra) to use federal military troops to assist in putting down lawlessness, insurrection, and rebellion.

[a]States may not maintain armed forces without the consent of the U.S. Congress: Article I, Section 10, of the U.S. Constitution provides that "No State shall, without the Consent of Congress . . . keep Troops, or Ships of War in Time of Peace." (See the appendix of this text for applicable sections of the U.S. Constitution.)

Figure 2.1 illustrates the power that stands behind the neighborhood police officer in the United States.

Indian Tribes within the United States

Of the almost 1.5 million Native Americans in the United States, more than half live on reservations located mainly in seventeen states. The U.S. Supreme Court has pointed out that the 310 recognized Indian tribes in the United States "possess those aspects of sovereignty not withdrawn by treaty or statute, or by implication as a necessary result of their dependent status."[30]

In 1975 and again in 1977, the U.S. Supreme Court held that

Indian tribes are unique aggregations possessing attributes of sovereignty over both their members and their territory, *Worcester v. Georgia*, 31 U.S. 6 Pet. 515, 557 (1832), they are "a separate people" possessing the power of regulating their internal and social relations. *United States v. Mazurie*, 419 U.S. 544, 557, 95 S. Ct. 710, 717 (1975).[31]

Indian tribal governments have Indian tribal courts and Indian police. However, criminal jurisdiction in Indian country and on Indian reservations is complex. Prior to the passage of Public Law 280 in 1953 (and its amendment in 1968), criminal jurisdiction in Indian country was shared between the federal government and Indian tribal governments.

Public Law 280 changed this and required that in six states, federal authority be transferred to those states. However, the law permitted any of the six states to return criminal jurisdiction to the federal government if that state so desired. This would have to be done with the approval of the local tribe members.

The National Institute of Justice Report #229886 of 2010 states that polls among tribal members rated the performance of tribal police higher than that of state, county, or federal law officers. Interestingly, a good number of tribal police are non-Indian, and often these officers are deputized not only as tribal police officers but also as state and federal officers.

THE TRIBAL LAW AND ORDER ACT (TLOA) OF 2010

Some of the more than 500 recognized Indian tribes are prosperous, owing to casino operations or because valuable mineral or oil deposits exist on their land. But many Indian tribes, particularly those located in the Southwest and the Northern Plains, are very poor. Crime has always been a problem in these poor tribal areas. The May 2012 *FBI Bulletin* entitled "Indian Country and the Tribal Law and Order Act of 2010" states that criminal victimization of Indians living in Indian country is 2.5 times greater than that of other ethnic or racial groups. Speaking to this problem, U.S. Senator Byron Dorgan of North Dakota stated that because of budget cuts and increased criminal caseloads, prosecutors decline to prosecute more than 50% of the murders in Indian country, and 75% of rapes and sexual assaults. (See *N.Y. Times*, 8/2/2012, "Tribal Law and Order.)

In response to these problems, Congress passed the TLOA in 2010. It provides, in part, that

- Federal departments and agencies (FBI, DEA, ATF, Justice Department, and others) "shall coordinate" with their tribal counterparts on the status of investigations and the use of relevant evidence in tribal courts. This is hoped to make it easier to obtain convictions in murder, rape, and other serious crimes.
- Tribal courts may now sentence convicted persons to up to 3 years in prison per offense, with a maximum of 9 years for multiple-offense convictions. There is a $15,000 limit on fines. Previously, tribal courts could only prosecute misdemeanors.
- Native Americans sentenced for felony convictions may now be imprisoned in tribal facilities (if approved by the Bureau of Indian Affairs) or federal facilities at federal expense under a pilot program that allows up to 100 inmates.
- Tribal law enforcement must now be notified whenever a prisoner convicted of a sex offense, drug trafficking, or a violent crime is released into Indian country. This was not previously required.
- If crimes are not prosecuted because of a lack of funds or interest, tribes may seek federal intervention and federal prosecution.

Indians who commit crimes while not on or within their reservation or Indian country are subject to the laws of the state or government where the crime was committed.

Summary

- Each state has general power to make criminal laws. The federal government has only the power delegated to it in the U.S. Constitution.
- The federal government has specific power to make laws including criminal laws under parts of the Constitution such as the Commerce Clause, as well as power to make criminal laws for federal territories, enclaves, military posts, and as applied to crimes against federal employees or officers.
- The Commerce Clause gives the federal government power to regulate actions by use of criminal laws only if the actions involve or affect interstate commerce.
- International conventions, treaties, and other agreements between nations can confer power on

the federal government to make criminal laws. All countries, including the United States, have the power to regulate their shores and the sea area around those shores.

- The federal domain consists of substantial land areas within the United States, Puerto Rico, and other territories and enclaves. It also includes sea and air approaches to the United States.

- U.S. citizens serving in the military may be prosecuted for crimes in military courts, including when they are serving in foreign countries.

- Indian tribal courts have power to try Indians charged with crimes on an Indian reservation. Crimes committed by Indians outside a reservation are subject to state or federal prosecution.

Key Terms

jurisdiction, p. 36
federal enclaves, p. 39
extradition, p. 41

United Nations Conventions, p. 42
maritime jurisdiction, p. 43
martial law, p. 45

posse comitatus, p. 46

Case Analysis and Writing Exercises

1. Assume state and federal officers raid a cockfighting facility located in Oklahoma, but on land held by the Kiowa tribe, and thus in "Indian country" under federal law. A non-Indian is arrested and charged with violation of an Oklahoma statute making it a crime to be a spectator at an illegal cockfighting venue. Which jurisdiction—federal, state, or tribal—has jurisdiction to prosecute the defendant? May a federal court exercise jurisdiction using the Assimilative Crimes Act? See *United States v. Langford*, 641 F.3d 1195 (10th Cir. 2011).

2. Congress has enacted a statute, 18 U.S.C. § 2285 (a), which makes it a federal crime to operate a submersible or semi-submersible vessel in international waters, if the vessel does not have a national marking. The statute is aimed at the illegal drug trade, which uses this type of vessel to move drugs around the world. Do federal courts have jurisdiction under the Constitution to prosecute persons operating such vessels in international waters? What article of the Constitution confers such authority on federal courts? See *United States v. Saac*, 632 F.3d 1203 (11th Cir. 2011).

3. **The thief of Baghdad case**. A resident of Jordan was hired to work in the U.S. embassy in Baghdad, supervising shipping and customs. He developed a scheme to defraud the embassy, and used the scheme to steal money intended for the embassy. When the F.B.I. discovered the scheme it tricked the defendant into coming to the United States, where he was arrested and charged with violating 18 U.S.C.A. § 641. At his trial, the defendant contended the federal statute did not apply to "extra-territorial" conduct such as his, and thus he could not be convicted under the statute. Was he correct? See *United States v. Ayesh*, 702 F.3d 162 (4th Cir. 2012), cert. denied 133 S. Ct. 1619 (2013).

4. The federal kidnapping statute, 18 U.S.C. § 1201, provides that it applies to kidnappings where the victim is "willfully transported" across state lines (hence the Commerce Clause connection). Typical cases under this statute involve situations where the kidnappers force the victim into a car and then drive to another state. Does a federal court have jurisdiction to prosecute a defendant where the victim crosses a state line because of a deceptive message left on his cell phone by the defendant? See *United States v. Wills*, 234 F.3d 174 (4th Cir. 2000), *cert. denied*, 533 U.S. 953 (2001).

Endnotes

1. *United States v. Dire,* 680 F.3d 446 (4th Cir. 2012).

2. *Rochin v. California,* 72 S. Ct. 204 (1952).

3. "[T]he Constitution . . . withholds from Congress a plenary police power." *United States v. Lopez,* 514 U.S. 549, 566. (1995).

4. 514 U.S. 549 (1995).

5. In *United States v. Lopez, supra,* the U.S. Supreme Court stated that

   > We have identified three broad categories of activity that Congress may regulate under its commerce power. . . . [First] "[T]he authority of Congress to keep the channels of interstate commerce free from immoral and injurious uses has been frequently sustained, and is no longer open to question." Second, Congress is empowered to regulate and protect the instrumentalities of interstate commerce, or persons or things in interstate commerce, even though the threat may come only from intrastate activities.
   >
   > . . . [F]or example, the destruction of an aircraft (18 U.S.C. § 32), or . . . thefts from interstate shipments (18 U.S.C. § 659). Finally, Congress' commerce authority includes the power to regulate those activities having a substantial relation to interstate commerce, Jones & Laughlin Steel, 301 U.S., at 37, that is, those activities that substantially affect interstate commerce. 514 U.S., at 558.

6. If federal property is intentionally damaged or destroyed, the federal government ordinarily has jurisdiction over the matter. When state property is intentionally damaged or destroyed within that state, the state government has jurisdiction. What about a situation in which the property is internationally owned, such as the United Nations building in New York City? In the 1976 case of *People v. Weiner* (85 Misc. 2d 161, 378 N.Y.S.2d 966), the defendant was charged with criminal mischief for having sprayed red paint on the outside wall of the UN headquarters. The New York Criminal Court held that it had jurisdiction over the person of the defendant and the offense.

7. This material was presented in the *Working Papers of the National Commission on Reform of Federal Criminal Laws,* vol. 2, p. 832.

8. The *National Geographic* magazine article "To Use or to Save" (October 1996) states that the federal domain "covers a third of the nation, more than 700 million acres, a public trust unmatched in the world."

9. 355 U.S. 286, 78 S. Ct. 291 (1958).

10. 118 S. Ct. 1135 (1998).

11. 615 F.3d 1162 (9th Cir. 2010).

12. Indeed, under international law, piracy has always been viewed as every nation's problem: "A pirate, under the laws of nations, is an enemy of the human race. Being the enemy of all, he is liable to be punished by all." *United States v. Ali,* 2012 WL 2870263 (D.D.C. 2012), quoting Chief Justice John Marshall.

13. *United States v. Georgescu,* 723 F. Supp. 912 (1989). The "special aircraft jurisdiction" also gives federal courts concurrent jurisdiction with a state over which an aircraft was flying when a crime is committed aboard the aircraft. *United States v. Moradi,* 706 F.Supp.2d 639 (D. Md. 2010).

14. See the *New York Times* article "Trying to Make Sure That War Crimes Aren't Forgotten or Go Unpunished," September 22, 1997.

15. The first person convicted for Balkan war crimes was a Croat. See the *New York Times* article "Croat Is First to Be Convicted (in The Hague) by Balkan War Crimes Panel," June 1, 1997. The article points out that of seventy-six people charged with Balkan war crimes, only nine were in custody.

    A Bosnian Serb who returned to live in Germany was sentenced to life imprisonment by a German court for war crimes committed in Bosnia. After the man was arrested in Germany, the German government agreed to try him under German law because the United Nations War Crimes Tribunal in The Hague stated it was overburdened. See the *New York Times* article "Bosnian Serb Is Sentenced to Life Term for Genocide," September 27, 1997.

16. The United Nations established the United Nations Tribunal for Rwanda in 1994. It was responsible for prosecuting persons suspected of committing the crime of genocide.

17. During Prohibition in the 1920s (when the consumption and sale of alcoholic beverages were illegal in the United States), European ships would sell liquor to Americans in "Rum Row," international waters off the East Coast of the United States. The U.S. Supreme Court upheld a Coast Guard vessel coming alongside Lee's ship and observing illegal whiskey on the deck. Lee's conviction was affirmed in the case of *United States v. Lee,* 47 S. Ct. 746 (1927).

18. *Singleton v. United States,* 789 F. Supp. 492 (D. Puerto Rico 1992).

19. Article I, Section 8, of the U.S. Constitution provides (in part) that

    > The Congress shall have Power . . .To define and punish Piracies and Felonies committed on the high Seas, and Offenses against the Law of Nations; To declare War . . . and make Rules concerning Captures on Land and Water; To raise and support Armies; . . . To provide and maintain a Navy; To make Rules for the Government and Regulation of the land and naval Forces; To provide for calling forth the Militia to execute the Laws of the Union, suppress Insurrections and repel Invasions; . . . To make all Laws which shall be necessary and proper for carrying into Execution the foregoing Powers, and all other Powers vested by this

Constitution in the Government of the United States, or in any Department or Officer thereof.

Article II of the U.S. Constitution provides in part that

Section 1. The executive Power shall be vested in a President of the United States of America. . . . Section 2. The President shall be Commander in Chief of the Army and Navy of the United States, and of the Militia of the several States, when called into the actual Service of the United States.

20. 10 U.S.C.A. §§ 801–940 (Supp. V. 1970) amending 10 U.S.C.A. §§ 801–940 (1964).

21. 395 U.S. 258, 89 S. Ct. 1683 (1969).

22. 483 U.S. 435, 107 S. Ct. 2924 (1987).

23. *United States v. Ali,* 70 M.J 514 (Army Ct. Crim. App. 2011).

24. The best-known SOFA (status of forces agreement) is that with the NATO countries, where there has been a large U.S. military commitment since 1945 in a continuous effort to keep the peace.

25. 720 F.2d 340 (4th Cir. 1983).

26. The military magazine "Stars and Stripes" reported in 2011 that military authorities were permitting Korean courts to prosecute soldiers charged with rape and other offenses, and that in 2011 a military curfew was reinstated in South Korea.

27. 437 F.2d 200 (4th Cir. 1971).

28. See the *New York Times* article "One Pleads Guilty to Okinawa Rape; 2 Others Admit Role," November 8, 1995.

29. 18 U.S.C. § 1385 (1878).

30. 430 U.S. 641, 645 (1977).

31. *United States v. Antelope*, 430 U.S. 641, 645 (1977).

Essential Elements of a Crime

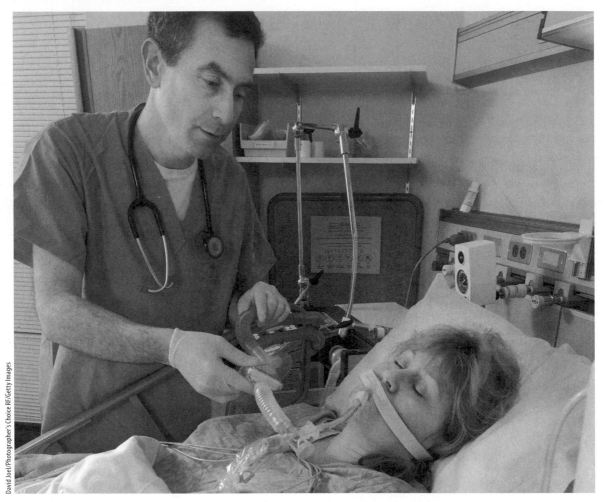

David Joel/Photographer's Choice RF/Getty Images

Victims of criminal assaults who lose essential brain functions may be kept alive by artificial means. Although the artificial means may be removed by physicians or family members, the death of the victim may still be treated as caused by the assault, resulting in a charge of murder.

OUTLINE

LEARNING OBJECTIVES

In this chapter we examine the acts or states of mind that constitute elements of a crime. The learning objectives for this chapter are the following:

- Learn the meaning of and difference between *actus reus* and *mens rea*.
- Identify when a criminal statute includes a requirement of a specific intent.
- Write a simple criminal charge that does not have as an element a specific intent.
- List the Model Penal Code degrees of culpability and their accompanying mental states.
- Distinguish between motive and intent.
- Identify some of the similarities of strict liability crimes.
- Explain why the year-and-a-day rule is a rule of proximate cause.
- Identify the relationship between use of presumptions in the prosecution's case and the Due Process Clause.
- Explain why a conclusive presumption is prohibited.

O n August 22, 2012, United States Secret Service agents arrested Anton Caluori, a Seattle, Washington resident, and charged him with violation of 18 U.S.C. § 871. That statute makes it a crime, punishable by up to 5 years in prison, to send messages (mail, telephone, or e-mail) stating the sender's intent to kill the president of the United States. Caluori was alleged to have sent e-mail messages to an open FBI e-mail address, stating he intended to use explosives to kill President Obama.

The statute discussed above is an exception; criminal statutes do not usually provide for punishment based only on intent, even if the intent is clearly expressed. Criminal laws focus on prohibited behavior. People usually cause harm by their actions, not just their thoughts or intentions. Moreover, in many situations it is appropriate to punish prohibited actions (called the *actus reus*) only if they are accompanied by a required mental state (called the *mens rea*). As the old saying goes, "even a dog knows the difference between being kicked and stepped on." Often, the required mental state for the crime to occur is "knowledge" about some aspect of the crime. For example, it is a federal crime to "knowingly"

use a fake identity belonging to another person. What must the defendant "know"? That an identity card is faked? That the identity belongs to another person? Or, under the laws in virtually all states making it a crime for a convicted felon to "knowingly" possess a firearm, when does a person "know" he is in possession of a firearm? What if a passenger in his car has a firearm in his possession? In this chapter we discuss the elements of crimes, focusing on both the physical act—the *actus reus*—and the mental state, the *mens rea*.

True Crimes and Strict Liability Crimes

From the development of common law until modern times, all crimes had two essential elements: (1) the physical act or omission and (2) a mental requirement known as criminal intent or purpose. Some writers refer to such crimes as *true crimes*. Today, true crimes continue to make up a considerable number of crimes in any criminal code.

In the 1920s and 1930s, state legislatures began creating criminal laws that did not require the mental element essential to true crimes. This relatively new type of crime is called a *strict liability crime,* or regulatory offense. Strict liability crimes can be found in criminal laws pertaining to traffic violations, narcotics, liquor, sanitation, hunting, and pure-food requirements. In strict liability crimes, the government does not have to prove intent or purpose and must show only that the accused performed the act or omission charged or brought about the results that are alleged and shown. Most crimes have some form of mental requirement as an element of the crime. The various forms of mental requirement found in those crimes are discussed in the following section.

Crimes Requiring Proof of Mental Fault

reasonable doubt Proof beyond a reasonable doubt means that it is not enough to prove it was more likely than not that an element of the crime was true. The proof must be such that a reasonable person could not conclude the element was not true.

actus reus The criminal act.

mens rea The criminal intent or state of mind.

Before a person may be convicted of a crime that requires proof of mental fault, the government must prove the following elements beyond a **reasonable doubt:**

- *The external physical act:* That the conduct or act forbidden by the law of the jurisdiction was in fact committed by the defendant.
- *The internal mental element:* That the act or omission was accompanied by a state of mind required by the criminal statute.

The Latin term **actus reus** ("guilty act") is used by courts and writers to describe the essential physical act, and the term **mens rea** ("guilty mind") is used to describe the essential mental requirement. State statutes vary on how they define the degrees of criminal intent. That is, with respect to an element of the offense, the mental state of the defendant as to that element can have various formulations. For example, to be convicted of the crime of possession of stolen property, almost all state statutes require that the defendant have knowledge that the property was stolen. The *actus reus* is the physical possession of the property; the *mens rea* is the intent to possess the property; the scienter (knowledge) element is knowledge that the property was stolen. (Scienter is discussed later in this chapter.) Other crimes might require only that the defendant was negligent about an element of the crime. For example, in most states the crime of vehicular homicide can be established by proof that the defendant unintentionally caused the death of another, while operating a motor vehicle recklessly or with gross negligence.

The **Model Penal Code (MPC)** is a proposed criminal code drafted by the American Law Institute, a group of lawyers, judges, and law professors. Many states have used parts of the MPC when drafting their own criminal codes. Section 2.02 of the MPC suggests the following formulation of the mental element:

> *Minimum Requirements of Culpability.* Except as provided in Section 2.05, a person is not guilty of an offense unless he acted purposely, knowingly, recklessly, or negligently, as the law may require, with respect to each material element of the offense.

The U.S. Supreme Court has never created or announced a doctrine requiring proof of *mens rea* in all crimes and in all cases before an accused can be held accountable for his or her acts [1] Therefore, the states are generally free to create criminal laws that do not require proof of *mens rea* or to create criminal laws requiring different degrees of mental fault or mental guilt. But if a degree of mental guilt is made an element of the crime by law, the prosecutor must then prove this essential element of the crime, as well as prove the acts taken together with this mental element.

Thinking of committing a crime without performing a criminal act is not a crime. If a person with criminal thoughts does nothing to carry out those thoughts, no crime has occurred. Government cannot punish thoughts alone. To show that a true crime has occurred, the state must show that the external physical act and the internal mental state essential to that crime occurred at the same time. Even crimes such as conspiracy, in which two or more people share their thoughts about a crime, generally require that the conspirators do at least one physical act in furtherance of the conspiracy (see Chapter 4).

In some instances, an act without the required mental state (guilty mind) is no crime. For example, a person incapable of entertaining the required criminal mind because of legal insanity has not committed a crime. A student who picks up someone else's book or briefcase by mistake has performed a physical act, but without the guilty or criminal state of mind necessary for the crime of theft, no crime has been committed. However, suppose that the student keeps the book or briefcase for two days and then, realizing the mistake, decides to keep the property. The taking and keeping of the property for two days has been a continuous act in the eyes of the law. The crime of theft occurred when the intent to deprive the true owner of permanent possession concurred with the act of taking and retaining possession.

The requirement that the mental fault and prohibited act must both be present in crimes requiring mental fault is usually called "concurrence." **Concurrence**

Model Penal Code (MPC) Proposed criminal law developed by the American Law Institute, a group of lawyers, judges, and teachers. Many states have modeled their criminal codes on the Model Penal Code.

Concurrence The requirement in crimes requiring proof of mental intent that the forbidden act and guilty mind must occur at the same time or otherwise be linked. For example, trustees, guardians, or lawyers might have possession of another person's money (physical act). However, for the crime of embezzlement to occur they must intentionally and wrongfully misappropriate this money (forbidden act and guilty mind).

requires a connection between the mental fault and the forbidden act, in the sense that the mental fault "drives" or "actuates" the forbidden act. For example, one who innocently enters a residence of another, but once inside decides to steal the occupant's property, cannot under most state statutes be convicted of burglary, because that crime requires the mental intent to enter the house for the purpose of committing a crime. The forbidden act occurred, but there was no concurrence of the required mental fault. Or, a person may both desire and make plans for the death of another, but if he subsequently and inadvertently kills that person in an automobile accident he cannot be guilty of murder. His mental state of wanting to kill the other person did not "drive" or "actuate" the act that caused the death.

Although the forbidden act and the guilty mind must concur, the resulting harm need not take place at the same time.

EXAMPLE ▶ While A is on vacation, X rigs a spring gun to A's front door (forbidden act), setting it with the intention that A be killed when he opens the door (guilty mind). Two weeks after the spring gun is set in place, A returns from vacation and is shot and killed when he opens his door.

In the example given, the *actus reus* and the *mens rea* concurred, but the results did not occur until A opened the door two weeks after the act with intent to kill was performed.

Actus Reus: The Forbidden Act or Omission

Most criminal laws forbid specific acts, and a few punish the failure (omission) to carry out a legal duty. The act forbidden or commanded by the law is described in the definition of each particular offense, usually in terms of the prohibited conduct and the harm or the wrong that occurs. In the crime of murder, the death of the victim caused by the defendant's forbidden act or omission is the harm and the wrong. In the crime of larceny, the loss of personal or movable property caused by the defendant's wrongful taking and carrying away is the harm and the wrong.

The manner in which the harm or wrong can be caused varies considerably. A murder can be committed by use of a gun, a knife, a blow, poison, or by any one of many other acts. The harm or the wrong done usually varies from crime to crime, but sometimes two crimes embody the same harm or wrong.

All criminal homicides share the same harm or wrong, which is the death of a person. Homicides differ from one another primarily because of the differing states of mind of the offenders at the time they cause the harm or wrong, which is the death of another person. Both murder and manslaughter involve the death of a person, but because of the different mental states required for a conviction, they are different crimes.

Just as different mental states may result in different crimes charged, so too may different acts be made criminal where more than one person is a party to a crime. As a result, the *actus reus* may be different for each party's involvement in the crime. A *party to a crime* could be (1) a person who actually and physically commits the crime, (2) a person who conspires in the planning of the crime or orders that the crime be committed, or (3) a person who aids and assists in the commission of the

ELEMENTS OF A CRIME: *ACTUS REUS*

Virtually every crime is defined in a statute. The statute describes the prohibited conduct, and in many cases also describes a prohibited result. The conduct (or omission) and result specified are the *actus reus* elements of the crime, and must be proved by the prosecution. In some cases, the statute may designate circumstances that accompany the prohibited conduct. These usually are called "attendant circumstances," and can also be elements of the crime.

EXAMPLE: A statute makes "discharging a gun in a public place" a crime. The conduct is discharging a gun, and "in a public place" is an attendant circumstance; both are elements of the crime and must be proved.

EXAMPLE: A statute makes it a crime to "drive a vehicle negligently so as to cause the death of another person." The result, the death of another person, is an element of the crime, and is part of the *actus reus* of the crime.

In addition to the *actus reus* elements of a crime, many statutes also require a particular mental state as part of the crime. In such cases, the required mental state must also be proved. The mental state requirement is discussed later in this chapter.

crime. All state criminal codes define parties to a crime and make each of the parties to a crime equally liable for the crime (see Chapter 4).

The different *actus reus* for parties to a crime are illustrated by the following example:

EXAMPLE

A hires B and C to murder X. A tells B and C how and where she wants X to be murdered. B is the vehicle driver and lookout while C commits the murder. A hired and ordered the killing.

C's act in killing X is the *actus reus* of the direct commission of the crime, murder. B's acts (driver and lookout) are the *actus reus* of aiding and abetting murder. A jury could easily find that all three parties (particularly A) conspired and agreed in the planning of the murder, which is the *actus reus* of the crime of conspiracy.

The state has the burden of proving beyond a reasonable doubt the *actus reus* element of every offense, and the jury must unanimously agree that the state has proved the *actus reus* elements before they may find a defendant guilty.

The criminal acts must be volitional; that is, the act must be the product of conscious though. Sleepwalking, experiencing a seizure, and many reflexive actions are not volitional and thus don't satisfy the *actus reus* requirement. This requirement of volition differs from *mens rea*, discussed below. Consider this example: A woman's arm lifts up and strikes another person. If the arm moved as a reflexive action, or during a seizure, or if another person caused the arm to move, the woman has not performed a conscious act, and the movement of her arm cannot satisfy the *actus reus* requirement of a criminal statute. However, if the woman made the conscious decision to raise her arm, she has acted volitionally, and satisfied any *actus reus* requirement. The *mens rea* requirement, if any, would depend on her mental state that accompanied her act in raising her arm. Did she intend to strike another person? Did she raise her arm in a crowded elevator, in reckless disregard of others? Or, did she reasonably believe she was alone in a room? These are *mens rea* questions.

A 2012 decision of the Washington Supreme Court illustrates a troublesome aspect of the volitional requirement. The prosecution must prove all the elements of a crime charged. In the example above, this would seem to mean the prosecution cannot simply prove the woman's arm *was raised*. It must prove the woman *raised her arm*. However, in *State v. Deer*[2] this was not the result. In that case, a woman was charged with having sex with a boy under the age of 16, a strict liability crime in Washington (and elsewhere). The woman did not contend the sexual acts did not occur, but asserted she was asleep during the sexual acts, and that thus the sexual acts were not volitional. The Washington Supreme Court agreed that proof she was asleep would make the sexual acts non-volitional; however, the court rejected her claim that the state was required to prove she was not asleep. All the state needed to prove, the court said, was that the sexual acts occurred. The woman's contention that she was asleep was an affirmative defense, the court said, and she carried the burden of proof on that defense.

Mens Rea: **The Guilty Mind**

A cardinal principle of criminal law pertaining to true crimes was long ago expressed in Latin as *actus non facit reum nisi mens sit rea* ("an act does not make a person guilty unless the mind is guilty").

WHEN FAILURE TO ACT IS A CRIME

State and federal criminal codes usually identify and prohibit specific, affirmative actions, called crimes of commission. Examples of these crimes are the prohibitions against murder, robbery, and similar crimes where the crime consists of taking defined actions.

A small percentage of crimes in criminal codes are crimes of omission—failure to act when a duty or obligation is imposed upon persons under certain circumstances. The following are examples of crimes of omission that can be found in state criminal codes. Using the statutes from your state's criminal code, find a section that defines and makes criminal the following crimes of omission:

1. Failure to report the death of a child
2. Failure to report the location of a human corpse
3. Failure by a parent or guardian to provide adequate food, clothing, shelter, or medical care to a child under the person's care and supervision
4. Failure to submit to a Breathalyzer or other similar test when lawfully requested to do so by a police officer
5. Failure of one involved in an accident to remain at the scene
6. Homicide by omission

FIGURE 3.1 Degrees of Mental Fault

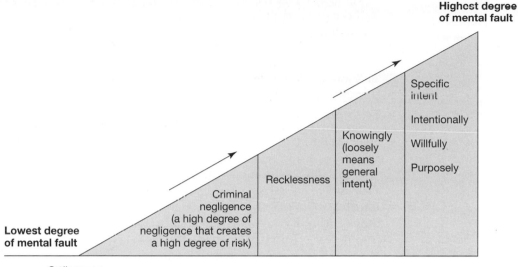

*All definitions are from § 2.02 of the Model Penal Code

The term *mens rea* means evil intent, criminal purpose, and knowledge of the wrongfulness of conduct. It is also used to indicate the mental state required by the crime charged, whether that is **specific intent** to commit the crime, recklessness, guilty knowledge, malice, or criminal negligence.

Criminal liability usually requires "an evil-meaning mind [and] an evil-doing hand."[3] However, while the phrase *evil-meaning mind* suggests an evil purpose for doing the evil act, a mind can be "guilty" without such evil purpose. For example, doing an act recklessly, but without the "evil" intent to harm another, may lack the *mens rea* for one crime but nonetheless satisfy the *mens rea* requirement of another. One's state of mind can range from being "purposeful"—that is, intending a particular result or consequence—to merely negligent—that is, failing to be aware of the probable results or consequences of an act. Figure 3.1 illustrates the degrees of mental fault.

The following example illustrates situations in which the harm done is the same in all cases, but the mental element varies. Consider the likely mental state of X in each situation:

specific intent The intent necessary for one or more elements of an offense. Murder, for example, requires the specific intent that the act be done intentionally or purposely.

EXAMPLE

X, a construction worker, is working on the fourth floor of a building under construction in the downtown area of a city. His conduct caused the death of W, who was hit on the head by a crowbar as she was walking on the sidewalk past the building.

1. X deliberately dropped the heavy crowbar so as to hit W on the head.
2. X did not want to kill anybody but wanted to see the people scatter when he dropped the crowbar to the sidewalk.

3. X threw the crowbar at another worker in a fight, but missed. The crowbar fell, killing W on the sidewalk below.
4. X came to work drunk and accidentally pushed the crowbar off the edge of the building, killing W.
5. Another worker called for the crowbar and X threw it to him, but the throw was bad and the crowbar hit W on the sidewalk below.
6. X was knocked unconscious when a crane collapsed, causing him to drop the crowbar, which hit and killed W.

Assuming a jurisdiction uses the mental fault classification similar to that suggested by the MPC, i.e., purposely, knowingly, recklessly, or negligently, what homicide crimes, if any, could X be charged with in each of these examples?

While the classification system suggested by the MPC distinguishes between each level of mental state, the distinction does not always make a difference. See *United States v. U.S. Gypsum Co.,* in which the U.S. Supreme Court stated that in the case of most crimes, "the limited distinction between knowledge and purpose has not been considered important."[4]

In *United States v. Bailey,* the U.S. Supreme Court stated that in a "general sense, 'purpose' corresponds loosely with the common-law concept of specific intent, while 'knowledge' corresponds loosely with the concept of 'general intent.'"[5]

The concepts of "general intent" and "specific intent" referred to in the *Bailey* decision were the common law's attempt to isolate and identify the different mental states required for various crimes. At common law, "general intent" referred to the intent of the defendant to do the forbidden act. If the act was done intentionally, it did not matter if the defendant had any particular purpose for doing the act. The crime of battery, for example, might be defined as the "wrongful application of force upon another." It would be a "general intent" crime, because the only intent required is the intent to do the act of applying force.

"Specific intent" refers to a required mental state (e.g., purpose, or reckless), which must be proved to have accompanied the prohibited acts. Thus, if a statute defined aggravated battery as "wrongful application of force upon another with the intent to cause fear or apprehension," the crime requires proof of the defendant's mental state when the force was applied.

For the most part, crimes are no longer classified as either "general intent" or "specific intent" crimes.[6] Rather, courts attempt, as in the following Case Close-Up, to determine what elements of a crime charged require proof of a specific intent.

"Specific intent" is thus understood today as referring to the intent that must accompany the forbidden act, over and above the intent to do the forbidden act. For example, the crime of burglary not only required the general intent to do the forbidden act of unlawfully entering the premises of another, but also the specific intent to steal or otherwise commit a felony within the premises. Other illustrations of the difference between general intent and specific intent might include the crime of "indecent exposure," which requires only the intent to do the forbidden act. It does not require the specific intent that any particular person should see the act. The crime of false pretenses requires not only the general intent to make a false statement, but also the specific intent to use the false statement to defraud another person of money or property.

CASE CLOSE-UP

Flores-Figueroa v. United States
United States Supreme Court
129 S. Ct. 1886 (2009)

Flores-Figueroa, a Mexican citizen, unlawfully entered the United States. In order to secure employment, Flores-Figueroa presented an employer with a counterfeit Social Security card and alien registration card ("green card"). The cards used his real name, but the numbers on the documents belonged to other people. Flores-Figueroa was charged with various immigration crimes, and was also charged with "aggravated identity theft" under 18 U.S.C. §1028A(a)(l), which upon conviction provides for a mandatory two years of imprisonment to be added to the sentences for the underlying crimes. Section 1028A(a)(l) states that it is a crime if one "knowingly transfers, possesses, or uses, without lawful authority, a means of identification of another person."

Flores-Figueroa was convicted of all charges, and he appealed the conviction and increased sentence under the aggravated identity theft statute. He alleged the prosecution failed to prove that he knew the numbers on the counterfeit cards belonged to "another person." Flores-Figueroa contended that §1028A(a)(l) required the government to prove he "knowingly" violated every element of the statute, including the use of a number belonging to another person. The trial court and court of appeals disagreed, and the Supreme Court granted review on that specific question. The Supreme Court agreed with Flores-Figueroa, and it reversed his conviction under the aggravated identity theft statute.

The government contended that "knowingly" modified only the actions of transferring or possessing counterfeit documents, and that Flores-Figueroa did so without lawful authority. It did not require, the government contended, knowledge that the counterfeit numbers belonged to "another" person. The Court rejected the government's position, mainly based on the way the statute was worded:

"There are strong textual reasons for rejecting the Government's position. As a matter of ordinary English grammar, it seems natural to read the statute's word 'knowingly' as applying to all the subsequently listed elements of the crime.... In ordinary English, where a transitive verb has an object, listeners in most contexts assume that an adverb (such as knowingly) that modifies the transitive verb tells the listener how the subject performed the entire action, including the object as set forth in the sentence." (129 S. Ct. at 1890).

Since the object of the sentence was the means of identification of "another person," the Court concluded the government must prove Flores-Figueroa knew the documents he used belonged to "another person." Since it did not, the conviction was reversed.

Justice Alito, in a concurring opinion, expressed concern that the majority decision was an "overly rigid rule of statutory construction." He identified some statutes where the lower federal courts had interpreted statutes differently, because of the context of the statute. For example, 18 U.S.C. § 2423(a), which makes it a crime to "knowingly" transport an individual under 18 years of age across state lines for the purpose of prostitution, has uniformly been interpreted by the federal courts of appeals as not requiring proof the defendant knew the individual transported was under 18 years of age. In the appropriate context, Justice Alito stated, such an interpretation would be correct. He concluded, however, that the present case did not have such a context, and thus agreed with the result.

At least one lower federal court has adopted Justice Alito's understanding of the limited holding in Flores-Figueroa. In United States v. Cox, 577 F.3d 833 (7th Cir. 2009), decided shortly after Flores-Figueroa, the Seventh Circuit Court of Appeals held that 18 U.S.C. § 2423(a) does not require proof that the defendant knew the individual transported was under the age of 18.

In *United States v. Bailey,* the U.S. Supreme Court stated that in "common law, crimes generally were classified as requiring either 'general intent' or 'specific intent.' This . . . distinction, however, has been the source of a good deal of confusion."

This confusion, the Court pointed out, had led to a movement away from the common law classifications of *mens rea.* Citing Section 2.02 of the MPC, presented earlier in this chapter, and LaFave and Scott's *Criminal Law,* 5th ed., Belmont, CA: West (2010), the Court suggested a better method would include using the following categories "in descending order of culpability: purpose, knowledge, recklessness, and negligence."

Proving Criminal Intent or Criminal State of Mind

When criminal intent or another mental element is an essential element of a crime, the state has the burden of proving the required *mens rea.* Proof of the mental element may be made by

- Showing the acts of the defendant and the circumstances that existed at the time of the crime. Because most people know what they are doing and also know the natural and probable consequences of their acts, a judge or jury may reasonably infer that the defendant intended the natural and probable consequences of his or her deliberate acts.[7] Thus, a person who pointed a loaded gun at another person and pulled the trigger knew what he or she was doing and desired the natural and probable consequences of the acts.
- Producing evidence to show the statements of the defendant at the time of the crime, as well as statements made after the crime. Statements of a defendant before or after a crime may be incriminating and may include admissions or a confession of guilt.

Only rarely is written evidence of the intent or purpose of a defendant available to the state. The following jury instruction on intent was approved by the Fifth Circuit Court of Appeals in the case of *United States v. Durham:*

> It is reasonable to infer that a person ordinarily intends the natural and probable consequences of his knowing acts. The jury may draw the inference that the accused intended all the consequences that one standing in like circumstances and possessing like knowledge should reasonably have expected to result from any intentional act or conscious omission. Any such inference drawn is entitled to be considered by the jury in determining whether or not the government has proved beyond a reasonable doubt that the defendant possessed the required criminal intent.[8]

Although one can reasonably infer that a person ordinarily intends the natural and probable consequences of his or her knowing and deliberate acts, one cannot extend that inference to conclude that a person intends results that are not the natural, reasonable, or probable consequences of a voluntary act. Moreover, this inference has sometimes been rejected as a basis for convicting a defendant who is charged with accomplice liability, such as aiding and abetting another in the commission of a crime, if the underlying crime requires a showing of specific intent. (Vicarious liability of aiding and abetting is discussed in Chapter 4.) Courts have held that convicting one who aids another person who has committed a crime that has a specific intent, like murder, based

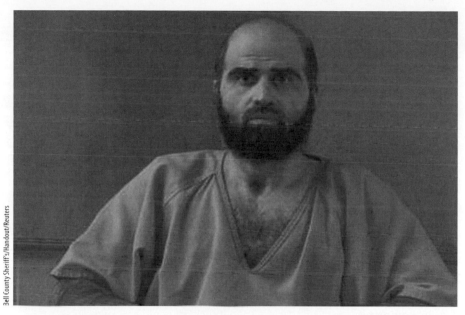

On November 9, 2009, Army Major Nidal Hasan, a psychiatrist, shot and killed thirteen soldiers and civilians at a military medical center at Fort Hood, Texas. Hasan was shot by police officers, and is paralyzed as a result. Hasan was being held in a military jail at Fort Hood, Texas awaiting trial for premeditated murder. In August 2013, Hasan was convicted of murder and sentenced to death.

only on the inference that the accomplice could foresee the other person might commit the specific intent crime, is not permitted, unless it is shown the accomplice intended to further the commission of the specific intent crime. In *Wilson-Bey v. United States,* 903 A.2d 818 (D.C. 2006), the court reversed the conviction for first-degree murder on an aiding and abetting theory because the government did not prove the aider had the specific intent to kill required by the statute.

The crime of murder generally requires proof of premeditation, which means not only that the killing was intentional, but also that the killer deliberated the killings for some (however short) period of time. Thus, prosecutors must prove Major Hasan, pictured here, not only intended to kill his victims, but also did so with premeditation. Proving the killings were intentional would likely follow from the act of pointing a loaded gun and a person and pulling the trigger. Proving premeditation would require additional evidence showing the acts were deliberated. In the tragic December 2012 killings by Adam Lanza in Newtown, Connecticut and William Spengler in Webster, New York, premeditation could be inferred from their actions prior to the killings. Lanza killed his mother before going to the Sandy Hook school, destroyed his computer's hard drive, arrived at the school wearing a camouflage vest and clothing, and killed most of his twenty-six victims with multiple bullet wounds. Spengler left a note indicating his intent to burn down his neighborhood and "do what he liked doing best: kill people." The firefighters shot by Spengler when they answered the fire alarm to put out the fire Spengler started were likely, it could be inferred, shot by Spengler to further his plan to burn his entire neighborhood.

INNOCENT ACTS THAT, IF DONE WITH FORBIDDEN INTENT, ARE CRIMES

Innocent Acts	Forbidden Intent	Resulting Crimes
Possessing a tool or other instrumentality	To use such a device to break into a depository or building and steal therefrom	Possession of burglary tools
Traveling in interstate or foreign commerce	To avoid prosecution for a state felony or to avoid giving testimony in such a prosecution	Fugitive felon or witness violation; 18 U.S.C.A. §§ 1073 & 1074 (a)
Traveling in interstate or foreign commerce	For the purpose of engaging in nonmarital sexual activity with a person under 18 years of age (21 countries now permit police to arrest for this offense in an effort to stamp out the sex trade in children between nations)	Mann Act; 18 U.S.C.A. § 2423
Traveling in interstate or foreign commerce	With intent to incite a riot (statute requires an overt act, but such act could be a lawful act)	18 U.S.C.A. § 2101 (a)(1)
Using U.S. mail, telephone, or interstate wire facilities	To participate through racketeering in a criminal enterprise	RICO violation; 18 U.S.C.A. §§ 1961–1968 (see Chapter 18)
Using U.S. mail	To advance a fraudulent scheme	Mail fraud; 18 U.S.C.A. § 1341
Using a fictitious name or address	To further a fraudulent mail scheme	18 U.S.C.A. § 1342
Association with other people or organizations	Knowing they advocate the overthrow of our government and that they intend to use force or violence to bring it about	18 U.S.C.A. § 2385
Entering a train	With intent "to commit any crime or offense against a person or property thereon"	18 U.S.C.A. § 1991
Going on "any military, naval, or Coast Guard reservation, post, fort, arsenal, yard, station, or installation"	"For any purpose prohibited by law or lawful regulation"	18 U.S.C.A. § 1382
Teaching or demonstrating the use, application, or making of a firearm, or making of a firearm, explosive, or incendiary device, or a technique capable of causing injury or death	"Intending that the same will be unlawfully employed for use in, or in furtherance of, a civil disorder which may in any way or degree obstruct, delay, or adversely affect commerce" or the performance of any federally protected function	18 U.S.C.A. § 231(a)(1)

Proving intent to kill under offenses like "assault with intent to kill" can be more difficult and often requires circumstantial evidence. As an example, in *State v. Wilds*[9] a defendant was convicted of assault and battery with intent to kill (ABIK) when he severely injured a victim he dragged under his car. An appeals court held that the jury could infer the required "malice aforethought" based on evidence the defendant knew the victim was in front of his car but accelerated anyway, repeatedly swerved the car with the victim under the car, and was observed laughing during the time the victim was being dragged.

The Requirement of Scienter

scienter A form of specific intent requiring a showing that the actor knew of the existence of certain facts. For example, one cannot be guilty of possession of stolen property if one does not know property is stolen.

Scienter is sometimes made an essential element of a crime that the state must prove beyond a reasonable doubt. **Scienter** is a legal term meaning possession of a degree of knowledge about facts material to a conviction of a crime. If a statute requires knowledge about the existence of a fact, that knowledge must be proved by the prosecution. Examples of crimes in which state statutes most often require scienter include the following:

- In battery or assault on a law enforcement officer, knowledge that the victim is a law enforcement officer
- In refusing to aid a law enforcement officer, knowledge that the person requesting assistance is a law enforcement officer
- In obstructing a law enforcement officer, knowledge that the person obstructed is a law enforcement officer
- In receiving stolen property, knowledge that the property received is stolen property
- In possession of obscene material, knowledge of the nature of the material
- In bribery of a public official or a juror, knowledge that the person is a public official or juror
- In harboring or aiding a felon, knowledge that the person aided is a felon

Whether or not a criminal statute has a scienter requirement depends on how the statute is written. In addition, it often matters whether a fact is an essential element of the offense, or whether the existence of the fact serves as the basis for sentence enhancement upon conviction of an underlying offense. For example, Georgia's aggravated assault statute, § 16-5-21, states that "A person who knowingly commits the offense of aggravated assault upon a peace officer . . . [while the officer is performing official duties]" is guilty of a felony. Because "knowingly" is made part of the offense, the statute has been held to require proof the defendant knew the person assaulted was a police officer.[10]

On the other hand, a California sentencing statute, West Ann. Cal. Pen. Code § 12022 (a)(1), which states that "any person who is armed with a firearm in commission of a felony . . ." shall receive an additional one-year sentence, does not require proof that all persons involved in the crime had knowledge one of them was armed with a firearm.[11]

Most state[12] and federal courts[13] have reached similar conclusions interpreting so-called "schoolyard" laws, which provide for imposition of additional sentences for certain crimes, such as sale of illegal drugs, committed near or on a schoolyard. These statutes generally have been interpreted as sentence enhancement statutes,

TO KNOW OR NOT KNOW: THAT IS THE QUESTION

In two 2012 decisions, separate panels of the Eighth Circuit Court of Appeals interpreted a federal statute, 18 U.S.C.A. § 1153, and reached different conclusions about the scienter requirement of that statute. (U.S. Circuit Courts hear cases in three-judge panels unless a court agrees to hear a case *en banc*, in which case all the judges participate.) The statute reads: "Whoever . . . knowingly . . . (2) engages in a sexual act with another person if that other person is (A) physically incapable of declining participation . . . in that sexual act" violates the statute.

In both cases, a defendant was convicted under this statute based on a sexual act with an intoxicated victim. Both defendants claimed the victim was conscious and consented to the sexual contact. However, in both cases the jury found that the victim was in fact incapacitated when the sexual act took place. Both defendants requested, but were refused, a jury instruction that required the jury to determine if the defendant "knew" the victim was incapacitated. Both were convicted.

Does the statute require that a person charged "know" the other person is incapacitated? Or, does the term "knowingly" modify only the "sexual act" element of the offense? In *United States v. Rouillard*, 701 F3d 861 (8th Cir. 2012), the court said the prosecution must prove the defendant acted knowingly with respect to the incapacitation of the victim, and reversed the conviction. In *United States v. Bruguier*, 703 F3d 393 (8th Cir. 2012), the court said the incapacitation element of the offense was strict liability, similar to statutes involving sex with minors, and affirmed the conviction. Both courts relied on the *Flores-Figueroa* case presented earlier in this chapter, as well as the *X-Citement Video* case discussed later in this chapter. Which panel decision is correct? The Eighth Circuit granted rehearing en banc in both cases. What do you think happened?

with no requirement of knowledge that the schoolyard was located near the place where the crime occurred.

A statute can of course add a scienter requirement by appropriate language. In *United States v. Thomas*[14] a defendant was charged with violation of 10 U.S.C.A. § 911, 912(a), which makes it a crime to "wrongfully introduce" illegal drugs into a military installation. The prosecution did not prove the defendant knew he was entering a military installation, but contended that knowledge was not required, citing the schoolyard cases discussed above. The court of military appeals disagreed, finding that while Congress intended strict liability in some federal statutes, such as the schoolyard drug-free zone statute, by adding the requirement of "wrongful" to 10 U.S.C.A. § 911, 912(a), Congress intended to make knowledge an element of the offense. The court thus held the statute applied only to those who knew they were introducing illegal drugs to a military installation.

Statutes can also dispense with the requirement of scienter as applied to an element of an offense. In such a case, with respect to that element the statute becomes one of "strict liability" (discussed more fully below). An example of such a statute is the federal assault statute, 18 U.S.C.A. § 111, which makes it an offense to "forcibly assault" a federal officer. In *Feola v. United States*[15] the U.S. Supreme Court held that the prosecution need not prove the defendant had knowledge the victim was a federal officer. All the statute required was an intent to assault, not an intent to assault a federal officer, the Court held.

The Motive for Committing a Crime

intent The mental purpose or design to commit a specific act (or omission).

Intent and *motive* are sometimes thought of as being one and the same. However, the law contains a clear distinction between the two. **Intent** is the mental purpose or design to commit a specific act (or omission), whereas **motive** is the cause, inducement, or reason why an act is committed.

Intent is an essential element of many crimes and must be proved beyond reasonable doubt when required. Motive is seldom made an essential element required for a criminal conviction. However, motive evidence can be used by the prosecution as an aid in obtaining a conviction or to rebut a defense offered by a defendant. For example, in the 2012 case of *State v. Laswell*,[16] the Arkansas Supreme Court held evidence that the defendant had expressed to a witness his desire to "live the thug life" was admissible to show the defendant's motive in robbing and killing the victim, and also to rebut the defendant's claim that he had no intent to rob the victim when he entered the victim's residence.

motive The cause, inducement, or reason why an act is committed.

Strict Liability Crimes

strict liability crime Crime that does not require proof of the mental element essential to true crimes.

In enacting statutes to enforce rules having to do with public safety—such as traffic, liquor, purity of food, hunting, and narcotics offenses—modern legislative bodies often choose not to create "true" crimes, but rather to enact statutes that do not require any proof of *mens rea*. In these areas, the legislature's interest in promoting public safety justifies strict regulation of acts that threaten that public safety. In such cases, the statute may dispense with the need to prove a defendant was aware his or her actions violated the statute or regulation. These statutory crimes are usually called **strict liability crimes**. Except for narcotics offenses, the penalties for strict liability offenses

ESSENTIAL ELEMENTS OF A TRUE CRIME

To obtain a conviction, the state must prove the following essential elements when charging a *true crime*:

- *The act element:* The forbidden act (or failure to act).
- *The mental element:* The state of mind required for the crime (the guilty mind); usually proved by use of inferences drawn from the acts of the defendant.
- *The harm element:* The wrong done (killing, physical injury, property damage, loss, and so on). Note that not all crimes have a harmful result element. For example, vehicular homicide requires proof that a person was killed; by contrast, drunk driving does not require proof of any harmful result be proved.
- *The cause element:* The harm done was the natural and probable result of the wrongful act.

Some crimes require proof of additional essential elements, such as scienter and possession (actual or constructive).

are usually lighter than those for "true" crimes. The offenders are often not considered "criminals" in the full sense of the word, and the state is not required to carry the burden of proving criminal intent or other mental fault. The defendant is liable based only on the acts taken, regardless of his or her state of mind at the time of the acts.

The motor vehicle codes, hunting regulations, and food and liquor laws of most states contain strict liability statutes that require no showing of any particular mental intent. Thus, a bartender cannot ordinarily use as a defense the fact that the person to whom he sold liquor looked 22 when in fact the person was only 17; the driver of an overweight truck cannot argue that the company scales were faulty; nor can an adult male, in most states, argue that he did not know the age of the 15-year-old girl with whom he had sexual intercourse.

In referring to strict liability crimes in these areas, the U.S. Supreme Court pointed out that "Congress has rendered criminal a type of conduct that a reasonable person should know is subject to stringent public regulation and may seriously threaten the community's health or safety."[17]

The following list shows laws that commonly have strict liability terms:

Firearms	Unregistered hand grenades
	Unregistered machine guns
	The offense of carrying a concealed weapon
Motor vehicle safety laws	Defective headlight
	Running a red light
Intoxicating liquor or beer	Sale to underage person
Drug-related deaths	A number of states have enacted so-called Len Bias laws that make people who illegally manufacture, distribute, or dispense illegal drugs strictly liable for drug-related deaths.
Public health laws	Corporation officers can be convicted of Federal Food and Drug Act violations even when "consciousness of wrongdoing [is] totally wanting."
Other laws	Prior to discharge from service, an Air Force colonel negotiated for a civilian job and was involved in contract negotiations that violated the laws against taking government action while having conflicting financial interest.

In the case of federal criminal statutes, the U.S. Supreme Court has stated that strict liability crimes are not preferred and that Congress must make it clear if it intends to eliminate the *mens rea* requirement from a criminal statute. For example, in *Staples v. United States*[18] the Court held that in a prosecution under the National Firearms Act (26 U.S.C. § 5801), which requires registration of automatic weapons that meet the definition of "firearms" under the act, the prosecution must prove that a defendant knew the weapon he or she possessed constituted a firearm under the act. The defendant was in possession of an automatic rifle, which qualified as a firearm that must be registered under the act.

The prosecution argued that because the statute stated simply that it was a crime to possess or receive a firearm that was not registered, the prosecution did not have to prove the defendant knew the weapon in his possession qualified as a firearm under the act. The Supreme Court disagreed. It held that where the act—possession of a rifle—was not clearly dangerous, the statute should be construed as requiring that the defendant know the weapon in his possession was one that must be registered. The Court distinguished cases involving firearms like hand grenades, on the basis that any person would know that a grenade was something inherently dangerous and liable to be the subject of regulations. That is not the case, the Court reasoned, for more standard weapons.

The maxim "ignorance of the law is no excuse" is generally applicable to most crimes. The U.S. Supreme Court has said that unless a statute provides otherwise, the use of a term such as "knowingly" in a statute refers only to knowledge of facts, not knowledge that conduct is illegal.[19]

In strict liability crimes, which often involve conduct that is not inherently "bad" or wrongful, that maxim may not always be applicable, and knowledge that an act is unlawful may be an element of the crime. This was the case in *Liparota v. United States*.[20] There the U.S. Supreme Court held that for a defendant to be convicted under 7 U.S.C.A. § 2024(b)(l) for the unlawful use of food stamps, the prosecution must prove the defendant knew that his use of food stamps was not authorized under the statute.

The result in *Liparota* is not the norm.[21] More common is the result in the 2012 case of *United States v. Zhou*.[22] There a research assistant at U.C.L.A. Health Systems

Stockbyte/Getty Images

If the young people shown here are not old enough to be drinking alcoholic beverages under the state laws setting the minimum drinking age, the bar or store that sold them the alcohol could be criminally liable under the state underage drinking laws, even if the bar did not know the young people were underage and even if the young people presented false identification showing them to be of drinking age. Underage drinking laws are examples of strict liability laws, which have no requirement that the person charged with violation of the law possess any particular mental state.

accessed patients' (mainly celebrities') health records after he had been terminated from employment, and thus was not authorized to access those records. There was no evidence the defendant intended to use or sell the records in any manner. He was convicted of a violation of the federal Health Insurance Portability and Accountability Act (HIPAA), which makes it a crime for a person "who knowingly and in violation" of HIPAA accesses patient health information.

The defendant appealed, contending the prosecution failed to prove he "knew" his actions violated the HIPAA statute. The court rejected that argument, holding that the only knowledge required under the statute was knowledge the defendant was obtaining individual patient health records.

Strict Liability Laws That Seek to Protect Children

The age of a minor is an essential element of such crimes as SIWAC (sexual intercourse with a child), contributing to the delinquency of a child, violating liquor laws or child pornography laws, and giving or selling a minor a pistol, drugs, cigarettes, and so on. Such laws seek to protect children. To provide further protection to children, many states take away the defense of "mistake of age" from some or all of the offenses that seek to protect children. When this defense is taken away, defendants cannot argue that they made an honest mistake about the age of a child. (See Chapter 7 for a discussion of the defenses of honest mistake of law or fact.)

By taking away the defense of honest mistake as to the age of a child, the state makes the offense a strict liability offense, and defendants can be proved guilty by showing only that they committed the forbidden act.

EXAMPLE

An adult has sex with a minor. The state has to show only that the sex occurred and the age of the parties. Consent cannot be used as a defense by the adult, as the minor is incapable of giving consent. Mistake as to the age of the minor cannot be used if this defense is prohibited by state law.

Proximate Cause or Causation

The material elements of crimes include conduct that is forbidden or required, and often the mental state existing at the time of the forbidden act or omission. In some crimes the result (the harm done or the wrong that occurs) of the conduct can also be a material element that must be proved by the prosecution.

In these crimes, the state must prove that the defendant's wrongful act or omission was the cause of the harm that resulted. In many cases this is an easy task. The harm to the victim could occur immediately, such as a bloody nose resulting from a blow to the face or death from being shot at point-blank range. In other instances, making the causal connection between the prohibited conduct and the harmful result of that conduct can be more difficult. This can be the case in homicide prosecutions, where the prosecution must prove the prohibited acts caused the resulting death. These causation problems are resolved by use of the **proximate cause** doctrine.

proximate cause The ordinary and probable cause of a result.

"PROXIMATE CAUSE" AND "CAUSE-IN-FACT"

Both the civil and criminal laws distinguish between "cause-in-fact" causation and "proximate cause." "Cause-in-fact" causation means the result would not have happened "but for" the prohibited conduct. Proximate cause (sometimes called "legal cause") refers to the ordinary and probable consequences that follow from actions.

Example: A slashes B's tires, stranding B on a highway. While B is waiting for help, C comes along and kills B. A's act of slashing B's tires is the cause-in-fact of B's death, because "but for" that act B would not have been stranded and subsequently killed by C. However, under the proximate cause doctrine, A is the legal cause of B's death only if B's death was the ordinary and probable result of A's action. Here, the actions of C would likely be called an "intervening" or "superseding" cause, and not the ordinary consequence of slashing a car's tires.

Causation problems in homicide crimes can occur when a substantial time gap exists between the criminal acts and the victim's death, or other factors contribute to the death. In these cases, the state must prove beyond a reasonable doubt that the unlawful and wrongful act of the defendant was the proximate cause of the death that resulted. The following cases illustrate court rulings in which the victim's death did not occur immediately or involved other factors that contributed to that death:

- In the 2010 case of *People v. Amigon*[23] the Illinois Supreme Court affirmed a murder conviction where the victim died 5 years after being shot by the defendant. The shooting caused the victim to be paralyzed from the shoulders down, and 5 years later he died from bacterial pneumonia, a condition common in paralyzed victims. The court said the pneumonia was an ordinary, probable result of the defendant's wrongful acts.
- In the 2011 case of *State v. Fox*[24] the Iowa Court of Appeals upheld a conviction of motor vehicle homicide where the victim chose to end life-support systems. The victim was paralyzed in an auto accident caused by defendant while defendant was intoxicated. After several days on life-support systems, the victim, who could communicate only by blinking his eyes, asked to have the life-support systems removed. They were, and he died at once. The court said the accident was the proximate cause of the death because the decision to terminate life support was an ordinary and foreseeable consequence of the accident.
- The court in the 2002 case of *State v. Kirby*[25] affirmed a conviction of second-degree murder where the victim of a terrible beating died while receiving medical treatment from personnel who did not discover damage to some of the victim's internal organs. The court said the beating was the proximate cause of the death because ordinary negligence of medical personnel treating a victim is not a superseding cause. Only gross negligence acts as a superseding cause.

The proximity between the distribution of illegal drugs such as cocaine or heroin and drug overdose deaths has led in to the enactment in some states of criminal statutes making the person who distributed the illegal drugs responsible for the resulting overdose death. For example, section 782.04(l)(a)(3) of the Florida Statutes (2001) states

MULTIPLE CAUSES OF DEATH IN HOMICIDE PROSECUTIONS

When a victim dies and there can be shown multiple causes of that death, application of the "but for" cause-in-fact test can be difficult in theory.

Example: A stabs V, inflicting a non-mortal wound that by itself would not cause V's death. Acting independently, B shoots V in the leg, causing a similar non-mortal wound. However, the two wounds combined cause V's death. Viewed independently, in theory neither A nor B was the "but for" cause of V's death, since V would not have died as a result of either independent wound.

Example: A stabs V, causing a mortal wound that will cause V's death. Before V dies, B independently shoots V in the head, which also inflicts a mortal wound from which V will die whether or not A had stabbed him. In theory, neither A nor B is the "but for" cause of V's death, since it cannot be said with respect to either A or B that V would not have died "but for" their actions.

Example: A stabs V, inflicting a mortal wound that will cause V's death in 30 minutes. Before that time ends, B shoots V in the leg, inflicting a non-mortal wound. The increased bleeding from B's wound causes V to die 20 minutes faster. While A's mortal wound is the "but for" cause of V's death, in theory B's actions are not.

Courts usually resolve these multiple "but for" causation problems as follows:

- **Joint action.** In many of these kinds of cases the defendants act in concert, and thus the actions of each are attributed to the other, making the "but for" applicable to each of them.
- **Concurrent causes.** In the first example, A and B, though acting independently, are concurrent causes of V's death, since V would not have died "but for" the combined actions of A and B. Both can be charged with murder.
- **Substantial factor.** In the second example, courts would hold that A and B are each the "but for" cause of V's death because their actions were each a substantial factor in that death. Both can be charged with murder.
- **Accelerated cause.** In the third example, courts would hold B also as the "but for" cause of V's death, because that death occurred earlier than it would have but for B's actions.[26] Both can be charged with murder.

that a person who distributes illegal drugs that cause death by overdose of the drugs is guilty of first-degree murder. In *Armuller v. State*[27] a drug distributor convicted of murder under this statute contended his actions were not the proximate cause of the overdose death because he sold the drugs (heroin) to friends of the victim, who then helped the victim to inject the drug. The court rejected his "intervening cause" argument, holding that the defendant initiated the distribution of the heroin, and that was sufficient under the statute to satisfy the causation requirement.

The Ancient Year-and-a-Day Murder Rule

The response by the common law to a significant lapse of time between the criminal act and the victim's death was the "year and a day" rule. Under this rule, death of the victim must occur within a year and a day of the criminal act in order to be the "cause" of the death. The rule goes back hundreds of years in the law to 1278,

CASES OF UNINTENDED HARM RESULTING FROM A MISDEMEANOR OR OTHER MINOR OFFENSE

In the following cases the defendants were convicted of manslaughter or negligent homicide based on unintended deaths that occurred during or following the defendants' unlawful actions. Courts there held that the defendants' unlawful actions were the cause of the death of the victims.

- *Freeman v. State*, 969 So.2d 473 (Fla. App. 2007). Defendant unlawfully failed to confine six dangerous pit bulls, which attacked and killed an elderly neighbor. Manslaughter conviction upheld.
- *State v. Rodriguez*, 804 N.W.2d 844 (Iowa 2011). Defendant permitted intoxicated brother to drive car after brothers fled from a gas station without paying for gas. Brother hit motorcycle, killing driver. Conviction for vehicular homicide affirmed.
- *State v. Rivera*, 291 P.3d 512 (Kan. App. 2012). Mother left 4-year-old child with boyfriend, despite her knowledge that boyfriend abused the child. The child died after boyfriend's abuse, and mother was charged with involuntary manslaughter based on a death that occurred while mother was violating child endangerment statute, a misdemeanor. Conviction for involuntary manslaughter upheld.
- *State v. Small*, 100 So3d 797 (La. 2012). Mother left 6-year-old child in apartment while she went out drinking. Accidental fire started, killing the child. Conviction for negligent homicide affirmed. (This case also appears in Chapter 10.)

when medical science was primitive.[28] Before the American Revolutionary War, Sir William Blackstone described the rule as follows: "In order . . . to make the killing murder, it is requisite that the party die within a year and a day after the stroke (blow) received, or cause of death administered; in the computation of which the whole day upon which the hurt was done shall be reckoned the first."[29]

When the colonies became states, they all adopted the common law of England, which included the year and a day rule. Because of changes in medical science, making it easier to show the relationship between an injury and a death that occurs much later, many, perhaps most, states, either by statute[30] or court decision,[31] have abandoned the year and a day rule. A few courts have rejected requests by defendants to judicially abrogate the rule, stating that is a legislative function.[32] California has developed a hybrid version of the rule: Cal. Penal Code § 194 (West 2007) states that there is a rebuttable presumption that a death that occurs more than three years after an injury was not caused by the injury. The state must then bear the burden of proving that causation.

Possession Alone as a Crime

All states make the possession of certain objects a criminal offense. Examples of such crimes are possession of illegal drugs, carrying a concealed weapon, possession of an instrument of a crime, possession of stolen property (vehicles, credit cards, and so on), and possession of graffiti instruments (in some cities and states). The following jury instruction defining *possession* is used in federal courts:

> [T]he law recognizes different kinds of possession. A person may have actual possession or constructive possession. . . . A person who has direct physical control of something on or around his person is then in actual possession of it. A person who is not in actual possession but who has both the power and the intention to later take control over something . . . is in constructive possession of it. . . . Whenever the word "possession" has been used in these instructions it includes actual as well as constructive possession.[33]

Because of public safety, virtually all states forbid carrying an unauthorized concealed weapon (see Chapter 9). *Carrying* requires a showing of actual possession. If a pistol is in the trunk of the car and not within the immediate reach and control of a person, it is not within actual possession.

Illegal drugs could be in actual possession of a defendant, or a defendant could have constructive possession of the drugs. The term *constructive possession* is used to indicate control over property and objects that the defendant does not have in actual possession. The object may be in his or her car parked two blocks away, in a home or office desk drawer, or in a suitcase stored somewhere for which he or she has a baggage claim check or key. Constructive possession would not be sufficient to sustain a conviction for carrying a concealed weapon, as a showing of actual possession is necessary. However, constructive possession would sustain a conviction for the possession of contraband, such as narcotics.

The mental element that must be proved in possession offenses is generally that of intention or "knowledge." These mental elements are usually easy to prove, because a person with a loaded revolver or a bag of marijuana in his pocket cannot argue convincingly that he did not know that the contraband was in his actual possession. The intent to possess, then, is a state of mind existing at the time the person commits the offense. In seeking to determine the state of mind of the alleged offender in order to decide whether an intent existed, the jury or the court may base its decision on the defendant's acts, conduct, and other inferences that can be reasonably deduced from all the circumstances.

Possession is one of the rights of ownership of property. Criminal statutes do not require that ownership be proved. A person who possesses heroin may or may not be the owner of the heroin. Possession of personal property is presumptive evidence of ownership, and possession accompanied by the exercise of complete acts of ownership for a considerable time is strong evidence of ownership. In the absence of evidence showing otherwise, the presence of objects and articles in a vehicle, dwelling, or business place leads to a strong inference that they are in the constructive possession of the person controlling the vehicle, dwelling, or business place. Therefore, heroin found in an apartment searched under the authority of a search warrant is in the constructive possession of the person controlling and occupying the apartment, unless the person can show otherwise (also see Chapter 16 on drug abuse).

The Possession of Illegal Contraband Inference

A strong inference of possession of illegal contraband (such as cocaine or an illegal gun) can be made when the contraband is found (1) under the front seat of a car

WHEN POSSESSION ALONE IS A CRIME

Possession May Be	Possession May Be	Possession of a Controlled Substance May Be
Actual or Constructive (not in actual possession)	In one person (sole); or Joint (in possession of more than one person)[a]	Of a *usable amount*; or Of a *trace amount*; or Within the body of the suspect; or A combination of any of the above

Most states will not permit a criminal conviction for drug possession based only on a showing of illegal drugs within the body of a defendant. Some states will not sustain a conviction of drug possession on a showing of a trace amount alone. The strongest cases are those in which a usable amount or a large amount (possession with intent to deliver) is proved (see Chapter 16 on drug abuse).

[a]Charges of joint possession are commonly brought in cases in which law enforcement officers seize a large amount of illegal drugs from a shared-occupancy dwelling. While "[t]he mere fact that a defendant is a joint occupant" of a residence where illegal drugs are found is not enough to establish constructive possession, evidence can be used to tie the occupant to the illegal drugs. An example of such evidence tying a wife to a husband's illegal drugs is the 2012 case of *United States v. Duenas,* 691 F.3d 1070 (9th Cir. 2012).

driven by the owner of the vehicle, (2) in the home of a person who is the sole occupant of the house or apartment, or (3) in other situations in which a reasonable inference of possession can be drawn.

However, unless a statute has eliminated the scienter requirement and made possession a strict liability offense, some knowledge of the nature of the things possessed must be shown. The U.S. Supreme Court in *United States v. X-Citement Video, Inc.*[34] used the following examples to illustrate this requirement, noting that innocent persons could be charged with possession without some knowledge requirement:

- A Federal Express courier delivers a box containing the illegal contraband.
- A new resident of an apartment receives mail (containing contraband) for the prior resident and stores the mail unopened.
- A retail druggist returns an uninspected roll of developed film to a customer, unaware that the film contains illegal sexually explicit child photographs.

In the 2013 case of *Commonwealth v. Romero*[35] the Massachusetts Supreme Judicial Court reversed a conviction for carrying a firearm without a permit. The defendant was the driver of a car carrying a passenger, who had placed a gun in his lap after the car was stopped for a traffic violation. The lower courts had held that the driver had "constructive possession" of the gun because of his proximity to the gun and his operation of the car. The Supreme Judicial Court reversed, holding that the state must prove the defendant exercised some control over the gun beyond the simple fact he owned and operated the car in which the passenger possessed the gun. Drivers are not strictly liable for all contraband brought into their cars, the court said.

The Use of Presumptions and Inferences in Criminal Law

Presumptions and inferences have long been hailed as a "staple of our adversary system of fact-finding."[36] Presumptions and inferences enable a fact finder to conclude that because some facts have been proved (usually called *predicate facts*), other facts may be inferred or presumed to be true. For example, if it is proved that a contractor failed to order materials needed to perform a home repair contract, it might logically be presumed or inferred that the contractor never intended to perform the home improvement contract.

In criminal prosecutions, use of presumptions and inferences can present due process problems, if the jury is permitted or required to find facts necessary to a conviction based only on inferences or presumptions drawn on other facts. Because the Due Process Clause requires the prosecution to prove every element of a crime beyond a reasonable doubt, the use of inferences or presumptions can violate that clause if the facts establishing the element of the crime are the result of a presumption or inference.

The Supreme Court of the United States has generally permitted the use of permissive inferences and permissive presumptions, because the fact finder need not reach the presumed conclusion. As a result, the prosecution continues to bear the burden of proof beyond a reasonable doubt, and the Due Process Clause is not violated. However, mandatory presumptions have been treated differently. Mandatory presumptions, generally referred to as *irrebuttable* or *conclusive* presumptions, can be unconstitutional under the Due Process Clause because such a presumption allows the prosecution to avoid proving an element of the crime charged.[37]

Some presumptions direct the fact finder to reach conclusions in favor of the defendant. The best-known presumption, and probably the oldest, is the presumption of innocence until proven guilty. The presumption of innocence until proven guilty is a *rebuttable* presumption, which means it may be overcome by evidence proving otherwise. The presumption of innocence may be overcome by evidence showing that a defendant is guilty beyond a reasonable doubt.

Sometimes a conclusive presumption is stated as a rule of substantive law that cannot be overcome with evidence showing otherwise. Of the few conclusive presumptions of this type, perhaps the best known is the rule of law that a person under a certain minimum age, usually 7 years, has not reached the age of reason and therefore is not capable of committing a crime. (Infancy as a limit on criminal responsibility is discussed more fully in Chapter 4.)

Figure 3.2 illustrates the different elements that may be essential to the proof of a crime.

Functions of Presumptions and Inferences

Both presumptions and inferences play an important role in trials. Presumptions are created to permit orderly civil and criminal trials.[38] The Supreme Court of Pennsylvania and the Supreme Court of Indiana defined the function and legal significance of presumptions as follows:

FIGURE 3.2 Essential Elements of Crimes

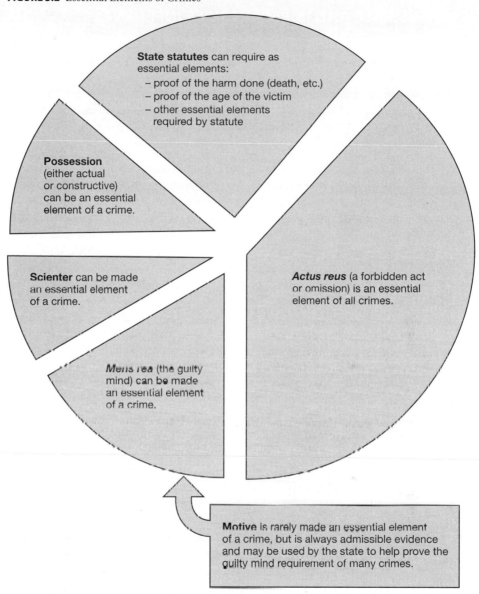

State statutes can require as
essential elements:
  – proof of the harm done (death, etc.)
  – proof of the age of the victim
  – other essential elements
    required by statute

Possession
(either actual
or constructive)
can be an essential
element of a crime.

Scienter can be made
an essential element
of a crime.

Actus reus (a forbidden act
or omission) is an essential
element of all crimes.

Mens rea (the guilty
mind) can be made
an essential element
of a crime.

Motive is rarely made an essential element
of a crime, but is always admissible evidence
and may be used by the state to help prove the
guilty mind requirement of many crimes.

A presumption of law is not evidence nor should it be weighed by the fact finder
as though it had evidentiary value. Rather, a presumption is a rule of law
enabling the party in whose favor it operates to take his case to the jury without
presenting evidence of the fact presumed. It serves as a challenge for proof
and indicates the party from whom such proof must be forthcoming. When the
opponent of the presumption has met the burden of production thus imposed,
however, the office of the presumption has been performed; the presumption is
of no further effect and drops from the case.[39]

PERMISSIBLE AND IMPERMISSIBLE INFERENCES

In criminal trials, fact finders may draw reasonable inferences from facts presented in a case. Stacking of inferences, or basing an inference solely upon another inference, is not permitted. For example, a jury could properly infer that a tire jack used with such force as to cause the victim to fall after being hit in the head and neck area was a deadly weapon, and that an intent to kill existed. This particular example was held not to be inference stacking in *State v. Jacks*, 63 Ohio App. 3d 200, 578 N.E.2d 512 (1989).

The table gives examples of permissible and impermissible inferences.

Defendant forced a young girl into a secluded area and forced her to take off her clothes and lie on the ground. He threatened her with a gun as he loosened his pants. Nothing was said of his intent, and he fled at this point.	Can an inference be made as to the intention of the defendant?	Yes, conviction for attempted sexual assault affirmed. See *Green v. Connecticut*, 194 Conn. 258, 480 A2d 526 (1984), *review denied* 469 U.S. 1191, 105 S. Ct. 964, 36 CrL 4178 (1985).
In the middle of the day, police saw defendant walking out of an empty warehouse. Defendant was cooperative, did not run, and had nothing in his possession. He told police that he had to go to the toilet and entered the building looking for a lavatory.	Can an inference of intent to steal be drawn to justify a conviction of burglary (illegal entry with intent to steal)?	No, see *Commonwealth v. Muniem*, 225 Pa. Super. 311, 303 A.2d 528 (1973).
Police with a search warrant stopped a United Parcel Service (UPS) truck carrying more than 200 parcels on city delivery. The warrant authorized the opening of one of the parcels, which was found to contain two pounds of heroin.	Can an inference be drawn, based on this information, establishing probable cause to justify an arrest of the UPS driver by the police?	No.
X is present in a store while the store was robbed.	Would mere presence at the scene of a crime justify an arrest?	No, further information would be needed.
A murder is committed, and only two people were at the scene of the crime. They could have committed the crime together, or one could be guilty and the other innocent.	Would these facts justify a conclusion that probable cause exists to arrest either or both?	Yes, see Restatement of Torts (2d) Sec. 119 (1965).
Defendant was one of the crew aboard a small boat carrying 22,000 pounds of marijuana on a long trip to the United States. Defendant claims he had no knowledge of the illegal enterprise.	From the facts, can inferences be drawn that defendant was a party to the illegal enterprise?	Yes, see *United States v. Guerrero-Guerrero*, 38 CrL 2235, 776 F.2d 1071 (1st Cir. 1985).

Police sought to catch a thief who had been stealing property at a Veterans Administration hospital. Money in a wallet was left in a room. The wallet was marked with invisible dye that dye became visible when it came in contact with moisture. Defendant was seen leaving the room with blue dye on her hands. The money in the wallet was gone.	Are these facts and the inferences drawn from them sufficient to sustain a conviction for petty theft?	Yes, see *United States v. Baker*, 769 F. Supp. 137 (S.D.N.Y. 1991).
Defendant was arrested with cocaine in his possession. He also had a scale for weighing the cocaine, baking soda for cutting it, more than $1,000 in 20-dollar bills, and other drug-related items. At his jury trial, a woman testified that she bought cocaine from the defendant on the day of his arrest.	Would this evidence justify the jury's finding of possession of cocaine with intent to deliver?	Yes, see *Sams v. State*, 197 Ga. App. 201, 397 S.E.2d 751 (1990).

Inferences of guilt cannot be drawn from the following:

- The fact that a defendant in a criminal case does not get on the witness stand and testify in his or her own behalf. *Griffin v. California*, 85 S. Ct. 1229 (1965); *Carter v. Kentucky*, 101 S. Ct. 1112 (1981).
- A Detroit Police Department policy providing for the automatic arrest of all occupants in a vehicle wanted in connection with a felony. The car in question was stopped 48 hours after a burglary, and all occupants were arrested. The policy based on impermissible inferences was condemned by Michigan courts. *People v. Harrison*, 163 Mich. App. 409, 413 N.W.2d 813, 42 CrL 2153 (1987).
- Prosecutors, judges, and police officers cannot comment on the fact that a defendant asserted his or her Fifth Amendment right to remain silent after being given *Miranda* warnings. *State v. Marple*, 98 Or. App. 662, 780 P.2d 772 (1989).

In a period of six months, four elderly women were sexually assaulted in their homes. The unique pattern of the crimes indicated that a single perpetrator was committing the crimes. After the defendant was arrested, the series of very similar crimes stopped. Most state and federal courts hold that evidence of the inference of guilt drawn from the fact that a series of similar crimes stopped when the defendant was arrested and held in jail was inherently unreliable to prove guilt. See *Commonwealth v. Foy*, 612 A.2d 1349 (Pa. 1992). An Arizona court disagreed with the Foy result, and held it was permissible to permit a police officer to testify that crimes fitting the defendant's modus operandi stopped after the defendant was arrested. *State v. Miller*, 156 P.3d 1145 (Ariz. App. 2007).

presumption A rule of law that the trier of fact shall assume the existence of a state of facts without evidence being produced. Presumptions are either rebuttable or irrebuttable.

A **presumption** is an assumption that the law expressly directs that the trier of fact (jury or judge) to make. Because most presumptions may be disputed, they may be outweighed or overcome with evidence showing otherwise. Unless a presumption is overcome with other evidence, judges and jurors *must* accept the presumption as true. It is this aspect of presumptions that creates due process problems in criminal cases, since placing the duty on a defendant to overcome a presumed fact can operate to relieve the prosecution from its duty to prove every element of a crime beyond a reasonable doubt.

The purpose of civil and criminal trials is to determine the truth of the issues presented to the fact finder. Criminal trials commence with the presumption that the defendant is innocent. To overcome this presumption, the state must present evidence proving the guilt of the defendant beyond a reasonable doubt in the minds of the jury. Each essential element of the crime charged must be proved beyond a reasonable doubt.

Inference A conclusion or deduction that a jury or judge may draw from a fact or a group of facts presented to them.

An **inference** is a conclusion or deduction that a jury or judge *may* draw from a fact or a group of facts presented to them. Fact finders must use good common sense and their knowledge of everyday life. In their reasoning process, juries and judges must use inferences. A common inference used in criminal trials is that persons intend (desire) the natural and probable consequences of their deliberate acts. The following example illustrates this.

EXAMPLE

X is charged with either attempted assault with a deadly weapon or attempted murder. X is a strong 30-year-old man who did the following:

Conduct of X	Inferences That Can Logically Be Drawn from X's Conduct
Reliable witnesses testify that X repeatedly at tempted to hit Y on or about Y's head with a baseball bat. Bystanders stopped X.	Fact finders can easily conclude that a baseball bat is a deadly weapon in the hands of a strong man who exhibited an intent to kill or seriously injure.
A rolled-up newspaper to strike at Y.	Fact finders cannot logically conclude that a rolled-up newspaper is a deadly weapon or that the defendant exhibited intent to kill; therefore, neither charge could stand.

The Presumption That All Persons Are Sane, Normal, and Competent

An important presumption is that all adults are sane, normal, and competent. Thus, adult witnesses in civil and criminal cases are assumed to be sane, normal, and competent. However, attorneys in civil or criminal proceedings may challenge this presumption if necessary, and show otherwise. Furthermore, before young children can testify, the trial judge questions them (*voir dire*) and then rules as to whether they meet these requirements of a witness.

California statutes, like those of most states, provide that defendants in criminal cases are presumed to be competent to stand trial. Thus, in most states a defense lawyer challenging this presumption has the burden of coming forward with evidence to prove that a defendant is incompetent and cannot be tried. In a very few states, the prosecution must prove by "clear and credible evidence" that the defendant is competent. See, e.g., Wis. St. Ann., § 971.14(4)(b). The U.S. Supreme Court held in *Medina v. California*[40] that it was not a constitutional violation for a state to use the presumption of competency. The defendant in *Medina* was convicted of three murders committed during robberies and shooting sprees. The U.S. Supreme Court followed the ruling of the California Supreme Court in holding that California Penal Code Section 1369(f), which makes a defendant prove incompetence by a preponderance of the evidence, does not violate any right granted or protected by the U.S. Constitution. However, in *Cooper v. Oklahoma*,[41] the Court reversed a conviction because an Oklahoma law required a defendant to prove incompetence by "clear and convincing" evidence, rather than the lesser standard of "preponderance of the evidence."

Summary

- *Actus reus* describes the physical acts making up the crime, while *mens rea* refers to any mental requirement for conviction of the crime.
- Not all crimes require proof that a defendant had a specific intent to achieve a specific end. In some cases, all that is required is that the defendant intended to do the prohibited act, sometimes known as general intent.
- An example of a crime that does not require a specific intent is second-degree murder, which under many state statutes does not require that the defendant act with the specific intent to cause death.
- The Model Penal Code, which some states have followed, lists the mental states for criminal liability as purposely, knowingly, recklessly, and negligently. If a statute requires a showing that the defendant acted purposely or knowingly, the defendant's mental state (intent or knowledge) is an element of the offense.

- Motive is the reason a defendant took action; intent is simply the mental state leading to the action taken.
- Strict liability crimes generally involve areas where a government has a strong interest in regulating conduct to promote public safety, such as food laws, or protect certain persons, such as school children.
- The year-and-a-day rule in murder cases, though no longer followed in many jurisdictions, is a rule of proximate causation that sets a limit on how far removed in time a death can be from acts causing harm to the victim and still be treated as a murder.
- Since the Due Process Clause requires the prosecution to prove every element of an offense beyond a reasonable doubt, a presumption that operated to mandate a jury finding on an element of an offense without such proof would violate the Due Process Clause. A conclusive or mandatory presumption is one that may not be rebutted by the defendant.

Key Terms

Case Analysis and Writing Exercises

1. The defendant was charged with violation of 18 U.S.C.A.§§ 2421 and 2422, transporting a person under the age of 18 across state lines for the purpose of engaging in prostitution. What must the prosecution prove under these statutes as elements of the offense? Must the prosecution prove the defendant knew the person transported was under the age of 18? *See United States v. Daniels*, 685 F.3d 1237 (11th Cir. 2012).

2. The defendant was charged with "sex trafficking of a minor" in violation of 18 U.S.C.A. § 1591. What, if any, is the mental element required under that statute? Is it a strict liability statute on the age of the victim, as is sometimes the case in crimes involving child victims? If not, how is the prosecution to prove the mental element required about the age of the victim? *See United States v. Robinson*, 702 F.3d 22 (2nd Cir. 2012), cert. denied 133 S. Ct. 1481 (2013).

3. It is generally true that it is not a defense to a crime that the defendant was intoxicated, at least if the intoxication was voluntary. However, under some circumstances even voluntary intoxication might be relevant in a criminal prosecution. Remembering that the prosecution must prove the *actus reus* of a crime charged, how did voluntary intoxication affect the outcome in *State v. Wells*, 139 Cal. Rptr. 3d, 422 (Cal App. 2012)? What are the *actus reus* elements of the crime of "DUI causing serious personal injury"?

4. A homeless person is charged with murder in the killing of another homeless man. The defendant admits hitting the victim with a blunt object, but plans to offer evidence he was drunk when the acts occurred. Is that evidence relevant in the case? Consider the *mens rea* for first-degree murder and second-degree murder. Is first-degree murder a specific intent crime? Is second-degree murder a specific intent crime? *See State v. Amos*, 823 N.W.2d 418 (Ia. App. 2012).

Endnotes

1. *Powell v. Texas,* 392 U.S. 514, 535, 88 S. Ct. 2145 (1968).
2. 287 P.3d 539 (Wash. 2012), *cert denied* 133 S.Ct. 991 (2012).
3. *Morissette v. United States,* 342 U.S. at 252 .
4. 438 U.S. 422 (1978).
5. 444 U.S. 394, 404 (1980).
6. The Court noted in the *Bailey* case that the use of the general intent-specific intent distinction had "been the source of a good deal of confusion." 444 U.S.394 (1980).
7. See 22 *Corpus Juris Secundum Criminal Law,* Sections 30–36.
8. 512 F.2d 1281 (5th Cir. 1975).
9. 584 S.E.2d 138 (S.C. App. 2008).
10. *Fedd v. State*, 680 S.E.2d 453 (Ga. App. 2009). Most states have similar statutes requiring knowledge that the person assaulted is a police officer.
11. *People v. Overton*, 34 Cal. Rptr. 2d 232 (Cal. App. 1994).
12. *See State v. Herman*, 474 N.W.2d 906 (Wis. App. 1991), *review denied*, 477 N.W.2d 286 (Wis. 1991), interpreting a Wisconsin statute similar to the federal "schoolyard" statute, 21 U.S.C. § 860.
13. *See United States v. Harris*, 313 F.3d 1228 (10th Cir. 2002).
14. 65 M.J. 132 (2007).
15. 420 U.S. 671 (1975). Congress amended the assault statute after the *Feola* decision, which some lower federal courts have regarded as limiting some aspects of the *Feola* decision. However, the scienter part of the decision does not seem to have been changed.
16. 2012 WL 1630878 (Ark. 2012).
17. See pages 242–250 of LaFave and Scott, *Criminal Law,* 2nd ed. Belmont, CA: West/Wadsworth (1986).
18. 511 U.S. 600 (1994).
19. *Dixon v. United States*, 548 U.S. 1 (2006).
20. 471 U.S. 419 (1985).
21. Indeed, in *Bryon v. United States*, 524 U.S. 184 (1998) the Supreme Court indicated the result in *Liparota* was required by the way Congress phrased the statute.
22. 678 F.3d 1110 (9th Cir. 2012).
23. 940 N.E.2d 63 (Ill. 2010).
24. 810 N.W.2d 888 (Iowa App. 2011).
25. 39 P.3d 1 (Kan. 2002).
26. A good discussion of these causation issues can be found in *State v. Jackson*, 697 S.E.2d 757 (Ga. 2010).
27. 944 So. 2d 1137 (Fla. App. 2006), *rev denied* 956 So. 2d 455 (2007).

28. See *People v. Stevenson,* 416 Mich. 383, 331 N.W.2d 143 (1982).

29. Blackstone, *Commentaries,* 197.

30. *See e.g.* Fla. Stat. § 782.035 (2007).

31. *See e.g. State v. Picotte*, 661 N.W.2d 381 (Wis. 2003).

32. *See Ex Parte Key*, 890 So.2d 1056 (Ala. 2003).

33. See *United States v. Winchester* (916 F.2d 601 (11th Cir. 1990)), having to do with people who cannot possess a firearm under the Federal Gun Control Act of 1968.

34. 115 S. Ct. 464, 467 (S. Ct. 1994).

35. 984 N.E.2d 853 (Mass. 2013).

36. *County Court v. Allen*, 442 U.S. 140 (1979).

37. *Sandstrom v. Montana*, 442 U.S. 510 (1979).

38. Because taxpayers have possession of their tax records, the burden of proof is on the taxpayers to prove the accuracy of their tax returns. Federal courts have held for many years that rulings of the commissioner of the Internal Revenue Service are presumed to be correct. See *Welch v. Helvering*, 290 U.S. Ill at 115 (1933). During the debate on the new federal tax code in 1998, changes were urged by members of Congress, and many writers predicted that this presumption and burden of proof would be changed in the new tax law. However, the 1998 Tax Reform Act modifies the old rules only slightly, and the presumption and burden of proof remain practically the same as they have been for many years.

39. *Commonwealth v. Vogel*, 440 Pa. 1, 17, 268 A.2d 89, 102 (1970); *Sumpter v. State,* 261 Ind. 471, 306 N.E.2d 95 (1974).

40. 505 U.S. 432 (1992).

41. 517 U.S. 348 (1996).

Criminal Liability

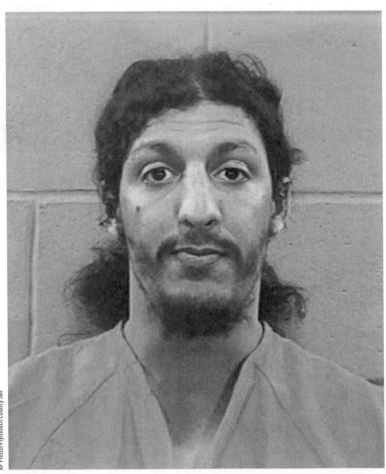

AP Photo/Plymouth County Jail

In 2003 Richard Reid, the "shoe bomber", pled guilty in Federal Court to 8 counts of terrorism based on his failed attempt to blow up a commercial airliner on which he was a passenger by detonating explosives hidden in his shoes. His crime resulted in the requirement that air passengers remove their shoes before going through gate security lines. Reid, a British citizen, is currently serving a life sentence in a Federal super-max prison in the United States.

OUTLINE

Preliminary, Anticipatory, and Inchoate Crimes

Solicitation or Incitement to Commit a Crime

Conspiracy to Commit a Crime

The Requirement of an Overt Act

The Crime of Attempt

Impossibility in Attempt Cases

Parties to the Principal Crime

Theories of Criminal Liability

Liability for Crimes Other than the Planned and Intended Offense

Post-Crime Offenses

LEARNING OBJECTIVES

In this chapter we examine the manner in which criminal liability is assessed, in particular for liability based upon acts and the relationship of those acts to crimes. The learning objectives for this chapter are the following:

- Identify when conduct has crossed the line between thinking about committing a crime and attempting to commit a crime.

- Explain the function of and need for corroborating evidence in solicitation prosecutions.

- Identify the steps that must be taken before one can be guilty of a conspiracy.

- Explain when, if ever, impossibility of committing the completed crime is a defense to a charge of attempt.

- Identify the circumstances when abandonment of the criminal purpose can have an effect on liability for an attempt, or liability for criminal acts done in a conspiracy.

- State the rule for liability of one conspirator for actions of another.

- List the parties who can be treated as principals for purposes of criminal liability.

A man and his girlfriend got in an argument in a parking lot in Wyoming. A third party interceded, and the man became abusive toward the third party. After a few blows were exchanged, the man jumped in his car, said, "I'll just run you over," and tried to hit the third party, but missed. He then stated he was going to "get his gun." The third party called the police, and shortly after they arrived at the parking lot the man was seen approaching in his car. The man turned and drove away after seeing the police, but when stopped he was found with a loaded gun in the car. The man said to the police "I lost it. I came back to kill him." He was arrested, charged with, and convicted of attempted first-degree murder.

The Wyoming attempt statute, Wyo. Stat. Ann. § 6-1-301, states that one is guilty of an attempt if "[w]ith the intent to commit the crime, he does any act that is a substantial step toward commission of the crime." In 2010 the Wyoming Supreme Court affirmed the conviction. At what point did the man's actions become "attempted murder"?

Criminal laws have long recognized that a person's conduct prior to or leading up to a substantive crime is often by itself blameworthy, even if the substantive crime is not committed. The same is true of actions taken after a crime that in some way aid the criminal, or obstruct law enforcement officers in their efforts to identify and apprehend the criminal. This chapter discusses many of these crimes and the elements that must be proved in the prosecution of them. Crimes such as solicitation, conspiracy, and attempt can be committed and punished quite independently from prosecution and punishment of the crime that was the intended outcome. We discuss many of the limitations on these crimes that have developed over the years, and continue to develop.

In some actions involving two people, such as an illegal drug transaction, the two parties may have earlier agreed between themselves that they would commit that crime. That agreement suggests they have also committed the crime of conspiracy, but as we will see, the Wharton rule prevents them from being convicted of that crime. We learn about this and other limiting doctrines in this chapter.

Preliminary, Anticipatory, and Inchoate Crimes

Professor Wayne LaFave, in his treatise on criminal law, uses the following example to illustrate the varieties of criminal charges that might result from criminal behavior, with the nature of the charge depending on the extent of the behavior:

> Suppose A wants B to kill C. If A hires B to do so, and B does kill C, B is guilty of murder, and so is A, either as an accessory, or as a principal. If B tries to kill C, but fails, A and B are both guilty of attempted murder. If B agrees with A to kill C, but does not attempt the murder, A and B are guilty of conspiracy to commit murder. However, even where B refuses A's request to kill C, and thus cannot be liable for any crime, A can be liable for solicitation.[1]

In this chapter we examine the basis for criminal liability, including liability for the preliminary crimes illustrated in the example above. In prosecutions for preliminary crimes it is not required that the underlying criminal act occurs; it is the planning or attempt to commit that crime that the law makes criminal.

Preliminary crimes are not always present when an underlying crime occurs, because not all crimes are planned in advance. Some crimes are committed impulsively, with the decision to commit the crime being made on the spur of the moment or almost simultaneously with the commission of the offense. Nor are all crimes completed. In some instances, the person who has carefully planned to commit a crime decides, for one reason or another, not to do so. Crimes are sometimes not completed because of events that prevent their completion. The problem in prosecuting preliminary crimes is determining when sufficient planning or attempt has occurred to justify the conclusion a crime has been committed.

In most situations, a person who has formulated the intent to commit a crime, but has taken no actions in furtherance of the crime, has not yet violated any law. He or she may even in some instances vocally express the intention to commit a crime without committing an offense. However, in some instances, such a person may be subject to arrest or to detention for expressing such intentions. One example we saw in Chapter 1 involved threats upon the life of the president of the United States.

It is possible for a person to commit a crime based on a statement of intention even though that person only intended a joke or hoax. For example, 18 U.S.C. § 35(b), the so-called Bomb Hoax statute, makes it a crime to make a false statement about the presence of a bomb in a civil aircraft. A person making such a statement can be convicted under the act, even if the person never intended to place a bomb on an aircraft, so long as the statement was made maliciously.[2]

The examples above illustrate areas where the simple statement of an intention is regarded as sufficiently dangerous or intrusive to justify criminal sanctions. They also demonstrate the need to prevent serious social harm before it occurs. To accomplish this goal, courts long ago created the three separate and distinct common law crimes of solicitation, conspiracy, and attempt. Although these offenses are crimes in themselves, each of these acts is **preliminary** or **anticipatory** to a more serious crime that the offender has in mind. These anticipatory crimes are commonly referred to as **inchoate crimes.**

> **preliminary, anticipatory, and inchoate crimes** Criminal acts that lead to or are attempts to commit other crimes.

In considering the preliminary offenses, the following questions always arise:

1. Where and when does non-criminal conduct become criminal conduct by a further act of the suspect?
2. Which of the preliminary offenses, if any, has the suspect committed?
3. When does the commission of the principal offense begin, so as to allow the state to charge either the preliminary offense or the principal offense?

Solicitation or Incitement to Commit a Crime[3]

By the early 1800s, English and American courts had recognized solicitation as a misdemeanor under the common law.[4] *Solicitation* may be defined as an attempt to get another person to commit a crime. It may also be described as an attempt to conspire to commit a crime. The solicitation does not have to be successful. The crime of **solicitation** or **incitement** (as it is called in England) is committed even if the person solicited refuses to cooperate and repudiates the proposal. It is also immaterial, in most instances, whether payment or reward is offered and whether it is accepted or refused. Evidence of the offer of payment or reward, however, can be important in proving solicitation.

> **solicitation or incitement crimes** Attempting to get another to commit a crime.

States commonly have both specific solicitation statutes—such as solicitation of prostitution or bribery—and general solicitation statutes applicable to other conduct. An example of a general solicitation statute is Wisconsin Statutes Annotated, Section 939.30, which states:

> (1) Except as provided in sub. (2) and § 961.455, whoever, with intent that a felony be committed, advises another to commit that crime under circumstances that indicate unequivocally that he or she has the intent is guilty of a Class H felony.

Prosecutions under solicitation statutes require a showing that the defendant has done more than make a casual suggestion that a crime be committed. In many cases the defendant's intent is shown by eliciting incriminating statements that are overheard by the police. For example, in a case prosecuted under the Wisconsin statute cited above, a defendant was charged with solicitation to commit murder. She told a friend that she had hired a co-worker to kill her ex-boyfriend. The friend permitted a police officer to listen in on a telephone conversation with the defendant, where she repeated those statements. Her conviction was upheld based on the testimony of the friend and the police officer, even though the defendant subsequently told the "hit man" not to go through with the crime.[5]

Some state statutes have specific corroboration requirements in the general solicitation statutes. For example, the Texas Penal Code Annotated, Section 15.03(b), states in part that "A person may not be convicted under this section on the uncorroborated testimony of the person allegedly solicited …"

The following cases further illustrate the crime of solicitation:

- A husband who solicited another person to kill his estranged wife's lover, and who also drove the "hit man" (an undercover police officer) around town showing him where the lover might be found, was properly convicted of both solicitation to commit murder and attempted capital murder for hire. *Ostrander v. Com.,* 658 S.E.2d 346 (Va. App. 2008)
- A defendant was convicted of solicitation to commit murder after he offered another man money to kill the main witness against the defendant in a fraud case. The conviction was upheld even though, in a subsequent "tapped" phone conversation with the other man, the defendant stated he "didn't need" to go through with the planned murder because "he had a good case." *People v. Houthoofd,* 790 N.W.2d 315 (Mich. 2010)
- In the two previous examples, the defendant was soliciting another to commit a crime as a perpetrator. Solicitation under specific-crime solicitation statutes can also apply to attempts by a defendant to involve a victim in illegal activity. In *State v. Arave,* 268 P.3d 163 (Utah 2011) the solicitation conviction of a man who offered an 11-year-old boy $20 to let the man perform oral sex on him was upheld.[6]

Conspiracy to Commit a Crime[7]

conspiracy: An agreement between two or more persons to engage in unlawful acts.

The crime of **conspiracy** is the oldest of the preliminary crimes. It received some legislative recognition as early as 1292, but it was not until the early 1600s that the English Court of the Star Chamber developed the crime of conspiracy into an offense of wide scope, capable of extensive application. This court was created in the late 1500s to try certain high crimes without a jury. Because of the ruthless methods used, the court is sometimes referred to as "the infamous Star Chamber." Modern critics of the crime of conspiracy sometimes recall the ancient unsavory use of the crime of conspiracy, as did former U.S. Supreme Court Justice Robert H. Jackson in his concurring opinion in *Krulewitch v. United States:*

> The crime comes down to us wrapped in vague but unpleasant connotations. It sounds historical undertones of treachery, secret plotting and violence on a scale that menaces social stability and the security of the state itself. "Privy conspiracy" ranks with sedition and rebellion in the Litany's prayer for deliverance. Conspiratorial movements do indeed lie back of the political assassination, the coup d'état, the putsch, the revolution and seizure of power in modern times, as they have in all history.[8]

The federal government (18 U.S.C.A. § 371) and all states have enacted statutes making conspiracy a crime in their jurisdictions. The reasoning behind such legislation generally is that when two or more persons plan a crime together,

(1) the extent of potential harm to the society is often increased considerably, (2) the possibility of the abandonment of the criminal plan is greatly reduced, (3) the chances of success in the criminal venture are greater than if only one individual were involved, and (4) their actions can be more difficult to detect than an individual's preparation to commit a crime.

The purpose, then, of criminal conspiracy statutes is to prevent and punish criminal partnerships in crime and to stop, if possible, such criminal combinations of people before attempts to commit substantive crimes are made.

Each state has its own definition of conspiracy, but most have language similar to that found in the Texas Penal Code: "A person commits criminal conspiracy if, with intent that a [crime] be committed: (1) he agrees with one or more persons that they or one or more of them engage in conduct that would constitute the offense; and (2) he or one or more of them performs an overt act in pursuance of the agreement" (V.T.C.A., Penal Code, § 15.02).[9]

Because conspiracy was looked on as a partnership in crime, the traditional view, known as the "bilateral approach," was that the state must prove the involvement of *two or more* guilty persons in the conspiracy.[10] One consequence of the bilateral approach was that if A and B were charged with conspiracy to murder and a jury found A guilty and B not guilty, the traditional view was that the conviction against A could not stand. The reasoning for the dismissal of the charge and conviction against A was that A could not conspire alone and that two or more guilty persons are necessary for the conviction to stand.

Influenced by § 5.03 of the Model Penal Code, a substantial number of states have limited or rejected the "two or more guilty persons" requirement for the crime of conspiracy.[11] The "bilateral" approach of conspiracy has largely been replaced by the "unilateral" approach. Section 5.03 (1) of the M.P.C. states a person is "guilty of conspiracy with another person" if the person "(a) agrees with such other person or persons that they or one of them will engage in conduct ..." that constitutes the agreed crime. The unilateral approach has two main differences from the bilateral approach: First, the crime is committed if the defendant agrees with another person, even if that other person is only feigning agreement, or lacks the capacity to make agreement; second, the person with whom the defendant agreed (such as an undercover police officer) need not be guilty in order to convict the defendant.

EXAMPLE ▶ A defendant used an Internet chat room to reach "agreement" with a woman to meet and have sex with the woman and her 13-year-old daughter. The woman was an undercover police officer, and there was no daughter. When the defendant arrived for the meeting he was arrested and charged with conspiracy to commit sexual assault on a child. In affirming his conviction, the Colorado Court of Appeals held in 2012 that the Colorado conspiracy statute adopted the "unilateral" approach, and thus it was not a defense that the other party to the agreement was an undercover officer.[12]

A conspiracy does not end if one of the conspirators dies before the object of the conspiracy is obtained or an overt act occurs.[13] Conspiracy can also be proved even if the co-conspirator cannot be found or cannot be identified. See *United States v. Thomas*.[14] (All that was required for a conspiracy conviction is that the existence of a co-conspirator is alleged and proved, even if he cannot be identified.)

A conspiracy, even under the "unilateral" approach, does require the agreement of two natural persons. Thus, an officer of a corporation acting for the corporation cannot be convicted of a conspiracy with the corporation. On the other hand, as long as another natural person was part of the agreement, even if not identified, conspiracy can be proved.[15]

The Requirement of an Overt Act

Under the common law conspiracy rules, proof of the criminal partnership was all that was required to prove the crime of conspiracy. There was no requirement that the prosecution prove that some overt act was done in furtherance of the conspiracy. Today, most states have written into their criminal conspiracy statutes the requirement of proof of an overt act by a defendant. The Model Penal Code, section 5.03(5) states that a conviction for conspiracy requires proof of an overt act, unless the underlying crime is a "felony of the first or second degree."

Virtually any act in furtherance of the conspiracy will satisfy this requirement. Moreover, the overt act need not be itself illegal. For example, making a telephone call[16] or obtaining guns to be used in a robbery[17] can satisfy the overt act requirement. However, some overt act must be alleged and proved. The agreement itself cannot be the overt act. In the 2012 case of *United States v. Lockhart*[18] the court dismissed an indictment charging conspiracy to sell prescription drug samples because the government failed to allege any overt act taken in furtherance of the conspiracy.

The overt act requirement exists in some federal conspiracy statutes, but not others. The general federal conspiracy statute, 18 U.S.C. § 371, expressly requires proof of an overt act done in furtherance of the criminal conspiracy that is charged. However, Congress has enacted specific conspiracy statutes that do not contain express overt act requirements. For example, 21 U.S.C.A. § 846, which applies to a conspiracy to violate federal drug laws, has no requirement of proof of an overt act, but only proof of a criminal conspiracy. The U.S. Supreme Court held in the case of *United States v. Shabani*[19] that the federal drug conspiracy statute was constitutional, stating: "[T]he language (of the federal statutes does not) require that a overt act be committed to further the conspiracy, and we have not inferred such a requirement from congressional silence in other conspiracy statutes."

Conspiracy prosecutions under the Federal Racketeer Influenced and Corrupt Organizations Act (RICO), 18 U.S.C. § 1962, have presented some problems in the overt act requirement. The RICO Act (discussed in Chapter 18) punishes persons who form criminal enterprises. Convictions under § 1962(c) require the prosecution to prove that a defendant committed at least two "predicate acts," that is, actions that were themselves criminal violations, in furtherance of the enterprise. When a defendant is charged under § 1962(d) with conspiracy to violate the RICO laws, the federal circuit courts were initially split on the need for proof that the defendant agreed to commit the two predicate acts.

However, in *Salinas v. United States*,[20] the U.S. Supreme Court held that § 1962(d) did not require proof that the defendant committed or agreed to commit the two predicate acts needed for conviction under § 1962(c). Salinas, a deputy sheriff, and his superior, the sheriff, were charged with accepting bribes in violation of the federal bribery law, 18 U.S.C. § 666; violation of the RICO law, § 1962(c); and conspiracy to violate the RICO law, § 1962(d). Salinas was acquitted of the substantive violation, but convicted under the conspiracy section. On appeal Salinas contended that because the jury did not find that he committed the two predicate acts needed for conviction under § 1962(c), and the prosecution did not prove he agreed to commit such acts, he could not be convicted of conspiracy.

The Supreme Court rejected his argument, noting first that § 1962(d), unlike the general conspiracy statute, had no overt act requirement. As a result, a person could be convicted of the conspiracy without having taken any acts, so long as he agreed to participate in the underlying crime. The Court said that while the underlying crime, the RICO violation, required two predicate acts, Salinas could be convicted under § 1962(d) without personally committing or agreeing to commit those two predicate acts:

> In the case before us, even if Salinas did not accept or agree to accept two bribes, there was ample evidence he conspired to violate subsection (c). The evidence shows that (the sheriff) committed at least two acts of racketeering activity when he accepted numerous bribes and that Salinas knew about or agreed to facilitate the scheme. This is sufficient to support a conviction under § 1962(d) (522 U.S. at 66).

In *Whitfield v. United States,* 543 U.S. 209 (2005) the Supreme Court held that 18 U.S.C. § 1956(h), the money-laundering statute, required no overt act for a conspiracy conviction. In discussing whether a statute has an overt act requirement, the Court in *Whitfield* stated that if the congressional statute was "modeled on 18 U.S.C. § 371" (the general conspiracy statute) it has an overt act requirement, but if it was "modeled on the Sherman Act, 15 U.S.C. § 1" (the antitrust statute) it dispensed with such a requirement. Based on this distinction, the federal district court in *United States v. Johnson,* 624 F. Supp. 2d 903 (W.D. Tenn. 2009) held that the federal murder-for-hire statute, 18 U.S.C. § 1958(a), required no proof of an overt act for a conspiracy conviction.

Overt acts are often very convincing evidence of the sincerity of a conspiracy agreement, and almost all strong conspiracy cases have evidence of overt acts.

The Wharton Rule Some crimes cannot be committed alone, but instead require two or more people. Examples of such crimes are dueling, bigamy, gambling, adultery, incest, pandering for prostitution, receiving a bribe, and distributing illegal drugs. As the crime of conspiracy punishes partnerships in crime because of increased danger to society, the **Wharton rule,** named after Francis Wharton, the author of an early treatise on criminal law, states that the crime of conspiracy cannot be charged if the number of people involved include only those necessary to commit the crime. In *Ianelli v. United States,*[21] the U.S. Supreme Court explained the place of the Wharton rule in federal conspiracy prosecutions. The Court stated that it applied, but only to those crimes that required multiple participants for their commission, and subject to clear legislative intent that Congress intended both prosecutions to be permitted. The Court in *Ianelli* held that Congress did intend prosecutions for conspiracy to violate federal gambling statutes, which require the participation of five persons, to be maintained together with prosecutions for the underlying crime.

Wharton rule The requirement that crimes needing more than one person for commission, such as bigamy, require three or more people for a conspiracy conviction.

| EXAMPLE | To distribute illegal drugs, there must be both a deliverer and a person receiving the drugs. Under the Wharton rule, if two persons engage in a one-time sale of a small quantity of an illegal drug, the seller and buyer cannot be charged with conspiracy.[22] |

Most states and the federal government use the Wharton rule and will not permit a conspiracy charge when only the people necessary to commit the crime are named as defendants. However, if more people than the number necessary to commit the crime were charged with conspiracy, the Wharton rule would not apply. For example, if three people conspire to sell illegal drugs all three can be charged with the conspiracy crime and also the underlying drug offense, if completed.

In the example given above of the drug deal, the Wharton rule could also be defeated if sufficient evidence showed that the buyer and seller have a long-standing criminal relationship involving repeated sales of large quantities of illegal drugs. The evidence would have to show an agreement beyond a simple one-time transaction. Most states would then permit substantive drug charges in addition to the conspiracy charge.

Impossibility, Abandonment, and Withdrawal

What effect, if any, should the impossibility of committing the criminal object of a conspiracy, the abandonment of the conspiracy by all the conspirators, or the withdrawal from the conspiracy of one conspirator have on the conspiracy charge?

In the case of impossibility, the U.S. Supreme Court in 2003 rejected a federal court of appeals ruling that included an impossibility defense. In *United States v. Jimenez Recio*[23] the Court reversed a Ninth Circuit Court of Appeals decision that conspirators could not be convicted of the crime if the "object of the conspiracy had been defeated" before the defendants had joined the conspiracy. In *Jimenez,* police officers seized a truck carrying illegal drugs and convinced the truck driver to lure the defendants to the scene. When they arrived and drove away with the truck, the police arrested them. The defendants argued that since the object of the conspiracy, possession of illegal drugs, was made impossible by the drug seizure by the police, the conspiracy was over before it began. The Ninth Circuit Court of Appeals agreed, but the Supreme Court did not. The Court stated that the essence of the crime is the agreement to commit a crime, not the crime to be committed. Citing the LaFave treatise and the Model Penal Code, it rejected the notion that impossibility is ever a defense to a conspiracy charge.

In the 2013 case of *United States v. Min*[24] the Fourth Circuit Court of Appeals rejected an impossibility defense to a conspiracy charge, where the defendants were charged with conspiracy to rob what they believed was a criminal "stash house" for illegal drugs. In fact, the house was part of an FBI sting operation aimed at drug dealers. The defendants contended it was impossible to complete the crime because the "stash house" didn't exist. The court rejected that argument, noting that the conspiracy crime is complete when the agreement is made, and thus it did not matter that the purpose of the agreement could not be realized.

The same reasoning applies to abandonment of the conspiracy or withdrawal by one conspirator. Even if the conspiracy is abandoned or one conspirator withdraws, the crime of conspiracy is nonetheless complete; "since the crime is complete with the agreement, no subsequent action can exonerate the conspirator of that crime."[25] However, if one conspirator withdraws from a conspiracy outside the limitations period for prosecution of the conspiracy, the withdrawal bars conviction. In the 2013 case of *Smith v. United States*[26] the U.S. Supreme Court held that the defendant carried the burden of proving he withdrew from a conspiracy prior to the limitation period. Under federal law, most prosecutions must commence within 5 years of the criminal acts. In *Smith*, the defendant was part of the conspiracy, but spent the 6 years prior to commencement of the prosecution in federal prison, which the defendant contended amounted to withdrawal from the conspiracy. The Court said it was the defendant's duty to prove that withdrawal, not the prosecution's duty to prove the defendant had not withdrawn.

The Model Penal Code provides a defense to a conspiracy charge where a conspirator "thwarted the success of the conspiracy, under circumstances manifesting a complete and voluntary renunciation of his criminal purpose." A few states have similar provisions. The New York Penal Code, Section 40.10 (4) states: "In any prosecution for criminal solicitation … or for conspiracy … in which the crime solicited or the crime contemplated by the conspiracy was not in fact committed, it is an affirmative defense that, under circumstances manifesting a voluntary and complete renunciation of his criminal purpose, the defendant prevented the commission of the crime."

The Crime of Attempt

Attempt is the most frequently charged of the three preliminary crimes, because "near" victims and witnesses generally report attempted rapes, robberies, murders, and other crimes to the police. Moreover, such victims and witnesses are generally more cooperative about appearing in court to testify to the attempted crimes.

attempt crimes Acts that are a substantial step toward the commission of a crime that is not yet completed.

Actus Reus of Attempt Crimes States can differ on how the act requirement in **attempt crimes** is defined, though as the box below notes, the "substantial step" test is probably the majority view. One method of defining the act requirement in attempt, which usually imposes a higher burden on the prosecution, is illustrated by the New York Criminal Code, which provides that "a person is guilty of an attempt to commit a crime when, with intent to commit a crime, he engages in conduct which tends to effect the commission of such crime."[28] New York courts have held under this statute that the state must show that the defendant performed acts that carried the "project forward within dangerous proximity of the criminal end to be attained."[29]

Bad thoughts alone cannot be charged as attempt or any other crime. The prosecution must show that the defendant attempted to commit the crime charged, and this requires showing an overt act or acts. The following cases illustrate conduct that courts ruled to be attempts to commit the crime charged:[30]

- Gathering addresses of witnesses, arranging for financing for a "hit man," and sending a letter to arrange for "hits" on witnesses constituted

THE *ACTUS REUS* OF ATTEMPT IN STATE AND FEDERAL COURTS

For many years courts differed greatly on the definition of the *actus reus* in attempt crimes. Terms such as "dangerous proximity test" (see below), "probability of desistence test," and "fragment of the crime test" as well as other terms were used by courts to describe the act requirement. That has changed. In the 2011 case of *United States v. Hernandez-Galvanithe*[27] the court noted that "The modern trend is a shift toward the 'substantial step' test from the Model Penal Code, which is now the majority view among the states and federal courts." Section 5.01 of the MPC states the requisite elements of attempt:

1. an intent to engage in criminal conduct, and
2. conduct constituting a "substantial step" towards the commission of the substantive offense that strongly corroborates the actor's criminal intent.

"Substantial step" means conduct that is strongly corroborative of the actor's criminal purpose. MPC § 5.01 (2). Later in this chapter we present several examples of "substantial steps" sufficient to support a conviction for an attempt.

substantial step in attempted murder. *United States v. Augustin*, 2011 WL 294281 (E.D. Tenn. 2011).

- Contacting potential accomplices, touring bank, and recruiting "getaway" driver were substantial steps for attempted robbery conviction. *United States v. Wesley*, 417 F.3d 612 (6th Cir. 2005).

- Defendant was stopped by police in possession of cold pills and ammonia, two of the six ingredients needed to "cook" methamphetamine. A container in his car also contained minute traces of meth residue. The court held that was enough to show a "substantial step" for attempted manufacture of methamphetamine. *State v. Stensaker*, 725 N.W.2d 883 (N.D. 2007).

- Defendant entered a convenience store and went into the bathroom, where he smoked some cocaine. He then exited the bathroom and walked to the front of the store carrying a knife. When he reached the cashier he swiped the knife in the air, but then collapsed in a corner, where he was subsequently arrested. In affirming the defendant's conviction of attempted armed robbery, the court said his actions were sufficient overt acts under the state's attempt statute. The court said an act need not be the "last requisite" act, but only must go beyond "mere preparation." *State v. Legins*, 645 S.E.2d 835 (N.C. App. 2007), *affirmed*, 653 S.E.2d 144 (N.C. 2007).

Mens Rea of Attempt   One element of most states' attempt statutes is the intent to commit a crime. Thus, even if a person engages in conduct that could result in the completed crime, coupled with that conduct must be the intent to complete that crime. In part, this is because the focus of attempt crimes is the dangerousness of the actor, and not the conduct, which need not by itself be illegal or criminal. Thus, an otherwise legal act can satisfy the "substantial step" test.

OVERT ACTS: CONSPIRACY VERSUS ATTEMPT

As we have seen, both conspiracy (under many statutes) and attempt require an "overt act" or "substantial step" before the crime is complete. Are the requirements for what constitutes the necessary act the same for both crimes? Based on what you know about conspiracy, is proof of the necessary "overt act" in conspiracy prosecutions easier or harder than proof of the necessary "substantial step" in attempt prosecutions? Why or why not? Consider the following two cases from the same jurisdiction, and decide if they are consistent.

1. Defendant stated to others that he planned to kill his estranged wife. Shortly after that, police found defendant in his car, parked in his wife's workplace parking lot near the door she used to exit the building. In his car he had an ice pick, a box cutter, and binoculars. Is he guilty of attempted murder? *See Collier v. State*, 846 N.E.2d 340 (Ind. App. 2006), *review denied*, 860 N.E.2d 585 (Ind. 2006).
2. Defendant and another person were arrested and charged with sale of illegal drugs. The two men discovered the name of the witness who turned them in, and agreed to kill her. They had a third person, a sister of one of the men, go to the witnesses' home and conduct surveillance so as to come up with a plan for killing the witness. Assuming the agreement to kill the witness was made, have the defendants taken the "overt act" needed for a conspiracy conviction? Would that act constitute a "substantial step" under attempt law? *See Conn. v. State*, 948 N.E.2d 849 (Ind. App. 2011).

What relevance, if any, does the kind of intent required by the completed crime have to a conviction for the attempt of that crime? That is, if the completed crime requires a specific intent, must the person charged with attempt have the same specific intent? The answer seems to be a qualified "yes."

As an example of this, courts have usually held that despite the fact that one could be convicted of the completed crime of murder even though one intended only to inflict serious bodily harm on the deceased, one could not be convicted of attempted murder if the victim did not die. That is because "attempted murder" requires the intent to bring about the result described in the completed crime of murder, which is the death of a person, and not merely serious bodily harm.[31]

This rule has led to inconsistent holdings in attempt convictions of crimes that do not have a specific intent. For example, the crime of voluntary manslaughter, and in many jurisdictions, the crime of second-degree murder, do not require proof that the defendant intended death to occur. As a result, some courts have held that there can be no crime of attempted manslaughter or attempted second-degree murder, because attempt crimes all require the intent to commit the base crime (death of another).[32] Others have held that proof that the defendant committed an act that would have resulted in death and was evidence of a "depraved mind" (the usual definition of second-degree murder—see Chapter 10), constituted proof of attempted second-degree murder.

In the case of strict liability crimes (see Chapter 3), it would seem logical to conclude that one cannot be convicted of strict liability attempt, because attempt is defined as doing an act with the intent to commit a crime. In strict liability, one can be convicted of the crime without either knowledge or intent to commit a crime if one engages in conduct that is made criminal. Merely attempting to engage in that conduct, the reasoning goes, cannot be an attempt crime, because it lacks the required intent.

In at least one kind of strict liability crime, unlawful sex with a child, courts have upheld attempt convictions. While statutes aimed at adults having sex with children have a variety of names (generally grouped under the name "statutory rape"), they all share one element: If the defendant had sexual intercourse with the victim, he could be convicted of the crime, even though he may have not known the victim was under age. These statutes thus require no intent with respect to the age of the victim.

Most courts uphold convictions of attempted sexual contact with a child, holding that all the state must prove is that the defendant intended to have sex with the victim.[33] In the 2012 Internet "sting" case of *State v. Washington*[34] the court held that where the defendant was attempting to have sexual contact with a police officer who was pretending to be a child, the state must prove the defendant believed the victim was a child.

Impossibility in Attempt Cases

Francisco Duran paced back and forth on the sidewalk in front of the White House in Washington, D.C., until he saw a man he believed to be President Clinton. Duran then pulled an automatic weapon from under his coat and began firing at the man through the White House wrought-iron fence until security forces seized him.

Duran was charged with the federal crime of attempted assassination of the president. Duran contended he could not be charged with the attempt because it was impossible to complete the crime. The man he saw and shot at was not the president, who was in fact not in Washington at the time of the attempt. The federal court rejected this defense and convicted Duran of the attempt charge.[35]

In a somewhat similar case, defendant Benny Curtis was charged with attempting to kill wild deer out of season when he shot at a deer decoy set up by game wardens in response to residents' complaints about illegal deer shootings. Curtis argued that it was impossible to complete the crime because he was shooting at a decoy, and therefore he could not be guilty of the attempt. The Supreme Court of Vermont rejected that contention, and Curtis was convicted of the charge.[36]

Courts formerly categorized impossibility defenses in attempt cases into two classes: factual impossibility and legal impossibility. Attempting to pick an empty pocket is an example of factual impossibility. The only thing that prevents the crime from being completed is the fact that the pocket is empty. Attempting to receive stolen goods that were not stolen has been characterized as an example of legal impossibility. Even if the defendants completed the intended act, they would not be guilty of a crime.

Most state courts and the federal courts have abandoned the distinction between factual and legal impossibility and have rejected the defense in both situations.[37] The Model Penal Code, Section 5.1, also rejects the impossibility defense, whether factual or legal, concluding that the culpability of the defendant should be judged by the circumstances as the defendant viewed them. Thus, in the examples above, the pickpocket believed he would find something in his victim's pocket, and the person receiving the goods believed they would be stolen property. Had their beliefs been correct, they would have committed the completed crime. As a result, they can be convicted of attempting that crime.

One form of the impossibility defense in attempt cases remains viable. If a defendant plans to engage in conduct that he believes to be a crime, but the conduct as planned is not a crime, the defendant is not guilty of an attempt.

EXAMPLE   Assume an adult plans to have sex with a female, believing her to be 16 years old, and also believing the age of consent in his state is 18 years of age. In fact, the age of consent is 16, so that having consensual sex with the female is not a crime. The man cannot be convicted of an attempt, even though he believed he was committing a crime.

LaFave, in *Criminal Law,* states that under the principle of legality (discussed in Chapter 1 of this text), "the defendant did not intend to do anything which had been made criminal, and what is not criminal may not be turned into a crime after the fact by characterizing his acts as an attempt."[38] For the same reason, one cannot be convicted of a conspiracy to commit a crime if the agreed objective is not criminal. See *In re Sealed Case,* 223 F.3d 775 (D.C. Cir. 2000).

Abandonment of the Criminal Purpose   In attempt, conspiracy, and solicitation, a person usually has time to change his or her mind and decide not to go ahead with the intended crime. The Model Penal Code, Section 501.04, states that it is a defense to the crime of attempt that the actor abandoned the attempt under circumstances "manifesting a complete and voluntary renunciation of his criminal purpose."

Many states now have statutes in their criminal codes on abandonment of a criminal effort. Important questions concerning abandonment of a criminal intent include these: Has a preliminary crime already been committed (how far along is the criminal effort)? Was the abandonment voluntary or involuntary? What was the reason for the abandonment (did the victim scream or police arrive at the scene or a burglar alarm go off)? The following cases illustrate:

- A liquor store video camera caught the defendant putting three bottles under his coat. The store manager then followed the defendant, who went into a bathroom where other men were located. The defendant was overheard saying "They're on us. We need to get out of here." He then left the bottles on the bathroom floor and exited the bathroom, where he was detained and arrested. His conviction of attempted theft was affirmed, the court stating that the Indiana statute on abandonment of criminal purpose, which applies to attempt and conspiracy crimes, requires the abandonment to be completely voluntary, based only on a change of mind not caused by external circumstances. Here, the renunciation was the result of fear of getting caught, which is not a proper basis for the abandonment defense. *Mumford v. State,* 923 N.E.2d 11 (Ind. App. 2011).
- A defendant and three other high school students went to police and informed them that another student, Kerns, was planning a Columbine-style attack at their high school. The police searched Kerns's home, and found explosives and other information showing the intent to bomb the high school. The information also showed the defendant had agreed to be a part of the attack. The defendant was convicted of conspiracy to commit murder. On appeal the court rejected his claim that he had abandoned the conspiracy and renounced his criminal intention, because when he went to the police he did not tell them he was part of

ATTEMPT CRIMES AND INTERNET CHAT ROOMS

One of the unfortunate side effects of the Internet boom is the use of so-called chat rooms by pedophiles to communicate with children. These sex-related communications are, by themselves, harmful to children and present the real possibility that the conversation could lead to actual contact between the adult pedophile and the child. As a result, states have passed legislation aimed at this conduct, generally making it criminal to entice a child into having unlawful sexual relations. As an example, Section 18.2-374.3 of the Virginia Code Annotated makes it a crime to use a communication system, including a computer, for the purpose of promoting unlawful sex with a child.

Police officers often enter these chat rooms and pass themselves off as young children to others using the chat room. When an adult pedophile connects with the officer, the officer engages in conversations that frequently lead to the arrest of the adult for attempted violations of these enticement statutes.

Two issues often arise in these cases. First, the defense of legal impossibility is often raised by these defendants. Courts virtually always reject that defense, as the courts in the following cases did:

- *U.S. v. Murrell,* 368 F.3d 1283 (11th Cir. 2004), *cert. denied,* 125 S. Ct. 439 (2004). Defendant was convicted of attempt to entice a child into having unlawful sexual relations. An investigator posed as the father of a minor child in chat room conversations with the defendant, although in fact no minor child existed. The defendant contended that he could not be convicted because he never communicated with a minor child. The court rejected this argument, saying the attempt crime required only that the government prove the defendant tried to entice a child into having sexual relations. It did not matter that no child ever heard those enticements.
- *State v. Patel,* 242 P.3d 856 (Wash. 2010). The defendant was convicted of attempted rape of a child under the age of 14. After chat room conversations in which the defendant proposed having sex with the "child," an undercover officer posing as a 13-year-old girl, the defendant

the conspiracy, and had renounced because of his fear of Kerns. *Commonwealth of Massachusetts v. Nee*, 935 N.E.2d 1276 (Mass. 2010).[39]

- The defendant approached a "hit man," actually an undercover police officer, and asked him to kill her ex-husband. The hit man agreed, and they discussed how it could be accomplished. Later, the defendant telephoned the hit man, and said, "Let's just hold off for a while." She was arrested and charged with solicitation to commit murder. Before trial, she moved to dismiss the charges, based on Alabama's abandonment statute, which states it is a defense if the defendant proves a "complete and voluntary renunciation of [his] criminal intent." The trial court agreed, and dismissed the charges, but the state appealed (generally permitted for dismissals before jeopardy attaches—see Chapter 7). On appeal, the court held that because the defendant did not clearly renounce all intention to have her husband killed, it was a jury question whether the abandonment defense was available. The case was remanded for trial on the solicitation to commit murder charge. *State v. Cromwell*, 33 So. 3d 31 (Ala. 2009).

agreed to meet the "child" at her apartment. When he arrived, police arrested him. The court rejected his argument that he could not be convicted of the crime of attempted rape of a child under the age of 14, holding that it did not matter that he never actually communicated with a child. It was sufficient, the court held, that he was attempting to do so.

Second, the question of the "substantial step" requirement is often involved in these attempt crimes, since getting close to the "completed act" is logically difficult because there is no child involved. The following two cases considered the proper substantial step requirement in Internet attempt prosecutions:

1. The defendant entered into Internet conversations with "Emily," who stated she was 14, though she was in fact a police officer. After several Internet conversations where defendant "groomed" Emily ("grooming" refers to recognized procedures pedophiles use to gain the confidence of their victims), defendant agreed to meet Emily at a motel to have sex. The defendant went to the motel, and later to a nearby park where he believed Emily was waiting, where he was arrested. His conviction was affirmed, the court saying his actions satisfied the substantial step requirement for attempted incitement of a child. *United States v. Young*, 613 F.3d 735 (8th Cir. 2010).
2. An Internet conversation by itself has been held insufficient to constitute an overt act. In *United States v. Winckelmann*, 70 M.J. 403 (U.S. Armed Forces 2011), an army officer was convicted of attempted enticement of a child. An adult believed the officer was a pedophile, and entered an Internet chat room that she knew the officer visited. Passing herself off as a 15-year-old boy, the adult had several sexually explicit conversations with the officer. At the end of one chat the officer asked "u free tonight," the adult said "yes," and they signed off. In reversing the officer's conviction for attempted enticement of a child the court said the Internet chat messages did not satisfy the substantial step requirement.

Parties to the Principal Crime

At the time of the American Revolution, more than 200 crimes were punished by death in England. Application of the death penalty depended on the degree of criminal participation in the completed crime. The following four common law categories were used to determine the penalty that would be applied after conviction to the **parties to the principal crime:**

parties to the principal crime Under common law, persons who either committed the crime, or aided or abetted the commission of the crime or the persons who committed the crime.

1. *Principal in the first degree* was the person (or persons) who actually committed the crime, and would receive the death penalty if applicable.
2. *Principal in the second degree* was a person who was present at the commission of the crime, was not involved in the planning of the crime, but aided and abetted in the actual commission of the crime. Under the common law this

offender could not be tried until the actual perpetrator had been apprehended and convicted of the offense.

3. *Accessory before the fact* was a person who, knowing that a crime was to be committed, aided in the preparation for the crime but was not present at the time the crime was committed.
4. *Accessory after the fact* was a person who knew that the crime had been committed and gave aid or comfort to the person who committed the crime. Neither an accessory before the fact nor an accessory after the fact could be tried until after the conviction of the principal in the first degree.

Today, most states have done away with the four common law categories, as has the federal government. Under 18 U.S.C. § 2, in prosecutions for violation of federal law any person who "commits" the crime or "aids or abets" commission of the crime may be convicted "as a principal." The Model Penal Code, § 2.06 (3), calls this "accomplice" liability. The **accomplice** to a crime has liability that derives from the actions of the principal, and can be prosecuted for the same crimes committed by the principal. Persons who aid a person after a crime has been committed are no longer treated as parties to the crime, and thus have no derivative liability. These persons can be charged with other crimes, such as Model Penal Code § 243.2, Hindering Apprehension or Prosecution.

The majority of jurisdictions have statutes that create the following two categories of criminal liability and make all principals or parties to the crime liable to the same punishment:

1. All people who knowingly are involved in or connected with the commission of a crime either before or during its commission are known as *principals, accomplices, or parties to the crime,* regardless of their connection. This category is a combination of the common law principal in the first and second degree and the accessory before the fact.
2. The person or people who render aid to the criminal after the crime has been committed were previously known under the common law as *accessories after the fact.* Legislative bodies have statutes identifying the criminal offenses in this category. This category is discussed in the section on post-crime offenses in this chapter.

The rule has been abolished that neither the principal in the second degree nor the accessories before or after the fact could be forced to trial before the trial of the principal in the first degree. Any participant in a crime may be tried and convicted, even though the person who actually committed the crime has not been apprehended and tried or even identified.[40]

Theories of Criminal Liability

Defendants may be charged as principals or parties to violations of criminal laws either because they committed the forbidden acts themselves, or because some other person did so and they are in some way liable for the acts of the other person. The following sections discuss the various ways one can incur criminal liability based on actions of another person.

Criminal Liability as an Aider and Abettor and/or a Conspirator   A person could be criminally liable for the conduct of another if he or she was a party to

accomplice One who aids another in the commission of a crime. An accomplice is generally treated the same as a principal.

a conspiracy to commit a crime and hired, urged, counseled, or planned with another to commit a crime. A person is also liable for the conduct of another if he or she is an **aider and abettor** to a person who committed a crime.

Aiders and abettors of a crime are usually at the scene of a crime and render aid and assistance to the person committing the crime, but the aid and assistance could also be rendered miles from the crime scene. The aider and abettor might also have been involved in the planning of the crime and therefore would also be a **conspirator.** Therefore, a conspirator could live in London, England (or elsewhere), hire the killing of a person in Los Angeles, and never go near the scene of the crime.

Fact finders (jury or judge) may draw reasonable inferences from the conduct of the offenders and make conclusions as to whether the people were aiders and abettors or conspirators to the crime, or both. In states using the common design rule, fact finders could infer from the facts of the case whether the defendants in a criminal case committed the crime (or crimes) under a common design or plan.

Criminal Liability Under the Common Design or Common Plan Rule Under the common design rule, when people have a common plan to do an unlawful act, whatever is done in furtherance of the **common design or plan** is the act of all, and they can all be punished for that act.

Thus, if one of the parties to an armed robbery wore a mask, then all the parties to the robbery wore a mask, and all are subject to the penalties of committing the crime of armed robbery while concealed. If one of the parties to a drug-trafficking offense carried a gun, then all the parties are subject to the penalties of carrying a loaded gun while trafficking illegal drugs.

A common design is a spoken or unspoken conspiracy to commit an unlawful act. Any member of the conspiracy (plan) could be held liable as a principal for any offense committed in the furtherance of the plan or conspiracy while he or she is a member of it. Latecomers cannot be convicted as principals for offenses that were committed before they joined the conspiracy or after they withdrew from the conspiracy.[41]

The following cases are illustrations of the principle **"what one did, they all did":**

- The defendant told two friends a woman he knew was holding drugs and money for a local drug dealer. The three men agreed to go to the woman's house, and have the defendant gain entry by greeting the woman at the front door, which he would then leave unlocked. The other two men would then enter the home, and steal the drugs and money. They did as planned, and when they entered one of the men shot and killed the woman. The defendant claimed that he did not know the killing was planned, but the court affirmed his conviction for murder.[42]
- Defendant Watts guarded the parents of a teenage girl while his two friends raped the girl. Watts was convicted of two counts of rape in concert because he aided and abetted both rapes. In affirming the California convictions for these and other crimes, the Federal Court of Appeals wrote,

  We hold that no violation of due process has occurred in this case. . . . The ancient and universally accepted principle of accomplice liability holds a defendant legally responsible for the unlawful conduct of others that he aids and abets.[43]

---

aider and abettor One who provides help to the person who commits a crime, either before or after the crime is committed.

conspirator A person who is a party to an agreement to commit an unlawful act.

common design or plan Scope of liability of persons who are party to a conspiracy or other agreement to do an unlawful act.

What one did, they all did The rule that all parties to a conspiracy or other agreement to perform an unlawful act are liable for every action taken by any party in furtherance of the conspiracy or agreement.

- In a 2009 case[44] the court upheld the manslaughter conviction of a defendant who had left an apartment he and two other men had entered with the intent to rob the occupant. After the defendant and one man found drugs and money, they ran out of the building. The remaining man shot at and killed the occupant of the apartment. Defendant's conviction was affirmed because the man who killed the victim stated prior to entering the apartment that he would use the shotgun he was carrying "if he needed to." The defendant could thus foresee that a killing might occur in the robbery.

Liability for Crimes Other than the Planned and Intended Offense

Pinkerton rule The rule followed in federal courts that one conspirator is liable for crimes committed by another conspirator, if foreseeable and done in furtherance of the conspiracy.

When the evidence demonstrates a common design or conspiracy to commit an unlawful act to which all the defendants agreed, whatever is done in the furtherance of the criminal plan is the act of all, if it is a natural and probable consequence of the intended crime. In prosecutions under the various federal conspiracy laws, courts commonly apply the so-called **Pinkerton** rule, taken from the Supreme Court's decision in *Pinkerton v. United States,* 328 U.S. 640 (1946). Under the *Pinkerton* rule a co-conspirator can be held liable for crimes committed by another conspirator, even if the co-conspirator did not know about the other crime, and did not agree to commit the other crime, so long as the crimes were committed in furtherance of the conspiracy and were foreseeable.

> EXAMPLE ▶

Several men agreed to enter into an illegal drug distribution conspiracy. When they were caught dealing drugs, one of the men was carrying a concealed weapon, which the other men claimed they did not know existed. They were all convicted of possessing a firearm while distributing illegal drugs. The court affirmed the conviction, stating that it is foreseeable that one member of an illegal drug conspiracy would be armed. *United States v. Vasquez-Castro*, 640 F.3d 19 (1st Cir. 2011).

Some but not all[45] state courts apply rules similar to the *Pinkerton* rule. For example, if guns are carried and a shot is fired by one member of the group, that shot is fired by all the defendants, and all of them must answer for the results.[46]

In *People v. Jones,* the California courts held that an accused who knew that his co-defendants were armed was responsible for all the consequences when a night watchman was killed in a robbery.[47] The defendant in the *Jones* case was unarmed.

The definition of the natural and probable consequences of the intended crime varies somewhat from jury to jury and court to court. The following example illustrates the problem:

> EXAMPLE ▶

X and Y conspire to burglarize a residence. X is the lookout and getaway driver while Y is in the house committing the burglary. Y commits the following additional crimes. For which of the crimes committed by Y may X be convicted?

1. Y is surprised by the homeowner and, in an attempt to get away, kills the man.
2. Y is surprised by an 11-year-old boy who lives in the house and needlessly kills the boy.

ACCOMPLICE LIABILITY AND THE *PINKERTON* RULE

The rules for making an accomplice (aider and abetter) liable for crimes committed by the principal actor are similar to liability under the *Pinkerton* rule in the sense that one person is liable for a substantive crime committed by another. However, the rules may have one important difference when applied to crimes that have a specific intent requirement. Consider the following two situations:

1. A and B enter into a conspiracy to rob a convenience store. B states he will carry a weapon, and A says "OK, but don't shoot anyone." In fact, B intentionally shoots and kills the cashier, a person disliked by B.
2. B asks A to give him a ride to a convenience store, and watch for police while B robs the store. B goes into the store, and during the robbery shoots and kills the store's cashier.

Can A be convicted of murder? In the first situation, probably yes under the *Pinkerton* rule, because the killing was both foreseeable and in furtherance of the conspiracy. Moreover, under "joint venture" or "common design" theory, courts have held that the prosecution need not prove a defendant/participant knew that any particular person carried a weapon, but only that one did, even if it was the defendant. *See Commonwealth v. Britt*, 987 N.E.2d 558 (Mass. 2013).

In the second situation, some states would not permit a conviction, because although A is clearly an accomplice to the crime of robbery, A lacked the specific intent to kill the store cashier. Those courts require for accomplice liability that the accomplice have the same mental state as the principal—here, intent to kill. *See Gonzales v. Beard*, 2012 WL 4510711 (E.D. Pa. 2012). Model Penal Code § 2.06 (3) and (4) points to the same conclusion.

3. In addition to stealing, Y comes upon a woman in bed and rapes the woman.
4. After stealing from the house, Y sees a gallon of gasoline in the back hall of the house, spills the gasoline around the house, and burns it down.

Prosecutors could charge X as a co-conspirator with all the additional crimes, but whether X would be convicted would depend on whether the finder of fact determined that the additional acts were a natural and probable consequence of the burglary.

X's defense could be that some of the offenses are not the natural or probable consequence of the intended crime of burglary, and therefore X would not be criminally liable for those offenses. In all cases, X would be charged with and convicted of the crime of burglary.[48]

Can Criminal Liability Result from an Accident?

Criminal liability can result from intentional, reckless, or grossly negligent conduct. However, can criminal liability result from accidental conduct? Criminals also have accidents. U.S. Supreme Court Chief Justice Roberts noted in the 2009 case of *United States v. Dean*, 129 S. Ct. 1849, "Accidents happen. Sometimes they happen to individuals committing crimes with loaded guns."

The famous English lawyer and writer Sir William Blackstone answered the question of criminal liability from accidents in his *Commentaries*, written in 1769, as follows:

IF THE STATE CAN PROVE ONE OF THE FOLLOWING BEYOND REASONABLE DOUBT, A PERSON CAN BE HELD CRIMINALLY LIABLE

For a preliminary or anticipatory crime:

- Solicitation
- Conspiracy
- Attempt

For the planned and intended crime (if completed):

- As the person who committed the crime, or
- As a person who intentionally aids and abets the person who committed the crime, or
- As a conspirator who advises, hires, counsels, or otherwise procures another to commit the crime

For a post-crime offense relating to the planned and intended crime:

- Party to a crime, in which the state would have to prove each person participated in one of the preceding categories
- Common design or plan
- Criminal liability under the complicity, accountability, or accomplice rules

"[I]f any accidental mischief happens to follow from the performance of a lawful act, the party stands excused from all guilt: but if a man be doing any thing unlawful and a consequence ensues which he did not foresee or intend, as the death of the man or the like, his want of foresight shall be no excuse … he is criminally guilty of whatever consequences may follow from the first misbehavior."

In the *Dean* case a defendant entered a bank carrying a weapon, intending to rob the bank. In the process, the firearm he carried discharged. The defendant was charged with violation of 18 U.S.C. § 924(c)(1)(A), carrying a firearm during the commission of a violent crime. Conviction under that statute results in a 5-year minimum sentence, which is increased to 7 years if the firearm is discharged. The defendant argued the discharge was an accident, but the Court said the enhanced sentence was still proper: "It is unusual to impose criminal punishment for the consequences of purely accidental conduct. But it is not unusual to punish individuals for the unintended consequences of their unlawful acts."

Post-Crime Offenses

post-crime offenses Actions taken after a crime has been committed, with knowledge that the crime was committed, which provide aid to the person who committed the crime.

Today, all states and the federal government have enacted many statutes regarding **post-crime offenses.** These statutes are meant to assist law enforcement officers in performing their duty of investigating crimes and apprehending criminals. Some statutes punish people who knowingly give police false information with the intent to mislead them. Other statutes are designed to permit the proper and efficient functioning of the courts and the criminal justice system. Some of these offenses existed under the common law, whereas others have been created in modern times. Examples are the following:

- Refusing to aid an officer while the officer is doing any act in his or her official capacity
- Obstructing or resisting an officer while the officer is doing any act in his or her official capacity (interfering with an officer)[49]
- Obstructing justice
- Compounding a crime: the making of an agreement (for a consideration) to withhold evidence of, or to abstain from prosecuting, a crime of which the accused has knowledge[50]
- Making false reports to an officer or law agency[51]
- Misprision of a felony (failure to report or prosecute a known felon)[52]
- Harboring or aiding felons
- Committing perjury
- Escaping from custody
- Bribing witnesses
- Jumping bail
- Communicating with jurors with the intent to influence them

Figure 4.1 illustrates the various stages of crimes, from the original idea of the crime to the offenses that can occur after the crime.

FIGURE 4.1

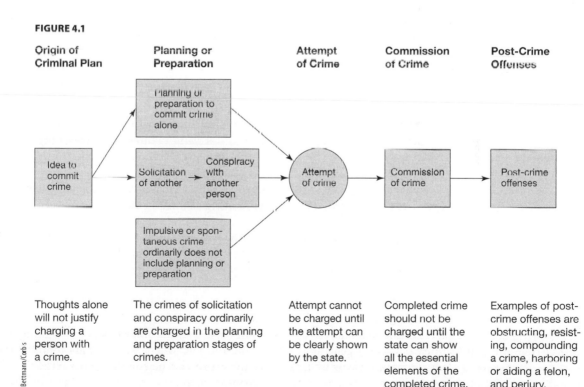

Origin of Criminal Plan	Planning or Preparation	Attempt of Crime	Commission of Crime	Post-Crime Offenses
Idea to commit crime	Planning or preparation to commit crime alone / Solicitation of another → Conspiracy with another person / Impulsive or spontaneous crime ordinarily does not include planning or preparation	Attempt of crime	Commission of crime	Post-crime offenses
Thoughts alone will not justify charging a person with a crime.	The crimes of solicitation and conspiracy ordinarily are charged in the planning and preparation stages of crimes.	Attempt cannot be charged until the attempt can be clearly shown by the state.	Completed crime should not be charged until the state can show all the essential elements of the completed crime.	Examples of post-crime offenses are obstructing, resisting, compounding a crime, harboring or aiding a felon, and perjury.

Bettmann/Corbis

STRICT LIABILITY DISTINGUISHED FROM VICARIOUS LIABILITY

Strict Liability

When a criminal statute imposes liability without requiring proof of mental fault, the offense is called a strict liability offense. If a statute requires proof of a mental element, the offense is not a strict liability offense.

To prove a strict liability offense, the state need prove only that the defendant did the forbidden act. The state does not have to prove a mental fault (*mens rea*). For example, in most states, it is not necessary for the state to prove a defendant knew the age of a victim of statutory rape.

Vicarious Liability

When a person becomes liable for the criminal act (or acts) of another, the liability is vicarious. Section 2.06 of the Model Penal Code lists the following categories of vicarious liability:

- Causing innocent or irresponsible people to do a criminal act
- Becoming a criminal accomplice of another person by:

  a. Soliciting the person to do a criminal act
  b. Aiding the other person in planning or committing the act
  c. Having a legal duty to prevent the act and failing to take reasonable steps to prevent the act
  d. Falling into a class of persons whose complicity for the crime is expressly established by statute

Summary

- Thoughts alone are not crimes. However, when actions are taken that are steps toward completing a crime, or persuading another to commit the crime, criminal liability is possible.
- In solicitation charges, corroboration is important to show the defendant unequivocally intended to convince another person to engage in criminal conduct.
- A conspiracy conviction requires as a minimum that two or more people agree to commit actions that are criminal. Most conspiracy statutes require the additional step of an overt act taken in furtherance of the conspiracy, but many federal conspiracy statutes have no overt act requirement.
- The fact that the completed crime could not have occurred, the impossibility defense, is generally not a defense to an attempt charge, unless what was being attempted was not a crime at all.

- Because the crimes of conspiracy, solicitation, or attempt are complete whether or not the underlying crimes ever are committed, abandonment of the conspiracy or attempt is generally not a defense. Some states provide an abandonment defense if a defendant prevents the underlying crime from occurring.
- One conspirator can be held liable for acts of another conspirator, including other crimes, if they are committed in furtherance of the conspiracy. The fact that one conspirator did not know of or agree to the commission of other crimes does not matter unless the other crimes were unforeseeable.
- Both those who commit the acts constituting the crime and thus who act to facilitate commission of the crime can be convicted as parties to the crime.

Key Terms

preliminary, anticipatory, or
inchoate crimes, p. 87
solicitation or incitement crimes,
p. 87
conspiracy, p. 88

Wharton rule, p. 91
attempt crimes, p. 93
parties to the principal crime, p. 99
accomplice, p. 100
aider and abettor, p. 101

conspirator, p. 101
common design or plan, p. 101
"What one did, they all did," p. 101
Pinkerton rule, p. 102
post-crime offenses, p. 104

Case Analysis and Writing Exercises

1. Can the victim of a sexual assault be an accomplice? Why not? *See People v. Gourley*, 2009 WL 529216 (Md. App. 2009). Why was defendant arguing that the victim, Berry, was an accomplice?

2. The defendant was charged with being an accomplice (called a "second-degree principal" in Virginia) to robbery, robbery with a firearm, and robbery to benefit a criminal street gang. Defendant drove the van while others robbed a convenience store. What must the state prove to convict the defendant on these charges? *See Lebron v. Com.*, 712 S.E.2d 15 (Va. App. 2011).

3. The federal statute 18 U.S.C.A § 2422(b) makes it a crime for an adult to entice or attempt to entice a minor into engaging in sexual activity "for which any person can be charged with a criminal offense." The circuit courts of appeal are split on whether under this statute a defendant must engage or attempt to engage in some physical contact with the minor. In *United States v. Taylor,* 640 F.3d 255 (7th Cir. 2011), the court held it did require physical contact. In *United States v. Fugit*, 703 F.3d 248 (4th Cir. 2012), the court held it did not. Assume an adult has a conversation (telephone or Internet) with

a child, and suggests the child engage in some sexual activity, such as touching his or her own genitals. Nothing more happens. Is the adult guilty of solicitation under the federal statute? Is this an example of attempted solicitation? Is attempted solicitation possible? Finally, how does this example differ from the Internet chat room attempt cases on p. 98–99, which require some substantial step beyond the Internet conversation? A petition for certiorari to the U.S. Supreme Court was filed in May 2013. Would you grant the petition if you were a Supreme Court Justice? Why or why not?

4. Assume two people enter into a conspiracy to distribute drugs. One person, A, is a convicted felon. The other, B, is not. During the conspiracy, but unknown to B, A obtains possession of a gun, a violation of a firearms statute prohibiting a convicted felon from owning or possessing a firearm. Can B be convicted of the crime of possession of a firearm by a convicted felon under the *Pinkerton* rule? Do you see problems with applying the rule here? See *United States v. Walls,* 225 F3d 858 (7th Cir. 2000).

Endnotes

1. See Section 11.1, Wayne LaFave, *Criminal Law,* 4th ed. (Belmont, Calif.: Thomson/West, 2003).
2. *See United States v. Hassouneh* , 199 F.3d 175 (4th Cir. 2000).
3. In the United States, the crime is generally called "solicitation"; in England the crime is called "incitement," as the term *solicitation* is used there for solicitation for prostitution. See *Moriarty's Police Law (Law and Regulations for the Use of Police Officers)*, 21st ed. (London: Butterworths, 1972).
4. The English parliament enacted the Incitement to Mutiny Act (English armed forces) in 1797. See *Moriarty's Police Law*, p. 12.
5. *State v. Hauk,* 652 N.W.2d 393 (Wis. 2002). Since the crime of solicitation is complete when the solicitation occurs, it does not matter if the defendant later recants the solicitation. Also, as the *Hauk* court held, the usual rule that one cannot be convicted of a crime based only on a confession is inapplicable where the confession is not made to the police, but to a friend.

See page 219, Thomas Gardner and Terry Anderson, *Criminal Evidence*, 6th ed. (Belmont, CA: Thomson/ Wadsworth, 2007).

6. The defendant was also convicted of attempted sodomy on a child, but the Utah Supreme Court reversed that conviction, stating that "Solicitation alone cannot constitute a substantial step toward commission of a crime." 268 P.3d at 168.

7. In 1925, Judge Learned Hand called conspiracy the "darling of the prosecutor's nursery," as prosecutors were using conspiracy as a weapon against organized crime and illegal business practices. See *Harrison v. United States* (7 F.2d 259, 263, 2d Cir. 1925). Today, the federal and state RICO statutes are much more effective in this type of criminal prosecution. See Chapter 18 for a discussion of the RICO statutes.

8. 336 U.S. 440, 445, 69 S. Ct. 716, 719 (1949).

9. The Texas conspiracy statute is actually limited to agreements to commit a *felony,* as opposed to a *crime.* In that respect, Texas is in the minority; most states have statutes making the crime of conspiracy applicable to an agreement to commit any crime. For those states retaining the common law definition of conspiracy, the agreement need only be to achieve some "unlawful purpose." See *Commonwealth v. Hunt* (45 Mass. (4 Mete.) Ill, 123 (1842)).

10. Under the old common law, a husband and wife were one person, with the wife being subject to the control and discipline of the husband. (See the discussion on the defense of duress and coercion in Chapter 7.) Because of this relationship, the common law rule held that *because* the husband and wife were one person, they could not conspire together and be charged as the two persons to a conspiracy.

This old common law rule was rejected by the U.S. Supreme Court in the 1960 case of *United States v. Dege* (80 S. Ct. 1589), in which the Court held that a wife is a person like anyone else and therefore is capable of entering into a criminal conspiracy with her husband or another person. Today, all states would follow this reasoning if the question were before a state court.

11. The general federal conspiracy statute, 18 U.S.C.A. § 371 retains the "bilateral" approach to conspiracy, and thus there must be two or more guilty persons before a conspiracy is formed.

12. *People v. Vecellio,* 2012 WL 866421 (Colo. App. 2012), *review denied,* 2012 WL 5384641 (Colo. 2012).

13. See *Alleyne v. California,* 98 Cal. Rptr. 2d 737 (2000), *cert, denied* 532 U.S. 958 (2001).

14. 348 F.3d 78 (5th Cir. 2003), *cert denied,* 540 U.S. 1207 (2004).

15. *See United States v. Giuseppe Bottiglieri Shipping Co. S.P.A.,* 2012 WL 1899844 (S.D. Ala. 2012).

16. *United States v. Fellabaum,* 408 F.2d 220(7th Cir. 1969).

17. *Burk v. State,* 848 P.2d 225 (1993).

18. 2012 WL 5866672 (E.D. Ky. 2012).

19. 115 S. Ct. 382 (1994).

20. 522 U.S. 52 (1997).

21. 420 U.S. 770 (1975).

22. See *United States v. Delutis,* 722 F. 2d 902 (1st Cir. 1983). The Wharton rule was held not to apply to the crime of possession with intent to distribute illegal drugs, as one person alone can commit this crime. See *Johnson v. State,* 587 A.2d 444 (Del. 1991).

23. See *United States v. Cohen,* 260 F.3d 68 (2d Cir. 2001).

24. 704 F.3d 314 (4th Cir. 2013).

25. LaFave, *Criminal Law,* 4th ed., p. 652 (Belmont, CA: Thomson/West, 2003).

26. 133 S. Ct. 714 (2013).

27. 632 F.3d 192, 198 (5th Cir. 2011).

28. Section 110.00, McKinney's *Consolidated Laws of New York, Annotated,* Book 39.

29. *People v. Warren,* 489 N.E.2d 240 (N.Y. 1985).

30. Examples of conduct that was mere preparation and did not amount to conduct to attempt to commit the crime charged include the following:
   - In *Comm. v. Bell,* 917 N.E.2d 740 (Mass. 2009) the court reversed an attempted rape conviction. The defendant had arranged to meet a woman, actually an undercover police officer, to discuss paying her to have sex with her "child." The defendant met the woman in a parking lot, and they agreed to meet later with the child. The defendant was then arrested, and later convicted of attempted rape. The Court of Appeals reversed, holding that under Massachusetts law an overt act must be either the "last act" before completion of the crime, or only a "narrow gap" must exist between the overt act and the completed crime.
   - In *United States v. Thornton,* 539 F.3d 741 (7th Cir. 2008) the court reversed a conviction for attempted bank robbery. The defendant was seen attempting to enter the bank's door, wearing a mask and dressed to disguise his appearance. The court said those acts were not a "substantial step" toward completion of the crime.

31. See Wayne, *Criminal Law,* 4th ed. Section 11.3b, p. 584. (Belmont, Calif.: Thomson/West, 2003).

32. Cases from many jurisdictions are collected in *State v. Gutierrez,* 172 P.3d 18 (Kan. 2007). More recent decisions, at least for attempted voluntary manslaughter and second-degree murder, hold there can be attempts of these crimes. *See Mendenhall v. State,* 82 So. 3d 1153 (Fla. App. 2012).

33. *See People v. Reyes,* 908 N.Y.S. 2d 14 (N.Y.A.D. 2010); *Maxwell v. State,* 895 A.2d 327 (Md. App. 2006); *State v. Sorabella,* 891 A.2d 897 (Conn. 2006), *cert denied,* 549 U.S. 821 (2006).

34. 270 P.3d 591 (Wash. 2012).

35. *United States v. Duran,* 884 F. Supp. 577 (D.D.C. 1995). Duran continued to fire his automatic weapon until the clip was empty. While Duran was replacing the empty clip, bystanders seized Duran on the sidewalk outside the White House and disarmed him.

36. *State v. Curtis,* 603 A.2d 356 (Va. 1991).

37. See page 38 of LaFave and Scott, *Criminal Law,* 2nd ed. (Belmont, Calif.: West/Wadsworth, 1986). Legal writers distinguish between legal and factual impossibility. However, the Supreme Court of Pennsylvania states that no American court has recognized factual impossibility as a defense to an attempt charge (*Commonwealth v. Henley,* 474 A.2d at 1116).

In addition to legal and factual impossibility, some courts write of "inherent impossibility." The committee drafting the revised Illinois Criminal Code in 1961 wrote this comment on the defenses of impossibility (Chapter 38, p. 513):

It is the intent of section 8-4(b) to exclude both factual and legal impossibilities as defenses to prosecution for attempt. However, inherent impossibility (attempts to kill by witchcraft such as repeatedly stabbing a cloth dummy made to represent the person intended to be killed) is not intended to be excluded as a defense. [Emphasis in original]

38. LaFave, *Criminal Law,* 4th ed., p. 600 (Belmont, Calif.: Thomson/West, 2003).

39. The court stated that it was not adopting an abandonment defense, which it said must be created by the legislature. It simply said that even if such a defense existed, the defendant would not be entitled to the defense. In Missouri, which has a conspiracy renunciation statute, the court held that the defense would not be available in attempt crimes until the legislature said so. *State v. Rollins,* 321 S.W.3d 353 (Mo. App. 2010).

40. In the 1980 case of *Standefer v. United States* (447 U.S. 10, 100 S. Ct. 1999) the U.S. Supreme Court held that a defendant may be convicted of aiding and abetting the commission of a federal crime, even though the person who actually committed the crime had been acquitted of the offense. Model Penal Code § 2.06 (7) has a similar provision.

41. The New Jersey accountability and accomplice liability law is presented in the 1992 case of *State v. Bryant,* 607 A.2d 1343 (N.J. 1992), as follows:

N.J.S.A. 2C:2-6a provides that a person is guilty of an offense "if it is committed by his own conduct or the conduct of another person for which he is legally accountable, or both." N.J.S.A. 2C:2-6b provides in part: b. A person is legally accountable for the conduct of another person when:* * *

(3) He is an accomplice of such other person in the commission of an offense; or

(4) He is engaged in a conspiracy with such other person.

c. A person is an accomplice of another person in the commission of an offense if:

(1) With the purpose of promoting or facilitating the commission of the offense, he

(a) Solicits such other person to commit it;

(b) Aids or agrees or attempts to aid such other person in planning or committing it; or

(c) Having a legal duty to prevent the commission of the offense, fails to make proper effort so to do; or

(d) His conduct is expressly declared by law to establish his complicity.

42. *State v. Turner,* 130 P.3d 1154 (Nev. 2009).

43. *Watts v. Bonneville,* 879 R2d 685 (9th Cir. 1989).

44. *State v. Coward ,* 972 A.2d 691 (Conn. 2009).

45. *State v. Nevanez,* 130 P.3d 1154 (Idaho App. 2005); *State v. Roberts,* 14 P.3d 713 (Wash. 2000).

46. *People v. Bracey,* 249 N.E.2d 224 (1969).

47. 29 P.2d 902 (1934).

48. In the 1991 case of *Ward v. State* (567 N.E.2d 85), no evidence showed that the defendant knew anything about the planned robbery. The defendant drove three men to the store they planned to rob and then left the area. Another car arrived carrying the weapons and ski masks used. During the robbery, a store clerk was killed. The Supreme Court of Indiana reversed the defendant's conviction of felony murder, pointing out that the defendant was not shown to have participated in either the planning or carrying out of the robbery, that he did not remain as a lookout but left the area, that he did not return to aid in the escape, and that he did not receive any proceeds of the robbery.

In the case of *Mumford v. Maryland,* 313 A.2d 563 (Md. App. 1974), a rape and murder occurred during a burglary. The defendant (a 15-year-old girl) stated that she was elsewhere on the premises when the rape and murder occurred and that she did not know these crimes were being committed. In reversing her conviction for first-degree murder (felony murder) and ordering a new trial, the court stated:

There must be a direct causal connection between the homicide and the felony. Something more than mere coincidence in time and place between the two must be shown; otherwise, the felony-murder rule will not be applicable.

(See Chapter 10 for material on the felony murder rule.)

49. Obstructing or interfering with an officer sometimes occurs during an accident or public disaster. Newspaper photographers were convicted in the following cases for seeking to obtain photographs of accidents after being repeatedly told to stay in the area where the general public was permitted. In both disasters, police had cleared the area so that emergency fire and medical vehicles could enter the area, control fire and explosions, and render aid to the injured and dying.

In the case of *State v. Peruta,* 591 A.2d 140 (Conn. App. 1991), a fatal car accident had occurred. The photographer was convicted of "interfering with an officer" because he repeatedly interfered with rescue efforts.

In the case of *City of Oak Creek v. King,* 436 N.W.2d 285 (Wis. 1989), a commercial airline had crashed, causing many deaths and injuries. King was convicted of disorderly conduct because he would not stay behind police lines. The Supreme Court of Wisconsin pointed out that reporters do not have special rights that the general public does not have and must obey reasonable police orders at the scene of a public emergency.

50. The South Dakota statute of compounding a crime is as follows:

Any person who accepts or offers or agrees to accept any pecuniary benefit as consideration for

1. Refraining from seeking prosecution of an offender; or

2. Refraining from reporting to law enforcement authorities the commission or suspected commission of any crime or information relating to a crime; is guilty of compounding. Compounding a felony is a Class 6 felony. Compounding a misdemeanor is a Class 1 misdemeanor.

51. For a false report case that went to the U.S. Supreme Court, see *United States v. Rogers,* 466 U.S. 475 (1984).

52. The drafters of the Model Penal Code state, "In general, our society does not use penal sanctions to compel reporting of crime" (§ 242.5, Comment at pp. 251–252, 1980).

Criminal Responsibility and the Capacity to Commit a Crime

James Holmes, the accused killer in the 2012 Aurora, Colorado movie theater homicides, in a pretrial court appearance. Holmes has raised the insanity defense in his trial on murder charges arising out of the killings.

OUTLINE

Ancient Concepts of Criminal Responsibility

Infancy and Criminal Responsibility

The Juvenile Court System

The Insanity Defense

Insanity at the Time of the Criminal Incident

Tests Used to Determine Insanity

The *M'Naghten* Case and the "Right and Wrong" Test

The "Product-of-Mental-Illness Rule" and "Irresistible Impulse"

The Model Penal Code "Substantial Capacity" Test

The Plea and Verdict of Guilty but Mentally Ill

Mental Conditions That Do Not Satisfy the Insanity Defense

The Defense of Diminished Capacity

The Requirement of Competency to Stand Trial

The Criminal Liability of Corporations

LEARNING OBJECTIVES

In this chapter we consider when a person has the capacity for criminal responsibility. The learning objectives for this chapter are

- Learn when a child can be held responsible for violation of a criminal law.
- Distinguish between the method of imposing criminal liability upon a child under age 7 and a child of age 14.
- List the two prongs of the *M'Naghten* rule.
- Describe the difference between the *M'Naghten* rule and the "substantial capacity" test.
- Identify the extent, if any, to which the voluntary use of drugs or alcohol may be used as an insanity defense or diminished capacity defense.
- Distinguish the "not guilty by reason of insanity" verdict from the "guilty but mentally ill" verdict.
- List factors that may present issues of a criminal defendant's competency to be tried on criminal charges.
- Explain why a defendant of questionable competency should not be tried for a criminal violation.

O n July 20, 2012 James Holmes, a 25-year-old former doctoral student at the University of Colorado, entered a movie theatre in Aurora, Colorado armed with an AR-15 rifle, a 12-gauge shotgun, and a .40 caliber pistol. Holmes opened fire at the audience, choosing random victims as he walked through the theatre. When he was done, he had killed twelve people and injured fifty-eight. Holmes has entered a plea of "not guilty by reason of insanity" in the murder charges filed against him. Holmes will be evaluated by Colorado mental health experts, and if they agree he was insane at the time he committed the homicides it is possible the prosecutors could decide the charges against him should be dismissed, and Holmes be committed to a mental institution. If the experts do not determine Holmes was insane, that defense would be determined at his murder trial. If he is successful in this defense he will not be convicted of first-degree murder, but instead will face confinement for treatment in a mental institution for some period.

In this chapter we examine the rules that determine when persons can be held criminally responsible for their actions. We also learn about the evolution of the insanity defense and its place in criminal law today.

Ancient Concepts of Criminal Responsibility

The law has undergone many changes over the centuries regarding how to determine criminal responsibility and how to assess who has the capacity to commit a crime. At the time of the Norman Conquest of England (1066), for example, trial by ordeal and trial by battle were commonly used to determine criminal responsibility. If a person was of noble birth or was titled, he could demand trial by battle if accused of a crime. In trial by battle, if the suspect or accused came out second, it was then determined that he was guilty of the offense with which he was charged. However, the question of guilt or innocence could become moot, because the accused might be killed or badly injured.

trial by ordeal A test used to determine criminal responsibility in ancient England involving subjecting the individual to a torturous ordeal. These ordeals were essentially appeals to God; surviving the ordeal was viewed as God's judgment of innocence.

In determining criminal responsibility in a **trial by ordeal**, the accused often was required to take a pound weight of red-hot iron into his hands or to plunge his hand, up to the wrist, into boiling water. Ordeal by fire and ordeal by water were also used. Sir James Stephen described trial by ordeal in his *History of the Criminal Law of England,* published in 1883:

> It is unnecessary to give a minute account of the ceremonial of the ordeals. They were of various kinds. The general nature of all was the same. They were appeals to God to work a miracle in attestation of the innocence of the accused person. The handling of hot iron and immersion of the hand or arm in boiling water were the commonest. The ordeal of water was a very singular institution. Sinking was the sign of innocence, floating the sign of guilt. As anyone would sink unless he understood how to float, and intentionally did so, it is difficult to see how anyone could ever be convicted by this means. Is it possible that this ordeal may have been an honourable form of suicide, like the Japanese happy despatch? In nearly every case the accused would sink. This would prove his innocence, indeed, but there would be no need to take him out. He would thus die honourably. If by accident he floated, he would be put to death disgracefully.[1]

Another form of superstition involved the concept that individuals deliberately became witches or practiced witchcraft. These individuals were thought to be capable of causing great social harm, such as crop failure, as well as causing serious injuries or illnesses and death to others. Witchcraft first became a crime under the Roman Empire. During the sixteenth, seventeenth, and eighteenth centuries, thousands of people were tried and put to death because they were believed to be either witches or to practice witchcraft. For example, Joan of Arc was charged with being a witch and condemned to death. She was burned at the stake in France in 1431.

Prosecution of such people in the American colonies occurred in Massachusetts, Connecticut, and Virginia. These trials reached a high point in 1692 in Salem, Massachusetts, where 19 persons were executed as witches, and 150 more were sent to prison. The Salem trials were the last American witchcraft trials; the last English witchcraft trials took place in 1712. In 1735, Scotland repealed all laws that made witchcraft a crime in that country.

Today the lack of criminal responsibility and capacity are generally seen as potential excuses for the commission of acts that would ordinarily be criminal, as opposed to defenses to criminal liability. That is, if one who commits criminal acts can show he lacked responsibility or capacity, his actions are excused from criminal liability. In this chapter we examine the specifics of the traditional tests for determining responsibility and capacity, mainly as they apply to infancy and insanity. In later chapters we examine the circumstances where one accused of criminal acts might have a defense to criminal liability.

The capacity and criminal responsibility doctrines discussed in this chapter are often labeled affirmative defenses, though if proved they serve not as justification for actions, but excuse of responsibility. In the case of infancy most states have adopted various presumptions about a child's criminal responsibility, as the materials below discuss. In the case of adults, in most states a defense of insanity requires the defendant to prove insanity by a **preponderance of the evidence**. The U.S. Supreme Court has long held that to require a defendant to prove insanity or other lack of criminal responsibility does not violate the Constitution.[2]

In only a very few states the prosecution must prove the presence of capacity or sanity, usually beyond a reasonable doubt. Most states treat lack of capacity or sanity as affirmative defenses, which must be proved by the defendant. However, in some of those states once some evidence of insanity has been introduced, the burden shifts to the prosecution to prove sanity. *See e.g., People v. Grenier,* 200 P.3d 1062 (Colo. 2008). Those states may have been influenced by the Model Penal Code, § 112 (1) and (2) (a), which requires the prosecution to prove an affirmative defense that relates to an element of the crime, once some evidence showing the defense has been introduced.

One aspect of criminal responsibility has seen recent developments. The U.S. Supreme Court held in *Atkins v. Virginia,* 536 U.S. 304 (2002), discussed in Chapter 8, that a mentally retarded person could not be subject to the death penalty. Following that decision, many states passed statutes establishing procedures for determining when a defendant is mentally retarded and thus not subject to the death penalty. Virtually all states placed the burden of proof of mental retardation on the defendant. While many state statutes only require proof by a preponderance of the evidence, others require proof by "clear and convincing" evidence. In *Stripling v. State,* 711 S.E.2d 665 (Ga. 2011), the Georgia Supreme Court held that the Georgia statute required the defendant to prove mental retardation by proof beyond a reasonable doubt.

Infancy and Criminal Responsibility

Under the civil law, an **infant (child)** is a person who has not yet reached the age of majority, whether that age is 18, 19, 20, or 21, as determined by the law of each

preponderance of the evidence The greater weight of the evidence, though not necessarily the amount needed to remove every reasonable doubt. It is proof sufficient to incline a reasonable person toward one side of an issue rather than the other.

infant (child) Under the civil law, a person who has not yet reached the age of majority, whether that age is 18, 19, 20, or 21, as determined by the law of each jurisdiction.

jurisdiction. Although infants, with some exceptions, are not able to enter into contracts, make wills, or vote, the law on children's criminal responsibility for their acts differs from the law governing the children's civil capacity.

The question of the criminal responsibility of children first came before courts in Western Europe in the Middle Ages. By the fourteenth century, the common law had determined that children under the age of 7 did not have the capacity to commit a crime. By that time, 7 had been established as the "age of reason" under ecclesiastical law and also as the age of responsibility under Roman civil law. In establishing the age of 7 as the lowest age of criminal responsibility, the common law concluded that a child under the age of 7 did not have the mental capacity to formulate the intent to commit a crime and that, therefore, for children under 7, the threat of punishment would not serve as a deterrent against crime.

Many states have codified some version of the common law rules on children's criminal capacity, though they vary on the age limits adopted.[3] An example of a typical state statute determining children's criminal responsibility is Section 9A.04.050 of the Washington Statutes, which provides in part:

> Children under the age of eight years are incapable of committing crime. Children of 8 and under 12 years of age are presumed to be incapable of committing crime, but this presumption may be removed by proof that they have sufficient capacity to understand the act or neglect, and to know that it was wrong.

The age selected by the jurisdiction as the minimum age for a child's criminal responsibility creates a conclusive presumption that a child under that age lacks the capacity to commit a crime. As the presumption is conclusive, evidence to the contrary may not be presented. People over a certain age—in most states, around 14 years of age—are inferred to be capable of formulating the necessary mental frame of mind to commit a crime. Evidence showing otherwise, however, can be used to show incapacity. Moreover, such children may be prosecuted through the juvenile court system, rather than in adult court.

A rebuttable presumption exists under most state statutes and the common law that children between the minimum age (usually around 7) and the maximum age (usually around 14) are presumed to be without criminal capacity to commit a crime. This presumption, however, may be overcome by the presentation of evidence by the state showing that the child has the mental capacity and the ability to formulate the necessary criminal intent.[4]

The U.S. courts look to a variety of factors when the capacity presumption is at issue, and they usually hold that the younger the child, the stronger must be the evidence of mental capacity. The Washington Supreme Court considered the presumption contained in the statute cited above in the 2004 case of *State v. Ramer*.[5] There, an 11-year-old boy was charged with first-degree rape of a child, a 7-year-old boy. The state unsuccessfully attempted to prove the child had the capacity to understand the nature of his acts and that the acts were wrong. In reviewing the trial court's decision, the Washington Supreme Court said,

> We have identified seven factors to consider in determining capacity: (1) the nature of the crime, (2) the child's age and maturity, (3) whether the child evidenced a desire for secrecy, (4) whether the child told the victim (if any) not to tell, (5) prior conduct similar to that charged, (6) any consequences that attached

to that prior conduct, and (7) whether the child had made an acknowledgment that the behavior is wrong and could lead to detention.[6]

The court also noted that in sexual charges against children, it is difficult to overcome the presumption, because it is hard to tell if children understand prohibitions on sexual behavior. Based on the testimony of two psychologists, who both stated the child did not understand that his conduct was wrong, the court agreed that the state failed to overcome the presumption of incapacity.

IS THE ROLE OF JUVENILE COURTS CHANGING?

When the first juvenile court was established in Cook County, Illinois, in 1899, the idea behind the court was to rehabilitate youths, rather than punish them for their wrongdoings. For the next 50 years or so, this was the guiding philosophy as the states created their own juvenile court systems. These courts tended to be very informal and treated the youths more like wayward children than criminals.

By the late 1960s and early 1970s, two forces began to exert a change on the prevailing juvenile court philosophy. First, in cases like *In re Gault*, 387 U.S. 1 (1967), the U.S. Supreme Court decided that juveniles were entitled to many of the same procedural protections available to adult offenders, such as the right to an attorney, the right to confront witnesses, and the right to remain silent. This change of emphasis from an informal, *in loco parentis* type of proceeding to an adversarial trial caused legislatures to rethink the rehabilitative ideal upon which juvenile courts were based.

Second, the rise of serious, violent juvenile crime in the 1980s and 1990s created an atmosphere of anxiety and fear among the general public. These events caused many state legislatures to modify the juvenile court system, mainly to make it easier for a juvenile to be waived out of the system and into adult court. These modifications took two forms. In one form, states' statutes listed crimes for which the juvenile courts had no jurisdiction. For example, Nevada Revised Statutes, Section 62B.330 (2003), exempts murder, sexual assault, use of a firearm in a crime, or any felony that results in death or serious bodily harm from the juvenile court's jurisdiction. California has a similar provision.[a]

The other way that these modifications came about was that states began expanding the circumstances under which a juvenile could be transferred from juvenile court to adult court. Most states now have some form of mandatory transfer statute, and the age of youths eligible for transfer has dropped significantly. For example, the Ohio transfer statutes, Ohio R.C. § 2152.10 and .12 make transfer mandatory where the crime charged is a category one crime (murder or attempted murder) and the child is 16 or 17. It also provides for mandatory transfer of a child who is 14 or 15 and has previously been declared delinquent in a category one or two (e.g., armed robbery) crime. For other crimes and younger offenders, transfer is discretionary and a hearing in juvenile court must occur. *State v D.W.*, 978 N.E.2d 894 (Ohio 2012).

Under mandatory transfer statutes, courts have held there is no right to a hearing before a juvenile court before a case is transferred to adult court, and the transfer must be made upon request by the prosecutor. *See e.g., State v. Fernandez*, 12 A.3d 925 (Conn. 2012). In discretionary transfer cases, a hearing must be held in juvenile court, where the court must consider the possibility of rehabilitation before transferring to adult court. *See e.g., People v. Moore*, 957 N.E.2d 555 (Ill. App. 2011).

[a]Cal. Wel. & Inst. Code, Section 602 (1998 & 2006 Supp.).

The Juvenile Court System

All states have enacted statutes governing the jurisdiction of children's (juvenile) courts. These courts deal with children who are delinquent and in need of supervision or with children who are neglected and dependent. "Delinquency" is usually defined by statute as conduct by a child that, if committed by an adult, would be a violation of the criminal code of that state. States vary on the maximum age for the jurisdiction of juvenile courts but usually set a limit around 18 years of age. State statutes also generally provide that juvenile courts may waive jurisdiction to the adult courts of children otherwise under the jurisdiction of the juvenile court.

In most jurisdictions, a juvenile court judge has the discretion to waive the juvenile court's jurisdiction, based on factors such as the age of the juvenile, the crime charged, and the extent of previous offenses. In some states, the prosecutor has the additional discretion to decide to file charges in either the juvenile court or adult court. A few states have "once-an-adult-always-an-adult" rules, where if a juvenile is once transferred to adult court, he will always be treated as an adult in further offenses.

The Insanity Defense

No subject in criminal law has received as much attention and debate as the insanity defense. The questions of what degree of insanity, mental defect, or mental disease renders a person blameless for acts or omissions and what **insanity tests** should be used in determining legal and moral liability have been debated for years.

insanity tests Tests to determine legal and moral liability.

Defense lawyers seldom use the insanity defense for minor criminal charges.[7] It is most often used in murder cases and for other serious felony charges in which the evidence against a defendant may be so strong that no other defense is available.

Studies have shown that the insanity plea is usually not an easy way out for criminal defendants and that only about 2 percent of defendants charged with serious crimes use the insanity plea.[8] The success rate among defendants using the insanity plea is not high when medical doctors differ as to the sanity of a defendant. Terrible and gross crimes by themselves are not likely to convince a jury to make a finding of "not guilty by reason of insanity."

In most jurisdictions the burden is on the defendant to prove the insanity defense, usually by a preponderance of the evidence.

Insanity at the Time of the Criminal Incident

The question of insanity (mental disease or defect) may be raised at specific stages during the criminal proceedings. If a defendant is found insane at the time the crime occurred, the court enters a judgment of not guilty by reason of insanity, and the defendant may never again be tried for that offense.

A defendant who is found not guilty by reason of insanity is almost always committed to a mental institution under the laws of that state (or the federal government). Such state and federal laws provide for the length of stay and the conditions under which the person may be eligible for release.[9]

In the case of *Foucha v. Louisiana*,[10] the defendant was found not guilty of burglary by reason of insanity. After four years in a state psychiatric hospital, a doctor at the hospital stated that Foucha was no longer mentally ill, but declined to certify that the defendant was no longer a danger to himself or others. Under Louisiana law at that time, Foucha had the burden of proving that he was no longer dangerous in order to earn his release from the hospital.

The U.S. Supreme Court held that the Louisiana law violated due process: "the State must establish insanity and dangerousness by clear and convincing evidence in order to confine an insane convict beyond his criminal sentence, when the basis for his original confinement no longer exists." The Court stated that since the State conceded Foucha was no longer insane, the only basis for holding him was his dangerousness. While "dangerousness" by itself can sometimes be a basis for confining a person, the Court said, it must be proved by the State, not disproved by the person confined.

The holding in *Foucha,* where the State conceded the defendant was no longer insane, should be contrasted to the burden of proof required for the release of a person committed after a finding of not guilty by reason of insanity. It is common for commitment statutes to place the burden of proving a person committed is no longer insane on that person, not the government. For example, in *United States v. Weed*,[11] a defendant was found not guilty by reason of insanity of the murder of a postal worker, a federal offense. Under the federal commitment statute, 18 U.S.C. § 4243, after such a verdict a hearing is held to determine if the defendant should be confined in a mental institution or released "because no longer dangerous" to others. At that hearing, section 4243(d) requires the defendant to prove by "clear and convincing" evidence that his mental condition does not present a risk to others. The court held that since the defendant had the benefit of a jury trial in which it was found he was insane, sufficient reason existed to confine him, and that it thus became his burden to show that the reason no longer existed.

Tests Used to Determine Insanity

If a state permits a defense to criminal charges based on insanity, it remains to be determined how the insanity decision is made. In *Clark v. Arizona,* 126 S. Ct. 2709 (2006), discussed in more detail later in this chapter, the U.S. Supreme Court reviewed the kinds of tests traditionally used to make that determination, and listed the states using the various tests. It noted that states are free to define insanity as they think proper. The Court found that the insanity tests have historically followed one or more of four approaches: (1) cognitive incapacity, (2) moral incapacity, (3) volitional incapacity, and (4) the product of mental illness.

Numbers (1) and (2) combined are the *M'Naghten* rule, number (3) is commonly called the "substantial capacity" rule, and number (4) is usually referred to as the "product" rule. The *Clark* Court stated that seventeen states and the federal government have adopted the *M'Naghten* rule. One state has adopted only the "cognitive incapacity" approach, and ten have adopted only the "moral incapacity" approach. Fourteen states have adopted the "volitional incapacity" approach, most using the Model Penal Code's "substantial capacity" as a model. Two states combine the

M'Naghten rule with "substantial capacity." Only one state, New Hampshire, has adopted the "product-of-mental-illness" approach. The following materials in this section discuss those rules in more detail. The verdict of "guilty but mentally ill" is also discussed in this section, while the "diminished capacity" test appears in the next section.

The *M'Naghten* Case and the "Right and Wrong" Test

It was not until the 1800s that English and American courts considered the question of whether insanity, mental disease, and mental defect should be factors in determining the criminal responsibility of people charged with crimes. The **"right and wrong" test**, which became the most widely used test to determine the question of legal insanity in the United States, was developed in 1843 in the aftermath of the famous English murder case of *Rex v. M'Naghten,* House of Lords, 1843.[12]

Daniel M'Naghten lived in London in the 1840s and believed that the British Home Secretary, Sir Robert Peel, was the head of a conspiracy to kill him. (Peel was the widely recognized founder of the British police, who thus received the nickname "bobbies.") In 1843, M'Naghten shot and killed Edward Drummond, private secretary to Peel, because he mistook Drummond for Peel. At his trial, the defense argued that M'Naghten was insane at the time of the shooting and that he should not be held responsible because his mental delusions had caused him to act as he did. The British jury agreed, and M'Naghten was found not guilty because of insanity.

The "right and wrong" test that emerged from the *M'Naghten* case has become the prevailing standard and test for insanity in U.S. courts. Under the *M'Naghten* rule, defendants are not legally responsible for their acts if at the time they were "laboring under such a defect of reason, from disease of the mind, as not to know the nature and quality of the act he was doing, or, if he did know it, that he did not know that what he was doing was wrong." 8 Eng. Rep. at 722. Under this rule, insanity is present either when a person, because of mental illness, either has "cognitive incapacity," that is, does not know what actions he is taking, or "moral incapacity," that is, he does not know the actions taken were wrong.

The *M'Naghten* **rule** established the burden of proof as follows:

> Every man is presumed to be sane and to possess a sufficient degree of reason to be responsible for his crimes, until the contrary be proved to (the jury's) satisfaction; and that to establish a defense on the ground of insanity, it must be clearly proved.

The "Product-of-Mental-Illness Rule" and "Irresistible Impulse"

After courts had for some time used the *M'Naghten* rule to determine insanity, many were critical of the rule. According to its critics, the principal fault of the *M'Naghten* rule was its narrowness and its restricted application to only a small percentage of the people who are mentally ill. The rule does not, critics said, recognize that mental illness is not limited to an inability to *know* that one is doing

"right and wrong" test An insanity test that claims that defendants are not legally responsible for their acts if, due to a defect of the mind, at the time of the crime they were unable to understand the difference between right and wrong.

M'Naghten rule The insanity defense rule requiring proof that because of mental disease or defect defendants did not know the scope or character of their actions.

wrong, but includes an inability to control one's acts even if known to be wrong. In response to this criticism, a few states adopted a form of "volitional incapacity" called the "irresistible impulse" and added it to the *M'Naghten* rule.[13] Under this test, defendants must prove that even if they knew what they were doing was wrong, mental illness prevented them from controlling their conduct.[14]

The irresistible impulse rule has not been widely adopted, mainly because courts and legislators have concluded that it lacks precision on the question of what an impulse is and when it is irresistible.

The "product-of-mental-illness" approach has had very limited adoption. In 1954, a form of this approach called the *Durham* product test was adopted by the U.S. Court of Appeals for the District of Columbia in the case of *Durham v. United States*.[15] The court stated that "an accused is not criminally responsible if his unlawful act was the product of mental disease or defect." The *Durham* case established a test for insanity based on a *substantial* lack of mental capacity rather than a complete lack of capacity. It has been criticized on the grounds that it is too broad and gives psychiatrists, rather than the jury, too much discretion in determining the legal issue of insanity. "Criminal responsibility is a legal not a medical question."[16]

In 1984 Congress passed the Insanity Defense Reform Act, 18 U.S.C. § 17. This act established a rule for federal criminal prosecutions that is virtually identical to the *M'Naghten* rule. The Act was designed to abolish both the "irresistible impulse" rule and the *Durham* test. Section 17 states:

> It is an affirmative defense to a prosecution under any Federal statute that, at the time of the commission of the offense, the defendant, as a result of severe mental illness or defect, was unable to appreciate the nature and quality or the wrongfulness of his acts. Mental disease or defect does not otherwise constitute a defense.

Congress also addressed the criticism that "criminal responsibility" is not a medical question by providing in Rule 704(b) of the Federal Rules of Evidence that a medical expert may not render an expert opinion on the ultimate question of a defendant's sanity under the statute. Most states that considered the "product-of-mental-illness" test ultimately adopted a test modeled on the "substantial capacity" test discussed next.

The Model Penal Code "Substantial Capacity" Test

About a year after the adoption of the *Durham* test by a few jurisdictions, the American Law Institute proposed still another test for determining criminal responsibility. In proposing the new test, the following comment was made:

> No problem in the drafting of a penal code presents larger intrinsic difficulty than that of determining when individuals whose conduct would otherwise be criminal ought to be exculpated (freed of guilt) on the grounds that they were suffering from mental disease or defect when they acted as they did. What is involved specifically is the drawing of a line between the use of public agencies and public force to condemn the offender by conviction. . . . [T]he problem is to discriminate between the cases where a punitive correctional disposition is appropriate and those in which a medical-custodial disposition is the only kind that the law should allow.[17]

"substantial capacity" test A test to determine criminal responsibility based on whether the defendant could (1) distinguish between right and wrong or (2) conform his or her conduct to the requirements of law.

The final draft of the American Law Institute (ALI) **"substantial capacity" test,** found in Section 4.01 of the Model Penal Code, states:

1. A person is not responsible for criminal conduct if at the time of such conduct as a result of mental disease or defect he lacks substantial capacity either to appreciate the criminality (wrongfulness) of his conduct or to conform his conduct to the requirements of law.
2. As used in the Article, the terms *mental disease* or *defect* do not include an abnormality manifested only by repeated criminal or otherwise antisocial conduct.

The Model Penal Code test (or the ALI "substantial capacity" test) reportedly has now been adopted by about half the states.

While the *M'Naghten* rule requires a defendant to show total mental impairment, the "substantial capacity" test puts less of a burden on defendants. Under the "substantial capacity" test, even if defendants "knew" what they had done, they are permitted to attempt to show that they did not have the "substantial capacity to conform their conduct to the requirements of law."

EXAMPLE

In March 2002, using the Texas version of the *M'Naghten* rule, Andrea Yates was found sane and guilty of the murder of her five young children in Houston, Texas. After an appeal to a Texas appellate court, her conviction was overturned because a prosecution witness had given false testimony. Yates was retried in 2006, and on July 26th of that

AP Photo/Steve Ueckert

In 2001 Andrea Yates confessed to the crime of filicide (the murder of a child by a parent). Despite the testimony of doctors that she was psychotic when she drowned her five children, a jury in Houston, Texas, initially found her sane under the M'Naghten rule. In July 2006, she was retried and found not guilty by reason of insanity.

year she was found not guilty by reason of insanity. She was committed to a state mental institution until it was determined she was no longer a "threat to society."

Because of the publicity surrounding many recent uses of the insanity defense, some states that have used the Model Penal Code "substantial capacity" test have returned to the stricter standards of the *M'Naghten* rule. In addition, five states—Idaho, Montana, Kansas, Nevada, and Utah—have passed legislation that abolished the insanity defense.

The Montana Supreme Court has held that the abolition of the insanity defense did not violate the Constitution *(Montana v. Cowan).*[18] The U.S. Supreme Court denied certiorari.[19] The Supreme Courts of Idaho, Kansas, and Utah[20] all reached the same result. However, in 2001 the Nevada Supreme Court reached the opposite conclusion and held the Nevada statute abolishing the insanity defense unconstitutional.[21] Nev. Rev. Stat. § 194.010 (2004) now follows the *M'Naghten* rule.

With or without an insanity defense, the state must prove mental fault *(mens rea)* in crimes that have as an element of the crime a specific intent, for example, first-degree murder. If mental illness or mental defect prevents a defendant from forming the required *mens rea,* a conviction for that crime could not be obtained, and the defendant could be found not guilty. Even the states identified above that have abolished insanity as a general defense each have statutes permitting evidence of insanity to negate a specific mental intent required for conviction of a crime. See, e.g., 18-207 Idaho Code and K.S.A. § 22-3220.

The Plea and Verdict of Guilty but Mentally Ill[22]

The incidence of people who are found not guilty because of insanity and who then go on to commit other violent crimes after release from mental hospitals has caused thirteen states to adopt the plea and verdict of **guilty but mentally ill.**[23] (Statutes authorizing this plea and verdict are often called "GBMI" laws.) The Michigan legislature was the first to do so in 1975, when it enacted Mich. Comb. Laws § 768.36 after several defendants found not guilty of earlier murders because of insanity committed additional murders.

The public outcry over the insanity defense can be illustrated by events arising in an insanity defense case in Illinois. In that case, Thomas Vanda killed a girl when he was 18 years old. While undergoing psychiatric treatment in Chicago, he was released and killed another girl. He was found not guilty because of insanity. When doctors concluded that his psychosis had disappeared, he was again released over objections from the trial judge and his own defense attorney. In 1978, when he was 25 years old, Thomas Vanda was again charged with murder. The third victim was a 25-year-old woman.

Illinois enacted a guilty but mentally ill statute in 1981. Former Illinois Governor James R. Thompson described the new statutory procedure as follows:

> Under this procedure, when an insanity defense is raised, the court, if the evidence permits, may instruct the jury on the alternative verdict of guilty but mentally ill.

When a person is not legally insane, he or she may be found guilty but mentally ill if, at the time of the offense, he or she suffered from a disorder of thought or

guilty but mentally ill A defendant may be found guilty but mentally ill if all the following are found beyond a reasonable doubt: (1) defendant is guilty of the offense; (2) defendant was mentally ill at the time the offense was committed; and (3) defendant was not legally insane at the time the offense was committed.

DEFENDANTS WHO WERE FOUND NOT GUILTY BECAUSE OF INSANITY

John Hinckley

In 1981 John Hinckley attempted to kill President Ronald Reagan. In a wild shooting spree in downtown Washington, D.C., Hinckley wounded the president and several other people. Hinckley entered a not guilty plea and a not guilty because of insanity plea.

At that time, the federal courts had broken away from the majority rule in the United States, and the government had the burden of showing that people such as Hinckley were sane and normal. Because of Hinckley's wild, bizarre behavior, the government was not able to carry the burden of showing that Hinckley was sane and normal, and Hinckley was found not guilty because of insanity. Within a short time, Congress passed a law changing the procedure, and now defendants pleading insanity have the burden of coming forward with evidence proving mental disease or defectiveness.[a]

Lorena Bobbitt

Lorena Bobbitt was charged with malicious wounding in 1993. She testified to repeated rapes, beatings, and sodomizing by her husband. On the night of the crime, she testified that her husband came home drunk, tore off her clothes, and forced himself on her. She said that her mind went blank and that only later did she realize that she had sexually mutilated her husband by cutting off his penis, which she threw in a field.

A Virginia jury found Mrs. Bobbitt not guilty under Virginia's insanity test, which holds that a defendant may be held blameless for an act he or she knows is wrong if "his [or her] mind has become so impaired by disease that he [or she] totally is deprived of mental power to control or restrain his [or her] act." After a four-week stay, Mrs. Bobbitt was released from a Virginia mental hospital on the condition that she get therapy. Her husband, John, had been acquitted earlier of marital sexual abuse.

[a]John Hinckley continues to be held in a Washington, D.C. hospital. He has requested permission to spend a limited number of three- and four-day visits at his parents' home outside Washington, D.C., and a federal judge has granted those requests. However, in September 2012 a federal judge denied Hinckley's request for a release from the hospital to live with his mother unless a local mental health institution came forward with a plan for treatment of Hinckley.

mood that does not represent a condition amounting to insanity in the legal sense. When a guilty but mentally ill verdict is returned, the court may impose any sentence that could have been ordered for a conviction on the crime charged. However, the prison authorities must provide necessary psychiatric or psychological treatment to restore the offender to full capacity in an appropriate treatment setting. If the mental illness is cured, the offender must be returned to prison to serve out his or her sentence.

Insanity determinations under existing law deal in absolutes; a defendant must be found totally sane or totally insane. This fails to reflect reality. It does not allow the jury to consider the degree of an individual's mental impairment, the quality of the impairment, or the context in which the impairment is operative. A mental impairment does not necessarily eradicate the state of mind required to make a person guilty of a crime, and the jury should be permitted to consider the gradations of a defendant's mental state.

CASE CLOSE-UP

Clark v. Arizona
Supreme Court of the United States
126 S. Ct. 2709 (2006)

As stated earlier in this chapter, the Supreme Court denied review in the cases from state courts that ruled on the constitutionality of abolition of the insanity defense. In *Clark* the Court considered the claims by a defendant convicted of murder under Arizona law that the Arizona insanity defense statute violated the Due Process Clause. Prior to 1993 Arizona had adopted both alternatives of the *M'Naghten* rule: a defendant could establish the insanity defense if a mental defect left the defendant unable to know what he or she was doing (the so-called cognitive capacity part); alternatively, the defendant could establish the defense if the defendant did not know what he or she was doing was wrong (the so-called moral capacity part of the rule). In 1993 the Arizona legislature changed the law so that only the second part of the *M'Naghten* rule could be used to establish the insanity defense.

The Arizona appellate courts rejected the defendant's claim that narrowing the grounds for establishing the insanity defense violated due process. The U.S. Supreme Court affirmed, holding that states have the traditional power to define crimes and defenses, and that the *M'Naghten* rule had not been elevated "to the level of fundamental principle."[a] Moreover, the Court concluded, as a practical matter, that evidence of a defendant's inability to know the nature of his or her actions would be relevant and admissible on the issue "Did the defendant know what he or she was doing was wrong?" If the evidence showed a mental defect prevented a defendant from knowing what he or she was doing, the Court concluded, that same evidence should establish the insanity defense

under the Arizona statute: "In practical terms, if a defendant did not know what he was doing when he acted, he could not have known that he was performing the wrongful act charged as crime."[b] As a result, the Court concluded, the Arizona insanity statute did not deprive Clark of due process.

The Court also held that Arizona's court-made rule that expert evidence of a defendant's mental disease or defect was not admissible on the question of *mens rea* did not violate due process. Under the Arizona rule, so-called observational evidence was admissible on the question of a defendant's ability to have the necessary *mens rea* required for a crime. Evidence of the defendant's actions—what he or she said or did—are examples of admissible evidence on the defendant's mental state. However, expert psychological testimony about the effect of a defendant's mental disease on his or her capacity to form the required *mens rea* was excluded. The Court addressed many claims a defendant might have for the admissibility of relevant evidence, but it ultimately held that Arizona's interest in preserving the integrity of the form of the insanity defense it had chosen justified excluding expert testimony evidence, which would otherwise be admissible on the insanity defense, when the question was the defendant's ability to form the required *mens rea*.

Finally, the Court stated it was not passing on the constitutionality of state statutes that abolished the insanity defense altogether: "We have never held that the Constitution mandates an insanity defense, nor have we held that the Constitution does not so require. This case does not call upon us to decide the matter."[c]

[a]126 S. Ct. at 2719.

[b]126 S. Ct. at 2722.
[c]126 S. Ct. at 2722, fn. 20.

The guilty but mentally ill verdict does not abolish the insanity defense. It simply recognizes that there are gradations in the degree of mental impairment; it provides accountability, promotes treatment, and eliminates the need to manipulate the system.

Most important, it is designed to protect the public from violence inflicted by people with mental ailments who previously slipped through the cracks in the criminal justice system.[24]

In most states, the statute authorizing a GBMI verdict allocates the burden of proof as follows: First, the prosecution must prove beyond a reasonable doubt that the defendant committed the crime charged. Second, the jury must determine if the defendant was legally insane. Typically, the defendant must prove insanity by a preponderance of the evidence standard, though a few states place the burden or proving sanity on the prosecution. If the jury finds the defendant was not legally insane, it must determine if the defendant was mentally ill—that is, whether the defendant suffered from some mental impairment that affected his ability to control or understand his behavior, but that did not amount to insanity. In most jurisdictions, the prosecution must prove mental illness beyond a reasonable doubt. See, e.g., Ga. Code Ann. § 17-7-131. A few jurisdictions demand only proof by a preponderance of the evidence. See, e.g., *Commonwealth v. Rabold,* 951 A2d 329 (Pa. 2008).

Defendants convicted with GBMI verdicts have frequently attacked the GBMI statute as unconstitutional under the Due Process Clause, contending the presence of the GBMI option permits the prosecution to effectively convict a defendant without proving guilt beyond a reasonable doubt. To date, no court has declared a GBMI statute unconstitutional. See 2 *Wharton's Criminal Law* § 105 (15th ed. 2007).

Opponents of the guilty but mentally ill verdict argue that it is nothing but a nice name for "guilty and going to prison." The National Alliance for the Mentally Ill opposes such legislation "because it would stigmatize insane offenders with a criminal conviction, compounding the handicaps already faced by those persons in obtaining employment and social acceptance."[25]

Mental Conditions That Do Not Satisfy the Insanity Defense

Many mental conditions do not rise to the level of "insanity" and thus do not provide a defense to criminal conduct. For example, the battered woman syndrome, discussed in Chapter 6, has rarely been successfully raised as a mental disease. Nor have claims like television intoxication, premenstrual syndrome, or so-called cultural defenses. The voluntary use of drugs or alcohol does not qualify as a mental disease, even if the drugs or alcohol make defendants unable to appreciate the nature or quality of their acts.

Defendants sometimes use the compulsive gambling defense against criminal charges such as theft, bank robbery, and embezzlement. They argue they would not have committed such crimes but were compelled to do so because of their gambling urges.[26] For example, in the case of *United States v. Lynch,* the defendant stole $7.5 million and unsuccessfully asserted compulsive gambling in an attempt to be found not guilty on his insanity plea.[27]

Prosecutors argue that accepting compulsive gambling as an insanity defense could set a dangerous precedent. In any state that would allow such a defense, thieves could claim kleptomania as a defense, arsonists could claim pyromania, perjurers could claim pathologic lying, drunk drivers could claim alcoholism, and prostitutes could claim nymphomania.

In all the reported cases, defendants using compulsive gambling as a defense have failed to be found not guilty because of insanity. There is no showing of acceptance in the mental health field that a compulsive gambler is unable to resist the impulse to steal or to commit other crimes.

The Defense of Diminished Capacity

diminished capacity defense A defense for criminal responsibility based on the fact that because of mental or emotional conditions, the defendant did not possess the required *mens rea* for conviction of crime charged.

In some states a defendant is permitted to assert what is usually called the **diminished capacity defense.** It applies when a defendant has introduced evidence of mental incapacity that does not satisfy the requirement for a finding of insanity under the relevant statute. A court may consider the evidence on the issue of the defendant's requisite *mens rea* for crimes that require a specific intent. Under this defense, it is possible that a defendant was not insane at the time he committed the crime charged, but that his mental condition made it impossible to entertain some specific intent required for conviction. This basis for this defense and its consequences were discussed in the case of *United States v. Fishman* as follows:

> The defense of "diminished capacity" is simply a label that identifies evidence introduced by a defendant to support a claim that he did not commit the crime charged because he did not possess the requisite *mens rea*. A diminished capacity defense varies from a legal insanity defense in several important respects. Whereas following a successful legal insanity defense the court retains control of the defendant and may order involuntary commitment, a successful diminished capacity defense results in a complete acquittal of the crime charged.[28]

The diminished capacity defense under the Federal Insanity Defense Reform Act, 18 U.S.C. § 17, is generally permitted in federal prosecutions. Section 17(a) of the Act adopts a test for insanity that is essentially the *M'Naghten* rule, and identifies it as an affirmative defense, which under § 17(b) the defendant must prove by clear and convincing evidence. Section 17(a) also states that except as set forth for the insanity defense, "Mental disease or defect does not otherwise constitute a defense." Courts applying this sentence to the diminished capacity defense generally conclude that Congress intended only to exclude evidence of mental incapacity as proof of any other test for insanity. Congress did not intend to exclude evidence of mental incapacity less than legal insanity on other issues, such as the absence of the required *mens rea* in a crime. Thus, diminished capacity is in fact not a "defense" at all, since it cannot be used to exonerate a defendant, as a true insanity defense could. It is better seen as an evidentiary rule, permitting a defendant to introduce evidence of diminished capacity as relevant to the presence or absence of any required specific intent in a statute.

Voluntary intoxication or drug abuse can sometimes lead to the same mental impairment that constitutes the classic insanity defense. Though voluntary intoxication might establish the diminished capacity defense by eliminating the defendant's ability to form a required specific intent (see Chapter 7), virtually all states reject such voluntary acts as a basis for the insanity defense. For example, in the 2011 case *State v. Hotz*, 795 N.W.2d 645 (Neb. 2011), the court held that a defendant who suffered a psychotic episode caused by ingesting hallucinogenic drugs could not use that mental state as proof of the insanity defense. Citing cases in other states, the court noted that some states permit the insanity defense where voluntary intoxication or drug use has created a "settled" psychotic mental state, that is, where prolonged use of drugs or alcohol has permanently altered the defendant's mental condition. The court did, however, permit evidence of the defendant's mental state on the issue of his diminished capacity to form the specific intent required under the Nebraska murder statute.

TESTS OR PROCEDURES USED TO DETERMINE CRIMINAL RESPONSIBILITY

Test or Procedure	Year When First Used	Type of Test	Current Extent of Use
M'Naghten "right and wrong" test	1843	Based on ability of defendant to know the difference between right and wrong.	Used by practically all U.S. courts until the 1970s. Now used, with variations, by about half of the states.
Model Penal Code "substantial capacity" test	1955	Did defendant have the "substantial capacity" to (1) distinguish between right and wrong or (2) conform his or her conduct to the requirements of law?	Used in some states, though California and the federal courts have returned to use of the *M'Naghten* rule.
Guilty but mentally ill alternative verdict and plea	1975	Defendant may be found guilty but mentally ill if all the following are found beyond a reasonable doubt: (1) defendant is guilty of offense; (2) defendant was mentally ill at time offense was committed; and (3) defendant was not legally insane at time offense was committed.	Used in thirteen states with either the *M'Naghten* rule or the "substantial capacity" test.
Diminished capacity defense	1957	Defense seeks to introduce evidence showing that because of mental or emotional conditions, the defendant did not possess the required *mens rea* for conviction of crime charged.	A finding that the state failed to prove the *mens rea* for the crime charged could result in a finding of not guilty of the more serious offense, but guilty of a lesser offense.

SEXUAL VIOLENT PREDATOR LAWS AND INVOLUNTARY CIVIL COMMITMENT LAWS

Type of Law	Examples
Sexual violent predator laws used to detain persons likely to be sexually violent	Sexual violent predators are persons who have been convicted of a sexual violent crime. Once released from confinement, such persons often revert to their previous actions. In May 2010 John Gardner, a convicted sexual offender released on parole in California, was sentenced to life imprisonment for the rapes and murders of Chelsea King, 17, and Amber DuBois, 14. In response to cases like this, most states have adopted Sexual Violent Predator Laws (SVP laws) that permit states to bring civil commitment proceedings against the offender based on a showing the person is a sexual violent offender, and poses a substantial risk of future violent sexual actions. In *Crane v. Kansas*, 534 U.S. 407 (2002), the U.S. Supreme Court held that in civil commitment proceedings under SVP statutes the state must prove not only that the person is a sexual violent offender who is a danger to others, but also that the offender lacks significant control over his actions. In *United States v. Comstock*, 130 S. Ct. 1949 (2010), the U.S. Supreme Court held that Congress possessed the power to pass a law permitting federal officials to bring civil commitment proceedings to keep dangerous sex offenders confined after their prison sentences have been served. In the 2013 case of *United States v. Kebodeaux*, 133 S. Ct. 2496, the U.S. Supreme Court held federal courts possessed jurisdiction to hear charges that defendants who had been released from federal custody after serving prison terms for sex offenses violated SORNA registration provisions.
	The U.S. Supreme Court has repeatedly affirmed state sexual violent predator laws that permit a state to hold for an indefinite period of time anyone "who has been convicted or charged with a sexual violent offense and who suffers from a mental abnormality or personality disorder which makes the person likely to engage in predatory acts of sexual violence." *Kansas v. Hendricks*, 117 S. Ct. 2072 (1997).
	If such laws are civil and not criminal, and not punitive in nature, they do not violate the *Due Process, Ex Post Facto,* or *Double Jeopardy* clauses. As treatment is not a constitutional requirement for civil commitment, such laws do not have to provide for treatment. See also *Allen v. Illinois,* 106 S. Ct. 2988 (1986).
Emergency mental detention laws and civil commitment to mental hospital laws	States have emergency mental detention laws under which persons who appear dangerous to themselves or others or are unable to care for themselves may be detained for mental observation for a short period of time, as provided by the statutes of that state. For example, a person who has attempted to commit suicide could be detained for medical observation for a time as provided by the statute of that state.

The Requirement of Competency to Stand Trial

A defendant must be competent (mentally fit) before the government can force him or her to go to trial on criminal charges. The U.S. Supreme Court has stated:

> A person whose mental condition is such that he lacks the capacity to understand the nature and object of the proceedings against him, to consult with counsel, and to assist in preparing his defense may not be subjected to a trial.[29]

competency to stand trial Defendants must have the ability to cooperate with their attorneys and the ability to understand the charges and proceedings against them.

The test for **competency to stand trial** originated in the common law and now has been codified in state and federal statutes. For example, 18 U.S.C. § 4241 provides procedures for determining competency for persons charged with federal crimes. When either the defendant or the prosecution requests, the court may order the defendant to submit to examination to determine competence. If the court finds by a preponderance of the evidence that the defendant lacks competence to stand trial, the defendant can be hospitalized for up to four months to try restore competence. If that does not happen, the defendant may be hospitalized for a longer period under 18 U.S.C. § 4246(d). Under that section, the court must find by clear and convincing evidence that the defendant has a mental defect that creates a substantial risk that the defendant might harm another person. If so, the defendant may be confined until he no longer presents such a risk.

A DEFENDANT MAY BE FOUND MENTALLY COMPETENT TO STAND TRIAL BUT INCOMPETENT TO ACT AS HIS OR HER OWN LAWYER

The U.S. Supreme Court held that a criminal defendant has a constitutional right to act as his or her own attorney unless it is shown that (1) the request was untimely, (2) the defendant abused the right of self-representation, (3) the request was made solely for the purpose of delay, (4) the case is so complex that it requires the assistance of a lawyer, or (5) the defendant is unable to voluntarily and intelligently waive his or her right to an attorney.[31] Does it therefore follow from that right that every person found competent enough to stand trial must be allowed to act as his or her own attorney?

This issue was before the Supreme Court in the 2008 case of *Indiana v. Edwards*, 554 U.S. 164. Edwards was charged with attempted murder, two additional felonies, and a misdemeanor. He was first found to be incompetent to stand trial, but after being committed to a state hospital he was found to be competent. However, he requested the right to represent himself at his trial.

The trial court found that while Edwards was competent enough to stand trial, he was not competent to act as his own attorney in a criminal case that with the potential to become a very complicated legal proceeding.

Edwards went to trial with an appointed lawyer representing him and was convicted of all charges. Edwards did not claim his attorney was ineffective or inadequate, but rather that he had the right to represent himself at his trial. The Indiana Supreme Court agreed, and ordered a new trial for Edwards. The state of Indiana appealed. The U.S. Supreme Court reversed the Indiana Supreme Court and sustained the trial court's ruling that Edwards was incompetent to act as his own attorney but competent to stand trial. The criminal convictions were affirmed.

The U.S. Supreme Court has repeatedly held that it is a violation of due process to try to convict a mentally incompetent person. Because most states place the burden on the party challenging the presumption of competency, the standard of proof on defendants to prove incompetency is that of the "preponderance of the evidence."[30]

A translator or an attorney who can speak the language of a defendant could solve the problem of a defendant who does not understand English. People skilled in sign language could communicate for a deaf person. But a defendant with the mental ability of a 5-year-old child or a defendant who is mentally disabled because of excessive use of drugs or alcohol present more difficult

MAY THE GOVERNMENT FORCE A DEFENDANT'S COMPETENCY?

In federal and state prosecutions, a defendant who has been found to be incompetent to stand trial because of his or her mental condition can be transferred to a medical facility for a reasonable time for examination and treatment.[a] If the defendant has a condition that is treatable by medications, may the government force the defendant to take those medications in order to render the person competent to stand trial?

In *Sell v. United States*, 539 U.S. 166 (2003), the U.S. Supreme Court held that although a defendant has a constitutional right to be free of involuntary medical treatment, medications can be forced on a defendant to render him or her competent if (1) the treatment is medically appropriate, (2) the medications will not have side effects that undermine the fairness of the trial, and (3) the medications are necessary to advance an important government interest.

Three cases illustrate how the *Sell* rule is applied in federal courts. In *United States v. Hardy*, 878 F. Supp.2d 373 (E.D. N.Y. 2012), the court ordered a defendant charged with murder to be involuntarily medicated to make him competent to stand trial. The court concluded that the medicine for treating the defendant's condition, paranoid schizophrenia, was appropriate and successful for most patients; that the medicine had no unmanageable side effects; and that prosecuting the defendant on the murder charge was an important government interest. The defendant had a history of violence and had assaulted medical personnel during treatment.

In *United States v. Grigsby*, 712 F.3d 964 (6th Cir. 2013) the court refused to order the involuntary medication of a defendant charged with bank robbery. The defendant was shown to suffer from a severe case of schizophrenia, and if not prosecuted for the robbery charges would very likely be civilly committed to a mental health facility for a substantial period, the court found. Given that the defendant raised a substantial insanity defense claim, the court concluded under *Sell* that it was not appropriate to force the defendant to take antipsychotic drugs.

In *United States v. Austin*, 606 F. Supp. 2d 149 (D. D.C. 2009), the court refused to order the involuntary medication of a defendant charged with threatening an attempt on the life of a judge. The court noted that while prosecuting an attempt on a member of the judiciary is a serious government interest, the government did not prove that administration of the antipsychotic medication would restore the defendant to competency. Among other factors, the court noted that the defendant committed the very crime he was charged with while under medication.

[a] 18 U.S.C. Section 4241 (d) has a 4-month limit; most states have similar limits, up to one year.

problems. If a defendant does not understand the charges and proceedings against him or her and cannot cooperate with the defense lawyers, that individual cannot be determined to be competent to stand trial. In such cases the criminal proceedings must be suspended.

A criminal defendant found to be incompetent might remain so either for a short time, or indefinitely. Under most state statutes, a defendant may be placed in an appropriate institution for treatment for a period of time to determine if he or she can become competent. For example, the Ohio statute, R.C. § 2945.38, provides that if the court determines that it is probable the defendant can be restored to competency within a year, the defendant can be sent to a treatment facility. However, if it is unlikely that competency will be restored within a year, either the defendant must be discharged, or the state must start civil commitment procedures.

Statutes like the Ohio law discussed above are patterned after the decision in *Jackson v. Indiana,* where the U.S. Supreme Court held that defendants could not be held for longer than a "reasonable period of time" to determine whether they will regain their competence and capacity to stand trial.[32] After this period of time, the state has these options:

- Try the defendant, if he or she is found competent and capable of standing trial.
- Dismiss the charges.
- Commence civil proceedings against the person for the purpose of committing him or her to a mental institution if he or she remains incompetent and cannot be tried criminally.[33]

The Criminal Liability of Corporations

A corporation is a legal entity created under the laws of a state or the federal government. Although a corporation is not a living person and thus would seem to lack the capacity to commit a crime, it acts through human beings. Thus, for a crime committed by a person to be attributable to the corporation, the person must be in control of the corporation's affairs or in the employment of the corporation.

Regarding the **criminal liability of corporations,** Sir William Blackstone wrote in his eighteenth-century *Commentaries* that "a corporation cannot commit treason or felony or other crime in its corporate capacity, though its members may in their distinct individual capacities."[34] Blackstone's statement reflected the early common law thinking that because a corporation had no mind of its own, it could not formulate a criminal intent, and because it had no body, it could not be imprisoned or executed. The early common law view was understandable because relatively few corporations existed in those days, and other ways were available to handle crimes that were committed in the names of corporations. The corporate officers (or employees) who committed the act (or acts) could be criminally charged. The corporation was civilly liable for the acts of its officers and employees, and therefore civil suits for damages could be brought. In addition, a corporation that had committed *ultra vires* acts (acts that are beyond the scope of the corporate charter or that violate the laws of the state) could have its corporate charter revoked by the state.

criminal liability of corporations The rules for making corporations liable for actions taken by officers, directors, or employees. Corporations can be vicariously criminally liable for actions of their agents if the offense is minor, a duty is specifically assigned to a corporation, a statute explicitly creates vicarious criminal liability, or the person committing the crime is acting in the interest of the corporation and is a high managerial agent.

This common law view changed as corporations became more numerous and as it became apparent that corporations should be made criminally responsible for some types of criminal acts. Today, corporations may be charged with many but not all crimes. The Model Penal Code, Section 2.07(l)(a)–(c), provides that corporations can have criminal liability for (1) specific duties assigned to a corporation, (2) violations of minor offenses that carry only a fine, and (3) an offense authorized or performed by a "high managerial agent."

Many states have reached similar conclusions. As an example, in *People v. Hock Shop,*[35] a corporation was charged with the crime of knowingly selling a firearm to a convicted felon. An employee of the corporation sold a firearm to a person known by the employee to be a convicted felon. The Michigan Court of Appeals held that though the corporation was a "person" for purposes of the criminal law, it could not have vicarious criminal liability for the acts of an employee who was not a high management agent unless the statute specifically imposed such liability, or the board of directors authorized or permitted the employee's acts. The state statute did not provide for criminal liability for violation of the firearm law, and the corporation's board of directors was not aware of the sale of the firearm to the felon, so the court affirmed a dismissal of the criminal charges.

Even if a state permits criminal liability for corporations based on authorized acts of employees, courts have held that the prosecution must prove an individual employee could be liable for the offense with which the corporation is charged. In *Com. v. Life Centers of America,* 926 N.E.2d 206 (Mass. 2010), a nursing home corporation was charged with involuntary manslaughter in the death of a nursing home resident. The elderly resident wheeled her wheelchair through the home's entrance doors, and fell down eight steps to her death. The victim had a history of tying to exit the home, and physicians had placed orders on her chart that she must wear a "WanderGuard" device that automatically would lock exit and entrance doors when approached by the wearer. Due to a combination of factors, including staff changes and unclear directives about auditing residents' charts, the duty nurses on the night in question did not know the resident was supposed to be wearing the safety device. As a result, the resident was able to exit the home, with the resulting fatal fall.

The prosecution did not charge any individual employee of the nursing home with involuntary manslaughter, conceding that no one person had been anything more than negligent in performing his or her duties. However, the prosecution charged the corporate owner of the nursing home on the theory of "collective knowledge" of all the employees. Under that theory, the liability of a corporation can be based on aggregating the knowledge and actions of multiple employees.

The Massachusetts Supreme Judicial Court held that the corporation could not be liable under the collective knowledge theory. The Court reasoned that since involuntary manslaughter was a crime that required "wanton or reckless" conduct, unless at least one individual acted in such a fashion, the corporation could not be liable. While many of the nursing home employees were negligent in connection with the death, multiples of simple negligence to not constitute "wanton or reckless" conduct, the court concluded. If no individual employee could be convicted of involuntary manslaughter, the court held, neither could the corporation.

CORPORATE LIABILITY FOR ENVIRONMENTAL CRIMES

Many corporations conduct business operations that have an impact on the environment. They are thus required to conform their operations to rules and regulations protecting the environment, including the criminal laws adopted to accomplish environmental goals. Many environmental crimes applicable to corporations include only fines as punishment for violations, and are often classified as misdemeanors. These statutes usually are aimed at some harm that an environmental interest suffered based on actions of the corporation. However, even though it can be shown the corporation's actions caused the environmental harm, attaching criminal liability for those actions can be unclear. The following cases involving criminal prosecutions under the federal Migratory Bird Treaty Act (MBTA) illustrate the difficulty.

The MBTA prohibits the "taking" (killing, catching, or causing death) of certain protected, migratory birds without a permit. As applied to corporations, it is a class B strict liability misdemeanor, providing fines for violations. The application of the act to commercial operations of corporations has had varied results.

In *United States v. Citgo Petroleum Corp.*, 893 F. Supp.2d 841 (S.D. Tex. 2012), the court held the act did apply to commercial activities that were not intended to kill or capture protected birds. There, the defendant corporations maintained open-air oil tanks in which migratory birds became entrapped and died. The court said the act applied because the corporations were the proximate cause of the birds' deaths, even though the commercial activity was not intended to cause those deaths.

On the other hand, in *United States v. Brigham Oil & Gas Co.*, 840 F. Supp.2d 1202 (D. N.D. 2012), the court held the act inapplicable to corporate commercial actions not intended to cause the death of the migratory birds. There, the defendants maintained oil reserve pits that were used to hold chemicals and other residue from oil drilling operations. Migratory birds landed in and died in the pits. The court dismissed prosecutions under the MBTA, saying the act applied only to intentional killing of migratory birds.

Courts have recognized the difficulty of applying environmental crime laws to corporate commercial activity that indirectly harms the protected environmental goals. An example of a court attempting to fairly apply these environmental crime laws to commercial activity is *United States v. Apollo Energies, Inc.*, 611 F.3d 679 (10th Cir. 2010). In that case the court affirmed corporate convictions under the MBTA where it was clear the corporation had knowledge that its equipment carried the probability of killing migratory birds, but reversed convictions of a corporation that lacked such knowledge.

Summary

- Children below a certain age, usually 7 or 8, cannot be convicted of a crime. Children between the minimum age and about 12–14 are presumed to lack capacity to commit a crime, but the presumption may be overcome.

- A child under the minimum age may not be convicted of a crime regardless of the evidence of his mental state. A child of 14 could be convicted if it can be shown the child had the mental ability and understanding to formulate the required criminal intent.

- The first prong of the *M'Naghten* rule requires a showing the defendant did know what he was doing (the cognitive capacity prong); the second prong requires a showing that the defendant did not know what he was doing was wrong (the moral incapacity prong).
- The *M'Naghten* rule differs from the substantial capacity test primarily on the magnitude of the defendant's understanding of events that made up the crime charged. The *M'Naghten* rule applies only if the defendant did not "know" the nature of his acts and that they were wrong. The substantial capacity test applies whenever the defendant cannot "appreciate" the nature of his acts, or that they were wrong, a lesser requirement.
- Voluntary intoxication or drug use is almost never the basis for the successful assertion of the insanity defense. However, in most states the defendant's intoxication or drug use may serve as the basis for a claim for diminished capacity.

- A verdict of not guilty by reason of insanity results in an acquittal of the defendant; a verdict of guilty but mentally ill is a conviction, but the defendant must be given treatment during his confinement.
- Mental illness, mental retardation, and many forms of physical illness may be the basis for finding a person incompetent to stand trial. Unless the condition is cured, the defendant cannot be tried for a crime. Defendants may be confined while competency is determined and treated.
- A person who lacks competency does not have the ability to understand what is happening at trial, and thus lacks the ability to participate in his own defense. Due process requires persons charged with crimes to be given an opportunity to consult with counsel, and assist in their own defense. Lack of competency makes that impossible, and thus trials of incompetent persons violate their due process rights.

Key Terms

Case Analysis and Writing Exercises

1. The insanity defense and the defense of diminished capacity generally involve the defendant claiming that while he did the criminal acts, his mental condition prevents him from being held responsible (or his responsibility should be diminished) for those acts. Does the defendant have to admit to the crime, or can these defenses be raised along with an "I didn't do it" claim? *See Com. v. Hutchinson*, 25 A.3d 277 (Pa. 2011). Note that this question arose in the context of a claim of "ineffective assistance of counsel." What did the defendant claim was "ineffective" about the lawyer who represented him? What did the appeals court say about that claim?

2. Section 4.01 of the Model Penal Code, the "substantial capacity" test, states in subsection 2 that mental disease or defect does not include "an abnormality manifested only by repeated criminal or antisocial conduct." This language was clearly adopted to exclude the psychopath, that is, a person who repeatedly manifests criminal conduct. Why should such a person be excluded? What must a defense lawyer prove to get a "psychopath" back within the test? See LaFave, *Criminal Law,* Section 7.5(b) (Belmont, Calif: West/Wadsworth, 2003).

3. Courts overwhelmingly hold that amnesia of criminal acts brought on by drugs or alcohol does not render a defendant mentally incompetent to stand trial. Why is that? When could amnesia result in a determination of incompetence? *See Gonzales v. State,* 313 S.W.3d 840 (Tex. App. 2010), *cert. denied* 131 S. Ct. 921 (2011).

4. Diminished capacity usually results in the defendant being convicted of a lesser offense than the crime charged, because the defendant lacked the capacity to have the specific intent needed for a conviction of the more serious charge. Is the defense available in cases where the statute is a "general intent" crime? What are the mental state requirements for a "general intent" crime? How does diminished capacity fit with those requirements? *See United States v. Frank,* 472 Fed Appx 431 (9th Cir. 2012).

Endnotes

1. Sir James Fitzjames Stephen, A *History of the Criminal Law of England*, vol. 1 (Macmillan & Co., 1883), p. 73.

2. *Leland v. State,* 343 U.S. 790 (1952).

3. An example of a state statute that codifies the common law is Mississippi Code Annotated, Section 43-21-151. This statute provides that no child under the age of 13 can be charged with a crime. Children over that age can be so charged, and apparently there is no presumption about their lack of capacity. See *Clemens v. State,* 733 So. 2d 266 (S. Ct. 1999), where a 14-year-old boy was convicted of killing three people and was given two life sentences, to run consecutively.

4. In 1994, a 10-year-old boy became the youngest child in a maximum-security juvenile prison when he and an 11-year-old were found to have thrown a 5-year-old out of the fourteenth floor of a Chicago housing project building. The 5-year-old, who died in the fall, had refused to steal candy for the older boys.

   See the 1991 case of *In re Devon T.,* 584 A.2d 1287 (Md. App. 1991), for a discussion of this law. Devon T. was almost 14 years old and a middle-school student in Baltimore when twenty plastic bags of heroin were found on his person. The Maryland courts held that the state produced sufficient evidence permitting a reasonable inference that Devon knew the difference between right and wrong and knew the wrongfulness of his acts.

5. 86 P.3d 132 (Wash. 2004).

6. 86 P.3d at 136–137.

7. A defense lawyer who entered an insanity plea for a client in a minor charge could find the client committed to an institution for a much longer time than if the client were found guilty of the offense charged.

   In *Lynch v. Overholser,* 369 U.S. 705, 82 S. Ct. 1063 (1962), a municipal court refused to accept a former mental patient's plea of guilty to a minor check forgery charge. Instead, the court found the defendant not guilty by reason of insanity. Because the defendant was a first offender, he would probably have not received a jail sentence. After the defendant served two years in a mental institution, the U.S. Supreme Court reversed the trial court's decision, holding that the trial court was not justified in committing the defendant to a mental institution on bare reasonable doubt concerning past sanity.

   Also note that prosecutors sometimes find that it is in the state's best interest to seek a civil commitment of a person when evidence shows that the individual is dangerous to him- or herself or others and in need of treatment.

8. The 1990 study done by Policy Research Associates of Delmar, New York, is one such study.

9. The federal Insanity Defense Reform Act of 1984 (the "Act") provides that a federal criminal defendant found not guilty by reason of insanity may not be released onto the streets. Justice Stevens of the U.S. Supreme Court summarized the act as follows in *Frank v. United States,* 113 S. Ct. 363 (1992):

   > It (the federal Act) provides that "the Attorney General shall hospitalize the person [found not guilty by reason of insanity] in a suitable facility" until a state assumes responsibility for his care and treatment or the Attorney General finds that his release would not create a risk of harm to people or property in 18 U.S.C. § 4243(e). The question presented by the petition for certiorari is whether a defendant who has pleaded not guilty by reason of insanity is entitled to a jury instruction explaining the effect of this statute. If such an instruction is not given, there is a strong possibility that the jury will be reluctant to accept a meritorious defense because of fear that a dangerous, mentally ill person will go free.

10. 112 S. Ct. 1780 (S. Ct. 1992).

11. 389 F.3d 1060 (10th Cir. 2004).

12. 10 CI. & R 200, 8 Eng. Rep. 718.

13. See, e.g., Georgia Code Annotated, Section 16-3-3; *Vann v. Commonwealth*, 544 S.E.2d 879 (Va. 2001).

14. The "irresistible impulse" rule became well known because of the book and film *Anatomy of a Murder*. There, a soldier escapes punishment for the death of his wife by pleading that an irresistible impulse caused him to act.

15. 94 U.S. App. D.C. 228, 214 R2d 862 (1954).

16. *Sauer v. United States*, 241 F.2d 640, 648 (9th Cir. 1957).

17. Commentary to Section 4.01, Model Penal Code.

18. 260 Mont. 510, 861 P.2d 884 (Mont. 1993).

19. 114 S. Ct. 1371 (1994).

20. Idaho: *State v. Searcy*, 798 P.2d 914 (Idaho 1996); Kansas: *State v. Bethal*, 66 P.3d 804 (Kan. 2003), *cert. denied*, 540 U.S. 1006 (2003); and Utah: *State v. Herrera*, 895 P.2d 359 (Utah 1995).

21. *Finger v. State*, 27 P.3d 66, (Nev. 2001) *cert, denied* 534 U.S. 1127 (2002).

22. An heir to the du Pont fortune, John E. du Pont, was found guilty of third-degree murder but mentally ill. World-class wrestlers were using du Pont's Pennsylvania estate for training. John du Pont shot Olympic gold medalist David Schulz three times at point-blank range without any apparent provocation. The defendant was found to be "actively psychotic" and was ordered to be treated in a mental hospital until cured, after which he will be sent to a prison for the remainder of his sentence. Du Pont was the wealthiest murder defendant in the history of the United States.

23. In 1998, the Federal Court of Appeals for the Tenth Circuit upheld the guilty but mentally ill law of New Mexico in the case of *Neely v. Newton* (1998 WL 33423). The court held that in clarifying the distinction between those individuals who are not guilty by reason of insanity and those who are mentally ill yet criminally liable, the law serves a legitimate state interest. State court decisions upholding the constitutionality of guilty but mentally ill laws are found in *State v. Neely*, 819 P.2d 249 (New Mex. 1991).

    However, in 1997 an Illinois appellate court held that the Illinois guilty but mentally ill law encouraged compromised verdicts in violation of due process and that the law seduced juries into settling on a middle ground between guilty and not guilty when in fact there is no middle ground. See *People v. Robles*, 1997 WL 342483 (111 App. 2 Dist. 1997). In *People v. Lantz*, 712 N E. 2d 314 (111, 1999) the Illinois Supreme Court reversed the Appellate Court, and found the GBMI act constitutional.

24. *The Journal of Criminal Law and Criminology* 73 (1982), pp. 867–874, contains the entire text of former Governor Thompson's remarks as co-chair of the National Violent Crime Task Force. Governor Thompson stated that "the insanity defense has been described as the chronic scandal of American criminal law."

25. "The Insanity Defense: Ready for Reform?" *Wisconsin Bar Bulletin*, December 1982.

26. A 1997 study conducted by the Harvard Medical School and financed by the gambling industry concluded that 1.29 percent of adults in Canada and the United States have compulsive gambling disorders. However, the percentage of problem gamblers among people with alcohol or drug abuse problems or mental disorders was found to be 14.29 percent.

    The need for money to gamble could cause compulsive gamblers to steal from employers, family, friends, and others. Compulsive gamblers also borrow money from other people, including loan sharks. Children of compulsive gamblers are often deprived of necessities needed for their well-being and education. (See the *New York Times* article "Compulsion to Gamble Seen Growing: Study Finds Legality Spreads the Problem," December 7, 1997.)

27. 699 F.2d 839 (7th Cir. 1982).

28. 743 F. Supp. 713 (N.D. Cal. 1990). It should be noted that many specific intent crimes, such as murder, have lesser offenses like manslaughter that have no specific intent requirement. A defendant using the diminished capacity defense may avoid the murder charge, but be convicted of the manslaughter charge.

29. See *Drope v. Missouri*, 420 U.S. at 171, 95 S. Ct. at 903–04 (1975) and *Pate v. Robinson*, 383 U.S. at 378, 86 S. Ct. at 838 (1966).

30. See the 1996 U.S. Supreme Court case of *Cooper v. Oklahoma*, 517 U.S. 348 (1996), in which the Supreme Court invalidated laws in Oklahoma, Connecticut, Rhode Island, and Pennsylvania and required these states to place the burden on defendants to prove incompetency by a "preponderance of the evidence." Laws in these states had previously used the higher burden of "clear and convincing evidence."

31. *Faretta v. California*, 422 U.S. 806 (1975).

32. 406 U.S. 715, 92 S. Ct. 1845 (1972).

33. A made-for-television movie aired in 1979 about Donald Lang, an 18-year-old totally illiterate deaf-mute. Lang could not talk, write, read lips, or understand sign language. In 1965, he was charged with the murder of a Chicago prostitute (Cook County criminal case #65-3421). Because he could not hear, speak, read, or write, he was declared incompetent to stand trial and was placed in a state mental hospital. After Lang was held for five years, the Illinois Supreme Court ordered him tried or released. Because witnesses were no longer available, he was released. In 1973, Lang was charged with killing another woman. After a conviction for the second murder, he was held to be incompetent and was committed in 1979 to a mental hospital. In 1992, Lang again was found unfit to stand trial and was denied release from the Illinois institution to which he was committed. *See People v. Lang*, 587 N.E.2d 490 (Ill. App. 1992).

34. 18 *Commentaries*, section 12.

35. 681 N.W.2d 669 (Mich. App. 2004).

The Law Governing the Use of Force

Scott Heppell/PA Photos/Landov

A police officer fires a Taser device, which propels wires carrying an electrical charge of over 1,200 volts. The wires are attached to darts, which can penetrate a suspect's clothing to cause temporary paralysis.

OUTLINE

Self-Defense and the Defense of Others

The Use of Deadly Force in Self-Defense or the Defense of Others

Loss of Self-Defense Privilege for a Wrongdoer or an Aggressor

The "Castle" Doctrine and the Minority Duty-to-Retreat Exception to That Doctrine

Battered Women and Domestic Homicides

The Use of Force in the Defense of Property

The Use of Force in Making an Arrest

Using Reasonable Force to Obtain Evidence of Drunk or Drugged Driving

Standards for the Use of Deadly Force Established by the U.S. Supreme Court

Definition of an Unreasonable Seizure Today

Use of Force in Resisting an Unlawful Arrest

The Use of Tasers and Other Force In Traffic Stops

Disciplining Children

LEARNING OBJECTIVES

In this chapter we consider the rules governing the use of force by private persons or police officers. The learning objectives for this chapter are

- Identify the three key points for determining when force is justified.
- Describe the "castle" doctrine and explain what it says.
- Determine how "stand your ground" laws affect the general rules for using force and the effect such laws have on the "castle" doctrine.
- List the circumstances that justify a police officer using non-deadly force in making an arrest.
- Explain why the Fourth Amendment applies to use of force by a police officer.
- Identify the circumstances that would justify the use of deadly force by a police officer.
- List the people who may use force in the discipline of children.

In November of 2011 students at the University of California-Davis organized a protest modeled on the "Occupy Wall Street" movement. The students erected tents and occupied the University Quad. University officials ordered the students to leave, but they refused. On November 18, 2011, university police officers surrounded the students, who had joined arms and were seated in a circle on the Quad grounds. After the students again refused to obey orders to leave, the officers walked around the circle and sprayed the students in the face with orange pepper spray. Some students were arrested, but later released. Police officers justified their actions, contending the students "cut off officers' movements." In September of 2012 the university settled a lawsuit brought by the injured students against the university.

In this chapter we discuss the rules governing the use of force, including the force law enforcement officers may use to arrest or control criminal suspects.

The use of force by one person against another is a violation of the criminal law unless some justification for the use exists. Justification means that the person using the force had a legally sufficient reason for doing so. Whether or not the use of force is justified often depends on the kind of force used, the person using the force, and the circumstances leading up to the use of force.[1] For example, the rules justifying the use of deadly force are different from those that apply to non-deadly force. The rules justifying the use of force in the protection of property differ from those that justify force to protect persons. Also, the rules justifying the use of force by law enforcement officers reflect the duties and risks facing such officers. As you study the materials in this chapter, consider how they apply to the following hypothetical situation:

A, the owner of a house, throws a graduation party for his daughter, D. B, an uninvited acquaintance of D, "crashes" the party by entering A's house. A orders B to leave the house, but B refuses, and starts knocking over party decorations. A twists B's arm behind his back, drags him out of the house, and throws B into the street. Incensed, B goes to his car and grabs a tire wrench, and runs at A. A, mistakenly believing the wrench is a machete, pulls a pistol and shoots B in the arm. B runs off as a police officer arrives at the scene. The officer orders B to stop, and when B refuses the officer fires his service revolver at B, hitting B in the leg.

Force has been used by each of the actors in this hypothetical situation. As you study the materials in this chapter, try to determine which, if any, use was justified.

Self-Defense and the Defense of Others

self-defense The elements to evaluate whether an act of force for self-defense is justified include the unlawfulness of the other's action, the necessity to defend oneself immediately, and the reasonableness of the act of self-defense under the circumstances.

defense of another The elements to evaluate whether an act of force for defense of another is justified include the unlawfulness of the action toward the other, the necessity to defend the other immediately, and the reasonableness of the act of defense under the circumstances.

Section 3.04 of the Model Penal Code provides that force can be used in self-protection "when the actor believes that such force is immediately necessary for the purpose of protecting himself against the use of unlawful force by such other person on the present occasion." In their criminal codes and in their court decisions, all states and the federal government have rules for the use of force. The state of New York, for example, provides in Public Law 35.15 that "one may use physical force upon another when and to the extent he reasonably believes necessary to defend himself or a third person from what he reasonably believes to be the imminent use of unlawful physical force by such other persons." The key points in determining the lawfulness of force in **self-defense** or the **defense of another** are

- *Unlawfulness:* Is what the other person doing unlawful? If the other's behavior is not unlawful, force is not justified.
- *Necessity:* Force must be immediately *necessary* to protect the person or another from the use of *unlawful* force or interference by another.
- *Reasonableness:* The amount of force used in self-defense or defense of another must be *reasonable* under the circumstances that exist.

In determining what force is reasonable in self-defense, a court or a jury will take into account the size and age of the parties in relation to one another, the instruments or weapons used, and the aggressiveness of the assault made. Ordinarily, if fists were used in the attack and the parties were about the same size and strength, then fists and the strength of arms and body would be the maximum force that could be used in defense.

Also, so long as the belief is reasonable, it does not need to be correct. Someone who reasonably believes another person is reaching for a weapon to use against her or him may respond with force, even if in fact the aggressor was reaching for something else.

A 70-year-old, 100-pound woman becomes angry with a 25-year-old, 200-pound man and begins to hit him with an umbrella. The man may defend himself by taking the umbrella away from the woman, but because he has such physical control of the situation, the amount of force that he would be justified in using against her ends there.

The rules for defense of another person mirror the rules for self-defense. A person may come to the aid of another and use necessary and reasonable force to defend the other person against unlawful force or interference. The person coming to the assistance or defense of another must reasonably believe that the facts are such that the third person would be privileged to act in self-defense and also must reasonably believe that his or her intervention is necessary to protect the third person against unlawful force or interference.

Good Samaritan laws Laws that encourage people to come to the aid of another or to defend another against unlawful force or interference.

Many states have enacted **Good Samaritan laws** that encourage, but do not require, people to get involved when they witness an assault. As an example, the Maryland statute states, "Any person witnessing a violent assault upon the person of another may lawfully aid the person being assaulted by assisting in that person's defense" (Art. 27, § 12A). Under these statutes a person may use force to protect another only if the threat of violence is occurring or imminent. Thus, in the 2011 case of *State v. Clinch*, 335 S.W.3d 579 (Mo. App. 2011) the court affirmed a murder conviction, holding that the defendant's belief that the victim would abuse the defendant's grandchildren once given visitation rights did not warrant a "defense of others" instruction to the jury.

Some states have enacted statutes that require people witnessing an assault to take limited action, such as calling the police. Violations of these laws usually are punished by a small fine.

The Use of Deadly Force in Self-Defense or the Defense of Others

The rules providing justification for the use of deadly force generally are similar to those governing the use of non-deadly force, with some important differences. **Deadly force** is force that is likely to cause or is capable of causing death or serious bodily injury. Firing a weapon at a person is the use of deadly force, whether the intent is to kill or to wound.

deadly force Force that is likely to cause or is capable of causing death or serious bodily injury.

All people, including law enforcement officers, may use deadly force, but only if such force is necessary to prevent imminent death or great bodily harm to themselves or others. Moreover, unlike the use of non-deadly force, where there is no duty to retreat, some states impose such a duty where deadly force is used. Section 3.04 (b)(ii) of the Model Penal Code, for example, states that deadly force is not justified if the actor knows he or she can retreat with "complete safety." (See Chapter 10 for a discussion of imperfect self-defense where unlawful force has been used in self-defense.)

ONE DAY CAN MAKE A DIFFERENCE

Many states have passed statutes eliminating the duty to retreat before using deadly force, either using the "castle doctrine" or "stand your ground" laws similar to the Florida statute that was the first of these laws. Those statutes are discussed in this chapter.

However, when a legislature passes a statute eliminating a duty to retreat, the statute generally applies only to cases that arise after the effective date of the statute. Thus, the date on which a use of deadly force occurs may make a difference between the presence and absence of a duty to retreat.

This was the controlling issue in the 2011 Case of *Krajcovic v. Statei*.[2] The defendant was charged with murder in the death of a person visiting the defendant's home. The defendant claimed self-defense, based on his fear that the victim was going to kill him or his child. At his trial, the trial court instructed the jury that the defendant had a duty to retreat before using deadly force, which was the law in Texas before September 1, 2007, the effective date of adoption of the "castle doctrine" by the Texas legislature. However, the facts did not clearly show whether the killing occurred on the last day of August or the first day of September. If it was the latter, the jury instruction was erroneous, because there would have been no duty to retreat. A Texas Court of Appeals reversed the defendant's murder conviction, stating the jury might conclude the killing occurred on September 1, and thus defendant would not have a duty to retreat. In 2013 the Texas Court of Criminal Appeals reversed the decision of the Court of Appeals, holding that there was no evidence upon which a "rational jury" could conclude the killing occurred on or after September 1, 2007. It affirmed the defendant's murder conviction.[3]

Under the common law, and some state statutes, a person was not permitted to use deadly force if retreat from an attack was reasonably possible and safe. Thus, even if an unlawful attacker threatened death or serious bodily harm, the law instructed the victim of the attack to "retreat to the wall" before employing deadly force against the attacker.

"stand your ground" laws Recent laws passed in many states that permit using deadly force in response to an unlawful attack, in contrast to the traditional "duty to retreat" policy.

The Florida "Stand Your Ground" Law   Perhaps because it was dissatisfied with the duty to retreat, in 2005 the Florida legislature passed this country's first **"stand your ground" law.** The Florida law states:

A person who is not engaged in an unlawful activity and who is attacked in any other place where he or she has a right to be has no duty to retreat and has the right to stand his or her ground and meet force with force, including deadly force if he or she reasonably believes it is necessary to do so to prevent death or great bodily harm to himself or herself or another or to prevent the commission of a forcible felony.[4]

Section 776.032 of the Florida law provides for immunity from prosecution if force, even deadly force, is used as authorized by this statute. Immunity means that if a judge determines a defendant used force under circumstances authorized by the statute, self-defense is not a jury question and the charges must be dismissed. In *State v. Gallo*, 76 So.3d 407 (Fla. App. 2011), the court affirmed a dismissal of second-degree murder charges against a defendant engaged in a gunfight "reminiscent of the 'Shootout at the OK Corral'" because the trial court determined the defendant was using lawful force under the statute.

In the 2009 case of *Hair v. State,* 17 So.3d 804 (Fla. App. 2009), the court held that a passenger in a car who shot and killed a person who unlawfully and forcibly entered the car could not be charged with a crime under the Florida "stand your ground" law, because the law states that any person making such a forcible entry is presumed to present a threat of imminent harm to the occupants of the car. The court also held that it did not matter that at the time the passenger fired the handgun the intruder was backing out of the car. After a highly-charged Florida trial, in July 2013, a six-person jury found George Zimmerman not guilty of murder or manslaughter in the death of teenager Trayvon Martin. Zimmerman argued he was acting in self-defense when he shot and killed the unarmed Martin.

Since the Florida statute was passed, at least twenty-nine other states have passed similar laws or are considering such laws. These laws have been criticized as "giving more rights to use deadly force than we give police officers"[5] and are really "shoot first" with a "license to kill."[6] See www.leg.state.fl.us/statutes for the full text of the Florida law.

Loss of Self-Defense Privilege for a Wrongdoer or an Aggressor

The right of a person to use force in self-defense arises from the unlawful force or activity encountered by that person. If the person asserting self-defense is engaged in unlawful activity such as the commission of a crime, or is himself the unlawful aggressor, the right of self-defense does not exist.

> **EXAMPLE** ▸ V, the owner of a car, discovers D unlawfully breaking into the car. V grabs D and tries to restrain him. To escape, D punches V and runs away. Since V was using reasonable force to protect his property, V was acting lawfully. As a result, D's use of force against V was unlawful.

> **EXAMPLE** ▸ D wrongfully starts a fight with V, pushing him to the ground. V fights back, striking D with his fists. To defend himself, D kicks V in the knee, severely injuring him. D was the initial aggressor, and thus had no right to use force in self-defense against V's use of force.

State statutes and court decisions recognize two situations in which the aggressor or wrongdoer can regain the right of self-defense:

1. A wrongdoer (X) begins an encounter with the unlawful use of his or her fists or some non-deadly weapon. The victim, however, unlawfully uses deadly force, which, under the circumstances, is unnecessary and unreasonable. Now, X may use force in self-defense but is not privileged to resort to the use of force intended or likely to cause death unless he or she has exhausted

   • every means of escape (under the duty to retreat) and
   • every means of avoiding death or great bodily harm to herself or himself.

2. A wrongdoer who is the initial aggressor may regain the right of self-defense by withdrawing in good faith from the use of force and giving adequate notice of that withdrawal to the victim. If the initial victim continues to use force, the victim becomes the aggressor, and the initial aggressor reacquires a right of self-defense.

"STAND YOUR GROUND" AND UNLAWFUL ACTIVITY

The "stand your ground" laws all apply to force used by "A person who is *not engaged in an unlawful activity...*" This language raises two questions: (1) what does "unlawful activity" include, and (2), what rule applies if the defendant uses force while engaged in an unlawful activity? Two 2011 decisions from states with "stand your ground" laws addressed these questions.

- *Dawkins v. State*, 252 P.3d 214 (Okla. App. 2011). Defendant was in a friend's home when the friend's former boyfriend entered the home and began hitting another occupant. Defendant had a sawed-off shotgun, and shot the former boyfriend. When he was charged with manslaughter, the defendant invoked the "immunity" provision of the Oklahoma "stand your ground" law. The appeals court affirmed his conviction, holding that because the sawed-off shotgun was illegal, defendant was "engaged" in illegal activity and thus lost the right to use deadly force under the statute. The court said the illegal activity did not have to relate to use of force, but did not include mere "technical" violations of the law.
- *Dorsey v. State*, 74 So.3d 521 (Fla. App. 2011). An appeals court held a defendant was not entitled to the "stand your ground" defense because he was a convicted felon in possession of a weapon, and thus engaged in unlawful activity when he used the weapon to kill another person. However, the court reversed the defendant's second-degree murder conviction because he used the weapon after being attacked by other guests at a "keg" party. The court said he was entitled to use deadly force in self-defense, even if he was engaged in unlawful activity so as to a make the "stand your ground" law inapplicable, if he could show that the force used against him was deadly and he could not have safely retreated. The case was remanded for a new trial on that issue.

The "Castle" Doctrine and the Minority Duty-to-Retreat Exception to That Doctrine

"castle" doctrine The doctrine permitting people who have been assaulted in their homes by a trespasser to stand their ground and use such force as is necessary and reasonable to defend themselves.

It has long been the law that people who have been assaulted in their homes by a trespasser have no duty to retreat or flee but instead may stand their ground and use such force as is necessary and reasonable to defend themselves or others. Because a person's home is his or her "castle," the privilege not to retreat in one's home is known as the **"castle" doctrine.** Even states that require retreat before using deadly force exempt dwellings from the duty, as does the Model Penal Code (see § 3.04(b)(ii)(A)). The U.S. Supreme Court decided long ago in the case *of Beard v. United States*[7] that under federal law a homeowner had no duty to retreat in the face of an unlawful assault in his home or on his property.

"make my day" rules Rules adopted by some states that put no limits on the use of deadly force by the occupant of a dwelling in response to a trespasser.

Also, some states have adopted **"make my day" rules,** which put no limits on the use of deadly force by the occupant of a dwelling. In *State v. Anderson,*[8] the court interpreted the Oklahoma statute (Tit. 21, § 1289.25) as intended to remove any requirement that the force used must be "reasonable" under the circumstances. An occupant who reasonably believes the intruder who has wrongfully entered a residence intends to use some force, however slight, is privileged to use any force, including deadly force.

EXAMPLE ▶ D trespassed in V's apartment, and V ordered him to leave. D did, but returned and jiggled V's doorknob. V followed D back to D's apartment, and entered without D's knowledge. D then came out of his bedroom with a machete, and injured V. D was convicted of first-degree assault. The appeals court reversed, saying that if the jury found that V was wrongfully in D's apartment, D would be entitled to the "make my day" defense. *People v. Zukowski*, 260 P.3d 339 (Colo. App. 2011), *cert. denied,* 2011 WL 3855726 (Colo. 2011).

Florida's "stand your ground" law, discussed above, also changes the law on the force permitted under the "castle" doctrine.[9] The Florida law creates a presumption that a homeowner has a reasonable fear of imminent peril or death whenever another person unlawfully and forcefully enters the dwelling. Under this law it is no longer necessary for the homeowner (or other legitimate occupant) to prove the intruder presented the threat of death or serious bodily harm.

The "castle" doctrine does not require a lawful occupant of a home to retreat when confronted by a trespasser or a person who does not reside in the home. However, state laws vary when the wrongdoer is also a co-occupant of the home (such as a spouse or domestic partner, housemate, or family member). The Florida "stand your ground" law, for example, states that the presumption that a person forcefully entering a residence will use deadly force does not apply if that person has a right to be there, such as a co-occupant.

HOW RULES ON USE OF FORCE EVOLVED

The common law rules on the use of force have evolved over time, mainly by statutory changes. In these columns we compare the common law rules to current rules on the use of force.

Common Law	Current Statutes
Non-deadly force: Reasonable force in response to unlawful force or activity. No duty to retreat.	Same
Deadly force: Only in response to unlawful, deadly force; duty to retreat.	"Stand your ground" laws: Only in response to deadly force or to prevent forcible felony; no duty to retreat.
In dwellings: Deadly force if intruder threatens deadly force; no duty to retreat.	Castle doctrine: Deadly force if intruder threatens deadly force; no duty to retreat.
	"Make my day" laws: Deadly force in response to any force by intruder. No duty to retreat.
	"Stand your ground" laws: Presumption that intruder in dwelling threatens deadly force, so deadly force permitted against any intruder. No duty to retreat.

EXAMPLE   D and V are co-owners of a house. After an argument, D leaves the house and stays in a hotel. The next night, D forces his way into the house, and appears to be drunk and violent. V shoots D. V is not entitled to the presumption that she has a reasonable fear of deadly force, even though D forcefully entered the house. V will be entitled to claim self-defense only if in fact D was threatening her with deadly force.

EXAMPLE   Assume the same facts as above, except that D is threatening V with a knife, and V is standing by the open back door. In most states V has no duty to retreat (the "castle doctrine"), and may use deadly force to defend herself.

In a few states the "castle" doctrine has a duty to retreat. The Supreme Court of New Jersey pointed out in the case of *State v. Gartland*[10] that New Jersey is now among the minority of states that require a lawful co-occupant to retreat (if possible) before using deadly force against another co-occupant. In the *Gartland* case, a trial court convicted the wife of manslaughter because she failed to retreat before shooting her husband, who was assaulting her in a bedroom of their home. The appeals court reversed the conviction and ordered a new trial, stating that although a duty to retreat existed, the jury did not consider if retreat was possible:

> Exactly where could she retreat? As we understand the record, there was no other way out of the bedroom other than the doorway where her assailant stood. The (jury) charge should have asked whether, armed with a weapon, she could have safely made her way out of the bedroom door without threat of serious bodily injury to herself.

Battered Women and Domestic Homicides

The National Clearinghouse for the Defense of Battered Women states that every year 500 to 750 women kill men who abused them and that "our prisons are filled with women with long histories of abuse, linked to the crimes they're in prison for."[11] The clearinghouse also estimates that a woman is abused in the United States every 13 seconds.

These estimates indicate the high levels of anger, fear, hatred, and humiliation in the households where such conditions prevail. Battered women (and those who allege they were abused) can be found in the prisons of every state. They are serving sentences ranging from assault and battery to voluntary manslaughter and first-degree murder.

To lawfully use deadly force in self-defense, a real or reasonable fear of imminent death or great bodily harm must exist. If no immediate threat is present, then, it is assumed that the abused woman has lawful alternatives to force, such as going to a shelter for battered women or going to a family member for help.

EXAMPLE   A woman is terrified as her husband or boyfriend comes toward her in a rage, screaming that he will use the knife in his hand to kill her. Witnesses state that the woman had no opportunity to retreat but was able to grab a gun, which she used to kill the man. Her action would be held to be lawful use of force in self-defense.

EXAMPLE   After years of beatings and many other abuses, the defendant kills her husband with a handgun as he is taking a nap. Her husband has been drinking for two days, and the defendant believed he would beat her again, as he had often done in the past, when he finished his nap and resumed drinking. The killing would be held to be "imperfect self-defense," and the defendant could be charged with voluntary manslaughter.

battered woman defense Evidence of past abuse offered by women charged with violence against their abusers to show its psychological effects as part of their claim of self-defense.

A 2007 trial in Tennessee that received national attention involved a **battered woman defense.** The defendant, a 33-year-old wife of a minister, was charged with murder after shooting her husband with a shotgun. She testified in her own defense and stated that her husband had abused her physically and sexually during their marriage. She also testified that the shotgun went off accidentally. The jury of ten women and two men convicted her of voluntary manslaughter, with a possible sentence of three to six years or less, instead of murder, with a possible sentence of 12 years to life. One of the men, the jury foreman, after expressing skepticism about the abuse claims, told reporters after the trial that "It was a room of 10 ladies … 10 ladies were going to have a tendency to see [the defendant's] view." In response, one of the female jurors stated, "You shouldn't kill, but you also shouldn't beat your wife."[12]

AP Photo/The Jackson Sun, Andrew McMurtrie

Mary Winkler (left) was accused of murdering her husband, a preacher, with a shotgun, and was tried for first-degree murder. At her trial she admitted shooting her husband but testified in her defense that her husband psychologically and sexually abused her. The jury found her guilty of voluntary manslaughter on April 19, 2007. Winkler was sentenced to three years in prison, which under state law required her to serve at least 210 days. The defense of spousal abuse, although usually not a complete defense to a crime charged, can often lead to a reduced charge or conviction for a lesser crime, as it did in Winkler's case.

WHEN FORCE *CANNOT* BE USED

Force in self-defense or in the defense of another person cannot be used under the following circumstances:

- The force is not immediately necessary to protect against unlawful force.
- The amount of force used is unreasonable compared to the unlawful force threatened.
- In states without a "stand your ground" law, the force is deadly and the person using deadly force had an opportunity to retreat.
- The person using the force is the aggressor or is acting unlawfully.
- The other person's actions are lawful.
- The force used cannot be based on a fear that another person means to do harm sometime in the future if there is no immediate fear of harm.
- Force cannot be used to punish or to retaliate for past harm or past injury, such as a sexual assault in the past.

Many states now permit abused women charged with violence against their abusers to introduce evidence of their abuse and its psychological effects as part of their claim of self-defense. Women in prisons who were abused or who claim they were abused have appealed to state governors for clemency. Gaile Owens, who was given the death penalty for the arranged murder of her husband, was scheduled to be executed on September 28, 2010, which would have made her the first woman executed in Tennessee in nearly 200 years. Owens had claimed she suffered from "battered wife" syndrome, though she did not introduce evidence of abuse at her trial. On July 14, 2010, Tennessee Governor Phil Bredesen commuted Owens's sentence to life imprisonment. Owens was granted parole on September 28, 2011, and released from prison. Governor Bredesen stated that part of the reason for his decision to commute Owens's sentence was the outcome in the Mary Winkler case, pictured here. Winkler, who also alleged the "battered wife" defense, was convicted but served only 67 days in a mental health facility.

Governors in all states receive many requests for pardons and clemency each year. Parole boards and governors review the records of women requesting clemency because they were abused. Chapter 10, on homicide, contains further material on battered women who kill.

The Use of Force in the Defense of Property

A person is privileged to threaten to or intentionally use non-deadly force to protect property that is lawfully in his or her custody or care. The interference with the property must be unlawful. Force may be used only when necessary to terminate the interference, and the amount of force must be reasonable under the circumstances.

EXAMPLE Y, a store employee, sees X snatch merchandise and run out of the store. Y may use *necessary* and *reasonable* force to prevent the *unlawful* taking of merchandise by X.

EXAMPLE X snatches W's purse and runs off. Y, who observed the crime, would be justified in using necessary and reasonable force to recover the purse. Theft from the person (or robbery, if force is used) is a felony in most, if not all, states, which would authorize Y, in most states, to make a citizen's arrest. Force could also be used under these circumstances under the state law governing the use of force in making an arrest.

Deadly force was at one time commonly used to protect property. On the American frontier, farmers and ranchers often used deadly force to prevent the theft of their horses, cattle, or farm equipment. This force was necessary in those times, because law enforcement officers were seldom readily available.

Today all states forbid the use of deadly force in the defense of property. The reasons for the change in the law can be summarized as follows:

1. On the frontier, a horse and many other items of property were important for survival. Today, few items of property are vital to survival because they can be replaced within a few days.
2. Today, many items of personal property (such as a car) are ordinarily insured against loss by theft. On the frontier, insurance was unknown, and the loss of major or personal items could be a tragedy to a frontier family.
3. Today, thanks to modern communication and transportation, law enforcement agencies are readily available to assist individuals confronted with theft.

The rule that a person cannot use deadly force to protect property applies whether the owner is present or uses an automated device, such as a spring gun, that is triggered by opening a door or otherwise engaging a spring attached to the property. Indeed, some U.S. jurisdictions, such as Oregon, and Wisconsin, and some countries, such as England, go so far as to punish separately the mere setting of a spring gun.

EXAMPLE A farmer who becomes exasperated because melons are being stolen from his fields is not justified in shooting the thieves with a shotgun. Neither can he set up a shotgun that is discharged when a thief brushes a wire attached to the trigger mechanism.

Virtually all states permit owners of real estate to use non-deadly force to evict trespassers from their property or protect the real estate from imminent harm. Most state statutes require the property owner to request that the trespassers leave the property before force is used. In the 2011 case of *State v. Starke*[13] the appeals court reversed a conviction for terrorist threats because the trial court failed to instruct the jury on the defendant's right to use force to protect his premises. The defendant, a 79-year-old man, ordered two men, whom he had paid to do some work, to leave his house, and when they refused the defendant threatened them with a handgun, a use of "force" under that state's law. The appeals court remanded the case for a new trial because a jury might find that the defendant had a reasonable belief the men would refuse to leave and damage his property.

SECTIONS OF THE U.S. CONSTITUTION CONTROLLING THE USE OF FORCE BY LAW ENFORCEMENT OFFICERS

Provision of the U.S. Constitution	Limit on Force Used
The Fourth Amendment forbids "unreasonable searches and seizures"; a "seizure" includes the use of unreasonable force.	The use of force, including deadly force by law enforcement officers, must be "objectively reasonable in light of the facts and circumstances confronting (the officer) … judged from the perspective of a reasonable officer on the scene. . . ." *Graham v. Conner*, 490 U.S. 386, 390 (1989)
The Eighth Amendment forbids "cruel and unusual punishment."	Once convicted and incarcerated, any use of force against an inmate is viewed as punishment and thus subject to the "cruel and unusual punishment" clause. Where force is used to maintain order in jails or prisons, the question becomes "whether force was applied in a good faith effort to maintain order … or maliciously and sadistically for the very purpose of causing harm." *Whitley v. Albers*, 475 U.S. 312, 320–321 (1986).
The Due Process Clauses of the Fifth and Fourteenth Amendments forbid governments from depriving any person of "life, liberty, or property without due process of law."	The U.S. Supreme Court has limited the use of the "due process" guarantee to those circumstances where there is no other source "of constitutional protection against a particular sort of intrusive governmental conduct." *Graham v. Conner*, 490 U.S. 386 at 395 (1989).

The Use of Force in Making an Arrest

Force may not be used legally in making an arrest unless the arrest is a lawful, custodial arrest made in good faith. This does not mean that the arrested person must be found guilty of the charge; however, it does mean that probable cause (reasonable grounds to believe) must exist to authorize the arrest.

In most arrests, force is unnecessary because the person arrested complies with instructions and offers no resistance. If force in making arrests should be necessary because of resistance or an attempt to escape, the officer may use only such force as is reasonably believed necessary to

1. Detain the offender, make the arrest, and conduct lawful searches.
2. Overcome any resistance by the offender.
3. Prevent an escape and retake the offender if an escape occurs.
4. Protect the officer, others, and the offender, if necessary.

The tests used in determining whether excessive force was used by a law enforcement officer in making an arrest were established by the U.S. Supreme

Court in the case of *Tennessee v. Garner,* discussed below for the use of deadly force, and the case of *Graham v. Connor.*[14] In *Graham* the U.S. Supreme Court held:

> Today we make explicit what was implicit in *Garner*'s analysis, and hold that *all* claims that law enforcement officers have used excessive force—deadly or not—in the course of an arrest, investigatory stop, or other "seizure" of a free citizen should be analyzed under the Fourth Amendment and its "reasonableness" standard, rather than under a "substantive due process" approach. Because the Fourth Amendment provides an explicit textual source of constitutional protection against this sort of physically intrusive governmental conduct, that Amendment, not the more generalized notion of "substantive due process," must be the guide for analyzing these claims.
>
> Determining whether the force used to effect a particular seizure is "reasonable" under the Fourth Amendment requires a careful balancing of "the nature and quality of the intrusion on the individual's Fourth Amendment interests" against the countervailing governmental interests at stake. (Citations omitted). Our Fourth Amendment jurisprudence has long recognized that the right to make an arrest or investigatory stop necessarily carries with it the right to use some degree of physical coercion or threat thereof to effect it.[15]

The question of what force is reasonable in making an arrest must make allowance for the fact that the police are making judgments in volatile situations. Common uses of force courts find reasonable include forceful application of physical restraints, like handcuffs; force used to place a suspect on the ground to be handcuffed; and force used to take away a weapon on the suspect's person. One area where courts differ is the use of Taser guns to make arrests, a subject discussed later in this chapter.

Using Reasonable Force to Obtain Evidence of Drunk or Drugged Driving

More than 10,000 persons are killed each year, and more than a million injured, in traffic accidents involving drunk or drugged driving (driving under the influence—DUI). This is about 31 percent of total traffic deaths from all causes. The National Highway Traffic Safety Administration (NHTSA) estimates the annual cost to Americans for alcohol or drug-impaired driving to be $45 billion. On October 2, 2012, the Centers for Disease Control and Prevention reported that although more than 1.4 million people were arrested for DUI in 2010, it estimated that there were over 112 million episodes that year where drivers operated vehicles while under the influence of alcohol or drugs.

All states make driving under the influence of alcohol or drugs a crime and have laws that require a driver to submit to breath, blood, or urine analysis when police officers have reasonable grounds to believe the driver is impaired. These laws have been upheld as reasonable regulation of an important and potentially dangerous activity. As these courts frequently point out, driving on public streets is a privilege, not a right.

In recent years an increasing number of drivers have refused to submit to standard breath tests. While all states have "refusal to consent" criminal statutes,

AMERICAN POLICE GET HIGH MARKS FOR RESTRAINT IN THE USE OF FORCE

There are more than 17,000 police and sheriff's departments in the United States, employing over 600,000 full-time officers with general arrest power. Some of these officers are daily first responders to armed robberies, home invasions, and tavern brawls, and sometimes to terrorist attacks and school shootings.

The question of whether American law enforcement officers, as a whole, use force wisely within constitutional limits has been asked in a number of studies. What follows are summaries of three of those studies:

1. A 1999 study ordered by the U.S. Congress, NCJ 184957, which concluded that the use of force by federal officers was very low compared with the many violent and potentially violent situations with which they were confronted.

2. A 2006 report by the U.S. Department of Justice, NCJ 210296, on citizens' complaints against law enforcement officers showed that only about 8 percent of the thousands of complaints filed against officers were sustained, and most of the complaints were not about use of force.

3. In the June 2012 issue of the *FBI Bulletin*, the article "Restraint in the Use of Deadly Force: A Preliminary Study" discusses a U.S. Department of Justice survey involving over 2,000 working law enforcement officers. The survey found that

   - 80 percent of the officers had been assaulted an average of seven times during their career. Some officers commented that assaults "come with the job," while other officers limited their comments to assaults where they required medical attention.
   - Approximately 70 percent of the officers who had been assaulted reported that they could legally have fired their weapons during the assault, but chose not to do so. In some of those situations, the officer did not have a clear shot at the suspect, and declined to shoot because of the possible danger to the public.
   - The restraint shown by police officers in not firing their weapons where they were justified in doing so "sharply contrasts with the public perception of police and others and [their] use of deadly force."

the penalties for failure to consent are generally less than for a DUI conviction, and defense lawyers might believe that defending a refusal to consent charge presents fewer obstacles than defending a DUI charge.

It is difficult, as a practical matter, to force an uncooperative driver to submit to a breath or urine test. As a result, police and prosecutors have begun taking forced blood samples from these uncooperative drivers. The U.S. Supreme Court upheld the constitutionality of taking a blood sample without the consent of a suspect in *Schmerber v. California*[16] but stated that the sample must be taken under reasonable circumstances. It should be noted that while the police did not have a warrant to draw the blood sample in *Schmerber*, the Supreme Court stated the warrant was not needed under the "exigent circumstances" exception to the Fourth Amendment's warrant requirement. (See Gardner & Anderson, *Criminal Evidence*, p. 370 (8th ed., 2013).) However, in the 2013 case of *Missouri v. McNeeley*[17] the U.S. Supreme Court held that the fact that alcohol in the bloodstream dissipates over time is not by itself "exigent circumstances" that justify drawing blood without consent or a warrant. Absent other facts that make it imperative for the blood sample to be taken before police obtain a warrant, the Fourth Amendment requires them to obtain the warrant.

Standards for the Use of Deadly Force Established by the U.S. Supreme Court

Deadly force is force that is likely to cause death or serious bodily injury. The law regarding the use of deadly force in making an arrest varies somewhat from state to state.

Police department regulations also vary in the language used to regulate and instruct officers as to the use of deadly force. State laws and police regulations must conform, however, to the requirements established by the U.S. Supreme Court in the case of *Tennessee v. Garner* (which follows) and the case of *Graham v. Connor* (discussed above).

The question of the reasonableness of the use of deadly force by a law enforcement officer frequently arises in a "1983" action, a civil action brought under 42 U.S.C. § 1983. That statute makes state officials liable if they violate a person's civil or constitutional rights. In the case of deadly force in an arrest, the representative of a person killed or an injured person may assert a cause of action against the officer employing the deadly force under the Fourth Amendment, since the use of force is a "seizure" and violates the Fourth Amendment if it is unreasonable. That was the claim in *Tennessee v. Garner*, which follows.

Definition of an Unreasonable Seizure Today

unreasonable seizure A seizure made by a government officer that is unreasonable under the circumstances and thus violates the Fourth Amendment.

In most states, an **unreasonable seizure** would occur if deadly force were used by law enforcement officers or private citizens under any of the following circumstances:

1. Deadly force may never be used to make the arrest of or to prevent the escape of a person who has committed a misdemeanor.

EXAMPLE

Deadly force should not be used to catch a "prowler" seen in someone's backyard in the middle of the night or to halt a shoplifter who has taken a $75 item and cannot be apprehended in any other way.

2. Deadly force may not be used in every arrest, but only where the arresting officers or others are threatened by the suspect.

EXAMPLE

In 2012, a federal court of appeals held that police officers were not entitled to qualified immunity when they used a stun gun and unleashed a police dog to attack a defendant following a car chase on a speeding violation.[19]

EXAMPLE

In 2012 a federal court of appeals held officers were justified in using roadblocks to capture speeding motorcyclists, where one of the motorcyclists was struck by a civilian car stopped by the roadblock, causing the cyclist to crash and die.[20]

3. Deadly force may never be used by law enforcement officers to arrest or prevent the escape of a person who has committed a nonviolent felony.

CASE CLOSE-UP

Tennessee v. Garner
Supreme Court of the United States
(1985) 471 U.S. 1, 105 S. Ct. 1694

At about 10:45 p.m. on October 3, 1974, Memphis police officers were dispatched to answer a "prowler inside call." Upon arriving at the scene, they saw someone run across the backyard. The fleeing suspect, Edward Garner, stopped at a six-foot-high chain-link fence at the edge of the yard. With the aid of a flashlight one of the officers was able to see Garner's face and hands. He saw no sign of a weapon. Garner was 17 or 18 years old and about five feet five inches or five feet seven inches tall. While Garner was crouched at the base of the fence, the officer called out "police, halt" and took a few steps toward him. Garner then began to climb over the fence. Convinced that if Garner made it over the fence he would elude capture, the officer shot him. The bullet hit Garner in the back of the head, killing him.

In using deadly force to prevent the escape, the officer was acting under the authority of a Tennessee statute and pursuant to police department policy. The statute provides that "[i]f, after notice of the intention to arrest the defendant, he either flee or forcibly resist, the officer may use all the necessary means to effect the arrest" (Tenn. Code Ann. § 40-7-108 (1982)). The department policy was slightly more restrictive than the statute but still allowed the use of deadly force in cases of burglary. The incident was reviewed by the Memphis Police Firearms Review Board and presented to a grand jury. Neither took any action.

Garner's father then brought this action in the U.S. District Court for the Western District of Tennessee, seeking damages under 42 U.S.C. § 1983 for asserted violations of Garner's constitutional rights. The complaint alleged that the shooting violated the Fourth, Fifth, Sixth, Eighth, and Fourteenth Amendments to the U.S. Constitution.[18] The District court dismissed the case. The Supreme Court said this about the Court of Appeals decision reversing the District Court:

> It reasoned that the killing of the fleeing suspect was a "seizure" under the Fourth Amendment and thus constitutional only if reasonable. The court concluded that the Tennessee statute failed to distinguish between degrees of felonies, and in the present case the use of deadly force was unreasonable.

On review the U.S. Supreme Court affirmed the conclusion of the Court of Appeals that "the facts, as found, did not justify the use of deadly force" and further held:

> While we agree that burglary is a serious crime, we cannot agree that it is so dangerous as automatically to justify the use of deadly force. The FBI classifies burglary as a "property" rather than a "violent" crime. See Federal Bureau of Investigation, Uniform Crime Reports, Crime in the United States 1 (1984). Although the armed burglar would present a different situation, the fact that an unarmed suspect has broken into a dwelling at night does not automatically mean he is physically dangerous. This case demonstrates as much…. In fact, the available statistics demonstrate that burglaries only rarely involve physical violence. During the 10-year period … 1973–1982, only 3.8 percent of all burglaries involved violent crime.

EXAMPLE ▸ In a 2008 Virginia case, *Couture v. Com*,[21] a police officer was convicted of manslaughter in the death of a motorist stopped after running a stop sign. The officer

THE SEARCH FOR NONLETHAL WEAPONS

Device	Description
Stun guns, stun shields, and stun belts	Devices deliver electrical charge meant to subdue without killing. The M26 Taser electric stun pistol shoots darts that stick to clothing and deliver up to 50,000 volts of electricity. Law enforcement agencies often use Tasers to incapacitate people without physical restraint. There is usually no long-term injury, though death has occurred in rare occasions.
Chemical sprays such as pepper spray, mace, and tear gas	Devices used to repel but not kill an assailant. Most states permit any person over age 18 to carry these products.
Crowd control devices	Water cannons and tear gas are commonly used; American law enforcement agencies are reluctant to use rubber bullets, which can be lethal under some circumstances. A new device known as the "Active Denial System" uses concentrated electromagnetic waves to control crowds. The waves, which can reach subjects from as far as a mile away, cause extreme temperature increases—as much as 122 degrees Fahrenheit—in the clothes and outer skin of those hit by the waves. The heat increase causes the person hit to move away at once, called "the goodbye effect." The waves can cause second-degree burns, but no permanent injury unless handled improperly.

and his fellow officer approached the stopped car, and the driver opened his door to exit the car. The officers ordered to driver to get back in the car, and when he did he reached his hands under the front seat. The defendant reached into the car to restrain the driver, and the driver put the car in gear and caused it to start moving. The officer, while struggling with the driver, then pulled his service pistol and shot the driver, whose hands were on the steering wheel. A gun was found under the seat. The court affirmed the officer's conviction, holding his actions were unreasonable and thus not justified.

Use of Force in Resisting an Unlawful Arrest

Under the common law, a person had a legal right to forcibly resist an unlawful arrest. This rule developed hundreds of years ago in England, when safeguards to protect a person from unlawful arrest did not exist. Today, there are many safeguards, and the old rule has been changed by court decisions and statutes in most states. California Penal Code, Section 834a, and Connecticut Statutes, Sections 53a-23, are examples of such statutes. The Connecticut statute is as follows: "A person is not justified in using physical force to resist an arrest by a reasonably identifiable police officer, whether such arrest is legal or illegal." A few states, however, retain the common law rule. For example, in 2012 the Michigan Supreme Court held that the common law right to

CASE CLOSE-UP

Scott v. Harris
Supreme Court of the United States,
127 S. Ct. 1769 (2007)

In March 2001, Harris was spotted driving his car 73 miles per hour in a 55 zone on a Georgia highway, and he was pursued by Officer Scott and other police officers. The chase lasted several minutes and took place mainly on a two-lane county road. Harris's speed sometimes exceeded 85 miles per hour, and at one point during the chase his car bumped a police vehicle. A videotape of the chase showed Harris passing cars in the left-hand turn lane, running red lights, and causing approaching cars to pull over to the curb to avoid being hit by Harris.

Scott radioed his superiors, seeking permission to execute a maneuver called a "precision intervention technique," in which the pursued vehicle is blocked by a police vehicle in a manner that causes it to slide to a stop. Scott was given that permission but determined the conditions did not make the technique possible. Instead, Scott rammed the Harris vehicle, causing it to crash and severely injuring Harris, who was rendered a quadriplegic as a result of the crash.

Harris sued Scott and the county that employed Scott under Section 1983, alleging that Scott's decision to ram his car was an exercise of unreasonable deadly force and violated the Fourth Amendment. The lower federal courts held that Harris had stated a claim against Scott that raised a factual question about the reasonableness of Scott's actions under *Garner v. Tennessee*. The Supreme Court granted review and reversed the Court of Appeals, holding that as a matter of law

Scott's actions were not unreasonable and did not constitute use of excessive force under the Fourth Amendment.

The Court first found that no real factual dispute existed about the nature of the police chase. It found, mainly in reliance on the police video of the chase, that no reasonable jury could have found that Harris was driving his car in a manner that did not present a serious risk of harm to other motorists or pedestrians. It then held that even though Scott's decision to terminate the chase by ramming Harris's vehicle with his bumper was a "seizure" under the Fourth Amendment, it did not violate Harris's rights. The Court concluded that the threat to the public created by Harris's actions outweighed the high likelihood that Scott's actions would injure Harris, and that as a result Scott's decision to "seize" Harris was reasonable under the Fourth Amendment. The Court observed that in making the "reasonableness" calculation here it was important to note that while the likelihood of injury to Harris was high, it lacked the near certainty of death created by shooting an escaping felon in the head in *Garner*.

Finally, the Court rejected Harris's argument that Scott should have abandoned the chase and that his failure to do so made his subsequent actions unreasonable. It said it was "loath to lay down a rule requiring the police to allow fleeing suspects to get away whenever they drive so *recklessly* that they put other people's lives in danger."

resist a police officer who had entered a defendant's home unlawfully to search for another suspect still existed. The court reversed a conviction for felony obstruction of a police officer. *People v. Moreno*, 814 N.W.2d 624 (2012).

The Use of Tasers and Other Force in Traffic Stops

When a motorist is stopped by police for a traffic violation, the common procedure is for the police to inform the motorist of the violation, issue a ticket, and obtain

USE OF PHYSICAL RESTRAINTS

When law enforcement officers come in contact with a suspect or a person who might become violent, they may decide to use some form of physical restraint to protect themselves or the person restrained. Use of such restraints can in some circumstances be an unreasonable use of force, as the following materials illustrate.

Use of neck choke holds	Could be held to be unreasonable and excessive use of force	The FBI Law Enforcement Bulletin article "Physiological Effects Resulting from Use of Neck Holds" (July 1983) states,
		Because of the organs involved, neck holds must be considered potentially lethal whenever applied. Officers using this hold should have proper training in its use and effects. Police officers should have continual in-service training and practice in the use of the carotid sleeper. They should not use or be instructed in the use of the chokehold other than to demonstrate its potential lethal effect. Officers should recognize that death can result if the carotid sleeper is incorrectly applied.
Use of handcuffs	When an arrest is made	Generally upheld as reasonable
Use of handcuffs	When an investigative stop is made	Would be held reasonable if circumstances justified use.
Use of handcuffs	In transporting mental patients	Would be unreasonable if there was no need to handcuff, but would be justified when there was a reasonable concern for safety.

the motorist's signature showing receipt of the ticket. However, when this common, usually peaceful transaction becomes a confrontation, officers sometimes use force on the motorist to compel the motorist to comply with the officer's commands. What level of force is permitted in these situations?

In 2009 and 2010, the Ninth Circuit Court of Appeals had occasion to consider two cases where officers used Taser guns to subdue persons stopped for traffic violations. Taser guns use compressed nitrogen to propel aluminum darts (probes), which are connected to wires that deliver a very painful, 1,200-volt electrical charge into the muscles of the person hit, causing pain and temporary paralysis in muscles hit. Subsequently, both motorists brought actions against the officers under 42 U.S.C. § 1983, the civil rights statute. The officers would have been liable only if the force they used was "excessive" under the principles discussed earlier in this chapter, so the court was required to evaluate the reasonableness of using Tasers in those cases.

In *Bryan v. McPherson*, 590 F.3d 767 (9th Cir. 2009), the court held that the police use of a Taser gun was excessive force. There, the motorist, Bryan, was stopped by a California police officer for failure to wear a seat belt. Bryan exited his car, wearing only boxer shorts and tennis shoes, and began slapping his thighs, yelling gibberish, and acting agitated. Bryan did not attack the officer, but the officer fired his Taser gun from about 20 to 26 feet away and struck Bryan, who fell to the ground and fractured four teeth. One of the Taser's probes had to be removed with a scalpel. The court found the use of the Taser to be excessive, noting that "traffic violations generally will not support the use of a significant level of force."

In *Brooks v. City of Seattle,* 599 F.3d 1018 (9th Cir. 2010), the court concluded that use of a Taser in a traffic stop was not excessive. There, a motorist, Brooks, was stopped by Seattle police for speeding in a school zone. When presented with a ticket, Brooks refused to sign the ticket and tried to grab her driver's license away from the officer. The officer called his supervisor, who came to the scene and instructed Brooks to comply with the officer's commands. Brooks again refused, refused to turn off her car, and refused to exit her vehicle. The officers opened the driver's door and exerted pressure on Brooks's left arm to gain compliance, but Brooks resisted efforts to remove her from the vehicle. The officers then stated they were going to use a Taser gun, but Brooks again refused, informing the officers she was pregnant. The officers then applied the Taser to Brooks's thigh, removed her from her vehicle, and arrested her.

The District Court found the officers had used excessive force. The Court of Appeals reversed, stating that under the circumstances the use of the Taser was not excessive. The court distinguished the *Bryan* case by noting that here, unlike in *Bryan,* the Taser was used in "drive-stun" mode, and applied directly to Brooks's body, causing only temporary, localized pain. In that mode, the court noted, the effect of the Taser was considerably less than in the "dart" mode used by the officer in *Bryan.* The court also noted that the Seattle Police Department Use of Force Training Guideline identified use of a Taser in "drive-stun" mode as a "level 1 Tactic." Since the officers were acting reasonably in arresting Brooks for obstruction, the use of "level 1" force was not excessive.

In the 2011 case of *McKenney v. Harrison*[22] the court held that use of a Taser by an officer to prevent a suspect wanted on misdemeanor charges from jumping out a window was not excessive, even though the suspect died when the Taser incapacitated him.

In a small, informal survey of ten police departments in five states, published in the September 2007 *FBI Law Enforcement Bulletin* and titled "The Dynamic Resistance Response Model—A Modern Approach to the Use of Force," the author who conducted the survey found that while most police departments require motorists to sign for tickets, all ten responded "no" to the question, "Would you use a Taser on a motorist who refused to sign a ticket?" Most of the officers stated that their practice was to hold the driver's license, but let the motorist go, assuming the motorist had no outstanding warrants and had proof of registration and insurance.

Disciplining Children

Under common law, parents and people who take the place of parents *(in loco parentis)* have a natural right to the custody, care, and control of their children. They have a duty to provide food, clothing, shelter, and medical care to the children and to educate and discipline them. Under the common law, a parent or a person *in loco* may use a reasonable amount of force in disciplining a child.

A 2001 study[23] reported that the majority of American families discipline their preschool children by using occasional mild to moderate spanking. The study reported no negative effects on children. However, the study also showed that 4 to 7 percent of parents fell into the "red zone" (danger zone) because they disciplined their children frequently and impulsively by such means as verbal punishment, using a paddle, hitting their children in the face or body, or throwing or shaking their child. These children were more likely to have behavioral problems or experience anxiety or depression.

All states have laws requiring school officials, health professionals (nurses, doctors, therapists), and law enforcement officials to report suspected child abuse. In determining the crime of child abuse, the following factors have to be considered:

- The age, size, and health of the child, as force used on a baby or a sick or helpless child is much different than the same force used on a healthy 14-year-old boy.
- The reason for the discipline, because spanking a child for unintentional bed-wetting or throwing up could lead to the conclusion that the parent was out of control and not rational.

The question of what amount of force is reasonable was presented to the Texas Court of Appeals (Houston) in the case of *Teubner v. State.*[24] The court held:

> Texas Penal Code section 9.61 permits the use of force against a child under a "reasonable belief" standard. However, force going beyond that which is necessary for discipline is prohibited. The question in this case is whether the appellants reasonably believed their use of force was necessary to discipline their child.

> From the evidence presented, no reasonable person could possibly believe the conduct was justifiable. The child was subjected to a savage beating with a leather belt on two successive nights. On the first night, Victoria Teubner took over the whipping when her husband tired himself. On the second night, they gagged their daughter to stifle her crying. The photographs admitted into evidence offer a grim record of the effects of the beating. The appellants could not have reasonably believed that the degree of force used was necessary for disciplinary purposes. Appellants' second point of error is overruled.

Besides the parents, any person taking the place of the parents and thus classified as ***in loco parentis*** may reasonably discipline a child in his or her care. This category includes legal guardians, foster parents, and public school teachers.

Because of the threats of lawsuits and pressure from anti-paddling groups, many states have forbidden corporal punishment in public schools within those states. In the states that continue to permit corporal punishment, many school boards forbid or limit the use of corporal punishment of students within the school district. The U.S. Supreme Court held in the case of *Ingraham v. Wright* that under common law, "a teacher may impose reasonable but not excessive force to discipline a child."[25] The U.S. Supreme Court noted:

> Where the legislatures have not acted, the state courts have uniformly preserved the common law rule permitting teachers to use reasonable force in disciplining children in their charge.

in loco parentis (Latin; "in place of the parents") Any person taking the place of the parents has the duties and responsibilities of the parents and may reasonably discipline a child in his or her care. This category includes legal guardians, foster parents, and public schoolteachers.

SUMMARY OF THE LAW ON THE USE OF FORCE

Situation	Less than Deadly Force	Deadly Force
In self-defense or in the defense of others	"The use of (reasonable) force upon or toward another person is justified when the actor (reasonably) believes that such force is immediately necessary for the purpose of protecting himself or herself (or another) against the use of unlawful force by such other person on the present occasion."[a]	"The use of deadly force is not justified unless such force is necessary to protect against death, serious bodily harm, kidnapping, or sexual intercourse compelled by force or threat."[b]
In the defense of property	"One may use physical force, other than deadly force such as may be necessary to prevent or terminate the commission or attempted commission of larceny or of criminal mischief with respect to property other than premises."[c]	Under the old common law, deadly force could be used in the defense of property. All states now forbid the use of intentional deadly force in the defense of property.
To apprehend a person who has committed a crime	"When an officer is making or attempting to make an arrest for a criminal offense, he is acting for the protection of public interest and is permitted even a greater latitude than when he acts in self-defense, and he is not liable unless the means which he uses are clearly excessive."[d]	Misdemeanor: Never. Fleeing felon: Deadly force could be used when officers "have probable cause to believe that the suspect (has committed a felony and) poses a threat to the safety of the officers or a danger to the community if left at large" (*Tennessee v. Garner*).
To stop a person for investigative purposes when only "reasonable suspicion" exists	Only such force that is reasonable and necessary under the circumstances that then exist.	Never
Disciplining children (corporal punishment)	Only parents and other people having a status of *in loco parentis* to a child may use reasonable force "reasonably believed to be necessary for (the child's) proper control, training, or education."[e] Other persons (such as strangers or neighbors) may not discipline a child.	Never

[a]Sections 3.04(1) and 3.05(1) of the Model Penal Code.
[b]Section 3.04(2) (b) of the Model Penal Code.
[c]State of New York, Public Law 35.25.
[d]*Restatement of Torts*, § 132(a).
[e]*Restatement of Torts*, § 147(2), as quoted by the U.S. Supreme Court in *Ingraham v. Wright*, 429 U.S. 975, 97 S. Ct. 481(1976).

Law enforcement officers, neighbors, and other adults who see children misbehave may not discipline a child (or children), although they may use reasonable force to prevent damage to property or injury to other persons or themselves.

Reasonable force to maintain order (as distinguished from discipline) may be used by personnel on airplanes, ships, trains, or buses and by ushers at theaters, sporting events, and other public gathering places. A disorderly child or adult may be ordered to leave if he or she is disturbing other people or has failed to pay the fare or admission fee. The test, again, is that of reasonableness. Did the provocation justify the action taken? Was the force reasonable under the circumstances?

Summary

- Use of force is justified only if (1) reasonable, (2) necessary, and (3) in response to unlawful actions by another.
- The "castle" doctrine states that a person in his home is justified in using reasonable force, including deadly force, in response to an assault in his home. There is no duty to retreat under this doctrine.
- The "stand your ground" laws generally give persons the absolute right to refuse to retreat and to respond to an attacker with reasonable force, including deadly force. Such laws change the "castle" doctrine in many states by adopting a presumption that a homeowner has a fear of imminent peril whenever he is attacked in his home.
- A police officer may use non-deadly force to detain a suspect, prevent his escape, overcome resistance to arrest, or protect the officer or others from harm.

- Actions by police officers using force to arrest a suspect are "seizures" of the suspect, and thus under the Fourth Amendment must be reasonable. State laws or regulations stating how and when police officers may use force must also comply with the Fourth Amendment.
- A police officer may, as may any person, use deadly force when faced with the threat of death or serious bodily harm to the officer or another. A police officer may also use deadly force to prevent the escape of a suspect in serious, violent felony arrests if the officer reasonably believes the escaped suspect presents a serious danger to the public.
- Parents, guardians, and those *in loco parentis* may use reasonable force in disciplining children in their charge.

Key Terms

self-defense, p. 138
defense of another, p. 138
Good Samaritan laws, p. 139
deadly force, p. 139

"stand your ground" laws, p. 140
"castle" doctrine, p. 142
"make my day" rules, p. 142
battered woman defense, p. 145

unreasonable seizure, p. 151
in loco parentis, p. 157

Case Analysis and Writing Exercises

1. Was the use of force justified in the following two true situations?

   a A 19-year-old woman was raped by two men. She subsequently invited them for a return date, at which time she killed one with a shotgun, while the other man fled. What facts do you think would be material to the outcome of this case?

   b A 62-year-old retired army officer was awakened by noise in his home. He got up and, armed with a pistol, walked into a hallway where he saw two men coming toward him. He fired his pistol, killing both men, who were in the act of burglary. Does it matter if the burglars were unarmed? Would a statute like the Florida "stand your ground" law apply to this situation?

2. Does the "castle" doctrine apply to an area outside the home (called the "curtilage")? See *People v. Riddle,* 649 N.W.2d 30 (Mich. 2002), where a homeowner claimed the "castle" doctrine permitted him to use deadly force against another person in his driveway, without first seeking a safe way to retreat. (When this case was decided, Michigan had a limited duty to retreat before deadly force may be used.) Does M.C.L.A. § 780.972, enacted in 2006, change the result in *Riddle?* Why?

3. Police officers surrounded an armed man in a building, who was holding an 18-month-old child as hostage. After the man threatened to kill the child, police charged the building, firing fifty-five shots at the man, and killing the hostage child. Was this the use of excessive force? *See Lopez v. City of Los Angeles,* 126 Cal. Rptr.3d 706 (Cal. App. 2011).

4. What is the status of a "security officer" working at a bar, in terms of use of deadly force? In *Lee v. State,* 996 A.2d 425 (Md. App. 2010) an armed security officer at a bar shot and killed a bar patron who was arguing with other patrons. Under what circumstances, if any, was the security officer entitled to sue deadly force?

Endnotes

1. When cases go before a criminal court, most states place the burden of proving there was no justification for the force (such as self-defense) upon the state. The U.S. Supreme Court pointed out in the 1987 case *of Martin v. Ohio* (480 U.S. 228, 107 S. Ct. 1098) that only two states continue to follow the common law "that affirmative defenses, including self-defense, were matters for the defendant to prove." Forty-eight states require "the prosecution to prove the absence of self-defense when it is properly raised by the defendant." Ohio and South Carolina continue to follow the common law rule. The Supreme Court held that the rule used in Ohio and South Carolina is constitutional. The Court pointed out that "the Constitution (does not) require the prosecution to prove the sanity of a defendant who pleads not guilty by reason of insanity."

2. 351 S.W.3d 523 (Tex. App. 2011).

3. 393 S.W.3d 282 (Tex. Crim. App. 2013).

4. Florida Statutes Section 776.013(3).

5. Paul Logli, president of the National District Attorney's Association.

6. See the *New York Times* article, "15 States Expand Victim's Rights on Use of Deadly Force," August 7, 2006.

7. 158 U.S. 550 (1895).

8. 972 P.2d 32 (Okla. Cr. 1998).

9. Florida Statutes Section 776.013 (1)

10. 694 A2d 564, 574 (N.J. 1997).

11. See the *New York Times* article, "More States Study Clemency for Women Who Killed Abusers," February 2, 1991.

12. *Pensacola News Journal,* April 20, 2007.

13. 800 N.W.2d 705 (N.D. 2011).

14. 490 U.S. 386, 109 S. Ct. 1865.

15. 490 U.S. at 395–396.

16. 384 U.S. 757 (1966).

17. 2013 WL 1628934 (2013).

18. The police officers in the U.S. Supreme Court case of *Tennessee v. Garner* could use the defense known as "qualified immunity." Under this defense, police officers or other public officials who

are sued for violating someone's constitutional rights cannot be held liable if either the law at the time of the incident was unclear or if they (the police officers) reasonably believed at the time that their conduct was lawful.

19. *Austin v. Redford Tp. Police Dept.*, 690 F.3d 490 (6th Cir. 2012).

20. *Terranova v. New York*, 676 F.3d 305 (2nd. Cir. 2012).

21. 656 S.E.2d 425 (Va. App. 2008).

22. 635 F.3d 354 (8th Cir. 2011).

23. See the *New York Times* article, "Finding Gives Some Support to Advocates of Spanking: Adding Fuel to Bitter Debate on Child Care," August 25, 2001.

24. 742 S.W.2d 57 (Tex. App. 1987).

25. 430 U.S. 651, 97 S. Ct. 1401 (1977).

Other Criminal Defenses

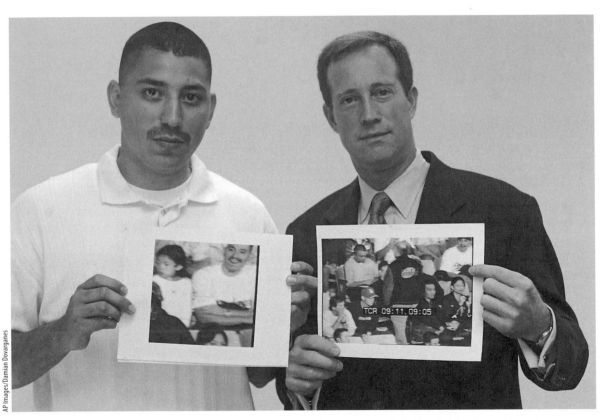

Juan Catalan was charged with murder in a homicide that occurred in San Fernando Valley, California, and served 5 months in jail after his arrest. He maintained that he and his 6-year-old daughter were attending a Los Angeles Dodgers–Atlanta Braves game at Dodger Stadium, 20 miles away from the murder site, at the time the victim was killed. Here, Catalan and his attorney hold prints from film of the TV show *Curb Your Enthusiasm*, which was shooting scenes during the Dodgers-Braves baseball game. The time-coded film showed Catalan and his daughter at the game, confirming his alibi. We examine other criminal defenses in this chapter, including alibi defenses like the one successfully raised by Catalan.

OUTLINE

LEARNING OBJECTIVES

In this chapter we present several defenses a defendant may assert in a criminal prosecution. The learning objectives for this chapter are the following:

- Identify the kinds of immunity to criminal prosecution available, and their limits.
- Determine when, if ever, a mistake of fact or law may provide a defense.
- Distinguish between the defenses of duress and necessity.
- State why the Double Jeopardy Clause prohibits successive prosecutions for the same crime.
- Distinguish between a prosecution for the same offense and one for a separate offense.
- Define "acquittal" for purposes of the Double Jeopardy Clause.
- Identify the tests that determine when government inducements become entrapment.
- List the factors that determine when a speedy trial violation has occurred.

On November 26, 2010, Mohamed Mohamud, a 19-year-old Somali-American college student living in Portland, Oregon, pushed a button on a cell phone that he believed would detonate an 1,800-pound bomb placed at a city Christmas tree lighting ceremony. In fact the bomb was a fake, supplied to Mohamud by FBI agents operating a terrorism sting.

Mohamud went on trial in January 2013, facing life in prison for attempting to use a weapon of mass destruction. His attorneys offered an "entrapment" defense, contending Mohamud was simply an angry Muslim college student and had no predisposition to commit terrorism acts, and would not have done so if the FBI had not made the "bomb" and given it to Mohamud. The prosecution maintained that Mohamud was actively seeking to engage in terrorist attacks, and the FBI merely made available the means to do so. On January 31, 2013, a jury convicted Mohamud of attempted bombing.

In this chapter we discuss the various affirmative defenses to prosecution available to a defendant, including immunity defenses, and the circumstances that must be shown for those defenses to be available.

Affirmative Defenses

corpus delicti In all criminal cases, the government must prove that the crime charged was committed (corpus delicti) and that the defendant was party to the crime (committed the crime or was an accomplice).

affirmative defense A defense to a criminal charge in which the defendant generally admits doing the criminal act but claims an affirmative defense such as duress (he or she was forced) or entrapment.

To prove the guilt of a person charged with a crime, the state must present evidence (1) that a crime was committed (**corpus delicti**) and (2) that the defendant committed or was a party to the crime charged. The U.S. Supreme Court has repeatedly held that "the requirement that guilt of a criminal charge be established by proof beyond a reasonable doubt dates at least from our early years as a Nation."[1]

Defendants in criminal cases may choose to sit quietly if they wish and place on the government the burden of coming forward with evidence proving guilt beyond a reasonable doubt. If the government does carry this burden, a defendant may then produce evidence showing actual innocence, justification, or other defenses, usually called affirmative defenses.

An **affirmative defense** is any defense that assumes the complaint or charges to be correct but raises other facts that, if true, would establish a valid excuse or justification or a right to engage in the conduct in question. An affirmative defense does not concern itself with the elements of the offense at all; it concedes them. In effect, an affirmative defense says, "Yes, I did it, but I had a good reason."

Defenses to a criminal charge provide either an excuse for the criminal conduct or a justification for that conduct. The insanity defense, for example, if proved, excuses the behavior that would otherwise be criminal. Self-defense, on the other hand, doesn't excuse the force used; if proved, the defense provides a justification for the use of the force. The distinction between excuse and justification is not of great importance, and the term "affirmative defense" is commonly used to refer to both kinds of defense.

It is generally agreed that a state may place the burden of proof for the establishment of an affirmative defense on the defendant. In *Leland v. Oregon*,[2] discussed in Chapter 3, the Supreme Court upheld a law that required a defendant to prove the defense of insanity beyond a reasonable doubt. Not all states do so; in the case of the insanity defense, a few states require the prosecution to prove the defendant was sane when the crime was committed.

It is also generally agreed that a state may not shift the burden of proof on an element of the crime to the defendant by designating the element as an affirmative defense.[3] However, it is not always clear that the state has made this improper designation. If the state has the power, as states usually do, to define what conduct is criminal, a statute that defines a crime broadly, and then makes affirmative defenses to the crime the burden of the defendant, is not a violation of the burden of proof principle. For example, in many states it is a strict liability crime to sell impure food; the prosecution need only prove that the food sold was impure. It would be permissible for a state to make it an affirmative defense that the seller used reasonable efforts to inspect the food sold, and then place the burden of proof on the defendant to prove the defense. On the other hand, a state would probably be prohibited from defining, as an example, first-degree burglary as any unprivileged entry of a dwelling, and then placing the burden on the defendant to show as an affirmative defense that the entry was not made at night, and thus only a second-degree felony. The fact "at night" is an element of the crime that makes the burglary a more serious crime (as it is in some jurisdictions; see Chapter 14). As a result, the state must bear the burden of proving that element.

Affirmative defenses come from various sources. Some, such as immunity or the alibi defense, are the product of state or federal statutes. Others, such as self-defense and duress, have evolved from the common law. Finally, a few affirmative defenses are mandated by the U.S. Constitution. The double jeopardy and speedy trial defenses are examples of defenses with their roots in the Constitution. In this chapter we identify the requirements for many of the affirmative defenses available in state and federal criminal prosecutions.

Immunity as a Defense

Under some circumstances, persons who have committed crimes are exempt from prosecution for their actions, either temporarily or permanently. The basis for their claim to immunity might come from a federal or state statute, an international agreement, or in one case from the U.S. Constitution. The principal forms of immunity are discussed in this section.

Diplomatic Immunity

In 1972 the United States ratified the Vienna Convention on Diplomatic Relations, an international agreement on the status of diplomats stationed in a foreign country. More than a hundred other countries have ratified this Convention. Article 31.1 of the Convention states that a "diplomatic agent" shall enjoy full **immunity** from the criminal jurisdiction of the receiving state. (In international law conventions, the word *state* means a "nation or country.") Article 37.1 extends this immunity to members of the diplomat's family. U.S. law (22 U.S.C. § 254(d)) states that any action brought against a person entitled to diplomatic immunity must be dismissed. Two federal cases illustrate the scope and limit of diplomatic immunity.

In the 2006 case of *United States v. Kuznetsov*,[4] a federal district court denied diplomatic immunity to a Russian citizen employed by the United Nations in New York City. Although the defendant was at one time certified as a member of the Russian Federation Mission, and therefore entitled to immunity, when he became

immunity An exemption from criminal prosecution based on the U.S. Constitution, statutes, or international agreements.

chairman of a UN committee the Russian Mission informed the State Department that the defendant was no longer part of the Mission. The court thus concluded that even though the defendant regarded himself as a "career Russian diplomat," during the years he worked for the UN, when the crimes he was charged with occurred, he was not a "diplomatic agent" and not entitled to immunity. The court also held that the defendant lacked immunity under the United Nations Convention on Privileges and Immunities. That convention applies only to "visiting foreign officials." The court concluded the defendant was not simply "visiting" the UN, but rather was a full-time employee. As a result, the only immunity the defendant enjoyed under the Convention was immunity for acts done in his official capacity. This immunity can be waived by the secretary general of the UN, who did so in this case.

In the 2004 case of *United States v. Al-Hamdi*,[5] a federal court of appeals held that the diplomatic immunity given to members of a diplomat's family ends at age 21. The Vienna Convention leaves it to member states to determine the extent of the family immunity, the court held, and since the State Department issued a regulation setting the 21 years of age limit (23 if enrolled in school), that regulation was conclusive on the issue. The defendant, 26 years old when indicted, was thus convicted of being a nonimmigrant alien in possession of a firearm.

Diplomatic immunity may be waived by the diplomat's home country, and in the case of serious crimes, the U.S. government frequently requests that waiver. An example of this waiver can be seen in *Van Den Borre v. State*,[6] in which Belgium waived immunity for a diplomat who was then convicted of a double murder.

Immunity for consular officers is not absolute, as it is for diplomats. Article 43 of the Vienna Convention provides that "[consular officers . . . shall not be amenable to the jurisdiction of [the host nation] in respect to acts performed in the exercise of consular functions." Criminal acts not so performed expose the consular offices to prosecution. For example, in *United States v. Cole*,[7] a consular officer was successfully prosecuted for smuggling money out of the United States in a diplomatic pouch. The court said the officer was not exercising consular functions.

Legislative Immunity

Article I, Section 6, of the U.S. Constitution provides that U.S. senators and representatives "shall in all Cases except Treason, Felony and Breach of the Peace, be privileged from Arrest during their Attendance at the Session of their respective Houses, and in going to and returning from the same." Most state constitutions extend the same or similar privileges to state legislators while the state legislature is in session.

Representatives, senators, and state legislators thus have a limited degree of temporary immunity while their legislative bodies are in session. Charges, however, could be held until the legislative body adjourns. Also, state legislators enjoy no immunity from prosecution for federal crimes.[8]

Article I, Section 6 also contains the "speech and debate clause," which provides that members may not be "questioned" for any "speech or debate" in their respective houses, which has been interpreted to bar prosecution for all "legislative acts" taken by a member and part of the "legislative process." This protection is limited. In the 2011 case of *United States v. Renzi*,[9] the court held that the clause did not bar prosecution of corruption charges against a House of Representatives member who promised to introduce legislation in exchange for a payment of money. The negotiations for the proposed legislation were not "legislative acts," the court held.

Witness Immunity

Federal and state prosecutors have the power to subpoena witnesses to give testimony to aid the prosecutors in investigations of crimes. Legislative bodies have a similar power. Under the Fifth Amendment, a witness cannot be compelled to testify against himself. A witness summoned to testify may thus refuse to testify by invoking his Fifth Amendment right. To resolve this conflict, both the federal government and the states have passed various immunity statutes, under which a witness can be given immunity from prosecution, thereby protecting his Fifth Amendment right, and be compelled to answer questions that might be incriminating.

The principal federal immunity statute is 18 U.S.C. § 6002, which requires a witness to testify if called before a court, federal agency, or legislative body, on the condition that his or her testimony may not be used against him in a criminal prosecution. Because of statements made by the Supreme Court in the early case of *Counselman v. Hitchcock*,[10] earlier versions of section 6002 had been interpreted as grants of total or **transactional immunity**. Under transactional immunity the witness cannot be prosecuted for any offense related to the subject matter of his or her testimony.

Congress was concerned that total immunity hampered federal efforts to combat crime. In 1970 Congress enacted the current version of section 6002, which grants only **use immunity**. Under use immunity, the statements made by the witness may not be used in subsequent prosecutions, but the witness can be prosecuted for the crimes about which them to the witness testified if other evidence is used to convict the witness. The U.S. Supreme Court upheld the constitutionality of section 6002 in *Kastigar v. United States*,[11] holding that the statute gives the same protection as the Fifth Amendment, and that is all the protection Congress is required to give a witness.

Many states have enacted both transactional and use immunity statutes, with the prosecution deciding which immunity to request. For example, Illinois has a transactional immunity statute, 725 ILCS 5/106-1, which provides that after a request by the state a court "may order" a witness to testify by granting immunity from prosecution for the crimes about which the witness testifies. The use immunity statute, 725 ILSC 5/106-2.5, provides that after a request by the State, the court "shall order" a witness to testify with immunity from use of his testimony. In *People v. Ousley,* 919 N.E.2d 875 (Ill. 2009), the Illinois Supreme Court reversed a decision of a district court judge who refused the prosecution's request to grant use immunity. In *Ousley,* three defendants were charged with murder, and the prosecution requested a grant of use immunity to one of the defendants so he could testify against the other two defendants. The trial court refused the request, stating concerns about the effect such testimony might have on the rights of the other defendants. On appeal, the Illinois Supreme Court held that the use immunity statutory was mandatory, and as a result the prosecution's request for an order granting use immunity should have been granted.

transactional immunity Total or full immunity for the criminal offense to which compelled testimony relates.

use immunity Prohibits prosecutorial authorities from using compelled testimony in a criminal prosecution, but does not make the witness totally immune from prosecution based on evidence other than the witness's testimony and not derived from that testimony.

Mistake or Ignorance of Fact as a Defense[12]

At times, a mistake of fact can serve as a defense to criminal liability. For example, suppose a man walking out of a restaurant takes the wrong coat from the coat rack. A few minutes later, the true owner of the coat angrily complains to a police officer. The officer stops the man with the wrong coat blocks away and brings him back to the restaurant. Investigation shows that the man does have a coat similar to the coat that he walked away in. Has the man committed a theft, or has he made an honest mistake of fact?

The common law rule is that an honest mistake or ignorance of fact is a defense if it negates the existence of a state of mind essential to the crime. A material element of the crime of theft is taking property of another with intent to deprive the owner of the property. Did the man take the coat with intent to deprive the owner of possession of his coat? If his honest mistake negated that intent, he is not guilty of the crime.

Other kinds of mistake of fact do not provide a defense. For example, the mistaken belief that property taken belongs to person A, when in fact it belongs to person B, does not serve as a defense to the crime of theft. That is because even if the circumstances were as believed, the person taking the property would be guilty of the crime.

One of the most often cited cases for the mistake defense is the case of *Morissette v. United States*[13] where the U.S. Supreme Court reversed a conviction for theft of government property. The defendant asserted the defense that he believed spent bomb casings on a government bombing range had been abandoned by the government, based on their condition and the fact that the defendant and other people routinely used the area for hunting. The Court said the jury should have been allowed to consider whether the defendant had the requisite "evil-meaning mind" necessary to convict him of theft.

The following cases are examples of application of the honest mistake of fact rule.

Mistake of fact defense allowed:

- *People v. Sojka*, 126 Cal. Rptr. 3d 400 (Cal. App. 2011): Defendant's honest and reasonable belief that female victim consented to sexual activity negated specific intent necessary for conviction of forcible rape.
- *Commonwealth. v. Claudio*, 978 N.E.2d 591 (Mass. App. 2012): Defendant's honest belief that check given her by a friend was genuine and not a counterfeit negated specific intent required in theft by cashing an invalid check statute.

Mistake of fact defense not allowed:

- *Ingram v. State*, 261 S.W.3d 749 (Tex. App. 2008): Mistaken belief, even if reasonable, that residence was abandoned not a defense to charge of burglary of a habitation. The burglary statute required specific intent on the element of intent to steal property in a residence, but only general intent on the fact that the building entered was a habitation. Thus, all the prosecution must prove is that in fact the building entered was habituated.

- *People v. Wilson*, 877 N.Y.S.2d 761 (N.Y. App. 2009): Honest belief that a shotgun's safety catch was on was not a good defense to a manslaughter charge, because the crime required only negligence.

Strict Liability Crimes and the Defense of Mistake

When a state legislature or the Congress of the United States creates a strict liability crime, the defense of mistake of fact cannot be used, because criminal liability comes from simply doing the forbidden act without any requirement for the state or government to prove any mental fault (see Chapter 3). Examples include the following:

- *State v. Jadowski*, 680 N.W.2d 810 (Wis. 2004): Defendant could not use defense of honest but mistaken belief as to the age of the victim in statutory rape charge, even though the victim misrepresented her age to defendant.[14]
- In assaulting a federal officer, the defendant cannot use the honest but mistaken belief that he or she did not know the victim was a federal officer: *United States v. Feola*, 420 U.S. 671; 95 S. Ct. 1255 (1975); *United States v. Goldson*, 954 F.2d 51 (2d Cir. 1992).
- In use of employment of a minor in Minnesota for nude dancing, the honest but mistaken belief as to the age of the child cannot be used: *State v. Fan*, 445 NW.2d 243 (Minn. App. 1989); *Minnesota v. White*, 464 NW.2d 585 (Minn. App. 1990), *review denied*, 502 U.S. 819, 112 S. Ct. 77 (1991).

Mistake or Ignorance of Criminal Law

The full scope of the Latin maxim *Ignorantia legis neminem excusat* ("Ignorance of the law excuses no one") may have caused Blackstone to change the phrase in his *Commentaries* (4 *Commentaries*, 27) to "Ignorance of the law which every one is bound to know, excuses no man." Blackstone's statement is a far better expression of the law, because courts will not allow a defendant who has committed an offense that is generally well known to the public to argue ignorance or mistake of that law. Serious offenses, such as murder, rape, robbery, and theft, are violations not only of the statutory law but also of moral and ethical laws. Courts would not seriously consider a defense of mistake or ignorance of such laws. Nor would courts ordinarily permit a person charged with a traffic violation in the state in which he or she is licensed to drive to argue ignorance of the traffic laws of that state. It is presumed that the holder of a license knows the traffic laws when the license is received or renewed.

But what of the hundreds of criminal laws that are not well known? In a now-famous publication, the President's Commission on Law Enforcement and Administration of Justice reported in *The Challenge of Crime in a Free Society* that the federal government alone has defined more than 2,800 crimes and observed that state and local governments have defined even more numerous offenses (p. 18). The following U.S. Supreme Court cases illustrate the complexity and great numbers of laws that exist today:

Cheek v. United States

Supreme Court of the United States (1991), 498 U.S. 192, 111 S. Ct. 604

Mr. Cheek was an airline pilot who did not file federal income tax returns for six years. Cheek argued that he did not "willfully" fail to file income tax returns and that he honestly believed his failure to file returns was lawful.

Because of the complexity of the U.S. tax laws, the Supreme Court held that the "willfully" requirement of the criminal charge against Cheek could not be met if the alleged violator was honestly confused about the meaning of the law.

Other courts now view this case as an exception to the general rule that ignorance of the law is no excuse. (See the 2009 case of *State v. Casper,* 297 S.W.3d 676 (Tenn. 2009), reviewing court decisions.)

Lambert v. California

Supreme Court of the United States (1957), 355 U.S. 225, 78 S. Ct. 240

The defendant was charged with and convicted of failing to register as required under a Los Angeles municipal ordinance that requires "any convicted person" who is in the city for longer than five days to register with local authorities. The defendant had been convicted of forgery and had lived in Los Angeles for more than seven years without registering. In a 5–4 decision, the U.S. Supreme Court held that the registration provision of the ordinance violated the due process requirement of the Fourteenth Amendment.

Justice William O. Douglas, writing for the majority, stated:

The rule that "ignorance of the law will not excuse" . . . is deep in our law, as is the principle that of all the powers of local government, the police power is "one of the least limitable." . . . On the other hand, due process places some limits on its exercise. Engrained in our concept of due process is the requirement of notice. Notice is sometimes essential so that the citizen has the chance to defend charges. Notice is required before property interests are disturbed, before assessments are made, before penalties are assessed. Notice is required in a myriad of situations where a penalty or forfeiture might be suffered for mere failure to act. . . .

This appellant on first becoming aware of her duty to register was given no opportunity to comply with the law and avoid its penalty, even though her default was entirely innocent. . . . Where a person did not know of the duty to register and where there was no proof of the probability of such knowledge, he may not be convicted consistently with due process. Were it otherwise, the evil would be as great as it is when the law is written too fine or in a language foreign to the community.

mistake of law A claim by a defendant that the defendant did not know the action taken violated the criminal law.

Sometimes what appears to be a **mistake of law** may nonetheless provide a defense. For example, in *United States v. Smith*,[15] a government employee was charged with violating the federal Espionage Act. That act makes it a crime to reveal classified information with the intent to cause injury to the United States. The defendant revealed classified information to two individuals the defendant believed were CIA officials. The defendant claimed he believed he was authorized by law to reveal the information to CIA officials, though in fact he was not authorized to do so. The court said his defense, if believed, negated the "intent to harm the United States" element of the crime, and could be raised.

The mistake of law in the *Smith* case provided a defense because the defendant's mistaken belief negated a required mental state, the "intent to harm" the United States. Where the mistake of law is simply that the defendant did not know the actions he or she took were against the criminal law, but the defendant otherwise had the required mental state, it is rare for the mistake to provide a defense.

Intoxication or Drugged Condition as a Defense

Voluntary intoxication or drugged condition as a defense to the commission of criminal acts is frequently raised unsuccessfully. Crimes that require only a general intent, that is, only the intent to do the act, do not permit an intoxication defense. For example, in the 2001 case of *United States v. Sewell*,[16] a defendant charged with robbery attempted to defend himself by offering evidence that he was high on crack cocaine when he committed the robbery. The court concluded that robbery was a general intent crime and rejected the defense.

Crimes that require a specific intent as to one or more elements of the crime do permit a defense based on voluntary intoxication or drugged condition. To assert the intoxication defense, the defendant must be charged with a specific intent crime, such as intentional murder, kidnapping, or arson. The degree of intoxication must be so great "as to render (the defendant) incapable of purposeful or knowing conduct."[17] *State v. Sexton,* discussed in Chapter 5, is an example of this use of a drugged condition defense.

Even if the intoxication defense successfully negates a specific intent, the defendant may still be convicted of a lesser offense requiring only general intent. For example, although defendants may lack the specific intent to commit murder, they could be convicted of a lesser general intent crime, such as second-degree murder or manslaughter.[18]

A few states have eliminated the defense of voluntary intoxication entirely. Montana not only did away with the defense of intoxication but also prohibited any consideration of the defense of intoxication by a fact finder (judge or jury). The Montana law was challenged before the U.S. Supreme Court in 1996. In the case of *Montana v. Egelhoff,* the Supreme Court found that the Montana law did not violate due process protections of the U.S. Constitution.[19]

The involuntary intoxication or drugged condition can be a defense to a criminal charge if the trier of fact (the jury or judge) believes the defendant's story, supported by credible evidence, that (1) he or she did not voluntarily take the drug or intoxicant and instead was tricked or forced into taking the substance and (2) the defendant became so intoxicated or drugged that he or she was not able to mentally form the specific intent necessary for the crime charged but was physically able to commit the crime.

Duress, Coercion, or Compulsion as a Defense

duress A defense to criminal prosecution on the grounds that the defendant was forced to commit the criminal act.

coercion A person who forces (coerces) another to commit a crime can be charged and convicted of the crime committed in addition to other offenses.

If a person charged with a crime can show his or her actions were the result of duress, coercion, or compulsion, under some but not all situations, a valid defense may be raised. In attempting to use the defense, defendants must admit that they committed the offense charged but assert that they were forced to do so to avoid death or serious bodily injury to themselves or others. Defining **duress** and **coercion** in *People v. Sanders,* the court stated:

> In order for duress or fear produced by threats or menace to be a valid, legal excuse for doing anything, which otherwise would be criminal, the act must have been done under such threats or menaces as show that the life of the person threatened or menaced was in danger, or that there was reasonable cause to believe and actual belief that there was such danger. The danger must not be one of future violence, but of present and immediate violence at the time of the commission of the forbidden act. The danger of death at some future time in the absence of danger of death at the time of the commission of the offense will not excuse. A person who aids and assists in the commission of the crime, or who commits a crime, is not relieved from criminality on account of fears excited by threats or menaces unless the danger be to life, nor unless that danger be present and immediate.[20]

One area where duress or coercion is offered as a defense involves escape from prison or other custody. The Supreme Court of Delaware has held that the general rule is that "intolerable conditions" were not by themselves justification for escape from prison, and that defendants must introduce other evidence for such justification existed.[21] The court stated that the tests used by California courts to determine if sufficient duress existed to justify an escape were useful in determining justification.

The California tests, established in *People v. Lovercamp,* hold that justification is available as a defense to the charge of escape from prison only when

1. The prisoner is faced with a specific threat of death, forcible sexual attack, or substantial bodily injury in the immediate future.
2. There is no time for a complaint to the authorities or there exists a history of futile complaints that make any result from such complaints illusory.
3. There is no time or opportunity to resort to the courts.
4. There is no evidence of force or violence used toward prison personnel or other "innocent" persons in the escape.
5. The prisoner immediately reports to the proper authorities when he or she has attained a position of safety from the immediate threat.[22]

The U.S. Supreme Court ruled as follows in the escape case of *United States v. Bailey:*

> We therefore hold that, where a criminal defendant is charged with escape and claims that he is entitled to an instruction on the theory of duress or necessity, he must proffer evidence of a bona fide effort to surrender or return to custody as soon as the claimed duress or necessity had lost its coercive force. We have reviewed the evidence examined elaborately in the majority and dissenting opinions below, and find the case not even close, even under respondents' versions

of the facts, as to whether they either surrendered or offered to surrender at their earliest possible opportunity. Since we have determined that this is an indispensable element of the defense of duress or necessity, respondents were not entitled to any instruction on such a theory. Vague and necessarily self-serving statements of defendants or witnesses as to future good intentions or ambiguous conduct simply do not support a finding of this element of the defense.[23]

Duress or coercion is generally not a defense to a charge of murder. Under the common law, the defense of duress was not available to a defendant in a murder or treason charge. Blackstone stated that the reason for this was that a man under duress "ought rather to die himself than escape by the murder of an innocent."[24] This apparently is the common law today in more than half the states and in the United Kingdom. About twenty states define the defense of duress by statute, and most do not allow the defense in murder cases (and sometimes in other serious crimes). A few states allow the defense in murder cases: *MacKool v. State,* 213 S.W.3d 618 (Ark. 2005); *State v. Heinemann,* 920 A.2d 278 (Conn. 2007). This is also the rule in the Model Penal Code, § 2.09. Finally, in a few states the defense of duress in a murder charge may be proved for the purpose of reducing the charge of first-degree murder to manslaughter.[25]

Even in those states that do not permit the defense of duress or coercion in murder cases, the defense is generally available to a charge of felony murder (see Chapter 10). In the treatise *Criminal Law* (2nd ed., West/Wadsworth, 1980 § 5.3 b, pp. 435–436), La Fave and Scott state, "The law properly recognizes that one is justified in aiding a robbery if he is forced by threats to do so to save his life; he should not lose the defense because his threateners *(sic)* unexpectedly kill someone in the course of the robbery and thus convert a mere robbery into a murder." In *McMillan v. State,* 51 A.2d 623 (Md. 2012), the court held that although Maryland does not permit the duress defense in murder cases, where the murder charge is based on the felony-murder rule the defendant may prove duress forced him or her to participate in the underlying felony. The court reasoned that if the duress would be a complete defense to the underlying felony (robbery), it would lead to "absurd results" if the defendant could then be convicted of murder. The *McMillan* court also concluded that the threat of imminent harm made by gang members who forced the defendant to help them secure entry for a home invasion was sufficient proof of the "imminent" threat to life required for the duress defense.

Necessity or Choice of Evils Defense[26]

A person who, because of necessity, performs an act that otherwise would constitute a crime may use the justification of **necessity** as a defense if the "harm or evil sought to be avoided by such conduct is greater than that sought to be prevented by the law defining the offense charged."[27]

necessity A defense to criminal prosecution on the grounds that the harm to be avoided outweighed the harm caused by the crime committed. Necessity will not justify taking another person's life.

EXAMPLE

An airplane crashes at night in an isolated area. It is very cold and rescue is not likely until daylight, so the survivors break into a summer cottage and use the food and blankets in the cottage to comfort the injured and sustain themselves until help arrives. In this example, the necessity of breaking into the cottage is obvious and serves as a justification for breaking into the cottage. It is likely the survivors would openly admit what they had done, and the owner of the cottage would be assured of compensation for the damages. Law enforcement officers and the prosecutor would not consider criminal charges, and the matter would not receive further attention.

While the common law recognized the necessity defense, and was thus incorporated into the law of most states, the existence of the defense in federal prosecutions is unclear. In *United States v. Oakland Cannabis Buyers' Co-op*, 532 U.S. 483, 490 (2001), the U.S. Supreme Court stated: "[W]e note that it is an open question whether federal courts ever have authority to recognize a necessity defense not provided by statute." There, the Court did not decide the question, simply holding that even if available, the necessity defense was incompatible with the Controlled Substances Act, and thus not available. A few lower federal courts have held that the defense is available in prosecutions under the felon-in-possession charge under 18 U.S.C. § 922(g), though the statute does not expressly state that such a defense exists. See *United States v. Alston*, 526 F.3d 91 (3d Cir. 2008).

Most courts that recognize a common law defense of necessity state the requirements for the defense to contain some or all of the following elements:

1. The emergency or threat of imminent harm must not have been caused by the defendant.
2. The situation must present the immediate and imminent threat of serious harm to the defendant or another.
3. There must be no reasonable alternative available to avoiding the harm other than breaking the law.
4. The harm to be avoided must be greater than the harm to be prevented by the law prohibiting the conduct.

State statutes that have codified the necessity defense generally have similar requirements, though they do not always include all four elements listed above. The Texas statute, VTCA Penal Code § 9.22, requires only that the actor reasonably believes the conduct is necessary to avoid immediate harm, the harm to be avoided "clearly outweighs" the harm sought to be prevented by the prohibited conduct, and a legislative purpose to exclude the defense does not plainly appear. The Illinois statute, 720 ILCS 5/7-13, requires that the defendant not have caused the circumstances that created the threat of imminent harm, that it was reasonable to believe serious harm was imminent, and that the harm to be avoided is greater than the harm to be prevented by the statute prohibiting the conduct.

Cases in which defendants unsuccessfully used the necessity defense include the following:

- Defendant grew marijuana to alleviate her son's suffering from leukemia and other medical conditions. The court said other alternatives to breaking the law existed, and the necessity defense was not available. *State v. Thayer*, 14 A.3d 231 (Vt. 2010).
- A homeless man charged with drunk driving raised the necessity defense, stating he was required to move his car to avoid obstructing a Salvation Army entrance. The court said the defense was not available because the defendant placed himself in that position by illegally parking on the Salvation Army premises. *Hoagland v. State*, 240 P.3d 1043 (Nev. 2010).

- Unlawful trespass on a naval installation by a protester who claimed he was attempting to cause the dispersion of nuclear submarines from the naval base and surrounding waters. The protestor unsuccessfully argued that such deployment was the "greater evil" and that his decision to trespass was the lesser evil.[28]

The necessity defense, like the duress and coercion defense discussed above, is not available to justify the death of another person.

Can One Kill to Save Oneself?

The question of whether a person can kill to save his or her own life came before courts many years ago in the following famous cases:

United States v. Holmes

Court of Appeals of the United States (1842), 26 Fed. Cas. 360

The defendant was a member of the crew of a ship that sank, leaving him and many others in an overcrowded lifeboat. Because the ship's mate feared that the boat would sink, he ordered the male passengers thrown overboard, leaving the women and the ship's crew. The defendant assisted in throwing sixteen of the men out of the boat to their deaths. A grand jury refused to indict him for murder, so he was charged with and convicted of manslaughter.

Rex v. Dudley and Stephens

Queen's Bench Division (1884), 14 Q.B.D. 273

The defendants and another man and a boy were shipwrecked and adrift in an open boat for eighteen days. After seven days without food or water, the defendants suggested that the men kill the boy, who was then very weak. When the other man refused, the defendants killed the boy, and all the men fed on the boy's body. Four days later, they were rescued. The jury, by a special verdict, found that the men would probably have died within the four days had they not fed on the boy's body. The jury also found that the boy would probably have died before being rescued. However, the defendants were convicted of murder, with the sentence commuted to six months' imprisonment.

These two cases have been debated by judges, lawyers, and law students throughout the English-speaking world for years. Few people urge that the doctrine of necessity be expanded to full forgiveness instead of the partial forgiveness of manslaughter used in both the cases given. In commenting on the problem, former U.S. Supreme Court Justice Benjamin N. Cardozo observed: "Where two or more are overtaken by a common disaster, there is no right on the part of one to save the lives of some, by killing of another. There is no rule of human jettison."[29]

THE USE OF THE DUDLEY CASE IN ETHICS CLASSES TODAY

The *Dudley* case discussed earlier, while decided in 1884, continues to be used in classrooms throughout the United States today. In 2009, a public broadcasting program featured the case in an ethics discussion with several hundred Harvard University students. The various choices open to the shipwrecked sailors in the lifeboat were discussed, including the ethical and legal implications of each choice.

Using the criminal code of your state, would police and prosecutors likely seek criminal charges today for the following choices made by the persons in the lifeboat?

1. A lottery was suggested in the *Dudley* case, but not used. Suppose the lottery idea was adopted, and the loser was killed. Would the remaining persons be subject to criminal charges? Would it matter if they did or did not feed on the dead person's body?
2. Suppose the boy (or another person) agreed to be killed in order to save the others. Would the others be charged with a crime?
3. Based on the facts of the *Dudley* case, should all the persons on board the lifeboat be charged, or only those who actually killed the boy?

The attitude of the British courts today is probably reflected by the 1971 case of *Southwark London Borough v. Williams:*

> [T]he law regards with the deepest suspicion any remedies of self-help, and permits these remedies to be resorted to only in very special circumstances. The reason for such circumspection is clear—necessity can very easily become simply a mask for anarchy.[30]

alibi A defense to criminal prosecution on the grounds that the defendant physically could not have committed the crime because at the time the crime was committed, he or she was at another place.

Alibi as a Criminal Defense

In using the defense of **alibi,** the defendant is asserting that he or she physically could not have committed the crime, because at the time the crime was committed, he or she was at another place.

EXAMPLE

X is charged with robbery and has been identified by two witnesses and the victim as the man who robbed a liquor store. X uses the defense of alibi and argues that it was physically impossible for him to rob the store because he was at his mother's home 100 miles away at the time of the robbery. His mother and his wife corroborate X's story, stating that they were there also.

Because an alibi can be easily fabricated, it must be carefully investigated. Many states have statutes requiring defendants who plan to use an alibi defense to serve notice on the prosecutor before trial. These statutes are meant to safeguard against the wrongful use of alibis, as they give law enforcement agencies and prosecutors necessary notice and time to investigate the merits of the proposed alibi.

Alibi Notice Statutes

Alibi notice statutes require defendants to make disclosures regarding their cases. Such disclosures include the place where the defendant claimed to have been at the time the crime was committed and the names and addresses of witnesses to the alibi, if known.

In the case of *Wardius v. Oregon,* the U.S. Supreme Court held that when a defendant is compelled to disclose information regarding his or her case, the state must also make similar disclosures. The U.S. Supreme Court held:

> [In] the absence of a strong showing of state interests to the contrary, discovery must be a two-way street. The State may not insist that trials be run as a "search for truth" so far as defense witnesses are concerned, while maintaining "poker game" secrecy for its own witnesses. It is fundamentally unfair to require a defendant to divulge the details of his own case while at the same time subjecting him to the hazard of surprise concerning refutation of the very pieces of evidence which he disclosed to the State.[31]

Alibi notice statutes now require disclosure by prosecutors as well as defendants.

An alibi presented to and believed by a jury constitutes a complete defense to the crime charged. Even if the alibi raises only a reasonable doubt in the mind of a jury, it becomes a good defense because the jury cannot convict if a reasonable doubt exists. If only two or three of the jurors believe the alibi, a hung jury may result. The burden is not on the defendant to show that he or she was not at the scene of the crime; it is on the state to show beyond reasonable doubt that the defendant *was* at the scene and committed the crime. Charges of perjury, solicitation to commit perjury, or subornation of perjury have resulted when it has been shown that alibi witnesses testified falsely or that attempts were made to persuade people to testify falsely.

The Defense That the Defendant Was Acting Under the Authority, Direction, or Advice of Another

A person who commits an act that is obviously criminal, such as arson or murder, and then attempts to use as a defense the fact that he or she was acting under the direction of a superior officer or on the advice of an attorney or another person would ordinarily be held fully liable for such an offense. The general rule is that one who performs a criminal act under the advice, direction, or order of another cannot use such a defense.

However, because hundreds of crimes are not well known to the general public, the U.S. Supreme Court quoted with approval a jury instruction stating that when a person

> [f]ully and honestly lays all the facts before his counsel, and in good faith and honestly follows such advice, relying upon it and believing it to be correct, and only intends that his acts shall be lawful, he could not be convicted of crime which involves willful and unlawful intent; even if such advice were an inaccurate

construction of the law. But, on the other hand, no man can willfully and knowingly violate the law and excuse himself from consequences thereof by pleading that he followed the advice of counsel.[32]

Where the advice that contemplated conduct would be legal comes from a government official, the defense called "entrapment by estoppel" (also known as "official misleading") has developed in federal prosecutions.[33] The following two U.S. Supreme Court cases are often cited as the origin of the defense:

Cox v. Louisiana

Supreme Court of the United States (1965), 379 U.S. 559, 85 S. Ct. 476

Among other charges, the defendant was convicted of demonstrating "in or near" a courthouse in violation of a Louisiana law modeled after a 1949 federal statute. The U.S. Supreme Court reversed the conviction, stating:

> The highest police officials of the city, in the presence of the Sheriff and Mayor, in effect, told the demonstrators that they could meet where they did, 101 feet from the courthouse steps, but could not meet closer to the courthouse. In effect, appellant was advised that a demonstration at the place it was held would not be one "near" the courthouse within the terms of the statute.[34]

Raley v. Ohio

Supreme Court of the United States (1959), 360 U.S. 423, 79 S. Ct. 1257

The U.S. Supreme Court held "that the Due Process Clause prevented conviction of persons for refusing to answer questions of a state investigating commission when they relied upon assurance of the commission, either express or implied, that they had a privilege under state law to refuse to answer, though in fact this privilege was not available to them." The Court stated that this would be to sanction an indefensible sort of **entrapment** by the State—convicting a citizen for exercising a privilege that the State had clearly told him was available to him.

entrapment The defense that a law enforcement officer used excessive temptation or urging to wrongfully induce the defendants to commit a crime they would not have ordinarily committed.

The requirements for the defense of entrapment by estoppel are (1) the official giving the opinion on legality is "empowered to render" that opinion, (2) the official knew all the facts giving rise to the request for the opinion, (3) the opinion was "affirmatively misleading," and (4) the defendant's reliance on the opinion was reasonable.[35]

In the 2007 case of *People v. Chacon*,[36] the California Supreme Court held that the defense of entrapment by estoppel was recognized in California, but was not available in the case before the court. The defendant, a city councilwoman, was charged with criminal conflict of interest. She alleged she relied on the advice of the city attorney that she was not in a conflict of interest situation. The court rejected the defense, holding that the city attorney was not in a position to render that advice.

The Defense of Double Jeopardy

The Fifth Amendment of the U.S. Constitution provides that "no person . . . shall . . . for the same offense . . . be twice put in jeopardy of life or limb." In the case of *United States v. Scott,* the U.S. Supreme Court, quoting other Supreme Court cases, held that the Double Jeopardy Clause ensures

> that the State with all its resources and power should not be allowed to make repeated attempts to convict an individual for an alleged offense, thereby subjecting him to embarrassment, expense and ordeal and compelling him to live in a continuing state of anxiety and insecurity, as well as enhancing the possibility that even though innocent he may be found guilty.[37]

THE MEANING OF ACQUITTAL

Michigan v. Evans
United States Supreme Court (2013),
133 S. Ct. 1069

Lamar Evans was charged with arson under a Michigan statute that applied to burning "other real property"; another statute applied to burning real property that was a dwelling. Penalties were higher for burning a dwelling than for burning "other real property. " After the prosecution rested the case against Evans, Evans moved for a directed judgment of acquittal. He contended the prosecution was required to prove, as an element of the offense, that the building burned was not a dwelling, and that the only proof introduced by the prosecution was evidence that the building was a dwelling. The trial court agreed, and entered a verdict of acquittal.

On appeal, the Michigan Supreme Court reversed and remanded the case for a new trial. That court held, and Evans agreed, that the trial court erred in holding that an element of the statute included proof that the burned building was not a dwelling house. The court rejected Evans's double jeopardy argument, holding that the trial judge's "acquittal" was based on an error of law that "did not resolve any factual element of the charged offense."

The U.S. Supreme Court granted review, and reversed the Michigan Supreme Court. It held that the trial court's judgment of acquittal, even though based on an erroneous interpretation of the statute, was nonetheless an "acquittal" for purposes of double jeopardy. Unlike a dismissal on a procedural ground, which does not generally present a double jeopardy issue, here the trial court evaluated the evidence and found it insufficient to prove the crime charged. The Court said that even though the trial court did so erroneously, it was still a resolution of the guilt or innocence of the defendant. Such a resolution can only occur once under the Double Jeopardy Clause, the Court said.

double jeopardy A defense, stated in the Fifth Amendment, to prosecution on the grounds that the defendant has been tried before on the same charge, and acquitted.

Therefore, **double jeopardy** means that a person who has been acquitted by a judge or a jury may not be tried again, even if subsequent investigation reveals evidence that proves conclusively that the defendant is guilty. If a defendant is found not guilty because of insanity, the person may not be tried again for the same crime, even if the person is later found sane and normal.

The Times When Jeopardy Attaches

In the case of *Press-Enterprise Co. v. Superior Court of California, Riverside County*,[38] the U.S. Supreme Court pointed out that jeopardy attaches when a jury is sworn.[39] In a nonjury trial, the Court stated that jeopardy attaches when the first witness is sworn.[40] Thus, if the defendant is acquitted of the charges after jeopardy attached, he cannot be tried again on the same charge, or on a lesser included crime.

Questions about the meaning of "acquitted" were raised before the U.S. Supreme Court in the 2012 case of *Blueford v. Arkansas*.[41] In that case a defendant was charged with capital murder, and the jury was instructed to consider lesser included charges such as manslaughter if it could not agree on the capital murder charge. After deliberating for some time, the jury told the judge it could not reach a verdict, because although it unanimously voted "not guilty" on the capital murder charge, it could not reach a decision on any lesser charge. As a result, the trial court declared a mistrial.

When the state filed new charges of capital murder, the defendant claimed the double jeopardy clause barred the prosecution because he was "acquitted" on the capital murder charge in the first trial. The U.S. Supreme Court rejected that claim. It said that in the case of a mistrial the double jeopardy clause does not bar another prosecution, because there has been no final decision by the jury. That was the case here, the Court held, because although the jury said it had voted not guilty on the capital murder charge, that was not final, and the jury could have gone back to deliberations and changed its mind. As a result, the defendant had not been acquitted of the charge of capital murder, and could be retried.

Prosecution by Both State and Federal Governments

Because most crimes are crimes only against a state, only the state may prosecute. Some crimes, however, are offenses against not only the state but also the federal government. The robbery of a federally insured bank or savings and loan association is an example.

The question of whether the state and federal governments may both prosecute for such offenses has come before the U.S. Supreme Court more than a dozen times. Justice Oliver Wendell Holmes, in noting that both state and federal prosecution in such cases is not in violation of the Fifth Amendment, stated that the rule "is too plain to need more than a statement."[42] The reasoning is presented in the case of *Bartkus v. Illinois* as follows:

> Every citizen of the United States is also a citizen of a State or territory. He may be said to owe allegiance to two sovereigns, and may be liable to punishment for an infraction of the laws of either. The same act may be an offense or transgression of the law of both. That either or both may (if they see fit) punish such an

WHEN IS A NEW TRIAL A "SECOND TRIAL" FOR DOUBLE JEOPARDY?

A criminal prosecution can "end" in a variety of ways: conviction, acquittal, dismissal of charges, mistrials, or hung jury. Moreover, the result in a trial may be changed on appeal. When any of these happen, can the government bring new charges, or would it amount to a "second trial," barred by the Double Jeopardy Clause? The following rules address some of these situations.

I. Re-prosecution after conviction, where conviction reversed on appeal.
  (A) Retrial not permitted if reversal was for failure to grant defendant's motion for judgment of acquittal.
  (B) Retrial permitted if reversal is for any other trial error.

II. Re-prosecution after "acquittal."
  (A) Pretrial: The government may appeal pretrial dismissal, because effect of reversal would not be a "second trial."
  (B) Mid-Trial
    1. Dismissal
      (a) The government may not appeal a verdict of not guilty or a pre-verdict grant of motion for judgment of acquittal, because effect of reversal on appeal would be a second trial after a determination of factual guilt/innocence.
      (b) The government may appeal a mid-trial dismissal on any grounds other than factual guilt/innocence. A retrial would not be a "second trial."
    2. Mistrials
      (a) Where the government moves for a mistrial, a retrial is permitted only if it shows a "manifest necessity" for mistrial.
      (b) Where the defendant moves for a mistrial, a retrial is permitted unless the government intended to provoke the mistrial motion.
    3. Hung jury
      (a) If the jury is unable to reach a decision and the case is dismissed, a retrial is permitted.
      (b) Post-trial

The government may appeal a post-trial dismissal of the charges because the effect of the reversal on appeal is simply reinstatement of the verdict of conviction, and does not require a second trial.

offender cannot be doubted. Yet it cannot be truly averted that the offender has been twice punished for the same offense; but only that by one act he has committed two offenses, for each of which he is justly punishable. He could not plead the punishment by one in bar to a conviction by the other.[43]

In *Bartkus v. Illinois,* the defendant was tried in a federal court and acquitted of robbing a federally insured bank. He was then indicted by an Illinois grand jury and convicted on substantially the same evidence used in the federal court. The Illinois court sentenced him to life imprisonment under the Illinois Habitual Criminal

Statute. The U.S. Supreme Court affirmed the conviction, holding that the second trial did not violate the Fifth Amendment of the U.S. Constitution.

Since *Bartkus v. Illinois,* however, many states, including Illinois, have passed legislation that forbids prosecution after another jurisdiction has prosecuted the defendant for the same crime. In such states, the law of the state, and not the Double Jeopardy Clause, forbids prosecution after prosecution in another jurisdiction.[44]

The Meaning of "Separate Offense"

Double jeopardy does not bar successive prosecutions of a defendant convicted of one offense if the subsequent prosecution involves a different or separate offense. The meaning of *separate* adopted by the U.S. Supreme Court has changed over time. In *Blockburger v. United States,* the Court adopted the following "different offense" rule:

> The applicable rule is that where the same acts or transaction constitutes a violation of two distinct statutory provisions, the test to be applied to determine whether there are two offenses or only one, is whether each provision requires proof of an additional fact which the other does not.[45]

This rule prevented, among other things, prosecutions for so-called lesser included offenses, that is, offenses whose elements were included in the greater offense. For example, in the 2011 Case of *State v. Marchi,*[46] the Washington Court of Appeals reversed a conviction of assault on a child because the state also charged the defendant with first-degree murder. The double jeopardy clause applied because the same act (drugging the child) constituted the *actus reus* for both crimes, and the same evidence would be used to prove both crimes, the court held.

In the early 1990s, the Supreme Court in *Grady v. Corbin* appeared to modify the *Blockburger* "same element" test, holding in one case that successive prosecutions arising out of the "same conduct" were barred by the Double Jeopardy Clause.[47] If the same conduct violated two criminal statutes, successive prosecutions were barred, even though the statutes had different elements. Such a rule would prevent some prosecutions that would be possible under *Blockburger.*[48] However, in 1993, the Supreme Court reversed *Grady v. Corbin* and the "same conduct" rule.[49] It held that the *Blockburger* "same element" test determined double jeopardy questions.

Other Times When the Defense of Double Jeopardy Could Not Be Used Successfully

The defense of double jeopardy could not be used successfully in the following situations:

When one legal action is civil and the other is a criminal action.	The O. J. Simpson case illustrates this principle of law. O. J. Simpson was acquitted of murder charges in a Los Angeles criminal case, but the families of the victims then commenced civil lawsuits against Simpson and won jury awards of more than $34 million.

When a hung jury occurs or in most cases in which a mistrial is declared before jeopardy is attached.

After two all-white juries were unable to reach verdicts in a criminal trial of Byron De La Beckwith, a white supremacist, he was convicted in a third trial for the murder of Medgar Evers, a civil rights activist. The third murder trial was 31 years after the first trial, but neither federal nor state laws have a statute of limitations for murder.

If there is serious fraud in the first trial, a defendant has not been placed at risk, so the defendant cannot claim double jeopardy.

It was shown in the 1997 U.S. Supreme Court case of *Illinois v. Aleman,* 519 U.S. 1128, that an Illinois judge accepted a $10,000 bribe to acquit Aleman of murder. In the first such case in American legal history, the second Illinois trial judge held that Aleman had never been placed in jeopardy and that "absent such risk, the claim of double jeopardy is more imagined than real."

If the prior legal action is an in rem civil forfeiture, the following criminal action is not barred (stopped) by double jeopardy.

The U.S. Supreme Court has held repeatedly that *in rem* (against a thing, a car, a house) civil forfeiture actions are neither "punishment" nor criminal for the purposes of the Double Jeopardy Clause if Congress or the state legislative body meant such actions to be civil and not punitive in form and effect. *United States v. Ursery,* 518 U.S. 267 (1996).

"dual sovereignty" doctrine A doctrine that different governments may each file separate criminal actions for the same criminal act.

Under the "dual sovereignty" doctrine, different governments may each file separate criminal actions for the same criminal act.

Unless a state statute forbids it, a state may charge and convict a person who has already been charged in a federal court, in another state, or in a foreign country, because the **"dual sovereignty" doctrine** permits different governments to each file separate criminal actions for the same criminal act committed against sovereign governments. In the 1996 case of *United States v. Guzman,* 85 F.3d 823 (1st. Cir. 1996), Guzman violated the drug laws of both the Netherlands and the United States and could be convicted for the same criminal acts by both countries.

Entrapment and Outrageous Government Conduct as Defenses

The defense of entrapment was recognized by the U.S. Supreme Court in the case of *Sorrells v. United States.*[50] In *Sorrells,* the Supreme Court ruled that entrapment occurs "when the criminal design originates with the officials of the government, and they implant in the mind of an innocent person the disposition to commit the alleged offense and induce its commission in order that they (the Government) may prosecute." The defense of entrapment therefore has two elements: (1) improper government inducement of the crime and (2) lack of predisposition on the part of the defendant to engage in the criminal conduct.

Defendants seeking to use the defense of entrapment carry the initial burden of coming forward with evidence of both the government's improper inducement and the defendant's lack of predisposition to commit the alleged offense. If a defendant makes a showing of improper inducement by the government and lack of predisposition by the defendant, the burden then shifts to the government. The government must then show "readiness" on the part of the defendant and that the "defendant was poised, was likely, to engage in criminal activity."[51]

The U.S. Supreme Court ruled in the case of *Mathews v. United States*[52] that a defendant "is entitled to an entrapment instruction (to a jury) whenever there is sufficient evidence from which a reasonable jury could find entrapment."

Courts throughout the United States have long recognized that law enforcement officers (or their agents) can properly create ordinary opportunities for a person to commit an offense if the criminal intent or willingness originated in the mind of the defendant. The fact that the officer afforded the opportunity or the facility for the defendant to commit the crime in order to obtain evidence does not constitute entrapment. In *Hampton v. United States,*[53] the Court held the entrapment defense was not available to a defendant who sold illegal drugs to undercover police officers, even though a government informer, acting for the government, supplied the drugs sold. The Court said the defendant must prove he did not have the criminal intention until it was implanted by the agent.

A sting operation is not improper inducement to commit a crime if it merely provides an opportunity to commit a crime. Thus, the Supreme Court held in *United States v. Russell* that infiltration into a drug ring, and supplying some of the items needed to produce the illegal drugs, does not amount to entrapment.[54] However, proof of a sting operation that includes additional conduct by police may amount to sufficient evidence to meet a defendant's burden. For example, in *Jacobson v. United States,*[55] the Supreme Court held that repeated attempts by government agents to entice a defendant to purchase child pornography through the mail constituted entrapment. Entrapment occurs, the Court said, "when the Government's quest for convictions leads to the apprehension of an otherwise law abiding citizen who, if left to his own devices, likely would have never run afoul of the law."

Although law enforcement officers may create and present the usual and ordinary opportunities for a person to commit a crime, they may not use excessive urging, inducement, temptation, or solicitation to commit a crime. For example, in the early case of *Sherman v. United States*,[56] the Court held that actions by a government informant to entice a drug addict to return to drug use and supply drugs to the informant constituted entrapment.

The Supreme Court quoted another court as follows in the *Sorrells* case:

> It is well settled that decoys may be used to entrap criminals, and to present opportunity to one intending or willing to commit crime. But decoys are not permissible to ensnare the innocent and law-abiding into the commission of crime. When the criminal design originates, not with the accused, but is conceived in the mind of the government officers, and the accused is by persuasion, deceitful representation, or inducement lured into the commission of a criminal act, the government is estopped by sound public policy from prosecution therefore.

States Are Free to Write Their Own Rules for Entrapment   The U.S. Supreme Court has held that the defense of entrapment is not of constitutional dimension. Therefore, the U.S. Congress and state legislative bodies may "adopt any substantive definition of the defense that [they] may desire."[57]

Some states have enacted statutes that define entrapment. Most states, however, use common law definitions created by their courts as the entrapment rules to be used within that state.

Most states and the federal courts use the "origin of intent" test in determining whether the defendant was predisposed to commit the crime charged. The test seeks to determine whether the defendant had the willingness and readiness to commit the crime *and* whether the police or a government agent only provided what appeared to be a favorable opportunity.

Denying the Criminal Act While Using the Defense of Entrapment
Until 1988, most states would not permit defendants to plead innocence, while at the same time using an affirmative defense such as entrapment. The innocent plea generally means, "I didn't commit the crime," whereas in the entrapment defense, the defendant is pleading, "I wouldn't have committed the crime if it had not been for the improper conduct of the police."

In the case of *Mathews v. United States*,[58] the U.S. Supreme Court pointed out that such inconsistent defenses have historically been permitted in federal prosecutions. But because it is not a constitutional issue, the Supreme Court held that it is up to each state to determine whether inconsistent defenses would be permitted.

In response to the *Mathews* decision, many states now permit inconsistent defenses (such as entrapment and denying the criminal act), and other states continue to require that criminal defenses be consistent.

A defendant who cannot claim entrapment may still be able to invoke the defense of outrageous government conduct. The U.S. Supreme Court first raised the concept of outrageous police conduct in the case of *United States v. Russell* (discussed earlier in this chapter), in which the Court stated:

STINGS AND SCAM OPERATIONS

The U.S. Supreme Court stated long ago that American "courts have uniformly held that in waging war against crime . . . traps, decoys and deception (may be used) to obtain evidence of the commission of the crime." *United States v. Sorrells,* 287 U.S. 435, 454 (1932).

Many of the "sting" and "scam" operations operated every year in the United States are triggered by tips or other information that criminal activity is taking place or being planned. For example, suppose the police are told that a man is offering $5,000 to have his wife or another person murdered. To determine whether this is true, an undercover officer or cooperative person might approach the suspect and pretend to be willing to undertake the murder. If the suspect agrees and solicits the undercover officer, police have sufficient evidence to arrest the man and bring criminal charges. The following are examples of the wide use of stings and scams today:

Pedophile and child enticement or Internet sex scams. These scams are commonly used to identify and apprehend adults who sexually prey on children. Police officers represent themselves, often through Internet chat rooms, as children, and the suspect communicates with them believing that to be the case. If the suspect attempts to entice the "child" into sexual contact, the suspect is arrested. (These scams are discussed more fully in Chapter 12.)

Storefront stings. Thieves, burglars, robbers, or shoplifters are tricked into bringing stolen goods to a store, where hidden video cameras and microphones record their transactions for subsequent use in criminal prosecutions.

Open-air drug dealing stings. These are set up on streets, alleys, or shopping centers where illegal drug dealing is suspected. Police pretending to be drug dealers offer to sell illegal drugs such as heroin to persons frequenting the area. These stings are upheld as not being entrapment; see *State v. J.D.W.,* 910 P.2d 1242 (Utah App. 1995).

[W]e may some day be presented with a situation in which the conduct of law enforcement agents is so outrageous that due process principles would absolutely bar the government from invoking judicial processes to obtain a conviction. . . . [59]

In the case *of Hampton v. United States,* Justice Powell stated that "police over-involvement in crime would have to reach a demonstrable level of outrageousness before it could bar conviction."[60] Thus, even if it is found that the government conduct was wrong or illegal, before dismissing charges based on that conduct a court must determine that the outrageous conduct violated due process rights of the defendant.

Outrageous Government Conduct That Violated the Due Process Rights of Defendants   The following conduct was held to fall within the shock-the-conscience or outrageous conduct exception so as to cause dismissal of the criminal charge:

- Using a defendant's attorney to gather information against him was held to violate not only due process but also the defendant's Sixth Amendment right to an attorney.[61]

Money-laundering stings. Undercover officers engage in transactions with suspected car dealers, real estate brokers, financial institutions, or other businesses to determine whether they are using the business to launder money obtained from criminal activities. (Chapter 18 discusses money-laundering crimes.)

Food stamp scams. Undercover police pose as food stamp holders and determine whether suspected persons are using the food stamps for wrongful purposes, like buying alcohol or cigarettes for minors, or wrongfully selling food stamps or food stamp debit cards for cash.

Fugitive felons scams. In order to apprehend some of the 1.2 million persons wanted on outstanding warrants, police often use a scam where they send letters or e-mails to addresses where the fugitives might be found, saying they have won a free trip or other prize. When the fugitives show up to collect their "prize," officers are there to arrest them.

FBI stings. The FBI investigates suspected bribes or other wrongdoing by elected state or county officials for violations of federal criminal laws. These stings usually involve an undercover FBI agent offering bribes to an official, which, if accepted, are criminal violations.

Stings to test the integrity of law enforcement officers. Police departments test themselves to make sure officers are acting with integrity. The New York Police Department, which has over 30,000 officers, conducts 600 or more stings designed to test those officers each year. The FBI also does this, but does not report the number and kind of stings it conducts each year.

The use of deer decoys. In states with substantial hunting regions, poaching and other kinds of illegal hunting are often the subject of decoy stings. A fake deer or bear is set up, and police arrest persons who shoot the decoy. Entrapment is generally not a successful defense to the charges of trespassing, shooting out of season, or other weapons violations.

- Manufacture of crack cocaine by the police for use in a reverse sting[62] operation caused dismissal of charges by the Supreme Court of Florida.[63]
- For two and a half years, government agents supplied many materials and showed defendants how to manufacture illegal alcohol, which the agents said they would buy. *Greene v. United States.*[64]

Conduct Held Not to Be Outrageous So as to Violate Defendant's Due Process Rights   In the following cases, courts held that the conduct was not so outrageous as to violate the defendant's due process rights:

- A civilian working with a police department had sex with a woman to obtain evidence necessary to convict her of prostitution. The Supreme Court of Hawaii affirmed the conviction, holding that it was not outrageous conduct, but it was also not the "ethical standards which law enforcement officials should be guided by."[65]
- Paying a defendant's former girlfriend's living expenses while she assisted in building a criminal case against the defendant was held not to be outrageous conduct.[66]

- In a 2011 decision, a California court held that while it was undoubtedly a serious misconduct for a prosecutor to give false testimony in a hearing involving a criminal trial, the false testimony did not violate the defendant's due process rights. The court reversed a trial court's dismissal of the criminal charges against the defendant.[67]

The Defense That Another Person Committed the Crime

There are a number of ways of proving the wrong person has been charged with or convicted of a crime. Providing exculpatory evidence to the prosecution or investigating officers is the easiest way to accomplish this result, in particular if the evidence is convincing, such as DNA evidence. Showing that an eyewitness wrongly identified the defendant or committed perjury can also be good exculpatory evidence. The Innocence Project, a national organization that works to free wrongfully convicted persons, estimates that 62 percent of single-witness identifications are incorrect. See the Innocence Project, "Eyewitness Misidentifications," info@ innocenceproject.org. Another defense that can be used is evidence that another person committed the crime. However, this defense can be abused. Defendants with ample money or power could find another person willing to "confess" to the crime in exchange for money or because of coercion. In a recent case in Milwaukee, Wisconsin, the brother of the defendant charged with murder appeared in the district attorney's office and asserted he was the person who committed the murder. Also, it is not unusual in criminal cases that receive media attention to find people calling prosecutors and "confessing" to the crimes, just to get attention. Allowing these people to testify would likely confuse the jury.

To deal with this situation, most states have rules similar to Rule 804(b) (3) of the Federal Rules of Evidence. That rule states that before a witness can be allowed to offer evidence to exculpate a defendant, there must be evidence of corroborating circumstances that clearly indicate the trustworthiness of the statement.

The Right to a Speedy Trial as a Defense

The Sixth Amendment of the U.S. Constitution provides that "in all criminal prosecutions, the accused shall enjoy the right to a speedy and public trial."[68] Most defendants charged with a serious crime do not wish either a speedy or a public trial, but unless the right to a speedy trial is waived with the consent of the trial court, the constitutional mandate of a speedy trial must be followed.

The four-factor balancing test used to determine whether a speedy trial violation has occurred was established by the U.S. Supreme Court in the case of *Barker v. Wingo*.[69] The factors that are weighed are (1) the length of the delay, (2) the reason for the delay, (3) the defendant's assertion of his or her right, and (4) the prejudice resulting from the delay.

In holding that the right to a speedy trial commences when a person "is indicted, arrested, or otherwise officially accused," the U.S. Supreme Court held in *United States v. Marion* that

> The protection of the Amendment is activated only when a criminal prosecution has begun and extends only to those persons who have been "accused" in the course of that prosecution. These provisions would seem to afford no protection to those not yet accused, nor would they seem to require the Government to discover, investigate, and accuse any person within any particular period of time.[70]

The Court stated that the purpose and "interests served by the Speedy Trial Clause" are as follows:

> Inordinate delay between an arrest, indictment, and trial may impair a defendant's ability to present an effective defense. But the major evils protected against by the speedy trial guarantee exist quite apart from actual or possible prejudice to an accused's defense. To legally arrest and detain, the Government must assert probable cause to believe the arrestee has committed a crime. Arrest is a public act that may seriously interfere with the defendant's liberty, whether he is free on bail or not, and that may disrupt his employment, drain his financial resources, curtail his associations, subject him to public obloquy, and create anxiety in him, his family and his friends.[71]

The U.S. Constitution does not identify a specific number of days necessary to satisfy the speedy trial requirement. Therefore, the federal government and states have enacted statutes establishing their own standards. For example, the federal government in the Speedy Trial Act, 18 U.S.C. § 3161(c)(1), requires that a person indicted for a felony be tried within 70 days unless the defendant waives his or her right to a speedy trial. Failure to try the person within that time could cause dismissal of the criminal charge if it were shown that the delay prejudiced the defendant under the *Barker v. Wingo* factors. In the 2010 case of *Bloate v. United States,*[72] the Court held that time delays caused by filing pretrial motions are not automatically excluded from calculating the 70-day period, but can be excluded if the trial court makes a specific finding that the time should be excluded.

Defendants already incarcerated in one state often have pending charges in another state. Obtaining a speedy trial under those circumstances can be difficult, and determining if a Speedy Trial Clause violation has occurred can also be a problem. To deal with this situation most states are party to the Interstate Agreement on Detainers Act. Under this Act, if a person detained in one state makes a request that charges against him pending in another state be brought to trial, the other state must bring the prisoner to trial within 180 days of the request. If that does not occur, the charges must be dismissed. The dismissal court has the discretion to make the dismissal with or without prejudice, depending on the circumstances. In the 2011 case of *United States v. Ferraira,*[73] the Sixth Circuit Court of Appeals reversed a trial court's decision that a dismissal should be without prejudice, so that the government could file new charges. The appeals court concluded that the 3-year delay in requesting transfer of the defendant to the district court for trial violated the defendant's Sixth Amendment right to a speedy trial, and that the appropriate remedy was dismissal of the indictment with prejudice.

The Statute of Limitations as a Defense

statute of limitations
A defense to a criminal prosecution based on a statute that sets the maximum time the government has to prosecute a violation of a criminal law.

The old English common law adopted the doctrine that "no lapse bars the King"; therefore, statutes limiting the time for criminal prosecutions are rare in England.

However, criminal **statutes of limitations** appeared in America as early as 1652. The federal government adopted time limits for the prosecution of most federal crimes in 1790, and the majority of the states have enacted statutes of limitations for most crimes.

The speedy trial requirements are constitutional mandates and therefore are imposed on all states. Statutes of limitations on criminal prosecutions are optional legislative enactments. Reasons given for limitations on criminal prosecutions are as follows:

> A limitation statute is designed to protect individuals from having to defend themselves against charges when the basic facts may have become obscured by the passage of time and to minimize the danger of official punishment because of acts in the far-distant past.[74]

> * * *

> The Speedy Trial Clause and the limitations statutes work in tandem to prevent pretrial delay: the statutory period insures against pre-accusation delays and the Sixth Amendment controls the post-indictment time span. . . . Both provisions shield defendants from endless anxiety about possible prosecution and from impairment of the ability to mount a defense. By encouraging speedy prosecution, they also afford society protection from unincarcerated offenders, and insure against a diminution of the deterrent value of immediate convictions, as well as the reduced capacity of the government to prove its case.[75]

Statutes of limitation generally permit a longer period for the prosecution of felonies than for the prosecution of misdemeanors. No time limit is generally placed on prosecution for murder. As discovery of some theft offenses may occur years after the theft, extensions of time are generally given, based on the time of discovery of the offense. The running of time under a criminal statute of limitation could be halted by

- Issuance of an arrest warrant or summons, an indictment, filing of information, or the commencement of prosecution.
- Statutory requirement that the person must be a public resident of that state for the time to toll.
- Acts by the suspect to avoid or to frustrate legal proceedings against him or her.

SPEEDY TRIAL, DOUBLE JEOPARDY, AND STATUTES OF LIMITATIONS AS DEFENSES

Double jeopardy and the requirement of a speedy trial are both mandated by the U.S. Constitution and must be complied with.

Speedy trial	Because the U.S. Constitution does not specify the time period within which a defendant must be tried, federal law or the law of each state establishes this time period. Defendants, however, often waive their right to a speedy trial. This is done in open court and most often in writing and signed by the defendant and the defense lawyer.
Double jeopardy	A criminal defendant cannot be retried if jeopardy has attached to the crime with which the defendant has been charged. The U.S. Supreme Court has held that jeopardy attaches when a jury is sworn and, in a non-jury case, when the first witness is sworn.
Statutes of limitation	These are not required by the U.S. Constitution and are optional state legislative enactments. The states of South Carolina and Wyoming have no criminal statutes of limitation.[a]

[a] "The Statute of Limitation in Criminal Law," 102 U. Pa. L. Rev. 630.

Summary

- Diplomatic immunity is limited to recognized diplomats and certain members of their families. Legislative immunity applies only to active legislators, and only during the time the legislature is in session. Witness immunity can be given to overcome the Fifth Amendment privilege a witness has. The immunity can be for prosecution for any charges related to the witness's testimony, or only for use of that testimony.

- A mistake of fact provides a defense when the mistake is honest and reasonable and nullifies a specific intent necessary for conviction of the crime charged. A mistake of law rarely provides a defense, unless the criminal law defining the offense is generally not known to reasonable people.

- The Double Jeopardy Clause serves as a limitation on the power of government to use its resources to subject a citizen to repeated exposure to the criminal laws, and it also guards against the conviction of innocent persons.

- Two offenses are the "same" for double jeopardy purposes if the same facts serve as a basis for each offense. If one offense requires proof of a fact that was not part of the other offense, each charge can be prosecuted. Prosecutions based on the same actions under both a state and a federal statute are not prosecutions for the "same" offense under the Double Jeopardy Clause.

- Acquittal under the Double Jeopardy Clause means a judgment of dismissal or not guilty made by the fact finder (judge or jury) based on an evaluation of the evidence and a finding that it was insufficient to prove the crime charged.

- Government inducements become entrapment when the actions of law enforcement officers are improper and the defendant had no predisposition to commit the crimes made the subject of the improper inducements.

- A speedy trial violation has occurred when there has been an excessive delay (made specific in statutes but not in the Constitution), no good reason for the delay exists, the defendant has asserted the right to a speedy trial, and the delay has caused prejudice to the defendant.

Key Terms

corpus delicti, p. 164
affirmative defense, p. 164
immunity, p. 165
transactional immunity, p. 167
use immunity, p. 167

mistake of law, p. 170
duress, p. 172
coercion, p. 172
necessity, p. 173
alibi, p. 176

entrapment, p. 178
double jeopardy, p. 180
"dual sovereignty" doctrine, p. 183
statute of limitations, p. 190

Case Analysis and Writing Exercises

1. Assume a defendant is convicted in federal court of murder for hire. Subsequently, California prosecutors charge him with capital murder, including committing a murder by "lying in wait," a capital offense in California. The murders committed are the same in both prosecutions. Does the Double Jeopardy Clause bar the California prosecution? If not, why not? See *People v. Homick*, 150 Cal. Rptr. 3d 1 (Cal. 2012).

2. Montana permits sale and use of marijuana for medical purposes. Authorized sellers may only sell certain amounts to patients with state-issued medical cards. An undercover officer applies for a medical card under a false name, visits a physician under an alias to verify his medical condition, and uses the card to purchase more than the permitted amount of marijuana from the defendant. Is this entrapment? Is it outrageous government conduct? Why or why not? See *State v. Fitzpatrick*, 291 P.3d 1106 (Mont. 2012).

3. Many of the defenses discussed in this chapter are created by legislatures, although some are the result of court decisions. When a defendant is convicted of a crime, but the conviction is reversed, the Ex Post Facto clause prohibits the legislature from abrogating a defense that was available when the defendant was initially tried and convicted. What is the result when a defense was available at the first trial, but between that trial and a retrial after a conviction was reversed the state supreme court abrogated the defense? May the defendant raise the defense in his retrial? Does the Ex Post Facto Clause apply? If not, how is this issue determined? See *Lancaster v. Metrish*, 683 F.3d 740 (6th Cir. 2012). The U.S. Supreme Court reversed the court of appeals in *Metrish v. Lancaster*, 133 S. Ct. 1781 (2013). What was the basis for the Court's decision to reverse the lower court?

4. Defendant and another person extorted money from a former married lover of the defendant by threatening to disclose the previous sexual relationship to the victim's wife. At her trial, defendant asked for an instruction on the defense of duress, claiming the other person threatened to kill her if she didn't cooperate in the extortion scheme, which lasted several months. The trial judge refused to give the instruction. Why not? Was the judge correct? See *United States v. Nwoye*, 663 F.3d 460 (C.A.D.C. 2011).

Endnotes

1. *In re Winship*, 90 S. Ct. 1068, 1071 (1970).
2. 343 U.S. 790 (1952).
3. *Mullaney v. Wilbur*, 421 U.S. 197 (1975).
4. 442 F. Supp. 2d 102 (S.D. New York 2006).
5. 356 F.3d 564 (4th Cir. 2004).
6. 596 So.2d 687 (Fla. App. 1992).
7. 717 F Supp. 309 (E.D. Pa. 1989).
8. *United States v. Gillock*, 445 U.S. 360 (1980); *U.S. v. Gonzalez De Modesti*, 145 F. Supp. 2d 171 (D.P.R. 2001).
9. 651 F.3d 1012 (9th Cir. 2011).
10. 142 U.S. 47 (1895).
11. 406 U.S. 441 (1972).
12. The fact that a law enforcement officer made an honest mistake about an important fact in making an arrest would not necessarily invalidate the arrest. In the 1971 U.S. Supreme Court case of *Hill v. California*, 401 U.S. 797, 91 S. Ct. 1106, police made an "honest mistake" in arresting the wrong man. In the 1980 case of *United States v. Allen*, 629 F.2d 51 (D.C. Cir.), the appellate court held that "the case law establishes that an arrest based on actual assumptions later found erroneous may be valid if there is adequate basis in the record to determine the reasonableness of the officer's conduct in making the arrest." The U.S. Supreme Court heard another honest mistake case in 1987. In *Maryland v. Garrison*, 480 U.S. 79, 107 S. Ct. 1013, police officers obtained a search warrant for the third floor of a building, believing that there was only one apartment on that floor. Before they discovered that there were two apartments on that floor, police found heroin and drug paraphernalia in the apartment of another man (Garrison). The Supreme Court held that the evidence was lawfully obtained, adding another case to what is known as the *honest mistake exception*.

The following three examples are found in the New York Criminal Code Annotated Practice Commentary to Section 15.20, Effect of Ignorance or Mistake Upon Liability:

- A police officer having a warrant for the arrest of A mistakenly arrests B, who resembles A, and holds him in a police station for an hour before ascertaining his mistake and releasing him. The officer is not guilty of "unlawful imprisonment" (Section 135.05) because his mistake of fact "negatives a culpable mental state necessary for the commission of the offense," namely, "knowledge that the restriction is unlawful" (Section 135.00(1)).
- M has sexual intercourse with F, a mentally ill woman whose condition is not always apparent and is not known to or realized by M. Although M would be guilty of third-degree rape if he had realized F's condition, his unawareness is, by statute, expressly made a defense to the charge (Section 130.10).
- During a heated argument between A and B, B, a man with a reputation for violence and rumored to carry a pistol on occasion, suddenly places his hand in his bulging pocket, and A strikes him in the face and breaks his nose. Although B did not have a pistol and was merely reaching for a cigarette, A is not guilty of assault because his factual mistake was of a kind that supports a defense of justification. Section 35.15 (1).

13. 342 U.S. 246 (1952).
14. In a minority of states the defense of mistake of a victim's age in statutory rape charges is allowed. Some states make the defense available in all statutory rape cases; *see, e.g.,* K.R.S. § 510.030. In other states the defense is good only in cases where the underage victim made reasonable declarations that her age was over the statutory minimum for consent; *see, e.g.,* R.C.W.A. 9A.44.030. In still other states, the mistake of age defense is available only for lesser sexual offenses where the age of the victim is over 16, and the defendant is no more than four years older than the victim.
15. 592 F. Supp. 424 (E.D. Va. 1984).
16. 252 F.3d 647 (2d Cir. 2001).
17. *State v. Cameron*, 514 A2d 1302 (1986).
18. *State v. Souza*, 72 Haw. 246, 813 P.2d 1384 (1991).
19. 116 S. Ct. 2013 (1996).
20. 82 Cal. App. 778, 785, 256 P. 251, 254 (1927).
21. *Johnson v. State*, 379 A.2d 1129 (Del. 1977).
22. 43 Cal. App. 3d 823, 118 Cal. Rptr. 110 (1974).
23. 444 U.S. 394, 100 S. Ct. 624 (1980).
24. Blackstone, *4 Commentaries*, 30.
25. See Wisconsin Statute 939.46.
26. In the 1980 case of *United States v. Bailey* (444 U.S. 394 100 S. Ct. 624), the U.S. Supreme Court pointed out the distinctions between the defenses of duress and necessity as follows:

> Common law historically distinguished between the defenses of duress and necessity. Duress was said to excuse criminal conduct where the actor was under an unlawful threat of imminent death or serious bodily injury, which threat caused the actor to engage in conduct violating the literal terms of the criminal law. While the defense of duress covered the situation where the coercion had its source in the actions of other human beings, the defense of necessity, or choice of evils, traditionally covered the situation where physical forces beyond the actor's control rendered illegal conduct the lesser of two evils. Thus, where A destroyed a dike because B threatened to kill him if he did not, A would argue that he acted under duress, whereas if A destroyed the dike in order to protect more valuable property from flooding, A could claim a defense of necessity. See generally LaFave and Scott, Criminal Law, 2nd ed. (Belmont, Ca.: West/Wadsworth, 1986), pp. 374–384.

27. Model Penal Code, Section 3.02 (Justification Generally).
28. *U.S. v. Maxwell*, 254 F.3d 21(1st Cir. 2001). Protesters violating criminal law frequently argue that the law they are

protesting is the "greater evil." Examples of such unsuccessful claims are *Cyr v. State,* 887 S.W.2d 203 (Tex. App. 1994) (abortion); *Troen v. Oregon,* 501 U.S. 1232 (1991) (nuclear power plants); and *State v. Marley,* 509 P.2d 1095 (Haw. 1973) (the Vietnam War).

One court, in *United States v. Schoon,* 955 F2d 1238 (9th Cir. 1991), held that necessity can never be a defense in so-called indirect civil disobedience cases. These are cases in which the law violated is not the law being protested. The "greater harm" is thus not caused by the law violated but instead by some other law or governmental policy. Direct civil disobedience, where the defense of necessity might be available, occurs when the protesters violate the very law they are protesting. For example, if a law requires citizens to use lead paint on their houses, the harm caused by lead paint would likely exceed the harm caused by violating the law.

29. *Selected Writings of Justice Cardozo,* 390.

30. 2 All E.R. at p. 181 (1971).

31. 412 U.S. 470, 93 S. Ct. 2208 (1973).

32. *Williamson v. U.S.,* 207 U.S. 425, 453, 28 S. Ct. 163, 173 (1908).

33. *United States v. Batterjee,* 361 F.3d 1210 (9th Cir. 2004)(Fla. App. 1975).

34. The defense lawyer missed the boat on this case. He or she could have also had the statute declared invalid as being "void for vagueness." Everybody has to guess about what is meant by "near." Modern statutes now forbid demonstrations "in" a courthouse or within 200 or 300 feet of a courthouse. Such statutes do not violate "void for vagueness" (see Chapter 1).

35. *Id,* 361 F.3d at 1216.

36. 150 P.3d 755 (Cal. 2007).

37. 437 U.S. 82, 98 S. Ct. 2187 (1978).

38. 464 U.S. 501, 104 S. Ct. 819 (1984).

39. *Downum v. U.S.,* 372 U.S. 734, 83 S. Ct. 1033 (1963).

40. *Wade v. Hunter,* 336 U.S. 684, 69 S. Ct. 834 (1949).

41. 132 S. Ct. 2044 (2012).

42. *Westfall v. U.S.* 274 U.S. 256, 47 S. Ct. 629 (1927).

43. 359 U.S. 121, 79 S. Ct. 676 (1959).

44. In 1993, the United States prosecuted several Los Angeles police officers for civil rights violations arising out of a beating they gave Rodney King. In a previous, very controversial state prosecution, the same officers were acquitted of state criminal charges. Two of the officers, Koon and Powell, were convicted, and two were acquitted. The Double Jeopardy Clause did not prevent those convictions because of the dual sovereignty rule.

The famous videotape of the King beating, which showed that beating in great detail, was extensively used by the federal court in its sentencing decision. See *U.S. v. Koon,* 833 F. Supp. 769 (C.D. Cal. 1993). Koon and Powell were sentenced to 30 months in prison, based on various sentencing guidelines that indicated a downward departure from the 80- to 87-month sentence guidelines for their convictions.

The Ninth Circuit Court of Appeals reversed the downward departure made by the federal district court (see 34 F.3d 1416), but the U.S. Supreme Court essentially restored the original sentences. See *Koon v. United States,* 518 U.S. 81 (1996).

45. *Blockburger v. United States,* 284 U.S. 299, 304 (1932). Thus, a prosecution for auto theft barred prosecution for the lesser offense of joyriding, and vice versa. See *Brown v. Ohio,* 432 U.S. 161 (1977).

46. 243 P.3d 556 (Wash. App. 2011), *review denied* 253 P.3d 393 (Wash. 2011).

47. *Grady v. Corbin,* 495 U.S. 508 (1990).

48. Ibid.

49. *United States v. Dixon,* 509 U.S. 688 (1993).

50. 287 U.S. 435, 454, 53 S. Ct. 210, 217 (1932), separate opinion.

51. *Jacobson v. United States,* 503 U.S. 540 (1992).

52. *Mathews v. United States,* 485 U.S. 58 (1988).

53. 425 U.S. 484 (1976).

54. *United States v. Russell,* 411 U.S. 423 (1973).

55. 503 U.S. 540 (1992).

56. 356 U.S. 369 (1958).

57. *U.S. v. Russell,* 411 U.S. 423 (1973).

58. 485 U.S. 58, 108 S. Ct. 883 (1988). Examples of inconsistent defenses that were permitted when the evidence justified it are the following:

- In an 1896 murder case arising out of a gunfight in Indian Territory, the defense of self-defense was used, along with an instruction on manslaughter. Killing in the heat of passion is inconsistent with self-defense. *Stevenson v. United States,* 162 U.S. 313, 16 S. Ct. 839 (1896).

- In a 1970 rape case, the defendant was permitted to argue that the act did not take place and that the victim consented. *Johnson v. United States,* 426 F.2d 651 (D.C. Cir. 1970), *cert. granted,* 400 U.S. 864(1970), *cert. dismissed,* 401 U.S. 846 (1971).

59. 93 S. Ct. at 1642–43.

60. 425 U.S. at 495, n. 7.

61. *United States v. Marshank,* 777 F.Supp. 1507 (N.D. Cal. 1991).

62. A reverse buy or reverse sting scheme is one in which the government sells or attempts to sell an illegal drug rather than buy it. Because this conduct by the police could cause defense lawyers to use the entrapment or outrageous government conduct defenses, great caution should be used by law enforcement officers.

63. *Metcalf v. State,* 635 So. 2d 11 (Fla. 1994).

64. 454 F.2d 783 (9th Cir. 1971).

65. *State v. Tookes,* 699 P. 2d 983 (1985).

66. See *United States v. Miller,* 891 F.2d 1265 (7th Cir. 1989). One area where such operations are used by police is Internet chat rooms, where police officers present themselves as children in order to lure adults attempting to initiate sexual meetings with children into the police net. These operations have commonly been upheld as appropriate government conduct.

67. *People v. Uribe,* 132 Cal. Rptr. 3d 102 (Cal. App. 2011).

68. In the 1992 case of *State v. James* (484 N.W.2d 799), an undercover officer was standing in an area known for high drug activity and "sold" crack only to people who approached him. Eight such locations were used in Minneapolis to discourage buyers who came into high drug activity areas to buy drugs. The Minnesota Court of Appeals affirmed the defendant's conviction, pointing out that the state carried the burden of showing predisposition by the defendant and that the officer did not solicit or encourage the defendant in any way. See also the case of *United States v. Cea,* 963 F.2d 1027 (7th Cir. 1992).

69. The Federal Speedy Trial Act (18 U.S.C.A. 3161) sets a 70-day limit, which begins to run on the date of indictment

(§3161(c)(l)). See *Henderson v. United States,* 476 U.S. 321, 106 S. Ct. 1871 (1986).

70. 407 U.S. 514 (1972).

71. 404 U.S. 307, 92 S. Ct. 455 (1971).

72. 130 S. Ct. 1345 (2010).

73. 665 F.3d 701 (6th Cir. 2011).

74. *Ibid.* at 320, 92 S. Ct. at 463.

75. See *Toussie v. U.S.,* 397 U.S. 112, 114–115, 90 S. Ct. 858, 859–60 (1970).

Criminal Punishments

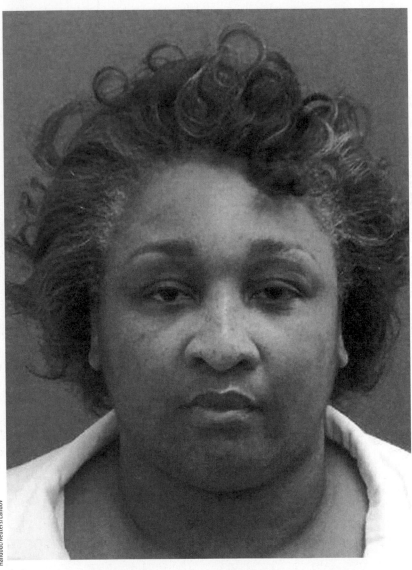

Kimberly McCarthy, sentenced to death for the 1997 brutal killing of a neighbor woman, was executed in Texas on June 26, 2013. She was the first woman executed in the U.S. since 2010. Since 1976, when the U.S. Supreme Court upheld the constitutionality of the death penalty, over 1,300 people have been executed in the U.S. Kimberly McCarthy was the 500th person executed in Texas since 1982, when the current Texas death penalty statute was enacted.

OUTLINE

LEARNING OBJECTIVES

In this chapter we examine the kinds of punishments that may be imposed for violation of a criminal law, and some limitations on those punishments. The learning objectives for this chapter are the following:

- Know the text of the Cruel and Unusual Punishment Clause.

- Explain the relationship between the Sixth Amendment and sentencing provisions that permit a judge to determine when an enhanced sentence should be given a criminal defendant.

- State the present status of the Federal Sentencing Guidelines.

- Identify the procedures a school official must follow before imposing corporal punishment on a student.

- Explain why the death penalty was declared unconstitutional in *Furman v. Georgia*.

- Identify at least three groups of persons who cannot be given the death penalty.

- State the present rule on the imposition of life without parole sentences for juveniles.

- Describe the kinds of evidence that must be produced if the prosecution seeks imposition of the death penalty after a jury has found the defendant guilty of the crime charged.

- Define "three strikes" laws and list the common characteristics of such laws.

On June 6, in Palmdale, California, Rodrigo Caballero, a 16-year-old member of the "Lancas" gang, opened fire on three boys he believed to be members of the "Val Verde Park" gang. He wounded one of the boys, who was seriously injured but survived the shooting. After a trial on three counts of attempted murder, and related gang offenses, Caballero was sentenced to consecutive prison terms that would make him eligible for parole after 110 years. A California appeals court affirmed the conviction and sentence.

In August of 2012 the California Supreme Court, relying on the U.S. Supreme Court's decisions in *Graham v. Florida* and *Miller v. Alabama* (discussed in this chapter), reversed the court of appeals, and remanded the case for resentencing in which Caballero would be provided with "a meaningful opportunity to obtain release based on demonstrated maturity and rehabilitation." The court also invited all other juveniles currently imprisoned in California under similar sentences to file the necessary court papers to have their sentences reviewed or changed where appropriate.[1]

In this chapter we learn the rules governing the imposition of various kinds of punishments, from simple fines to the death penalty. We will also learn some of the limitations the U.S. Constitution places on punishments for violation of criminal laws.

Punishments Used in Early England

The criminal punishments used hundreds of years ago in England and elsewhere in Europe were very severe. In England alone, more than 200 offenses were punishable by death. Condemned criminals were usually hanged, although occasionally they were beheaded, quartered, or drawn (dragged along the ground by the tail of a horse). Until 1790 burning continued to be the punishment inflicted on women for treason, high or petty (which later included not only the murder by a wife of her husband and the murder of a master or mistress by a servant but also several offenses against the king). In practice, women were strangled before they were burned; this, however, depended on the executioner. In one notorious case, a woman was actually burned alive for murdering her husband, the executioner being afraid to strangle her because he was caught by the fire.[2]

For lesser offenses, various forms of mutilations—such as cropping (clipping of the ears), blinding, amputation of the hand, and branding—were common. The whipping post and the pillory were often used, as were fines and imprisonment. The pillory is a frame erected on a post. The offender's head and hands are placed in the open holes, and the top board is then moved into place, immobilizing the offender in a standing position.

Practices Used in England to Avoid Severe Penalties

benefit of clergy A medieval limit on capital punishment. People convicted of a capital crime entitled to claim the benefit of clergy (by the fifteenth century, anyone who could read) could not be executed for their offense. By the end of the eighteenth century, the privilege had been eliminated for most crimes.

For various reasons, including the severity of penalties, England developed procedures to avoid severe penalties. By usage and custom, the following came into practice.

Benefit of Clergy[3]　In the twelfth century, a controversy arose about whether priests accused of felonies should be tried by the royal courts or the ecclesiastical courts. It was decided that the royal courts could try priests but could not put them to death for the first felony conviction. This privilege was known as the **benefit of clergy,** and by the end of the Middle Ages, it was extended to all laypeople who could read.

Colonial Americans followed the lead of the English in terms of punishment. As punishment for lesser offenses, various forms of mutilation, such as cropping (clipping of the ears), blinding, amputation of the hand, and branding were common. The whipping post and the pillory were often used, as were fines and imprisonment. Stocks like the one shown here were situated in very public places so that shame and ridicule by the community were a strong part of the punishment.

The test to determine who could claim the privilege of benefit of clergy was a person's ability to recite the first verse of Psalm 51: "Have mercy upon me, O God, after Thy great goodness." This came to be known as the *neck verse* because it saved the accused from hanging. The only punishment that could then be inflicted was imprisonment for one year and an *M* branded on the brawn of the left thumb to prevent the criminal from claiming the privilege again. For many years, only three crimes were excluded from benefit of clergy (high treason, highway robbery, and the willful burning of a house), but in 1769, Blackstone noted that "among the variety of actions which men are daily liable to commit no less than 160 have been declared by Act of Parliament to be felonies without benefit of clergy."[4]

sanctuary In the Middle Ages in England, a sanctuary was a religious place where criminals could take refuge. The concept of sanctuary later broadened to include asylum for refugees.

The Law of Sanctuary and the Right of Asylum   In the Middle Ages, **sanctuary** was common. The place of sanctuary was generally a church or other religious place. Criminals who were permitted to take refuge in a church or monastery could not be removed from it. Even after sanctuary as an institution was abolished, a system developed in England by which the refugee took an oath of abjuration before a coroner, admitted guilt, and swore to leave the country for life to an agreed-upon place (often the American colonies or, later, Australia). Sanctuary was abolished in England in 1623; however, a modified form reportedly continued in England for another century.[5] Sanctuary never became part of the legal system of the American colonies or of the newly formed United States of America.

The United States, however, recognizes and grants right of asylum to refugees from other countries who can show a "well-founded fear of persecution."[6] Over the last fifty years, the United States has granted asylum to many thousands of refugees. Two famous refugee cases illustrate this practice:

- After the Soviet invasion of Hungary in 1956, the United States gave asylum to Jozsef Cardinal Mindszenty in the American embassy in Budapest for 15 years until the Soviets permitted the cardinal to leave Hungary.
- In April 2102 a Chinese dissident, Chen Cuangcheng, escaped from house arrest in China and was granted asylum by the U.S. Embassy in China. On May 19, 2012, after negotiations with the Chinese government, Chen was permitted to leave China for the United States to attend college.

Transportation   People convicted of crimes in England could be pardoned if they agreed to be transported to a colony to do hard labor for a number of years. The first convicts were sent abroad to America in 1655. By the time of the American Revolution, England was sending overseas some 2,000 convicts a year.

After the American Revolution, Australia became the principal place to which prisoners were sent under the condition of the pardon. Over the years, approximately 100,000 prisoners were sent to America and an equal number to Australia.[7] Australia and other British colonies strongly objected to the practice of transporting convicts, which was gradually abolished between 1853 and 1864. Imprisonment in England and hard labor on public works were then substituted as punishment.[8]

Punishment Used in Early America

Blackstone points out that English criminal law and punishments before the American Revolution were fairly civilized by comparison with those of the rest of Europe. U.S. Supreme Court Justice Thurgood Marshall made the following observations in comparing **capital punishment** in the American colonies with its use in England:

capital punishment
Inflicting deadly injury as punishment for criminal conduct.

> Capital punishment was not as common a penalty in the American Colonies. "The Capitall Lawes of New-England," dating from 1636, were drawn by the Massachusetts Bay Colony and are the first written expression of capital offenses known to exist in this country. These laws make the following crimes capital offenses: idolatry, witchcraft, blasphemy, murder, assault in sudden anger, sodomy, buggery, adultery, statutory rape, rape, man stealing, perjury in a capital trial, and rebellion. Each crime is accompanied by a reference to the Old Testament to indicate its source. It is not known with any certainty exactly when, or even if, these laws were enacted as drafted; and, if so, just how vigorously these laws were enforced. We do know that the other Colonies had a variety of laws that spanned the spectrum of severity.

> By the eighteenth century, the list of crimes became much less theocratic and much more secular. In the average colony, there were 12 capital crimes. This was far fewer than existed in England, and part of the reason was that there was a scarcity of labor in the Colonies.[9]

The Constitutional Limitation on Punishment

The Eighth Amendment of the U.S. Constitution, ratified in 1791 as part of the Bill of Rights, provides that "excessive bail shall not be required, nor excessive fines imposed, nor cruel and unusual punishments inflicted." Two members of Congress opposed passage of this amendment. One stated,

> What is meant by the term excessive bail? Who are to be the judges? What is understood by excessive fines? It lies with the court to determine. No cruel and unusual punishment is to be inflicted; it is sometimes necessary to hang a man, villains often deserve whipping, and perhaps having their ears cut off; but are we in the future to be prevented from inflicting these punishments because they are cruel? If a more lenient mode of correcting vice and deterring others from the commission of it could be invented, it would be very prudent in the Legislature to adopt it; but until we have some security that this will be done, we ought not be restrained from making necessary laws by any declaration of this kind.[10]

cruel and unusual punishment Under the Eighth Amendment, a limitation on punishment for criminal conduct.

About **cruel and unusual punishment**, Justice William J. Brennan stated in 1972,

> [T]he Cruel and Unusual Punishments Clause, like the other great clauses of the Constitution, is not susceptible of precise definition. Yet we know that the values and ideals it embodies are basic to our scheme of government. And we know also that the Clause imposes upon this Court the duty, when the issue is properly presented, to determine the constitutional validity of a challenged punishment, whatever that punishment may be.[11]

proportionality An objective evaluation of the appropriateness of a punishment for a particular crime.

The basis courts have used to evaluate the "constitutionality of a challenged punishment" historically has been the **proportionality** principle. In the case of *Pulley v. Harris*, the U.S. Supreme Court defined the manner of evaluating the appropriateness or proportionality of a punishment for a particular crime:

> Traditionally, proportionality has been used with reference to an abstract evaluation of the appropriateness of a sentence for a particular crime. Looking to the gravity of the offense and the severity of the penalty, to sentences imposed for other crimes, and to sentencing practices in other jurisdictions, this Court has occasionally struck down punishments as inherently disproportionate, and therefore cruel and unusual, when imposed for a particular crime or category of crime. See, e.g., *Solem v. Helm*, 463 U.S. 277 (1983); *Enmund v. Florida*, 458 U.S. 782 (1982); *Coker v. Georgia*, 433 U.S. 584 (1977). The death penalty is not in all cases a disproportionate penalty in this sense.[12]

The *Solem* case cited above by the Supreme Court appeared to have held that the Cruel and Unusual Punishment Clause required courts to conduct a proportionality review in all cases, including those in which there was an imposition of a non-capital sentence. Such a review, *Solem* said, included considerations of (1) the gravity of the offense and the harshness of the penalty, (2) sentences imposed for similar crimes in the same jurisdiction, and (3) sentences imposed for the same crime in other jurisdictions.

Decisions of the U.S. Supreme Court since *Solem* was decided cast some doubt on the status of the proportionality test set forth in that case. In *Harmelin v. Michigan*,[13] and *Ewing v. California*[14] the Supreme Court expressed disagreement on the continued force of the *Solem* holding. Two members of the Court in each case took the position that the Eighth Amendment did not require proportionality review in non-capital cases. While the other justices disagreed with that position, they nonetheless agreed that before the tests adopted in *Solem* can be applied to a non-capital sentence, a court must first determine that the sentence meets the "grossly disproportionate" test. Only if it does is the sentence then subjected to the tests set forth in *Solem*. Moreover, in *Harmelin* the Court also held that courts reviewing non-capital sentences need not make the kind of inter-jurisdiction comparison suggested by the Court in *Solem*.

Since the decision in *Solem,* decisions reversing prison sentences under a proportionality review have been rare, and none have been issued by the U.S. Supreme Court. While the Supreme Court did in 2010 and 2012 reverse life sentences imposed on juvenile offenders under an Eighth Amendment analysis, it did not base the decision on proportionality. See *Graham v. Florida,* 130 S. Ct. 2011 (2010), and *Miller v. Alabama*, 132 S. Ct. 2455 (2012), discussed later in this chapter. As a result, though *Solem* has not been reversed, its continued viability is unclear.

Sentencing and Jury Trials

In 2000, the U.S. Supreme Court decided the case of *Apprendi v. New Jersey* (530 U.S. 466). In *Apprendi,* the Court held that any fact that increases the penalty for the crime charged must be submitted to the jury and proved beyond a reasonable doubt. It thus held unconstitutional a New Jersey hate crime statute that permitted the trial judge to increase the sentence of a convicted defendant if the judge found by a preponderance of the evidence that the defendant acted in a manner intended to intimidate the victim. The *Apprendi* opinion caused many changes in sentencing procedures and also resulted in many reversals of sentences handed down by trial judges. Many state sentencing systems, as well as the Federal Sentencing Guidelines, permitted a judge to make fact findings on questions that determined whether the sentence for the crime charged would be enhanced or reduced. After *Apprendi,* judges could make fact findings, but only if they were "sentencing factors" used to determine a sentence within a range provided in the statute establishing the minimum and maximum sentences that could be imposed for the crime charged: "… judge-found sentencing factors cannot increase the maximum sentence a defendant might otherwise receive based purely on the facts found by the jury." *United States v. O'Brien,* 130 S. Ct. 2169, 2175 (2010).

In *O'Brien* the U.S. Supreme Court stated that a fact was a "sentencing factor" only if it was not an "element" of the offence charged. In *O'Brien* defendants were charged with four counts in violation of 18 U.S.C. § 924(c), which prohibits the use or carrying of a firearm in a crime of violence or drug trafficking offense.

The minimum sentence for a violation is 5 years in prison. However, § 924(c)(1)(B)(ii) provides that if the firearm is a "machine gun," the minimum sentence is 30 years in prison. The prosecution dismissed one of the counts, the count that alleged use of a machine gun. After the defendants pled guilty to the remaining counts, the prosecution contended the fact that the defendants used a machine gun could be determined by the judge as a "sentence enhancement" factor, and if found by the judge would make the 30-year minimum sentence applicable. The trial judge disagreed, and sentenced the defendants within the 5-year minimum statute.

The prosecution appealed, but the Supreme Court agreed with the trial court. It held the "fact" of the use of a machine gun was an "element" of the offense, and not merely a "sentencing factor." The Court found that the immense danger of a machine gun, the moral depravity of a person choosing to use such a weapon, and the substantial increase in the maximum possible sentence meant the use of a machine gun was an element of the offense, and must be proved by the prosecution beyond a reasonable doubt. 130 S. Ct. at 2175.

Finally, in a June 2013 decision, the Supreme Court used the reasoning of the *Apprendi* decision to reverse *Harris v. United States*, 536 U.S. 545 (2002), which had held that facts that increase the mandatory minimum sentence, but not the maximum sentence, could be treated as "sentencing factors" and found by the trial judge, not the jury. In *Alleyne v. United States*, 133 S. Ct. 2151, the Court held that a fact that increases the mandatory minimum sentence (in *Alleyne* "brandishing" a weapon during a robbery), but not the maximum sentence possible, must be determined by the jury using the reasonable doubt standard.

Blakely v. Washington, 124 S. Ct. 2531 (2004), applied the reasoning of *Apprendi,* which involved specific statutory language that permitted a judge to find facts that increased the maximum sentence for a crime, to state sentencing systems. In *Blakely,* a defendant pled guilty to second-degree kidnapping and use of a firearm. After 3 days of hearings before the trial judge, the defendant was sentenced to a prison term more than 3 years longer than the maximum sentence for the crime charged, based on the trial judge's finding that the defendant acted with "deliberate cruelty." Under Washington State sentencing guidelines, a finding of deliberate cruelty permitted the sentencing judge to increase the sentence. The Washington Court of Appeals affirmed the conviction and sentence (47 P.3d 149). The Supreme Court granted certiorari.

The Supreme Court held the sentence was invalid under the Sixth Amendment, because the sentence imposed exceeded the maximum sentence possible based solely on the facts found by the jury. The Court held that the defendant was entitled to a jury trial on the facts supporting the finding that he acted with deliberate cruelty. Because the trial judge, rather than the jury, made the finding that the defendant acted with deliberate cruelty, the resulting sentence was invalid, the Court held.

In 2005 the Supreme Court decided the case of *United States v. Booker,* 125 S. Ct. 738. In *Booker,* the Court held that under the holdings of *Apprendi* and *Blakeley,* the Federal Sentencing Guidelines violated the Sixth Amendment's right to jury trials in criminal cases.

U.S. SUPREME COURT CASES STATING THE CONSTITUTIONAL LIMITATIONS ON PUNISHMENT

Coker v. Georgia
Supreme Court of the United States (1977), 433 U.S. 584, 97 S. Ct. 2861

The defendant escaped from a Georgia prison where he had been serving sentences for murder, rape, kidnapping, and aggravated assault. While committing an armed robbery and another offense, he raped an adult woman. The defendant was convicted of rape, armed robbery, and other offenses and was sentenced to death on the rape charge. The U.S. Supreme Court reversed the sentence of death, holding as follows:

> That question, with respect to rape of an adult woman, is now before us. We have concluded that a sentence of death is grossly disproportionate and excessive punishment for the crime of rape and is therefore forbidden by the Eighth Amendment as cruel and unusual punishment.

State of Louisiana ex rel. Francis v. Resweber
Supreme Court of the United States (1947), 329 U.S. 459, 67 S. Ct. 374

Because of an accidental failure of equipment, the defendant was not executed in the first attempt. The Court held that there was no intention to inflict unnecessary pain, and even though the defendant had been subjected to a current of electricity, this did not prevent the state from executing him in the second attempt. In the 1972 case of *Furman v. Georgia*, the U.S. Supreme Court stated that "had the failure been intentional, however, the punishment would have been, like torture, so degrading and indecent as to amount to a refusal to accord the criminal human status."

Robinson v. California
Supreme Court of the United States (1962), 370 U.S. 660, 82 S. Ct. 1417

California enacted a law making narcotics addiction in itself a crime. The defendant received a ninety-day sentence for being a narcotics addict. The Court held that a state may not punish a

A majority of the Court concluded that the mandatory provisions of the Guidelines, which required judges to enhance sentences when certain facts were found by the judge, such as the quantity of the drug possessed by a defendant in a drug case, were unconstitutional. A different majority held, however, that federal judges could use the non-mandatory provisions of the Guidelines as reference points to help reach a sentencing decision.

As a result, sentences may raise a problem under *Blakely* or *Booker* in either of two ways: in one, the sentencing judge may use facts found only by the judge to enhance the defendant's sentence; in the other, the judge may use the Federal Sentencing Guidelines as mandatory rather than discretionary. The first result is unconstitutional under *Blakely*; the second is prohibited by *Booker*. See, for example, *Villafranco v. United States,* 2006 WL 1049114 (D. Utah 2006).

Lower courts have addressed one question left open in *Booker,* namely, the extent the decision applied retroactively to sentences handed down before *Booker* was decided. While the Court held that the decision was applicable to person for being "mentally ill, or a leper, or ... afflicted with a venereal disease" or for being addicted to narcotics. "Even one day in prison would be a cruel and unusual punishment for the 'crime' of having a common cold."

Roberts v. Louisiana
Supreme Court of the United States (1977), 431 U.S. 633, 97 S. Ct. 1993

The Supreme Court held that the fact that the murder victim was a police officer performing his regular duties may be regarded as an aggravating circumstance. The Court held that there is a special interest in affording protection to those public servants who regularly risk their lives to safeguard other people and property. However, a Louisiana statute that provided for a mandatory sentence of death for the crime of first-degree murder of a police officer and that did not allow consideration for particularized mitigating factors was held unconstitutional. The Supreme Court held that such a statute invites "jurors to disregard their oaths and choose a verdict for a lesser offense whenever they feel the death penalty is inappropriate."

Woodson v. North Carolina
Supreme Court of the United States (1976), 428 U.S. 280, 96 S. Ct. 2978

In holding a North Carolina death penalty statute unconstitutional because it provided for an automatic death penalty in all first-degree murder cases, the Court held that "the Eighth Amendment draws much of its meaning from 'the evolving standards of decency that mark the progress of a maturing society.'" The Court concluded that North Carolina's mandatory death penalty statute varied "markedly from contemporary standards."

all sentences that were not final when the decision was handed down, it did not decide what application the decision had for other sentences. Most courts considering the constitutionality of sentences that were final before *Booker* was decided have held the decision was not applicable to such sentences when collateral review was sought under statutes like 28 U.S.C. § 2255, the federal post-conviction relief statute. Generally speaking, when the Supreme Court announces a new rule of constitutional dimension like that in *Apprendi* or *Booker,* unless the Court holds that the rule is retroactive, it is not applicable to cases already final when the rule was announced.

Except for the constitutional dimension limitations on sentencing discussed above, each state has its own system of determining the appropriate sentence for one convicted of a crime. These systems usually give the sentencing judge some discretion within a range set by the legislature. Some common characteristics of state sentencing systems include the following:

Sentences Can Be

Concurrent or Consecutive Sentences A defendant ordered to serve two years consecutively for conviction of two counts of a crime must serve the sentences one after the other, for a total of 4 years. If the sentences are to be served concurrently, they are served at the same time, for a total of two years for the two-count conviction.

Determinate or Indeterminate A sentence of a specific period (e.g., 30 days in jail) is a determinate sentence, and must be fully served, less time off for good behavior. A sentence of 3 to 5 years in prison is an example of an indeterminate sentence, with the minimum and maximum time to be served.

Suspended Sentence A person receiving a sentence like 3 to 5 years in prison could have the sentence suspended based on the person's agreement to commit to the completion of a drug treatment program and not be arrested or convicted of any other crime. Failure to comply with any of the conditions could result in the imposition of the original sentence.

Aggravating and Mitigating Factors Pre-sentence reports prepared by a state agency play an important role in the final sentence. These reports will present the defendant's background and detail aggravating and mitigating factors. A long criminal record would be an aggravating factor while no previous criminal record would be a mitigating factor.

Other Sentencing Laws

Truth in Sentencing Laws In 1984 the federal government passed the Truth in Sentencing law (TIS), which encouraged states, by providing money for prison costs, to pass sentencing laws that guaranteed a defendant sentenced to, for example, a 10-year prison term would serve close to that entire time rather than just a few years. Under TIS laws, parole is abolished and an offender would be given a set determinate prison sentence, followed by a period of extended supervision similar to parole. If a violation of the supervision rules occurred, a reconfinement hearing could be held, and the person could be returned to prison.

The Florida Anti-Murder Act In 2007 Florida passed the Anti-Murder Act, Ch. 2007-2, § 5, Laws of Florida, March 12, 2007. Under the terms of this act, any violent offender on probation who violates the terms of his or her probation or commits another felony is immediately arrested and detained until a hearing is held on the violation. If the violation is upheld, the offender is returned to prison. Florida allocated $21.8 million to pay the expected increases in prison costs this new act would cause over the next 3 years. The law also expanded the authority of Florida judges to impose maximum prison sentences under Florida sentencing guidelines.

Corporal Punishment

corporal punishment
Inflicting nondeadly physical injury as punishment for criminal conduct.

Corporal punishment was used as criminal punishment in the early history of the United States. Mutilations, such as cutting off ears and various types of branding, were discontinued many decades ago. Whipping, however, continued in some states into the early 1900s. The Eighth Circuit Court of Appeals observed that in 1968 only two states permitted the use of the strap as punishment. As a result of the Eighth Circuit Court's decision in the case of *Jackson v. Bishop,* whipping as a form of punishment was discontinued in the remaining two states. In the *Jackson* case, the court held:

> We have no difficulty in reaching the conclusion that the use of the strap in the penitentiaries of Arkansas is punishment which, in this last third of the 20th century, runs afoul of the Eighth Amendment; that the strap's use, irrespective of any precautionary conditions which may be imposed, offends contemporary

concepts of decency and human dignity and precepts of civilization which we profess to possess; and that it also violates those standards of good conscience and fundamental fairness enunciated by this court in the *Carey* and *Lee* cases.[15]

The Use of Corporal Punishment in Schools

In the case of *Ingraham v. Wright,* the U.S. Supreme Court considered the relationship between the Cruel and Unusual Punishment Clause and the use of corporal punishment in public schools. The Court first observed that no general rule prohibited corporal punishment in schools: "The prevalent rule in this country today privileges such force as a teacher or administrator 'reasonably' believes to be necessary for [the child's] proper control, training or education."[16]

In holding that the Eighth Amendment's Cruel and Unusual Punishment Clause is not applicable to the use of corporal punishment for disciplinary purposes in the public schools, the Court held:

> The schoolchild has little need for the protection of the Eighth Amendment. Though attendance may not always be voluntary, the public school remains an open institution. Except perhaps when very young, the child is not physically restrained from leaving school during school hours; and at the end of the school day, the child is invariably free to return home. Even while at school, the child brings with him the support of family and friends and is rarely apart from teachers and other pupils who may witness and protest any instances of mistreatment.
>
> The openness of the public school and its supervision by the community af ford significant safeguards against the kinds of abuses from which the Eighth Amendment protects the prisoner. In virtually every community where corporal punishment is permitted in the schools, these safeguards are reinforced by the legal constraints of the common law. Public school teachers and administrators are privileged at common law to inflict only such corporal punishment as is reasonably necessary for the proper education and discipline of the child; any punishment going beyond the privilege may result in both civil and criminal liability.... As long as the schools are open to public scrutiny, there is no reason to believe that the common law constraints will not effectively remedy and deter excesses such as those alleged in this case.
>
> We conclude that when public school teachers or administrators impose disciplinary corporal punishment, the Eighth Amendment is inapplicable.

Ingraham continues to be the law today, and corporal punishment continues to be meted out in schools. Eighteen states continue to permit the use of corporal punishment, usually paddling with a wooden or plastic paddle. The most recent state to abolish the practice, New Mexico, did so in 2011. The U.S. Department of Education, Office for Civil Rights, collected data for 2008, and estimates that about 223,190 children are subjected to corporal punishment in public schools each year.

In *Sandin v. Conner,*[17] the U.S. Supreme Court stated that although the Eighth Amendment may not apply to school punishments, where children are sent to public schools "arbitrary corporal punishments represents an invasion of personal security." Since that decision, some lower federal courts have interpreted the *Ingraham* decision as applying only to Eighth Amendment cruel and unusual punishment claims. Other claims based on Fourteenth Amendment procedural and substantive due process may be possible, these courts hold. See, e.g., *Preschooler II v. Clark County Bd. of Trustees*,[18] where the court held that a teacher's slapping of an autistic child could qualify as excessive force and a violation of the Fourth and Fourteenth Amendments.

procedural due process A claim under the Fourteenth Amendment that there is an absence of fair procedures regulating state conduct.

Procedural due process claims under the Fourteenth Amendment are based on the absence of fair procedures regulating state conduct. For example, if a school district permitted corporal punishment without a prior determination of some violation of school rules by the student, the student's procedural due process rights would be violated.[19] Moreover, even if the school had fair procedures regulating such punishment, procedural due process could be violated if the state had no adequate means for a student to seek redress from a school or teacher who violated those procedures.[20]

substantive due process A claim under the Fourteenth Amendment that state conduct is so brutal, demeaning, and harmful as to shock the conscience.

Substantive due process claims under the Fourteenth Amendment are based on state conduct that is so brutal, demeaning, and harmful as to shock the conscience.[21] Almost all the federal courts of appeal have concluded that excessive corporal punishment by a school official can give rise to a Fourteenth Amendment substantive due process claim.[22]

An example of a substantive due process claim can be found in *Neal v. Fulton County Board of Education*, a decision of the Eleventh Circuit Court of Appeals. In *Neal*, a student was seriously injured when the varsity football coach struck him in the eye with a metal weight lock as punishment for fighting with another student. The court concluded that the coach intentionally used an excessive amount of force that presented a reasonably foreseeable risk of serious bodily injury.[23]

In *Garcia v. Miera*, the U.S. Court of Appeals for the Tenth Circuit summarized the law concerning school punishments:

> We thus envision three categories of corporal punishment. Punishments that do not exceed the traditional common law standard of reasonableness are not actionable; punishments that exceed the common law standard without adequate state remedies violate procedural due process rights; and finally, punishments that are so grossly excessive as to be shocking to the conscience violate substantive due process rights, without regard to the adequacy of state remedies.[24]

The Use of Corporal Punishment in Prisons

The use of corporal punishment against inmates of prisons is subject to Eighth Amendment cruel and unusual punishment claims. Unlike school students, prison inmates have none of the "community and legal constraints" that provide safeguards against the sort of abuses the Eighth Amendment prohibits.[25]

Eighth Amendment claims by prison inmates have both objective and subjective requirements. The inmate must show that the punishment failed the Eighth Amendment's proportionality test (the objective test) and also that the official administering the punishment possessed the requisite mental intent (the subjective test).[26] An example of such a punishment can be found in *Hope v. Pelzer*,[27] where the U.S. Supreme Court held that chaining a prisoner to a hitching post for seven hours without a water break or bathroom break violated the Eighth Amendment. The Court held that safety concerns were not present once the inmate had been subdued, and that the conduct of the guards supervising the punishment showed the gratuitous infliction of wanton and unnecessary pain.

Capital Punishment

The death penalty was widely accepted at the time the U.S. Constitution and the Bill of Rights were ratified. The only reference to capital punishment in the Constitution is found in the Fifth Amendment, which reads: "No person shall be held to answer for a capital, or otherwise infamous crime, unless...." In the 1972 case of *Furman v. Georgia,* death penalty laws in all states were struck down as "arbitrary and capricious" by the U.S. Supreme Court.[28] The Court found that the imposition of the death sentence varied greatly from case to case, and that it was being administered without any reasonable standards for determining when it would be imposed. The Court stated that states wishing to use the death penalty must establish objective standards for determining when the death penalty will be imposed.

By 1976, when the Supreme Court upheld the death penalty statute passed by the Georgia legislature, thirty-five states had enacted capital punishment statutes, and in one state, California, the voters adopted a constitutional amendment authorizing capital punishment. The state statutes enacted responded to *Furman v. Georgia* by addressing these issues:

- The state statute must determine which crime (or crimes) may be punished by the death penalty, whether it will be the trial judge or jury who will make the decision to impose it, by what method it will be inflicted, and the appellate process used to review the sentence.
- The statute must require juries or judges considering the death penalty to make findings of statutory **aggravating circumstances** to justify the imposition of the death penalty and also make findings of the **mitigating circumstances** that would weigh against the imposition of the death penalty.

aggravating circumstances A consideration in imposing the death penalty that judges and juries must make a finding of statutory aggravating circumstances to justify the penalty.

mitigating circumstances A consideration in imposing the death penalty that judges and juries must make findings of the mitigating circumstances that would weigh against the imposition of the death penalty.

Death Penalty Laws After *Furman v. Georgia*

Furman v. Georgia invalidated death penalty statutes in forty-one states, as well as the death penalty in federal crimes for which the death penalty could then be imposed. In a 1984 case, the U.S. Supreme Court observed that

> In responding to (*Furman v. Georgia*), roughly two-thirds of the States promptly redrafted their capital sentencing statutes in an effort to limit jury discretion and avoid arbitrary and inconsistent results. All of the new statutes provide for automatic appeal of death sentences. Most, such as Georgia's, require the reviewing court, to some extent at least, to determine whether, considering both the crime and the defendant, the sentence is disproportionate to that imposed in similar cases. Not every State has adopted such a procedure. In some States, such as Florida, the appellate court performs proportionality review despite the absence of a statutory requirement; in others, such as California and Texas, it does not.[29]

In 1976, the U.S. Supreme Court reviewed the new death penalty statutes of Georgia,[30] Florida,[31] and Texas.[32] In the 1984 California death penalty case of *Pulley v. Harris,*[33] the U.S. Supreme Court quoted from its 1976 *Jurek v. Texas* decision in affirming the death penalty procedure used by California:

IMPORTANT RECENT U.S. SUPREME COURT DEATH PENALTY DECISIONS

- In *Ring v. Arizona,* 536 U.S. 584 (2002), the Court held that a state capital sentencing procedure that permitted the sentencing judge to make the factual determination of the aggravating and mitigating circumstances present violated the Sixth Amendment's right of trial by jury. Factual questions bearing on the imposition of the death sentence or life imprisonment must be decided by the jury, the Court held.

- In *Smith v. Spisak,* 558 U.S. 139 (2010), the Court stated the procedure to be followed when deliberating the death sentence: The jury must unanimously find that the prosecution proved each aggravating circumstance beyond a reasonable doubt, but each juror may consider any relevant evidence of mitigating factors. The jury must then unanimously find the aggravating circumstances proved outweigh the mitigating circumstances.

- In *Ford v. Wainright,* 477 U.S. 399 (1986), the Court held that the Eighth Amendment prohibits the execution of a prisoner who is insane at the time of the execution.

  Courts differed on what constitutes "insane" for Eighth Amendment purposes, though most followed a two-part test referenced in *Ford:* a defendant is not competent to be executed unless (1) he is aware of the punishment he is about to suffer, and (2) he knows why he is to suffer the punishment. In *Panetti v. Dretke,* 448 F.3d 815 (5th Cir. 2006), the Fifth Circuit Court of Appeals held that a defendant on Texas's death row was not insane, even though he suffered from severe paranoid delusions and believed the state really wanted him executed as punishment for preaching the Gospel. The Court concluded *Ford* did not require that the defendant "rationally understand" the reason for his execution. It is enough, the Court said, that he was "aware" of those reasons. The Supreme Court reversed, holding that the District Court should have considered the defendant's claims of delusions before concluding he was competent and sane. See *Panetti v. Qurterman,* 127 S. Ct. 2842 (2007).

- In *Atkins v. Virginia,* 536 U.S. 304 (2002), the Court held that the Cruel and Unusual Punishment Clause of the Eighth Amendment prohibited imposition of the death penalty on

Texas' capital sentencing procedures, like those of Georgia and Florida, do not violate the Eighth and Fourteenth Amendments. By narrowing its definition of capital murder, Texas has essentially said that there must be at least one statutory aggravating circumstance in a first-degree murder case before a death sentence may even be considered. By authorizing the defense to bring before the jury at the separate sentencing hearing whatever mitigating circumstances relating to the individual defendant can be adduced, Texas has ensured that the sentencing jury will have adequate guidance to enable it to perform its sentencing function. By providing prompt judicial review of the jury's decision in a court with statewide jurisdiction, Texas has provided a means to promote the evenhanded, rational, and consistent imposition of death sentences under law. Because this system serves to assure that sentences of death will not be "wantonly" or "freakishly" imposed, it does not violate the Constitution.

Since states restored the death penalty in 1976, 1,321 people have been executed in the United States. In that same period 142 inmates have been exonerated based defendants with mental retardation.[a] In 2004, the Court held in *Tennard v. Dretke* (124 S. Ct. 2562) that evidence of mental retardation is inherently mitigating in a capital case, whether or not the defendant has shown a nexus between his mental capacity and the crime committed.

- In *Baze v. Rees,* 553 U.S. 35 (2008), the Court upheld the validity of the lethal injection method of execution. The thirty-seven states using the lethal injection method all use a three-step "cocktail" for the execution. The first drug is an anesthetic, the second causes muscle paralysis, and the third causes cardiac arrest.

- In *Sattazahn v. Pennsylvania,* 537 U.S. 101 (2003), the Court held that the Double Jeopardy Clause does not bar a state from imposing the death sentence after a defendant convicted of murder and sentenced to life imprisonment appeals the conviction and gets the conviction reversed. On retrial and subsequent conviction, the death sentence may be imposed.

- In *Kennedy v. Louisiana,* 128 S. Ct. 2641 (2008), the Supreme Court invalidated a Louisiana statute permitting imposition of the death penalty for the rape of a child. Because the rape did not result in death, and was not intended to cause death, the Court said the cruel and unusual punishment did not permit imposition of the death penalty. The Court noted that since Louisiana adopted the statute in 1995, only six other states followed suit, indicating a national consensus existed against use of the death penalty in such cases.

[a] The *Atkins* court did not determine Atkins was retarded. Rather, it remanded the case to Virginia state court for a factual hearing on that issue. Atkins committed the murder for which he was sentenced to death in 1996, when he was 18 and had just dropped out of high school, having failed for the third time to pass the tenth grade. When Atkins was tested during his first trial in 1998 he scored 59 on an IQ test used in Virginia criminal cases, well below the cutoff score of 70 used for determination of retardation. However, when tested in November 2004 he scored 76 on the prosecution's test and 74 on the defense's test. Atkins's mental competency was submitted to a jury in 2005, and the jury concluded he was not retarded. In 2006 the Virginia Supreme Court reversed that decision, finding that the trial court erred by admitting improper expert testimony by the prosecution's expert witness, and by telling the jury the consequence of finding Atkins retarded would be to overturn a decision of another jury to give Atkins the death sentence. The case was remanded for another hearing on Atkins's competency. See *Atkins v. Com.,* 631 S.E.2d 93 (2006). A circuit judge subsequently commuted Atkins's sentence to life imprisonment, which was upheld on appeal.

on proof of innocence. Forty-three prisoners were executed in 2011, and the same number in 2012; the highest number was ninety-eight in 1999. While California has the highest number of prisoners on death row, 724, it has executed only 13 since 1976. Texas has 304 prisoners on death row, and has executed 492 since 1982. The United States government has executed three people since 1976.[34]

Although polls show that the American public continues to generally support the death penalty, the number of death sentences handed out by juries has declined markedly since 1998, when 294 people were sentenced to death. In 2011, 78 people were sentenced to death.[35]

Reasons given for the decline in the use of death penalty by juries include the following:

- Fears by jurors that they are executing the wrong person. Most people are well aware that DNA evidence has proved innocent persons have been convicted in the past.

- States, such as Texas, have passed laws giving juries the option of sentencing the defendant to life without parole. In the past Texas averaged thirty-four death penalties per year, but in 2011 juries handed down only eight death penalties.
- In 2009 New Mexico became the fifteenth state to repeal the death penalty. The governor of New Mexico stated this was due in part to tight budgets and the high cost of death penalty appeals.
- Distrust of the death penalty by state officials. In November of 2011 the governor of Oregon stopped a pending execution and declared there would be no more executions during his term of office.

FEDERAL CRIMES FOR WHICH THE DEATH PENALTY CAN NOW BE APPLIED

When President Clinton signed the 1994 Violent Crime Control and Law Enforcement Act, the number of federal crimes for which the death penalty could be applied increased significantly. The following is the 1994 list of federal death penalty crimes:

Assassination of the president, vice president, a member of Congress, cabinet member, or Supreme Court justice

Drug trafficking of large amount of drugs

First-degree murder on federal land or property

Genocide

Gun murders during federal crimes of violence and during drug trafficking crimes

Killing a person in a federal witness protection program

Killing (or attempted murder) by a drug kingpin of a public officer or a juror to obstruct justice

Murder at a U.S. international airport

Murder by a federal prisoner or escaped prisoner who is (or was) serving a life sentence

Murder for hire (when a federal crime)

Murder in aid of racketeering activity (federal)

Murder in a federal facility involving a firearm

Murder of federal witness, victim, or informant

Murder of a state correctional officer by an inmate

Murder of a U.S. citizen abroad by another U.S. citizen

Murder of a court officer or juror

Murder of a federal law enforcement official

Murder of a foreign official or internationally protected person on U.S. soil

Murder of a state or local official assisting federal law officers

Murder within the special maritime and territorial jurisdiction of the United States

Treason and espionage

Where death results:

- Aircraft hijacking (domestic or international)
- Alien smuggling
- Carjacking (federal)
- Destroying federal property with explosives
- Destruction of aircraft, motor vehicles, or their facilities (federal)
- Drive-by shooting (federal)
- Hostage taking (federal)
- Kidnapping (federal)
- Mailing injurious articles (such as explosives)
- Robbery of a federally insured bank
- Sexual abuse (federal)
- Sexual exploitation of children (federal)
- Torture (federal)
- Train sabotage (federal)
- Transporting explosives with intent to kill
- Use of weapons of mass destruction (poison gas, biological, and so on)
- Violating federally protected rights based on race, religion, or national origin

- Improved performance by defense counsel, coupled with the U.S. Supreme Court's requirement that juries be told life without parole is an option.
- Concern by juries that lethal injection as a method of execution lacks reliability.

Prosecutors have in the past used the threat of seeking the death penalty to obtain guilty pleas, or information about the crime. For example, when James Earl Ray assassinated Martin Luther King, his crime was extremely well planned, and he was able to obtain a Canadian passport in another person's name and escape to Europe before he was apprehended by police. Prosecutors, believing others might be involved in the assassination, used the threat of the death penalty to try to convince Ray to provide information about the involvement of others. Ray did not cooperate, and prosecutors did not seek the death penalty. Ray never provided any information about a possible conspiracy, and he died in prison after one escape attempt.

Imprisonment as Punishment

Under early Roman law, imprisonment was illegal as punishment and was used for detention only.[36] Imprisonment is as old as the law of England, but only rarely did statutes in early England provide for imprisonment as punishment for crime. Nearly every English court had its own particular prison, and the right of keeping a gaol (jail) in and for a particular district was a franchise the king granted to certain people, just as he granted other rights connected with the administration of justice in England. In addition to the franchise prisons were the Fleet, the prison of the Star Chamber, and the prison of the Court of Chancery.[37]

Because of the filthy, unsanitary conditions of the early English prisons and the corruption and brutality that arose from the franchise system, reform movements began in England as early as 1773, when John Howard became sheriff of Bedfordshire. When he saw the disgraceful conditions in his jail, he proposed that salaried gaolers replace the franchise system. The condition of U.S. prisons has also been the subject of many reform movements, and the use of prisons for the purpose of punishment has been subject to much debate.

While conditions in prisons in the United States have improved over these early models, one severe problem is overcrowding. The Government Accountability Office reported in September 2012 that the federal prison system is 39 percent over capacity. There are many reasons for the increase in the number of prisoners, but drug-related crimes are at the core of the problem. At the end of 2011 there were 218,000 prisoners in federal prisons; 48 percent of these inmates were there on drug charges.[38]

State prisons face similar overcrowding problems. In the 2011 case of *Brown v. Plata*[39] the U.S. Supreme Court found that California state prisons, which were designed to hold 80,000 inmates, had double that number incarcerated. Finding this violated the Eighth Amendment, the Court ordered California to reduce the prison population to 137 percent of design capacity by the middle of 2013. If new construction does not cure the problem, it is likely California will be forced to release prisoners before the end of their sentences.

LIFE IMPRISONMENT WITHOUT PAROLE FOR JUVENILE DEFENDANTS

The Cruel and Unusual Punishment Clause of the U.S. Constitution has a "proportionality" principle, but the U.S. Supreme Court has generally used that principle only in reviewing capital punishment cases. Where the sentence was a term of years, or life imprisonment, the Court has been reluctant to reverse a sentence because it was out of proportion to the crime committed, or to sentences imposed in similar cases.

In two recent cases involving juvenile defendants the Supreme Court declared that sentences of life imprisonment without possibility of parole (LWOP) for juvenile defendants violated the Cruel and Unusual Punishment Clause. The first case was *Graham v. Florida*, 130 S. Ct. 2011 (2010).

In 2003, at the age of 16, Terrance Graham and two friends attempted to rob a restaurant in Jacksonville, Florida. Graham was arrested, and tried as an adult for attempted robbery. He pled guilty, and was sentenced to 3 years of probation, the first year of which was to be spent in jail. In December 2004, 6 months after his release from jail and while still on probation, Graham and two friends undertook a home invasion, where they assaulted the homeowner, holding a pistol against his chest while the home was ransacked. Later that night Graham and his friends attempted another robbery, during the course of which one of the friends was shot. Graham took the friend to a hospital, and was subsequently arrested and charged with armed robbery. At the time, Graham was 34 days short of his 18th birthday.

Because Graham was on probation, a court held a hearing on the state's claim that Graham had violated his probation by engaging in criminal conduct and possessing a weapon. The court held him in violation of probation, finding Graham committed the crimes charged. Based on these charges, the judge could impose a sentence from 5 years to life. Although the pre-sentence report prepared by the probation office suggested a 4-year prison sentence, the judge sentenced Graham to life in prison. Because Florida had dropped its parole system, see Fla. Stat. § 921.002, this sentence amounted to a sentence of life without possibility of parole. That meant the only chance for Graham to be released was executive clemency. The Florida appellate courts affirmed the sentence. The U.S. Supreme Court granted certiorari, and reversed.

The Court first stated that some sentences for a juvenile should be reviewed using the "categorical" approach. This approach considers "the particular type of sentence," either the nature of offense and the sentence imposed or the characteristics of the defendant. An example of this kind of review is review of the death penalty for juveniles or the mentally retarded, where the Court has said "categorically" the death penalty violates the Eighth Amendment.

The Court then said sentences of life without any possibility of parole for juvenile offenders in non-homicide cases categorically violated the Eighth Amendment. The Court said that the undeveloped maturity of a juvenile made him less culpable than an adult who committed the same

Can Indigents Be Held in Jail to Work Off Their Money Fines?

In the case of *Williams v. Illinois*,[40] the question of whether a person who was indigent (without money) could be imprisoned for the inability to pay a fine was presented to the U.S. Supreme Court. In the *Williams* case, the Illinois courts had ruled that Williams would be held in prison and work off his fine at the rate of $5 per day. Williams asked to be released so he could get a job and pay the fine and court costs.

crime, and a juvenile's greater capability for rehabilitation made the denial of any chance of parole more damaging. It therefore reversed the decisions below and remanded the case for resentencing. In 2012, Graham was re-sentenced to 25 years in prison. He could be released in 13 years under the Florida "Gain-time" prison rules.

In the second case, *Miller v. Alabama*, 132 S. Ct. 2455 (2012), the Court held that a mandatory sentence of life without possibility of parole for a juvenile violated the Eighth Amendment even in homicide cases, an area that the Court in *Graham* was careful to exclude from its holding in that case.

In *Miller* and a companion case, 14-year-old boys were involved in robberies where the victim was killed. Each boy received a sentence of life imprisonment without any possibility of parole, which under state law was the mandatory sentence the judge was required to impose with no discretion to do otherwise. The Supreme Court held that mandatory life sentences without any chance for parole in homicide cases "categorically" violated the Eighth Amendment for the same reasons stated in *Graham*. It therefore reversed the cases for resentencing.

One significant difference between *Graham* and *Miller* is the resentencing that will occur. Juveniles sentenced to life without parole for non-homicide crimes must be resentenced with some realistic possibility they will not spend the rest of their lives in prison. Courts after *Graham* have differed on the application of that case's rule to very long sentences of juveniles in non-homicide cases. Some, like the California court whose decision was discussed in the beginning of this chapter, have concluded such sentences are tantamount to life without parole, and declared them invalid. Others, like *Angel v. Commonwealth*, 704 S.E.2d 386 (Va. 2011), and *State v. Brown*, 2013 WL 1878911 (La. 2013), have held that it is permissible for courts to sentence juveniles to "stacked" non-parole terms for multiple offenses that are in total longer than the juvenile's expected life.

Juveniles in homicide cases given a mandatory sentence of life without possibility of parole also must be resentenced, but they may still be sentenced to life without the possibility of parole if the sentencing judge determines that is the proper sentence, taking into account the fact that the defendant is a juvenile. An example of such a sentence can be found in *People v. Gutierrez*, 147 Cal. Rptr. 3d 249 (Cal. App. 2012), where the court affirmed a sentence of life without parole for a 17-year-old juvenile who murdered his aunt with "special circumstances" (aggravating circumstances). The Court held *Miller* did not prohibit the sentence, because the trial judge had discretion to include parole and chose not to do so. In the 2013 case of *Commonwealth v. Batts*, 66 A.3d 286 (Pa. 2013) the Pennsylvania Supreme Court held that on remand a trial court could sentence a 14-year-old juvenile convicted of murder to LWOP, so long as the relevant factors set forth in *Miller* were properly evaluated.

In the case of *Tate v. Short*[41] the indigent defendant owed fines of $425 on nine traffic offenses and was ordered to serve 85 days in a Texas prison farm to work off the fines at the rate of $5 per day.

The U.S. Supreme Court held that other ways of collecting fines are available and that permitting a person with money to pay fines, but requiring a person without money to work off a fine in jail or prison violates the Equal Protection Clause of the U.S. Constitution.[42]

Fines as Punishment

Money fines payable by the convicted offender are frequently used as an alternative to incarceration or together with incarceration. In most states, the maximum fine for any designated criminal act is set by statute. Also, it is common to limit the amount of a fine each level of court within a state may assess against a defendant. A municipal court that handles minor offenses has a lower fine limit than a district court with the jurisdiction to hear major crimes.

Fines must not be excessive. The Eighth Amendment to the U.S. Constitution prohibits "excessive fines imposed" as punishment. Generally, analysis of punishment under the Cruel and Unusual Punishment Clause requires application of the proportionality test. In excessive fines cases, that means comparing the fine assessed with the nature of the offense charged.

Fines can be difficult to collect if the offender is unemployed or has a low-paying job. To improve the rate of collection of fines, some or all of the following methods are used:

- Allowing offenders to pay their fines on an installment plan, which is usually worked out by a clerk, taking into account the offender's income and the amount due.
- Accepting credit cards for payment.
- Computerizing record-keeping systems.
- Telemarketing (use of the telephone to contact people and remind them of payments due).

FINES, FACT-FINDING, AND THE SIXTH AMENDMENT

Corporations can only be punished for criminal violations by fines. In the case of violations of environmental crimes, computing the fine can require findings of fact that have the potential for greatly increasing the punishment. In *Southern Union Co. v. United States*, 132 S. Ct. 2344 (2012), the U.S. Supreme Court considered the requirements of the Sixth Amendment when fines as punishment are determined.

The defendant corporation was convicted of violating the federal Resource Conservation and Recovery Act by storing hazardous waste without a permit. The statute provides for a fine of $50,000 for each day the defendant violated the statute. The jury convicted the defendant on one count, but made no finding of exactly how many days the violation lasted. The trial judge imposed a $6 million fine and a "community service obligation" of $12 million. The corporation appealed, contending the Sixth Amendment was violated because the jury must make every factual finding that increases a criminal punishment.

The U.S. Supreme Court agreed, and reversed the conviction and fine. It held that since the potential fine facing the defendant was serious enough to require a jury trial under the Sixth Amendment, the *Apprendi* line of cases (discussed earlier in this chapter) required the jury to find facts that determine the severity of the fine.

- Turning collection over to private collection agencies that can pursue debtors across state lines and often have access to databases that allow them to track the movements of an offender. Collection agencies often routinely notify credit bureaus of delinquent accounts, a practice that is reported to be an important factor in recovering overdue fines.

Forfeiture as Punishment

forfeiture Going back to early English law, the concept and use of seizing the property that was used to commit a crime.

The concept and use of **forfeiture** go back to early English law. Seizing the property that was used to commit a crime is a strong deterrent to crime. Seizing the profits of crime is also a deterrent in crimes committed for profit.

Forfeiture was first used in customs violations such as smuggling. In addition to the traditional criminal punishments of death and fines, the economic sanction of forfeiture was imposed through seizure of ships, implements, and the goods being smuggled.

Forfeiture not only punished the wrongdoers by depriving them of ships (or boats), implements, and goods, but also rewarded the king and government, who benefited from the use and sale of these items.

The concept of forfeiture came to America with English common law. It was used over the years in various forms. During Prohibition, forfeiture was used extensively to deter and discourage the manufacture, sale, and use of illegal alcohol.

While forfeiture is not "punishment" for many purposes, such as application of the Double Jeopardy Clause, it remains an important part of law enforcement's efforts to combat crime. Federal statutes today authorize the forfeiture not only of contraband property but also of instrumentalities used in narcotics, gambling, and untaxed alcohol and tobacco. For example, Section 55 of the Uniform Controlled Substance Act, which has been adopted by many states and the federal government, provides for forfeiture not only of controlled substances in violation of the law but also of all raw materials, all vehicles "used, or intended for use," weapons, records and books, and all property, "including money" and profits. Section 55.5 of the act details forfeiture proceedings.[43]

Important U.S. Supreme Court and other federal court cases regarding civil forfeitures are as follows:

- *United States v. Ursery,*[44] The Supreme Court held that "*in rem* civil forfeitures are neither 'punishment' nor criminal for the purposes of the Double Jeopardy Clause"; therefore, the government can commence both a criminal action and a civil forfeiture action without violating double jeopardy.
- *Austin v. United States,*[45] The Supreme Court held that the civil forfeiture provision of 21 U.S.C. § 881(a)(4), providing for forfeiture of property used in drug transactions, was "punishment" for purposes of the Eighth Amendment excessive fines clause. Whether termed civil or criminal, the Court stated a forfeiture provision is a "punishment" if it has a purpose other than remedial action.
- *Bennis v. Michigan,*[46] In this case, the Supreme Court held that a state forfeiture law could provide for forfeiture (seizure) of property from an owner who was unaware of the illegal use of the property. (Bennis was convicted of a sex act with a prostitute

in a car owned by Bennis and his wife, who was unaware of the illegal use of the car.) The U.S. Supreme Court held that under such a state statute, "the innocence of an owner (Bennis's wife) has almost uniformly been rejected as a defense to forfeiture."

- *United States v. 785 Nicholas Ave.*[47] Under 21 U.S.C.A. Section 881(a)(7), the federal government may seize real estate being used for illegal activity such as drug dealing. To defend against such a forfeiture action, the owners must demonstrate a lack of consent to the illegal activities and that they did all that reasonably could be expected to prevent the illegal activities once they learned of them.

18 U.S.C.A. § 983(d)(1), the Civil Asset Forfeiture Act, now provides an "innocent owner" defense applicable in all federal forfeiture cases. The owner must show either lack of knowledge of the illegal activity in which the property was involved, or that the owner did all that reasonably could be done to prevent the use of the property in the illegal activity.

Under federal law today and under the provisions of the forfeiture statutes of many states, the following can now be seized under court order:

- Instrumentalities of the crime (vehicles, watercraft, and the like used in the commission of the crimes)
- Profits of the crime (money from drug dealing, stolen goods, and so on)
- Proceeds of the illegal acts (farms, yachts, cars, homes, and other luxury goods purchased with profits of illegal acts)

The Internal Revenue Service can also seize under court order the property of people charged with or convicted of crimes. Because people involved in the sale of marijuana, cocaine, and narcotics often make huge profits without paying proper taxes, tax liens may be filed against them. Property belonging to such people may be seized for payment of taxes, including homes, furniture, cars, stereo equipment, video games, gems, and real estate.

Under the Mandatory Victims Restitution Act, 18 U.S.C. § 3663A, Federal judges must order restitution as part of the sentence in certain crimes, such as crimes of violence or fraud, where an identifiable person has suffered a loss. In *Dolan v. United States,* 130 S. Ct. 1047 (2010), the Supreme Court held that while the Act requires a judge to determine the amount of restitution to be paid no later than 90 days after sentencing, the 90-day limit may be extended if the judge determines restitution will be ordered, but cannot within the time limit determine the exact amount to be ordered.

Career Criminals and the Repeat Offender

Law enforcement priorities are most often determined by the crime itself. High priority is most often given when crimes involve injury or death or when important aspects of public interest are involved.

Attention is focused on the person committing the crime rather than on the crime when it is determined that the person is a career criminal or a repeater (or habitual criminal). Recidivism is a major problem in the United States. In a 2009 report published by the Office of Justice Program, Bureau of Statistics, titled "Re-Entry Trend in the United States: Recidivism," statistics showed that nationwide 67.5 percent of persons released from prison in 1994 were rearrested within 3 years of their release, and 51.8 percent of those released were back in prison within 3 years.

By taking such offenders off the street, the incidence of crimes can be considerably lessened. Many cities and states have created career-criminal programs. Such programs ordinarily

- Operate under statutes providing additional and longer sentences for repeat offenders.
- Establish special career-criminal units in the offices of police and prosecutors that vigorously investigate frequently committed crimes or crimes following patterns.
- Speed up prosecution of career criminals.
- Discourage plea bargaining, which could lessen prison terms, unless the suspect incriminates associates.

recidivist One who is a habitual criminal.

Several repeater (**recidivist**) cases have come before the U.S. Supreme Court in recent years, with different results. One of the earliest cases was the 1980 Texas case of *Rummel v. Estelle*. In that case a defendant had received a life sentence under the Texas repeater statutes for three nonviolent crimes that netted the defendant a total of $230. The Court affirmed the conviction and sentence, holding that the sentence did not violate the Eighth Amendment.

In the case of *Solem v. Helm*[48] the U.S. Supreme Court decided another recidivism case. Helm lived in South Dakota and had a serious problem with alcohol. By 1975, he had committed six nonviolent felonies. In 1979, he pleaded guilty to uttering (passing) a "no account" check for $100 (his seventh felony). Under the South Dakota recidivist statute, his crime was classified as a "class I" felony, and he was sentenced to life imprisonment.

Unlike the Texas statutes in the *Rummel* case, South Dakota statutes forbade parole in recidivist cases. Murderers and rapists were eligible for parole in South Dakota, but Helm would never be eligible for parole. The Supreme Court held that the sentence violated the Eighth Amendment, stating

> The Constitution requires us to examine Helm's sentence to determine if it is proportionate to his crime. Applying objective criteria, we find that Helm has received the penultimate sentence for relatively minor criminal conduct. He has been treated more harshly than other criminals in the State who have committed more serious crimes. He has been treated more harshly than he would have been in any other jurisdiction, with the possible exception of a single State. We conclude that his sentence is significantly disproportionate to his crime, and is therefore prohibited by the Eighth Amendment.

The absence of the possibility of parole appeared to be the basis for the distinction between *Solem* and *Rummel;* the defendant in *Rummel* could be eligible for parole in 12 years, whereas the defendant in *Solem* would never be paroled. However, in *Ewing v. California*, 538 U.S. 11 (2003), the Court upheld a sentence of 25 years to life under the California "Three Strikes" law (discussed in the next section). The statute provided that parole could not be considered until the 25-year term had passed, but the Court did not identify the possibility of parole as the basis of its decision. Rather, the Court held that a state has a legitimate interest in incarcerating repeat offenders who have demonstrated an inability to conform to the criminal laws.

In *Lockyer v. Andrade* (discussed in the next section) a companion case to *Ewing*, the Court upheld a sentence of two consecutive 25-years-to-life terms under the

California three strikes law. While dissenting justices noted that a 50-year minimum sentence for a 37-year-old defendant amounted to life without parole, the majority did not make the presence or absence of parole the basis for its decision.

"Three Strikes" Laws

For many years, most states and the federal government have had laws that provide for increased punishment for multiple felony convictions. For example, The Armed Career Criminal Act, 18 U.S.C. § 924(e)(1) (ACCA), mandates a sentence of 15 years in prison for any felon convicted of violation of 18 U.S.C. § 922(g)(1), the felon in possession of a firearm statute, if the felon had three previous convictions for drug offenses or "violent crimes." In *Begay v. United States,* 453 U.S. 137 (2008) the U.S. Supreme Court held that "violent crimes" under § 924(e)(1) did not include previous

PRISONS AND JAILS IN THE UNITED STATES; 2009–2011

Every year thousands of inmates are released from U.S. prisons. Unfortunately, many of these inmates are back in prison within a few years of their release. This result, called *recidivism,* has for years been a serious problem in the United States. The causes of this high recidivism rate have been debated for years in Congress and in the states. There is general agreement that two of the major factors contributing to that high rate are the serious mental health problems of about one in six inmates and the scarcity of programs for helping an ex-convict find a job and start a new life.

Because states must spend nearly $30 billion each year to maintain prisons, new efforts are being made to deal with the recidivism problem.

During the 40 years from 1969 to 2009, prison and jail populations have grown every year in the United States, to a present total of about 2 million prisoners. This is far more than the combined total number of inmates incarcerated in the thirty-six European countries.[a]

At present, each year about 650,000 inmates are released from prisons, but unfortunately between one-half and two-thirds of these inmates are back in prison within a few years of their release. Recidivism continues to be a very serious problem in the United States, and state and federal officials are very concerned about that problem. U.S. Attorney General Eric Holder stated before the American Bar Association in 2009 that "[t]here is no doubt that we must be tough on crime. But we must also commit ourselves to being smart on crime … we need to adopt what works."[b]

At the end of 2011 there were 1,598,780 inmates in state and federal prisons. In 2011 688,384 inmates were released from state and federal prisons. Also, at the end of 2011 there were 853,900 ex-convicts on parole from prison. During 2011, about 12 percent of parolees were reincarcerated.[49]

There remain important questions to answer. Will crime rates go up because of unemployment and other problems in the United States? Will recidivism continue at the present high rates? How will the state and federal governments react to these situations?

[a]See the *New York Times* article of April 23, 2008, entitled "U.S. Inmate Count Far Exceeds Those of Other Nations."
[b]See the *New York Times* op-ed article of August 15, 2009, entitled "Getting Smart on Crime."

ALTERNATIVES TO PRISON FOR OFFENDERS BELIEVED TO BE NONVIOLENT

Alternative Punishment	Description	Probable Use
House arrest or confinement with electronic monitoring	Monitoring is done with an ankle or wrist bracelet or a telephone device that monitors the detainee's presence in the house.	Used as a mixture of penalties tailored to the offender. Person must agree as condition of parole, probation, or work release program.
Agreement to take a drug such as Antabuse or to commit to a drug treatment program	When the cause of the criminal conduct is alcohol abuse, drugs are available to suppress or eliminate the urge to drink. Drug and alcohol treatment programs are available in all states.	Person agrees to take suppressant medication "voluntarily" as condition of probation or parole, usually to avoid imprisonment.
"Intensive sanctions" or "shock" probation or parole	Usually used for nonviolent, non-drug user. Can be sentenced by court or enter a program from a correctional institution. Used in overcrowded jails or prisons to free space for new inmates.	The overcrowding of jails and prisons causes use of this type of program.
"Therapy courts"	There are about 2,000 "therapy courts" in the United States dealing with drug, alcohol, and spousal abuse problems. A few courts dealing with gambling addiction have recently been formed.	Because of lack of adequate home facilities, house arrest is not used. Persons committing crimes caused by their addictions or to fund their addictions are likely to be repeat offenders unless they successfully complete treatment programs. In these courts, they are given the choice of correcting their problems or going to prison.
Mandatory deportation	Under stricter immigration laws enacted by the U.S. Congress, immigrants who have been convicted of a broad range of felonies (from murder to drug possession) must be deported to their country of origin.	From 1997 to 2007, more than 672,593 people were deported under the stricter legislation. In *Carachuri-Rosendo v. Holder*, 130 S. Ct. 2577 (2010), the court held mandatory deportation improper for minor drug offenses.
Banishment to another city or state	Giving an unwanted person the choice to "get out of town" or go to jail was not uncommon 50 years ago. Some cities even provided bus fare. Another practice was to suspend a criminal sentence if the defendant joined the military. It was much easier to get into the military in those days.	Today, the banishment order must be reasonably related to the offense and to rehabilitation. In the 1991 rape case of *McCreary v. State* (582 So. 2d 425), the Supreme Court of Mississippi reviewed cases from other states where banishment was part of a punishment package that the defendant agreed to (usually in a plea bargain agreement).

[a]The eventual success of the program is discussed in the *New York Times* article, "U.S. Deports Felons but Can't Keep Them Out," August 11, 1997.

fourth-offense convictions for drunken driving, even though they were treated as felonies under state law. The Court reasoned that Congress intended to limit the kind of prior felonies that resulted in the increased sentence to crimes that were in their nature violent or created the possibility of violence. For similar reasons, the Supreme Court held in *Johnson v. United States,* 130 S. Ct. 1265 (2010), that a conviction under the Florida battery statute, which defines the crime as "actually and intentionally touching" another person, was not a violent felony under the ACCA.

In the mid-1990s laws called "three strikes and you're out" laws gained prominence when the U.S. Congress incorporated a "three strikes" provision into the Violent Crime Control and Law Enforcement Act of 1994. Many states followed suit.[50]

"three strikes" laws Laws that impose increased penalties for multiple felony convictions.

In November 1994, California voters adopted Proposition 184, a "three strikes" law, in part as a response to the murder of Kimberly Reynolds, an 18-year-old fashion student, by a paroled drug dealer with a long history of violent crime. California's law is among the harshest **"three strikes" laws** for three reasons: (1) the third or "trigger" conviction may be any felony, not necessarily one for a violent crime; (2) the first two strikes may be convictions for any "serious" felony, though not necessarily a violent crime; and (3) a sentence of 25 years to life must be assessed on each count, with multiple counts served consecutively. Parole may not be considered until the entire mandatory sentence is served.[51]

SENTENCE ENHANCEMENT STATUTES

All states and the federal government use sentence enhancement statutes that increase criminal penalties. The following are some of the usual conditions that cause enhancement:

- The crime is a hate crime, or the victim is elderly or handicapped.
- The person is a repeat offender (habitual criminal statute).
- A dangerous weapon is used committing the crime.
- A bulletproof garment is used in committing the crime.
- Concealment of identity (such as a mask) is used.
- Drugs or a weapon are used or sold within 1,000 feet of a school.

Another form of enhancement used to protect people having duties within the criminal justice system increases a misdemeanor battery to a felony battery if committed against the following persons:

- A law enforcement or firefighting officer if the officer is acting in an official capacity
- A witness or juror
- A public official or officer
- A prison guard, another prisoner, or a visitor

In the 1997 case of *United States v. Gonzales,* 121 F.3d 928 (5th Cir. 1997), the defendant carried a machine gun during a drug transaction. The 30-year additional sentence enhancement under the federal enhancement statute (18 U.S.C.A. § 924[c]) was held not to violate the Eighth Amendment because machine guns are uniquely associated with drug trafficking and crimes of violence and present a grave danger to the public.

In 2003 the U.S. Supreme Court decided *Lockyer v. Andrade,* 538 U.S. 63. Andrade was convicted under California's "three strikes" law and sentenced to two terms of 25 years to life, meaning Andrade would not be eligible for parole until 2046. The crimes Andrade committed to invoke the "three strikes" law were mainly minor theft crimes, not crimes of violence. The Ninth Circuit Court of Appeals found the "three strikes" statute unconstitutional, because the sentence was so disproportionate to the crimes committed it violated the Eighth Amendment. The Supreme Court reversed the Ninth Circuit, holding that under established law the sentence was not so grossly disproportionate as to violate the Eighth Amendment.

The *Andrade* decision provides no clear answer to the "gross disproportionality" problem for sentences under "three strikes" laws. However, the last paragraph in the majority opinion suggests the approach the Supreme Court will take to that problem when presented again: "The gross disproportionality principle reserves a constitutional violation for only the extraordinary case."

State courts may, notwithstanding the holding in *Lockyer v. Andrade,* overturn a sentence under state constitutional provisions. California, as an example, has a "cruel or unusual" prohibition in its state constitution, Article 1, section 17. In *People v. Carmony,* 26 Cal. Rptr. 3d 365 (2005), the court held a 25-to-life sentence imposed under the California three-strikes law for defendant's failure to register as a sex offender within 5 days of his birthday violated the state constitution.

Summary

- The text of the Eighth Amendment prohibits excessive bail, excessive fines, and cruel and unusual punishment.
- The Sixth Amendment requires that factual findings made for the purpose of enhancing a sentence must be made by a jury.
- The Federal Sentencing Guidelines are no longer mandatory, but federal courts imposing sentences must consider the guidelines and the factors stated in the Federal Sentencing Act, 18 U.S.C. § 3553 when imposing a sentence.
- School officials may impose corporal punishment on a student only if (1) it is not excessive, and (2) it follows a prior determination that the student violated a school rule.
- *Furman v. Georgia* held that imposition of the death penalty without an established procedure to determine which defendants should live and which die was arbitrary and capricious, and thus a violation of the Eighth and Fourteenth Amendments. It was not the death penalty that was unconstitutional, but rather the "lightning-like" way in which it was imposed.

- Mentally retarded defendants, juveniles under the age of 18, and insane persons may not be given the death penalty.
- Juveniles may never be given life without possibility of parole for non-homicide crimes. For homicide crimes juveniles may not be given mandatory life sentences without possibility of parole, but a sentencing court may in its discretion do so after considering all relevant factors, including the fact that the defendant was a juvenile.
- State statutes must identify aggravating circumstances, and the jury must find such circumstances exist, before the death penalty may be imposed. Jurors must also be instructed on mitigating factors to be integrated into the decision to impose the death penalty.
- "Three-strikes" laws provide for the automatic enhancement of a prison sentence, often to life imprisonment, upon the conviction of a third felony or violent crime. Parole generally is not available until the minimum term of years is served.

Key Terms

benefit of clergy, p. 198
sanctuary, p. 199
capital punishment, p. 200
cruel and unusual punishment, p. 201

proportionality, p. 201
corporal punishment, p. 206
procedural due process, p. 208
substantive due process, p. 208
aggravating circumstances, p. 209

mitigating circumstances, p. 209
forfeiture, p. 217
recidivist, p. 219
"three-strikes" laws, p. 222

Case Analysis and Writing Exercises

1. A finding of "gross disproportionality" in a term-of-years sentence is, as the U.S. Supreme Court said, "exceedingly rare." What was it about the circumstances in *State v. Bruce*, 796 N.W.2d 397 (S. D. 2011) that convinced the court the "grossly disproportionate" standard had been met? Simply the 100-year sentence? Or were other factors important?

2. Assume a defendant was convicted in 2000 for robbing a bank. After his release in 2003 he robs a bank in July and again in September of 2003. He is arrested and charged with the July 2003 robbery. He is convicted, and sentenced to 5 years in prison. Upon his release he is indicted for the September 2003 bank robbery, and is convicted. Should he be sentenced to life imprisonment under the federal three-strikes law? Why not? *See United States v. Davila-Felix*, 667 F.3d 47 (1st Cir. 2011).

3. When joint owners of a residence face forfeiture because the residence was used in criminal activities, the federal Civil Asset Forfeiture Reform Act permits the "innocent" joint owners to avoid forfeiture of their joint interest. What if neither is completely innocent, but one is more culpable than the other? Can the less culpable person avoid forfeiture? If so, when? Compare *United States v. Sabhnani*, 599 F.3d 215 (2nd Cir. 2010), with *vonHolte v. United States*, 492 F.3d 175 (2nd Cir. 2007).

4. Under the federal Armed Career Criminal Act, a person convicted of a firearm offense, such as possession of a firearm by a convicted felon, can have the sentence enhanced to 15 years in prison if he has three prior convictions for violent felonies. Should attempting to escape by driving away from police who seek to pull over a driver for improper headlights constitute a "violent felony"? If so, how does the Supreme Court define "violent felony"? *See Sykes v. United States*, 131 S. Ct. 2267 (2011).

Endnotes

1. *People v. Caballero*, 282 P.3d 291 (Cal. 2012).
2. *A History of the Criminal Law of England* (three volumes) by Sir James Fitzjames Stephens, Judge of High Court of Justice, Queen's Bench Division (England 1883) 1: 477.
3. In 1996, John Silber, president of Boston University, wrote an op-ed article for the *New York Times* titled "Students Should Not Be Above the Law: Judging Crimes Is a Job for Courts, Not Colleges" (May 9, 1996). He pointed out that colleges and universities are "circumventing the courts (to) bury serious criminal cases in their own judicial systems." Because crime victims are talked out of reporting their cases to the police, students are receiving special treatment, just as people did who qualified under the "benefit of clergy" exception centuries ago. Silber cited as an example a man who graduated in 1996 from Miami University in Ohio, a private university. After the man was accused of sexually assaulting an 18-year-old freshman as she was sleeping, the man was allowed to graduate on "student conduct probation" instead of having Ohio police and prosecutors handle the matter.
4. Blackstone 4 *Commentaries*, 18.
5. *A History of the Criminal Law of England*, chapter 13, pp. 491–492.
6. The treatment of refugees from Cuba, Haiti, Mexico, Central America, and other parts of the world has been a

continuing problem in the United States. The Immigration and Naturalization Service (INS) most often concludes that the refugees are fleeing from poverty in their countries and thus are not eligible for legal entry into the United States. Transporting, smuggling, or harboring aliens in violation of the Refugee Act of 1980 (Public Law 96-212) is a criminal offense. The defendants in the case of *United States v. Aguilar et al.*, 871 F.2d 1436 (9th Cir. 1989), *opinion amended and suspended* 883 F.2d 662 (9th Cir. 1989), ran a "modern-day underground railroad" that smuggled Central Americans across the border between Mexico and Arizona. The defendants in the *Aguilar* case were convicted of violations of the immigration laws (smuggling, transporting, and harboring aliens) arising from their participation in a "sanctuary movement."

7. Radzinowicz, *A History of English Criminal Law and Its Administration* (London: Stevens, 1948); Chute and Bell, *Crime, Courts, and Probation* (New York: Macmillan, 1956).

8. "Transportation" was used by a number of countries. The Roman Empire transported prisoners to Romania; the Soviet Union transported hundreds of thousands of political prisoners to Siberia. In addition, people fleeing from the law or political trouble have always used the frontiers of the world as a refuge.

9. *Furman v. Georgia*, 408 U.S. 238, 92 S. Ct. 2726 (1972).

10. Annals of Congress, 782 (1789).

11. *Furman v. Georgia*, 408 U.S. 238 at 258, 92 S. Ct. 2726 at 2736 (1972).

12. *Pulley v. Harris*, 465 U.S. 37, 104 S. Ct. 871 (1984).

13. 501 U.S. 957 (1991).

14. 538 U.S. 11 (2003).

15. 404 F.2d 571 (8th Cir. 1968), where the court presents reasons why whipping is unconstitutional as a punishment.

16. 429 U.S. 975, 97 S. Ct. 481 (1977).

17. 515 U.S. 472 (1995).

18. 479 F.3d 1175 (9th Cir. 2007).

19. Most school districts that permit corporal punishment require it to be administered only after the principal has approved it, in the presence of another adult, and not with an instrument that could cause physical injury to the student.

20. See *Garcia v. Miera*, 817 F.2d 650, 656 (10th Cir. 1987).

21. *County of Sacramento v. Lewis*, 523 U.S. 833 (1998).

22. *Neal v. Fulton County Board of Education*, 229 F.3d 1069, 1075 (11th Cir. 2000).

23. *Ibid*, at 1076.

24. 817 F.2d 650, 656.

25. *Ingraham*, 429 U.S. 975 (1977).

26. Because of state and federal sentencing guidelines, a convicted defendant is very unlikely to be sentenced by a court to receive corporal punishment. Such a sentence would be judged solely by the objective proportionality test of the Eighth Amendment. Other unusual sentences likewise can run afoul of the Eighth Amendment. For example, in *Williams v. State*, 505 S.E.2d 816 (Ga. App. 1998), a convicted sex offender was required to walk in the area where he committed his crime while wearing a sign that said, "BEWARE HIGH CRIME AREA." The appellate court said this sentence constituted cruel and unusual punishment

because the defendant was put in harm's way from other criminals frequenting the designated area.

27. 536 U.S. 730 (2002).

28. 408 U.S. 238, 92 S. Ct. 2726 (1972).

29. *Pulley v. Harris*, 465 U.S. 37, 44. In *Pulley v. Harris* the Supreme Court also defined and explained the use of proportionality. *Id.* at 42–43.

30. *Gregg v. Georgia*, 428 U.S. 153, 96 S. Ct. 2909 (1976).

31. *Proffitt v. Florida*, 428 U.S. 242, 96 S. Ct. 2960 (1976).

32. *Jurek v. Texas*, 428 U.S. 262, 96 S. Ct. 2950 (1976).

33. 465 U.S. 37, 104 S. Ct. 871 (1984).

34. Report, Death Penalty Information Center, January 17, 2013.

35. *Id*, based on Bureau of Justice Statistics.

36. Rubin, *The Law of Criminal Corrections* (St. Paul, Minn.: West, 1963).

37. England also had debtors' prisons in which people who owed civil debts could be imprisoned until the civil debt was paid. England abolished the practice of debtors' prisons in 1869. Such imprisonment would not be lawful under the U.S. Constitution, and some state constitutions specifically forbid this form of imprisonment. Most of the democratic world has abolished the practice.

38. General Accountability Office, *Growing Inmate Crowding Negatively Affects Inmates, Staff, and Infrastructure* (September 12, 2012).

39. 131 S. Ct. 1910 (2011).

40. *Williams v. Illinois*, 90 S. Ct. 2018 (1970).

41. 915 S. Ct. 668 (1971).

42. In footnote 19 of the *Williams* case, the Court stated: " We wish to make clear that nothing in our decision today precludes imprisonment for willful refusal to pay a fine or court costs. See *Ex parte Smith*, 97 Utah 280, 92 P.2d 1098 (1939)." Therefore, a person who has money or an income may be imprisoned for refusal to pay either a fine or court costs.

43. Other federal statutes that have forfeiture provisions are the Controlled Substance Act, 21 U.S.C.A. § 881; Organized Crime Control Act of 1970, 18 U.S.C.A. §§ 1963 and 1955(d); Copyrights Act, 17 U.S.C.A. §§ 506(b) and 509(a); and Child Protection Act of 1984, 18 U.S.C.A. §§ 2253 and 2254.

44. 116 S. Ct. 2135 (1996).

45. 509 U.S. 602 (1993).

46. 116 S. Ct. 994 (1996).

47. 983 F.2d 396, *review denied*, 113 S. Ct. 2349 (1993).

48. 463 U.S. 277.

49. National Reentry Resource Center, Council of State Governments Justice Center, 2012.

50. A driver's license may be revoked (or suspended) not only for traffic violations but also, depending on state law, for sex crimes, failure to pay child support, failure to pay non-traffic fines, underage drinking, truancy, or other reasons specified by the law of the state.

51. Between 1993 and 1995, twenty-four states enacted "three-strikes" laws. See *State v. Oliver*, 745 A.2d 1165, 1169 (N.J. 2000).

52. California Penal Code § 1170.12.

Free Speech, Public Order Crimes, and the Bill of Rights

Scott Olson/Getty Images

These members of a religious group that is avowedly anti-homosexual make it a practice to demonstrate or protest at funerals of soldiers killed in Iraq or Afghanistan. The group's leader, Rev. Fred Phelps, has been sued by the father of a marine killed in Iraq. Phelps and his followers contend the soldiers are killed because they serve a country that permits homosexuality. A jury initially gave the father a judgment of $5 million against Phelps, but that was reversed on appeal by a federal circuit court. The U. S Supreme Court affirmed the decision of the court of appeals in 2011.

OUTLINE

LEARNING OBJECTIVES

In this chapter we examine the extent to which the Bill of Rights, mainly the First Amendment, serves as a limit on the power of government to make criminal laws regulating conduct, such as speaking or assembling in public places. The learning objectives for this chapter are the following:

- Read and remember the First Amendment.
- Identify the difference between fighting words and merely rude language.
- Define a "clear and present danger."
- List the circumstances that permit government to regulate speech based on content.
- Define obscenity.
- State when a threat becomes a "true threat."
- Describe some ways one person might stalk another person in violation of a criminal law.
- Identify when an assembly becomes unlawful.
- State the basis for the Supreme Court's decision that the Second Amendment is binding on the states.

In 2007 Xavier Alvarez was elected to the board of the Three Valleys Water District in California. At a board meeting Alvarez stated he had been awarded the Congressional Medal of Honor for heroism in 1987. This statement was false, and local newspapers quickly discovered that Alvarez had lied, publicly condemning his actions.

Federal prosecutors then filed charges against Alvarez, charging violations of the Stolen Valor Act, legislation passed by Congress in 2006 in response to incidents similar to the Alvarez statement. That statute makes it a misdemeanor to "falsely represent" one has been awarded a medal or decoration authorized by Congress for the Armed Forces of the United States. For falsehoods about most medals the punishment was up to 6 months in prison; if the medal was the Medal of Honor, the sentence could be increased to one year in prison.

Alvarez pled guilty to the charges, reserving the right to contest the constitutionality of the law on appeal. The Ninth Circuit Court of Appeals reversed his conviction, holding the law violated the First Amendment. While this decision was pending on appeal to the Supreme Court, another federal court, the Tenth Circuit Court of Appeals, upheld the law, stating it did not violate the First Amendment. The U.S. Supreme Court in 2012 agreed with the Ninth Circuit, finding the Stolen Valor Act violated the First Amendment as an impermissible "content-based" restriction on free speech. (That decision is discussed more fully later in this chapter.)

The relationship between the rights of free speech—as well as the freedom of assembly, privacy, and religion—and criminal laws is very important but very complicated. In this chapter we learn about the extent to which governments can pass laws that make certain kinds of speech or assembly a crime, or criminal laws that invade a person's rights of privacy or religion. Also discussed are many of the limits placed on such criminal laws by the U.S. Constitution.

Crimes such as those against the person, or against property rights, rarely present conflicts with other private or public goals. That is, there generally is no accepted policy or goal that is advanced by assaulting an innocent person or stealing his or her property. That is not the case with many of the crimes presented in this chapter. Some of them involve the written or spoken word, and thus raise First Amendment issues. Others are "public order crimes"—that is, violations of criminal statutes or ordinances that seek to maintain public order by regulating the activities of persons on public streets and property and that rub against the freedom of movement. This chapter examines the power of government to use the criminal laws to regulate these activities, and the limitations placed on that power by the U.S. Constitution.

Belief—Speech—Action: When Speech May Be Regulated

The First Amendment of the U.S. Constitution provides that "Congress shall make no law … abridging the freedom of speech, or of the press." Courts have repeatedly pointed out that "freedom to speak one's mind is not only an aspect of individual liberty—and thus a good unto itself—but also is essential to the common quest for truth and the vitality of society as a whole."[1]

Human communications take many forms. Pure speech includes words spoken face to face or through one of the many media. Written communication includes books, magazines, newspapers, billboards, bumper stickers, and so on. Picketing, protest marches, and boycotts are also forms of communication. Symbolic speech such as uniforms, religious garb, black armbands, and hand gestures express messages and ideas and are protected by the First Amendment.

Speech and other forms of communication are not absolute rights, as they can seriously clash with the rights of others and the need for public order. The U.S. Supreme Court has pointed out that such regulation is necessary or the freedoms of an organized society could be "lost in the excesses of unrestrained abuse."[2]

In creating the "narrowly limited classes of speech" that can be forbidden and punished, the U.S. Supreme Court has repeatedly stated that "the line between speech unconditionally guaranteed and speech which may be regulated, suppressed, or punished is finely drawn."[3] The following are five categories of speech that the First Amendment does **not** protect:

1. Obscenity, which when identified by a state can be punished as a crime.
2. Fighting words.
3. Inciting or urging unlawful conduct (including "true" threats that clearly and unequivocally threaten the life or safety of another person).
4. Defamation (libel or slander).
5. Public nuisances, which require a "showing that substantial privacy interests are being invaded in an essentially intolerable manner"[4] (for example, loud noises in the middle of the night while others are sleeping).

Criminal statutes that have some effect on speech raise First Amendment issues. Generally speaking, if a statute is directed at the **content** of the speech (e.g., banning a book, a film, or a photograph), the statute is presumptively invalid under the First Amendment, and subject to strict scrutiny. Under strict scrutiny, the state must show a "compelling interest" served by the statute, and that the means used to achieve that interest are the "least restrictive" possible.

However, if the statute is "content neutral," it violates the First Amendment only if the government lacks a substantial interest in adopting the statute. For example, so-called adult movies and books generally cannot themselves be outlawed because of the limitations of the obscenity test. A statute banning specific books or videos would be directed at the content of those books or videos, and be subjected to strict scrutiny. However, reasonable regulations on the location or number of adult bookstores or theaters could be content neutral, and not a violation of the owners' First Amendment rights.[5]

The "Clear and Present Danger" Test

"clear and present danger" test One of the tests used to judge government restrictions on speech.

One of the principal tests used to judge government restriction of speech based on its content is the **"clear and present danger" test.** Local, state, and federal governments in the United States cannot forbid or suppress speech and punish the speaker unless the speech is likely to bring harm to people or property. Justice Oliver Wendell Holmes announced the "clear and present danger" doctrine in the 1919 case of *Schenck v. United States*:

The most stringent protection of free speech would not protect a man in falsely shouting "Fire" in a crowded theater, causing panic. It would not even protect a man from an injunction against uttering words that may have all the effect of force. The question in every case is whether the words are used in such circumstances that are of such a nature as to create a clear and present danger that they will bring about the substantive evils that Congress has a right to protect. It is a question of proximity and degree. When a nation is at war many things that might be said in time of peace are such a hindrance to its efforts that their utterances will not be endured so long as men fight and that no court could regard them as protected by any constitutional right.[6]

Using Justice Holmes's example, one could yell "fire" in an open field or a public park without fear of prosecution, because anyone hearing the words would feel no need for panic. The words would thus not present a "clear and present danger" of harming anyone. On the other hand, communicating a threat to take the life of the president is inherently dangerous, so much so that Congress passed 18 U.S.C. § 871(a), which makes it a federal crime to knowingly threaten the life of the president.[7]

Fighting Words

All states and cities have enacted laws and ordinances that are called disorderly persons, **disorderly conduct,** breach of the peace, or disturbance of the peace laws. These laws and ordinances forbid speech or conduct that either causes a public disorder or tends to cause a public disorder. **Fighting words** are communications that could either cause a public disorder or tend to cause a public disorder.

In 1942 the U.S. Supreme Court in *Chaplinsky v. New Hampshire* defined *fighting words* as "those words which by their very utterance . . . tend to incite an immediate breach of the peace."[8] Since that case was decided, the Supreme Court has not upheld a conviction based on the "fighting words" doctrine.[9] However, some state courts have done so. If a defendant were to be charged with a criminal violation based only on the words used, a judge or jury would have to determine if

disorderly conduct
Loud, obnoxious, or other offensive conduct in a public place.

fighting words
Speech which, because it will likely incite immediate violence, is not protected by the First Amendment.

David McNew/REUTERS

While obscene gestures like the one pictured here are vulgar and in bad taste, rarely do gestures alone result in arrests or prosecutions. Such gestures are not generally seen as "fighting words."

the insulting or vulgar language tended to incite a breach of the peace in an ordinary person, thus amounting to fighting words. The examples following the next "Case Close-Up" illustrate the fighting words doctrine and its limits.

CASE CLOSE-UP

United States v. Alvarez
Supreme Court of the United States,
132 S. Ct. 2537 (2012)

18 U.S.C. § 704(b), The Stolen Valor Act (the "Act"), was enacted by Congress in 2006. Senate and House Reports supporting the adoption of the statute stated that fraudulent claims about military medals and decorations damaged the "reputation and meaning" of the decorations, and that legislative action was needed to permit law enforcement officers to protect the reputation and meaning of the medals.

In 2007 Xavier Alvarez attended his first meeting of a water commission in California, to which he had just been elected. At that meeting, he publicly stated he had been awarded the Congressional Medal of Honor in 1987. This claim was quickly discovered to be false, and Alvarez was indicted and charged with violating the Stolen Valor Act. He pled guilty in the district court, but reserved the right to appeal his conviction based on his claim that the Act violated the First Amendment. The Ninth Circuit Court of Appeals agreed with him, and reversed his conviction. In part because another federal court of appeals subsequently upheld the Act in a similar case, the Supreme Court agreed to review the *Alvarez* decision.

The first words of the Supreme Court's opinion (there was no consensus majority opinion; six justices believed the Act was unconstitutional, but only four joined in the opinion written by Justice Kennedy) disclosed the Court's view of the defendant's conduct: "Lying was his habit," referring to other brazen lies told by the defendant, such as that he played hockey with the Detroit Red Wings. However, the Court said, that did not end the inquiry.

Because the Act was directed to the content of the defendant's false statements, the Court said it must meet the strict tests used to uphold content-based prohibitions. It specifically rejected the Government's contentions on this point: "The Court has never endorsed the categorical rule the Government advances: that false statements receive no First Amendment protection."

Under strict scrutiny applied to content-based prohibitions, the government must show a compelling reason for the statute, and that it is not overly restrictive of speech. The Court held that while the goal of the statute in upholding the importance and meaning of military decorations was clearly appropriate, the government made no showing the outright prohibition of speech was necessary to achieve that goal. The Court noted that within days of the defendant's false statement the local press uncovered his lie, and publicly condemned him as contemptible. This public condemnation protected the medal's reputation, the Court said: "The remedy for speech that is false is speech that is true."

The Court also found the statute to have an improper "chilling effect" on speech, since on its terms it applied to false statements "whether shouted from the rooftops or made in a barely audible whisper." The Court feared that giving such authority to the government would lead to a long list of subjects about which a false statement would lead to criminal sanctions. Such a result, the Court said, was exactly the "chill" the First Amendment was designed to avoid.

Finally, the Court did say that the decision placed no limits on prohibiting false statements designed to commit fraud or secure illegal ends. In those cases it is not the speech that is prohibited but the speech's illegal purpose.

EXAMPLE   One resident of a neighborhood kept a large RV parked in his yard. Other neighbors complained, but he refused to move the vehicle. The neighbors then convinced the town council to pass an ordinance banning the practice. While the ordinance was pending, the resident placed several mock tombstones in his yard, graphically and rudely describing the "deaths" of the complaining neighbors. A town police officer ordered the resident to remove the tombstones. He refused, and a fight broke out between the neighbors. The resident was arrested for disorderly conduct. He subsequently sued the police officer, alleging a civil rights violation under 42 U.S.C. § 1983, claiming his arrest and the order to remove the tombstones violated his First Amendment rights. The trial court applied the fighting words doctrine, and found for the police officer. On appeal, the circuit court held that the fighting words doctrine did not apply, because while the words on the tombstones might be likely to cause injury to the neighbors, they were not the kind of words that would incite a breach of the peace. Thus, the tombstones were protected under the First Amendment, and could not be ordered to be removed. *Purtell v. Mason*, 527 F.3d 615 (7th Cir. 2008), *cert. denied*, 129 S. Ct. 411 (2008).

EXAMPLE   During an angry exchange of words in a Washington restaurant, a 35-year-old man called 70-year-old Texas Congressman Henry Gonzalez a "communist." Gonzalez "nailed the man with his fist," causing a black eye and facial cuts. Both men were cited for disorderly conduct. Calling a congressman a communist in 1986, at the height of the Cold War (as was done in this example), was very provocative, and most juries in those days would probably have found that a fighting words violation had occurred.

But one wrong does not justify another wrong, and Gonzalez committed a misdemeanor battery when he struck the other man. The police properly issued citations to both men, as two crimes had occurred.

To prove a fighting words violation, the city, county, or state would have to prove the following in most jurisdictions:

- That the defendant addressed very insulting and abusive language.
- To another person face-to-face (Causing a likelihood that "the person addressed will make an immediate violent response)."[10]
- If the charge is a public disorder, then the statute or ordinance would probably require a showing that the offense occurred in a public place.

Note that words sent in an e-mail, or spoken over the telephone, rather than face to face, would not be fighting words. In the 2010 case of *State v. Drahota*[11] the Nebraska Supreme Court reversed a conviction for breach of the peace based on e-mails sent by the defendant to a former teacher that called the teacher a "traitor" and "Al Qaeda sympathizer."

When Does Vulgar, Insulting Language to a Police Officer Constitute Fighting Words?

Many state courts have imposed higher standards for "fighting words" directed at police officers, reasoning that police officers are expected to exercise greater restraint when foul, insulting language is directed toward them. After reviewing hundreds of state cases, the *FBI Law Enforcement Bulletin*[12] listed the following generally accepted concepts to assist law enforcement officers in deciding whether to arrest for speech directed at them:

1. Direct threats to the safety of an officer "generally constitute 'fighting words' unprotected by the first amendment." However, if the speech falls short of a direct, outright threat and is only harassing and nasty, state courts have held that such communications do not fall under the threat exception.

2. When a crowd is present and the *speech is likely to incite the crowd* (or some of the people in the crowd) to violence, state courts will hold that such speech is not constitutionally protected.

3. Speech that obstructs and hinders police in the performance of their duty generally has been held to justify an arrest. Probably all states have codified the common law crime of obstructing and hindering police officers in the performance of their public duty. However, state statutes vary considerably in defining the crime of obstruction. A few states limit the crime to "resisting." Other states use the words *resist, obstruct,* or *oppose,* and still other states use *resist, obstruct,* or *abuse.*

The following four cases all involved convictions based only on words spoken to a police officer, and no physical confrontation. Two convictions were upheld on appeal and two were not.

Convictions Upheld

- Defendant was attempting to enter an anti-immigration rally. Because of the expected large crowds, police had posted "no parking" notices in some areas. The defendant parked in such an area, and when told to leave called the African-American police officer a "n-----" and engaged in loud and abusive language. His conviction for disorderly conduct was affirmed. *State v. Mitchell*, 343 S.W.3d 381 (Tenn. 2011), *cert. denied*, 132 S. Ct. 244 (2011).

- Defendant was crossing a crowded street at midnight. The defendant called a police officer sitting a nearby parked car a "f------ pig." After the defendant finished crossing the street, the officer went to the defendant and asked what the problem was. The defendant said "f---off asshole." Police arrested the defendant and he was convicted of disturbing the peace. His conviction was affirmed, the court holding the words were "fighting words" and not protected speech. *State v. Robinson*, 82 P.3d 27 (Mont. 2003), *cert. denied*, 541 U.S. 1037 (2004).

Convictions Overturned

- A police officer siting in his police vehicle saw a woman videotaping him. The officer ran a license check on an automobile next to the woman, and then exited his vehicle to ask her who owned the car. She stated her grandfather owned the car. The officer returned to his vehicle, and the defendant approached its passenger-side open window and asked why the officer ran the license check. The officer said he "could run a check if he wanted to," and the defendant walked away, hurling profanities at the officer. The officer exited his vehicle and arrested the defendant for disorderly conduct. A resulting search uncovered crack cocaine in the defendant's pocket. He was convicted of possession of cocaine and disorderly conduct.

On appeal, the court reversed both convictions. It held the abusive language was not accompanied by any threat of "public harm," and did not put the officer in any fear for his safety. Moreover, the court said, the officer was trained to deal with emotional situations such as this and was expected to respond with reserve. The disorderly conduct charge was reversed, and because the search that uncovered the cocaine was the result of an improper arrest, the cocaine should not have been admitted at the defendant's trial. *People v. Baker*, 984 N.E.2d 902 (NY 2013).

- National Park Service rangers were attempting to arrest a suspect in Yosemite National Park. A crowd gathered, and hurled insults at the rangers. The defendant, when told to disperse, said "f--- you" and refused to leave the

VERBAL OFFENSES

Type of Verbal Offense	To Constitute the Verbal Offense, There Must Be
Fighting words[a]	1. Insulting or abusive language 2. Addressed to a person face to face 3. Causing a likelihood that "the person addressed will make an immediate violent response"
Obscenity	1. A communication that, taken as a whole, appeals to the prurient (lustful) interest in sex 2. And portrays sexual conduct in a patently offensive way 3. And the communication, taken as a whole, does not have serious literary, artistic, political, or scientific value
Inciting or urging unlawful conduct	1. Language or communication directed toward inciting, producing, or urging 2. Imminent lawless action or conduct, or 3. Language or communication likely to incite or produce such unlawful conduct
Obstruction of a law enforcement officer or of justice	1. Deliberate and intentional language (or other communication) that hinders, obstructs, delays, or makes more difficult 2. A law enforcement officer's effort to perform his or her official duties (the scienter element of knowledge by the defendant that he or she knew the person obstructed was a law enforcement officer is required) 3. Some states require that "the interference would have to be, in part at least, physical in nature" (see the New York case of *People v. Case*)
Abusive, obscene, or harassing telephone calls	1. Evidence showing that the telephone call was deliberate 2. And made with intent to harass, frighten, or abuse another person 3. And any other requirement of the particular statute or ordinance
Loud speech and loud noise	Cities and states may: 1. Forbid speech and noises meant by the volume to disturb others, and 2. Forbid noise and loud speech that create a clear and present danger of violence

[a]Many state courts apply a higher fighting words standard to law enforcement officers.

area. The next day he was arrested and charged with violation of the federal disorderly conduct statute. He was convicted and appealed. The Ninth Circuit Court of Appeals reversed the conviction for disorderly conduct, holding the words were not "fighting words," nor were they likely to incite the crowd to violence. *United States v. Poocha*, 259 F.3d 1077 (9th Cir. 2001).

Obscene Communications

obscenity Communication that the average person, using contemporary community standards, would find appeals to the prurient interests or depicts sexual conduct in a patently offensive manner and, taken as a whole, lacks serious artistic, literary, political, or scientific value.

Obscenity is not protected by the First Amendment and may be forbidden by government. Defining obscenity, however, has been the subject of many court rulings and debates. The U.S. Supreme Court established the following guidelines for American courts to define obscenity in the famous case of *Miller v. California* [13]:

- Whether "the average person applying contemporary community standards" would find that the work, taken as a whole, appeals to the prurient interest.[14]
- Whether the work or communication depicts or describes, in a patently offensive way, sexual conduct specifically defined by the applicable state law.
- Whether the work or communication, taken as a whole, lacks serious literary, artistic, political, or scientific value.

Inciting and Urging Unlawful Acts

inciting The offense of urging another to commit an unlawful act.

Inciting or urging another person to commit a crime or perform an unlawful act was a misdemeanor at common law. The offense is committed even though another person does not commit the suggested act. The First Amendment does not protect speech and other forms of communication that encourage others to commit crimes. To be unlawful, the speech or other communication must be "directed to inciting or producing *imminent* lawless action and [must be] likely to produce such action."[15]

The U.S. Supreme Court cases of *Hess v. Indiana*[16] and *Brandenberg v. Ohio*[17] involved convictions for inciting violence based on statements to crowds that seemed to urge others to commit violent acts ("we'll take the f------ streets later"; "there might have to be some revenge taken"). The U.S. Supreme Court held that the words of the defendants in both cases did not urge imminent (immediate) lawless action, and therefore neither defendant could be convicted of disorderly conduct or inciting. In neither case did the words of the defendant constitute a clear and present danger.

Defamation: Libel and Slander

defamation The offense of injuring the character or reputation of another by oral or written communication of false statements. Defamation consists of libel (written offense) or slander (oral offense).

The crime and the civil offense of defamation go back more than 700 years in the law. As early as 1275, the English Parliament enacted a libel statute that forbade false news and tales. The colonies and the original thirteen states undoubtedly all had laws concerning libel and slander. Over the years, the laws of England and the United States developed into the libel, slander, and defamation laws of today.

Defamation is the offense of injuring the character or reputation of another by oral or written communication of false statements. Defamation consists of the twin offenses of *libel* and *slander*. Libel is generally a written offense, whereas slander is generally an

THE FORMER CRIMES OF BLASPHEMY, PROFANITY, AND INDECENT LANGUAGE

People in the United States have become accustomed to hearing profanity in both public and private settings. The F-bomb gets dropped far more than it should, most people believe, but they also believe (correctly) that it is generally not a crime to drop it. In this box we discuss the cases that led to the current rules on profanity in public places.

Prior to the 1970s, most American cities and counties had ordinances that made it an offense to use profanity or vulgar language in a public place. The 1970 ruling of the U.S. Supreme Court in the case of *Cohen v. California* made major changes in this area of criminal law.

Cohen was arrested in the Los Angeles courthouse because he was wearing a jacket with "F___ the Draft" printed on the back to protest the Vietnam War. Cohen would not have been arrested if he had voiced his opposition with the message "Darn the Draft" or "To Heck with the Draft." The U.S. Supreme Court reversed Cohen's conviction for disorderly conduct, ruling that a state "may not, consistent with the First and Fourteenth Amendments, make the simple public display here involved of this single four-letter expletive a criminal offense."

The *Cohen* case established the following two concepts regarding the public use of vulgar, profane, or indecent language:

1. The U.S. Supreme Court defended Cohen's use of the admittedly vulgar word *f___*. The Court refused to allow a state "to cleanse public debate to the point where it is grammatically palatable to the most squeamish among us," because, the Court concluded, "one man's vulgarity is another's lyric." This ruling makes it difficult to define any vulgar, profane, impolite, or other language as a crime, in and of itself.

2. The U.S. Supreme Court also held that people "in the Los Angeles courthouse could effectively avoid further bombardment of their sensibilities simply by averting their eyes." In the 1975 case of

oral offense. Although most states probably have one or more criminal defamation or libel statutes, charges under these statutes are rarely filed, in part because of the First Amendment conflicts and the Supreme Court's decision in *Garrison v. Louisiana*,[18] which struck down a Louisiana criminal libel statute as unconstitutional. A recent case illustrates some aspects of the problems with filing criminal libel prosecutions.

Colorado has a criminal libel statute, Colo. Rev. Stat. § 18-13-105, which makes it a class 6 felony to utter false statements about a person with the intent to damage his reputation or hold the person up to public ridicule or contempt. In *Mink v. Suthers*,[19] a college student was arrested based on a complaint that the student had violated this statute by publishing rude and false stories about a professor in the student's Internet magazine. Because of First Amendment concerns, the state prosecutor decided not to prosecute the student, although the prosecutor did authorize the issuance of a search warrant. The Court of Appeals upheld the student's right to bring a case for damages against the district attorney for her decision to authorize a search warrant to seize the student's computer.

States have sometimes repealed criminal libel statutes after a court has found the statute to be overbroad. In *Parmelee v. O'Neil*, 186 P.3d 1090 (Wash. App. 2008), a court of appeals held the Washington Criminal Libel statute, RCW p.58.010,

Erznoznik v. City of Jacksonville, the Supreme Court held that "the burden normally falls upon the viewer to avoid further bombardment of [his] sensibilities simply by averting his eyes."[a]

The following bumper sticker cases illustrate the efforts in a few states to regulate language seen on bumper stickers:

- The state of Georgia attempted to stop use of a bumper sticker stating "Shit Happens." The Georgia Supreme Court held that the statute used was overbroad, because it regulated protected speech as well as unprotected speech. The court held that because people were not compelled to look at the bumper sticker and could turn their eyes away, there was no captive audience. And because the law was not written to protect children, the relaxed standard of review for the protection of children could not be used. See *Cunningham v. State,* 400 S.E.2d 916 (1991).
- The 1991 case of *Baker v. Glover,* 776 F. Supp. 1511 (M.D. Ala.), concerned an Alabama law forbidding obscene bumper stickers and signs. "Warning tickets" were issued for the first violation of the new obscenity statute. Baker was a truck driver and received a warning for a bumper sticker on his truck that read, "How's My Driving? Call 1-800-EAT-Shit." After Baker was warned that he would be fined if he did not remove the bumper sticker, he commenced a lawsuit in federal court alleging violation of his First Amendment right of freedom of expression. The federal court held that because the message on the bumper sticker did not appeal to a "prurient interest," the state could not forbid the message as obscene. The bumper sticker also was held to have a serious literary or political value as a protest against the Big Brother mentality of urging the public to report bad driving by truck drivers.

[a]91 S. Ct. 1788.

unconstitutional as overbroad and a violation of the First Amendment. In 2009 the Washington legislature repealed the statute.

Most victims choose to rely primarily on the civil actions of libel and slander that are available to them. Money awards to both compensate and punish can be obtained through the civil suits. The burden of proof is also lower in civil actions.

The "fighting words" doctrine is limited to face-to-face confrontation involving a communication that either causes violence or tends to cause a violent reaction by a person to whom the words are addressed. The law of defamation requires that the communication be made to people other than the victim and that the victim's reputation be lowered in the esteem of any substantial and respectable group. It is possible that words spoken could be not only fighting words but also the basis for civil libel and slander suits.

Law enforcement officers and other public officials carry a heavier burden if they file a lawsuit for defamation. Law enforcement officers have been defined by case law as public officials. To succeed as plaintiffs in a defamation proceeding, as public officials they must plead and prove that the person or newspaper publishing the defamation did so with a reckless disregard as to the truth or falsity of the statements.[20]

Symbolic Speech and the First Amendment

Symbols, along with gestures, conduct, and speech, have always been used to communicate between human beings. The symbol can be used alone or with other forms of communication.

Uniforms and the way people dress are types of symbols. People often communicate by their dress who they are, what their lifestyles are, and, to some extent, what they think and believe. The following seminal **symbolic speech** case came before the Supreme Court in 1969:

symbolic speech
Nonverbal expressions that convey a belief or idea.

During the Vietnam War, a group of Iowa students wished to communicate their opposition to the war by wearing black armbands in school. However, the high school principal forbade the armbands, which led to the lawsuit *Tinker v. Des Moines Independent Community School District*.[21] Because the black armbands did not disrupt classes or school, the U.S. Supreme Court in *Tinker* sustained the students' action, holding

> The wearing of an armband … was closely akin to pure speech, which we have repeatedly held is entitled to comprehensive protection under the First Amendment. Students or teachers [do not] shed their constitutional rights of freedom of speech or expression at the schoolhouse gate.

Flag Burning and Cross Burning as Symbolic Speech

Flags are symbols. The American flag has symbolic meanings that are cherished by most Americans. This, however, has sometimes caused protesters and demonstrators seeking to make a political statement to burn or otherwise defile an American flag in an attempt to communicate the message.

In past years, states had statutes that made this type of defilement of the American flag a crime. If the demonstrators burned their own flag as a means to communicate a political message, the symbolic act was held to have the protection of the First Amendment in the two U.S. Supreme Court cases of *Texas v. Johnson*,[22] and *United States v. Eichman*.[23]

Cross burning can also be a symbolic act that seeks to communicate a message, and therefore it can also have First Amendment protection. A statute that prohibited all forms of cross burning would be unconstitutional. In the case of *R.A.V. v. St. Paul, Minnesota*, the U.S. Supreme Court struck down a St. Paul ordinance making it a crime to burn a cross[24] with an intent to communicate a hate message. The Court found the ordinance invalid because the ordinance forbade the symbolic conduct "based on its [the ordinance's] hostility to the underlying (hate) message."

However, in the 2003 case of *Virginia v. Black*,[25] 538 U.S. 343 (2003), a majority of the U.S. Supreme Court held that a Virginia statute that made it criminal to burn a cross on public property or property of another "with the intent of intimidating any person or group of persons" was not unconstitutional on its face. The Court distinguished *R.A.V.* because there the focus of the ban on cross burning was the content of the message intended to be communicated by the burning. In *Black* the ban on

CASE CLOSE-UP

United States v. Stevens
United States Supreme Court,
130 S. Ct. 1577 (2010)

Defendant Stevens was charged with violation of 18 U.S.C. § 48, which makes it a crime for anyone who knowingly "creates, sells, or possesses a depiction of animal cruelty" if done for commercial gain. A depiction of animal cruelty is defined in the act as one "in which a living animal is intentionally maimed, mutilated, tortured, wounded, or killed" if the act violates state or federal law. The legislative history of the statute makes it clear Congress was intending to punish those who create, sell or possess so-called "crush videos," where women are filmed while crushing small animals such as cats, monkeys, or mice with either their bare feet or wearing high heels. Such videos were often accompanied by the sounds of anguish emitted by the animals, or dominatrix patter by the women.

Stevens was convicted of violating § 48 based on sales he made of videos showing pit bull dogfights, and attacks made by pit bulls on other animals. The trial court dismissed Stevens's claim that the statute violated the First Amendment, holding that depictions defined in § 48, just as in the case of child pornography and obscenity, were not protected by the First Amendment. On appeal, the Third Circuit Court of Appeals reversed the conviction, holding that the conduct covered by § 48 was covered by the First Amendment.

On appeal, the Supreme Court affirmed. It rejected the government's argument that animal cruelty depictions should be treated the same as child pornography, and not protected by the First Amendment. (See the discussion of *United States v. Williams*, 553 U.S. 285 (2008), where the Court declined to apply the overbreadth doctrine to a child pornography statute. That case is discussed in Chapter 12, pages 351-352.) In the 2012 case of *United States v. Alvarez*, 132 S. Ct. 2537, the Court rejected the government's argument that false statements, like child pornography, are never protected by the First Amendment. (That case is discussed earlier in this chapter.) The Court decided the case based on the "overbreadth" doctrine. The Court stated that Stevens's objection to the statute was based on its "facial" overbreadth, that is, that the statute as written can be applied to conduct that is clearly lawful and ordinary, and by making such conduct a crime violates the overbreadth doctrine. The Court agreed, noting that under the statute a depiction of any "killing" or "wounding" of an animal would be a violation, so long as the conduct was unlawful in the state where the sale or possession of the depiction occurred. The statute does not require that such "killing" or "wounding" be done cruelly. As a result, the Court said, the statute would make criminal the "humane slaughter" of a stolen cow, or a video depicting killing an animal during recreational hunting that was legal in the state where the killing occurred, but illegal where the depiction was sold or possessed. The United States argued that prosecutions would be limited to "crush" video depictions, noting that President Clinton issued a signing statement when he signed the bill into law that prosecutions should be limited to depictions of wanton cruelty to animals to appeal to prurient interests in sex. The Court rejected that argument, stating that notwithstanding the signing statement, here the prosecution was based on depictions that had no prurient sexual connotations. Because lawful, protected conduct could be made criminal under the terms of the statute, the overbreadth doctrine rendered the statute unconstitutional. The Court did suggest that a statute properly limited to apply to "crush" videos might pass constitutional muster.

cross burning focused on the intended intimidating effect the burning had on people, regardless of the content of the message the cross burners intended. Taking action, even though it might involve symbolic speech, with the intent to intimidate another is not a protected activity. The Court also concluded, however, that the Virginia statute was unconstitutional as applied, because the statute contained a provision that made burning a cross prima facie evidence of an intent to intimidate another person. This provision, the Court said, invites a jury to punish based solely on the fact of the cross burning, without specifically finding an intent to intimidate.

Threats of Violence as Crimes

A threat becomes a crime if it is explicit and likely to result in imminent lawless action. Threats can be charged as various crimes, such as disorderly conduct, inciting violence, or even racketeering if made repeatedly (see Chapter 18). If accompanied by "physical menace," the Model Penal Code, Section 211.1(l)(c), makes **threats of violence** an assault.

Many states have specific statutes making "terroristic threats" a crime.[26] The First Amendment provides no protection for threats of violence because the purpose of the speech is not to communicate ideas but to put another person in fear of imminent physical harm.

In the following examples courts considered if speech was a **true threat** and not protected by the First Amendment, or protected speech:

threats of violence
Statements or actions that unequivocally convey the message that violent actions will be taken.

true threat A serious expression of an intent to inflict bodily harm.

- *Threats against public officials:* In particular, threats against the president of the United States. Such threats are a violation of federal law (18 U.S.C § 871). That statute requires only that the threat be made, and does not require proof that the defendant had the ability or intent to carry out the threat. In the 2013 case of *United States v. Turner*, a federal court of appeals held that blog postings advocating the murder of federal judges were not protected speech.[27] Most states have laws making it a crime to threaten a state official, and require proof similar to the federal statute. In *Abbott v. State*, 989 A.2d 795 (Md. App. 2010), the court reversed a conviction under Md. C. L. § 3-708, threats against public officials. The defendant sent a threatening e-mail to the website maintained by the governor of Maryland, which solicited comments from citizens. The court found that the trial court did not properly instruct the jury on whether a reasonable person would have believed the threat was serious.
- *Threats by schoolchildren against teachers or other students:* Because of the number of school killings in recent years, officials have begun taking students' threats very seriously. However, to be the basis of a criminal conviction (as opposed to school discipline), the threat must be a "true threat." In *In re Douglas D.*,[28] the Wisconsin Supreme Court overturned the conviction of a high school student under Wisconsin's disorderly conduct statute. The student wrote an essay in class in which the main character (clearly the student) stated he would come to school the next day and cut off the teacher's head. The court held the essay was not a true threat, because the student could not reasonably understand that a reasonable person would view the statement as a serious expression of intent to inflict bodily harm, which is the definition of a "true threat."

- In *Fogel v. Collins,* 531 F.3d 824 (9th Cir. 2009) the court held that painting a sign on the back of a van that said "I am a f——g suicide bomber communist terrorist" was not a true threat, and thus was protected speech. The court stated that a reasonable person viewing the van, which was covered with clearly political statements, would not find the "threat" to be a serious expression of intent to inflict bodily harm.

- *Terrorist threats:* Since the events of September 11, 2001, state and federal governments take terrorist threats seriously. The Model Penal Code, Section 211.3, makes it a third-degree felony to make threats designed to cause the evacuation of public buildings or public conveyances. Many states have also passed "false bomb report" laws, which make it a crime to give a false statement to a police officer or airline employee about concealing a bomb. In *Levin v. United Airlines,*[29] the court held that Cal. Penal Code § 148.1 was constitutional and required only that a person making a false statement about a concealed bomb do so knowing the statement was false. The court stated that "true threat" rules did not apply, because the statute was not directed to the content of the statement, but simply made the **act** of making the false statement a crime. The statute in effect was a codification of Justice Holmes's famous example of yelling "fire" in a crowded theater, the court said.

- *Violations of restraining orders:* Restraining orders directed against former spouses, boyfriends, girlfriends, and family members are routinely issued in an attempt to prevent violence and harassment. Violation of a restraining order can subject the violator to a contempt charge or other criminal liability. In *Cobble v. State,*[30] a defendant was convicted under the Georgia terroristic threat statute when he stood outside his former girlfriend's house and yelled obscenities directed at her. When the police arrived and subdued him, the defendant stated that as soon as he was released, he would return and kill the girlfriend. Even though the girlfriend did not hear those threats, the court found the defendant guilty under the terroristic threat statute.

Using the U.S. Mail, Telephones, the Internet, or E-Mail to Threaten Another Person

Whether speech constitutes a threat is usually a question of state law. However, when the threat is made by U.S. mail, telephones, the Internet, or other interstate communication devices, the threat can also result in a federal charge. Such threats include the following:

Telephone threats   The defendant, a member of the White Aryan Peoples Party, was convicted in 2004 of knowingly transmitting a threat in interstate commerce when he telephoned three synagogues and left a threatening voicemail message: "We're going to blow up your f------ synagogue this coming week and send you f-----s to the gas chambers." He was convicted of three counts of violating 18 U.S.C. § 844(e).[31]

U.S. Mail threats   In 2006 two defendants were convicted of violating 18 U.S.C. § 876 by mailing threatening communications to judges hearing litigation claims the defendants were asserting in the judges' courts. The letters sent included references to Judge Joan Lefkow, a judge whose family had been murdered by a disgruntled litigant, with the note "Be Aware Be Fair." The court of appeals affirmed the conviction, rejecting defendants' claim that they did not intend to threaten the judges. The court said that the statute does not require the government to prove intent, only that the letter was threatening, and that it was sent knowingly.[32]

E-mail and Internet threats   Using e-mail or the Internet to express a threat of violence is also a federal crime. In 2012 a defendant was convicted of violating 18 U.S.C. § 875(c) by posting a music video on YouTube and a Facebook link. The video was addressed to the judge hearing a child custody case in which the defendant was involved. The video's lyrics included the words "Take my child and I'll take your life." The appeals court affirmed the defendant's conviction, rejecting his claim that he didn't really mean the words. The court said the statute does not have a subjective intent requirement; all the government had to prove is that a reasonable observer would regard the video as a true threat.[33]

Many states have passed statutes making it a crime to use e-mails or the Internet to harass a person. In *Massimo v. State*,[34] a defendant was convicted of violation of Texas Penal Code Section 42.07(a)(2), unlawful harassment by electronic communication, when she sent repeated e-mails to a former friend threatening to kill her and her children.

Bullying: Not a Crime, but It Can Consist of Criminal Conduct

In 2010 the State of New York became the forty-third state to enact an "anti-bullying" law. This law requires schools to ban bullying practices, train their staffs to combat bullying, and to formulate anti-bullying programs. While bullying itself is not a crime, the conduct associated with bullying can be criminal.

The U.S. Department of Justice, Office of Community Oriented Policing Services (COPS), defines bullying as having two components:

1. Repeated harmful acts which involve physical, verbal, or psychological attacks of intimidation
2. Directed against victims who cannot properly defend themselves because of size or strength, or because they are outnumbered or less psychologically resilient.

The director of COPS stated that while bullying was once viewed as harmless adolescent behavior, it is now known that bullying can have a long-term effect on both the bully and the victim, and can lead to other forms of violence. The increased use of the Internet has also created cyberbullying, which can exacerbate consequences. In the legislative history to § 814, McKinney's New York Education Statutes (2008), the New York legislature cited a U.S. Department of Justice survey that found one out of every five children ages 10 to 17 received sexual exploitation advances over the Internet. The survey also quoted findings by I-SAFE, a non-profit youth Internet safety organization, that 42 percent of children using the Internet have been subjected to bullying when online.

Municipal and county law enforcement offices regularly respond to calls from local schools, and they often place officers within schools to monitor student conduct and enforce state laws. Under the U.S. Supreme Court ruling in *Tinker v. Des Moines School District,* discussed in this chapter, schools may impose discipline on students when the student's speech or conduct, including bullying behavior, substantially interferes with the school's educational mission. However, schools cannot control the bullying that occurs outside of school, or on the Internet.

The consequences of a combination of in-school bullying and Internet harassment can be deadly. On January 14, 2010, Phoebe Prince, a 15-year-old student at South Hadley (Massachusetts) High School, hanged herself after months of bullying at school and over the Internet. Five of her classmates pled guilty to criminal harassment, and received sentences of probation and community service. In March 2010 Alexis Skye Pilkington, a 17-year-old Long Island, N.Y. high school student, killed herself after receiving vicious attacks on the social networking website FormSpring.me.

Additional material on bullying in schools can be found on the U.S. Department of Justice COPS website at http://cops.usdoj.gov.

Loud Noise or Nuisance Speech

The U.S. Supreme Court has stated that "it can no longer be doubted that government has a substantial interest in protecting its citizens from unwelcome noise" in *Ward v. Rock Against Racism*.[35] The *Ward* case upheld a New York City regulation that gave city officials broad authority to regulate sounds from Central Park performances.

City ordinances regulating private parties often present both First Amendment and overbreadth problems. In the 2011 case of *U.R.I. Students v. Town of Narragansett*[36] a federal court of appeals upheld a town ordinance that imposed criminal penalties on owners and users of private property where loud or drunken parties were held. Students at the nearby University of Rhode Island often rented housing in Narragansett, and then had loud parties. The city council passed an ordinance that provided that once a property had been "posted" for a loud gathering, a subsequent "loud gathering" on the property was a crime punishable by a fine. The landowners and student renters claimed the ordinance violated their First Amendment and due process rights, but the court of appeals disagreed. It said the ordinance was valid because it required as a precondition to liability a showing that persons at a gathering had violated some other law, such as public intoxication or public urination.

In *Kovacs v. Cooper*, the U.S. Supreme Court upheld a city ordinance that prohibited the use of sound trucks that emitted "loud and raucous" noise on city streets:

> City streets are recognized as a normal place for the exchange of ideas by speech or paper. But this does not mean the freedom is beyond all control. We think it is a permissible exercise of legislative discretion to bar sound trucks with broadcasts of public interest, amplified to a loud and raucous volume, from the public ways of municipalities.[37]

Regulating the Use of Public and Private Places

The First Amendment guarantees "the right of the people peacefully to assemble and to petition the Government for a redress of grievances." First Amendment freedoms and the rights of expression in public places, however, are not absolute. They may be limited or restricted in order to insure public safety and order. Figure 9.1 illustrates the balance that must be maintained between First Amendment freedoms and public welfare.

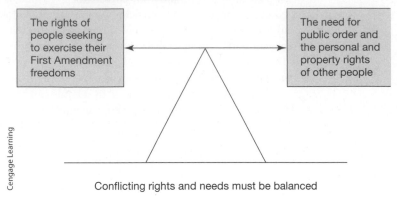

FIGURE 9.1   Balancing Tests Used by Courts to Determine the Limits of First Amendment Freedoms

When a city, state, or federal agency restricts or limits conduct, it must show the following:

1. The government has significant interest (or good reason) based on the nature of the property or some other source.
2. The restriction or limitation can be no greater "than is essential to the furtherance of that (substantial) interest." See *United States v. O'Brien*.[38]
3. A government (federal or state) may regulate property "under its control for the use for which it is lawfully dedicated" *Adderley v. Florida*,[39] where defendants trespassed in an area of a jail closed to the public.
4. Where there is communication (for example, yelling at a basketball game in a public arena as distinguished from yelling in a library or during a city council meeting), the U.S. Supreme Court has said, "[T]he crucial question is whether the manner of expression is basically incompatible with the normal activity of a particular place at a particular time." See *Grayned v. City of Rockford*.[40]

Under these guidelines, governments may regulate picketing, whether it be at a city hall, a factory, or an abortion clinic; demonstrations, whether against some government action or in celebration of winning the World Series, parades;[41] and door-to-door canvassing and passing out handbills, whether for political or commercial purposes. The next sections in this chapter discuss some of the crimes charged under a city or state's power to regulate streets and public places.

The Crimes of Unlawful Assembly and Rioting

Under the common law, an **unlawful assembly**[43] was a gathering of three or more people for any unlawful purpose or under such circumstances as to endanger the public peace or cause alarm and apprehension.

An unlawful assembly became a **riot** under the old common law when those assembled began to execute their enterprise by a breach of the peace. A riot was

---

unlawful assembly
Under the common law, a gathering of three or more people for any unlawful purpose or under such circumstances as to endanger the public peace or cause alarm and apprehension.

riot   Under the common law, a tumultuous disturbance of the peace by three or more people assembled with a common purpose to do an unlawful act.

PERJURY, SUBORNATION OF PERJURY, AND THE FEDERAL FALSE STATEMENT ACT

The crime of perjury consists of knowingly and materially testifying falsely while under oath. It applies to false statements made under oath to judicial courts, grand juries, or legislative bodies such as the U.S. Congress. The crime of subornation of perjury is committed when a person induces, urges, or knowingly permits another to testify falsely.

People who lie to a federal investigator can be charged with a crime under the Federal False Statement Act, even if they are not under oath. In the case of *Brogan v. United States*,[42] federal investigators from the Labor Department and the Internal Revenue Service asked Brogan during an investigation whether he had received any illegal cash or gifts in the matter they were investigating. Brogan was not in custody, nor did the federal agents intend to take him into custody. But the federal agents did know and had evidence that Brogan had received illegal payments.

When Brogan denied receiving illegal payments and said "no" to the question of the federal investigators, his lie became the basis for federal prosecution under the Federal False Statement Act, which forbids "false, fictitious, or fraudulent statements or representations." Brogan's statement was found to be a deliberate falsehood, and he was convicted of violating the act.

In another case, celebrity Martha Stewart was questioned by federal investigators in regard to her sale of stock just prior to the collapse of the stock's price. Based on her answers, she was charged with the crime of making false statements to the investigators. In 2004, she was convicted of that crime, and sentenced to five months in prison, five months of home confinement, and a $30,000 fine.

In 2011 baseball player Barry Bonds was convicted of obstruction of justice based on false statements he made to a grand jury investigating the use of steroids in professional sports. He was acquitted of a charge of perjury. Bonds was sentenced to 30 days of house arrest, 2 years of probation, and 250 hours of community service. Bonds is appealing his conviction.

a tumultuous disturbance of the peace by three or more people assembled with a common purpose to do an unlawful act.[44] Riot was a misdemeanor at common law, and all persons who encouraged, promoted, or took part in a riot were criminally liable.

States have by statute adopted one or both of these common law crimes. The state of New York, for example, has enacted the following offenses:[45]

- Section 240.10 Unlawful assembly (class B misdemeanor)
- Section 240.08 Inciting to riot (class A misdemeanor)
- Section 240.06 Riot in the first degree (class E felony)
- Section 240.05 Riot in the second degree (class A misdemeanor)

The present federal riot control statute, § 2102, Title 18, United States Code Annotated, provides in part as follows:

As used in this chapter, the term "riot" means a public disturbance involving (1) an act or acts of violence by one or more persons part of an assemblage of three or more persons, which act or acts shall constitute a clear and present danger of, or shall result in, damage or injury to the property of any other person or to the

OBEYING LAWFUL POLICE ORDERS

Failure to obey a lawful, valid police order is punished as an offense in all states. For example, Section 843.02 of the Florida Criminal Code forbids resisting an officer: "Whoever shall obstruct or oppose any such officer … in the execution of legal process or in the lawful execution of any legal duty … shall be guilty of a misdemeanor of the first degree." The following cases illustrate the rule:

Case	Facts of Case	Ruling
City of Oak Creek v. King, Wisconsin Supreme Court, 436 N.W.2d 285 (1989)	When a commercial airline crashed near an airport, the site was sealed off so that emergency equipment and personnel could assist the injured and dying. The defendant and other employees of a newspaper were repeatedly ordered to leave the area, but the defendant wanted to take pictures of the crash site and stated that he would not leave unless he was arrested. The defendant was arrested and convicted of disorderly conduct (not the charge of refusal to obey the police order). The Wisconsin Supreme Court affirmed his conviction and $40 fine.	"We conclude that the appellant's repeated refusal to obey Detective White's reasonable order, combined with his continued penetration into a nonpublic restricted area in the presence of the general public, was conduct of a type which tends to cause or provoke a disturbance, under the circumstances as they then existed. Therefore, we affirm the decision of the circuit court finding the appellant guilty of disorderly conduct."
Georgia v. Storey, Court of Appeals of Georgia, 351 S.E.2d 502, *review denied*, 107 S. Ct. 1895 (1987)	The defendant and others disrupted the Georgia legislature by shouting opposition to the death penalty. They then refused to obey orders of police and security persons to leave the state capitol building.	Convictions for disrupting the legislature and refusal to obey orders were affirmed, and the U.S. Supreme Court denied review.
State v. Jaramillo, New Mexico Supreme Court, 498 P.2d 687 (1972)	The defendants sat and lay on the floor in the governor's waiting room. They refused to leave when the office closed at 5:00 p.m., and again refused to leave when the building closed at 6:00 p.m. They were convicted under the New Mexico "wrongful use of public property" statute.	The convictions were affirmed, and the statute was held to be constitutional. The court stated: "There is no question but that a State may regulate the use and occupancy of public buildings."
Daniel v. Tampa, Florida, Federal Court of Appeals, 11th Cir., 38 F3d 546, *review denied*, 115 S. Ct. 2557 (1995)	Because of serious crime problems in public housing projects, canvassing was forbidden. Defendant was warned and refused to leave the building. Conviction for trespass was affirmed.	Florida's trespass-after-warning statute was sustained, and because this was a neutral restriction on speech, it was held to be a reasonable means of combating crime in the public housing project. No First Amendment violation occurred.

person of any other individual or (2) a threat or threats of the commission of an act or acts of violence by one or more persons part of an assemblage…. where the performance of the threatened act or acts of violence would constitute a clear and present danger of, or would result in, damage or injury to the property of any other person or to the person of any other individual.

In *United States v. Markiewicz,*[46] a federal court of appeals upheld the conviction under the Riot Act of six members of the Oneida Indian tribe. The defendants gathered on tribal lands to confront other tribal members over control of a bingo parlor on tribal property, and subsequently burned down the parlor.

Obstruction of the Law Enforcement Process

The crime of obstruction can be committed in many different ways. Failure to identify oneself when there is a legal obligation to do so is a frequent problem. In 2004 the U.S. Supreme Court upheld a state statute that required individuals to identify themselves when they were the subjects of a lawful investigative detention or police stop. There, a police officer who was investigating a report of an assault on a woman asked the suspect, Hiibel, to identify himself eleven times. When Hiibel, who appeared intoxicated, refused to do so, he was arrested and later convicted of the crime of "willfully resisting, delaying, or obstructing a public officer in discharging … any duty of his office." The U.S. Supreme Court held that "stop and identify" laws go back hundreds of years and were a staple of English and American law. In affirming Hiibel's conviction, the Court stated that it had never had an obstruction of justice case come before it in which disclosure of a person's name would violate the Fifth Amendment right to remain silent.[47]

The following are some of the many incidents that could result in a charge of obstruction or other similar crime.

- A witness to a felony or serious accident refusing to identify himself when questioned by the police investigating the crime or accident.
- Making false material statements or providing false information to a law enforcement officer or other investigation (18 U.S.C. § 1038 makes this a federal crime).
- Tampering with a witness, victim, or informant (a federal crime under 18 U.S.C. § 1512).
- Giving false identifying information to an officer that obstructs a computer records search.
- Obstructing a crime scene, such as by destroying evidence (e.g., erasing fingerprints), planting false evidence, or altering evidence to make the incident appear to be an accident.
- Failing to identify a known offender. For example, a Wisconsin attorney had a friend drive her home in her car from a late-night party because she had been drinking. The friend drove the car on a sidewalk, and when police spotted the car, the friend drove off at high speeds to evade arrest, a felony. The friend

ultimately ran off, and the attorney refused to identify him. However, when faced with a contempt charge, the attorney identified the driver, who was arrested and convicted of fleeing from the police.

Public Nuisances as Civil or Criminal Offenses

Under common law, a public nuisance was a civil offense. More than 200 years ago Blackstone, the famous English lawyer, described *nuisances* as "anything that unlawfully worketh hurt, inconvenience, or damage" (Blackstone 3 *Commentaries,* 216).

Today, cities and states continue to use the civil law of public nuisances to correct problems. By going into a civil court and filing a civil lawsuit, a city can petition the court to declare a public problem to be a nuisance and urge civil remedies. Public nuisance laws have been used to

- Seize and tear down crack houses and property owned by slumlords who allow their properties to be used by gangs or drug dealers.
- Seize and take title to the motor vehicles of people who commit offenses such as having sex with a prostitute on a public street.[48]
- Obtain court orders against repeat offenders, such as people who blocked the entrances to abortion clinics. After some people were arrested more than fifty times, a Wisconsin court issued a court order forbidding this conduct and made violations of the court order punishable by a fine of up to $5,000 and a jail sentence of up to 1 year.
- Obtain court orders against prostitutes with five or more convictions, ordering them not to loiter in specific areas of a city or to flag down cars. Violation of the court order is a much more serious offense than the conviction for prostitution or loitering for the purpose of prostitution and can be punished by a larger fine and longer jail sentences.
- An apartment building, a bar, or other building can be declared a "chronic nuisance" if law officers are repeatedly called to quell a disturbance at the premises. Many ordinances permit the city to bill the owner of the building for the cost of the police calls and other necessary city or county services performed.

The Crime of Stalking and Violation of Protective Orders

stalking   A crime involving activities such as spying on the victim, following the victim, or attempting to communicate with the victim through the telephone or mail. Cyberstalking through the Internet is also a crime.

Stalking has become a serious problem in the United States and in Europe. Stalkers have attacked musician John Lennon, tennis star Monica Seles, and some former U.S. presidents. Margaret Mary Ray, the woman who for years stalked TV host David Letterman, committed suicide in 1998 by kneeling in front of a speeding train. Often stalking involves offenders who had a previous relationship with the victim. Stalking has now been made criminal in most states, whether or not the stalker ever commits some other crime against the victim, such as assault or battery. Activities such as spying on the victim, following the victim, or attempting to communicate with the victim through the telephone or mail can be charged as stalking.[49]

Authorities encourage victims to carefully document the stalker's activities, such as in a daily log or journal. This makes it possible for the police to conclude a crime is being committed and gives evidence to the prosecution to satisfy its burden to prove to a court the crime was committed.

The federal government has a general stalking statute, 18 U.S.C. § 2261, which prohibits crossing state lines to intimidate or threaten a person. Part B of the statute applies to cyberstalking, which prohibits using the mail or any computer service, such as the Internet, to place another in fear of his life or serious bodily injury. In the 2010 case of *United States v. Grob*[50] the defendant was convicted under this statute when over the course of several weeks he sent twenty-two e-mails and fifty text messages to a former girlfriend stating he would track her down and make her pay for ending the relationship and having a miscarriage.

State courts have the power to issue protective orders in the appropriate circumstances, such as in a divorce case where one spouse will not leave the other spouse alone. Stalking or harassing a person would be another appropriate situation where a protective order could be obtained. Some states have passed statutes specifically directed at stalking, such as the Kansas Protection from Stalking Act, which permits a person who proves the elements of stalking or harassment set out in the statute to obtain a protective order. In 2007 Gwen Wentland, the 2005 U.S. indoor high-jump champion, used this act to obtain a protective order against John Uhlarik, who had stalked Wentland for years.

In the California case of *People v. Grams*,[51] a court had issued a protective order against Grams. Grams was charged with violating the order by stalking his estranged girlfriend. The California law provided that protective orders remained enforceable, notwithstanding the acts of the parties, until the order was changed by the order of the court. Grams argued that he could be entrapped if his girlfriend invited him over and then called the police. The California appellate court held that the California legislature could reasonably provide that only the court could lift the order, as the victim's consent is often misguided. (For further material on harassment and protective orders, see Chapter 11.)

Crime on City Streets

City governments, understandably enough, wish to minimize the amount of street crimes that occur. The use of criminal laws directed at conduct or persons believed to be related to criminal acts is common, but they must be tailored to avoid infringing on individual rights. Some such laws include the following:

- *Anti-cruising laws:* Fines for prohibited cruising—driving cars on designated routes on certain streets during late-night hours—can be as high as $1,000 in some places and may also include short jail sentences. The *Milwaukee Journal Sentinel* reported on April 24, 2007, that the city's new anti-cruising laws resulted in the issuance of 658 tickets and 86 arrests in one weekend. Four shootings occurred on that same weekend.
- *Truancy arrests or detentions:* State laws vary on the treatment of truancy, but in many states authorities are authorized to detain a school-age child not attending

This man is purchasing a firearm for personal use, which under recent Supreme Court decisions discussed in this chapter is his right under the Second Amendment. While he has the "right to bear arms," the right is not absolute. States and the federal government can pass reasonable laws regulating firearms; for example, if this man is ever convicted of a felony he may lose the right to own firearms.

school and in some cases obtain criminal convictions of the child's parents. Enforcement of truancy laws has been shown to cut down on crimes such as burglary, criminal damage to property, theft, and criminal graffiti.

- *Juvenile curfew laws:* Daytime curfew laws are aimed at keeping children in school, while nighttime curfews seek to minimize teen drinking, drug use, fighting, vandalism, and gang activities. Such curfews have generally been upheld if they are not overbroad, that is, written to prohibit conduct that is permitted, like attending school or church events in the evening.
- *Laws directed at homeless persons:* There are close to a million homeless persons on our cities' streets. Some of their conduct can violate criminal laws, such as disorderly conduct, public drinking, and unlawful panhandling. Laws directed specifically at homeless persons—such as prohibitions against sleeping on public streets or parks or in public buildings such as libraries—are generally upheld. (See Chapter 1 for material on homeless persons and status crimes.)

Gun Ownership and Registration Laws

The federal government, the states, and local governments all have power, to some degree, to regulate the ownership, registration, and use of guns, including through the criminal law. All have done so. For example, 28 U.S.C. § 5841 requires the registration of weapons with silencers, sawed-off shotguns, and similar weapons, on the reasoning that these weapons are much more likely to be involved in crimes than other, more ordinary, guns. Violation of this statute can result in a prison sentence of up to 10 years. California Penal Code § 12280(b) bans ownership of assault weapons. District of Columbia Code § 7-2502.02(a)(4) bars registration of handguns, except by retired D.C. police officers.

Prior to 2008 there was uncertainty in courts and legislatures about the limits, if any, on state or federal power to regulate firearms by the Second Amendment to the U.S. Constitution. That amendment states, "A well regulated Militia, being necessary to the security of a free State, the right of the people to keep and bear arms shall not be infringed." Some regarded this as a private right available to all citizens, while others viewed it as a public right, available only to state governments.

In *District of Columbia v. Heller,* 128 S. Ct. 2783 (2008), the U.S. Supreme Court held that the Second Amendment was a private right, and that as a result the District of Columbia could not ban the home possession or ownership of handguns. The Court stated, however, that the District of Columbia could pass reasonable regulations on firearms, such as barring convicted felons from possessing firearms, or passing laws aimed at controlling the sale of firearms.

In *McDonald v. City of Chicago,* 130 S. Ct. 3020 (2010), the Court held that the Second Amendment applied to the states under the Fourteenth Amendment, because the right to bear arms was "firmly rooted" in our nation's history, and was thus a "fundamental right" made binding on states by the Due Process Clause. The Court struck down a Chicago ordinance that (1) banned possession of a firearm without a registration certificate, and then (2) prohibited virtually all citizens from registering handguns. The *McDonald* Court reiterated the statements in *Heller* that reasonable regulation of gun use and ownership was permitted. Because of its virtual prohibition of gun ownership, the Chicago ordinance was not reasonable, the Court said.

Regulating Guns After *Heller*

The federal government, states, and cities have continued to try to regulate ownership and possession of guns after the *Heller* and *McDonald* cases were decided. Some degree of regulation is permitted, since in both cases the Supreme Court was careful to say the Second Amendment right is not unlimited. Certain aspects of the opinion in *Heller* have served as guidelines for courts considering the constitutionality of gun regulations.

First, the actual holding in *Heller* was this: "We hold that the District's ban on handgun possession *in the home* violates the Second Amendment." (Emphasis added) 554 U.S., at 635. Thus, strictly speaking the decision does not address regulations effective *outside* the home.

Second, while the Court said it was not conducting an "exhaustive analysis" of the Second Amendment right, it made it clear that nothing in its decision should cast doubt on prohibitions such as (1) possession of guns by felons and the mentally ill, (2) carrying guns in "sensitive" places like schools and government buildings, (3) placing conditions on the commercial sale of guns, and (4) possession of "unusual weapons" that are not in common use.

Third, the Court said about gun regulations: "And whatever else it leaves for future evaluation, it surely elevates above all other interests the right of law-abiding responsible citizens to use arms in the defense of hearth and home." 554 U.S., at 635.

The following cases applied *Heller* and the Court's statements set out above to claims that gun regulations violated the Second Amendment that were made after *Heller* and *McDonald* were decided.

- *Moore v. Madigan*, 702 F.3d 933 (7th Cir. 2012). The court held the Second Amendment right extended to ownership and possession of guns outside the home. It also held that the Illinois law that prohibited most persons other than police and security guards from carrying "ready-to-use" firearms violated the Second Amendment, because the law was not based on reasonable limitations that satisfy a legitimate governmental interest.

- *United States v. Masciandaro*, 638 F.3d 458 (4th Cir. 2011), *cert. denied,* 132 S. Ct. 756 (2011). The court upheld a conviction under a federal law that made it a crime to carry a loaded gun in a car in a national park. The court held that outside the home the Second Amendment right is subject to regulation, and that such regulations were to be judged by "intermediate scrutiny," not strict scrutiny. All the regulation need do is to regulate the use or possession of guns consistent with a legitimate government purpose. Here, the court said, safety of the general public using a national park was sufficient to justify the limit on the defendant's Second Amendment right. The Fourth Circuit reached a similar decision in the 2013 case of *Woollard v. Gallagher*, 712 F.3d 865 (4th Cir. 2013), where it upheld a Maryland regulation that required citizens to show a "good and substantial reason" for a permit to carry a gun in public for personal protection.

- *Kachalasky v. Westchester County, N.Y.*, 701 F.3d 81 (2nd Cir. 2012). The court upheld New York State's requirement that any person seeking a license to carry a handgun must "demonstrate a special need for self-protection distinguishable from that of the general community." The court said that while Second Amendment protections are at "their zenith" within the home, they do extend outside the home. However, outside the home the government may pass reasonable restrictions. Using "intermediate scrutiny," the court said that limiting the right to carry a concealed gun in public to people who have an actual, not speculative, need for self-defense is a reasonable method to achieve the state's legitimate interest in public safety. A petition for certiorari was filed in January 2013.

- *United States v. Reese*, 627 F.3d 792 (10th Cir. 2011), *cert. denied* 131 S. Ct. 2476 (2011). The court upheld a federal statute making it a crime for an individual under a domestic protection order to possess guns. Using intermediate scrutiny, the court said it was reasonable for the government interest in public safety to keep guns out of the hands of persons with a propensity for violence.

- *United States v. Marzzarella*, 614 F.3d 85 (3rd Cir. 2010), *cert. denied* 131 S. Ct. 958 (2011). The court upheld a federal law making it a crime to possess a gun, in or out of a home, with an obliterated serial number. The court said that while the law applied to the defendant's possession of a gun in his home, it did not bar him from possessing *any* gun, as was the case in *Heller*, but only certain kinds of guns. The court said this was not a prohibition of the core right of the Second Amendment. As a result, the court said intermediate scrutiny was appropriate, and agreed that the government's legitimate interest in being able to trace and identify dangerous articles like guns made the law permissible.

- *United States v. Huitron-Guizar*, 678 F.3d 1164 (10th Cir. 2012), *cert. denied,* 133 S. Ct. 289 (2012). The court upheld the federal statute that makes it a crime for an illegal alien to possess a gun. The court did not hold that illegal aliens have no Second Amendment rights (as some other courts have done, *see United States v. Flores*, 663 F.3d 1022 (8th Cir. 2011), *cert. denied*, 133 S. Ct. 28 (2012)), but did say the kind of rights available to citizens and lawful aliens can be greater than those available to illegal aliens. The court then held that the government's purpose is keeping guns out of the hands of persons who are not easily identified by the government, and who show a willingness to violate the law, was legitimate.

- *National Rifle Association of America v. McCraw*, 719 F.3d 338 (5th Cir. 2013). The court upheld a Texas law that barred most persons under the age of 21 from obtaining a concealed handgun permit because age limitations were one of the "longstanding limitations" courts have upheld.

Forty-nine states permit law-abiding residents to carry concealed handguns. Most do so by requiring applicants to obtain permits, though three states allow residents to carry without a permit. Illinois was the only state with a complete ban on ordinary citizens carrying concealed handguns, and that law was struck down in 2012 (see above). The Seventh Circuit Court gave the Illinois legislature until June 2013 to pass a law consistent with the Second Amendment rights. On July 10, 2013, the Illinois legislature overrode the Illinois Governor's veto of legislation permitting ordinary citizens to carry concealed handguns.

The Free Exercise of Religion

The U.S. Supreme Court stated in 1990: "We have never held that an individual's religious beliefs excuse him from compliance with an otherwise valid law prohibiting conduct that the State is free to regulate." [52]

Freedom to believe is absolute; freedom to act is not. The U.S. Supreme Court has stated that it has never held that an individual's religious belief excuses compliance with an otherwise valid law regulating conduct. When a statute forbids a specific action or conduct, one who engages in that action or conduct because of a religious belief may be prosecuted for the violation. The following chart illustrates some of the conduct not protected by the Freedom of Religion clause:

CONDUCT NOT PROTECTED [53]	CASE
Multiple marriages in violation of state polygamy laws (crime of bigamy).	*Reynolds v. United States*, U.S. Supreme Court (1879) 98 U.S. 145, 25 L. Ed. 244.
Handling poisonous snakes in a public place in violation of the state law [54] as part of a religious ceremony.	*State v. Massey*, North Carolina Supreme Court (1949) 229 N.C. 734, 51 S.E.2d 179.
Requirements at airports, state fairs, and so on that religious, political, and other groups distribute or sell literature only from booths provided for that purpose.	*Heffron v. International Society for Krishna Consciousness*, U.S. Supreme Court (1981) 452 U.S. 640, 101 S. Ct. 2559.

(continued)

CONDUCT NOT PROTECTED[53]	CASE
Violation of child labor laws. Religious order used 9-year-old child to distribute religious pamphlets.	*Prince v. Massachusetts,* U.S. Supreme Court (1944) 321 U.S. 158, 64 S. Ct. 438.
An Air Force officer continued to wear his yarmulke (Jewish skullcap) after repeated orders to remove it. He was dropped from the service. Judgment for Air Force affirmed.	*Goldman v. Weinberger,* U.S. Supreme Court (1986) 475 U.S. 503, 106 S. Ct. 1310.
Members of the Old Order Amish, who do not use motor vehicles but travel in horse-drawn buggies, would not obey a state law requiring reflecting triangles on the rear of all slow-moving vehicles. Held not exempt from complying with this highway safety law.	*Minnesota v. Hershberger,* U.S. Supreme Court (1990) 495 U.S. 901, 110 S. Ct. 1918, *vacating* 444 NW.2d 282 (Minn. 1989).

The Right of Privacy

The U.S. Constitution has no explicit right of privacy. However, the Supreme Court has in various cases found such a right to exist by implication from notions of personal liberty found in the Constitution. Where a right to privacy exists, governments may not pass criminal laws that impinge upon the right, unless the laws have a reasonable, legitimate government purpose and are tailored to advance that interest with the least restriction on the right. In other words, like the freedom of speech, the right of privacy is not absolute.

Some criminal laws have been found to unlawfully impinge on the right of privacy. In *Griswold v. Connecticut,*[55] the case where the right of privacy was first articulated, the Court struck down a state statute that prohibited providing medical information on birth control to a married woman. In *Lawrence v. Texas,*[56] the Court struck down a Texas statute that made criminal consensual homosexual acts done in private, holding that the statute violated the concepts of personal liberty in the Fourteenth Amendment.

The right of privacy or personal liberty also resulted in the famous abortion decision *Roe v. Wade,*[57] 410 U.S. 113, 153 (1973). In that case the Court declared a state abortion law unconstitutional as a violation of a woman's right of privacy. It said,

> This right of privacy, whether it be founded in the Fourteenth Amendment's concept of personal liberty and restrictions on state action, as we feel it is, or, as the District Court determined, in the Ninth Amendment's reservation of rights to the people, is broad enough to encompass a woman's decision whether or not to terminate a pregnancy.

The Court also held, however, that the right was not absolute: "We, therefore, conclude that the right of personal privacy includes the abortion decision, but this right is not unqualified and must be considered against important state interests in regulation."

The Court then held that during the first trimester of a pregnancy the abortion decision was solely up to the woman; after the first trimester and before viability the state could regulate the abortion procedures, but could not ban abortions; and after viability the state could ban abortions, so long as an exception was made for the mother's health.

Summary

- The First Amendment protects freedom of religion, freedom of speech, free assembly, freedom of the press, and the right to petition the government for redress of grievances.
- Fighting words differ from ordinary rude language because they carry the possibility of inciting another to violence. It is not enough that the words cause injury.
- A clear and present danger is the possibility that some speech or conduct will bring harm to people or property immediately, not some time in the future.
- Laws directed at the content of speech are subjected to strict scrutiny, meaning the government must have a compelling interest in achieving some goal, and that the limit on the speech is necessary.
- Obscenity is speech or other communication that appeals to a reasonable person's prurient interest, describes in an offensive manner specific defined sexual conduct, and has no redeeming social value.

- A true threat is a threat that a reasonable person would believe was a serious expression of the intent to take violent, unlawful actions.
- A person can stalk another by physically intruding into the other person's life, by sending harassing messages, or through telephone conversations or the Internet.
- An assembly becomes unlawful when three or more people gather and make a public disturbance that includes acts that present a clear and present danger of harming people or property.
- The basis for finding the Second Amendment binding on the states was the Due Process Clause of the Fourteenth Amendment. Under the Supreme Court's incorporation rules, a right that was deeply embedded in our nation's history and was a fundamental right is made binding on the states.

Key Terms

"clear and present danger" test, p. 229
disorderly conduct, p. 230
fighting words, p. 230
obscenity, p. 235

inciting, p. 235
defamation, p. 235
symbolic speech, p. 238
threats of violence, p. 240
true threat, p. 240

unlawful assembly, p. 244
riot, p. 244
stalking, p. 248

Case Analysis and Writing Exercises

1. The Stolen Valor Act case, *Alvarez*, held that making a lie a crime simply because it was a lie violated the First Amendment. Is the same true for a statute that makes it a crime to impersonate a police officer by telling another person one is a county sheriff? What if the person to whom the lie is told is an officer who has stopped a motorist for a traffic violation? *See United States v. Chappell*, 691 F.3d 388 (4th Cir. 2012), *cert. denied*, 133 S. Ct. 965 (2013).

2. In *Heller* the Supreme Court stated that its decision did not change long-standing prohibitions on possession of "dangerous and unusual weapons." The Court was referring to an earlier decision upholding a law that outlawed sawed-off shotguns. Does the Cook County, Illinois (Chicago) ban on "assault weapons" satisfy the "dangerous and unusual weapons" exception to the Second Amendment right? How does the statute define "assault weapon"? Why does this matter? *See Wilson v. County of Cook*, 968 N.E.2d 641 (Ill. 2012).

3. The First Amendment prohibits the government from banning speech, including recorded speech such as tape recordings. Does the First Amendment apply to government attempts to prohibit the act of recording a conversation? Illinois (and many other states) makes it a criminal violation to make audible recordings of conversations between other people, including between citizens and police officers. Is that a violation of the First Amendment? Do you see problems with holding that it is? *See American Civil Liberties Union of Illinois v. Alvarez*, 679 F.3d 583 (2012), *cert. denied*, 133 S. Ct. 651 (2012).

4. It is not a crime simply to urge others to evade taxes, and if a statute were to make it so the First Amendment would prohibit it. What if the defendant publishes a book and holds seminars where specific methods of tax evasion are taught? Is that enough to support a conviction for fraud? *See United States v. Meredith*, 685 F.3d 814 (9th Cir. 2012). Does the Supreme Court's decision in *Alvarez* suggest an answer?

Endnotes

1. *Hustler Magazine v. Falwell*, 485 U.S. 46 (1988), quoting *Base Corp. v. Consumers Union*, 466 U.S. 485 (1984).
2. *Cox v. New Hampshire*, 312 U.S. 569 (1941).
3. *Speiser v. Randall*, 357 U.S. 513 (1958).
4. *Hustler v. Falwell*.
5. *City of Los Angeles v. Alameda Books, Inc.*, 535 U.S. 425 (2002).
6. 249 U.S. 47 (1919).
7. *Watts v. United States*, 394 U.S. 705 (1969).
8. *Chaplinsky v. New Hampshire*, 315 U.S. 568 (1942).
9. See *State v. Drahota*, 788 N.W.2d 796, 803 (Neb. 2010), citing "Demise of the *Chaplinsky* Fighting Words Doctrine," 106 Harv. L. Rev. 1129 (1993).
10. *Ibid.*
11. 788 N.W.2d 796 (2010).
12. *FBI Law Enforcement Bulletin*, "The Fighting Word Doctrine," April 1992.
13. 92 S. Ct. 2607 (1973).
14. The term *prurient interest* is generally defined as appealing "to a shameful, unhealthy, unwholesome, degrading ... interest in sex." *County of Kenosha v. C&S Management Inc.*, 588 N.W.2d 236 (1999).
15. *Brandenburg v. Ohio*, 89 S. Ct. 1827 (1969).
16. 94 S. Ct. 326 (1973).
17. 89 S. Ct. 1827 (1969).
18. 379 U.S. 64 (1964).
19. 482 F.3d 1244 (10th Cir. 2007).
20. See *New York Times v. Sullivan*, 376 U.S. 254 (1964).
21. 89 S. Ct. 733 (1969).
22. 109 S. Ct. 2533 (1989).
23. 110 S. Ct. 2404 (1990).
24. 112 S. Ct. 2538 (1992). Many communities have ordinances regulating the manner and time burning can occur. Burning a flag could also be cited as a violation of these ordinances.
25. 538 U.S. 343 (2003).
26. See, for example, West's Georgia Code Annotated Section 16-ll-37(a) and Nebraska Revised Statute Section 28-311.01 (1995).
27. *United States v. Dysart*, 705 F.2d 1247 (1983); *United States v. Turner*, 2013 WL 3111139 (2nd Cir. 2013).
28. 626 N.W.2d 725 (Wis. 2001).
29. 70 Cal. Rptr.3d 535 (Cal. App. 2008).
30. 603 S.E.2d 86 (Ga. App. 2004).
31. *United States v. Corum*, 362 F.3d 489 (8th Cir. 2004).
32. *United States v. Floyd*, 458 F.3d 844 (8th Cir. 2006), *cert. denied*, 549 U.S. 1236 (2007).
33. *United States v. Jeffries*, 692 F.3d 473 (6th Cir. 2012).
34. 144 S.W.3d 210 (Tex. App. 2004).
35. 109 S. Ct. 2746, 2756 (1989).
36. 631 F.3d 1 (1st Cir. 2011).
37. 336 U.S. 77 (1949).
38. 391 U.S. 367 (1968).
39. 385 U.S. 39 (1967).
40. 408 U.S. 104, 92 S. Ct. 2294 (1972). The U.S. Supreme Court held:

   The nature of a place, "the pattern of its normal activities, dictates the kinds of regulations of time, place, and manner that are reasonable." Although a silent vigil may not unduly interfere with a public library, making a speech in the reading room almost certainly would. That same speech should be perfectly appropriate in a park. The crucial question is whether the manner of expression is basically incompatible with the normal activity of a particular place at a particular time. Our cases make clear that in assessing the reasonableness of regulation, we must weigh heavily the fact that communication is involved; the regulation must be narrowly tailored to further the State's legitimate interest. "Access to [the streets, sidewalks, parks, and other similar public places] for the purpose of exercising [First Amendment rights] cannot constitutionally be denied broadly." Free expression "must not, in the guise of regulation, be abridged or denied."

41. Ku Klux Klan demonstrations and parades cost local communities a lot of money. Fewer than two dozen Ku Kluxers generally show up, but many more people will appear to protest against the Ku Klux Klan. The likelihood of violence and disorderly conduct is very great. Therefore, adequate police protection must be provided, which means allocating sufficient money for the necessary extra law enforcement and other costs.

    Because of such additional expenses, some communities passed laws and ordinances permitting the imposition of a fee, based on anticipated costs. This would mean that a local administrator would have to estimate the costs for a specific group. The U.S. Supreme Court struck down an ordinance that provided for a fee in the case of *Forsyth County v. Nationalist Movement* (a Ku Klux Klan group), 112 S. Ct. 2395 (1992). The U.S. Supreme Court pointed out that to estimate the fee, the local official had to consider who the group was and the contents of the message they were communicating.

    Requiring prepayment of an $85 fee for the processing of a parade permit application and the cost of traffic control was upheld by the courts in the case of *Stonewell Union v. City of Columbus,* 931 F.2d 1130 (6th Cir. 1991), *review denied* U.S. Supreme Court 112 S. Ct. 275 (1991).

42. 118 S. Ct. 805 (1998).
43. States generally statutorize the crime of unlawful assembly, as does Florida in Section 870.03 of the Florida Criminal Code. But some states provide that the crime of unlawful assembly is committed when the person gathered in the unlawful assembly fails to leave the area after law enforcement declares the gathering to be an unlawful assembly and orders the group or crowd to disperse and leave the area.
44. Under the old common law, if a number of people met together and suddenly quarreled and fought among themselves, this would constitute an "affray." An affray differs from a riot in that an affray is not premeditated. Under the old common law, a riot required three or more people, whereas an affray required two or more.

45. Under New York statutes, four or more people plus the person charged are needed for the crime of "unlawful assembly." To convict a person of any of the riot offenses, it must be shown that there were ten or more people gathered, plus the person charged.
46. 978 F.2d 786 (2nd Cir. 1992).
47. *Hiibel v. Sixth District Court of Nevada,* 542 U.S. 177 (2004).
48. In the case of *Bennis v. Michigan,* 134 L. Ed. 2d 68 (1996), Mr. Bennis's vehicle was forfeited after he was convicted of this offense. But Mrs. Bennis was an innocent co-owner of the car and appealed to the U.S. Supreme Court. The Supreme Court held that as the vehicle was an abatable nuisance, it could be forfeited without an offset for the innocent co-owner and without a showing that the innocent co-owner knew or consented to the public misuse of the vehicle.
49. California's stalking statute, Penal Code Section 646.9, reads: "Any person who willfully, maliciously, and repeatedly follows or harasses another person, and who makes a credible threat with the intent to place the person in reasonable fear of death or great bodily injury is guilty of the crime of stalking."
50. 625 F.3d 1209 (9th Cir. 2010).
51. 60 Cal. Rptr. 2d 423 (Cal. App. 2d 1997).
52. *Employment Division v. Smith,* 494 U.S. 872 (S. Ct. 1990).
53. The Freedom of Religion Clause could not be used as a defense for destroying government property (760 F.2d 447); extortion and blackmail (515 F.2d 112); racketeering (695 F.2d 765, review denied, 460 U.S. 1092); refusal to testify before a grand jury (465 F.2d 802; see 409 U.S. 944); refusal to be photographed after being arrested (848 F.2d 113); putting a logging road through an area sacred to Native American tribes (108 S. Ct. 1319); refusal to have children vaccinated (25 S. Ct. 358); and refusal to participate in the Social Security system (102 S. Ct. 1051), although in 1988 Congress enacted 26 U.S.C. § 3127, which permits members of certain religious groups, such as the Amish people, to elect to opt out of the employee portion of Social Security taxes.
54. According to the New Testament in Mark 16:16-18, "He that believeth and is baptized shall be saved. . . . [T]hey shall speak with new tongues; they shall take up serpents; and if they drink any deadly thing, it shall not hurt them." In *State v. Massey,* the defendant was convicted of handling poisonous snakes in a religious ceremony, taking literally these words from the New Testament. The Court ruled that the state law forbidding the handling of poisonous snakes was a valid use of the police power of the state of North Carolina and held that the public safety factor outweighed the right to religious freedom.
55. 381 U.S. 479 (1965).
56. 123 S. Ct. 2472 (2003).
57. 410 U.S. 113 (1973).

Homicide

William Melchert-Dinkel, a nurse who engaged in on-line chats with persons who later committed suicide, was convicted of the crime of assisting suicide based on encouragements he gave the suicide victims. He has appealed his conviction to the Minnesota Supreme Court, alleging the conviction violated his right of free speech.

OUTLINE

Homicide in General

The Corpus Delicti Requirement

Proving Corpus Delicti in "No Body" Cases

Body Without Proof of the Cause of Death Cases

The Common Law "Born Alive" Requirement and the Crime of Feticide (Fetal Murder)

Proof That the Victim Was Alive at the Time of the Defendant's Unlawful Act

When Is a Person Legally Dead?

The Causation Requirement

Causation and Proximate Cause

The Year-and-a-Day Rule

Murder

Intent-to-Kill and Premeditated Murder

The "Deadly Weapon" Doctrine

Transferred Intent

Intent-to-Do-Serious-Bodily-Harm Murder

Depraved-Mind or Depraved-Heart Murder

Felony Murder

Manslaughter

Definition of Manslaughter

Voluntary Manslaughter

Heat of Passion Manslaughter

Imperfect or Unlawful Force in Self-Defense Charged as Manslaughter

Involuntary Manslaughter

Suicide, Assisting Suicide, and Euthanasia

Murder, Suicide, or Neither?

The Oregon "Death with Dignity" Law

LEARNING OBJECTIVES

In this chapter we discuss the various kinds and degrees of criminal homicide. The learning objectives for this chapter are

- Know the meaning of corpus delicti and its role in criminal prosecutions.
- State the current status of the year-and-a-day rule and why its acceptance has waned.
- State the elements of the "born alive" requirement.
- Explain the doctrine of transferred intent.
- List the homicides that do not require proof of intent to kill.
- Identify which deaths that occur during the commission of a felony qualify as felony murder.
- State the difference between voluntary and involuntary manslaughter.
- List circumstances that could be sufficient to reduce a charge of murder to manslaughter.
- Explain why the U.S. Supreme Court upheld the Oregon Death with Dignity Law.

S atonia Small left her children, ages 6 and 7, alone in their apartment one evening about 10:00 P.M. while she visited at a friend's house. Around midnight a fire broke out in her apartment. One child was able to get out of the apartment, but one could not, and died from asphyxiation. Small was charged with murder under the Louisiana felony-murder law, which makes a death that happens during the commission of a felony crime murder (here the felony was "cruelty to a juvenile"), without the necessity of proving intent to kill. In 2010 Small was convicted of felony murder, and was sentenced to life in prison at hard labor without the possibility of parole.

In 2012 the Louisiana Supreme Court reversed Small's conviction. It stated the Louisiana felony-murder law did not apply unless the underlying felony directly, as opposed to proximately, caused the homicide. Here, the court said, Small's actions were only the proximate cause of her child's death, and she could only be liable for negligent homicide. It remanded the case to the trial court for resentencing for negligent homicide.

In this chapter we learn the various charges that may be brought against a person or persons when a homicide occurs and what the prosecution must prove in order to obtain a conviction on those charges. We learn what different mental states and circumstances can surround a particular homicide that could result in a charge of murder, or of voluntary manslaughter, or of involuntary manslaughter. We will also learn about the evolving treatment of cases such as assisted suicide and euthanasia.

Homicide in General

homicide The killing of one human being by another. There are three types of homicide: justifiable, excusable, and felonious.

Homicide, the killing of one human being by another, is not always criminal. Sir William Blackstone wrote in the eighteenth century that there were three kinds of homicide—justifiable, excusable, and felonious. He wrote that the first involved no guilt, the second involved little guilt, and the third was the worst crime that humans were capable of committing against the law of nature.

Justifiable homicide is defined in the common law as an intentional homicide committed under circumstances of necessity or duty without any evil intent and without any fault or blame on the person who commits the homicide. Justifiable homicide includes state executions, homicides by police officers in the performance of their legal duty, and self-defense when the person committing the homicide is not at fault.

Excusable homicide is the killing of a human being, either by misadventure or in self-defense, when there is some civil fault, error, or omission on the part of the person who commits the homicide. The degree of fault, however, is not enough to constitute a crime.

Criminal (or *felonious*) *homicide* occurs when a person unlawfully and knowingly, recklessly, or negligently causes the death of another human being. The common law and the states have divided criminal homicide into the crimes of murder, manslaughter, and negligent homicide.

This chapter deals with criminal homicide and the circumstances that give rise to specific charges. Criminal homicide encompasses a wide variety of acts. The acts and the intent with which they were committed determine whether the homicide is intentional or unintentional. Such determination is relevant, because penalties are more severe when the killing was intentional rather than as a result of recklessness, negligence, or carelessness.

The Corpus Delicti Requirement

Corpus delicti means the body or substance of the crime (proof that a crime has been committed). The prosecution must prove in all criminal cases that the crime charged has been committed. For example, if the prosecution cannot prove a fire was deliberately set or that a building actually burned, it cannot prove arson. If it cannot prove a death was not accidental, it cannot prove murder. If both parties were competent adults and consented to sex, rape or sexual assault has not occurred.

In some cases the principal evidence against the defendant is a confession. If no other evidence exists to corroborate the confession, courts often hold that the defendant cannot be convicted of the crime that is charged. Court decisions have noted that confessions can be the result of mistake, mental problems, coercion, or even a friend trying to take the blame for another person.

The corpus delicti rule is often court created, and as a result the rule can be changed by a court, without legislative action. This was the case in Colorado, where in 2013 the Colorado Supreme Court abandoned the 100-year-old court-created corpus delicti rule that out-of-court confessions alone could not support a criminal conviction. In *People v. LaRosa*[1] the defendant confessed over the telephone to police officers that he had sexually assaulted his infant daughter. The only evidence at his trial was his out-of-court confession. He was convicted of sexual assault crimes, and appealed. The Colorado Supreme Court said that the corpus delicti rule, which would ordinarily apply in this situation, no longer played a useful role, and should be abandoned. The court noted that in many kinds of crimes, like sexual assault on a young child, direct evidence of the crime might not exist. In future prosecutions, out-of-court confessions alone may be sufficient, if the confessions are proved by the prosecution to have trustworthiness.[2]

In states where corroborating evidence is required, courts differ on the kind and quality of the evidence sufficient to corroborate a confession and prove that the crime charged did occur. See *People v. Jennings*,[3] where the court held that the state had produced sufficient corroborative evidence to verify "bragging" by the defendant that he had murdered prostitutes and then took back the money he had given them.

Proving Corpus Delicti in "No Body" Cases

Virtually every American city has active cases of persons reported missing. In 2009 the U.S. Department of Justice launched the NamUs (National Missing and Unidentified Persons System) database. In May of 2011 the Department of Justice reported that since then, over 15,000 cases have been reported to NamUs. Most missing persons are missing for a short period of time, or they are living elsewhere and not communicating with their families and friends. Some, however, are victims of murders and other crimes.

Usually, if no body is found, there is no criminal case to prosecute, because evidence needed to prove corpus delicti is ordinarily proved in homicide cases by evidence obtained from the body of the victim or from witnesses to the crime. The corpus delicti rule requires that the prosecution prove (1) that the missing person is dead, and (2) that the defendant killed that person. In "no-body" cases, corpus delicti can be proved by circumstantial evidence or by confessions that have been corroborated and affirmed by other evidence.

In the following two "no body" cases, the body of the victim was not found, but corpus delicti was proved by circumstantial evidence. In each case, a murder conviction was affirmed.

Tetso v. State

Maryland Court of Appeals, 45 A. 3d 788 (2012), *cert. denied* 52 A.3d 979 (Md. 2012)

On March 6, 2005, Tracey Tetso was to attend a Motley Crue concert with a man with whom she was having an affair. She did not attend the concert, and was never seen again. In 2010 her husband, Dennis, was tried and convicted of second-degree murder of Tracey, based only on circumstantial evidence. On appeal, the court affirmed his conviction, stating there was sufficient evidence to support the jury verdict of guilty. The court pointed to the fact that Tracey was excited to go to the concert, that her dogs were left alone in her house, that she normally was in constant contact with her friends and family, and that her credit cards had not been used since her disappearance, was evidence sufficient to prove she was dead, the first corpus delicti requirement.

The court said defendant's knowledge of the affair and that Tracey wanted a divorce, that he was seen driving Tracey's car after March 6, that he was unwilling to help in the search for Tracey, and that a short time after her disappearance he made plans to buy a boat, telling others he would use money from a life insurance policy on Tracey, supported the jury finding that he killed Tracey, the second corpus delicti requirement.

State v. Watkins

New Jersey App. Court, 2011 WL 5573771, *cert. denied*, 43 A.3d 1168 (N.J. 2012)

On February 23, 1990, Craig White disappeared, and was never seen again. His body was never found, and no physical evidence surrounding his disappearance was discovered. Nineteen years later a jury convicted his cousin, Jesse Watkins, of murdering him. Watkins appealed that conviction, claiming insufficient evidence existed to support the jury's verdict.

On appeal the court affirmed his conviction. It held sufficient circumstantial evidence was introduced to support the jury verdict. The victim had a young son he was caring for, and the court said that it would be unlikely the victim would disappear without any communication with the son. The fact that the defendant's girlfriend had an affair with the victim, that the defendant had previously assaulted the victim over the affair, that the defendant was the last person to be seen with the victim on the day he disappeared, that the defendant left his home state right after the victim disappeared and did not return, and told a subsequent wife and girlfriend he had killed the victim, was sufficient to support the jury verdict of guilty of murder, the court held.

ATTEMPTS TO IDENTIFY AND MINIMIZE VIOLENCE AGAINST CHILDREN

The 2011 report of The National Centers for Disease Control, based on the 2011 National Health Survey, produced these statistics on child (ages 1–14) deaths: in 2010, 34,181 children in this age group died. Of that number, 957 died from assaults listed as homicides, about 40 percent of which involved victims under 1 year old. It is likely many other deaths were the result of abuse or neglect, but not reported as homicides.

The following systems have been created to deal with violence against children.

Child Death Review Teams

The United States (all fifty states), Australia, and Canada now have child death review teams to review deaths of children from violence, child abuse or neglect, motor vehicle accidents, child suicide, and natural or undetermined causes.

Safe Haven Laws for Unwanted Babies

For years, tragic stories of illegally abandoned babies found dead or in unsafe places have appeared in the news. Because of the continuing, sad, attention-getting cases, states began to enact safe haven laws to save the lives of babies. These laws allow a person (usually the mother) to leave an unwanted baby, anonymously and without fear of prosecution, at a hospital, fire station, or other designated place. Most states (if not all) have now enacted safe haven laws.

Mandatory Child Abuse Reporting Laws

Most states have laws that require persons who "know or have reasonable cause to suspect" child abuse, abandonment, death, or neglect to report that information to authorities. Under the Florida statute, for example, hotlines are established for communicating the information, and failure to do so is punishable as a misdemeanor.

Body Without Proof of the Cause of Death Cases

The body of the deceased is available in most criminal homicide cases. But if doctors are not able to testify specifically that the cause of death was an unlawful act, corpus delicti has not been proved. Unexplained deaths are unusual but not rare in medical history. If doctors are unable to determine the cause of death, or if they are uncertain and unable to state whether the death resulted from criminal acts or from natural causes, then a reasonable doubt may have been created.

Corpus delicti has historically been difficult to prove in sudden infant death syndrome (SIDS) deaths of babies between 2 months and 1 year old because doctors did not know the reason for the cause of death in many of the cases. Today, with more medical knowledge, physicians and medical journals have called into question the SIDS explanation for the deaths of some infants, particularly when multiple deaths occurred in one family. Prosecutors in many states reopened the death investigations of some infants that earlier had been classified as SIDS. For example, a woman in New York was convicted of the murder of five babies, which earlier had been classified as SIDS deaths, and in Philadelphia a woman was charged with the deaths of eight babies, which had earlier been thought to be SIDS deaths.[4]

The testimony of doctors that they "suspected" or had a "hunch" that a criminal act was the cause of death is not sufficient to prove corpus delicti. The *People v. Dendel* case illustrates how the corpus delicti requirement that proof of the cause of death must be established can be met.

People v. Dendel

Michigan Court of Appeals, 797 N.W.2d 645 (2010), *review denied*, 802 N.W.2d 618 (Mich. 2011)

The defendant was the long-time domestic partner of Paul Burley. Burley suffered from many medical problems, including dementia, and was HIV positive. The defendant was the sole caregiver for Burley. When Burley died, the medical examiner initially ruled the death was from "natural causes," since tests conducted on the body showed no presence of foreign substances. Although the defendant insisted on an immediate cremation, police investigators ordered an autopsy before the body could be cremated. Autopsy results showed damage to brain cells brought on by hypoglycemic shock, which can be caused by an injection of insulin in a person without diabetes. Defendant was then charged with murder. After a bench trial (one in which the judge finds the facts) she was convicted of second-degree murder and sentenced to 7–15 years in prison.

On appeal, the court affirmed her conviction. It held that sufficient circumstantial evidence supported the verdict of guilty. The court said that evidence included the following: the victim was not diabetic, and thus would not have insulin-related body signs; the victim was unable to give himself medication, so it was unlikely he committed suicide; the defendant was a diabetic, and knew insulin could not be discovered in a body after death; the defendant stated a week before the victim's death, "I feel like giving him a shot of insulin"; the defendant did not tell the victim's family he had died, and pushed for immediate cremation; the defendant objected to conducting an autopsy. The defendant's conviction for second-degree murder was affirmed.

The Common Law "Born Alive" Requirement and the Crime of Feticide (Fetal Murder)

Under the common law, the killing of a fetus (unborn baby) was not a homicide. Because most criminal homicide statutes prohibited only the killing of a "person" or a "human being," these statutes did not include the killing of a fetus, which was not a "person" under the common law. In the leading case of *Keeler v. Superior Court*[5] the California Supreme Court said the "born alive" rule prevented a conviction for the death of a fetus. After the *Keeler* decision California statutes were amended to define murder as the "unlawful killing of a human being, *or a fetus*, with malice aforethought" (Title 8, Section 187). This statute made the killing of a fetus in California "with malice aforethought" murder and changed the common law.[6]

"born alive" requirement To be able to charge homicide of a newborn baby, the prosecution must be able to prove that the child was living at the time it was killed.

feticide Murder of an unborn child.

In response to cases like *Keeler*, at least thirty states have abandoned the **"born alive" requirement**, and make the death of a fetus in a mother's body a homicide. The question of whether or not the fetus must be "viable" for conviction under such a statute often depends on the statutory scheme adopted. For example, Ind. Code § 35-42-1-1 (4) defines "murder" to include killing a fetus "that has attained viability." It is a Class A felony. Ind. Code § 35-42-1-6 makes it a crime to unlawfully "terminate a pregnancy" and requires no showing of viability of the fetus. It is a Class C felony. Many states have adopted similar "**feticide**" statutes, which treat the death of an unborn fetus outside the usual definitions of homicide. Under these statutes, there is no requirement that the fetus be born alive, or in most cases even be viable. The Arizona statute, for example, punishes for manslaughter anyone who "(k)nowingly or recklessly causes the death of an unborn child by any physical injury to the mother." A.R.S. § 13-1103.

In 18 U.S.C. § 1841, passed in 2004, the federal "Protection of Unborn Children" statute makes it a crime separate from murder to unlawfully take the life of a child that is "*in utero.*" A child that is *in utero* is defined as "a member of the species homo sapiens, at any stage of development, who is carried in the womb." However, if the circumstances show an intention to kill the fetus, the defendant can be charged under the general murder statute, 18 U.S.C. § 1111.

Eighteen states still have the "born alive" rule, and in most of those jurisdictions some showing that the fetus was alive when it left the mother's body must be made. In *State v. Lamy*, 969 A.2d 451 (N.H. 2009), the court reversed a manslaughter conviction because the state could not show the fetus displayed any signs of living on its own without life-support machines, and thus the state did not prove the fetus was born alive. In *State v. Courchesne*, 998 A.2d 1 (Conn. 2010), the Connecticut Supreme Court remanded a capital murder conviction for a determination of whether an infant kept alive for 42 days on life support after the defendant stabbed her mother to death was "alive."

Proof That the Victim Was Alive at the Time of the Defendant's Unlawful Act

Because criminal homicide is the unlawful killing of a living human being, the state has the burden of showing that the victim was alive at the time of the unlawful act. All people have a right to life, and whether they have 10 minutes or 10 years left to live makes no difference in the eyes of the law.

Whether or not the victim was alive when a sexual assault occurred is sometimes an issue in felony murder cases. In felony murder, discussed in more detail later in this chapter, a defendant convicted of one crime can also be convicted of murder if a person dies as a result of the crime. In such cases, it is necessary for the prosecution to prove the original crime, usually called the "predicate" crime. If for some reason the defendant cannot be convicted of the predicate crime, he or she cannot be convicted of felony murder.

In sexual assault cases, some jurisdictions hold that one cannot be guilty of sexual assault if the victim was dead at the time the assault occurred. See *People v.*

Hutner,[7] where a conviction for first-degree felony murder was reversed because the victim was dead when sexual penetration occurred. Other jurisdictions hold that so long as the victim was alive when a sexual assault began, it does not matter for felony murder purposes whether the person was alive when sexual penetration occurred. See *State v. Jones*,[8] where a felony murder conviction was affirmed even though the victim may have died before sexual penetration occurred.

When Is a Person Legally Dead?

Until the 1950s and 1960s, the heart was considered the body's most vital organ, and therefore death was defined in terms of cessation of heart and respiratory functions. When doctors became able to keep the heart and other organs alive for transplanting to other patients, medical science recognized that the body's real seat of life is the brain.

Court and state legislative bodies followed the medical profession in defining death in terms of "brain death." For example, the Indiana Supreme Court has defined death as the "permanent cessation of all brain function" and joined other states in holding that "for the purposes of the law of homicide proof of the death of the victim may be established by proof of the irreversible cessation of the victim's total brain function."[9]

End-of-Life Decisions   On an average day in the United States, more than 6,000 people die. Doctors estimate that at least several hundred of these deaths occur after doctors, patients, and family members agree to withhold life-sustaining treatment and allow the inevitable to occur.

To stay within the law and to avoid criminal prosecution, the decision to withhold treatment or to "pull the plug" on persons in deep continuous comas (persistent vegetative states) should be made only when the following can be shown:

1. Terminally ill patients who are mentally competent can instruct that treatment or life-support systems be withdrawn. Courts have held that the individual's right to refuse treatment must come before the interests of the state in keeping the individual alive.
2. Life-support systems or treatment may be withheld from patients who are comatose or in a persistent vegetative state if one of the following is clearly shown:

   a. That the patient left prior explicit written instructions that this be done (a *living will*) or
   b. That the patient had legally appointed another adult to make such health care decisions, should the patient be unable to do so (*medical power of attorney*), or
   c. Clear and convincing evidence is presented to a court showing that the withdrawal of treatment or of a life-support system is in accordance with the patient's own wishes or best interests.[10]

The population in the United States is growing older. The Census Bureau estimates that between the years 2000 and 2050 the percentage increase in the number of people over 65 will be 147 percent, compared to the estimated overall population increase of 49 percent. Aging diseases such as Alzheimer's and dementia can cause many older people to suffer conditions that are not comas, but are nonetheless destructive of the quality of life. For example, many people with these diseases have lost their ability to swallow food, and as a result they are required to be fed by tubes inserted in their bodies, much the same as those actually in a vegetative state. The application of the criminal laws to decisions shortening or prolonging life in this complex, unsettled, and controversial area remains unclear.

The Causation Requirement

Causation and Proximate Cause

Causation and proximate cause are discussed in Chapter 3 of this text. Causation is an essential element of all crimes. The state must show that what the defendant did (or failed to do) was the direct and proximate cause of the harm that occurred. The following two examples illustrate the law of causation:

EXAMPLE ▶ After loading a gun with live ammunition, X points the gun at Y and pulls the trigger. The firing pin comes down hard on the back of the live cartridge that X has placed in the chamber of the gun. The blow of the hammer detonates the primer in the cartridge, and the primer detonates the powder in the cartridge. The powder burns so rapidly that hot gases immediately build up tremendous pressure in the chamber of the gun. This pressure forces the propellant (the bullet) out of the muzzle of the gun at a high rate of speed. Because of rifling in the barrel of the gun and the direction in which X is pointing the gun, the bullet travels through the air and strikes Y in the head, killing Y immediately.

EXAMPLE ▶ After being shocked by seeing the defendant smash her door open and then rip her telephone cord out of the phone, an elderly woman dies of a heart attack. The defendant argues that he wanted to burglarize the woman's home but had no intention of harming her.

A jury can easily conclude in Example 1 that X intended the natural and probable consequences of the deliberate act; it would then find that X intended to kill Y. In Example 1, X's acts were the direct and proximate cause of Y's death. The chain of events that occurred after X pulled the trigger was expected and desired by X. Therefore, X can be held criminally responsible for Y's death.

In Example 2, the Nebraska Supreme Court affirmed the defendant's conviction for felony murder in the case of *State v. Dixon*[11]:

> Dixon admitted to Detectives Circo and Wade that Jourdan was alive when he entered the house. The implosion of window glass and part of the wooden kitchen door would startle the most imperturbable individual. Seeing Dixon coming through the doorway into the kitchen probably would stir one to "stare" at him, visual fixation founded in fear intensified by Dixon's ripping the "cord out of the phone." All that unfolded before Susan Jourdan, 76 years old and living alone. What total terror likely seized and constricted Susan Jourdan's heart may be beyond another's comprehension. What the jury did understand was Dr. Roffman's explanation of the cause of Susan Jourdan's death, "emotional

trauma of having her door kicked in and stimulating her heart to beat abnormally, causing her collapse and ultimate death."

When there is a substantial time gap between an injury and the victim's death, causation may become contested based on actions of the victim after the injury. For example, in the 2010 case of *Brown v. State*[12] the defendant doused his girlfriend with gasoline and started her on fire. After months in the hospital to treat her severe burns, the victim returned home. After 2 weeks at home she developed pneumonia. She refused to go to the hospital, and died within a few days. The Georgia Supreme Court affirmed the defendant's murder conviction and life imprisonment sentence. The court said expert medical testimony established that the pneumonia was the result of the burns inflicted by the defendant, and that the victim would have died even if she had gone to the hospital as directed by her physician. The court therefore held the defendant was the proximate cause of the death.

The Year-and-a-Day Rule

The year-and-a-day rule is also discussed in more detail in Chapter 3. The common law rule stated that a person could not be convicted of a murder unless the victim died within a year and a day from the time of the wrongful act. The Michigan Supreme Court pointed out that the year-and-a-day rule dates back to 1278 and that the "original rationale for the rule was probably tied to the inability of 13th century medicine to prove the cause of death beyond a reasonable doubt after a prolonged period of time."[13]

Common law rules became part of a new state's criminal law because virtually all states included in their constitution a clause that adopted the "common law of England" in place when the United States was formed. Subsequent changes to that common law, usually by state legislatures, were called "abrogation" of the common law. Courts also possess the power to abrogate a common law rule, which many have done in the case of the year-and-a-day rule.

The Michigan Supreme Court, in the case cited above, and many other state courts or legislatures, have abolished this rule. When the common law rule is abrogated by a state supreme court, the court must determine whether to make the abrogation retroactive, or only prospective. In *State v. Picotte*,[14] the Wisconsin Supreme Court abrogated the common law year-and-a-day rule but made the abrogation prospective. As a result, the defendant's conviction for reckless homicide of a victim who died more than one year after the crime occurred was reversed.

A few courts have not abolished the rule. In *Ex Parte Key*,[15] the Alabama Supreme Court reversed a conviction of a defendant for murder of a victim who died 18 months after the injury. The court held that the year-and-a-day rule was still part of the common law in Alabama.

Some states continue to use a variation of the rule. For example, Title 8, Section 194 of the California Penal Code provides that "To make the killing either murder or manslaughter, it is not requisite the party die within three years and a day after the stroke received or the cause of death administered. If death occurs beyond the time of three years and a day, there shall be a rebuttable presumption that the killing was not criminal."

Murder

The first murder to be reported in the American colonies occurred 10 years after the Pilgrims landed at Plymouth Rock. In 1630, John Billington, one of the original band of 102 Pilgrims to come over on the *Mayflower,* fired his blunderbuss at a neighbor and killed the man at close range. John Billington was charged with the common law offense of murder under the English law and, after a prompt trial and conviction, was hanged.[16]

Only one degree of murder existed under the common law, and it was punishable by death. After the American Revolution, some state legislative bodies began creating other degrees of murder, perhaps motivated by a desire to separate homicides to be punished by death from homicides that they believed did not warrant a sentence of death. In addition, there was distrust of adoption by the new states of the harsh English criminal penalty rules. The first Pennsylvania state constitution, adopted in 1776, included the statement that penal laws should be reformed, and that punishment should be proportionate to the crime. Pennsylvania was the first state to have degrees of murder based on culpability.

By the year 1900, virtually all the states had two or three degrees of murder. At that time, the degree system was a useful and meaningful method of distinguishing murder that was punished by capital punishment and that which was not. With the decline in the use of the death penalty in this century and its virtual nonuse in the 1960s and 1970s, the utility of the degree system declined considerably.

The degree system is still meaningful today, when first-degree murder carries a mandatory life imprisonment sentence or the death penalty. The degree system is also used as part of plea bargaining when the state finds advantage in allowing the defendant to plead guilty to second degree murder or to some other lesser offense if a reduction is appropriate.

State murder statutes vary in how they define first- and second-degree murder. An example of a first-degree murder statute that incorporates the common law "malice" requirement is Nebraska Revised Statutes § 28-303: "A person commits murder in the first degree if he kills another person (1) purposely and with deliberate malice. . . ." Second-degree murder is defined in § 28-304: "A person commits murder in the second degree if he causes the death of a person intentionally, but without premeditation."

The Illinois statute is an example of a statute that has a broader definition of first-degree murder:

> (a) A person who kills an individual without lawful justification commits first degree murder if, in performing the acts which cause the death, (1) he either intends to kill or do great bodily injury to that individual or another, or knows that such acts will cause death to that individual or another; (2) he knows that such acts create a strong probability of death or great bodily harm to that individual or another, or (3) he is attempting to commit a forcible felony other than second degree murder.[17]

Second-degree murder is defined as doing an act that constitutes first-degree murder, but under intense passion caused by serious provocation, or under an unreasonable belief that the killing was justified.

CLASSIFICATIONS OF COMMON LAW MURDER

- *Intent-to-kill murder:* The most common murder, the intentional killing of another human being, is considered the most serious offense in the criminal law.
- *Intent-to-do-serious-bodily-harm murder:* In this type of murder, the defendant intended to do serious bodily harm short of death, but his or her acts resulted in death.
- *Depraved-mind or depraved-heart murder:* When a death results from conduct that shows a wanton disregard for human life and when there is a high probability the conduct will result in death, the homicide is classified as this type of murder.
- *Felony murder:* At common law, one who caused another's death while committing a felony was guilty of felony murder. However, when the doctrine was created, only eight felonies were recognized, and all were punished by death. Because states now have many felonies that do not carry the death penalty, the felony murder rule is generally limited to crimes of violence.

Intent-to-Kill and Premeditated Murder

The unlawful, intentional, premeditated killing of another human being is considered the most serious criminal offense. It is in most states called first-degree or capital murder. The weapon used to implement the murder can be anything from a firearm to bare hands. The type of weapon used or the manner in which the fatal blow is delivered is not necessarily significant. Rather, the presence or absence of the specific intent to take the life of another human being separates this crime from all other degrees of homicide. The type of weapon and the manner in which it is used, however, may give rise to the legal inference that a person intends the natural and probable consequences of his or her deliberate acts.

murder Unlawful homicide with malice aforethought.

Murder under the common law and as enacted by the statutes of many states as first-degree murder is often defined as an "unlawful homicide with malice aforethought." The phrase *malice aforethought* signifies the mental state of a person who voluntarily, without legal excuse or justification, does an act that ordinarily will cause death or serious injury to another. Although the word *malice* ordinarily conveys the meaning of hatred, ill will, or malevolence, it is not limited to those meanings in "malice aforethought" but can include such motives as a mercy killing, in which the homicide is committed to end the suffering of a loved one. *Aforethought* has been interpreted to mean that the malice must exist at the time of the homicidal act. Courts have held that if the design and intent to kill precede the killing for even a moment, the person can be convicted of first-degree murder.[18]

Other states have defined first-degree murder as causing "the death of another human being with intent to kill that person." The American Law Institute Model Penal Code, § 210, uses the words *purposely* and *knowingly* causing the death of another person as the basis for a charge of murder.

A federal criminal statute, 18 U.S.C. § 1111, defines "murder" as follows: "Murder is the unlawful killing of a human being with malice aforethought." If the killing is done by poison, during the commission of certain identified crimes, or is "willful, deliberate, malicious and premeditated," it is murder in the first degree. All other murders are murder in the second degree. The meaning of "premeditated" was the issue in the following case.

In the 2011 case of *United States v. Begay*[19] the Ninth Circuit Court of Appeals, sitting *en banc,*[20] reversed a decision of a circuit court panel and affirmed the first-degree murder conviction of the defendant, Begay. A Ninth Circuit Court of Appeals panel of three judges had agreed with Begay's claim that the prosecution had failed to prove he killed the victim with premeditation. That court said the statute requires that "at some point *after* the defendant forms the intent to kill the victim, he has the time to reflect on the decision to commit murder, that he in fact does reflect on that decision, and that he commits the murder with a 'cool mind' after having engaged in such reflection."[21]

The panel had concluded the evidence did not support the jury finding of premeditation. It noted that Begay had no previous relationship with either victim, he had no shown motive for the killings, he engaged in no planning activity, and he didn't have a "cool head," because even though he was a skilled marksman, he missed with many of the rifle shots from a short range, which showed he was agitated and excited.

The *en banc* court held the evidence was sufficient to prove premeditation. That court thought it significant that after deciding to kill the victim, Begay walked back to his car, got his rifle, walked back to the car in which the victim was a passenger, walked around to the passenger window, and shot the victim at close range. A jury could reasonably conclude Begay had time then to consider the nature of his conduct, and still went through with the killing. The *en banc* court thus reversed the panel decision, and affirmed the jury verdict of guilty of first-degree murder. The U.S. Supreme Court denied certiorari, 132 S. Ct. 754 (2011).

The "Deadly Weapon" Doctrine

Committing a crime by use of a "deadly weapon," such as assault with a deadly weapon, is commonly a separate and more serious crime. In a murder case, the use of a deadly weapon can also be used to prove "malice" or other intent. Because direct evidence is rarely available to show the actual intent of a person charged with a crime, the fact finder, judge or jury, must draw inferences about intent from the conduct of the accused and the circumstances surrounding the crime to determine if the intent to kill existed. The use of a deadly weapon creates an inference of the user's intent. For example, if a defendant pointed a weapon he or she knew to be loaded at another person and pulled the trigger, no direct evidence of intent exists, but intent can be inferred by the defendant's conduct.

The "deadly weapon" doctrine is related to and part of the inference that a person intends the natural and probable consequences of his or her deliberate acts. A loaded revolver is certainly a deadly weapon when aimed and fired at close range. Under such circumstances, a jury can easily infer an intent to kill, because the natural and probable consequences of this act are death or serious bodily harm.

Determining what constitutes a deadly weapon depends on the object used and the circumstances that existed at the time of the homicide. One area where courts are split on this question involves whether human body parts—fists, feet, or teeth—can be deadly weapons. See *Parts of the Body as Dangerous Weapons,* 8 ALR 4th

1268 (1981; 2010 Cum. Supp.). Some jurisdictions hold that parts of the body cannot be a deadly weapon for purposes of conviction of crimes requiring the presence or use of a deadly weapon. For example, in the 2010 case of *McMillian v. State*,[22] the defendant used his teeth to bite out his girlfriend's left eye. The court held that using teeth to injure another cannot be "use of a deadly weapon" for purposes of a domestic assault statute. That appears to be the position of the Model Penal Code, § 210.0 (4).

On the other hand, in the 2009 cases of *Dasher v. State*[23] and *State v. Wallace*,[24] the courts held that fists or feet could be deadly weapons depending on how they were used, and the relative size of the assailant and victim. Most courts do agree that if an assailant is wearing heavy boots during an assault, the boots themselves are an extra-bodily object and can thus be a deadly weapon.[25]

Therefore, in determining what a deadly weapon is, a jury considers the instrument used, who used it, and how it was used. Some items, such as knives, clubs, or guns, are almost always considered deadly weapons because of the potential harm they can cause. Other instruments, such as automobiles, have to be viewed in light of their uses. The U.S. Supreme Court ruled in the early case of *Allen v. United States* that a lower court erred when it withdrew the question of self-defense from a jury on the ground that sticks and clubs were not deadly weapons.[26] Sticks and clubs can be deadly weapons, depending on their size, who is using them, and how they are used. The same is true for boots used to kick a victim in the head, a hardwood floor on which an infant's head was battered, and a nail gun.

Transferred Intent

If a killer is a poor shot and misses the intended victim but hits and kills another person, he or she could argue that there was no intent to kill that person. If there was a mistake of identity and the killer kills the wrong person, the same argument could be made. Defense lawyers have used these arguments for hundreds of years, arguing that because there was no ill will and malice toward the victim killed by accident, the defendant should not be convicted of intent-to-kill murder but, at the most, negligent or reckless homicide.

To accept such arguments would allow killers to benefit because of their poor marksmanship or because they killed the wrong person in a mix-up. The common law rejected that argument by creating the doctrine of **transferred intent**. This doctrine became part of the common law before the American Revolution and was recognized as early as 1766 by Blackstone in 4 *Commentaries* 200–201.

transferred intent A doctrine used when the intention to harm one individual inadvertently causes a second person to be hurt instead. The individual causing the harm will be seen as having "intended" the act by means of the "transferred intent" doctrine.

The transferred intent doctrine rests on the sensible foundation that where one has demonstrated the intent to take another person's life, it should not matter whose life is taken. The culpability of the killer remains the same: a life was taken intentionally. The law achieves this result by "transferring" the intent to kill the intended victim to the victim that actually is killed.

It does not alter the "transferred intent" doctrine if the killer manages to kill both the intended victim and another person. In the 2011 case of *Henry v. State*,[27] the defendant fired several rifle shots into a group of men fighting each other. The defendant hit the intended victim seven times, killing him. He also hit a bystander, killing her as well. The Maryland Supreme Court held that even if the defendant succeeded in killing his intended target, the doctrine of transferred intent would apply to the other person killed.

The transferred intent doctrine also may be used to prove the required "premeditation" for a first-degree murder conviction. Thus, if A aims a gun at B in a premeditated act to kill B, but instead strikes C, A can be convicted of the **premeditated murder** of C. See Wayne R. LaFave, 2 *Substantive Criminal Law,* § 14.7(a) (2nd Ed. 2003). However, the transferred intent doctrine *by itself* cannot be used to prove premeditation if the defendant in fact intended to kill the person who died. In such a case, the defendant's premeditated intent to kill **another person** does not "transfer," because the defendant had some kind of actual intent with respect to the actual victim. The nature of that intent must be proved by the prosecution. In the case of *State v. Hall,*[28] the defendant left an apartment with a gun, saying he planned to kill three unidentified people. In fact, the defendant walked to gas station and fired four shots point-blank at the station clerk. The trial court instructed the jury that under the transferred intent doctrine the premeditation to kill the three unidentified people satisfied the premeditation requirement for the killing of the clerk. The Minnesota Supreme Court reversed, saying that because there was no evidence the clerk was an unintended victim, the prosecution needed to prove the defendant premeditated the clerk's death.

premeditation Mental determination to unlawfully kill another person after planning or reflection on actions causing death.

Intent-to-Do-Serious-Bodily-Harm Murder

English courts under the common law long ago decided that a death at the hands of one who intended to do only serious bodily harm was nevertheless murder. The following famous English cases illustrate this type of murder:

Rex v. Errington

2 Lew. C.C. 148, 217 (1838)

The defendants covered a drunken man, who was sleeping, with straw, on which they threw a shovel of hot cinders. The man burned to death in the fire that resulted. The court instructed the jury that if they found that the defendants intended to do any serious harm to the deceased, the crime was murder under the common law; if the defendants' only intent was to play a joke or frighten the deceased, the crime was manslaughter.

Holloway Case

79 Eng. Rep. 715 (K.B. 1628)

The defendant tied a boy to a horse's tail and hit the horse to make it run. The boy was killed. The defendant was convicted of murder even though it was found that there was no intent to kill.

Many states follow this common law approach, and include "intent-to-do-serious-bodily-harm" as a class of murder. For example, Tex. Penal Code Ann. § 19.02(b)(2) includes in the definition of murder a person who "intends to cause serious bodily harm and commits an act clearly dangerous to human life that causes the death of an individual." In the 2012 case of *Cavazos v. State*,[29] the Texas Court of Criminal Appeals held that a man who pulled a gun at a party, pointed it at a person taunting him, and pulled the trigger twice could be found guilty of murder, even though no evidence of intent to kill was presented. Pointing a gun at another person and pulling the trigger is "clearly dangerous" the court held, even if no intent to kill was shown. The court affirmed the jury verdict of guilty of murder.

State murder statutes vary on the inclusion of "serious bodily injury" as a class or type of murder. Those that retain that class generally include it as second-degree murder, although Illinois continues to include it in the first-degree murder statute, 720 ILCS 5/9-1. The Model Penal Code, § 210.2 omits any reference to "intent to do serious bodily harm" in the classification of murder. Rather, the fact that a defendant intended to inflict serious harm would be a factor in showing the kind of "extreme indifference to the value of human life" that is included in the definition of murder.

Depraved-Mind or Depraved-Heart Murder

"Depraved heart" murder, which in some states is called second-degree murder, is similar in some aspects to intent-to-do-serious-bodily-harm murder. The primary difference is that depraved-heart murder includes no specific intent to injure or harm. However, if the conduct of the defendant were so reckless as to create a high risk of death, he or she would, in many instances, be found guilty of depraved-heart murder.

Since intent to kill is not an element of depraved-heart murder, the crime can be proved by evidence of extremely reckless actions. The distinction between "recklessly causing a death," which in most cases would be classified as involuntary manslaughter, and "depraved heart" murder, is not always clear. "Reckless" homicide generally means acting without regard to a substantial risk that death could ensue. "Depraved heart" homicide, similar to the Model Penal Code's definition of murder, means acting with "extreme indifference to the value of human life."

In the 2012 case of *Hawkins v. State*[30] the Mississippi Supreme Court affirmed a jury verdict of "depraved heart" murder under Miss. Code § 97-2-19(1)(b), which defines depraved heart murder as taking a life with actions "evincing a depraved heart, regardless of human life." The defendant got in a fight with his girlfriend, and struck her forcefully in the head at least once. Medical experts testified the victim had severe heart disease, and died from a trauma-induced heart attack. It was not clear if defendant was aware of the victim's heart condition. The court said defendant's actions satisfied the definition of depraved heart murder, and affirmed the jury verdict.

California is one of the states that define extremely reckless homicides as second-degree murder, not "depraved heart" murder. In the 2012 case of *People v. Cravens*[31] the California Supreme Court stated that this kind of murder requires a showing of "implied malice," which has both a physical and mental component.

The physical component is "an act, the probable consequences of which are dangerous to life." The mental component is acting "with a conscious disregard for life." In that case the defendant struck a violent fist-blow to an impaired victim, causing the victim to hit the concrete pavement with his head, causing his death. The court said that while a blow with a fist would not ordinarily show implied malice, it did here. The court noted the victim was intoxicated, and was reeling from blows administered by defendant's friends. After knocking the helpless victim to the ground the defendant laughed, and made no attempt to summon medical help. The court affirmed the jury verdict of guilty of second-degree murder.

Felony Murder

felony murder Most states and the federal government have felony murder statutes that punish as murder the causing of death of another while the defendant is committing a felony of violence. A felony murder conviction does not require a showing of malice or deliberate intent to kill

The **felony murder** rule became part of the common law of England many years ago. The rule initially stated that if a death occurs while a person is committing or attempting to commit any felony, the person could be convicted of felony murder even if the death was unintended and accidental. The theory behind the rule was that the intent to commit the underlying felony sufficed to show the intent to kill.

In the United States, courts and legislatures have limited the scope of the felony murder rule. The most frequent method of limiting the rule is illustrated by the federal murder statute, 18 U.S.C. § 1111. That statute includes as murder only a killing that occurs during the commission of certain enumerated crimes, such as arson, robbery, or sexual assault. If a person is killed during the commission of a felony not listed in § 1111, it is not murder **solely** because of the felony committed. In such a case, the prosecution would need to prove the required intent.

Other methods of determining when the felony murder rule is appropriate include a requirement that the killing was the "natural and direct consequence" of the felony, or that the act that caused the death occurred while the felony was in progress. In *People v. Klebanowski*,[32] the Illinois Supreme Court held the felony-murder rule, which applied to killings that occurred "during the commission" of a felony, applied when one of two robbers was killed by the victim (an off-duty police officer) during the robbers' attempt to escape. In *State v. Beach*,[33] the Kansas Supreme Court held that unless the defendant showed that an intervening force caused a death during the commission of a crime, there was no duty on the prosecution to prove otherwise that the death was a "direct result" of the commission. The court reasoned that the absence of an intervening force by itself established the causal connection between the felony and the killing.

Many states also have a version of the "continuous transaction" doctrine. Under that doctrine, a death triggers the felony murder rule only if the death was part of a continuous transaction with the underlying felony. In the 2013 case of *People v. Wilkins*, 295 P.3d 903 (Cal. 2013), the California Supreme Court reversed the conviction of a burglar who was found guilty of felony murder. The defendant had stolen several large appliances from a construction site, loading them in the back of his pickup, but forgot to shut the tailgate. While he was driving on the interstate sixty miles away from the burglary site an appliance fell off the pickup, causing an accident where a motorist was killed. A jury convicted the defendant of first-degree felony murder. The California Supreme Court reversed, holding that under the "escape" rule, once the burglar had reached a "place of safety" away from the crime scene, any subsequent death could not be part of a continuous transaction with the burglary.

The Model Penal Code's definition of murder in section 210.2 omits any reference to the felony murder rule. Instead, that section states that if a homicide occurs during one of the listed crimes (e.g., robbery, rape, arson, kidnapping) it is presumed that it was the result of "extreme indifference to the value of human life" and thus constitutes murder under § 210.2(b). Some state murder statutes, such as the statute in Kentucky, K.R.S. § 507.020, follow the Model Penal Code and drop the felony murder rule, instead using the "extreme indifference" language of the MPC.

In most states, though not all, it has been held that the death of a person, including a co-felon, that occurs during a felony but is caused by a third person—such as a person who was the intended victim, a passerby, or a police officer who confronts a felony in progress—does not qualify as felony murder. These states subscribe to what has been called the "agency" foundation of the felony murder rule. That is, if one of several persons committing a felony causes a death, the "malice" of that person is imputed to the others. However, where the death is caused by a third person, there is no "malice" to impute to the persons committing the felony.

Thus, if the police confront two robbers, and kill one of the robbers, the other robber is not guilty of felony murder. In New York, Penal Law § 125.25 states the felony murder rule applies when the defendant or "another participant" in the crime kills another person "other than a participant." In the 2012 case of *Davis v. Fox*[34] the West Virginia Supreme Court held that the killing of one of two persons committing a burglary by the owner of the building did not subject the surviving burglar to the felony murder rule. The court said that the purpose of the felony murder rule was to substitute the "malicious" intent underlying the felony for the "malicious" intent for the killing. When multiple defendants are involved in the felony, and one kills a third party, the malicious intent of the killer is transferred to the other defendant. However, when a death occurs that is not caused by either of the defendants, the requisite malice needed for a murder charge is not present, the court held. Citing other cases, the court said that "the thing that is imputed to a felon for a killing incidental to his felony is *malice and not the act of killing.*" It ordered the dismissal of the felony murder charge.

In other states, as the *Klebanowski* case discussed earlier shows to be the result in Illinois, the death of a co-felon makes the remaining felon guilty of felony murder. These courts follow the "proximate cause" theory of the felony murder rule, not the "agency" theory of implied malice illustrated above.

The Oklahoma Appellate Court reached that conclusion in *Kinchson v. State.*[35] The court affirmed the murder conviction of one of two robbers when the other robber was killed by the intended victim of the robbery. The court said that the felony murder rule applies because it was foreseeable that committing the crime of armed robbery could result in death of a person, including one of the perpetrators of the robbery. This also appears to be the rule in prosecutions under 18 U.S.C. § 1111. In *United States v. Garcia-Ortiz,* 528 F.3d 74 (1st Cir. 2008), *cert. denied* 129 S. Ct. 254 (2008), the court held that a defendant could be convicted of felony murder when an accomplice was killed by a third party.

In those states that do not apply the felony murder rule to the killing of a co-felon by a third party, a co-felon could be charged with provocative act murder. That doctrine applies if the co-felon took some action that was likely to provoke the third party into using deadly force. For example, in *People v. Concha*,[36] the California Supreme Court held a defendant could be convicted of first-degree murder under the "provocative act" murder doctrine when the victim of an attempted murder killed a co-felon. The court stated that in California even though a co-felon could not be guilty of felony murder in connection with either the death of another felon or death caused by a third party, if the underlying crime was the proximate cause of the death, the provocative act murder doctrine applied. Moreover, rejecting the defendant's argument to the contrary, the court held that if a jury found the attempted murder was premeditated, then the resulting death of the co-felon would be first-degree murder.

Manslaughter

Definition of Manslaughter

manslaughter Criminal homicides other than murder. Most states provide for two degrees of manslaughter: voluntary and involuntary.

Manslaughter was defined by common law as a classification of criminal homicide that is less than murder. The common law divided manslaughter into two categories: voluntary and involuntary. Most U.S. jurisdictions follow the common law classifications, but a few states have created three categories. For example, Section 192 of the California Penal Code creates the three classifications of voluntary, involuntary, and vehicular manslaughter. A few states have only one degree of manslaughter. Another form of classification identifies manslaughter by degrees (first, second, and so on)[37] rather than voluntary and involuntary.

Reasons given for a manslaughter conviction rather than a murder conviction are as follows:

1. The victim may have provoked the killing, or his or her unlawful conduct set into motion a chain of events that resulted in the killing.
2. The circumstances of the killing are not bad enough to be charged as murder, but the defendant's criminal conduct should be punished.
3. In some cases, the jury cannot unanimously agree on a finding of murder, and compromises on a manslaughter conviction.

Manslaughter is a crime that is generally considered to be separate and distinct from murder. Because the penalties are less severe than for murder, defense lawyers who are unable to obtain an acquittal for clients seek a conviction of manslaughter rather than murder.

Voluntary Manslaughter

The crime of voluntary manslaughter requires proof of an intentional killing. It differs from murder in that the killing is not accompanied by premeditation or malice. Thus, in any case where the defendant intentionally killed another person, circumstances must be examined to determine if the defendant lacked the required malice for a murder charge. Absence of malice can be shown in most states by either evidence of a "sudden quarrel" or "heat of passion" that directly preceded the intentional killing, or evidence of "imperfect" self-defense.

EXAMPLES OF MANSLAUGHTER

Heat of Passion Manslaughter

Example: D and V, a married couple, are separated. D arrives at V's residence and observes V having sex with another man. D becomes enraged, and kills V. Although D's actions show an intentional killing, the "heat of passion" likely would be seen as eliminating the "malice" need for a murder conviction.

Heat of passion manslaughter would be likely because

1. There was adequate provocation, which caused
2. Extreme anger and rage in a reasonable person,
3. There was no opportunity to cool off, and
4. There was a causal connection between the provocation, anger, and the fatal act.

Imperfect Self-Defense Manslaughter

Example: Defendant unlawfully started a fistfight with another person. The other person pulled out a knife, which under the circumstances was excessive force. Seeing the knife, the defendant pulled a gun and shot the other person, killing him. Since defendant was the wrongful aggressor, his claim of self-defense is "imperfect": self-defense only applies if the other person is the wrongful aggressor. However, even though the killing was intentional, it lacks the "malice" required for a murder conviction, because the defendant was responding to excessive force.

Example: Defendant honestly but unreasonably believed a person approaching him was about to strike him with a knife. In fact, the person was holding a flashlight. Defendant shot the person, causing his death. If the defendant actually had the mistaken belief, the killing was intentional, but the defendant lacked the malice required for murder. The defendant would not be entitled to claim self-defense, because he used unlawful force under the circumstances. His belief about the attack would permit the imperfect self-defense to lower the killing to manslaughter.

Involuntary Manslaughter (Also Called Unintended Manslaughter)

Example: A defendant repeatedly allowed vicious dogs to run loose, even though the dogs had on past occasions attacked people they encountered. If the dogs attacked and killed a person, the killing would not be murder, because the defendant did not intend the killing to occur. However, because allowing the dogs to run loose created an unusually high risk of injury or death, involuntary manslaughter could be charged.

Heat of Passion Manslaughter

All states provide for lesser charge of voluntary manslaughter where an intentional killing occurs in the "heat of passion." This crime is commonly charged when the actions of the victim cause the defendant to become enraged and angered to the point of losing normal self-control and, in the heat of passion, kill another person.

In 2 Wayne R. LaFave, *Substantive Criminal Law*, § 15.2(A), at 492 (West 2003) it is said,

There are four obstacles for the defendant to overcome before he can have his intentional killing reduced from murder to manslaughter: (1) There must have been a reasonable provocation. (2) The defendant must have been in fact provoked. (3) A reasonable man so provoked would not have cooled off in the interval of time between the provocation and the delivery of the fatal blow. And (4), the defendant must not in fact have cooled off during that interval.

In the 2012 case of *United States v. Jack*[38] a defendant convicted of murder appealed, contending the jury should have been given instructions on "heat of passion" manslaughter. The defendant killed his wife, but contended it occurred in a heat of passion brought on by her admission she was having an affair with another man. The appeals court held that although under some circumstances knowledge of an affair can be sufficient provocation for a heat of passion claim, those circumstances were not present here. The court noted that no evidence linked the time defendant found out about the affair to the killing, and in any case the evidence established that after arguing with his wife the defendant's father calmed him down, and the killing occurred several hours later. The court affirmed his murder conviction.

Sufficient and Adequate Provocation   Sufficient provocation naturally and instantly produces in the mind of an ordinary person the highest degree of exasperation, rage, anger, sudden resentment, or terror. The provocation must be of such a nature and be so great as to overcome or suspend an ordinary person's exercise of good judgment. The provocation must be such as to cause the person to act uncontrollably. The killing must occur immediately during or after the provocation and during the intense heat of passion. Only a few categories of provocation have been recognized by the law as legally sufficient and adequate to justify reduction of a murder charge to that of manslaughter.

In the United States, there is an almost uniform rule that words and gestures are never sufficient provocation to reduce a charge of murder to that of manslaughter. The U.S. Supreme Court stated in the early case of *Allen v. United States* that "mere words alone do not excuse even a simple assault. Any words offered at the time [of the killing] do not reduce the grade of the killing from murder to manslaughter."[39]

Although words and gestures alone are never sufficient provocation, if other acts, such as a battery, accompany the verbal provocation, then it might be held to be sufficient. In *People v. Rice*, the deceased slapped the defendant's child and a quarrel resulted.[40] This was held to be sufficient provocation. In the Georgia case of *Lamp v. State,* a minor and technical battery accompanied by words was held to amount to a sufficient provocation to justify reducing the conviction from murder to manslaughter.[41] But in *Commonwealth v. Cisneros,* the Pennsylvania Supreme Court arrived at an opposite conclusion.[42]

Many U.S. courts have held that when a married person finds his or her spouse in an act of adultery, this amounts to sufficient provocation if it causes a genuine heat of passion.[43] However, this rule may not apply if a girlfriend is caught cheating on her boyfriend (or vice versa).[44]

Trespass, like battery, depends on the facts and circumstances in each particular case. A homeowner certainly does not have sufficient and adequate provocation to

CRIMINAL HOMICIDE IN THE UNITED STATES

The criminal homicide that kills the most people	Drunk and drugged drivers kill over 12,000 people each year. Lower blood alcohol standards (0.08) and tougher enforcement have helped reduce that number.
The highest number of murder victims in one day	More than 2,800 people died in the terrorist attacks of September 11, 2001; 168 people died in the Oklahoma City bombing in 1995.
The nation's deadliest serial killers	Gary Ridgway (called the "Green River Killer") pleaded guilty in December 2003 to killing 48 women in the Seattle area over a 21-year period. This exceeds other serial killers: John Wayne Gacy (33, Chicago area, 1972–78); Ted Bundy (30, Washington State and Florida, 1970s); and Jeffrey Dahmer (17, Milwaukee area, 1978–92).
School-age children killed	In the 1992–1993 school year, 2,719 school-age children were murdered in the United States. Thirty-four of these murders occurred at school. In 2008–2009, 1,579 school-age children were murdered, a drop of 42%. Seventeen were murdered at school. D.O.J. report, February 2012. The twenty children murdered at Sandy Hook Elementary School in 2012 exceeded the national total for 2009 or 2010.

kill someone who walks across a lawn, yard, farm, or field in the middle of an afternoon. But snowmobilers who broke onto a farmer's land in Wisconsin and were circling the farmhouse at midnight caused a Wisconsin prosecutor to charge manslaughter when the farmer, in a terrible anger and rage, shot and killed one of the trespassers.

Courts often hold that mercy killing is not a defense to a murder charge (see the euthanasia section in this chapter). In a similar way, courts have also held that a request by a dying person to be killed is not adequate provocation to support the reduced charge of manslaughter. In the 2011 case of *State v. Goulding*[45] the court held that killing the victim at the victim's request, because the victim failed in an attempt to take his own life, was murder, not manslaughter or assisted suicide.

Heat of Passion and the Test of the Reasonable Person　The test of sufficiency or adequacy of provocation must be made in view of how the average or reasonable person would react to such provocation. Some people have extraordinary self-control and could endure much provocation before an uncontrollable rage would cause them to use deadly force. Others have short tempers and fly into a rage with little provocation.

A jury cannot give any special considerations to a defendant who has an extraordinarily bad temper. If the provocation is such that it would not cause the average reasonable person to explode in a sudden outburst of rage, it is not adequate or sufficient provocation to reduce murder to manslaughter. California courts have quoted with approval the statements of the court in the case of *People v. Logan*:

> The fundamental . . . inquiry is whether or not the defendant's reason was, at the time of his act, so disturbed or obscured by some passion—not necessarily fear and never of course the passion of revenge—to such an extent as would render *ordinary men of average disposition* liable to act rashly or without due deliberation and reflection, and from this passion rather than from judgment.[46] [Emphasis added.]

In the 2013 case of *People v. Beltran*, 301 P.3d 1120, the California Supreme Court, again basing its reasoning on the *Logan* decision, held that "heat of passion" requires only a showing that a reasonable person would under the circumstances act without rational thought but in response to the provocation. The court rejected the state's argument that the provocation must be such that it would move an ordinary person to *kill* another person. All that must be shown, the court said, is provocation that would "cause an emotion so intense that an ordinary person would simply react, without reflection." The focus of heat of passion must be on the mental state, not the act, the court said.

The case of *Bedder v. Director of Public Prosecutions* received considerable attention throughout the English-speaking world.[47] The defendant, who knew that he was impotent, attempted to have sexual intercourse with a London prostitute in a quiet courtyard. She jeered when he was unsuccessful and attempted to get away from him. He tried to hold her, and she slapped him in the face and punched him in the stomach. When he grabbed her shoulders, she kicked him in the groin. He took a knife from his pocket and stabbed her twice, killing her. The House of Lords affirmed both the finding of the jury that there was not sufficient or adequate provocation and the following jury instruction given by the trial court:

> The reasonable person, the ordinary person, is the person you must consider when you are considering the effect which any acts, any conduct, any words, might have to justify the steps which were taken in response thereto, so that an unusually excitable or pugnacious individual, or a drunken one or a man who is sexually impotent is not entitled to rely on provocation which would not have led an ordinary person to have acted in the way which was in fact carried out.

Cooling of the Blood   Cooling of the blood, also known as *cooling time* or *reasonable time to cool off,* is a factor that must be considered if there is an interval between the provocation and the killing. Assume that after Y provokes X into a heat of passion, X, who has lost his self-control, runs to get his gun. If it took X two minutes to get his gun, was this sufficient time for X to cool off? If it took X a half hour or an hour to obtain his gun, was this sufficient time for the heat of passion to cool off? These questions would have to be answered by a court and jury that would consider the type and degree of the provocation that caused the heat of passion.

Third Party Provocation   Under the common law, the heat-of-passion/provocation claim could be asserted to reduce a murder charge to manslaughter only if the victim was also the one doing the provocative acts. This was explained as the requirement that there be a "causal" connection between the provocation and the fatal acts.

> **EXAMPLE** ▶ Defendant and his estranged wife were arguing. The wife's brother intervened and fought the defendant to the ground. The defendant became enraged, and got away. He ran into his house, grabbed a knife, came outside, and stabbed his wife, who died. The court held the defendant was not entitled to a manslaughter instruction, because the victim, his wife, did not supply the provocation. *Commonwealth. v. LeClair*[48] (Mass. 2006).

The Model Penal Code, § 210.3 (Comment 5), would make provocation by a third party sufficient to reduce a murder to manslaughter, if the other requirements have been met. Under the MPC approach, it is the extreme mental state of the defendant, not the source of the provocation, which is important. Only a few states have adopted the MPC's approach. One is Minnesota, where in the case of *State v. Stewart*[49] the court held that the provocative action of a third party—telling defendant she was HIV positive—could be used to reduce a charge of murder to manslaughter of another victim. However, the court held in that case that the defendant killed the victim, a child, in order to keep his crying from alerting the police. Thus, the victim was not killed as part of the rage brought on by the news the defendant's girlfriend was HIV positive. It affirmed the defendant's murder conviction.

Imperfect or Unlawful Force in Self-Defense Charged as Manslaughter

perfect self-defense
A homicide in which the killer subjectively believes that his or her conduct was necessary and reasonable and that, by objective standards, a reasonable person would believe it was lawful and complied with the requirements of the law. The homicide is either justifiable or excusable, and it carries no criminal liability.

imperfect self-defense
A homicide in which the killer subjectively, but unreasonably, believes that his or her conduct was necessary. It may be unlawful if the killing was done with excessive or unnecessary force. An unnecessary killing in self-defense, in defense of another, or to prevent or terminate a felony of violence could be imperfect self-defense.

Homicide in **perfect self-defense** is either justifiable or excusable, and it carries no criminal liability. Perfect self-defense not only requires that the killer subjectively believe that his or her conduct was necessary but also that, by objective standards, a reasonable person would believe it was lawful and complied with the requirements of the law.

To use deadly force in self-defense, a person must reasonably believe he or she is (1) under threat of *imminent* death or great bodily harm, from (2) unlawful deadly force, and (3) that use of deadly force is necessary. If the belief in the imminent threat is not reasonable, and the person has other options available, deadly force is not legally justified.

If deadly force is used but not justified, and results in a death, the death could be treated as murder. However, one who kills with an actual, but unreasonable, belief that one is acting in self-defense differs from other intentional murders: "malice" is not present. That difference led many courts and legislatures to develop the mitigating doctrine known as **imperfect self-defense**.

In imperfect self-defense, the killer subjectively believes that his or her conduct was lawful and necessary, but that belief is unreasonable. If the killing was done with excessive or unnecessary force in self-defense, it is unlawful. An unnecessary killing in self-defense, in defense of another, or to prevent or terminate a felony of violence could be imperfect self-defense.

In imperfect self-defense cases the belief that use of deadly force was justified can occur in two types of situations, illustrated by the following two examples:

EXAMPLE ▶ D actually believes V is attacking him with deadly force, and D responds by using deadly force in "self-defense," killing V. In fact, D's belief that V was attacking with deadly force was unreasonable (either because the attack was not imminent, or the force used was not deadly). D's claim of perfect self-defense will fail.

EXAMPLE ▶ D attacks V with non-deadly force. V responds with deadly force. To counter V's threat of deadly force, D uses deadly force and kills V. Because D was the initial aggressor, and didn't retreat or use all efforts to avoid using deadly force, in most states his perfect self-defense claim would fail.

In the first example most states would permit the defendant to raise imperfect self-defense to mitigate a murder charge to manslaughter. For example, in *State v. Head*[50] the Wisconsin Supreme Court said that under W.S.A. § 940.01, a defendant who actually but unreasonably believed she needed to use deadly force to defend herself from her husband's physical abuses could raise imperfect self-defense to reduce the crime from first degree intentional homicide (murder) to second degree intentional homicide (manslaughter):

> We conclude in this case that [defendant's] offer of proof established a sufficient factual basis for a claim of unnecessary defensive force (imperfect self-defense), and that she should have been allowed to present evidence of [the victim's] violent character and past acts of violence at trial in an effort to mitigate the charge of intentional first degree homicide.

In the 2012 case of *People v. Lopez*[51] the California appeals court reached a similar result. It said that imperfect self-defense is permitted under California law:

> "Manslaughter is an unlawful killing without malice. (Citation omitted). The element of malice is negated, and a killing reduced from murder to voluntary manslaughter, when a defendant kills in the actual but unreasonable belief that he or she is in imminent danger of death or great bodily injury."

In the second example given above, where the defendant was the initial aggressor, some state courts have held imperfect self-defense is not available. Illinois is such a state.[52] However, even courts that have held that imperfect self-defense is not available in this situation note that some situations where the defense is claimed are situations where the prosecution may be unable to prove the malice required for a murder conviction, resulting in a manslaughter conviction without imperfect self-defense. For example, in the 2012 case of *People v. Reese*, the Michigan Supreme Court said,

> "Although we reject the doctrine of imperfect self-defense, many circumstances that involve what the Court of Appeals called 'imperfect self defense' can nevertheless provide grounds for a fact-finder to conclude that the prosecution has not proved the malice element that distinguishes murder from manslaughter."[53]

Involuntary Manslaughter

Involuntary manslaughter—sometimes called *unintentional* or *unlawful act manslaughter*—was discussed in Chapter 3 in relation to proximate cause or causation.

Involuntary manslaughter is often charged when extreme negligence or wanton or reckless conduct by the defendant brings about an unintended or accidental death. Two examples of cases in which defendants were charged and convicted of involuntary manslaughter follow. (For further cases on involuntary manslaughter, see Chapter 3.)

- *Extreme negligence and failure to act:* In the 2010 case of *Whitfield v. Commonwealth*[54] the Virginia Court of Appeals affirmed a conviction of involuntary manslaughter when a day-care driver placed a 13-month-old child in a van to go to the day care, but left the child in the van the entire day while he went home to sleep. The outside temperature reached 84 degrees, and all the van windows were closed. The child died before anyone discovered the child was in the van.
- *Reckless conduct:* A congressman from South Dakota with a history of careless driving was convicted of involuntary manslaughter when, traveling 16 miles per hour over the speed limit, he ran a stop sign and struck and killed a motorcyclist.

Most states have a vehicular manslaughter/homicide statute that can be used to charge a person who operates a vehicle in a grossly negligent manner and people are killed as a result. These statutes usually distinguish ordinary automobile-accident deaths from homicide crimes by requiring the prosecution to prove aggravating circumstances, such as intoxication or extremely reckless driving. In the 2012 case of *Otuwa v. State*[55] the Georgia appeals court affirmed a defendant's conviction for first-degree vehicular homicide. The defendant drove his car on a residential road at speeds up to 93 miles per hour. He lost control of the car and rolled it, killing two passengers. The defendant's blood alcohol level was twice the legal limit. The court said that under the Georgia statute, a person is guilty of first-degree vehicular homicide if he is (1) driving while intoxicated, or (2) driving recklessly, and causes a death. Second-degree vehicular homicide requires only a showing the defendant committed some other traffic offense, such as speeding.

Suicide, Assisting Suicide, and Euthanasia

In common law, suicide was considered to be self-murder and was a felony. Because the person who committed such a crime was beyond the reach of the law, the punishment was forfeiture of the deceased person's estate to the king and burial off the highway.

Assisting a suicide is a crime in most states. A person could assist another to commit suicide by conduct (or words) that a trial judge or a jury finds to amount to "assisting."

Euthanasia—or mercy killing—is murder. However, the motive for the murder is love, or concern for the suffering of the victim. In the case of *State v. Forrest*[56] the defendant was convicted of first-degree murder and sentenced to life imprisonment for the mercy killing of his terminally ill father, who was suffering from a number of untreatable illnesses. In such cases, appeals are made to the governor of the state for clemency, which is frequently granted after a number of years.[57]

euthanasia A killing of a terminally sick or injured individual with only a short time to live. Also called mercy killing.

Murder, Suicide, or Neither?

When one person participates in the death of another, that participation may constitute the crime of murder or assisted suicide. It may not be a crime at all, depending on the degree of participation and the laws of the state having jurisdiction over the acts.

assisting suicide The act of furnishing the means of a suicide, pursuant to a statute that permits such assistance.

The difference between murder and **assisting suicide** was explained by the California Supreme Court in *In re Joseph G.* as follows:

> The key to distinguishing between the crimes of murder and of assisting suicide is the active or passive role of the defendant in the suicide. If the defendant merely furnishes the means, he is guilty of assisting a suicide; if he actively participates in the death of the suicide victim, he is guilty of murder.[58]

The difference between participation that constitutes the crime of assisting suicide and participation that is not criminal is harder to draw. A doctor who, at the patient's or family's request, removes a life-support machine obviously hastens death but does not furnish the means of that death. On the other hand, a doctor who, like Dr. Jack Kevorkian, furnishes a person with a "suicide machine" clearly does furnish the means. Kevorkian admitted in 1997 to "being present" at more than 100 deaths.[59]

So-called passive euthanasia in hospitals does not fall easily into either category. A doctor who "sends a patient home" with a morphine drip and stops all other treatment is, in one sense, only letting nature take its course. On the other hand, the doctor knows that the morphine will shorten the patient's life, so that in prescribing large doses of the morphine he or she is providing the means for death.

Because of the ambiguities surrounding physician-assisted suicide, and because many patients have asserted a "right" to choose physician-assisted suicide, various constitutional attacks on state assisted-suicide statutes have been made. In *Washington v. Glucksberg*[60] and *Vacco v. Quill,*[61] the U.S. Supreme Court upheld the constitutionality of statutes in New York and Washington making physician-assisted suicides criminal. The Court rejected the contention that the Fourteenth Amendment prohibited states from making such conduct criminal. The concept of "liberty" in the Constitution, which spawned the right to marry, to have children, and to an abortion, does not, the Court held, include a right to assistance in choosing the time and manner of one's death.

The Internet has played a role in this controversy. Among the many "chat rooms" accessible on the Internet are sites where groups provide information and assistance on both sides of the assisted-suicide issue. Some "rooms" provide information about preventing suicide, while others share thoughts and information about suicide.

In the 2012 case of *State v. Melchert-Dinkel*[62] the Minnesota appeals court affirmed the conviction of William Melchert-Dinkel of two counts of "urging suicide." Dinkel, a former nurse who had his Minnesota license revoked in 2009, was obsessed with suicide, and under various identities participated in suicide chat rooms. While there, he often both provided information on committing suicide, and encouraged others to commit suicide. He was charged in the deaths of Mark Drybrough, 22, of Coventry, England, and Nadia Kajouji, 18, of Brandon, Ontario. Dinkel urged both people to commit suicide by hanging, and in the case of Kajouji attempted to convince her to do so with a webcam filming the event. Kajouji instead drowned herself in a river in Ontario. Dinkel told investigators he was a party to at least ten suicide "pacts," and that to his knowledge five of the other participants actually killed themselves.

In the case *of Baxter v. State,* 224 P.3d 1211 (Mont. 2009), the Montana Supreme Court held that it was not a criminal homicide for a physician to assist a terminally ill patient by giving him a prescription for a lethal drug. Because suicide is not a crime in Montana, the court said assisting the patient to do so was not a crime. Although section 45-5-102(1) MCA made it a crime to unlawfully "cause" another person's death, section 45-2-211(1) provided that consent of the "victim" was a defense, unless such consent was against public policy. The court held consent of a mature, aware, terminally ill patient was not against public policy.

The Oregon "Death with Dignity" Law

Most states make assisting a suicide a crime. Oregon, however, enacted a "death with dignity" law, which became effective in November 1997. The controversial law, which permits assisted suicides, is the first of its kind in the United States. The state of Washington followed with a similar law in 2008.

To qualify under either state's law, a patient must be found to be terminally ill and have less than six months to live. Patients must have the mental capacity to fully understand the situation that confronts them. There is a 15-day waiting period after the patient applies and is found to have qualified for physician-assisted suicide. A physician may then prescribe drugs to end the patient's life, but the physician does not administer the drugs. The physician is granted immunity from liability for her or his role in the process. Since it was enacted, about thirty people a year have used the provisions of the Oregon law. Each year about 30,000 people die in Oregon. There have been no serious efforts to repeal the law.

The Clinton administration decided not to challenge the Oregon "death with dignity" law, but the Bush administration moved to overturn it, contending physicians acting under the law were doing so in violation of the Federal Controlled Substances Act (CSA). In 2004, the Ninth Circuit Court of Appeals upheld the law, noting that the CSA was designed to fight drug abuse, not to regulate medicine and physicians.[63] On review, the U.S. Supreme Court upheld the Oregon law, reasoning that the CSA was directed at drug abuse and that treating a physician writing a prescription for a mercy killing as "drug abuse" was unreasonable.[64]

Summary

- *Corpus delicti* means the body of the crime. It must be proved by the prosecution before a defendant can be convicted of a crime.
- The year-and-a-day rule was adopted as a "bright line" rule of causation in homicide cases. A death beyond that period was not "caused" by the criminal acts. Today, medical science makes

proving the connection between actions and a resulting death much easier and clearer, so most states have dropped the year-and-a-day rule.

- The "born alive" requirement under the common law excluded the death of unborn children as murder. Many states have dropped the requirement, and make the death of an unborn child a crime separate from murder. In those states that still have the requirement, a fetus must by born "alive," that is, show some signs of brain function, before its death can be murder.

- Under the doctrine of transferred intent, the intention formed by the perpetrator of a homicide as to an intended victim is "transferred" to the killing of an unintended victim, thereby satisfying the intent requirement of the applicable homicide statute.

- Involuntary manslaughter and reckless homicide do not require proof of intent to kill. Second-degree murder based on intent to do serious bodily injury does not require specific intent to kill. In felony murder convictions, the intent to commit the underlying crime satisfies the intent requirement for murder.

- In all states, the death of the victim of a listed felony, and that of a third person killed by the felon, constitute felony murder. In some, but not all, states, the death of innocent persons killed by a third party or co-felons killed by a third party do not constitute felony murder.

- In voluntary manslaughter, the killing was intended, but occurred under circumstances where the defendant, though not excused, is not as culpable as in murder. In involuntary manslaughter the death was not intended, but arose out of severely reckless conduct.

- A charge of murder could be reduced to manslaughter if provocation existed to cause the criminal conduct, or if insufficient evidence exists to prove malice or premeditation.

- The state of Oregon has the power to determine what conduct is criminal in that state, unless it contravenes some federal law. The U.S. Supreme Court held that the Death with Dignity Law did not violate the Federal Controlled Substance Law, and thus was a permissible exercise of state power.

Key Terms

homicide, p. 260
"born alive" requirement, p. 265
feticide, p. 265
murder, p. 270

transferred intent, p. 272
premeditation, p. 273
felony murder, p. 275
manslaughter, p. 277

perfect self-defense, p. 282
imperfect self-defense, p. 282
euthanasia, p. 284
assisting suicide, p. 285

Case Analysis and Writing Exercises

1. Prosecutions for homicides that arise out of "passive" misconduct have their own special problems. "Passive" misconduct involves failure to take action when such action is needed and required to avoid some harmful result. Parental inaction that results in the death of a child is a frequent basis for a criminal prosecution. In *People v. Lewie*, 953 N.E.2d 760 (N.Y. 2011) a mother left her 8-year-old child with an abusive boyfriend, who had a history of abusing both the child and the mother. When the child died from that abuse, the mother was charged with both involuntary manslaughter and child endangerment under New York law. Can she be convicted of either or both of these charges? What are the tests used?

2. In states that include "intent to cause serious bodily injury" homicides in the definition of murder, there must be some definition of what constitutes "serious" injury, and what the defendant who causes such injury intended. New Jersey is such a state. What did the court say must be proved for a conviction based on serious bodily injury in the case of *State v. Merlain*, 2012 WL 986998 (N.J. A.D. 2012), *cert. denied* 53 A.3d 662 (N.J. 2012).

3. Can a mother who elects to deliver her baby at home, with no outside help, ever be convicted of

involuntary manslaughter? If so, what must the prosecution prove? See *Commonwealth v. Pugh,* 969 N.E.2d 672 (Mass. 2012).

4. Several members of the Vatos Locos gang were sitting in or standing near a car parked in South Minneapolis, part of the "territory" of the Surenos 13 gang. The defendant Cruz, a member of the Surenos 13 gang, arrived as a passenger in another car, and upon exiting asked "Que barrio?" meaning "what gang are you?" Before anyone could answer, Cruz pulled out a semi-automatic pistol and began firing at everyone. One person, Hernandez-Leon, was killed, and three others wounded. What homicide crimes did Cruz commit? Can Cruz, in reliance on *State v. Hall,* discussed in this chapter, successfully contend the doctrine of "transferred intent" does not apply to prove the necessary intent for a murder conviction? Why or why not? See *State v. Cruz-Ramirez,* 771 NW 2d 497 (Minn. 2009).

Endnotes

1. 293 P.3d 567 (Colo. 2013).
2. The court gave the change only prospective effect, and reversed the defendant's conviction under the corpus delicti rule that was in force when he was convicted. It also said the trustworthiness could be shown by proof of facts that corroborated the confession.
3. 807 P.2d 1009 (Cal. 1991).
4. See the *Newsweek* article "Death of the Innocent," August 17, 1998; the *New York Times* article "Mother Goes from Martyr to Defendant in Infanticides," August 7, 1998; and the *Chicago Tribune,* p. 20, September 25, 1997.
5. 470 P.2d 617 (Cal. 1970).
6. In 1994, the California Supreme Court held that the state could punish fetal murder without regard to the viability of the fetus. *People v. Davis,* 872 P.2d 591.
7. 530 N.W.2d 174 (Mich. App. 1995).
8. 705 A.2d 805 (N.J. App. 1998).
9. *Swafford v. State,* 421 N.E.2d 596 (Ind. 1981).
10. Of the many court cases involving brain-dead victims, two young women received a great amount of public attention. Nancy Cruzan received severe injuries in an auto accident, and Karen Ann Quinlan was brain dead because of a drug overdose. After years in vegetative states, the parents of both young women went into courts to obtain permission to withdraw life-support systems. In both cases, the parents carried the burden of showing that their incompetent daughters would not have wanted to go on living in vegetative states. See *In re Quinlan,* 70 N.J. 10, 355 A.2d 647 (1976), *review denied,* 429 U.S. 922, 97 S. Ct. 319 (1976) and *In re Cruzan,* 497 U.S. 261, 110 S. Ct. 2841 (1990).

    In the 1990 *Cruzan* case, the U.S. Supreme Court held that states could establish standards such as the Missouri "clear and convincing" evidence requirement showing that Nancy Cruzan would have wanted to die. The state of Missouri, which was paying about $112,000 per year to keep Cruzan alive in a "persistent vegetative state," had opposed efforts by her parents to have life-support systems withdrawn. In a hearing after the Supreme Court's decision, a Missouri court heard new evidence presented by three of Cruzan's co-workers, who testified that Nancy had stated she would never have wanted to live "like a vegetable." Cruzan's doctor testified that her existence was a "living hell." After eight years on life-support systems, the feeding tube was removed, and Nancy Cruzan died.

11. 387 N.W.2d 682 (Neb. 1986).
12. 703 S.E.2d 609 (Ga. 2010), *cert. denied,* 131 S. Ct. 2454 (2011).
13. *People v. Stevenson,* 416 Mich. 383, 331 N.W.2d 143 (1982). See also *State v. Hefler,* 60 N.C. App. 466, 299 S.E.2d 456 (1983), *affirmed* 310 N.C. 135, 310 S.E.2d 310, 34 CrL 2374 (1984), in which the North Carolina court stated: "For the courts to remain judicially oblivious of these advances [in medical science] when considering whether to extend an ancient common law rule would be folly."
14. 661 N.W.2d 381 (Wis. 2003).
15. 890 So.2d 1056 (Ala. 2003).
16. See Jay Robert Nash, *Bloodletters and Badmen: A Narrative Encyclopedia of American Criminals from the Pilgrims to the Present* (New York: M. Evans & Co., 1974).
17. 720 ILCS 5/9-1.
18. In a case in which the defendant shot a 15-year-old gasoline service station attendant in the head, neck, and back six times, the Minnesota Supreme Court held:

    > Extensive planning and calculated deliberation need not be shown by the prosecution. The requisite "plan" to commit a first-degree murder can be formulated virtually instantaneously by a killer . . . . Moreover . . . premeditation can be inferred from either the number of gunshots fired into the victim . . . or the fact that a killer arms himself with a loaded gun in preparation. State v. Neumann, 262 N. W.2d 426 (Minn. 1978).

19. 673 F.3d 1038 (9th Cir. 2011).
20. Federal Circuit Courts of Appeal hear cases in panels of three judges. When there is disagreement with a panel decision a request can be made for the case to be reheard in front of all the judges in that circuit. When this rehearing is held it is called *en banc.*

21. 567 F.3d 540, 546 (9th Cir. 2009).

22. 58 So.3d 849 (Ala. App. 2010).

23. 676 S.E.2d 181 (Ga. 2009).

24. 676 S.E.2d 922 (N.C. App. 2009).

25. See, e.g., *Commonwealth. v. Rumkin,* 773 N.E.2d 988 (Mass. App. 2002).

26. 157 U.S. 675, 15 S. Ct. 720 (1895).

27. 19 A.3d 944 (Md. 2011).

28. 722 N.W.2d 472 (Minn. 206).

29. 382 S.W. 3d 377 (Tex. Crim. App.).

30. 101 So.3d 638 (Miss. 2012).

31. 267 P.3d 1113 (Cal. 2012).

32. 852 N.E.2d 813 (Ill. 2006).

33. 67 P.3d 121 (Kan. 2003).

34. 735 S.E.2d 259 (W. Va. 2012).

35. 81 P.3d 681 (Okla. Crim. App. 2003).

36. 218 P.3d 660 (Cal. 2009).

37. See the New York Penal Code, Section 125.20.

38. 483 F. Appx. 427 (10th Cir. 2012).

39. 157 U.S. 675, 15 S. Ct. 720 (1895).

40. 351 Ill. 604, 184 N.E. 894 (1933).

41. 38 Ga. App. 36, 142 S.E. 202 (1928). In this case, the deceased used profane and insulting language and made threats to cut the defendant's throat.

42. 381 Pa. 447, 113 A.2d 293 (1955).

43. Years ago, Texas, New Mexico, and Utah enacted laws that provided that if a husband killed a man caught in an act of adultery with his wife, the killing was a justifiable homicide. Critics of these statutes argued that this permitted an "open shooting season" on paramours if they were caught by husbands in the act of adultery. Women's groups in these states angrily demanded that the statutes be either repealed or amended to give wives the same rights. All three states have repealed these statutes and probably have gone back to the common-law rule.

44. In a case where a fiancée was killed after she admitted infidelity, and in another case where a spouse was killed after confessing to adultery, the question before two state supreme courts was whether "mere words" justified reducing murder charges to voluntary manslaughter. Neither the Ohio Supreme Court nor the Michigan Supreme Court would reduce the murder charges to manslaughter because of mere words. See for Ohio *State v. Shane* (590 N.E. 2d 272) and for Michigan *State v. Pouncey* (471 N.W. 2d 346).

45. 799 N.W.2d 412 (S.D. 2011).

46. 175 Cal. 45, 164 P. 1121 (1917).

47. House of Lords, 2, All Eng. R 801 (1954).

48. 840 N.E.2d 510 (Mass. 2006).

49. 624 N.W.2d 585 (Minn. 2001).

50. 648 N.W.2d 413 (Wis. 2002).

51. 132 Cal. Rptr. 3d 248 (Cal. App. 2012).

52. *People v. Morgan,* 719 N.E.2d 681 (Ill. 1999).

53. 815 N.W.2d 85, 99 (Mich. 2012).

54. 702 S.E.2d 590 (Va. App. 2010).

55. 734 S.E.2d 273 (Ga. App. 2012).

56. 362 S.E.2d 252 (Ga. 1987).

57. The *Roswell Gilbert* case caused a national debate on euthanasia in 1985. Mr. Gilbert killed his wife, who was suffering from terminal debilitating diseases. He was 76 years of age at the time and received a sentence of 25 years' imprisonment without parole. After serving 5 years, he was granted clemency by the Florida governor and returned to Fort Lauderdale.

58. 667 P.2d 1176 (1983). In the case of *In re Joseph G.,* a minor (Joseph G.) and his friend made a mutual suicide pact. The two males drove a car over a cliff to carry out the suicides. Joseph G. survived, but his passenger was killed. The California Supreme Court reversed the first-degree murder conviction, holding that Joseph G. should be charged with assisting a suicide.

59. In April 1999, when he was 70 years old, Dr. Kevorkian was convicted of the crime of murder by a Michigan jury and sentenced to 10–25 years in prison, with the possibility of parole after 6 years and 8 months. He was released in 2007.

60. 117 S. Ct. 2258 (1997).

61. 117 S. Ct. 2293 (1997).

62. 816 N.W.2d 703 (Minn. App. 2012).

63. *Oregon v. Ashcroft,* 368 F.3d 1118 (9th Cir. 2004).

64. *Gonzales v. Oregon,* 546 U.S. 243 (2006).

Assault, Battery, and Other Crimes Against the Person

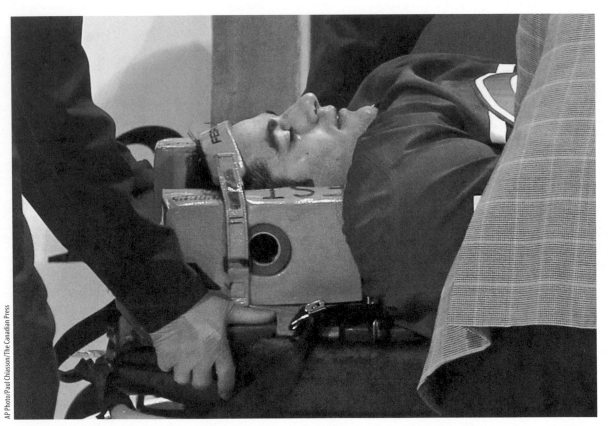

The Montreal Canadiens hockey player Max Pacioretty is wheeled off the ice after taking a severe hit from a Boston Bruins player. Physical contact in athletic contests, even that which causes severe injury, is generally not a crime unless the contact falls dramatically outside the kind of physical contact normally encountered in the athletic contest.

OUTLINE

The Crime of Assault

Assault with a Deadly or Dangerous Weapon

Battery

Offensive Touching Under Sexual Assault and Sexual Battery Statutes

Sports Injuries When Force Exceeds the Rules of the Game

Other Physical Contact Without Consent

Felonious and Aggravated Assaults and Batteries

Mayhem and Malicious Disfigurement

Hate Crime Laws

Child Abuse and Neglect

Offenses Against the Liberty of a Person: Kidnapping

Kidnapping and Hostage Taking

False Imprisonment

Parental Kidnapping or Child Snatching

The National Child Search Assistance Act

Family Violence and Disturbances

Domestic Violence and Women

Abuse of the Elderly

Violence in the Workplace

Road Rage: Violent Aggressive Driving

LEARNING OBJECTIVES

In this chapter we examine assaults and related crimes against the person. The following are the learning objectives for Chapter 11:

- Identify the different elements that must be proved for conviction of an assault or a battery.

- Know what kind of nonconsensual touching constitutes an assault or a battery.

- Describe circumstances that warrant a charge of aggravated assault or battery.

- List the various laws designed to protect children from assaults and other similar crimes.

- List some of the defenses available to a charge of assault or battery.

- Identify the "movement" requirement for a kidnapping conviction

- State how the crime of hostage taking differs from kidnapping.

I n May 2009 Elner Ferguson, an African-American woman, and her one-year-old grandson moved into a house in Wilmington, California. Two rival criminal street gangs, the "East Side Wilmas," a Hispanic street gang, and the "Ghost Town Bloods," an African-American gang, claimed "territory" in Wilmington, with the Pacific Coast Highway (PCH) as the dividing line between the claimed territories.

In late May Jose Mario Chavez, a member of the East Side Wilmas, confronted Ms. Ferguson and her grandson on the porch of their home. Pointing a cocked pistol at Ms. Ferguson, Chavez said, "Ain't no N------ allowed to live over here. The N------ live on the other side of PCH." He then said, "You have two days to be gone and out of here. If you call the cops, I'm going to burn down your house." Terrified, Ms. Ferguson and her grandson went into their house and called the police. That night, she packed up and moved to another city.

Police arrested Chavez, and prosecutors charged him with two counts of aggravated assault, and one count of dissuading a witness from reporting a crime, all with hate crime and criminal street crime enhancements. Chavez was convicted and sentenced to 47 years to life. In 2011 the California Court of Appeals affirmed his conviction, though it modified his sentence to 41 years to life.

In this chapter we will study the rules governing assault, as well as other crimes against the person such as kidnapping and domestic violence.

The Crime of Assault

assault In many instances, an assault is an attempt to commit a battery, but many states also make other conduct an assault. It could be combined with a charge of battery to constitute the crimes of "assault and battery."

battery A successful assault, in which the victim is actually and intentionally (or knowingly) struck by the defendant.

Under common law, **assault** and **battery** were two separate crimes. Today, however, the phrase *assault and battery* is sometimes used to indicate one offense. Because an assault is often an attempt to commit a battery, the California courts point out that an assault is an attempt to strike, whereas a battery is the successful attempt. A battery cannot be committed without assaulting a victim, but an assault can occur without a battery.

States have codified the common-law crime of assault. Included in the crime of assault today are (1) an attempt to commit a battery in which no actual battery or physical injury resulted, and/or (2) an intentional frightening (such as pointing a loaded gun at a person or menacing with a fist or knife). Generally, in an assault, the state must show apprehension or fear on the part of the victim if no blow, touching, or injury occurred.

In many states, the crime of assault also includes battery. For example, the state of New York does not have a crime of battery.[1] Therefore, in New York, a person who swings a knife at another with intent to cause serious physical injury is guilty of first-degree assault if successful but is guilty only of attempted assault if no injury occurs. (See New York *Commentaries,* Art. 120, p. 331.)

Section 240 of the California Penal Code (enacted in 1872) defines *assault* as "an unlawful attempt, coupled with a present ability, to commit a violent injury on the person of another." Chapter 38, Section 12-1, of the Illinois Statutes provides that "a person commits an assault when, without lawful authority, he engages in conduct which places another in reasonable apprehension of receiving a battery."

In some states (including California), the lack of "present ability" to commit the injury or battery is a defense to an assault charge.[2] The defendant in the case of *People v. Miceli* attempted to use this defense.[3] He used a semi-automatic rifle to club a victim. When charged with "assault with a firearm," the defendant contended he could not be guilty of an assault, because the firearm was not loaded, and as a result he lacked the "present ability" to injure that victim. The court disagreed, both because evidence existed that the firearm might have been loaded, and because the firearm was used as a club, which satisfied the "present ability" requirement.

Other, perhaps most, states, and the Model Penal Code § 211.1, have adopted the common-law definition of assault. Under that definition, an assault occurs *either* when one does an overt act that is intended to inflict bodily harm (the "attempted battery" assault), *or* when the overt act is intended to put another person in fear of bodily harm (the "reasonable apprehension of fear" assault).

The 2012 case of *United States v. Acosta-Sierra*[4] illustrates both these aspects of the common-law meaning of assault. The defendant was walking across the border from Mexico to the United States. A U.S. Customs officer passed the defendant as he walked on the other side of the walkway. The defendant picked up a baseball-sized rock and threw it at the officer, missing him by two feet. The officer did not see the defendant throw the rock, but heard it land behind him. The defendant was charged with assault against a federal officer. Based on the judge's understanding of assault requirements, the defendant was convicted of "reasonable apprehension of fear" assault.

On appeal, the court held the government had failed to prove the customs officer had a reasonable fear of injury, since the officer did not actually see the defendant throw the rock. It therefore reversed the trial judge's verdict of guilty on the assault charge. However, the court held that sufficient evidence existed to convict the defendant under the "attempted battery" prong of assault, and remanded the case for a new trial.

Under the present Federal Criminal Code, the crime of assault is directed toward certain situations over which the federal government has jurisdiction, such as assaults on a federal officer or assaults on a federal reservation. In the most general assault statute, assault within the territorial jurisdiction of the United States, assault also includes an actual battery; 18 U.S.C.A. § 113(a)(4) forbids "assault by striking, beating, or wounding." Thus, in addition to the two common-law aspects of assault discussed above (present ability or fear of infliction), the statute includes a third aspect, in which the crime of assault is committed by actually inflicting injury on another person.

The following two cases illustrate application of the assault against a federal officer statute and the general federal assault statute:

United States v. Drapeau

U.S. Court of Appeals, 644 F.3d 646 (8th Cir. 2011)

A Bureau of Indian Affairs officer followed defendant to his house, based on a complaint the defendant was disturbing the peace. The defendant refused to allow the officer to enter, and the officer heard a child crying in the house. The officer put his arm through an open window to obtain entry, but the defendant slammed the window down on the officer's arm. The court affirmed a conviction for assault under the federal assault statute, 18 U.S.C. § 111.

United States v. Lewellyn

U.S. Court of Appeals, 481 F.3d 695 (9th Cir. 2007), *cert. denied*, 128 S. Ct. 154 (2007).

Defendant spit in the face of a patient at a Veterans Administration Hospital, a "federal reservation" and thus governed by federal law. The court affirmed the defendant's conviction for "simple assault" under 18 U.S.C. § 113, holding that spitting on another person constituted "offensive touching" under the common law, and thus violates the statute. The court noted that because section 113 does not define "assault," the common-law meaning of the term is followed in federal courts, and includes "offensive touching."

Assault with a Deadly or Dangerous Weapon

A simple assault is a misdemeanor or ordinance charge. The criminal charge of assault with a deadly or dangerous weapon is a felony charge. A gun or a dangerous knife is certainly a deadly weapon if it is used to threaten or harm.

As pointed out in Chapter 10, the issue of what is a dangerous or deadly weapon is a question of fact for the fact finder (jury or judge). New York courts have held that something as common as a handkerchief can, under certain circumstances, be a deadly weapon, and many courts have also held that hands can be dangerous or deadly weapons, even if the assailant has no training in martial arts or boxing.

The relative size and strength of the assailant as compared with the victim, the manner and duration of the assault, and the severity of the injuries are all facts that must be taken into consideration in determining whether hands are dangerous or deadly weapons. Fact finders would surely find the hands of an adult man who punched a baby to be dangerous or deadly weapons under the circumstances.[5]

The defendant in *State v. Zangrilli* broke his ex-wife's jaw in two places, grabbed her by the throat and strangled her until she could feel her "eyes bulge," dragged her through several rooms in her house, punched her several times in the face and neck, and shoved her into a bathtub.[6] The Rhode Island Supreme Court affirmed his conviction of assault with a dangerous weapon, quoting the trial judge's holdings:

> The manner in which he used his hands on her throat constituted use of his hands in such a way that it could easily have led to her death.
>
> For that reason, I have concluded that his assault upon her was done with a dangerous weapon. As I say, hands are not *per se* dangerous weapons, but they are a means to produce death. And they were used, even though briefly, in a manner and in such circumstances as could be reasonably calculated to produce death.

Some things, such as guns or large knives, are treated as "inherently" deadly weapons. The "dangerousness" of other things depends on their use. For example, while a rock is not inherently a deadly weapon, it can become one. In the 2011 case of *State v. Baranovich*[7] the defendant and her 13-year-old brother attacked a former roommate of the defendant. The brother hit the female victim on the head with a rock, causing the victim to fall to the ground. The court affirmed the defendant's conviction for assault with a dangerous weapon.

Some states have created a separate crime of committing a felony while armed with a dangerous weapon, whereas other states enhance (increase) penalties of people who commit a felony while armed. What constitutes "armed" is most often a question of law.

A person who actually carries a pistol on his or her person is armed. However, it is less clear if one who commits a felony with a pistol in his or her *vicinity* is armed. The following two Illinois cases illustrate this problem.

In *People v. Board*[8] an appeals court upheld a conviction for armed violence in which the defendant was sitting on a sofa that had a gun under one of the cushions. Although the defendant made no attempt to get the gun, the court held that its accessibility sufficed to support the armed violence conviction. Conversely, in *People v. Shelato*,[9] the court reversed a conviction for armed violence when the defendant's gun was in the same room with the defendant but hidden in a zippered bag underneath sixty bags of marijuana. The court stated that it "defied common sense" to believe the defendant could have gotten this gun under the "watchful eyes of several police officers," and vacated the conviction.

Battery

For an offense to constitute assault, the victim must ordinarily be apprehensive of the impending harm or danger. This is not necessary in a battery. A blow from behind is a battery whether or not the victim is aware that it is coming. Battery is a crime that, like murder and manslaughter, is defined in terms of the conduct of the offender and also in terms of the harm done.

Most state battery statutes define battery to include either physical conduct or actual bodily injury. For example, Florida's battery statute, F.S.A. § 784.03, states a person commits battery if he either (1) "actually and intentionally touches or strikes another person against the will of the other" or (2) "intentionally causes bodily harm." Many other states have a statute similar to the Kansas battery law, K.S.A. § 21-3412. It includes as a battery "intentionally or recklessly" causing bodily injury. However, the "physical contact" form of battery must be done in "a rude, insulting or angry manner." Thus, if one intentionally causes another bodily harm, whether by directly striking the person, or indirectly doing so by acts like throwing an object at the person, the crime of battery has been committed. Batteries can be committed with fists, feet, sticks, stones, or other objects used to inflict injury. Under some circumstances, dogs or other animals can be used to commit a battery if they are used to injure another person illegally.[1] If there is physical contact without bodily injury, the contact must be offensive or unwanted.

Section 211 of the Model Penal Code combines the common-law crimes of assault and battery under the crime of assault. That section does not include "offensive touching" without bodily injury. The MPC limits simple "physical contact" to sexual offenses, as discussed below.

All states that make battery a crime require that the act to commit a battery must be intentional (or must be done knowingly), because an accidental physical contact or injury is not a battery. However, most states, as in the Kansas statute quoted above, include recklessly causing bodily injury in the definition of battery.

Offensive Touching Under Sexual Assault and Sexual Battery Statutes

Many states have enacted sexual assault statutes to replace or add to their old rape statutes. These statutes generally provide three or four degrees of sexual assault. In addition to defining sexual intercourse broadly, these statutes also forbid and punish **offensive touching**.

Before the enactment of the sexual assault statutes, offensive touching was ordinarily charged under the general assault statute or as a battery or disorderly conduct. Although offensive touching may continue to be charged under the old statutes, the sexual assault statute is now available. However, under the sexual assault statutes, the offensive touching generally must be of an "intimate part" or

offensive touching
Unpermitted physical contact with another person, usually limited to "private" or genital parts.

"private part" of the body and for the purpose "of arousing or gratifying sexual desire of either party" (§ 213.4 Model Penal Code).

The rape charge in the case of *People v. Margiolas* was dropped because of lack of evidence of resistance. However, the defendant admitted that he unbuttoned the victim's blouse, despite her verbal as well as physical objections. The defendant was convicted of sexual battery in forcibly unbuttoning the blouse.[11] Under such a statute, a prosecutor with a weak case might also issue a sexual battery charge when it is apparent that the rape charge has defects that might be insurmountable. (See Chapter 12 for more material on sexual assault and sexual battery statutes.)

Sports Injuries When Force Exceeds the Rules of the Game

A hard tackle in football or a blow to the jaw in boxing would be within the rules of the sport being played. Players in body contact sports consent to such conduct as part of the game. This is commonly referred to as the "voluntary participant" rule.

But if the conduct is beyond the rules of the game—such as a deliberate elbow to the face or a knee to the groin in basketball, the deliberate use of spikes by a runner in baseball, eye gouging in football, or other violence that causes unnecessary injuries—is it a battery or an assault? In one recent case, the Washington Court of Appeals held that an assault was committed when, during a game, one basketball player intentionally punched another player.[12] In the 2004 case of *State v. Guidugli*[13] the court upheld the conviction for assault where the defendant, the starting quarterback for the University of Cincinnati football team, hit an opposing player in the head with a fist during an intramural basketball game. The court noted that the defendant "wound up" before delivering the punch, which caused some harm to the other player's face. That was enough, the court said, to support the conviction.

Spectator violence and parental rage are occasionally a problem at sporting events. During a July 6, 2012, Little League game in Georgia that became well known on YouTube, two dads got into a fight during the game, and both were charged with disorderly conduct.

Other Physical Contact Without Consent

Pushing, pinching, biting, scratching, touching, kissing, punching, spitting, and tackling are all forms of physical contact in which the person initiating the contact could be acting in a friendly, joking, or loving manner. Alternatively, the contact could be hostile, angry, or belligerent.[14]

If such contact were intentional (not accidental) and done without any legal justification, it could cause a great amount of anger or concern in the person not consenting to such physical contact. If the physical contact were made in an obviously hostile or belligerent manner, the physical contact could also provoke a verbal or physical reaction.

If it is shown that the conduct provoked or tended to provoke a disturbance or a disorder, the offender could be charged with disorderly conduct.

EXAMPLE

A strange man roughly grabs a woman or a girl in a public place and kisses or touches her in the presence of her husband, boyfriend, other member of her family, or friends. Because such conduct is highly likely to cause a public disturbance or disorder, it can be charged as disorderly conduct (or disorderly person).

One defense to a charge of touching or physical contact could be that the touching was accidental. Implied consent could also easily be inferred if the touching was done to pull a victim away from danger or if mouth-to-mouth resuscitation was necessary to restore breathing to a victim of an accident. The defense of necessity could also be used if the physical contact was necessary to prevent and avoid a greater harm.

menacing Intentionally placing or attempting to place another in fear of immediate serious physical injury.

Some states have enacted the crime of **menacing**, which is defined as follows in Public Law 120.15 of New York:

[P]hysically menacing, intentionally placing or attempting to place another person in fear of imminent serious physical injury. (New York class B misdemeanor)

Other states have extended the scope of the crime of assault to include intentional scaring or menacing if a victim is apprehensive of immediate bodily harm.

A fierce look with intent to frighten would not amount to menacing or intentional scaring. Section 211.1 of the Model Penal Code provides,

(1) Simple Assault … (c) attempts by physical menace to put another in fear of imminent serious bodily injury.

New York City has passed a "jostling" law in response to the pickpocketing problem that exists in crowded public places such as subways. The procedure used by most pickpockets is to bump or shove the victim (or have a partner distract the victim by bumping and shoving) to permit entry into a pocket or purse for the theft. Jostling is defined by New York Public Law 165.25 as follows:

In a public place, intentionally and unnecessarily:

1. Placing one's hand in the proximity of a person's pocket or handbag, OR
2. Jostling or crowding another person at a time when a third person's hand is in the proximity of such person's pocket or handbag.

Felonious and Aggravated Assaults and Batteries

aggravated assault Assault made more serious by presence of a firearm or as part of intent to commit a felony.

Misdemeanor assault and misdemeanor battery are classified as class A or B misdemeanors in most states. The degree of these crimes and the penalties are increased by aggravating factors used by state legislatures. All states have enacted **"aggravated assault"** or **"aggravated battery"** statutes, which increase an assault or battery from a misdemeanor to a felony. In the case of assaults, the aggravating factors usually are (1) use of a firearm or (2) intent to commit a felony. *See* F.S.A. § 784.021.

aggravated battery Battery that causes serious bodily injury or is committed with a deadly weapon.

The most common aggravating factors for battery charges are (1) causing serious bodily injury or (2) using a deadly weapon in the battery. Vernon's Texas Penal Code § 22.02 is an example of such a statute. In some states circumstances in addition

DEFENSES TO AN ASSAULT OR BATTERY CHARGE

The Aggressor Defense

The defendant may assert that the other party was the aggressor, and the defendant acted in self-defense. Perfect or imperfect self-defense can then be argued by attempting to show that force was necessary and the amount of force used was reasonable.

Lack of Specific Intent

Although assault is usually regarded as a general intent crime, in some states the "intent to cause fear" form of assault requires the specific intent to cause the result, that is, fear or apprehension in the victim. In such prosecutions, it would be a defense that a defendant did not intend his acts to cause fear or apprehension. In the 2012 case of *State v. Fleck*[15] the Minnesota Supreme Court held that the "assault-fear" form of assault was a specific intent crime, and intoxication could be used to prove lack of specific intent. "Assault-harm" was a general intent crime, and required only a showing the defendant intended to do the act constituting the assault, the court held. Thus, intoxication was not relevant to a conviction.

Other Defenses

- That the other party consented within the rules of the sport being played.
- That it was reasonable discipline of a child by a parent, guardian, or a person acting in place of the parent.
- That in an "offensive touching" battery, the touching was accidental, or consented to, or necessary under the circumstances.
- That the conduct was necessary and lawful:
  - in the accomplishment of a lawful arrest
  - when necessary to lawfully detain or hold a person in custody
  - when necessary to prevent an escape of a person lawfully in custody
  - when necessary to prevent a suicide
  - for any other reason when the conduct is privileged by the statutory or common law of that state

to the two just stated constitute aggravated battery. For example, in Florida, F.S.A. § 784.045 makes it aggravated battery if the victim of a battery is pregnant and the defendant knew of should have known that fact. In Kansas, K.S.A. § 21-3414 makes it aggravated battery to cause physical contact in a rude or insulting manner with a deadly weapon. Oregon's statute, O.R.S. § 163.175, adds as an aggravating circumstance "recklessly" causing serious physical injury under circumstances that demonstrate "extreme indifference to human life."[16] In applying that statute to injuries arising out of an automobile accident, the Oregon Supreme Court stated:

> Witnesses testified that prior to the accident defendant was swerving across the road, tailgating so closely he almost hit the car in front of him and passing on a curve. The overwhelming weight of the evidence indicated that the accident occurred because defendant was across the center line in the oncoming lane of traffic. He sideswiped

CHAPTER 11: Assault, Battery, and Other Crimes Against the Person   **299**

the first oncoming vehicle, bounced or swerved into his own lane and then swerved back across the center line into the second oncoming vehicle, causing serious injury to the passenger. Defendant had a blood alcohol content of .24 percent two hours after the accident. He was belligerent at the scene of the accident, threatening to hit the passenger of the first car he sideswiped. Because of his intoxication he was not only unable to assist the victim, but at one point interfered with the assistance. The degree of intoxication, defendant's erratic driving and his conduct at the scene of the accident are circumstances the jury could properly consider in determining whether defendant was extremely indifferent to the value of human life.

We hold that the circumstances which exist in this case suffice to establish defendant's extreme indifference to the value of human life.[17]

Aggravated assault/battery cases often are complicated by an assertion of self-defense. Using force is justified for self-defense purposes, but only under certain circumstances. A person is not entitled to use force for self-defense if he is engaged in a crime when confronted by force. This has sometimes led to confusion in aggravated assault cases. For example, in the 2005 Florida case of *Williams v. State*,[18] a defendant charged with aggravated battery under the Florida statute cited above contended he struck the victim in self-defense. The trial court instructed the jury that self-defense was not available if the defendant used force while committing an aggravated battery. The Florida appeals court reversed the conviction, stating that the instruction negated the self-defense claim, because if self-defense was proper, the defendant was not guilty of aggravated battery.

Mayhem and Malicious Disfigurement

mayhem and malicious disfigurement Willfully inflicting an injury on another so as to cripple or mutilate the person.

Mayhem and malicious disfigurement (or malicious wounding) have been distinguished by federal courts as follows. "[M]ayhem involves disablement of normal functioning of a human body, by contrast with malicious disfigurement which focuses on willful permanent disfigurement."[19]

Lorena Bobbitt was convicted of malicious wounding in Virginia when, in a rage, she cut off her husband's penis and threw it in a field. Believing Mrs. Bobbitt to be a battered woman, a Virginia jury found her not guilty under Virginia's insanity test. She spent four weeks in a Virginia mental hospital and was released on the condition that she receive therapy.

States also follow the common-law definition of mayhem, which is the unlawful and violent depriving of the victim of full use of any functional member of the body (hand, arms, feet, eyes, legs, and so on) that would make the victim less able to defend himself or herself.

Article 1166 of the Texas Penal Code provides that "whoever shall willfully and maliciously cut off or otherwise deprive a person of the hand, arm, finger, toe, foot, leg, nose, or ear, or put out an eye or in any way deprive a person of any other member of his body shall be confined in the penitentiary not less than two nor more than ten years."[20]

Hate Crime Laws

The U.S. Supreme Court has repeatedly held that states may not silence "speech on the basis of its content,"[21] as was done in the flag-burning and cross-burning U.S. Supreme Court cases (see Chapter 9). But states may enact hate crime laws that enhance and increase penalties for crimes if it is proved that the defendant intentionally selected the victim because of the victim's race, religion, color, disability, sexual orientation, national origin, or ancestry.

An example of a hate crime law is the New York Hate Crime Act of 2000, N.Y. Penal Law § 485.05. That act makes it an enhanced crime with added penalties to commit any of several specified crimes if the defendant "intentionally selects" the victim "in whole or in substantial part" because of the defendant's "belief or perception" of the victim's race, religion, gender, age, national origin, sexual orientation, or disability. The specified crimes include virtually all the crimes against the person, as well as many crimes against property.

Proving that the defendant actually "hated" the victim is not generally an element of a hate crime offense. Under the New York law cited above, the prosecution must only prove that the race, religion, or one of the other listed characteristics, was a "substantial" factor in the decision to commit the crime. In this sense, the New York statute is drafted to make the "hate" feature part of the elements of the crime, which under the *Apprendi* decisions discussed in Chapter 8 means the prosecution must prove the "hate" element beyond a reasonable doubt.

Section 485.05(2) states that proof that the victim possessed one of the listed characteristics does not by itself satisfy the "people's burden" to prove the elements of a hate crime. Some other corroborating evidence is thus required. In *People v. Fox,*[22] the court found the required corroborating evidence in the fact the defendants used Internet chat rooms used by gay men to lure a victim to the robbery location.

Many other states have similar hate crime laws. In the 2010 case of *State v. Hennings*[23] the Iowa Supreme Court upheld a defendant's conviction for assault intended as a hate crime. The Iowa hate crime statute requires that the prosecution prove that the crime, here assault, was committed "because of the race" (or other listed factors, such as religion, gender, or sexual orientation) of the victim. The defendant, after an expletive-filled exchange with five African-American boys walking on a street, drove his vehicle at the boys, severely injuring one of them. The defendant, a member of a family well known in the community for its racist views, contended the mere fact that he held those views did not satisfy the hate crime requirements. The Iowa Supreme Court agreed, but held there was ample evidence to support his conviction of the hate crime. The court noted that in his statements to police, the defendant said, "What . . . f------ N------ don't have enough sense to stay out of the f----- road…they deserve to get hit." These comments showed the defendant targeted the boys because of their race, the court held.

Hate crime laws can be useful tools for prosecutors. For example, the district attorney for Queens, New York uses the hate crime law in prosecutions against criminals who single out old people, become their "friend," and then steal their life savings. Prosecutors have found that using the enhanced penalties in the hate crime law gives them extra leverage in plea bargaining, and makes sure the criminals get stiffer jail sentences. See *New York Times,* June 23, 2010, "A Novel Twist for Prosecution of Hate Crimes."

The Wisconsin hate crime statute was challenged on constitutional grounds in 1993. The U.S. Supreme Court upheld the constitutionality of the statute in the following case.

If a defendant selects a victim based on a prejudice against the perceived race of the victim, it is not necessary that the victim in fact be a member of that race.

Mike Stewart/Sygma/Corbis

On October 28, 2009, President Obama signed the Matthew Shepard and James Byrd, Jr. Hate Crimes Prevention Act. This Act was named in honor of Matthew Shepard, pictured above, a gay man, and James Byrd, Jr., a Black man, who were killed in separate hate crimes in 1998 that received national attention. The act makes it possible for federal prosecutors to expand the use of existing hate crime laws. The HCPA makes several additions to the federal hate crime laws, among them removing the previous requirement that the victim be engaged in some federally protected activity, like voting or attending school. It also gives federal prosecutors the ability to investigate suspected hate crimes that local authorities may not want to pursue. Finally, it requires the FBI to maintain statistics on hate crimes involving transgender victims.

In *Martinez v. Texas*,[24] the court affirmed a hate crime sentence enhancement of a defendant who killed a child, believing the child to be part African American. The court said if prejudice against a particular race of people caused the defendant to select the child as a victim, it did not matter that the child was in fact not a member of that race.

Child Abuse and Neglect

Child abuse, child neglect, and sexual abuse are serious problems throughout the United States. Based on statistics compiled by the U.S. Department of Health and Human Services, the national ChildHelp Foundation reported in 2011 that 3.3 million child abuse cases are reported each year, involving over 6 million children;

HATE CRIMES 2011

In the December 2012 Justice Department Report by the Federal Bureau of Investigation's Uniform Crime Reporting Program, the FBI provided the following hate crime statistics for 2011, the most recent year for which statistics are available: Law enforcement agencies reported 6,222 single-bias incidents, involving 7,254 criminal offenses, in 2011. 4,623 of these offenses were crimes against a person, and 2,611 were crimes against property, such as destruction or defacement. The statistics showed the following:

Why? (motivation)	Where? (place of crime)	Type of Crime Committed	Victims' Characteristics
Race 46.9%	Residence 32%	Intimidation 45.6%	Black 71.9%
Religion 19.8%	Highway/street 18.1%	Simple assault 34.5%	White 16.3%
Sexual orientation 20.8%	School/college 9.3%	Aggravated assault 19.4%	Asian 4.8%
Ethnicity 11.6%	Parking lot 5.9%	Murder, rape 0.2%	Multiple race 5.2%
Victim disability 0.9%	Church/synagogue 4.4%	(4 murders, 7 rapes)	Native American 1.9%

Sexual Orientation Crimes (1,572 victims)

Anti-male homosexual 56.7%
Anti-homosexual 29.6%
Anti-female homosexual 11.1%
Anti-bisexual 1.5%
Anti-heterosexual 1.2%

Religious Bias Crimes (1,318 victims)

Anti-Jewish 63.2%
Anti-Islam 12.5%
Anti-Catholic 5.7%
Anti-Protestant 3.4%
Multiple religions 4.4%
Anti-atheists 0.3%

Source: U.S. Department of Justice, 2012.

Wisconsin v. Mitchell

Supreme Court of the United States, 508 U.S. 476, 124 L. Ed. 2d 436 (1993)

A group of black youths including Mitchell viewed a scene from the motion picture *Mississippi Burning*, in which a white man beat a young black boy who was praying. The group then moved outside and Mitchell asked if they were "hyped up to move on some white people." When a white boy was seen, Mitchell said, "There goes a white boy; go get him." The group ran after the boy, beat him severely, and stole his tennis shoes. The victim was in a coma for four days.

Mitchell was convicted of aggravated battery in a trial before a jury. The maximum penalty for the crime of aggravated battery was two years. But because the jury found that the defendant had intentionally selected his victim because of the victim's race, the trial judge imposed a sentence of four years of imprisonment under the Wisconsin penalty-enhancement statute, known as the hate crime statute.

The U.S. Supreme Court affirmed the conviction and defendant's sentence, upholding the Wisconsin hate crime statute. The Court pointed out that the ordinance struck down in the hate crime case of *R.A.V. v. St. Paul* (112 S. Ct. 2538) was "explicitly directed at expression (i.e., speech or message) . . . where the statute in this case is aimed at conduct unprotected by the First Amendment." Finally, the Supreme Court held that in the *Mitchell* case, there was no First Amendment violation on the basis of a "chilling effect" on protected speech (overbreadth).

78.3 percent were neglect cases; and 80 percent involved children under the age of four. The report noted the dramatic increase in child abuse or neglect deaths. In 1998, 3.13 child abuse deaths occurred each day. In 2012, more than five such deaths occurred each day. According to the report, the United States has the worst child abuse/neglect record of any industrialized nation. Moreover, estimates of child deaths were probably low, because many child deaths are not reported as resulting from abuse or neglect.

Thousands of children in the United States suffer head injuries; broken bones from beatings, burns from cigarettes, stoves, and hot liquids; ruptured internal organs (such as liver, spleen, kidneys, and bowels) from blows to the abdomen; missing teeth; multiple scars; knife and gunshot wounds; and bruises and lacerations.

People who inflict such injuries on children may be charged with assault, battery, assault with a dangerous weapon, aggravated battery, and other offenses under the criminal code of the state in which the offense occurred. Criminal codes also have child abuse statutes and statutes forbidding the neglect of children. These statutes seek to protect children from injury and trauma inflicted on them by parents, stepparents, paramours, relatives, babysitters, and other adults.

Parents and others responsible for children have a duty to protect children and provide food, clothing, shelter, medical care, education, and a reasonable physical and moral environment for them. Child neglect is the failure to provide adequate food, clothing, shelter, sanitation, medical care, and supervision for a child. In extreme cases of child neglect, criminal laws are violated.

Religious beliefs that cause parents to refuse to obtain medical treatment for a child are controversial. In some states, parents can be charged under criminal homicide laws. For example, in 2009 a Wisconsin couple was convicted of reckless homicide in the death of their 11-year-old daughter. The child was suffering from diabetes, but rather than obtain medical treatment the parents relied on "faith healing." The parents appealed their convictions, relying on Wisconsin Statute 948.03(6), which they contended made them immune from prosecution.

The Wisconsin statute, like similar statutes in some other states, carves out an exception to prosecutions for neglect of a child for circumstances where the parents had a good-faith belief in healing by spiritual means or prayer. See, e.g., Minn. Stat. Ann. § 609.378, but even in those states the exception does not apply if the child dies. See Oregon R. Stat. § 163.206.

CRIMINAL AND CIVIL LAWS THAT SEEK TO PROTECT CHILDREN

Under early Roman law, children were considered to be the property of their father, who could discipline them as he saw fit: he could sell them or even condemn them to death.

This law changed slowly over the years, and by the early 1800s, mothers were the primary custodians of their children when a divorce occurred. The *tender years presumption* held that only a mother has the nurturing qualities needed to love and care for a child through the early part of the child's life, or the tender years.

The tender years presumption also changed, and today more than thirty states offer joint custody and shared parenting arrangements to parents who are divorcing or have never married. Most criminal laws seek to protect all parties (children and adults alike). States have sought to provide additional protection to children by the enactment of most (if not all) of the following statutes: (Students should complete blanks)

Laws Forbidding	Statute # in Your State
■ child abuse	_____
■ child neglect	_____
■ abandonment of a child	_____
■ contributing to the delinquency of a child	_____
■ child snatching from the lawful custody of a guardian of the child	_____
■ child endangerment	_____
■ child enticement	_____
■ exposing children to sexually harmful material	_____
■ sexual exploitation of a child	_____
■ statutory rape (children cannot consent to sexual intercourse or sexual contact) under age _____ is (*crime*) _____	_____
■ other	_____

Compulsory School Attendance Laws | _____ |
■ imposing duty on parents until age _____	_____
■ making student offense of skipping school truancy	_____
■ authorizing police to take truant into custody	_____

The parents convicted of reckless homicide of their 11-year-old daughter in the case discussed above initially appealed their convictions to the Wisconsin Court of Appeals. In 2012 the Wisconsin Court of Appeals certified the question of the application of the "faith-healing" exception to cases of death of a child to the Wisconsin Supreme Court. In a July 2013 decision, the Wisconsin Supreme Court affirmed the reckless homicide convictions of the parents of the 11-year-old girl. *State v. Neumann*, 832 N.W.2d 560 (Wisc. 2013).

The child abuse that often appears in courts is physical abuse, such as deliberate injuries inflicted on children. Such injuries may result from excessive and unreasonable force used in disciplining children. The U.S. Supreme Court pointed out in *Ingraham v. Wright* that parents and people taking the place of parents may use force "reasonably believed to be necessary for [the child's] proper control, training, or education."[25] What is "reasonable" is determined in view of the child's age and sex; the physical, emotional, and mental health of the child; and the conduct that prompted the punishment.

Unfortunately, most children who are victims of abuse are under age 5 and are helpless to protect themselves.

Child abuse as a crime has both an active and a passive element. Physical abuse—hitting, burning, cutting, kicking—of children is obviously the active part of child abuse crimes. But action is not always required for child abuse convictions. Most states have statutes making it a crime for one responsible for a child's welfare to endanger the life of the child. This can be done by failing to adequately feed or clothe a child, by leaving a child unattended at home, by leaving a child in an automobile on a hot day, or by failing to intervene when the child is being sexually molested.[26]

In response to the national problem of child abuse, the following have occurred:

- *Mandatory reporting laws* have been enacted by all states to require doctors, nurses, teachers, day-care workers, and other people coming in contact with children to report suspected child abuse. It is likely there is still tremendous underreporting of abuse.
- *Increased authority has been given to social workers* by some states to permit them to interview children without notifying their parents. Increased numbers of trained social workers are needed to handle growing caseloads.
- *New criminal laws* have been enacted, such as Washington's homicide by abuse statute, which makes child abuse resulting in death the equivalent of first-degree murder. Under this statute, prosecutors no longer have to prove premeditation or intent to kill for a conviction. Instead, the state must show that the defendant displayed "extreme indifference to human life." The writer of the bill stated, "Premeditation in child abuse cases is almost impossible to prove. This [law] gets around that oft-heard defense—I didn't mean to kill the boy; I just wanted to discipline him."

Sexual abuse and sexual exploitation of children are discussed in Chapter 12. Sexual abuse may be combined with physical abuse or child neglect. Abuse or neglect in any form may have a severe emotional and psychological effect on a child, causing behavioral problems that could have great impact on the child's life.

Offenses Against the Liberty of a Person: Kidnapping

Kidnapping and Hostage Taking

kidnapping False imprisonment coupled with movement of the victim.

Kidnapping was a crime at common law, punishable by life imprisonment. All states and the federal government, with some variations, have enacted statutes making kidnapping a crime. Section 212.1 of the Model Penal Code defines **kidnapping** in part as follows:

> A person is guilty of kidnapping if he unlawfully removes another from his place of residence or business, or a substantial distance from the vicinity where he is found.

One common motive for kidnapping is to obtain monetary ransom, as occurred in 2010 when two defendants confined a family of illegal aliens the defendants were smuggling into the United States, and demanded a ransom to release them. In *People v. Eid*[27] the court held that the California kidnapping for ransom statute does not require movement of the victim, though other types of kidnapping do require such movement. The court also held that the crime of kidnapping for ransom requires proof that the victim did not consent to the confinement. It reversed the convictions for a new trial on that issue.

Other kidnappings occur as part of crimes of rape, robbery, murder, and other felonies. Kidnappings have also taken place to terrorize, blackmail, or obtain a hostage for escape.

As the M.P.C. section quoted above states, in most states kidnapping requires that the victim unlawfully be "removed" from his residence or place of business, or a "substantial distance" from where he was found. This "moving" aspect of the kidnapping crime has frequently been an issue in kidnapping prosecutions, as the cases discussed here illustrate.

Two recent decisions involved one aspect of the "movement requirement" in kidnapping statutes, that is, what it means to "move" a victim. In a 2010 decision, *State v. Mejia*,[28] the Oregon Supreme Court affirmed the kidnapping conviction of a defendant who entered his former girlfriend's apartment and held her there for 90 minutes. The defendant contended he did not "move" the victim and thus could not be convicted of kidnapping. The Oregon Supreme Court rejected that argument. It held that under the Oregon kidnapping statute, Ore. Rev. Stat. Ann. § 163.225(l)(a), the crime is committed when a person "moves" or "constrains" another person "with the intent to interfere with another person's personal liberty." It is this interference that the statute makes criminal, the court said. The act of moving a person a "substantial distance" against her will is required only when no other evidence exists showing the intent to interfere with another's personal liberty. When, as the court found was the case there, other evidence showing that intent is present, the statute's "act" requirement is satisfied with any movement, including from room to room.

In a 2009 decision, *State v. Latham*,[29] the Arizona Court of Appeals held that the "moving" requirement under the Arizona kidnapping statute, A.R.S. § 13-1304, was satisfied even though the kidnapper did not physically move the victim. The defendant entered a married couple's home and held a gun on the husband until the man's wife returned from work. The defendant then said he would shoot the husband if the wife did not go to the bank and cash a check for $10,000. The wife

OFFENSES AGAINST THE LIBERTY OF A PERSON

Offense	Usual Definition	Usual Motivation and Use of Offense
False imprisonment	False imprisonment is the unlawful restraint of another and is committed when a person is detained unlawfully.	False imprisonment most often occurs when a retail store employee makes an improper detention for shoplifting or a peace officer makes an improper arrest. These incidents are brought in civil courts and often are called "false arrest" lawsuits.
Kidnapping	Kidnapping is a false imprisonment that is aggravated by the movement of the victim to another place.	Motives could be to obtain ransom or as part of rape, robbery, or murder; to terrorize; to blackmail, and so on. Kidnapping is punished severely, as it is one of the most serious crimes against a person.
Hostage taking	Used to gain an advantage and compel others to comply with demands.	"Taking hostage" is often a tactic used as part of an escape attempt. The crime does not require forcible movement of the victim "some distance."
Parental kidnapping or child snatching (includes former live-ins, lovers, and family)	This crime is often a kidnapping by a parent who has lost (or will lose) custody of the kidnapped child.	This serious crime is committed to retaliate, to harass, to use as leverage in determining support payments, or to control and maintain custody of the child. Some children are never seen again by the other parent.
Abduction	The English enacted the first abduction statute in 1488. For many years, the crime forbade taking a female for any sexual purposes.	States using abduction as a crime generally limit it to a natural parent taking a child from a person having lawful custody.
Slavery and involuntary servitude	The Thirteenth Amendment forbids "slavery … [and] involuntary servitude, except as a punishment for crime."	Slavery, serfage, peonage, debt bondage, and exploitation of children still exist in parts of the world. In 2008 a federal court upheld the involuntary servitude convictions of a man who forced mentally retarded "patients" into working on his farm in the nude. *United States v. Kaufman*, 546 F.3d 1242 (10th Cir. 2008), *cert. denied*, 130 S. Ct. 1013 (2009).

did so, and after arrest the kidnapper was charged with several crimes, including kidnapping the wife. The court of appeals affirmed the conviction, noting that no other case had been found with similar facts, but that the concept of "moving" the victim under the kidnapping statute applied when the victim "moved" because of the kidnapper's threat to kill her husband if she did not "move."

Another aspect of the "movement" requirement that has come before many courts is whether movements of short distances incident to the commission of such crimes as rape or robbery constitute kidnapping. According to California Jury Instruction 652,

> To constitute the crime of simple kidnapping, . . . there must be a carrying, or otherwise forceful moving, for some distance of the person who, against his will, is stolen or taken into custody or control of another person, but the law does not require that the one thus stolen or taken be carried or moved a long distance or any particular distance.

In interpreting "some distance," the California courts have held that "movement across a room or from one room to another" is not sufficient movement to justify a kidnapping conviction.[30] The general rule seems to be that movement "merely incident to the commission of the robbery [or rape]" is not kidnapping.[31]

In *People v. Washington,*[32] the court reversed a conviction for kidnapping during a bank robbery. The defendant took the teller and bank manager away from their posts to the bank vault room, distances of 15 and 25 feet, respectively. The manager opened the vault, and the robbers took the money and left the bank. The court said that under the California kidnapping statute, Cal. Penal Code § 209, the movement of a victim in a robbery must be more than incidental to the commission of the robbery, and must increase the risk of harm to the victim. Here, the court said, the only reason the manager and teller were moved to the vault area was to enable them to gain access to the cash in the vault. Moreover, the risks to the victims were not increased by this movement. However, in the 2010 case of *People v. Hernandez,*[33] the court affirmed a conviction of kidnapping during the robbery of a Chevron station. The court found the requirements of § 209 were satisfied by the movement of the store clerk to a back room, because there the robbers assaulted the clerk and robbed him of his personal money. Taking the clerk to the back room, which could not be seen by the public, dramatically increased the risk that harm would come to him, the court said.

In 2006 the California Supreme Court attempted to eliminate some of the uncertainty surrounding the amount or kind of movement necessary to support a kidnapping conviction in other contexts. In *People v. Dominquez,* 47 Cal. Rptr. 3d 575 (2006), a defendant was convicted of rape, kidnapping to commit rape, and felony murder. The defendant took the victim against her will from a street to an orchard located about 25 feet from the street but visible from the street. There the victim was raped by the defendant and killed by either the defendant or by another man present at the scene who had since died. The court of appeals reversed the kidnapping conviction, holding that the movement of the victim to the orchard was incidental to the rape. The Supreme Court disagreed. It held that movement of the victim is sufficient to support a kidnapping charge if the movement is substantial and increases the risk that the underlying crime might occur. Because the orchard provided the defendant with an easier site to commit the rape, even though visible from the street, movement of the victim to that site increased the risk of harm and was enough to support the kidnapping charge.

In the case of *State v. Masino,* the defendant dragged his victim from her car and down an embankment, out of sight from passersby, before sexually assaulting her.[34] The New Jersey Supreme Court affirmed the convictions of sexual assault and kidnapping.

The Florida Supreme Court has stated that there is a "definite trend" toward allowing a kidnapping conviction "where the purpose in confining or moving another person is to use that person as a hostage." In *Mobley v. State,* the defendants were inmates in a jail.[35] They took two guards and an attorney captive in the course of an escape attempt. In affirming the convictions of the defendants for kidnapping and other offenses, the Florida Supreme Court held that the "confinement was not incidental to the attempted escape once [defendants] began using [the victims] as hostages and threatening physical harm."

Because kidnapping usually requires a forcible movement of the victim "some distance" or a "substantial distance," some states have created the crime of **"hostage taking"** to eliminate those requirements. A movement of the victim is not required to prove this offense. In creating this new offense, the state legislature can require all the elements of the serious felony of kidnapping except movement of the victim. They can require the state to prove "intent to use the person as a hostage."[36]

Because hostage taking is a serious and dangerous offense, it is often made a class A or B felony. To encourage offenders to release victims unharmed, some states reduce the offense to a class B or C felony if the hostages are released "before the actor's arrest." In *State v. Warfield,*[37] the Wisconsin Court of Appeals held that a defendant who held four children hostage in an attempt to compel their mother to assist in a robbery of the check-cashing business where she worked was not entitled to the benefit of the "release" provision of the Wisconsin Hostage Statute. It rejected the defendant's arguments that he "released" the boys when he escaped from the house when police arrived. The court said the decision to escape was not the same as releasing the hostages.

False Imprisonment

Under the common law, **false imprisonment**[38] was a crime that, like kidnapping, was punishable by life imprisonment. Many states have enacted statutes making false imprisonment a crime. The usual elements are as follows:

1. The defendant must have confined or restrained the liberty or freedom of movement of another.
2. Such act must have been intentional and without the consent of the victim.
3. The defendant had no lawful authority to confine or restrain the movement of the victim.

False imprisonment differs from kidnapping in that, in kidnapping, the victim must be moved to another place. In false imprisonment, the confinement or restraint may be at the place of the false arrest or unlawful detention of the victim. Under the old common law, it was also required that kidnapping be done secretly; this is not required for false imprisonment. However, the requirement of secrecy for kidnapping has probably been eliminated by most state statutes.

Many false imprisonment actions today are civil actions alleging false arrest or the improper detention of a person. Law enforcement officers and retail store employees should not interfere with the liberty of a person unless authority exists that

hostage taking The use or threat of use of force to restrain or confine a person with the intent to use the person as a hostage to compel another person to perform some act.

false imprisonment Unlawful restraint or detention of a person.

justifies the restraint of a person. Many civil false imprisonment lawsuits concern detention of people believed to be shoplifters. Chapter 13 presents the law governing detentions and arrests in shoplifting cases.

Parental Kidnapping or Child Snatching

Child snatching is the abduction of a child by one parent without the consent of the other parent. It may occur before the parents have commenced a divorce action, while a divorce action is pending, or after a divorce judgment has been granted. Child snatching is also known as parental kidnapping, child abduction, and child stealing.

Thousands of children disappear each year as a result of parental kidnapping. Although the offending parent may state that he or she seeks to protect the child's welfare, other motives for child snatching are

MISSING CHILDREN IN THE UNITED STATES

The FBI maintains a database of annual reports of missing persons. The National Crime Information Center published these missing-person statistics for 2011: 550,424 children (persons under age 21) were reported missing, about an equal number of male and female children. Of those reported missing, 9,611 were missing under circumstances the FBI classifies as "involuntary," meaning the person was either abducted or kidnapped.

Studies show that the missing-children problem is really a set of at least five very different, distinct problems.[a] These problems, which are reported to law enforcement agencies, are identified as follows:

- *Family Abductions:* Those abductions in which a family member took (or failed to return) a child in violation of custody rights or an agreement. More than 150,000 family abductions are reported each year in which a child was absent at least one night. In the group studied, most of the missing children were under age 11. About half the abductions involved an unauthorized taking, whereas half involved a failure to return a child after an authorized visit. Sexual abuse was reported in 1 percent of the cases, whereas neglect or abandonment of the child was of greater concern. The motive for taking the children was generally revenge and retaliation. Family abductors were not limited to parents but also included other family members, lovers, and former live-ins. To deal with this growing problem, Congress passed the Parental Kidnapping Prevention Act in 1980.
- *Runaways:* Runaway age does not commence until 9 or 10. Physical or sexual abuse in the home could cause the runaway. Home conditions could be deplorable, or the child could have become involved in crimes, drugs, sexual relations, or a gang (sometimes all). Most of the reported runaways return home after being missing for one night or more. Runaways from juvenile facilities tend to be more serious than household cases. More than half leave the state, one-third are picked up by the police, and about one-tenth are jailed.
- *Throwaways:* These children are abandoned, deserted, told to leave the home, or not allowed to return to the home, or no effort is made to locate them. These children experience more

- Retaliation against and harassment of the other spouse
- As a means to bargain for reduced child support or reduced division of property in the divorce settlement
- An attempt to bring about a reconciliation of the marriage

Children who are kidnapped by a parent experience changes that may lead to emotional damage. First, the child is often told that the parent who had custody is either dead or no longer loves the child. Second, in most instances, the child begins a lifestyle in which he or she grows up with only one parent. Third, the child is frequently exposed to life on the run, because parental kidnapping is a felony in most states. The pain, fear, guilt, anger, and anxiety from these experiences can cause severe, irreparable psychological harm.

Most states are generally prepared to extradite the offending parent back to the state in which the offense was committed, if he or she can be located. Before the passage of the Uniform Child Custody Jurisdiction Act (UCCJA), a fleeing child

violence within the family and more sexual and physical abuse away from the home. Shelters for runaway and throwaway children report a high rate of exposure to AIDS and other diseases.

- *Lost:* Generally lost children are so young that they cannot identify themselves or give a home address. However, older children could become lost in a rural or wooded area, causing extensive searches. A "lost" child could be a runaway, a throwaway, or the victim of an abduction. Lost children are found and returned home in most cases.
- *Abduction by Strangers or Victims of Other Crimes:* Statistics show that about 100–150 children are kidnapped by strangers in the traditional sense every year in the United States. About fifty of those children are killed by their kidnappers. Strangers who abduct children are broadly categorized by the Behavioral Science Department of the FBI Academy as follows:

a. *The Pedophile:* The pedophile abducts a child primarily for sexual purposes. The Center for Child Advocacy and Protection states that pedophiles are generally young and middle-aged men who seek to control children rather than injure them. They will, however, murder children, and perhaps account for the highest number of abducted-child deaths.

b. *The Serial Killer:* The killings of twenty-nine young persons in Atlanta, Georgia, after their abductions, shocked the nation. Wayne Williams was convicted for the murders of two of the older victims.

c. *The Psychotic:* The psychotic is often a woman who has lost a baby or cannot conceive. To solve her problem, she abducts another family's child.

d. *The Profiteer:* This person seeks to make money by stealing children. The child may be used by a baby adoption ring, pornographers, or, in rare instances, as a kidnapping for ransom.

[a]*See the National Incidence Studies on Missing, Abducted Runaway, and Thrown-away Children in America: The Parental Abduction Prosecutor's Handbook,* available at the National Center for Prosecution of Child Abuse, 1033 N. Fairfax Street, Alexandria, VA 22314.

snatcher could run to another state, establish residence there, and seek a custody order from the courts of the new state. Under UCCJA, the home or resident state would continue to have jurisdiction.

Because the federal kidnapping statute (the Lindbergh Act)[39] specifically excludes parents from its scope, a federal Parental Kidnapping Prevention Act was passed by Congress in 1981. This act facilitates interstate enforcement of custody and visitation determinations. The act also declares that the Fugitive Felon Act applies in state felony parental kidnapping cases, giving the FBI jurisdiction when the child snatcher crosses state lines.[40]

The National Child Search Assistance Act

Because of increasing concern about child kidnapping by strangers, there are voluntary programs to fingerprint children for identification throughout the nation. The parents or legal guardians retain the fingerprint cards for use if the child, at a later date, gets lost or becomes missing.

The National Child Search Assistance Act of 1990[41] requires all federal, state, and local law enforcement offices to maintain reports of missing children, and transmit any information relating to missing children to the National Crime Information Center computer system, so that information can be exchanged with the National Center for Missing and Exploited Children. The act thus gives parents, legal guardians, or next of kin access to the information in the FBI National Crime Information Center's (NCIC) missing persons file.

The parental kidnapping act does not confer on the FBI any new investigative jurisdiction. The FBI can participate in investigation of parental kidnapping cases through the Fugitive Felon Act if the following conditions exist:

1. A state arrest warrant has been issued charging the parent with a felony violation.
2. Law enforcement officers have evidence of interstate flight.
3. A specific request for FBI assistance has been made by state authorities, who agree to extradite and prosecute.
4. A U.S. attorney authorizes issuance of an unlawful flight warrant.

The National Center for Missing and Exploited Children coordinates efforts to recover missing children. A telephone hotline and other facilities are available to aid in these efforts.

Family Violence and Disturbances

A study conducted for the National Institute of Mental Health concluded that "physical violence occurs between family members more often than it occurs between other individuals or in any other setting except wars and riots." The disturbance is often a quarrel between family members. It may start with a few angry words, or it could be a simmering dispute that explodes into violence. Destruction, damage, or taking of property may occur. One or both (or all) the parties may be under the influence of alcohol or drugs. Job stress or unemployment may contribute to the situation.

Hitting, pushing, choking, or wrestling, combined with other abusive behavior, may occur. Insulting and offending language is almost always used. Injuries can range in severity from minor to critical and life threatening.

RESPONSES TO DOMESTIC VIOLENCE

The following are some of the responses available to violent family situations:

1. Arrest of the offending person (or people)
   - If the state or city has a mandatory arrest law
   - Or at the discretion of the officer (or under the policy of the officer's department)
2. Obtaining a protective court order under the statutes of that state
3. Seeking shelter for the victim (spouse, children, parent, or others) under the shelter program available in that community
4. Commencing a divorce action and obtaining temporary or permanent court orders that could protect by
   - Removing offending spouse from premises
   - Forbidding communication or contact by offending spouse
   - Restricting visitation rights with children and enforcing other restrictions
5. Issuance (or threatened issuance) of a civil citation with a substantial money fine
6. Use of the emergency detention section of the state mental health act (if applicable) to place the offending party into custody for observation
7. Revocation of probation or parole if the offender has violated terms of a probation or parole agreement

Both parties could be at fault, or one party could be the agitator and the offender. The offender may have a prior record of violence and may be under a court order (divorce) or restraining order (criminal) forbidding such conduct. Or the offender may be on probation or parole, and his or her domestic conduct may violate the terms of that probation or parole. The offender's presence on the premises may be in violation of a court order or a condition of probation or parole. In addition to these violations, the offender may also be a trespasser.

Family units include not only male–female relationships (married or unmarried) but also homosexual relationships (married or unmarried), and single-parent and multigenerational households. The disturbance or violence could include not only adults but also children within the family unit.

Past experience has demonstrated that family-trouble calls can be dangerous for law enforcement officers. Approximately one-fifth of police deaths and almost one-third of assaults on officers occur when they respond to family quarrels and domestic disputes in which a weapon is used.

In past years, unless serious injury occurred or a clear violation of a court order or probation (or parole) existed, an arrest would ordinarily not be made. Police officers would attempt to mediate the dispute. However, studies by the Police Foundation have shown that police arrests sharply reduce violence in the home. The police commissioner of New York City stated that because of these studies and because of his own experience as a "cop on the street," he concluded that past police efforts to mediate have done little to stop a growing problem.

The commissioner stated that arresting violent members of a household would be more effective than attempts at mediation in protecting other family members and would help to safeguard police officers who are called to intervene in situations where violence could occur.

Some states have responded to domestic violence by passing criminal laws that address domestic violence directly. The terms of these statutes vary, but the following three state laws are representative. Nevada's domestic violence statute, N.R.S. 200.485, makes it a misdemeanor for a person to commit an assault or battery against a spouse, a former spouse, a person living with him or her, or a person in a dating relationship with him or her. The first offense is a misdemeanor with limited penalties; the second offense within 7 years is also a misdemeanor, but penalties are enhanced. The third and subsequent offenses within 7 years are felonies. The statute also provides that if the penalty is greater under the general assault and battery statutes—for example, because of the seriousness of the injury—the defendant can be sentenced under those statutes.

Indiana Code § 35-42-2-1.3 incorporates common-law assault and battery language, and it defines domestic violence to include "touching" in a "rude or insulting manner" that causes bodily injury. Persons covered by the statute include spouses, former spouses, persons who are cohabiting, or a person with whom the person charged has had a child. First-offense domestic violence is a misdemeanor. Subsequent offenses are class D felonies. It is also a class D felony if the domestic violence occurs in the presence of a child under 16 years of age.

Idaho Code § 18-918 defines domestic violence as committing an assault or battery as defined in the general criminal statutes for those crimes against a "household member," which includes a spouse, former spouse, a person living with the person charged, or a person with whom the person charged has a child. Assaults are punished as misdemeanors. If a battery results in a "traumatic injury," it is a felony. If not, it is a misdemeanor. "Traumatic injury" means any wound, or any "external or internal injury," regardless of how serious the injury is, caused by physical force.

In past years, it was not uncommon for police departments to receive calls from women asking for protection from men who had threatened them or from wives who expected to be beaten by their husbands when they came home from a tavern. Threats to injure can be the basis of a criminal charge. If the threat was made over a telephone, the charge of unlawful use of a telephone may be made.

Because of the battered woman problem, crisis counseling centers and shelters have been established throughout the United States to assist victims and their families. These centers provide shelter when needed, counseling, support, and emergency food and clothing. Shelter locations are generally not disclosed to the public, to prevent further confrontation of the victim by the offender.

Domestic Violence and Women

Physical abuse of women, usually by husbands, ex-husbands, or boyfriends, is a crime that is likely to go unreported and, if reported, is rarely prosecuted. Frequently, the victim refuses to press charges against the abuser. Although in theory the prosecutor may continue to prosecute a case even after the complainant wants charges dropped, in practice such cases become hard to prove and are usually dismissed.

FBI studies show that refusals by the battered spouse to cooperate with prosecutors rarely lead to better relations with the abusive spouse. This is because domestic abuse follows a familiar cycle of violence. In the first phase, the tension-building phase, the abusive spouse becomes hostile and belligerent and heaps verbal abuse on the partner.

This phase almost always leads to the next phase, the acute-battering phase. Injury and death can be the result in this phase. Following a severe battering, the abusive spouse will shower the partner with flowers, affection, and contrite behavior. This is called the honeymoon phase, but like all honeymoons, it always ends. The next phase is the tension-building phase, and the cycle continues from there.[42]

In 1994, Congress passed the Interstate Domestic Violence Act, as part of the Violence Against Women Act.[43] The VAWA and IDVA created new federal domestic violence crimes and also provided millions of dollars for battered women's shelters and child care. The IDVA applies when any person forces a "spouse, intimate partner, or dating partner" to travel across state lines, and commits a crime of violence against that person. The following cases illustrate prosecutions under the Interstate Domestic Violence Act:

- *United States v. Larson:*[44] The defendant beat his ex-wife in his home in Wisconsin, stuffed her in a garbage can filled with snow, took her to Illinois, and left her in an unheated self-storage facility. She was found near death the next day. In 2010 a court of appeals affirmed his conviction and sentence of life imprisonment.
- *United States v. Dowd:*[45] In 2005 a defendant was convicted under the interstate domestic violence statute for forcing his girlfriend to accompany him on an extended three-state trip during which he abused her both physically and psychologically.

Abuse of the Elderly

The National Center on Elder Abuse within the Bureau of Justice Statistics reported that for 2010, there were 5,961,568 reported cases of elder abuse, or about 9.5 percent of the elder population of the United States. Neglect accounted for 58.5 percent of the

THE BROOKE ASTOR CASE

In 2007 Brooke Astor died at the age of 105. She was the heir to a $200 million fortune she inherited from her third husband, Vincent Astor, who died in 1959. He in turn had inherited from his father, who died on the Titanic in 1912. The Astor family owed its wealth to their famous ancestor John Jacob Astor, a nineteenth-century industrialist who was, when he died in 1848, the United States' wealthiest person. From 1959 to the end of the twentieth century Brooke Astor famously lived as a socialite and philanthropist in New York City.

During the last five years of her life Brooke Astor suffered from Alzheimer's disease and was under the financial care of her son, Anthony Marshall. In 2009 Marshall, then 85, and his attorney were convicted of elder abuse and fraud in New York. While managing Brooke Astor's affairs they stole millions of dollars from her investments and fraudulently changed her will to increase her son's share of her estate. Marshall and his attorney were each sentenced to 1–3 years in prison for their crimes.

SCHOOL SHOOTINGS

From 1966 to 2013 there have been several instances of school-related shootings in the United States. While schools at all levels have generally been safe for students and faculty members, these events are especially tragic because of the children involved. The following list chronicles the major fatal shootings in the past 50 years:

- *1966—Austin, Texas:* In an incident known as the Texas Tower killings, a recent graduate of the University of Texas barricaded himself in a tower on the UT campus, and for 96 minutes fired his rifle at passing pedestrians, killing fourteen and injuring thirty-one before being killed by police.
- *1997—Paducah, Kentucky:* A 14-year-old boy killed three classmates and injured five others at a high school prayer meeting.
- *1998—Jonesboro, Arkansas:* Two cousins, ages 13 and 11, dressed in camouflage, killed four girls and a teacher, and wounded eleven other people, outside a middle school. The killers were released from juvenile corrections in 2005 and 2007. The older boy was recently arrested for carrying a loaded weapon (a pistol).
- *1998—Springfield, Oregon:* After being suspended from school for bringing a gun to school, a 15-year-old boy killed three and wounded twenty-three other students before other students subdued him, and the police arrested him.
- *1999—Littleton, Colorado:* Two Columbine High School students, ages 17 and 18, killed twelve students and a teacher and wounded twenty-three other individuals before killing themselves.
- *2005—Red Lake, Minnesota:* A 16-year-old boy killed his grandparents, five fellow students, a teacher, and a security guard before killing himself on a Native American reservation.
- *2006—Nichol Mines, Pennsylvania:* A 32-year-old man entered an Amish school and shot eleven girls—killing four and wounding seven—before killing himself.

reported cases, and physical abuse 15.7 percent. About 66 percent of the abusers were adult children or spouses.

A July 2001 report of federal and state inspections of the nation's 17,000 nursing homes showed that 30 percent were cited over a two-year period for physical, sexual, or verbal abuse of residents. About one in ten of the citations was a serious incident that either put the victim at great risk of harm or killed the patient. The report contained examples of nursing home residents being punched, choked, or kicked by staff members or by other residents.[46]

Under the assault statutes in many states, felony elder abuse is treated as a separate offense. For example, in the 2011 case of *People v. Gross,*[47] the defendant walked down a city street, randomly striking others with his fist. He knocked down a female victim, age 84, causing severe injuries. He was convicted of felony elder abuse under California law, and sentenced to 9 years in prison. The California Court of Appeals affirmed his conviction and sentence.

Because elder abuse frequently involves abuse by caregivers charged with caring for an elderly person, many states have enacted laws aimed at elder abuse committed by caregivers. An example of these laws is the Nebraska Adult Protective

- *2007—Blacksburg, Virginia:* A Virginia Tech student killed thirty-two students and teachers in a university building on the 26,000-acre campus of Virginia Tech. The student then killed himself. This was the worst mass shooting in the United States since 1991, when George Hennard killed twenty-three people in a cafeteria in Killeen, Texas.
- *2008—DeKalb, Illinois:* A 27-year-old student at Northern Illinois University killed himself and five other students, and wounded sixteen others. In the same year in *Baton Rouge, Louisiana,* a nursing student opened fire in a classroom at a technical college, killing two students before killing herself.
- *2009—Coral Gables, Florida:* A 17-year-old student was stabbed to death at 9:00 a.m. in the school courtyard by another student. In *Tyler, Texas,* a 16-year-old student stabbed to death a special education teacher in the classroom.
- *2010—Madison, Alabama:* A ninth-grade student was shot and killed in the school hallway by another ninth-grade student.
- *2010—Huntsville, Alabama:* A female faculty member who was bitter at being denied tenure at the University of Alabama killed three colleagues at a faculty meeting, and wounded three others.
- *2011—Omaha, Nebraska:* Two school administrators were shot by an expelled student. One died, and the student killed himself.
- *2012—Oakland, California:* A student at Oikos College ordered a class of nursing students to line up against a wall in a classroom, and shot them. Seven died before the shooter fled. One L Goh subsequently surrendered to police.
- *2012—Newtown, Connecticut:* After first killing his mother, Adam Lanza killed twenty children and six other adults at the Sandy Hook Elementary School before taking his own life. It was the second worst school massacre, after the killings at Virginia Tech in 2007.

Services Act (Neb. Rev. Stat. § 28 348 387). This act broadly defines *elder abuse* as an act or omission by a caregiver that causes physical injury, cruel punishment, sexual abuse, confinement, or denial of essential services to a vulnerable adult. The act treats violations as class V felonies. It also requires those who treat elderly people, such as physicians and nurses, to report evidence of abuse. Law enforcement agencies are then required to investigate such reports and take steps to protect the elderly person being abused.

California has been a leader in responding to elder abuse. Its law states that it is a crime—a misdemeanor or a felony, depending on the dangerousness of the situation—for any person charged with the duty of caring for an elder person to "willfully cause or permit the elder or dependent adult to be placed in a situation such that his or her person or health is endangered."[48]

In *People v. Heitzmann*[49] the California Supreme Court reversed the conviction of a daughter under this statute. Her 68-year-old father died from neglect while the father lived with the defendant's brothers. The court held that the filial relationship between the daughter and the father was not by itself enough for conviction under the statute. The state needed to prove the daughter had some legal duty to control the actions of the brothers who were neglecting the father, which the court said the state failed to do.

Violence in the Workplace

The U.S. Department of Justice reports that each year 1 million people become victims of violent crimes while at work. Most of such victims are robbed, are victims of felonious assault, or are raped.[50]

While newspapers and television depict scenes of crazed co-workers or fired employees coming back to wreak carnage, statistics show that about a thousand people are killed by violence in the workplace each year.

Is the workplace violent? Should we fear our fellow workers? Statistics show that we have little to fear. In 2011, the Occupational Safety and Health Administration (OSHA) reported that 780 occupational deaths occurred from workplace violence. Most assailants were not co-workers of the person killed. For example, 39 percent of women killed at work were killed by relatives; 36 percent of men killed at work were killed by robbers. Only a small number were killed by co-workers.

Road Rage: Violent Aggressive Driving

Vehicle traffic-related injuries and deaths are the ninth leading cause of death worldwide, and combined with the crime of driving while under the influence of alcohol they are the leading cause of criminal homicide in the United States. Moreover, common driving violations have led to the greater frequency of aggressive driving, known as "road rage."

The National Highway Traffic Safety Administration reported to the U.S. Congress that "violent aggressive driving" had increased 7 percent a year during the late 1990s. Violent aggressive driving was described as aggressive behavior like tailgating, weaving through busy traffic lanes, honking, screaming at other drivers, exchanges of insults, gunfire, and even murder.

Driving violations lead to accidents, which often can help trigger road rage. For example, a 2006 study by the University of Wisconsin showed that in the city of Milwaukee there were more than 1,000 vehicle accidents caused by drivers running stop signs or traffic lights. To combat this problem, about one-half the states have laws permitting red-light cameras, which photograph vehicles and their license plates.

In the 2002 Texas case of *Feldman v. State* (71 S.W.2d 738), a motorcyclist became enraged when a trucker passed him on the highway and nearly hit him. The motorcyclist chased the trucker, pulled up alongside the truck, and shot the driver. The motorcyclist was convicted of murder.

In 2007 motorists became so enraged at delays caused by construction work on a California state highway that they began verbally abusing, throwing objects, and even firing BB guns at the workers. The state highway department finally closed the highway until completion of the construction.[51]

Summary

- An assault conviction requires acts intended to cause bodily injury, or instill fear of such injury. Using a weapon to cause fear is an assault. A battery conviction requires intentional infliction of bodily harm or unlawful touching in a rude or offensive manner.
- Virtually any kind of physical contact can constitute a battery, so long as it is done in a manner that is non-consensual and in a hostile or belligerent manner.
- An assault or battery becomes aggravated if a deadly weapon is used to commit an assault or a battery, or there is an intent to commit a felony. In the case of a battery, if serious bodily injury results it is aggravated battery. Sometimes other circumstances, such as the fact that the victim is pregnant, make a battery aggravated.
- All states have laws that focus on child abuse, neglect, or endangerment. It is also a crime to expose a child to sexually harmful material, or involve a child in sexual activities. Contributing to the delinquency of a child can be used as the basis of prosecution for other forms of child neglect.
- Self-defense is a common defense asserted in assault and battery charges. Under some circumstances, the conduct may be justified, as in the case of a law enforcement officer using force. In some activities, like sports, consent is given to some use of force.
- Most states require that a kidnapping victim be "moved" as part of the crime. Generally, the movement must be substantial, and not just moving a person from one room to another. However, where it is clear the purpose of the action was to constrain the victim against that person's will, any movement of the victim will suffice.
- Hostage taking differs from kidnapping in that it lacks a "movement" element. The crime does require that a victim be held against his will in some fashion, and that the purpose of doing so is to force another to take some act, like pay a ransom, or allow the criminals to escape.

Key Terms

assault, p. 292
battery, p. 292
offensive touching, p. 295
menacing, p. 297

aggravated assault, p. 297
aggravated battery, p. 297
mayhem and malicious
  disfigurement, p. 299

kidnapping, p. 306
hostage taking, p. 309
false imprisonment, p. 309

Case Analysis and Writing Exercises

1. Parents can be convicted of kidnapping. However, parents are obviously in a different position than strangers who abduct a child. What must the prosecution show to convict a parent of kidnapping? *See Davila v. State*, 75 So.3d 192 (Fla. 2011).
2. Many crimes, such as armed robbery of a store or bank, involve the robbers ordering persons in the building to move to a different location. When is the movement sufficient to constitute kidnapping, so that the defendants can be convicted and sentenced for both robbery and kidnapping? *See United States v. Reynos*, 680 F.3d 283 (3rd Cir. 2012). [Note that after the panel decision the entire court initially ordered rehearing *en banc*, but then changed its mind and ordered reinstatement of the panel decision.]
3. Aggravated assault, or aggravated battery in many states, is a more serious crime than "simple" assault. It is charged based on factors such as the existence of serious injury, permanent disability, or use of a deadly weapon. Prosecutors must be careful to make sure the crime charged in the indictment matches the

evidence and jury questions, so that a defendant is not "convicted of a crime he was not charged with." Compare two Florida cases, *Calloway v. State*, 37 So.3d 891 (Fla. App. 2010), *cert. denied*, 51 So.3d 1154 (Fla. 2010), and *Reddick v. State*, 56 So.3d 132 (Fla. App. 2011). Why did the appeals court reverse the conviction in *Reddick* but not in *Calloway*?

4. In many states offensive touching sexual assaults are punished more severely if multiple sexual assaults are committed against the same underage victim. In *Schweiner v. State*, 2012 WL 3126810 (7th Cir. 2012), *cert. denied* 133 S. Ct. 796 (2012) a defendant was convicted under the Wisconsin "repeated sexual assault on a child" statute, which requires three sexual assaults within a specified period. The defendant on one occasion took some children swimming, throwing the children up in the air to land in the water. One of the children, a 13-year-old girl, testified when the defendant threw her he touched both her buttocks and her vagina. Is that one sexual contact or two, for purposes of the "three assaults" requirement?

Endnotes

1. A few states (including Wisconsin) have not statutorized the common-law crime of assault. Disorderly conduct and attempt to commit a battery are substituted for assault in charging.

2. Most states have passed statutes that criminalize the conduct of pointing an unloaded gun at a victim who does not know if the gun is loaded or unloaded and becomes apprehensive and frightened. The New York crime of menacing (§ 120.15) by placing "or attempting to place another in fear of imminent serious physical injury" is an example of such a criminal statute.

3. 104 Cal. App. 4th 256, 124 Cal. Rptr. 2d 888 (2002).

4. 690 F.3d 1111 (9th Cir. 2012), *cert. denied* 2013 WL 140373.

5. In the 1991 case of *Ray v. State* (580 So. 2d 103), the Alabama Court of Appeals quoted another court as to an adult man's fists being used to beat a baby:
   Certainly the use of an adult man's fists to beat a seventeen-month [old] child may appropriately allow those fists to be classified as a deadly weapon or a dangerous instrument.

6. 440 A.2d 710 (R.I. 1982).

7. 249 P.3d 1284 (Ore. App. 2011).

8. 534 N.E.2d 312 (Ill. App. 1989).

9. 592 N.E.2d 585 (Ill. App. 1992).

10. Other batteries and assaults include a running leap onto a woman's back as assault in *Russell v. State*, 814 S.W. 2d 871 (Tex. App. 1991); poking a teacher in the chest as assault in *People v. Dunker*, 577 N.E.2d 499 (Ill. App. 1991); a profane threat of physical violence as assault in *Wells v. State*, 418 S.W.2d 437 (Ga. App. 1992); grabbing the victim by his coat and punching him in the face as assault in *State v. Waltrip*, 484 N.W.2d 831 (Neb. 1992); holding the victim against her will as battery in *Bamette v. State*, 217 S.W.2d 20 (1949); head-butting the victim as disorderly conduct and assault in *State v. McKenzie*, 605 A.2d 72 (Maine 1992); attempting to film under victim's dress with camcorder as simple battery in *Fitzgerald v. State*, 411 S.E.2d 102 (Ga. App. 1991); and throwing rocks at moving cars on highway as several counts of assault, battery, and malicious destruction in *Ford v. State*, 603 A.2d 883 (Md. 1992).

11. 117 Ill. App. 3d 363, 73 Ill. Dec. 17, 453 N.E.2d 842. The Illinois Appellate Court cited the following:

    Other instances of conduct held to be simple battery based solely on insulting or provoking physical contact [include]: *People v. Hamilton*, ... 401 N.E.2d 318 ... (where defendant reached around the female complainant and placed his hand over her mouth); *People v. Siler*, ... 406 N.E.2d 891 ... (where defendant lifted up complainant's dress during a confrontation having sexual overtones).

12. *State v. Shelly*, 929 P.2d 489 (Wash. 1997).

13. 811 N.E.2d 567 (Ohio App. 2004).

14. The Federal Aviation Act of 1958, 49 U.S.C.A. § 1472(j), forbids assault, intimidation, or threatening of a flight crew member and punishes such conduct by imprisonment for up to 20 years.

    In the 1991 case of *U.S. v. Tabacca*, 924 F.2d 906 (9th Cir.), the defendant continued to smoke a cigarette after airline flight attendants requested that he extinguish the cigarette. After addressing vulgar language to the attendant, Tabacca grabbed her arm "and jerked and twisted her arm, causing her to strike the bulkhead of the seat across the aisle." The defendant's conviction was affirmed.

15. 810 N.W.2d 303 (Minn. 2012).

16. *State v. Boone*, 294 Or. 630, 661 P.2d 917 (1983).

17. *Id.*

18. 901 So. 2d 899 (Fla. App. 2005).

19. *Whitaker v. U.S.*, 616 A.2d 843 (D.C. App. 1992).

20. Vernon's Penal Code of the State of Texas Annotated.

21. 508 U.S. 476 (1993).

22. 844 N.Y.S.2d 627 (Sup. Ct. 2007).

23. 791 N.W.2d 828 (Iowa 2010).

24. 980 S.W.2d 682 (Tex. 1998).

25. 429 U.S. 975, 97 S. Ct. 481 (1976). The 1997 U.S. Department of Justice publication *In the Wake of Child Abuse and Childhood Maltreatment* states that more than 3 million children are reported to Child Protective Services each

year as being abused. Of these 3 million reported cases, 1 million are found to be abused children. The majority of abused children (85 percent) are under age 5, and nearly half of the victims (45 percent) have not reached their first birthday. More than three children die each day as a result of parental maltreatment. Abuse is the most common cause of death (48 percent), followed by neglect (37 percent), and a combination of abuse and neglect (15 percent). Child abuse is a crime that cuts across all walks of life and all social classes.

26. In *Commonwealth v. Miller,* 600 A.2d 988 (Pa. Super. 1992), the court discussed the endangerment statute's requirement that the defendant "knowingly" endangered a child's welfare. The court said the defendant must know he or she has a duty to care for the child, be aware the child is in a dangerous situation, and have either failed to act or acted in so meager a way that it could not reasonably be believed the actions would be effective. Thus, a mother who leaves her child unattended while she goes out to a nightclub can be convicted of endangerment of a child, but a mother who believes, wrongly and perhaps unreasonably, her boyfriend's statement that another person is watching her child probably would not.

27. 114 Cal. Rptr. 3d 520 (Cal. App. 2010).

28. 227 P.3d 1139 (Ore. 2010).

29. 219 P.3d 280 (Az. App. 2009).

30. See *People v. Daniels,* 71 Cal. 2d 1119, 80 Cal. Rptr. 897, 459 P.2d 225 (1969).

31. See *People v. Williams,* 2 Cal. 3d 894, 88 Cal. Rptr. 208, 471 P.2d 1008 (1970).

32. 127 Cal. App. 4th 290 (Cal. App. 2005).

33. 2010 WL 2857046 (Cal App. 2010).

34. 94 N.J. 436, 466 A.2d 955 (1983).

35. 409 So. 2d 1031 (Fla. 1982).

36. Section 940.305, Wisconsin "taking hostage" felony.

37. 728 N.W.2d 374 (Wis. App. 2007).

38. The tort of false imprisonment is sometimes called *false arrest.* False arrest is a wrongful arrest made either by a law enforcement officer or by a private person. Arresting, detaining, and holding a person in custody without authority is false imprisonment and gives the victim the basis for a civil lawsuit to recover for the false arrest and false imprisonment. In a civil lawsuit (tort action) for false arrest, the plaintiff alleges that there was no authority or legal justification for the defendant to interfere with the plaintiff's freedom of movement.

39. 18 U.S.C.A. § 1201.

40. 18 U.S.C.A. § 1073.

41. In October 1984, President Ronald Reagan signed the Missing Children's Assistance Act, now amended and known as the National Child Search Assistance Act of 1990, 42 U.S.C.A. § 5779, which provides for the operation of a national toll-free telephone line for exchanging information on missing children through a national resource center and clearinghouse. The administrator of the program will "facilitate effective coordination among all federally funded programs relating to missing children." Section 5775 of the act provides,

> The Administrator is authorized to make grants to and enter into contracts with [National Center for Missing and Exploited Children] and public agencies or nonprofit private organizations, or combination thereof, for research, demonstration projects, or service programs designed—(1) to educate parents, children, and community agencies and organizations in ways to prevent the abduction and sexual exploitation of children; (2) to provide information to assist in the locating and return of missing children; (3) to aid communities in the collection of materials which would be useful to parents in assisting others in the identification of missing children; (4) to increase knowledge of and develop effective treatment pertaining to the psychological consequences, on both parents and children.

42. *FBI Law Enforcement Bulletin,* July 1, 1996, p. 15.

43. 18 U.S.C.A. §§ 2261–2266. The Act incorporates the criminal violations parts of the Violence Against Women Act of 1994. In the May 2000 case of *U.S. v. Morrison,* the U.S. Supreme Court declared the civil remedy provisions of the Violence Against Women Act unconstitutional. Just as in the Gun-Free School Zones Act case of *U.S. v. Lopez* (115 S. Ct. 1624), violence against women and firearms in a school zone do not affect interstate commerce, and therefore the federal government has limited authority to enact the civil law portions of laws. Courts commonly upheld the criminal portions of the VAWA, which specifically require movement of the victim in interstate commerce. The VAWA expired in 2011. On February 11, 2013 the Senate voted to continue the VAWA. That bill must pass in the House of Representatives to become law. All states have criminal laws forbidding violence against women, and most states have gun-free school zone laws.

44. 615 F.3d 780 (7th Cir. 2010), *cert. denied,* 131 S. Ct. 681 (2010).

45. 417 F.3d 1080 (9th Cir. 2005), *cert. denied,* 126 S. Ct. 816 (2005).

46. See *Milwaukee Journal Sentinel* article, "30% of Nursing Homes Cited for Abuse," July 31, 2001.

47. 2011 WL 4357778 (Cal. App. 2011).

48. California Penal Code § 368(a).

49. *People v. Heitzmann,* 886 P.2d 1229 (1994).

50. NCJ 148199, U.S. Department of Justice, July 1994.

51. See *Milwaukee Journal Sentinel* article, "Road Rage Closes California Highway," July 27, 2007.

Sexual Assault, Rape, Prostitution, and Related Sex Crimes

Aaron Josefczyk/Reuters/Landov

In 2013, three Cleveland, Ohio women escaped from captivity after being held in sexual slavery for more than 10 years in a home owned by Ariel Castro. One woman had a six-year-old daughter fathered by Castro. Castro, shown here, pleaded guilty in July of 2013 to numerous counts, including aggravated murder for the brutal death of an unborn child carried by one of the victims. Castro was sentenced to life in prison without parole plus 1,000 years. Castro hanged himself in his prison cell on September 3, 2013.

OUTLINE

LEARNING OBJECTIVES

In this chapter we discuss sexual assault crimes and crimes related to sexual conduct. The learning objectives for Chapter 12 are the following:

- Identify the degrees of sexual assault, and the conduct that distinguishes them.

- Learn the areas of questioning of a sexual assault victim that are prohibited by the rape shield law.

- List two exceptions to the rape shield law's prohibitions.

- State the *mens rea* requirement for a conviction for statutory rape.

- State the conditions that must be shown for civil commitment of a sexual predator.

- Explain the reasons child pornography laws have been found unconstitutional.

- State the current status of federal acts such as the Child Online Protection Act.

Nonconsensual sex is virtually always a crime. In addition, every state has a "statutory rape" law, under which it is a crime to have sex with a child under a specified age, usually 13–16 years of age. Consent of the child is not a defense; a child is deemed to lack the capacity to give consent. In the case of an adult defendant, it is clear the law has made it the adult's duty to recognize the actions are wrong, regardless of the child's actions. It is also clear that the adult is the offender, and the child the victim protected by the statute.

In a 2011 case the Ohio Supreme Court was asked to decide what happens when both the "perpetrator" and the "victim" are under the specified age, in Ohio 13 years of age. Two boys aged 12 had anal sex, with one boy, D.B., initiating the sexual contact. D.B. was charged with violating the Ohio statutory rape statute, and was adjudicated a delinquent. On appeal, the Ohio Supreme Court reversed the delinquency adjudication, reasoning that in the case of non-forcible sex, neither child can be the "perpetrator," because both qualify as "victims." One cannot be both the victim and the offender, the Court held.[1]

In this chapter we will study the elements of sexual assault crimes, in particular the rape of women. We will also learn about the rules and procedures put in place to preserve the reputation and emotional well-being of the victim, such as the rape shield laws.

Sexual Relations in the United States Today

Sexual relations (non-marital) become a crime in the United States if

- There is a lack of consent.
- They are with a minor incapable of legally consenting.
- They are with a mentally deficient person or an adult otherwise deemed by the law to be incapable of consenting.
- They are performed in public.
- They are performed for profit (prostitution).
- They are between a therapist and a patient and in violation of the laws of that state.

Rape or Sexual Assault

Sex crimes occur often in the United States. The term *sex crime* includes a broad classification of offenses that range from serious offenses to nuisance offenses and private offenses between consenting adults. Historically, the term *rape* was used to identify the crime of nonconsensual sexual relations obtained by force or threat of force. The National Institute of Justice (NIJ), the research and development branch of the U.S. Justice Department, defines **rape** as vaginal, oral, or anal penetration achieved through the use of force or threat of force. Rape includes penetration of the vagina or anus by penis, finger, tongue, or some other object manipulated by the rapist. Many state criminal codes use a similar definition.

rape Anal, vaginal, or oral penetration by force or threat of force.

The criminal codes of the fifty states use the terms *rape, sexual assault,* or *sexual battery* when dealing with what the common law called rape and do so in a variety of ways. All the states probably treat "ordinary" rape in much the same way as did the common law, though often listing ordinary rape as a second-degree offense and punishing it as a class B felony.

Aggravated rape, however, is handled differently in different states. For example, gang rape, which is rape committed against a single victim by multiple offenders, is an aggravated offense under the Florida sexual battery statutes. Section 794.0233 of the Florida Statutes provides for enhanced penalties and punishes the offense as a first-degree felony (life felony). Other states simply classify gang rape as a first-degree felony.

Other factors that states use as aggravating factors to elevate a rape or sexual assault to a first-degree or class A felony include inflicting serious bodily harm on the victim, using a deadly weapon such as a knife or gun in the rape, causing the victim to become pregnant, infecting the victim with AIDS or another sexually transmitted disease, anal penetration, or raping a very young child.

sexual assault The crime in most states that includes the crime of rape, as well as other lesser degrees of assault.

The NIJ has estimated that rape (or first-degree **sexual assault**) with female victims occurs over 300,000 times each year, and nearly 93,000 times with male victims. In the 2006 National Violence Against Women Survey, the results of which were published by the NIJ,[2] telephone interviews conducted nationwide with 8,000 women and 8,000 men disclosed the following information:

- In the United States, one out of every six women has experienced either rape or attempted rape at some time in her life; one out of every thirty-three men has experienced either rape or attempted rape at some time in his life.
- Rape or attempted rape frequently involves young victims, with most victims being under the age of 12 when the rape occurred.
- Most rape victims are women, and most offenders are men.
- When the victim of rape or attempted rape is 18 years of age or older, physical injury is caused to 31.5 percent of female victims and 16.1 percent of male victims.
- Only 19.1 percent of the female victims of rape or attempted rape, and 12.9 percent of male victims, over the age of 18, reported the incident to the police.
- The reasons given for failure to report a rape or attempted rape were "fear of retaliation by the offender," "too ashamed or embarrassed," "thought the matter was a minor incident," or "not a police matter."
- Where female victims reported the rape or attempted rape, 37 percent resulted in prosecutions, with convictions in 46.2 percent of the prosecutions. Thirteen percent of the female victims sought and obtained restraining orders against the offenders; 69.9 percent reported that the restraining order was violated.

In an October 2012 report entitled "Criminal Victimization" by the Federal Bureau of Justice Statistics, National Crime Victimization Survey stated that in 2011 there were 243,800 reported rapes/sexual assaults in the United States. The report also estimated that more than 50 percent of sexual assaults go unreported to law enforcement authorities.

The Importance of Corroborative Evidence in a Rape Case

corroborative evidence Physical evidence or witness testimony other than from the victim that supports the claim that a crime occurred.

Today, in virtually every state, a rape conviction can rest solely on the uncorroborated testimony of the victim.[3] However, **corroborative evidence** (evidence affirming and supporting statements of the victim) is very important in most cases.

Statistics show that in as many as 40 percent of the cases that come into the offices of prosecutors in large cities, rape charges are not issued. Lack of corroborating evidence is probably the principal reason. Statements of the complaining witness can be corroborated and affirmed by the following:

- Scratches, bruises, injuries, torn clothing, or blood stains from either the victim or the suspect.

- Witnesses who heard screams or the sounds of a struggle, or observed either party before, during, or immediately after the assault.
- Color photographs of bruises, black-and-blue marks, lacerations, cuts, scratches, or other injuries to either party, as these injuries will disappear within a few days through the healing process.
- Blood, semen, saliva, or nail scrapings taken from the victim or suspect, as well as pubic and head hair obtained at the scene of the crime and from the bodies of the victim and suspect. Such genetic material may result in a positive DNA identification of the offender.
- Weapons or instruments that may have been used to force the victim to submit to the assault.
- Buttons, torn clothing, or other items that the victim or suspect may have lost in the struggle.
- Soiled or stained clothing of the suspect and victim that contains blood, seminal stains, or other evidence of the crime.
- Fingerprints found at the scene of the sexual assault or elsewhere that can be used to corroborate or to identify the suspect.
- Observations by doctors and nurses and samples of fluids from vagina, rectum, or oral cavity showing that forcible intercourse had occurred.
- If DNA evidence from blood, semen, saliva, and so forth is available, it could prove the identity of the offender almost conclusively.

In a rape case, whether the state has a strong or a weak case in going to trial depends on the physical evidence available and the ability of the complaining witness to testify. Lack of corroborative physical evidence and/or the inability of the complaining witness to testify effectively could cause the case to be viewed as weak.

Possible Responses to a Threat of Rape

Studies show that most women, especially young women, fear rape more than any other crime. How should a woman respond to an imminent threat of rape?

- *Should she scream, fight back, and try to escape?* Studies show that women who resist decrease the odds of completed rape by 80 percent. But they increase the likelihood of being physically injured. Experts say that it is better to be raped than to risk being permanently injured or killed.
- *Should she try to talk the man out of it?* Women have tried many different tactics in trying to avoid rape. They have pretended to be pregnant, or have stated they have a sexually transmitted disease, or have AIDS. They have fainted, cried hysterically, acted insane or vomited, urinated, or acted very ill.
- *Should she grit her teeth and bear it?* This is an available option that the victim might choose. Or the victim may be able to combine one or both of the above two in an effort to avoid being raped.

The "Force" Required in Rape or Sexual Assault

William Blackstone, the author of the famous "Commentaries on the Laws of England," published in 1895, said the English common law defined rape as "the carnal knowledge of a woman forcibly and against her will." When the American states adopted their own criminal laws, virtually all defined rape in a similar manner. As a result, rape statutes required a showing of both lack of consent ("against her will") and physical force. Early on, most statutes were amended to include the "threat of force" as a substitute for the "forcible compulsion" element, where actual force was not present.

Forcible Compulsion   In many states the prosecution was required to prove force "compelled" the victim to engage in the sexual acts, by introducing proof the victim "resisted" the acts. Absence of proof of resistance by the victim was fatal to the prosecution's case. That has changed dramatically. Sexual assault and rape statutes in the fifty states are worded in many different ways, but in most states that require proof of "forcible compulsion," there is no need to prove resistance by the victim, and the force used need only be sufficient to "overcome" the victim's will. Even where "resistance" is part of the definition of forcible rape, courts usually require only proof that the victim voiced her objection to the acts but was forced to comply.

In some states, sexual assault is defined generally to include any sexual penetration obtained "against the will" of the victim. If force is used, the sexual assault is classified as a more serious felony. The Colorado sexual assault statute, Col. Stat. § 18-3-402(4)(a), is such a statute. In *People v. Keene,* 226 P.3d 1140 (Colo. App. 2009), the court held that the defendant's own body weight can be the "physical force" that triggers the increased severity of the assault, if in fact the victim struggled and the weight prevented her from escaping.

The following two cases illustrate the meaning of "force" in two different rape statutes:

Case and State	Facts of the Case	Requirement of the State Statute
People v. Griffin, Supreme Court of California, 94 P.3d 1089 (2004)	The defendant told the victim to lie down on the floor. She did, and he held her wrists while he sexually penetrated her. The victim did not otherwise resist. The conviction for forcible rape was affirmed.	The California forcible rape statute, which had been amended to eliminate any need of showing resistance by the victim, required only a showing that the rape was "accomplished against a person's will by means of force, violence, or fear of immediate and unlawful bodily injury," the Court held.
State v. Jones, 299 P.3d 219 (Idaho 2013).	Defendant was charged with two counts of forcible rape of the victim. In one, the only force by the defendant was pushing the victim off her elbows and putting his body on her back. In the other, the victim pretended to be asleep, and offered no resistance. The court affirmed the conviction in count I but reversed the conviction in count II.	The Idaho rape statute defined forcible rape as occurring when the victim "resists, but her resistance is overcome by force or violence." The court said that under this type of forcible rape statute, some "extrinsic force" beyond the physical act of intercourse must be proved, though it need not be of any specific kind or degree. Since no extrinsic force was shown in the second rape, it was not forcible rape.

Non-Consent   There has long been a demand by rape victims and groups supporting them for reform of the traditional forcible rape laws. Reform groups sought the elimination of any requirement of force or threat of force, and instead urged legislators to make rape a purely "consent/non-consent" question. In a 2011 article in the *Journal of Criminal Law and Criminology*[4] the authors suggest that this reform movement has been only partially successful. They note that while twenty-eight states have true "non-consent" rape statutes, which require no proof of "forcible compulsion," only seventeen of them apply that standard to sexual penetration rapes. The other eleven states limit true "non-consent" sexual assaults to crimes involving sexual contact, without penetration. Sexual penetration rapes still must be accompanied by force. Fifteen states have no form of "non-consent" sexual assault, and the remaining states have statutes that incorporate force or threat of force into the meaning of "consent."

Threats of Force   Where force is still part of the rape requirement, threats or fear of force will normally serve as a substitute for actual force. The Maryland Court of Appeals has noted that the "vast majority of jurisdictions have required that the victim's fear be reasonably grounded in order to obviate the need for either proof of actual force on the part of the assailant or physical resistance on the part of the victim."[5] Pointing out that the reasonableness of a victim's apprehension or fear was plainly a question of fact for a jury to determine, the Maryland Court of Appeals held,[6]

> It was for the jury to observe the witnesses and their demeanor, and to judge their credibility and weigh their testimony. Quite obviously, the jury disbelieved Rusk [defendant] and believed Pat's [victim] testimony.
>
> * * *
>
> Just where persuasion ends and force begins in cases like the present is essentially a factual issue, to be resolved in light of the controlling legal precepts. That threats of force need not be made in any particular manner in order to put a person in fear of bodily harm is well established. . . . Indeed, conduct, rather than words, may convey the threat.
>
> * * *
>
> That a victim did not scream out for help or attempt to escape, while bearing on the question of consent, is unnecessary where she is restrained by fear of violence.

Defenses in Acquaintance Rape or Date Rape

More than half of the forcible rapes that are reported are committed by friends, acquaintances, or relatives. The after-the-date rape (or date rape) case can be particularly difficult to prove unless evidence of actual physical violence exists. Because of the friendly and sometimes close relationship that existed between the parties, defendants could use the following arguments in court:

Yes, We Had Sex, But . . .

She consented . . .	and her conduct shows she consented (after all, she invited me up to her apartment, or she came up to my apartment late at night).

I honestly thought she consented. . . .	"It is a defense to a charge of forcible rape that the defendant entertained a reasonable and good faith belief that the female person voluntarily consented to engage in sexual intercourse" (California Jury Instruction 10.23).[7]
She never did say "no". . .	and I thought that because she didn't say "no," she was consenting.
She consented, then changed her mind during the sex . . .	and did not clearly communicate her change of mind.
She consented, but later developed guilt feelings and regretted what she did . . .	but before and during the sex, she consented. (This defense is sometimes used with the "groupie" defense. Athletes and performers charged with rape often use this defense, arguing that the victim pursued them.)

The Report of Rape Rule and the Effect of Delay in Reporting

After a sexual assault, the victim may be confused and fearful of her assailant. This could result in a delay in reporting the crime. A long delay could raise questions of the credibility of the victim, it could substantially diminish the possibility of obtaining physical evidence of the rape, and it could prevent the person receiving the report of rape from testifying as to the statements and circumstances. The Model Penal Code, § 213.6(4) (the report of rape rule), states that no prosecution may be brought if the complainant fails to report the sexual assault within three months of its occurrence or, if the victim is less than 16 years old, within three months of the time a parent or other competent adult learns of the assault.

A person to whom a rape victim has excitedly reported a rape can testify as to the statements and circumstances under the report of rape or excited utterance exceptions to the hearsay rule.[8] Such testimony is important corroborative evidence in proving a rape charge. It also counteracts what has been called the "timing myth" that assumed rape victims who do not immediately "cry out" and alert others have not been raped.

In many states the "fresh complaint" rule permits the prosecution to introduce evidence the victim spontaneously reported the rape within a reasonable time. In the case of children, courts generally permit, as a reasonable time, a much longer interval between the rape and the report than found in the MPC section discussed above.

For example, in the 2011 case of *State v. W.B.*[9] the New Jersey Supreme Court affirmed a conviction for aggravated sexual assault on a child. The court held the trial court was correct in admitting under the "fresh complaint" rule evidence that the child victim, 14 years of age when the sexual assault occurred, spontaneously reported the sexual assault 15 months after it occurred. That period was reasonable, the court held, given the age of the victim, and her fear of the defendant, her stepfather.

NATIONAL PROBLEMS IN THE SEX CRIME AREA

Reports of Sexual Assaults and the Anonymous Reporting Option

It is generally agreed by those involved with domestic violence and sexual assault that a very high percentage, perhaps as much as 80 percent, of rapes and other sexual assaults go unreported. Many victims of sexual assaults are afraid or too embarrassed to inform law enforcement officers of the assault. The failure to report is a problem for law enforcement, both because the sexual assailant remains at large and may commit more sexual crimes, and because the failure to make a prompt report can result in lost evidence of the sexual assault, in particular DNA evidence. To alleviate victims' concerns and facilitate more reports of sexual assaults, the Violence Against Women Act, 18 U.S.C. § 2261 *et seq.*, requires states to make forensic medical exams available to victims of sexual violence and establishes a grant program to provide funds to pay for the medical examinations. Victims taking these examinations have no obligation to report the sexual assault or the examination's results to law enforcement, but they may do so on a voluntary, anonymous basis. A formal investigation by law enforcement will be undertaken only if the victim requests such an investigation. See the May 2010 *FBI Law Enforcement Bulletin*, "Options for Reporting Sexual Violence," at the FBI website, http://www.fbi.gov.

Failure of States to Test Rape Kits

When a sexual assault victim receives medical attention, medical professionals are trained to collect forensic evidence in "rape kits," which are then forwarded to the police to aid in their investigation of the sexual assault. For a variety of reasons, most states have a huge backlog of these kits that remain untested. A report of Human Rights Watch published July 7, 2010, states that in Illinois, of 7,494 rape kits turned over to police since 1995, only 1,474 have been tested, which suggested that 80 percent of rape kits are not being tested. In Los Angeles, a city audit conducted in 2009 found over 7,000 untested rape kits in the LAPD freezer, many of them more than 10 years old.

Failure to use the evidence in rape kits has a direct effect on arrests and convictions, studies show. In Illinois, the arrest rate for sexual assault crimes was about 11 percent. In New York City, once a mandatory rape-kit testing rule was put in place, the arrest rate climbed from 40 percent to 70 percent. In July 2010 the Illinois legislature passed the 2010 Sexual Assault Evidence Submission Act, PL 096-1011. Pursuant to this statute, police departments must within 10 days of the receipt of a rape kit submit it for tests, and the tests must be performed and results reported within 180 days.

Sexual Assaults in Prisons

In response to the growing problem of sexual assaults in prisons, in 2003 Congress passed the Prison Rape Elimination Act, 42 U.S.C. § 15602 (the "Act"). The stated purpose of the Act was to provide the means and funds to reduce the incidence of sexual assaults in prisons in the United States. Based on studies done in 2007 under the Act, in March 2008 the Department of Justice's

National Institute of Justice published a report of the Bureau of Justice Statistics (NIJ # 259). The report concluded that over 60,500 sexual assaults occur in U.S. prisons every year and only about 6,500 of these assaults are reported to prison officials. Of the reported cases, 47 percent involved assaults by other inmates, and 53 percent were assaults by corrections staff members. The report had several recommendations, including training programs for prison officers and methods of facilitating corroboration of assaults, a major problem for inmates who do report assaults.

Monitoring Sex Offenders in the United States

Since the first sex offender registration acts were passed (see discussion in this chapter), the number of persons required to register has mushroomed each year. In a June 2010 report the Center for Missing and Exploited Children stated that 716,750 individuals had registered as sex offenders. The number of sex offenders on state lists makes the lists almost useless: a state the size of Georgia might have as many as 18,000 individuals on its list, including rapists, kidnappers, flashers, and even juveniles who had consensual sex. Each state requires all sex offenders to register, and it also requires persons on the list to give the state a new address when they move. The federal SORNA Act requires all registered sex offenders who move from state to state to register in a new state; it is a crime punishable by up to 10 years in prison to fail to register. Notwithstanding these requirements, it is estimated that over 100,000 paroled sex offenders have failed to register or have given false information. It has been a sometimes-overwhelming task for local law enforcement agencies to keep track of these sex offenders. See the September 2, 2009 *New York Times* article entitled "Plenty of Data on Offenders, but Little on Its Effects."

Sex Offenders and State Licensing Laws

One question sex offender registration laws present to state officials is the effect, if any, sex offender status has on the granting of state licenses. Millions of work and professional licenses are granted each year to individuals, including security guards, locksmiths, real estate brokers, barbers, funeral directors, lawyers, and medical professionals. For some professionals, such as physicians, elaborate licensing provisions help answer that question. The Missouri physician license statute, V.A.M.S. § 334.100, permits the licensing agency to deny the issuance or renewal of a physician's license if the applicant has been convicted of a sexual offense. This section was used to deny a license to a physician in the case of *State v. Hartenbach*, 216 S.W.3d 158 (Mo. App. 2007). In many other areas, the licensing criteria make no mention of sex offender status or convictions; as an example, the South Carolina requirements for a funeral director's license, Code 1976, § 40-1-140, make a prior criminal conviction the basis for license denial only if the crime related to the profession. It is questionable whether denial of a license without specific statutory or regulatory reference to sex offender status is permitted.

It is true that a significant number of reports of rape or sexual assault turn out to be unfounded, though that is true of other crimes as well. Where the alleged victim has made prior false reports of sexual assaults, defendants often try to introduce evidence of those false reports, to attack the credibility of the complainant. These attempts raise an issue under rape shield laws, which are discussed in the next section.

Rape Shield Laws

rape shield laws Laws passed by many states to limit the extent to which defense attorneys in a rape case can inquire into the victim's past sexual life.

Most states have enacted **rape shield laws** that forbid the use of evidence of a rape victim's past sexual conduct with others and evidence of her reputation. Under the protection of rape shield laws, victims appearing as witnesses in a sexual assault case therefore do not have to defend their reputations or past sexual conduct.

Rule 412 of the Federal Rules of Evidence is an example of a rape shield law and is similar to many such laws adopted by states. It provides that in a criminal trial of a sexual assault charge, evidence (1) offered to prove the victim engaged in other sexual behavior, or (2) offered to prove the victim's sexual predisposition, is inadmissible. There are three exceptions to this rule: evidence is admissible if it is (1) evidence of specific sexual behavior of the victim offered to prove another person was the source of semen or other physical evidence; (2) evidence of specific past sexual contact between the victim and the accused, if offered to prove consent; or (3) evidence the exclusion of which would violate the constitutional rights of the accused. In *United States v. Pumpkin Seed*[10] the court upheld a trial court's decision to exclude evidence that the defendant was not the source of semen and pubic hair found on the victim. The court reasoned that since the prosecution did not offer the semen or pubic hair as evidence of the rape, that evidence was not relevant to any issue in the trial.

Before rape shield laws, defense lawyers deemed a victim's reputation "fair game," and the victim could be forced to defend her entire sexual history. Rape shield laws were enacted to encourage the reporting of sexual assaults and to forbid introduction of evidence that would prejudice a jury. Such evidence is also irrelevant to the issue of guilt or innocence before the court. Rape shield laws apply to male victims as well as female victims. Evidence offered to prove that the victim was a homosexual, or had engaged in past homosexual acts, would be inadmissible under most rape shield laws.[11] In the 2010 case of *State v. Rackliffe,*[12] the court rejected the contention of a defendant convicted of sexual assault on a male victim that proof of the victim's sexual orientation was relevant on the issue of consent to the sexual assault.

However, exceptions are made in rape shield laws to allow the introduction of relevant, probative evidence at trial. In the U.S. Supreme Court case of *Olden v. Kentucky,*[13] the defendant sought to prove that the victim made up her charge of sexual battery against him in order to protect her relationship with her boyfriend. The U.S. Supreme Court reversed the defendant's conviction, holding that his Sixth Amendment right to conduct reasonable cross-examination had been violated.

The presence or absence of consent by the victim is an important issue in a rape case. As a result, almost all rape shield laws permit defendants to introduce evidence of "past sexual contact between the victim and the accused, if offered to prove consent." The fact that an alleged victim had sexual contact with the defendant in the past can support the inference that the claimed sexual assault was consensual. In a highly charged 2012 case, the Sixth Circuit Court of Appeals was required to determine if a state court's refusal to introduce evidence of past sexual contact with the victim violated his Sixth Amendment rights:

Gagne v. Booker

United States Court of Appeals for the Sixth Circuit, 680 F.3d 493, *cert. denied*, 133 S. Ct. 481 (2012).

The defendant, the victim, and a third person had "threesome" sex. The victim claimed she had not consented to a threesome, and defendant was charged with forcible rape under Michigan law. (The third party was also charged with rape, and convicted. His appeal is not included in this case.) At his trial, defendant sought to admit evidence that he and the victim had engaged in threesome sex with other third parties in the past. He claimed such evidence was admissible under the "prior sex with victim" exception of the Michigan rape shield law. The trial court refused to admit the evidence, and the defendant was convicted of forcible rape. A Michigan appeals court affirmed the conviction, holding that evidence of threesome sex with a third party other than the third person who participated in the alleged rape has no probative value, because the fact the victim consented to the prior, different three-party sex acts does not support the claim she consented to the present threesome. Rather, the court concluded, such evidence tends to show the victim's predisposition to threesome sex, which is not permitted under the rape shield law. The Michigan Supreme Court affirmed the appeals court's decision.

The defendant then filed a habeas corpus petition in federal court, alleging that the Michigan application of the rape shield law violated his Sixth Amendment rights. A federal district court and a panel of the Sixth Circuit agreed, and granted the petition for relief. The Sixth Circuit then granted *en banc* review, and held the refusal to admit the evidence of other threesome sex acts did not violate the defendant's Sixth Amendment rights. It concluded the Michigan court's reasoning under the rape shield act was not an unreasonable determination of the probative value of the evidence, and thus did not violate existing Sixth Amendment law.

In the 2012 case of *Perry v. Commonwealth*[14] the Kentucky Supreme Court stated that under the Kentucky rape shield law, as in the majority of state courts, a defendant in a rape case is permitted to offer evidence that the victim had in the past made false rape claims against others. Such evidence is not about past sexual behavior, the court said, and thus the rape shield law was inapplicable. However, the court also said evidence of false reports is potentially very prejudicial, and as a result the defendant wishing to introduce such evidence must make a preliminary showing that the prior reports were "demonstrably false." Colorado's Rape Shield Law, C.R.S.A. § 18-3-407, specifically provides that evidence of past false reports

OLD RAPE LAWS AND NEW SEXUAL ASSAULT LAWS

Under Old Rape Laws and the Common Law

- Only females could be the victims of rape.

- Only a male could directly commit the crime.

- A husband could not rape his wife. (Under the common law, however, the husband could be charged with assault and battery.)

- Rape was defined in one degree (or at most a few degrees).

- Rape was defined only as the insertion of the penis into a vagina by force and against the will of the female.

- Common law rape did not include the crime of offensive touching (however, this could be charged either as disorderly conduct or assault and sometimes battery).

- "Utmost resistance" and resistance were required under the old common law.

- Rape was classified as a crime against sexual morality.

Statutory Changes Enacted in Most States Since the 1970s

- Any person (male or female) may be a victim.

- Any person (male or female) can directly commit the crime. See the 1986 case of *State v. Stevens,* 510 A.2d 1070 (Me.), in which the court held that an adult woman could be charged with having sexual intercourse with a 13-year-old boy.

- A husband can be charged with the rape of his wife under the law of states that have made this change from the common law.

- A variety of degrees of criminal conduct are defined in more specific language. "Ordinary" rape, which is often second-degree rape, is the most common criminal charge, while "aggravated" rape, such as gang rape or rape with use of a deadly weapon, or rape resulting in physical injury or pregnancy, is usually first-degree sexual assault.

- Sexual intercourse is broadly defined not only as vaginal intercourse but also as "cunnilingus, fellatio, anal intercourse, or any other intrusion, however slight, of any part of a person's body or of any object into the genital or anal opening of another, but emission of semen is not required." See Section 940.225(5)(c) of the Wisconsin Criminal Code.

- Many modern sexual assault laws include the offense of offensive touching in that they forbid "sexual contact" (intentional touching of an intimate part of another person's body without consent for sexual gratification). (See, e.g., Neb. Rev. Stat. § 28-319.)

- "Utmost resistance" is no longer required for the crime of rape. Instead, many states require proof that the sex act was done "without consent" and "against the will" of the victim. Wisconsin, for example, eliminated the requirement of utmost resistance in the 1970s.

- Sexual assault is more often classified as a crime against a person.

is admissible. However, in *People v. Weiss,*[15] the Colorado Supreme Court held that the defendant must "by a preponderance of the evidence" show the past rape reports were "in fact" false. It reversed the decision of a trial court that permitted a defendant to introduce evidence of previous rape reports by the victim, holding that just because no charges were filed based on the reports did not make them "in fact" false under the rape shield exception.

Exceptions vary from state to state, and the rape shield law of each state must be consulted to determine the exact nature of the exceptions.

Statutory Rape

statutory rape Sexual intercourse with a minor under a certain age, usually 16–18. Consent and, generally, mistake as to age are not defenses to this crime.

All states have statutes that make sexual intercourse with a person who is not the spouse of the perpetrator a criminal offense if the person is under the age stated by the state criminal code. This crime is called **statutory rape**.

OTHER TYPES OF RAPES OR SEXUAL ASSAULTS

Type of Rape	Characteristics	Most Common Defense Used
Rape in which the victim was mentally defective or diseased and incapable of giving consent	This type of criminal statute seeks to protect people who are mentally incompetent and incapable of giving consent to sexual acts. The offense usually requires that the state show that the defendant knew or had reason to know of the mental incapacity of the victim. See, e.g., *Comm. v. Fuller,* 845 N.E.2d 434 (Mass. App. 2006), *cert, denied* 848 N.E.2d 1211 (2006).	Defendant denies that he knew of the mental incapacity of the victim or that any sex act occurred.
Rape by use of a date rape drug	Rohypnol ("roofies") and GHB are odorless, nearly tasteless, and potentially lethal to a victim. They are slipped into a drink to drug and sexually assault women.	The woman has no memory of what happened, and most often there are no other witnesses. With no witnesses, it is important to obtain a urine sample immediately to prove the presence of a date rape drug.
Sexual intercourse obtained by threats other than threats of violence, which would be forcible rape	In the few states that have enacted a statute such as this, the threat might be to disclose information that the victim did not want disclosed, or it could be a job-related threat that the victim would be fired or lose a promotion if she refused to have sex. Employment and sexual harassment laws also provide civil remedies for such acts.	No threat was made or implied, or no sexual act occurred.

The origin of current U.S. statutes goes back to the English statute of 1275, when the age of consent was set at 12 years. In 1576, the age was reduced to 10 years. California, for example, enacted its first statute in 1850 making the age 10. In 1913, it was fixed at 18, where it remains.

Honest mistake as to the age of the minor is not permitted as a defense in virtually all states that forbid statutory rape. See, for example, the case of *State v. Jadowski,*[16] where the court held that even if the child intentionally misled the defendant about her age, it is no defense to a charge of statutory rape. Nor is consent by the child a defense, even if investigation shows that the child was a willing participant in the sex acts.

There are a few exceptions to the honest mistake rule. Some decisions by courts in California have said that in some circumstances a good-faith belief in the age of the child is a defense to statutory rape, but it is questionable if that is still the law.[17] Tennessee has a "criminal intent" statute that appears to require proof of intent in statutory rape. As a result, it has been held that failure to permit a jury to consider a mistake-of-age defense is reversible error.[18] Finally, at least one state, Washington, has a statute that allows a good-faith mistake in the age of a child as a defense, but only if (1) the defendant's belief was based on "declarations as to age by the alleged victim" and (2) the defendant proves the defense by a preponderance of the evidence.[19]

The Crime of Incest

incest Sexual relations between persons closely related.

The crime of **incest** may be committed by adults within a family, but the public concern and prosecution are generally for cases involving children. Like statutory rape, the crime does not require a showing that force was used (or threatened) or that the victim did not consent.

Incest was not a crime under common law, nor was it made a statutory crime in England until 1908. Before that time, the offense was dealt with by ecclesiastical (religious) courts. Today, all the states have statutes making the offense a crime. Generally, incest in the first degree involves sexual intercourse. Incest in the second degree involves sexual contact without penetration. Under most state statutes, incest is limited to sexual relations with a descendant, ancestor, brother, or sister of the offender. The category of "descendant" usually includes adopted children or stepchildren.

Most experts believe that an estimated 60,000 to 100,000 female children are sexually abused annually and that 80 percent of sexual abuse is not reported. It is believed that incest affects more than 10 percent of all American families, with at least 5,000 cases of father-daughter incest.

Penalties for incest range from 90 days to life imprisonment. Enforcement, however, is practically impossible unless a member of the family cooperates. Unfortunately, the credibility of the child victim is often attacked and severely questioned.

In 90 percent of cases, the victim is female, and the abuse may commence while the child is too young to realize the significance of the problem. When the child becomes knowledgeable about what has happened, or is happening, the child is apt to feel guilt, betrayal, confusion, and fright.

As stated above, incest is similar to statutory rape in that consent is not a defense, nor is use of force required for conviction. Unlike statutory rape laws, however, in most states the incest statute requires proof that the defendant knew the person was related to the defendant in the statutorily proscribed manner. Thus, a reasonable belief that the other person is not related to the defendant would be a defense to a charge of incest. This belief must relate to the absence of a biological relationship between the defendant and the other person.

In *State v. Hall*,[20] 48 P.3d 350 (Wash. App. 2002), the court affirmed a conviction for second-degree incest of the defendant with his biological daughter. The court rejected the defendant's argument that because he had surrendered his parental rights when the girl was 4 years old, he did not believe she was his daughter, and thus he lacked the knowledge required by the incest statute. The court said all the statute required was knowledge that the girl was his biological daughter, because that fact made her the defendant's descendant.

HIV and AIDS-Related Crimes

HIV is the virus that causes acquired immune deficiency syndrome (AIDS). When AIDS first became known to the medical establishment in the 1970s, there were few medications or treatments for AIDS patients, and in most cases death occurred within a few months of diagnosis of the disease. During the AIDS epidemics of the 1980s and 1990s, widespread fear of the spread of this disease led many states to enact criminal laws specific to the spread of the disease.

However, in the past 10 to 15 years, knowledge and treatment of AIDS and HIV have improved substantially, and the fear of infection has subsided somewhat. Notwithstanding those medical changes, the criminal laws adopted by more than thirty states remain on the books and continue to be enforced.

In virtually all states, knowingly, recklessly, or (in some) negligently exposing a person to or infecting a person with the AIDS virus is a felony. This is often charged under a specific AIDS or HIV statute; an example is the Missouri statute, V.A.M.S. 191.677. In the 2012 case of *State v. Sykes*,[21] an HIV-positive defendant was convicted under the Missouri statute of knowingly exposing his girlfriend to the HIV virus without telling her he was HIV-positive. The defendant had previously been convicted of the same offense, but did not tell his girlfriend about that conviction. The girlfriend became HIV-positive. The defendant was sentenced to life in prison as a repeat offender, and the appeals court affirmed his conviction and sentence.

The U.S. Center for Disease Control and Prevention states in its publication "*Basic Information About HIV and AIDS*" that HIV is primarily spread through sexual contact or the exchange of blood. That publication states that the virus cannot be transmitted through tears, sweat, or saliva. It also states that as of the publication date of March 2010, "There has been no documented case of HIV being transmitted by spitting." Severe bites can transmit the virus, but only if the bites involve severe trauma and include the presence of blood. The publication states that HIV cannot be spread if the skin is not broken. In the 2012 case of *State v. Ingram*[22] the court of appeals reversed a conviction for criminal exposure to HIV based on the defendant's spitting in the face of a police officer. The court said the state failed to prove spitting created a significant risk of HIV infection, which is a required element of the offense.

Laws That Require Registration for Sex Offenders (Megan's Law)

In the case *McKune v. Lite,* the U.S. Supreme Court stated,

> Sex offenders are a serious threat in this nation. . . . Between 1980 and 1994 the population of imprisoned sex offenders increased at a faster rate than for any other category of violent crime. . . . Victims of sexual assault are most often juveniles . . . nearly four in ten violent sex offenders said their victims were 12 or younger. [When released from prison] sex offenders are more likely than any other type of offender to be rearrested for a new rape or sexual assault.[23]

Megan's laws Laws passed in many states requiring convicted sex offenders to register with a state or local registration office. Named after a young girl killed by a convicted sex offender.

In response to these grim statistics, in the 1990s states began passing registration laws for sexual offenders. These laws, called **Megan's laws** after the name of a child killed by a sexual offender in 1994, require sex offenders to register their name and address when released from prison. In 2006 Congress passed the federal Sex Offender Registration and Notification Act (SORNA), 42 U.S.C. § 16913; additionally, 18 U.S.C. § 2250 authorizes up to a 10-year prison sentence for failure to register.

State laws usually list offenses for which registration is mandatory and those for which registration is within the discretion of a sentencing judge. Such laws commonly include some or all of the following features:

- Sex offenders are prohibited from living in a residence located within a specified distance from schools, day-care facilities, or other places where children gather; zoning or other local laws might have a similar restriction.
- Sex offenders are required to personally notify authorities when they change their place of employment or change their address. Failure to give this notification is a crime.
- Sex offenders are required to provide a DNA sample to authorities to be placed in a state and national DNA database.
- A website is to be accessible to the public that includes current information about sex offenders registered in the system. In 2006 Congress created the National Sex Offender Registry, 42 U.S.C. § 16919. This law requires the FBI to maintain a national registry available to law enforcement and the public that contains the names and addresses of all persons required to register in any state's sex offender registration system.

At least one state, Utah, includes in the sex offender registration requirements that a sex offender must list all "Internet identifiers" used by the offender in any "Internet communication," such as a chat room. Utah Code § 77-27-21.5(14)(i)(j). In the 2010 case of *Doe v. Shurtleff,*[24] a federal court upheld this part of the Utah sex offender registration law against a claim it violated the First Amendment, noting that information placed in the registry could only be used in investigation of sex offenses.

In hearings on the National Sex Offender Registry Act, the House Judiciary Committee of the U.S. Congress reported that there were 500,000 convicted sex offenders in the United States but that 100,000 of these offenders were not currently registered or were missing and could not be located.[25] Some prosecutors have stated that state registration laws have caused an increase in the number of sex offenders who disappear, leaving no information about their whereabouts. This creates an increased burden for law enforcement agencies, which must under state and federal laws track down released sex offenders and obtain the required information.

Civil Commitment of Sexually Dangerous Offenders

For many years states have had in place laws that permit the state to bring civil commitment proceedings for the involuntary, temporary commitment of persons who pose a threat to themselves or others. For example, a man who attempted suicide could be temporarily held for mental observation based on the demonstrated danger to his own life. If long-term civil commitment were needed, these laws required a court hearing to determine the need and justification for such commitment.

As an additional response to the threat posed by sexual predators, in the 1990s some states enacted sexual predator laws. These laws permitted the state to obtain civil commitment of convicted sexual offenders after the offenders were released from prison.[26] In *Kansas v. Crane,*[27] the U.S. Supreme Court held that before a state may commit a sex offender under a civil commitment statute, it must prove that not only was the offender dangerous and likely to commit more sex crimes but also that the offender had "serious difficulty in controlling [his] behavior." The Court noted that pedophilia was a mental abnormality that made it difficult for an offender to control his behavior and would thus properly be a basis for civil commitment.

In 2006 Congress passed 18 U.S.C. § 4248, which authorizes civil commitment of sexually dangerous federal prisoners following the expiration of their prison sentence. That section was upheld by the U.S. Supreme Court in the 2010 case of *United States v. Comstock,* 130 S. Ct. 1949.

It is estimated that about 2,700 pedophiles, rapists, and other sexual offenders are being held indefinitely under sexual predator laws enacted in twenty states. Because the goal of civil commitment is to furnish treatment to the sex offender, rather than punish the offender for criminal conduct, it is generally held that these civil commitments do not violate the Double Jeopardy Clause or Ex Post Facto Clause of the U.S. Constitution.[28]

Once committed under these programs, many sex offenders are never released. In a study of these programs published in the *New York Times,*[29] it was reported that virtually all those committed were men; only three women have been committed to date. The costs of commitment under these programs averaged more than four times the cost of keeping an inmate in prison. Ages of those committed varied greatly; under Wisconsin's sexual predator law, the youngest of the 283 persons committed was 18, and the oldest 102.

Critics of the need for civil commitment of sexual offenders have offered statistical support for their criticism. They note that only about 5.3 percent of sexual offenders commit sexual offenses within three years after release from prison. As of August 2012, the federal government has sought certification of sexually dangerous prisoners in only 136 cases, and 61 of them have been dropped. Only fifteen prisoners have been certified. Graydon Comstock, the prisoner involved in the Supreme Court case discussed above, was determined not to be sexually dangerous, and was released in 2011.[30]

Prostitution

prostitution Providing sex for money or other value.

The crime of **prostitution** can be one of at least three non-marital acts:

1. Engaging in sexual relations with another person for a fee or something of value
2. Offering (or soliciting) to engage in sexual relations with another person for a fee or something of value
3. Requesting (or agreeing) to pay a fee or something of value to another person for sexual services and acts

The fee or something of value is most often money. Members of either sex may now be convicted of prostitution, as distinguished from in the past, when only women could be convicted. Most (if not all) state prostitution statutes forbid males from selling sexual services to other males. Males who offer to pay a woman to engage in sex acts may also be charged with the crime.

Prostitution is often referred to as the world's oldest profession and is described in history's earliest written records. The Bible, for instance, makes many references to whores and whoremongering. Prostitution is an activity that grows and recedes, depending on the changing mores and morals of a particular civilization. Many believe that, like the poor, it will always be with us.

Throughout the world, efforts have been made to suppress, control, organize, or discourage prostitution, with varying degrees of success. Prostitutes range from the common streetwalker to the privately kept woman or man. In the United Kingdom and France, prostitution is legal, but publicly soliciting customers is against the law. In some countries, particularly in Asia, government-inspected houses of prostitution are allowed.

Efforts to decriminalize prostitution in the United States have met with little success. Only one state (Nevada) has legalized prostitution. In Nevada, each county has the option to legalize prostitution. Fifteen of Nevada's seventeen counties have decided to remove the legal restraints against prostitution.

The Crimes of Procuring, Promoting, and Pimping for the Practice of Prostitution

Many prostitutes operate without pimps or other people procuring or promoting for them. Some prostitutes, however, have pimps, who procure customers and provide protection and bail as needed. In addition to pimps, other people obtain money by procuring and promoting prostitution.

JUVENILES WHO COMMIT SEX OFFENSES AGAINST CHILDREN

A 2009 Department of Justice Juvenile Bulletin reported statistics from recent studies of sex offenses generally and sex offenses targeting children. Children, boys and girls, are the victims of nearly 70 percent of all sex crimes committed each year. Older children commit more than 25.8 percent of all reported sex offenses, and 35.6 percent of sex offenses against children. The report also stated:

- The criminal incidents in the study were rape (26.4 percent), sodomy (11.9 percent), sex assault with object (4.2 percent), fondling (47.2 percent), and non-forcible sex offenses (10.5 percent).
- 88 percent of the offenders were between the ages of 12 and 18.
- The offenses occurred mostly in a home/residence (68.1 percent); 12.1 percent occurred at a school.
- Of the victims, 64.5 percent were acquainted with the offender; 23.8 percent were family members.
- The juvenile offenders differed from the adult offenders in that (1) they were more likely to offend in groups, 24 percent versus 14 percent; (2) more likely to have male victims, 25 percent versus 19 percent; and (3) more likely to target younger children as victims, 59 percent versus 39 percent.
- Most juvenile offenders were male; only 7 percent of juvenile offenders were female.
- Juvenile offenders commit more than one in four of all sex offenses, and more than one in three of sex offenses against children.

procuring, promoting, and pimping Actions taken to provide services of a prostitute

Procuring, promoting, and pimping for prostitution are forbidden by state criminal codes. However, because of the potential financial gains, these people have a motive to encourage and coerce young people into prostitution. They increase the volume and extent to which prostitution is practiced and often gain a vicious hold over the prostitutes who work for them.

Most state procurement statutes apply to persons who "promote" prostitution, that is, engage in acts designed to aid unlawful sexual acts between prostitutes and third parties. As a result, some courts have held these laws do not apply to "consumers" of prostitution. In the 2010 case of *State v. Varga-Torres*[31] the court reversed a conviction under the Oregon "compelling prostitution" statute, which makes it a crime to "induce or cause a person under 18 years of age to engage in prostitution." The defendant gave car rides, cigarettes, and alcohol to a young girl in exchange for sex. The court said that since none of these "payments" were intended to induce the girl to have sex with others, the statute did not apply.

The federal government has a statute similar to state procuring laws, called the "2000 Trafficking Victim Protection Act." It prohibits sex trafficking in interstate commerce, including enticing minors to engage in commercial sex acts. It applies to any person who "entices . . . or obtains . . . any person" under the age of 18 who is caused to engage in a "commercial sex act." While the law is aimed at commercial sex ventures, those people who would be called "procurers" in similar state laws, the federal statute has a broader scope. In a 2013 case the law was held to apply to "consumers" as well as "providers" of child prostitution. In *United States v. Jungers*[32] the court held that a defendant who tried to "buy" time with a child for sexual acts in an FBI sting operation could be convicted under the trafficking act.

Crimes That Require Proof That the Crime Was Committed in a Public Place

Private sex acts between consenting adults are rarely charged as crimes, even if they violate specific sections of criminal codes. In the case of *Lawrence v. Texas,* 539 U.S. 558, the U.S. Supreme Court struck down a Texas statute that made it a crime for two male adults to have prohibited sex acts in the privacy of their home.

OLD OFFENSES THAT ARE NO LONGER CRIMES OR ARE SELDOM CHARGED

Offense	Definition	History
Bigamy (or polygamy)	Marriage to two or more spouses at the same time.	Statutorized in 1604 (prior to that time, it was an ecclesiastical crime in England). In recent years, it has seldom been prosecuted in the United States.[a]
Adultery[b]	Voluntary sexual intercourse in which one or both parties are married to another person (parties not married to each other). About half the states continue to make adultery a crime, but these old laws are rarely enforced.	Goes back in history to old Roman law. A Wisconsin woman admitted in a contested divorce hearing in 1990 that she had an affair; she received national attention when she was charged with the felony crime of adultery, which carried a possible two-year prison sentence as punishment. Charges were later dropped.
Homosexuality	Sexual relations between persons of the same sex.	For many years, this was a crime in all states. In *Lawrence v. Texas*, 123 S. Ct. 2472 (2003), the U.S. Supreme Court held a Texas sodomy statute unconstitutional because individuals have a right to engage in private consensual sexual conduct without government intervention.
Fornication	Voluntary sexual intercourse between two unmarried people.	Formerly a crime in all states. Most states have removed this offense from their criminal codes.
Seduction	Enticement by a male of an unmarried woman of prior chaste character to have sexual intercourse.	Was a crime in early English law and in many states.

Public sex acts, however, can be charged as criminal conduct. The statute defining the crime often requires proof that the crime was committed in a public place, as well as some intent to obtain sexual gratification. For example, in the 2010 case of *People v. Honen*[33] a California Court of Appeals distinguished the elements of the crimes of indecent exposure and lewd conduct under California statutes. While both crimes require proof that they were committed in "public view," "lewd conduct," such as sexual intercourse in public, has no requirement that the acts be done with the intent to have the public see them. Indecent exposure, the court said, requires proof that the person's private parts were exposed for sexual gratification with the intent they would be seen by the public.

Offense	Definition	History
Miscegenation	Intermarriage (and in some states living together) of people of different races (generally white and black).	Was a crime in some of the states. Such statutes were declared unconstitutional by the U.S. Supreme Court. See the case of *Loving v. Virginia* in Chapter 1.
Buggery (or sodomy)	Any type of sexual intercourse with an animal.	A statutory offense in England until 1967.
Abortion	Causing the expulsion of a human fetus prematurely.	Previously a crime in all states. States may not now make abortion a crime until the third trimester of pregnancy. Some states no longer have a crime of abortion.
Blasphemy, profanity, and indecent language	Cursing or reviling God; unbecoming, indecent, impious language.	Can no longer punish for language violations unless the language falls within one of the crimes listed in Chapter 9.
Crimes against transgender people	The term *transgender* covers cross-dressers, homosexual drag queens, and persons who believe they are both male and female.	An assortment of criminal laws were used in past years against transgendered persons (persons who either believe they were born in the wrong body or are intersexed).

[a] Utah banned polygamy as a required precondition to becoming a state in 1890, but over the years the practice of polygamy in Utah has failed to completely disappear. An estimated 37,000 fundamentalist Mormons still practice polygamy.
[b] Adultery remains a crime in the U.S. armed forces, Art. 134 U.C.M.J. Dismissal from the service is often the punishment. In *U.S. v. Orellana*, 62 MJ. 595 (N.M. Ct. Crim. App. 2005), *review denied*, 63 M.J. 295 (2006), a Marine corporal was convicted of adultery for having consensual sex with a woman while married to another woman. The court rejected the defendant's argument that *Lawrence v. Texas* (cited above) rendered Art. 134 of the U.C.M.J. unconstitutional.

PROSTITUTION (MALE AND FEMALE)

Type of Operation	Type of Complaint Received by Law Enforcement Agencies
Streetwalkers (and prostitutes who operate out of taverns and bars)	This is the form of prostitution most visible to the public. It is also the most dangerous for women because they are exposed to violence and robbery by strangers and to arrest by police. Female and male police decoys have been very effective in apprehending "johns" soliciting sex from males or females.
Public toilets and parks	When complaints of loitering for prostitution are received, police sometimes set up sting operations. In 2007 police did so at the Minneapolis/St. Paul Airport. During a three-month period, forty men including a U.S. senator were arrested and charged with crimes. The senator pled guilty to disorderly conduct and interference with privacy, gross misdemeanors. Others pled guilty or were convicted of loitering or indecent exposure.
Call girls (or boys) and other organized prostitution services	This could involve the crime of pandering through pimps, bartenders, cab drivers, and others who refer customers to call girls. A 1988 *FBI Enforcement Bulletin* noted that the crimes of theft, robbery, assault, battery, and illegal drug transactions are frequent products of organized criminal prostitution.
Online, Internet, escort services, and massage parlors	Online prostitutes say the Internet is a natural medium for selling sex because it is anonymous and connects with many potential customers. The Cook County (Chicago) sheriff filed a civil lawsuit against Craigslist in 2009, charging that the popular online ad site promoted and facilitated prostitution on a huge basis. Many law enforcement agencies are using Craigslist in sting operations, where they often make more arrests than in street prostitution. One online escort business, Emperor's Club V.I.P., charged up to $4,300 per hour for its prostitution services. Eliot Spitzer, the governor of New York, resigned from office after it was disclosed he used prostitutes from that service. See "4 Arrests, then 6 Tumultuous Days That Ended in a Governor's Resignation," *New York Times,* 3/13/08.
"Sex-for-drugs" prostitution	Public health officials are very concerned about the spread of disease linked to sex-for-drugs prostitution.
Brothels and houses of prostitution	State laws forbid houses of prostitution. In the case of *State v. Mueller,* 671 P.2d 1351 (1983), one woman was selling sex in her apartment with no street or public solicitation and only consenting adults involved. She argued that she had a right of privacy in her home to do as she wished. The Supreme Court of Hawaii affirmed her conviction, holding she had no right to practice prostitution.
Combining prostitution with con games, robbery, extortion, theft of money, credit cards, and so on	*FBI Law Enforcement Bulletin* article, "Knock-Out Dates: Flirting with Danger," January 1993, describes women who pick up men in hotels, restaurants, and bars to rob them or steal from them after placing a drug in their drink to incapacitate them. For an example, see the case of *U.S. v. Pasucci,* 943 F.2d 1032 (9th Cir. 1991), where a businessman was caught by an extortion ring.

A young woman, perhaps only a teenager, engages in the dangerous business of street prostitution.

"BECAUSE PROSTITUTION FUELS THE ILLEGAL DRUGS TRADE, CITIES USE ONE OR MORE OF THE FOLLOWING TO DISCOURAGE THE CRIME"

- Increased fines and jail sentences for prostitutes and johns.
- Cracking down on johns to discourage this activity.
- Increased use of the "loitering to solicit prostitution" ordinance or statute.
- Filing a civil lawsuit against people with five or more prostitution or loitering for prostitution arrests, as was done in San Diego and Milwaukee. The civil court would then declare loitering by such people in certain areas of the city to be a public nuisance and also forbid them from flagging down cars and loitering at bus stops throughout the city. Violations would lead to a civil forfeiture of up to $2,000 or jailing if the forfeiture was not paid. One of the defendants in Milwaukee had 18 arrests for prostitution and 124 arrests for loitering for prostitution. Police in San Diego reported that the lawsuit virtually eliminated street prostitution in specific areas of San Diego.
- Confiscation of the johns' cars under forfeiture statutes.
- City placing newspaper ads listing names of prostitutes and johns (a few cities also place pictures of the johns in the ads).
- Compulsory AIDS tests for convicted prostitutes and johns (a California statute mandating the testing for AIDS of people convicted of prostitution was upheld in the 1990 case of *Love v. Superior Court*, 226 Cal. App. 3d 736, 276 Cal. Rptr.).

A court officer in charge of a female prisoner had sex with the prisoner in a holding cell in the basement of a courthouse. A closed-circuit camera covered the courthouse, including the holding cell. The court held the sex occurred in a public place. See *Com. v. Merrill*, 864 N.E.2d 1235 (Mass. App. 2007).

Touching or Other Conduct Done to Arouse Sexual Desire

Touching a private part of another person's body could be (1) accidental, (2) consented to by the other person (children are not capable of consenting to sexual touching), or (3) necessary in the care of the person or for medical reasons. Touching could be in a friendly, joking, or loving manner, or the contact could be to discipline a child (spanking) or in a hostile or angry manner.

Most states have degrees of "sexual assaults," with the most serious involving sexual penetration. Sexual contact without penetration ("sexual touching") generally requires the state to show that the touching was done on "sexual or intimate

REGULATION OF NUDITY BY STATES OR MUNICIPALITIES

Nudity by itself is not obscene, lewd, or indecent but may be regulated by specific statutes and ordinances as follows:

Place of Nudity	Manner in Which Nudity May Be Regulated
Public nudity (public beach or public place, such as street)	May be forbidden or regulated by a specific statute or ordinance.
Nude entertainment or nudity in a place licensed to serve alcoholic beverages	May be forbidden or regulated under the authority given to states by the Twenty-First Amendment to the U.S. Constitution to regulate the sale and use of alcohol. The U.S. Supreme Court stated that "the broad sweep of the 21st Amendment has been recognized as conferring something more than the normal state authority over public health, welfare, and morals"; see *California v. LaRue,* 409 U.S. 109, 93 S. Ct. 390 (1972).
Nudity in a private place (a nudist camp, for example), a stage play, or a movie (the musical *Hair,* the play *Oh! Calcutta!,* and the opera *Salome* have nude performers)	May not be regulated unless the conduct or display is obscene. Nudity, by itself, is not obscene, lewd, or indecent.
Nudity used for sexual gratification	For example, see the case of *People v. Garrison,* 82 Ill. 2d 444, 45 Ill. Dec. 132, 412 N.E.2d 483 (1980), in which the defendant stood behind a storm door in his home exposing his penis to a woman standing outside. The Supreme Court of Illinois held that this was not private conduct and that the defendant had no right of privacy. If a jury found that the defendant exposed his body "with intent to arouse or to satisfy (his) sexual desire," the defendant could be found guilty of the Illinois public indecency statute.

parts," and for the purpose of sexual gratification. Lewd and lascivious conduct or behavior with a child statutes often require showing that the defendant "had the specific intent to arouse or gratify either child's sexual desires or his own."[34]

Following are examples of crimes that require showing that the conduct was intended to arouse sexual desire:

- The California lewd and lascivious acts with a child statute requires that the touching be done "with the specific intent to arouse, appeal to, or gratify the sexual desire of either party"; see *People v. Carson,* 890 P.2d 1115 (1995). The California Supreme Court also held that lewd touching can occur through the victim's clothing and does not require contact with the bare skin or with "private parts" of the defendant or victim. See *People v. Martinez,* 1995 WL 641969 (1995).
- Most state statutes include the buttocks as an intimate part of a person's body. To be a sexual battery or disorderly conduct or another sex crime, it must be shown that the touching was intentional, was without consent, and was for purposes of sexual gratification. See, for example, *State v. Osborne,* 808 P.2d 624 (N. Mex. 1991).
- The defendant offered a teenage boy a ride, made sexually suggestive inquiries of the boy, and then pressed his entire hand on the inner thigh of the boy in a manner suggestive of an intimate massage. The Massachusetts Court of Appeals affirmed the conviction of the defendant for indecent assault and battery. See *Commonwealth v. Lavigne,* 676 N.E.2d 1170 (1997).

Protecting Children Against Sexual Exploitation: Child Pornography

The U.S. Supreme Court has repeatedly held that states have a compelling interest in "safeguarding the physical and psychological well-being of a minor" and that "the use of children as subjects of pornographic materials is harmful to the physiological, emotional, and mental health of the child."[35]

Because of these reasons, **child pornography** is treated differently from adult **pornography**. Adult pornography is sold openly in many communities throughout the United States, but child pornography is outlawed by the federal government and most states.

The child pornography laws of the majority of states and the federal government do not require obscenity as an element of the crime.[36] If an actual child or children are depicted in a photograph or video as engaged in sexually explicit conduct, possession of such material is a crime under the federal pornography law and the laws of most states, even if the photograph or video would not meet the obscenity test applicable to adult pornography. In this sense, child pornography laws are viewed as outside the usual protection for "content-based" laws given by the First Amendment.

Five categories of conduct and attempted conduct are made crimes under the federal law and the laws of most states. The crime of child pornography broadly includes the following:[37]

child pornography Movies, pictures, or drawings that depict children in explicit sexual relations. Unlike adult pornography, child pornography need not be obscene to be criminal.

pornography Movies, pictures, writings, and other expressions that are intended to arouse sexual incitement and have no artistic merit or redeeming social value.

- Production of child pornography (for example, filming a child or children engaged in sexually explicit conduct)
- Advertising child pornography
- Possession of material, knowing that it depicts minors in sexually explicit conduct
- Trafficking in child pornography (importation, distribution, sale, loan, gift, exchange, receipt, or transportation of material, knowing that it depicts minors engaged in sexually explicit conduct)
- Procurement of child pornography (buying, selling, or transporting child pornography or inducing, coercing, or kidnapping a minor for the purposes of producing child pornography)

Child pornography includes depictions in magazines, books, motion pictures, and videos, and by other means. Most state statutes forbid live performances, and some specifically forbid the use of computers. The federal government and some

FIGHTING THE INTERNATIONAL CHILD SEX TRADE

Representatives of 134 countries met in Yokohama, Japan, in December 2001 to fight the fast-growing world sex trade in children. The first international meeting was held in Stockholm in 1996. UNICEF estimates that every year 1 million children (girls and boys) are forced into the sex trade.

Most of these children are from poor countries or are poor illegal immigrants living in industrial countries. Using the Internet and cell phones, pedophiles can reach the children online. The governments of the 134 countries pledged increased efforts to stamp out the thriving sex trade by tougher laws and by coordinating police efforts against the child sex trade.

In the United States, in 2003 Congress passed as part of the PROTECT Act (discussed in this chapter) 18 U.S.C. §§ 1591 and 2423, which are directed at international "sex trafficking" and "sex tourism." Section 1591 is aimed at "trafficking" and makes any person guilty of the crime that entices or transports a child under 18 in interstate or foreign commerce knowing the child will be forced to engage in a commercial sex act. In *United States v. Chang Da Liu*, 538 F.3d 1078 (9th Cir. 2008) the federal government used this statute to shut down a "teahouse" operated by the defendants in the Northern Mariana Islands, a territory within the jurisdiction of the federal government by virtue of an agreement between the United States and the Islands. The defendants lured Chinese girls to the Islands, promising them work as waitresses, and charging each one $6,000 in "broker fees." When the girls arrived, they were forced to engage in commercial sex. The Ninth Circuit upheld their conviction.

Section 2423 identifies three so-called sex-tourism crimes. Subsection (a) applies to a person who knowingly "transports" a child under 18 across state of international borders for the purpose of engaging in "illicit sexual conduct," which means sex with a child under 18 that would be illegal under federal law, or any commercial sexual act states forbid visual depictions or advertisements of child pornography "by any means including by computers."

Schools and libraries using federal funds are obligated to use computer filters to block pornographic material available on the Internet. Such filters are also available for parents to use on computers used by children. Child pornography from many countries, including the United States, Russia, and others, is available on websites and can be accessed from anywhere in the world. The National Center for Missing and Exploited Children estimates that the number of child pornography websites increased by 400 percent between 2001 and 2005.

Prosecutions for child pornography have also increased dramatically because of Internet sites. In a February 2013 report to Congress the U.S. Sentencing Commission said that in the year 2000 there were 700 federal child pornography prosecutions; in 2010 there were over 2,000. The Commission report also noted that the average sentences for convictions—5 years for possession and 11 years for

with a child under 18. Subsection (b) applies to persons who travel in interstate or foreign commerce with the purpose of engaging in illicit sexual conduct with a child under 18. Subsection (c) applies to any U.S. citizen who travels interstate or to a foreign country and engages in illicit sexual conduct with a child under 18. Subsections (a) and (b) are similar to prior law and require only that the defendant have the purpose of engaging in illicit sexual conduct. It is not a defense to prosecutions under either section that the individual the defendant intended to have illicit sex with was not under 18; it is enough the defendant believed that was the case. *United States v. Spurlock*, 495 F.3d 1011 (8th Cir. 2007), *cert. denied*, 552 U.S. 1054 (2007).

Section 2423(c) represents a change from former law and is expressly directed at "sex tourists." Under subsection (c), the government need not prove the defendant traveled to a foreign country for the purpose of having illicit sex. Thus, in the 2010 case of *United States v. Pendleton*, 658 F.3d 299 (3rd Cir. 2011), the defendant was convicted under § 2423(c) when he traveled to Germany from the United States, and while in Germany he was arrested for having sex with a 14-year-old boy. When the defendant finished a 2-year prison sentence in Germany, he was deported to the United States in January 2008; in March 2008 he was arrested and charged under § 2423(c) and was convicted.

The section also has what is called an "extraterritorial" effect on U.S. citizens. In *United States v. Clark*, 435 F.3d 1100 (9th Cir. 2006), a retired U.S. military member who resided in Cambodia but traveled between the United States and Cambodia was charged under § 2423(c) when he was arrested by Cambodian police for having sex with two 14-year-old boys and extradited to the United States. The court held that under the statute, all the government needed to prove was the illicit sexual conduct and the citizenship of the defendant.

More than two dozen states have passed criminal laws aimed at local brothels and sweatshops that bring people into the country, including children, and force them to work as sex slaves or in sweatshops. Most federal legislation in this area is directed at organized trafficking rings.

distribution—had doubled during that same 10-year period. The Commission report expressed doubt about the fairness of sentences given in federal courts. It noted that in 2004, only a few child pornography sentences (16 percent) fell outside the sentencing guidelines. In 2010, over 50 percent of the sentences were outside the guidelines. The Commission believed this indicated federal judges were not satisfied with the weighted factors in the guidelines for sentencing child pornography defendants, mainly because the culpability of those defendants varied so greatly. The Commission advised Congress to amend the child pornography laws and sentences to take into account the traffic volume of a child pornography website, the images depicted, the ages of the child victims depicted, and how long the defendant has had a child pornography collection.

Federal legislation directed at use of the Internet to exploit children has met with attacks on the legislation's constitutionality. In response to the use of the Internet for dissemination of pornography and the effect of such pornography on children, Congress passed two significant pieces of legislation in 1996: the Communications Decency Act (CDA) of 1996 (47 U.S.C. § 223) and the 1996 Child Pornography Prevention Act (CPPA) (18 U.S.C. § 2256). The CDA prohibited any use of the Internet to post material that was "indecent" or "patently offensive" and made available to children. The CPPA prohibited Internet use to post any picture "that appears to be" of a minor engaged in sexually explicit conduct. Both laws were found to be unconstitutional by the U.S. Supreme Court:

- In *Reno v. American Civil Liberties Union,* 521 U.S. 844 (1997), the Court held that the CDA was unconstitutional because it failed to clearly identify what constituted "indecent" or "patently offensive" material and as a result prohibited speech that was protected under the First Amendment.
- In *Ashcroft v. Free Speech Coalition,* 122 S. Ct. 1389 (2002), the Supreme Court held that the CPPA was overbroad and unconstitutional. The Court concluded that the CPPA did not limit its prohibition to only obscene materials but included all depictions of sexual conduct between children, including depictions of "simulated sex" between children. It noted that the movie *Traffic,* which won an Academy Award, had depicted sexual conduct of a 16-year-old girl.

In response to these decisions, Congress passed legislation designed to eliminate the problems in the earlier legislation. The Child Online Protection Act (47 U.S.C. § 231 of 1998) (COPA) prohibits any commercial Internet communication that is "harmful to minors." *Harmful to minors* is defined in a manner that tracks the obscenity test of *Miller v. California* (discussed in Chapter 9), including the "community standards" test. In *ACLU v. Gonzales,* 478 F. Supp. 2d 775 (E.D. Pa. 2007), a federal judge held that the COPA statute was unconstitutional because it did not use the least restrictive means to achieve the desired result. The Third Circuit affirmed that decision in 2008 (534 F.3d 181), and the U.S. Supreme Court denied certiorari, 129 S. Ct. 1032 (2009).

In 2003 Congress passed the PROTECT Act, 18 U.S.C. § 2252A(a)(3), which included several specific crimes directed at children through the Internet. In *United States v. Williams,* 444 F.3d 1286 (11th Cir. 2006), a federal court of appeals held the "pandering" provision of the PROTECT Act unconstitutional because it was vague and overbroad and did not solve the problems presented

CASE CLOSE-UP

United States v. Williams
Supreme Court of the United States,
553 U.S. 285 (2008)

18 U.S.C. § 2252(A) of the 2003 PROTECT Act added a new pandering and solicitation section to the child exploitation provisions of that act. It makes it a crime for any person to knowingly advertise, promote, present, distribute, or solicit through the mails or the Internet any material in a manner "that reflects the belief, or that is intended to cause another to believe" that the material contains (a) an obscene visual depiction of a minor engaged in sexually explicit conduct, or (b) a visual depiction of an actual minor engaged in sexually explicit conduct. In other words, the Act made it a crime to "pander" *obscene* child sexual depictions, regardless of whether the child pictured was an actual child or a simulated child. It also made it a crime to "pander" *any* image of a child, actual or simulated, engaged in sexually explicit conduct if the person pandering the image believes it to be an actual image of a child, or intends another to have such a belief.

The legislative history of the Act made it clear Congress was concerned that the decision in *Ashcroft v. Free Speech Coalition*, which seemed to limit non-obscene child pornography prosecutions to material that involved only actual children, would make it impossible to prosecute many pornographers who would allege their "depictions" were made by "virtual" imaging. To address this concern, Congress did not in the Act attempt to prohibit the possession of "virtual" child pornography. Rather, it prohibited a person from "pandering" material he believed to be either *obscene* virtual child pornography (which can always be prohibited) or depictions of *actual* children engaged in sexually explicit conduct (which can be prohibited only if not overbroad). It was the pandering provision that was under review in this case.

The defendant Williams conducted an online conversation in an Internet chat room with a person calling herself "Lisa n Miami." Lisa was in fact a Secret Service Agent working undercover. Williams posted a message that said, "Dad of toddler has good pics of her" for swap of "your toddler pics, or live cam." The agent exchanged some non-pornographic pictures with Williams. After some discussion, in which Williams demanded proof in the form of additional pictures which the agent refused to furnish, Williams posted a message stating "I CAN PUT UP CUZ IM FOR REAL" that contained a hyperlink that when followed led to seven pictures of actual children engaging in explicit sexual conduct. The Secret Service then obtained a warrant, seized Williams's computer, and found at least twenty-two pornographic images of actual children. He was charged with possession of child pornography under § 2252A(a)(5)(B) and pandering under § 2252A(a)(3)(B). After conviction under both statutes, Williams appealed only the pandering conviction, alleging the statute was overbroad. The court of appeals agreed, and reversed his conviction under that section.

On review, the Supreme Court upheld the statute, and reversed the court of appeals. It said that the pandering section is directed at persons who are attempting to engage in an illegal transaction, and such conduct is not protected by the First Amendment:

> Offers to engage in illegal transactions are categorically excluded from First Amendment protection.... One would think that this principle resolves the present case, since the statute criminalizes only offers to provide or requests to obtain contraband—child obscenity and child pornography involving actual children, both of which are proscribed and the proscription of which is constitutional, see *Free Speech Coalition*, 553 U.S., at 245–246, 256. *Williams*, 553 U.S. 285, at 297.

(Continued)

CASE CLOSE-UP *(Continued)*

Since the conduct proscribed (distributing or soliciting material believed to be depictions of actual children) was not protected, the Supreme Court said the circuit court was wrong to hold the statute up to the "strict scrutiny" test. That test only applies if a statute attempts to regulate protected speech or conduct. The Supreme Court also stated that the statute does not, unlike the statute in *Ashcroft v. Free Speech Coalition*, impinge on legitimate depictions of child sexual conduct, such as

advertisements for mainstream Hollywood movies that depict underage characters having sex. The Court thought it "implausible" that either the producers or the distributors either "believed" the scenes depicted actual children having sex, or "intended to cause" others to believe that was the case. The Court stated that the "average person" knows sex scenes in movies use non-child actors or depict sex scenes in a way that does not rise to the explicit level covered by the statute. Id. at 301, 302.

by the earlier statutes. The U.S. Supreme Court granted review of this decision, 127 S. Ct. 1874 (2007). In *United States v. Williams,* the subject of the previous Case-Close Up, the Supreme Court upheld the child pornography provisions of the PROTECT Act.

Movies, Videos, and Photographs

X-rated videos are a multibillion-dollar business in the United States. European and Asian producers also have large sales throughout the world. Are producers of X-rated videos and films, who pay adults to perform sexual acts that are filmed for movies and videos, engaged in the business of prostitution? This issue was before the courts in the case of *California v. Freeman.*[38]

Freeman was convicted of pandering under the California Criminal Code for hiring adults to perform sex acts, which he filmed and sold. The Supreme Court of California reversed the conviction, holding that Freeman's conduct was not prohibited by the California prostitution and pandering laws. The court held that hiring actors to perform sexual acts to be filmed in a private place is not "procuring" prostitution, because the payment to the actors was not made for the purpose of sexual gratification, a necessary part of the definition of prostitution. The court also noted that the film made was not obscene, and thus the prosecution under the pandering statute amounted to an improper "end run" around the First Amendment.

Because a new law expanding the California pandering and prostitution statute has not been enacted, California has become the capital of the United States for the production of X-rated and pornographic films and videos.[39]

"Sexting," and Nude Photos of Children Taken by Family Members

Many family photo and video collections have pictures of young nude children. But when children are no longer babies and have begun to develop sexually, is photography of them by parents and stepparents sexual abuse? This question has been before a number of U.S. courts, with results similar to the following case.

The defendant took color photos of his physically mature 14-year-old stepdaughter, showing her fully exposed breasts. He was convicted in a jury trial and sentenced to 10 years in prison. The Massachusetts Supreme Judicial Court reversed the conviction, holding the statute to be overbroad. The U.S. Supreme Court vacated the Massachusetts Supreme Court ruling and remanded the case for further hearings. On remand, the Massachusetts Supreme Judicial Court upheld the defendant's conviction, holding that although his photographs were not obscene, the state had a legitimate interest in protecting minors from such practices and that interest was more compelling than the defendant's "restrictive speech" interest under the First Amendment.[40]

Convictions of other defendants in similar situations have been affirmed. In *Perry v. State*, 568 So. 2d 339 (Ala. Cr. App. 1990), the defendant photographed not only his 15-year-old daughter but also her 14-year-old friend. In *Brackins v. State*, 578 A.2d 300 (Md. App. 1990), the court affirmed defendant's conviction for child sexual abuse based on the semi-nude photographing of a 12-year-old stepdaughter.[41]

Nude home photos can also result in prosecution under the federal child pornography statutes, including the PROTECT Act. In a 2010 case the Sixth Circuit Court of Appeals upheld the conviction under 18 U.S.C. §§ 2251 and 2252 of a defendant charged with possession of child pornography based on home pictures. The defendant took nude photographs of his 10-year-old daughter and her friends. He did not distribute the photographs or show them to other people. Because the pictures showed actual children in sexually suggestive positions, the court said the pictures were child pornography and violated the statutes. The court also held that Congress had power to regulate the activity under the Commerce Clause because of the possibility that homemade child pornography would hinder the purpose Congress has in regulating national child pornography.[42]

In the July 2010 issue of the *FBI Law Enforcement Bulletin*, an article entitled "Sexting: Risky Actions and Overreactions" discusses the problems related to juveniles "sexting" naked or near-naked pictures of themselves to others. Sexting is defined as "sending or posting sexually suggestive messages and images, including nude or semi nude photographs, via cellular telephones or over the Internet." The article suggests that juveniles consider the consequences of sexting, and offers this advice:

> Before hitting send, remember that you cannot control where this image may travel;
>
> If you forward a sexual picture of someone underage, you are responsible for this image as the original sender.
>
> Think about the consequences of taking, sending, or forwarding a sexual image of yourself or someone else under age.

One of those consequences could include criminal charges. In the 2009 case of *State v. Canal*, 773 N.W.2d 528 (Iowa 2009), the Iowa Supreme Court upheld the conviction of an 18 year old man who sent a cell phone picture of his erect penis to a 14-year-old girl. He was convicted under a statute that made it a crime to send obscene material to a minor.

Voyeurism and Other Criminal Invasions of Privacy

Until recent years, Peeping Toms who trespassed or were not in a public place were often charged as a disorderly person (or with disorderly conduct). Many states now have voyeurism or invasion of privacy laws in their criminal codes. An example of such law is Ohio Criminal Code Section 2907.08(A), which reads:

> No person, for the purpose of sexually arousing or gratifying himself or herself, shall commit trespass or otherwise surreptitiously invade the privacy of another, to spy or eavesdrop upon another.

These laws have been toughened in many states by provisions forbidding video voyeurism or video stalking. The terms *upskirting* and *downblousing* describe offenses that are charged under invasion of privacy statutes. Examples of conduct charged under these laws are as follows:

- A California man videotaped three different women at three different times as he had sex with them. The women did not know and did not consent to the filming. Police learned of the tapes when the man showed the videos to friends. He was convicted under California's invasion of privacy law, which forbids filming or recording confidential communications without the consent of participants. See *People v. Gibbons*, 263 Cal. Rptr. 905 (1989).
- An apartment manager secretly installed a video camera in a shower used by college women living in his building. After several months of filming the women taking showers, the camera was discovered, and the man was criminally charged under the Wisconsin Criminal Code.

Summary

- Most states divide sexual assault into two or more degrees. Factors that can increase the degree of the crime include force used, a weapon used, or bodily injury inflicted.
- Rape shield laws prohibit questioning of a rape victim if the purpose of the questions is to expose the victim's previous sexual history.
- Rape shield laws do not prevent the introduction of evidence of past sexual conduct of the victim if it is offered to prove either consent of the victim, or that another person was the source of semen or other physical evidence used as part of the case against the defendant.
- Statutory rape requires no specific intent to have sex with a minor. It is not a defense to the charge that the defendant reasonably believed the person was not a minor.
- Civil commitment is permissible only if it can be shown the person is a dangerous sexual predator who poses a substantial threat to commit sexual offenses in the future, and that the person cannot control his behavior.
- Child pornography can be regulated either because it is obscene, and thus prohibited even if it did not involve a child, or because it depicts actual children in sexually explicit conduct. The federal and state governments have a legitimate interest in keeping children away from such sexual conduct.
- The Child Online Protection Act has been found unconstitutional by a circuit court of appeal, and

the Supreme Court has denied review of that decision. Provisions of the PROTECT Act that apply to child pornography have been upheld by the Supreme Court.

Key Terms

rape, p. 324
sexual assault, p. 325
corroborative evidence, p. 325
rape shield laws, p. 332

statutory rape, p. 335
incest, p. 336
Megan's laws, p. 338
prostitution, p. 340

procuring, promoting, and
  pimping, p. 341
child pornography, p. 347
pornography, p. 347

Case Analysis and Writing Exercises

1. It is not a categorical defense to a charge of rape that the victim was the defendant's spouse, nor that the parties were still living in the same residence. Forcible rape of a spouse is still rape. However, the question of consent can be more difficult, since the willingness of the victim to engage in sex might change during the act. Also, since as married persons the victim and the defendant undoubtedly have a history of sex together, the relevance of "past sexual contact" between them, which is normally admissible on consent, presents a problem. How should these questions be answered? For one court's view, *see People v. Hernandez*, 2011 WL 4503335 (Cal. App. 2011). Are you satisfied with all aspects of the decision?

2. Many state appellate courts have created exceptions to the state's rape shield law based on constitutional rights claims. These permit the admission of evidence of the victim's past sexual conduct in addition to the usual exceptions set out in the rape shield statute. In Massachusetts, such an exception relates to past sexual conduct that shows the victim had a motive or reason to fabricate the charges against the defendant. In *Commonwealth v. Mountry*, 972 N.E.2d 438 (Mass. 2012), the defendant tried to introduce evidence that (1) the victim had sex with her boyfriend a few days before the alleged rape, and (2) the victim's motive in alleging the rape was to conceal those facts from her parents. The trial court refused to permit the defendant to introduce that evidence, and the appeals court agreed. Why?

   On a different issue, of what relevance was it to the defense that the defendant claimed he was intoxicated during the alleged rape?

3. Virtually every rape shield law permits a defendant to introduce evidence of "specific instances of sexual activity to show the origin of semen" found on the victim or her clothes. When is this section applicable? In *State v. Patterson*, 291 P.3d 556 (Mont. 2012) the victim had semen stains on the shirt she was wearing on the night of the alleged sexual assault. Tests showed the defendant was not the source. The trial court refused to permit the defendant to cross-examine the victim about the source of the semen, and the Montana Supreme Court agreed. Why? In what situation may a defendant introduce such evidence?

4. The Internet has magnified the child pornography problem in many ways, as stated in this chapter. Consider this problem: If someone were to show you a child pornographic photograph and you looked at it (don't do that!), you would not have committed a crime. Child pornography statutes are aimed at possession, control, or distribution of pornographic images. Have you done more if you click on and look at images on a child pornographic website, knowing it was such a site? Is it significant that your computer's web browser automatically stores the website in a temporary "cache" file, so that it can be easily found if you try to click on the site again? *See State v. Barger*, 247 P.3d

309 (Or. 2011). What if you have a program that downloads images from a peer-to-peer network to your computer? Is that like "looking at a magazine," as one defendant contended? *See State v. Urbina*, 278 P.3d 33 (Or. App. 2012),

review denied, 353 Or. 103 (Or. 2012). These two opinions from Oregon courts also help illustrate how courts struggle with new issues presented by the widespread use of computers and the Internet.

Endnotes

1. *In re D.B.*, 950 N.E.2d 528 (Ohio 2011), *cert. denied* 132 S. Ct. 846 (2011). The court did say that a juvenile under 13 could be convicted of forcible rape, but that fact was not present in this case.

2. The title of this report is "Extent, Nature, and Consequences of Rape Victimization: Findings from the National Violence Against Women Survey," NCJ 210346 (2006).

3. See *Gilmore v. State,* 855 P.2d 143 (Okla. Cr. 1993); *Cole v. State,* 818 SW.2d 573 (Ark. 1991); *Wealot v. Armontrout,* 740 F. Supp. 1436 (W.D. Mo. 1990); and *Case v. State,* 458 N.E.2d 223 (Ind. 1984).

4. John Decker and Peter Baroni, *"No" Still Means "Yes": The Failure of the "Non-Consent" Reform Movement in American Rape and Sexual Assault Laws,* 101 JCRLC 1081 (2011).

5. *State v. Rusk,* 289 Md. 230, 424 A.2d 720 (1981).

6. See also *State v. Reinhold,* 123 Ariz. 50, 597 P.2d 532 (1979); *People v. Hunt,* 72 Cal. App.3d 190, 139 Cal. Rptr. 675 (1977); *State v. Dill,* 3 Terry 533, 42 Del. 533, 40 A.2d 443 (1944); *Arnold v. United States,* 358 A2d 335 (D.C. App. 1976); *Doyle v. State,* 39 Fla. 155, 22 So. 272 (1897); *Curtis v. State,* 236 Ga. 362, 223 S.E.2d 721 (1976); *People v. Murphy,* 124 Ill. App.2d 71, 260 N.E.2d 386 (1970); *Carroll v. State,* 263 Ind. 86, 324 N.E.2d 809 (1975); *Fields v. State,* 293 So. 2d 430 (Miss. 1974); *State v. Beck,* 368 SW.2d 490 (Mo. 1963); *Cascio v. State,* 147 Neb. 1075, 25 NW.2d 897 (1947); *State v. Burns,* 287 N.C. 102, 214 S.E.2d 56 (1975), *cert. denied* 423 U.S. 933, 96 S. Ct. 288 (1975); *State v. Verdone,* 114 R.I. 613, 337 A.2d 804 (1975); *Brown v. State,* 576 SW.2d 820 (Tex. Cr. App. 1978); *Jones v. Commonwealth,* 219 Va. 983, 252 S.E.2d 370 (1979); *State v. Baker,* 30 Wash. 2d 601, 192 P.2d 839 (1948); *Brown v. State,* 581 P.2d 189 (Wyo. 1978).

7. However, "if as a result of self-induced intoxication, the defendant believed that the female was consenting, that belief would not thereby become either reasonable or in good faith" (California Jury Instruction 4.20).

8. Report of rape could also be made to a medical professional and be admissible under statements for the purposes of medical diagnosis or treatment. Report of rape is also known as the *fresh complaint* or the *outcry rule.*

9. 17 A.3d 187 (N.J. 2011).

10. 572 F.3d 552 (8th Cir. 2009).

11. See, e.g., *Comm. v. Battista,* 1995 WL 864097 (Pa. App. 1995).

12. 1 A.3d 438 (Me. 2010).

13. 488 U.S. 227 (1988).

14. 2012 WL 5274733 (Ky. 2012).

15. 133 P.3d 1180 (Colo. 2006).

16. 680 N.W.2d 810 (Wis. 2004).

17. *See People v. Branch*, 109 Cal. Rptr. 3d 412 (Cal. App. 2010).

18. *State v. Ballinger,* 93 S.W.2d 881 (Tenn. App. 2001).

19. Wash. RCWA 9A.44.030.

20. 48 P.3d 350 (Wash. App. 2002).

21. 372 S.W.3d 33 (Mo. App. 2012).

22. 2012 WL 5355694 (Tenn. App. 2012).

23. 536 U.S. 24, 32 (2002).

24. 628 F.3d 1217 (10th Cir. 2010).

25. See the *Milwaukee Journal Sentinel* article, "Sex Offender Database Passes House," July 26, 2006.

26. U.S. Supreme Court cases on sex offenders found to be sexual predators include *Kansas v. Crane,* 122 S. Ct. 867 (2002); *Kansas v. Hendricks,* 521 U.S. 346 (1997); *Conn. v. John Doe,* 123 S. Ct. 1160 (2002); *Foucha v. Louisiana,* 112 S. Ct. 1780 (1992); *Smith v. Doe,* 538 U.S. 84 (2003).

27. 534 U.S. 407 (2002).

28. *Hendricks v. Kansas,* 521 U.S. 346 (1997).

29. *New York Times,* March 4–March 6, 2007.

30. *Prison Legal News,* Vol. 23, No. 8 (August 2012).

31. 242 P.3d 619 (Ore. App. 2010).

32. 702 F.3d 1066 (8th Cir. 2013).

33. 111 Cal. Rptr. 3d 351 (Cal. App. 2010).

34. *State v. Rollins,* 581 So. 2d 379 (La. App. 1991).

35. *Osborne v. Ohio,* 110 S. Ct. 1691 (1990).

36. In 1977, the U.S. Congress enacted the Protection of Children Against Sexual Exploitation Act (18 U.S.C.A. § 2252). The federal child pornography law was upheld as constitutional by the U.S. Supreme Court in the case of *U.S. v. X-Citement Video, Inc.,* 115 S. Ct. 464, and the state of New York child pornography law was upheld in the case of *New York v. Ferber,* 458 U.S. 747, 102 S. Ct. 3348 (1982).

37. This material is adapted from the U.S. Department of Justice publication entitled *Child Sexual Exploitation: Improving Investigations and Protecting Victims* (1995).

38. 758 P.2d 1128 (Cal. 1988), *cert. denied,* 109 S. Ct. 1133 (1989).

39. In the 1990 Arizona case of *State v. Taylor* (808 P.2d 314), the Arizona courts distinguished between "prostitution and theatre." The defendant was convicted of four counts under the Arizona prostitution statute for paid performances in

which "sexual contact" occurred. The Arizona case distinguishes this case and statute from the California *Freeman* case.

In defending a criminal or civil obscenity case, defense counsel often use pay-for-view sex movies available at local hotels, erotic films available from cable or satellite providers, the number and location of X-rated video stores, X-rated material available on the Internet, and local nightclubs that feature nude or semi-nude entertainment as a way to prove the "contemporary community standards" requirement.

40. *Massachusetts v. Oakes,* 109 S. Ct. 2633 (1989); *on remand* 551 N.E.2d 910 (1990).

41. See the *New York Times* article, "Family Photos or Pornography? A Father's Bitter Legal Odyssey," January 30, 1995, which tells of a 45-year-old businessman who was arrested, handcuffed, and taken from his home. The man took 110 photographs of his nude 6-year-old daughter for an art class he was taking. The article tells of similar incidents in Ohio and California.

42. *United States v. Bowers,* 594 F.3d 522 (6th Cir. 2010).

Theft

Lon C. Diehl/PhotoEdit

Someone forgot to tell this shoplifter about the surveillance camera.

OUTLINE

LEARNING OBJECTIVES

In this chapter we discuss the various forms of larceny or theft. The learning objectives for Chapter 13 are the following:

- List the property concepts that underlie property theft crimes.
- State the "money" rule and why it is an exception to general property rules.
- List four ways the taking element can be proved.
- Define "property of another" as it applies to theft of jointly owned property.
- Identify ways the taking requirement can be met in shoplifting.
- Advise a hypothetical merchant on how best to proceed when a suspected shoplifter is identified.
- Explain the ways credit card theft can be proved.
- Distinguish between forgery and uttering a forged instrument.
- Describe how a check-kiting scheme works.

D uring a one-week period, Bachar Youssef withdrew over $16,000 from his account at Chevy Chase Bank, losing much of the money gambling in Atlantic City casinos. He made twenty-nine withdrawals at AIM machines in various amounts. Youssef was able to make these withdrawals because during the same week he deposited in his Chevy Chase Bank account checks payable to himself that he wrote on bank accounts he maintained in other banks. However, as Youssef knew, all the other bank accounts had negative balances, and the checks drawn on them ultimately bounced.

Youssef was able to make the withdrawals because Chevy Chase Bank, like many other banks, permitted customers to withdraw funds deposited in an account before the deposited check cleared the bank on which it was drawn. When Youssef's checks bounced, the bank informed the police, and Youssef was arrested. He was tried and convicted of fraud, based on the "systematic scheme" followed during the week, and theft, based on the individual withdrawals from the ATM machines. In 2011 the District of Columbia Court of Appeals affirmed his conviction.

In this chapter we will learn about several property crimes committed against individuals, government, and businesses, such as shoplifting, fraudulent use of credit cards, and check forgery. We will also learn about the rise of computer-related crimes and the use of computers in committing crimes. In shoplifting cases we will learn the rules that determine when a business is justified in detaining and questioning a suspected shoplifter and the risks associated with such a decision that turns out not to be justified.

General Property Concepts

Understanding the criminal law as it relates to property or interests in property requires some understanding of property law concepts. The following paragraphs illustrate some of these concepts.

- *Property* is divided into two types: real property and personal property. Real estate is real property; everything else is personal property.
- Two important rights to property are (1) the right of ownership and (2) the right of possession of the property. A person may have the lawful possession of property but not necessarily be its owner. Possession of personal property is presumptive evidence of ownership if no evidence to the contrary is shown. Possession accompanied by the exercise of the complete acts of ownership for a considerable period is strong evidence of the ownership of property.[1]
- Property ownership may be in the form of sole ownership. It could also be in the form of joint ownership, as between husband and wife, business partners, or friends or relatives. The property may be owned by a corporation or a business partnership. Property ownership may be vested in a government unit, such as a city, a county, a state, or the national government.
- Lawful possession of property takes many forms. The owner may have the possession of property or may permit another person to have lawful possession and use of the property. An employee or agent of the owner of the property may have possession.

    Bailees and pledges also have the lawful possession of property that belongs to others. A bailment exists, for example, when people take their car into a garage for repairs. The owner of the car retains title and ownership to the vehicle but gives possession to the garage so the repair work may be done. State statutes give the garage a right to a lien on the vehicle in the amount of the work that was done on the car. The garage then has a superior right of possession of the vehicle until the owner satisfies the amount lawfully due the garage. In many states, the owners of the property can be charged with theft if they intentionally and unlawfully take possession of such property from a pledgee or bailee who has a superior right of possession.[2]

- A thief lacks the lawful right either to possession or to ownership of stolen property. Therefore, in almost all situations, a thief cannot convey lawful title to stolen property to another person, even if that person is an innocent good-faith purchaser of the property. Known by the Latin phrase *nemo dat quod non habet* ("one cannot give what one does not have"), this principle, together with the phrase *caveat emptor* ("let the buyer beware"), requires the innocent purchaser to be very wary of buying from strangers.

- One exception to the *nemo dat* rule involves the transfer by a thief of stolen money or negotiable securities, such as bearer bonds, which are securities payable to any person in possession of the bonds. Called the "money" rule, it provides that

Bakalar v. Vavra

Court of Appeals of the United States for the Second Circuit, 500 Fed. Appx. 6 (2nd Cir.2012), *cert. denied*, 133 S. Ct. 2038 (2013).

During the 1930s and early 1940s the Nazi government in Germany "confiscated" hundreds of millions of dollars of property from Jewish owners who had the misfortune to be under Nazi control. This included some of the great works of art in Europe. Following the war, the owners and the heirs of many other owners who perished in Nazi death camps, sought return of the stolen art. This was sometimes possible, because the art-collection world has long been accustomed to carefully mark the "provenance" of important artworks, detailing the purchase and sale of the art. These attempts continue today, as this case shows.

Fritz Grunbaum, an Austrian art collector, owned several drawings made by the artist Egon Schiele. In 1941 Grunbaum was seized by the Nazis, and he died at the Dachau death camp. In 1942 his wife died in another concentration camp in Minsk. Grunbaum's art collection disappeared.

In 1956 one drawing appeared in a Swiss art gallery. In 1963 the drawing was sold to a New York gallery, who sold it to David Bakalar for $4,300 in 1963. In 2005, Bakalar consigned the drawing to Sotheby's auction house, where it received a bid of $675,000. However, before the sale could close, the Grunbaums' heirs brought an action to determine the ownership of the drawing.

The trial court found that under New York law, which applied, it was Bakalar's duty to prove the drawing had not been stolen by the Nazis. If the drawing was stolen, he did not get title when he bought it, even if he acted in good faith. Bakalar was able to show that Grunbaum's sister-in-law sold the drawing in 1956, but was unable to show how she acquired it from her sister, Grunbaum's wife. However, the court nonetheless awarded the drawing to Bakalar, holding the heirs failed to assert their claim in a timely manner once they were aware Bakalar possessed the drawing. The Court of Appeals affirmed the decision and the U.S. Supreme Court denied review.

362 PART 3: Crimes Against Property

a person who receives money in good faith and for value given takes title to the money. For example, in *City of Portland v. Berry,*[3] a thief stole nine $1,000 bills and eighteen $500 bills from her employer and took them to her bank, where she converted the large bills to bills of smaller denomination. When the theft was discovered, the bank still had possession of the large bills, and the owners sought their return. The court said no, because the bank had given value for the bills in good faith; that is, it had no reason to suspect the bills were stolen.

Theft or Larceny[4]

Historically, the common law recognized a broad and often confusing number of theft of property crimes. Today, virtually all states have consolidated these many crimes under the heading of **theft or larceny**.[5] A great number of these crimes remain, however. The federal government alone has more than 100 separate statutes in Title 18 of the U.S. Code that deal with theft or theft-related activity.[6]

A typical theft or larceny statute today would require an unlawful (1) taking of (2) property of another with (3) intent to deprive the owner of possession thereof. In this section, these requirements are discussed in detail.

The Taking

Taking refers to the act of obtaining physical possession or control of another's property. A taking can occur by acts of a stranger, by a trusted employee, or even by a spouse. It can be by one having no right to possess the property or by one with limited rights to that possession. The key to taking is that the thief exercises unauthorized dominion over the property.

Direct Taking   The most easily understood taking is direct taking, where the thief directly takes physical possession of another person's property. Examples of this include purse snatching, pickpocketing, shoplifting, and car theft. This kind of taking requires the thief to obtain actual physical possession of the property, even if for a short time.

> **EXAMPLE**

A stranger walks into your backyard and up to your locked bike. He attempts to break the lock, but before he can do so, he is stopped by a passing police officer. He has not yet taken the bike and is not guilty of theft.

> **EXAMPLE**

The same facts, except that the stranger breaks the lock. While he is turning to wheel the bike out of your yard, the police stop him. Even if he has moved only a few feet, he has taken the bike and is guilty of theft.

The common law and some states today require both a taking ("caption") and carrying away ("asportation") of the stolen property. Carrying away requires that the property be moved in some manner. However, even the slightest change of position of the property satisfies this requirement. Thus, in the example, in a state that retains a carrying away requirement, the smallest movement of the bike would be sufficient.[7]

theft or larceny
Stealing property of another with the intent to deprive the owner of possession.

taking The act of obtaining physical possession or control of another's property. The key to taking is that the thief exercises unauthorized dominion over the property.

The Taking of Lost and Mislaid Goods or Goods Delivered by Mistake A taking may also occur where the initial physical possession of the property of another is not unlawful but where the person in possession acts in a manner showing an intent to deprive the owner of ownership rights.

> **EXAMPLE** A woman found a purse under a bush near a walking path. Inside the purse she found $500 in cash. The woman put the cash in her pocket. At this point, she had not taken the cash, because her possession was not yet unlawful. Later, she used the cash to buy herself a new coat. At this point, she had taken the cash.

> **EXAMPLE** A man deposited a federal income tax return check in the amount of $1,907 into his checking account. His bank mistakenly credited his account in the amount of $10,907. When he discovered the mistake, the man withdrew over $7,000 of the money. He was convicted of theft.[8]

> **EXAMPLE** A man leaving the U.S. Army was to receive a severance check for $183.00, but to his surprise, the check he received was for $836,728.19. The man immediately deposited the money and began spending it. After the error was discovered, legal action was taken against the man.[9]

Sometimes in situations like these examples, the person in possession of lost or misdirected property does nothing about it. For example, the owner of a checking account may do nothing when he discovers that his bank has credited his account with too much money. Proving a taking in those cases may be difficult, even though the account's owner plans to wait and see if the bank discovers the mistake and, if not, keep the money. Some states have followed the Model Penal Code's approach to this problem. Section 223.5 makes one guilty of theft if "with purpose to deceive the owner thereof, he fails to take reasonable measures to restore the property to a person entitled to it." Other states, following the common law rules, find the person guilty of theft only if at the time the person learned of the mistake he or she formed the intent to appropriate the funds. In those states, the taking must occur at the same time the intent to steal is formed.[10]

A person who finds lost property and promptly makes an attempt to return it to the true owner is not guilty of theft, even if a reward is asked for the return of the property. However, at some point failure to make the return would become "appropriation" for the finder's own purpose, and a taking would occur. In the 2010 case of *People v. Zamani*[11] a company lost two valuable circuit boards while they were in transit in California. A buyer bought the boards on eBay for $74.95, though he knew they were worth "thousands." The defendant acquired the boards from that buyer, ostensibly to return them to the owner. When the defendant contacted the owners, he demanded a "reward" of $10,000, and refused repeated requests for their return for a smaller reward of $1,000. Finally, the owners turned the case over to the police. The defendant was arrested, charged with, and convicted of felony theft of lost property. The California appeals court affirmed the conviction.

If property is not lost, and a person takes it and subsequently demands a reward for its return, a taking does occur. For example, in *People v. Stay,*[12] a defendant was convicted of theft when he collected shopping carts owned by various supermarkets that customers had removed from the owners' premises. The defendant then offered to return the carts upon payment of a "finder's" fee. If the fee was not paid, the defendant sold the carts. The court held that because the carts were left within a few blocks of each store, in front of customers' houses, the markets knew where they were and routinely collected them. The carts were not lost, and therefore the defendant had no right to a finder's fee. The defendant was convicted of grand theft.

Taking by Trick, Deception, or Fraud   Taking has been achieved by the use of many tricks, deceptions, and **fraud**. The owner of the property may be deceived by false representations that cause the owner to give up possession of the property. Con games fall into this category. Modern theft and larceny statutes specifically define these forms of taking as elements of the crimes of theft and larceny.

fraud Use of deceit or trickery to obtain profit or advantage.

Confidence games and schemes (con games) have been used for hundreds of years. The pigeon drop was reportedly used more than 1,000 years ago in China. The deception has always been the same. The con man or woman wins the confidence of the victim, talking fast enough to keep the victim confused while dangling enough temptation to appeal to the victim. Unfortunately, a large percentage of the victims are elderly.

Phone call thefts are also common in the United States. The Federal Trade Commission (FTC), which monitors and investigates interstate telemarketing scams, reported that Americans lose nearly $1 billion each year in phony telemarketing schemes. The FTC reported that telephone swindlers are increasingly defrauding the elderly in telephone frauds. The chance of victims' recovering their money from con games and phone call thefts, unfortunately, is low.

The following cases illustrate two examples of theft by fraud or deception: insurance fraud and deceiving buyers of goods.

State v. Penalver

New Jersey Superior Court, 2006 WL 709839 (2006)

Defendants, mother and son, filed an insurance claim for $160,000, based on a fire that destroyed a residence owned by the mother. The fire insurance company paid the defendants $10,000 for living expenses while the fire was investigated. The insurance company concluded the cause of the fire was arson, denied the claim, and turned the case over to the police. The defendants ultimately were convicted of arson for starting the fire, and theft by deception for taking the $10,000 from the insurance company. (On review by the N.J. Supreme Court the convictions were affirmed, but the case was remanded to cure some sentencing irregularities. 901 A.2d 953 (N.J. 2006)).

Embezzlement[13]   Many employees have money and property that belong to their employer. Lawyers, stockbrokers, business partners, and bailees also have money or property that belongs to clients and business associates. Because bank clerks and cashiers in restaurants and stores already have possession of money belonging to their employers, they do not have to take the money in the physical sense in order to steal.

> ## Commonwealth. v. Pappas
>
> Pennsylvania Superior Court, 845 A.2d 829 (2004), *appeal denied*, 862 A.2d 1254 (2004)
>
> Defendant, a used car dealer, bought used cars, repaired them, and sold them to buyers. Many of the cars had undergone substantial (and faulty) repairs, and this was known to the defendant. However, when the cars were sold to buyers, the defendant stated that the cars had never been repaired and were as good as new. He was charged with theft by deception, based on his false statements about the fact of repair, and the appeals court held this was sufficient to support his conviction.

embezzlement To wrongfully appropriate money or property entrusted to one for one's own use.

To fill in this large gap left in the criminal codes, the crime of **embezzlement** was created by statutes in England and the United States. It forbids a person already in lawful possession of money or property from fraudulently converting the money or property to his or her own use.

Many states have also solved this problem by expanding the "taking" in their theft or larceny statutes to include use, transfer, concealment, and/or retaining possession. Under such a statute, a stockbroker, lawyer, or cashier who stole money could be charged with theft or larceny.

Defining What Property Can Be Stolen

Under the common law, only tangible personal property could be stolen. Real estate and items attached to the land could not be stolen, because of the "asportation," or "carrying away" requirement. Documents such as stocks, bonds, checks, or promissory notes were not subject to theft, because they are intangible personal property.

All states and the federal government have broadened the original common law definition of property that can be stolen. Some modern criminal codes include any sort of property of value that can be moved. Illinois defines *property subject to theft* as "anything of value," including real estate, money, commercial instruments, tickets, and written documents.[14] Minnesota defines *property* to include documents and things growing on or affixed to land.[15] Section 223.2 of the Model Penal Code defines "theft by unlawful taking or disposition" as

1. *Movable Property:* A person is guilty of theft if he takes, or exercises unlawful control over, movable property of another with purpose to deprive him thereof.
2. *Immovable Property:* A person is guilty of theft if he unlawfully transfers immovable property of another or any interest therein with purpose to benefit himself or another not entitled thereto.

As the above definition of "immovable property" suggests, in order to convict a person of theft of real estate there must be a "transfer" of the property, or of an interest in the property. Because an interest in real estate is transferred by the owner

FORMS OF TAKING AND TYPES OF THEFT

Shoplifting (Retail Theft) or Price Altering
- Shoplifting—the most common form of theft in retail stores—is the taking by concealment to avoid payment for goods.
- Price altering avoids payment of the full price of an object by lowering the amount on the price tag.

Taking by Employee, Bailee, or Trustee
- Employee theft of money and other objects from business premises causes large losses.
- Embezzlement of funds or negotiable securities that are in the custody of employees, bailees, or trustees.

Snatch and Run
- The taking is observed, and the offender flees to avoid apprehension.

Till Tap
- The thief opens a cash register unobserved and takes cash and coins.
- While store employee has cash drawer open, thief grabs money and flees (snatch and run).

Taking by Trick, Deception, or Fraud (Stings, Scams, and Swindles)
- Con games and operations.
- Deceptions and tricks to obtain property illegally.
- Obtaining property by false pretenses.

Taking from a Person
- Purse snatching (a form of snatch and run).
- Pickpocketing.
- Rolling a drunk (taking from a person incapacitated by alcohol, drugs, or other means).

Taking of Lost or Mislaid Goods or Money

Taking of Objects or Money Delivered by Mistake
- Example: a check for too much money is mailed to a person by mistake.

Looting
- Taking property from or near a building damaged, destroyed, or left unoccupied following a tornado, fire, physical disaster, riot, bombing, earthquake, or similar event.

signing a deed, the theft offense is usually committed by the thief deceptively persuading the owner to sign a deed transferring the property. For this reason, most state theft statutes that include theft of real estate define theft to include obtaining property by deception. *See, e.g.,* Cal. Penal Code § 484(a). However, executing a purported deed by forging the owner's signature and recording the deed is not theft, since absent a lawful deed nothing has been taken. The California Court of Appeals reversed a conviction under the theft statute based on a forged deed, holding that forged deed cannot convey title. The person forging the deed could be charged with forgery, or fraudulently recording a forged deed, the court said.[16]

Taking by Failure to Return a Leased or Rented Object

- Example: failure to return a rented car or DVD within the time specified by state statutes or city ordinance.

Taking by Illegal Entry into Locked Coin Box

- Vending machine, pay telephone, parking meter, and so on.

Smash and Run

- A store or other window is broken, and after snatching objects, the thief runs to avoid apprehension. (This can also be charged as burglary.)
- Women drivers waiting at stoplights are sometimes subjected to this tactic. The thief breaks the car window, takes the woman's purse from the front seat, and runs.[a]

Taking by Illegally Obtaining or Using Information

- Stock market insider trading scandals are examples of illegally using information.

Taking by Illegal Use of a Credit Card or Credit Card Number

Taking from a Person with a Superior Right of Possession

- People may acquire a superior right of possession over the owner of property because of a bailment, pledge, or contract. State criminal codes may make taking from a person with a superior right of possession a crime.

Theft by Possession of Stolen Property

- A person who receives stolen property, knowing it was stolen, commits theft.

Ordinary Theft

- Taking occurs observed or unobserved by owner or other people.

[a]The "bump" technique is also used. An expensive car occupied only by its driver is usually targeted. While the victim is waiting at a stoplight, the victim's car is bumped intentionally. When the victim gets out of the car to view the damages, one of the thieves distracts the victim while the other thief sneaks around to get into the victim's car. Because the victim generally leaves the keys in the ignition, the thief drives off in the victim's car. The other thief jumps in his or her car and also speeds away, leaving the victim stranded.

© Cengage Learning

In addition to documents, information from computers, files, and other places may be stolen.[17] Under fraud statutes and other specific statutes, telephone and computer services may be stolen. In a 2008 case, the Wisconsin Court of Appeals held that the Wisconsin theft statute, WSA 943.20(2)(b), applied to theft of phone services. An inmate serving a 133-year term in a Wisconsin prison set up several telephone accounts in fictitious names and then used the telephone numbers to make collect calls totaling over 40,000 minutes. The court held that the definition of "property" in the theft statute included "electricity," and that electricity includes telephone service. The court also held that the defendant could be prosecuted under the general theft statute, even though Wisconsin has a specific statute, WSA § 943.45, for telecommunications theft.[18]

Contraband, such as illegal drugs, can be stolen, even though people losing such property are not likely to report such thefts to the police. In *Ceballos v. State*,[19] the Arkansas Court of Appeals held that the Arkansas theft statutes included contraband. The defendant broke into a residence to steal illegal marijuana held there by the residence's owner. When charged with theft, the defendant argued illegal contraband is not "property of another," because no one can own contraband. The court disagreed, stating that the theft statutes define "property" as anything of value that can be possessed, and that illegal marijuana satisfies both of those requirements.

Value of Property   If the property has no intrinsic value, a prosecution for theft or larceny would be hard to sustain. A single sheet of paper worth a penny or less has little intrinsic value. If, however, a signed promissory note for $1,000 were on the sheet of paper, the value of the paper would increase considerably. In charging theft or larceny, the state must introduce evidence showing the value of the property alleged to have been stolen.

The value of the property stolen, in most instances, determines whether the charge is a misdemeanor or a felony. The value of the property must be determined by the court or jury. Statements by the owner concerning what he or she paid for the property, how long it was possessed, its replacement cost, and its condition are admissible in determining value. Evidence of the value of comparable property in comparable condition is admissible to show the value of the property at issue. Experts and appraisers may, in some instances, be called into court to testify as to value. (Sentimental value can generally not be considered.)

In the New York case of *People v. Harold,* the defendant was convicted of grand larceny for the theft of a water pump that had been purchased five days before the theft. However, the pump had been damaged before the theft by two men, Crego and Terpening, who had attempted to install the pump. In ordering a new trial, the court stated:

> The question presented by this appeal pertains to the value of the stolen pump… [T]he market value of a stolen item is to be measured by what the thief would have had to pay had he purchased the item instead of stealing it. . . . In the instant case, the value of the pump must be reduced to reflect the mechanical prowess of Crego and Terpening. Additionally, an allowance must be made for the fact that the pump, when taken, was no longer new.
>
> Many state statutes provide that *value* means the market value at the time of the theft or the cost to the victim of replacing the property within a reasonable time after the theft. The replacement value to a retail store is the replacement cost to the store, not the retail price of the item.[20]

As the New York court pointed out in the *Harold* case, the value in New York would be "market value" or "what the thief would have to pay had he purchased the item instead of stealing it." Colorado[21] and many other states also follow this rule in determining value. Other states use the replacement value rule—the replacement cost to a retail store to replace a stolen item.

Property of Another

To prove theft or larceny, the state must show that the property belonged to another, whether that is an individual, a corporation, or a governmental unit. Because the consent of the owner would constitute a total defense to a theft or larceny charge, the owner (or a representative of the owner) must testify that the taking was without his or her consent. A showing that the owner did not consent to the conduct of the defendant is also necessary in criminal damage to property, in trespass, and in arson of either real property or personal property.

Under modern law, a husband and wife are not treated as a single entity for many purposes, including the criminal law of theft. As a result, in most states one spouse can be guilty of theft of the other spouse's property, because that property qualifies as "property of another." However, the property must belong to the spouse from whom it is taken, and it cannot be the kind of property that is "normally accessible" to both spouses. A refrigerator, for example, even if bought by one spouse, cannot be stolen by the other spouse if the couple is still living together.

An example of theft by a spouse is *State v. Krinitt,*[22] a decision of the Supreme Court of Montana. In *Krinitt,* a husband was convicted of stealing his wife's trust fund check. The husband had a history of wasting the couple's finances, so the wife instructed the trust fund to send the check to her attorney. When the check was delivered to their home by mistake, the husband cashed it and spent the money. He was convicted of theft because the trust fund check was not "accessible" to both spouses.

In some states "property of another" is defined to exclude property owned by a spouse or owned jointly by a husband and wife. That is the case in Georgia under Ga. Code Ann. § 16-8-1. In the 2010 case of *Keathley v. State*[23] a husband was convicted of burglary when he broke into his estranged wife's apartment and stole some of her jewelry and a television set they jointly owned. The appeals court reversed the conviction, holding that burglary requires proof of intent to commit theft, and the husband could not have that intent because he intended to take only property of his wife or jointly owned property.

Many people hold property jointly with others. Suppose a business partner steals $1,000 from the partnership checking account and uses it for his personal needs. Or suppose a wife runs off with another man and takes $500 out of a savings and loan account that is in the name of her husband and herself. Is this stealing the property of another? Whether this constitutes theft or larceny would be determined by how the statutes of that jurisdiction define "property of another."

The Model Penal Code Section 233(7) defines "property of another" to include property in which the defendant has an interest, so long as the interest of the other person is one the defendant "is not privileged to infringe." Although each partner in a partnership, or each holder of a joint checking account, may have access to partnership funds or the checking account, they are not privileged to infringe on the others' rights and can be guilty of theft. In *State v. Mora,*[24] the court upheld a conviction for theft of funds in a checking account. The defendants convinced the mother of one of them to place their names on her checking and savings accounts. They then withdrew more than $50,000 from those accounts. When charged with theft, they contended that they did not steal property of another, because they were authorized to make the withdrawals. The court rejected their defense, stating that while a good-faith belief that a person had a right to take property was a good defense, the defendants could not have that belief based only on the fact their names were on the accounts. They knew the funds belonged to the mother, and that she had no intention of giving them any interest in the funds.

The question of the meaning of "property of another" also came up in the 2011 Hawaii case of *State v. Taylor*.[25] The defendant dug up some graves on public land, which contained artifacts of Native Hawaiians that had been repatriated by the state and reburied. He was charged with theft, and defended by contending the artifacts were not "property of another" because they were owned by no one. The appeals court affirmed his theft conviction, holding that under Hawaii law, all "historic property on lands and under the waters" was the property of the state, and thus the artifacts were the property of another under the theft statute.

Difficulties in Identifying Property   Some property is difficult for owners to identify. Diamonds and other valuable stones are an example. Valuable stones may be easily identified by their settings, but once they are removed, they are difficult to distinguish. The four Cs of the diamond business—cut, clarity, carat, and color—provide only the roughest means of identification. An owner's testimony of "it looks like my property, but I am not sure" is not sufficient identification. Because of the difficulty of identification, in some situations the police have been forced to return property to a known thief because of lack of evidence that the property was stolen.

The stolen property must be identified by introducing evidence showing no reasonable doubt as to its identity. For this reason, law enforcement agencies urge marking property in such ways that the identification marks cannot be easily removed or obliterated.

Abandoned Property   If the property has been abandoned or if the owner of the property cannot be located, then theft or larceny cannot be proved. *Abandonment* has been defined as the relinquishment or surrender of property or the rights to property. Most states permit the defense if in fact the property was abandoned, or the defendant had an honest, reasonable belief the property was abandoned. That was the reasoning of the U.S. Supreme Court in the case of *Morissette v. United States*,[26] discussed in Chapter 7.

Whether property is abandoned can depend on the way a state defines that term. In the 2009 case of *Hamilton v. Noe*[27] the defendant was arrested taking scrap metal from a demolition site. The city had torn down the pool house at a city pool, and the debris was left on the site. The defendant entered the site and carried away some of the scrap metal found in the debris. He was charged with theft, and contended the scrap metal was abandoned property. The city parks director testified the city planned to "junk" the debris. The appeals court affirmed the defendant's theft conviction, holding that under Ohio theft law, abandoned property requires a showing of intent by the owner to abandon *and* actions implementing that intent. The parks director's testimony showed intent to abandon, but no actions were taken to implement that intent.

Intent to Steal

Theft or larceny requires a specific intent to deprive the owner of possession of the property. The intent to steal may be proved by direct evidence or by circumstantial evidence. Generally, the fact finder (jury or judge) concludes and infers an intent to steal from the conduct and acts of the defendant. In the following shoplifting case, the California Court of Appeals directed that the described California jury instructions on intent to steal be given to the jury.

Frequently, defendants attempt to defeat the intent to steal requirement by contending that they intended only to borrow the property. In many cases, the jury gives little credence to this defense, sensibly concluding that the defendants' actions show a different intent. However, if proved, an intent to return the property negates guilt of theft, unless the return date is unusually far in the future. For example, taking a neighbor's lawn mower in April and intending to return it in November may be enough to prove theft, unless the theft statute of that state requires a showing that the taker intended to permanently deprive the owner of possession.

In some states, the "borrowing" problem has been solved by establishing a separate theft offense for taking property without the intent to deprive the owner of "permanent" possession. For example, the Kansas "Criminal deprivation of property" statute, KSA § 21-3705, makes a theft crime of any "obtaining or exerting unauthorized control over property of another, with the intent to deprive the owner of the temporary use thereof." In Texas, VTCA Penal Code § 31.01 includes within the meaning of "deprive another" of property keeping the property for "So extended a period of time that a major portion of the value . . . of the property is lost to the owner."

In some cases, even short-term borrowing can be a crime. Many states have statutes that make it a crime to use or operate another person's automobile, motorcycle, or other motor-propelled vehicle without permission of the owner, even if the person intends to return the vehicle after a short joyride. The Model Penal Code, Section 223.9, makes this conduct a misdemeanor.

Shoplifting

Theft has always been a problem for retail stores in the United States. Annual studies done jointly by the National Retail Federation and the University of Florida indicate that the cost of retail theft and fraud every year in the United States runs into billions of dollars. Preliminary results from the most recent survey, released by the National Retail Federation on June 22, 2012, show national retail inventory "shrinkage" (inventory losses) was $34.5 billion for 2011, down from $37.1 billion in 2010. Of that total, employee theft accounted for 43.9 percent of the total. Shoplifting was responsible for 35.7 percent. The balance of the shrinkage was due to administrative error (12.1 per cent), and vendor fraud (5.0 per cent).[28]

The most common form of employee fraud and theft is called "sweethearting," which occurs when cashiers fail to scan goods or ring up sales for goods brought through a checkout line or to a register by friends or relatives. Stealing from the till continues to be a problem, as does manipulation of store computers to issue gift cards or other fraudulent schemes. When stolen or fake credit cards are used to purchase inventory, the retail store owner can suffer losses if the credit card company does not honor the credit card.

The crime of **shoplifting**, or retail theft, is a form of theft and larceny. Shoplifting has the same essential elements as theft and larceny: (1) a taking and carrying away (2) of the property of another (3) without consent and (4) with intent to steal and deprive the owner of possession of the property.

shoplifting Stealing goods from retail stores by concealment, generally on the person of the defendant. Commission does not require removal of the goods from the store.

Taking and Carrying Away in Shoplifting

In modern self-service stores, customers are invited to examine merchandise on display. Garments may be taken to dressing rooms and tried on. Customers carry about merchandise either in their hands or in shopping carts provided by the store. The New York Court of Appeals pointed out in the case of *People v. Olivo* that stores therefore consent "to the customer's possession of the goods" for limited purposes.[29]

Stores do not consent, however, to concealment of their merchandise by customers. The merchandise is offered for sale, and if customers are not going to purchase an object, they are obligated to return the merchandise to the display counter in good condition.

If customers take the merchandise, they have a legal obligation to pay the purchase price. The highest court in New York State held in the *Olivo* case:

> If the customer exercises dominion and control wholly inconsistent with the continued rights of the owner, and the other elements of the crime are present, a larceny has occurred. Such conduct on the part of a customer satisfies the "taking" element of the crime.
>
>   * * *
>
> A taking of property in the self-service store context can be established by evidence that a customer exercised control over merchandise wholly inconsistent with the store's continued rights. Quite simply, a customer who crosses the line between the limited right he or she has to deal with merchandise and the store owner's rights may be subject to prosecution for larceny. Such a rule should foster the legitimate interests and continued operation of self-service shops, a convenience which most members of the society enjoy.[30]

Proving the Crime of Shoplifting When the Suspect Has Not Left the Store

There is a common belief that shoplifting has not occurred until the merchandise has been taken from the store premises. The Criminal Court of the City of New York discussed this belief in *People v. Britto:*

> There are a number of myths about the criminal law, comfortably shared and nourished by those in the street, the business community and sometimes, the courts. One of these is the belief that an observed shoplifter acts with impunity

unless and until he or she leaves the store with the goods. So strong is this belief that the majority of store detectives are instructed to refrain from stopping the suspect anywhere inside the premises; although the likelihood of apprehension is thus enormously decreased.[31]

Courts are virtually unanimous in holding that goods need not leave the store for theft to occur. The New York Court of Appeals explained that result as follows:

> Case law from other jurisdictions seems unanimous in holding that a shoplifter need not leave the store to be guilty of larceny. . . . This is because a shopper may treat merchandise in a manner inconsistent with the owner's continued rights—and in a manner not in accord with that of a prospective purchaser—without actually walking out of the store.[32]

Inconsistent actions might include hiding the goods under the shopper's coat or other clothes. As the Maryland Court of Special Appeals held in *Lee v. State,* if merchandise is secreted under clothing, it meets the requirement of concealment, and it does not matter if the concealment was for a short time or the shopper did not leave the store.[33]

CASE CLOSE-UP

Holguin v. Sally Beauty Supply, Inc.
264 P.3d 732 (N.M. App. 2011), *cert. denied,*
269 P.3d 903 (N.M. 2011)

The "willful concealment" form of shoplifting, where a merchant believes a shopper still in the store has concealed goods with the intent of leaving the store without paying, often results in detention by the merchant of the suspected shoplifter. When that happens, most state shoplifting statutes provide some, but not total, protection to the merchant from accusations of wrongful detention. This Case Close-Up illustrates the relationship between shoplifting criminal laws and merchant detentions of suspected shoplifters.

Patricia Holguin entered the Sally Beauty Supply store carrying a personal "eco-friendly" canvas shopping bag. While shopping, she placed a can of hair mousse in her bag, and started walking toward the cash register. A store manager stopped her and asked what was in her bag. Holguin said

she placed the mousse in her bag because she was going to the cash register to ask a question about the can's contents. The store manager detained her, telling her placing the mousse in her bag constituted concealment and shoplifting. The police were called, and the defendant was arrested and charged with shoplifting. Holguin ultimately pled guilty to shoplifting charges.

She then sued Sally Beauty Supply for false imprisonment. The trial court dismissed her case, concluding that under the New Mexico "conditional privilege" statute, NMSA § 30-16-23, the merchant was immune from civil or criminal liability. The "privilege" statute protects merchants who detain persons with "probable cause" to believe the person had "willfully concealed" merchandise. The trial court interpreted the

(Continued)

CASE CLOSE-UP *(Continued)*

"privilege" as incorporating the presumption in the New Mexico shoplifting criminal statute, 30-16-22, that it is "prima facie" evidence of intent to steal that goods had been "concealed on the person" of a suspect.

On appeal, the Court of Appeals reversed the trial court. It held that the presumption in the criminal statute, that concealment is presumed

to be evidence of intent to steal, applies only in criminal prosecutions. As a result, in order for the merchant to claim the protection of the "privilege" statute, the merchant must show it had "probable cause" to believe the concealment was done "willfully," that is, with intent to steal. The case was remanded to the trial court for a trial on that issue.

The Requirement of Probable Cause Based on Personal Knowledge

Private security officers and retail store employees are often told, "If you have not seen it, it has not happened." Customers are not to be treated like shoplifters until hard, firsthand information demonstrates that shoplifting has occurred. The Criminal Court of New York emphasized the **probable cause** requirement in *People v. Britto:*

probable cause
Reasonable grounds to believe.

> It must be emphasized that this court's holding in no way lessens the burden of proof on the People in shoplifting cases. On the contrary, there is, and should be, a higher standard of proof upon the People in self-service situations than in other larceny cases, because the mere fact of possession may not be used to demonstrate larceny. This remains true even when such possession is accompanied by suspicious or equivocal actions, such as placing unpaid goods directly into the defendant's shopping bag (citation omitted). It is only when the trier of fact concludes, beyond a reasonable doubt, that defendant's actions were totally inconsistent with and clearly adverse to the owner's interests that a conviction may lie. If the facts are sufficient to support such a conclusion *before* the defendant leaves the store, the fact that he has not left is wholly irrelevant and should not absolve him from the consequences of his acts.[34]

The U.S. Supreme Court defined *probable cause* as "facts and circumstances within their knowledge and of which they had reasonable trustworthy information [that] were sufficient in themselves to warrant a man of reasonable caution in the belief that the suspect had committed a crime."[35] The Supreme Judicial Court of Massachusetts has held:

> Historically, the words "reasonable grounds" and "probable cause" have been given the same meaning by the courts.
>
> * * *
>
> The Oregon Supreme Court construed the meaning of the words "reasonable grounds" in its "shoplifting statute" as having the same meaning as they have in a statute authorizing arrest without a warrant and applied the probable cause standard to the facts before it.[36]

EXAMPLE

On a hot July day, a woman customer stated to a clerk in a large food store, "I suspect that young man of shoplifting." She pointed at a young man wearing a jogging suit. The clerk relayed the statement to the assistant manager of the store, who confronted the young man, accusing him of shoplifting in a voice overheard by other people. The young man was detained, and the police were called. Did probable cause exist to justify this action?

defamation Wrongful injury to another's reputation.

When the police arrived, they questioned the store employees and the woman customer. The woman customer stated that she had not witnessed a shoplifting but had only "suspected" that a theft had occurred. The police then realized that probable cause did not exist from the facts known to the store employees, and they released the young man. In the civil lawsuit that followed, a jury awarded the young man money damages for false imprisonment and **defamation** (slander).

Criminal or Civil Prosecution of Shoplifters?

Shoplifting cases can be handled in a variety of different ways, depending on the circumstances of the case. Following are some of the alternatives for handling shoplifting cases:

- When the amount stolen is very small or the offender is very young or very old, a scolding and warning might be used. Parents of children could be called, or the police could take the child home and inform the parents of the problem. Many states have laws making parents liable in a civil action for goods damaged or taken by a minor in a theft.
- More than thirty states have passed laws giving merchants and retailers authority to extract payments and fines from thieves they catch in the act. The offender could sign an agreement under a civil settlement of shoplifting law, acknowledging guilt and agreeing to make the payments to the merchant. In this way, the merchant can save time and expenses by bypassing the police and the courts. The advantages to the shoplifter are that a criminal record is avoided and the incident is taken care of without a court appearance.
- Because criminal courts are very crowded, shoplifting cases are not ordinarily charged criminally unless the amount taken is very large. Civil citations are issued in many cases, and offenders can pay the fine in the same way as parking tickets are paid. Or the offender can be ordered to appear in a municipal court, where the case will be heard by a judge in the same way speeding and other traffic violations are heard.
- Criminal charges are likely to be issued in shoplifting cases when

  - The shoplifter commits a serious assault or battery in resisting detention or in attempting to escape. Assault on a law enforcement officer is a felony in probably all states.
  - Escape is made from a law enforcement officer while the defendant is in custody, which is a crime. Some states also forbid escape from a merchant who has lawfully detained a shoplifter. See Ohio R.C. 2921.34.
  - The shoplifter has a concealed weapon or illegal drugs on his or her person, or is in possession of a criminal tool or a shoplifting device. See *State v. Lee* 2012

HANDLING A SHOPLIFTING INCIDENT

1. Make sure you have probable cause and a good solid case before you restrain the freedom of movement of a person for shoplifting. Probable cause (or "reasonable grounds to believe") must be based on personal knowledge (firsthand information)—either yours or that of another reliable adult employee. Remember: "If you did not see it, it did not happen. When in doubt, let them go."

2. Observing a person concealing "something" or putting "something" in his or her pocket or purse is not sufficient to establish probable cause. The person may be putting a handkerchief or glasses back in a pocket. You must have "reasonable grounds to believe" (probable cause) that the object is unpaid-for merchandise and that the item belongs to the store. If you do not have probable cause, you may

   - Keep the person under observation.
   - Engage in voluntary conversation ("May I help you?" "Are you looking for something?").
   - Ask the person what they put in his or her pocket, or whether the person has a receipt for merchandise in his or her possession, under circumstances in which there is no restraint of their freedom of movement.

3. After a person is observed shoplifting, the following options are available to store employees or a security officer:

   - Confront the person immediately, and ask that he or she produce the item. Always ask if the person has a receipt showing that he or she paid for the item. Under these circumstances, you may seek only recovery of the item and deterrence, rather than prosecution in court.
   - You may be under instructions to allow the person to go beyond the last pay station (or, in some cases, even out of the store). Under these circumstances, the person should be kept under surveillance. A person who becomes aware of your surveillance may attempt to discard the shoplifted item or pass it onto another person. If you fail to observe the

WL 5333542 (Ariz. App. 2012), where the court held a reusable shopping bag was a shoplifting device under the Arizona shoplifting statute.

- The shoplifter causes considerable damage to the merchant's property in an effort to escape. Many states make criminal damage to property a crime if the damage is done either "intentionally" or "recklessly."
- The shoplifter obstructs and hinders a law enforcement officer by giving the wrong name and date of birth, as in the 2012 case of *State v. Collins*.[37]
- The shoplifter has a long prior record of theft and/or has a serious drug or alcohol problem, which the person is stealing to support. (Prosecutors can encourage such people to enter drug treatment programs by threatening jail sentences.)

Other Retail Theft Crimes

- *Tag Switching:* A lower price tag is placed on a store item.
- *Undercharging by Checkout Clerk* (under ringing schemes): The checkout clerk undercharges a friend or co-conspirator.

"discard" or "pass-on," you may then be unable to explain why the stolen property was not recovered. If it appears that the person may outrun you and other store employees, it may be wise to position yourself between the exit door and the person.

4. If your state has a civil settlement of shoplifting law, you should know the requirements of this law and also any guidelines that your employer has established for using the law.

5. Shoplifting cases are handled by your local law enforcement agency (police or sheriff), prosecutor, and judges. Consult a knowledgeable official to determine whether any specific standards are required, such as

- Whether the local judges require that the person observed shoplifting be allowed beyond the pay station (or out of the store) before being detained. (A young man in gym shoes who gets near a door or out of the store is going to outrun most store security people.)
- Whether cases will be prosecuted when
  - The value of the merchandise stolen is small. (What is the minimum for prosecution?).
  - The merchandise or item stolen has not been recovered.
  - The offender is very young or very old.
  - Other factors are considered.

6. Absolute defenses to civil suits are

- That the person either voluntarily stayed in the area or that the restraint of movement was made in good faith on probable cause based on personal knowledge.
- That if any force was used, it was necessary and reasonable either
  - In self-defense.
  - To detain the person.
  - To prevent the theft of the property.

© Cengage Learning

- *"Storming" or Mass Shoplifting:* Two or many more people storm an all-night or late-night convenience store, take items, and then leave. If force is used or threatened, this could be charged as robbery.
- *Till Tapping:* A person reaches into a cash register after distracting the employee, or grabs money from an open cash register ("snatch and run").
- *Boosting:* This is an organized form of shoplifting used by gangs, in which goods in large quantities are placed in booster bags (ordinary bags lined with aluminum foil to avoid store detectors) and then sold by the gangs at huge discounts.

Fraudulent Use of Credit Cards

Credit cards are a means of extending short-term credit. The three parties ordinarily involved in a credit card transaction are (1) the issuer of the credit card, which could be a bank or an organization, such as American Express or MasterCard; (2) the credit card user, who is the holder of the card and the person purchasing the merchandise or service; and (3) the seller of the merchandise or provider of the services.

A person holding a valid credit card signs for the receipt of the goods and commits himself or herself to pay for the service or the property that has been received. The merchant or business organization supplying the goods or services is then reimbursed for the amount of the billing by the issuer of the credit card. The credit card issuer then bills the credit card holder.

Credit Card Theft and Obtaining Credit Cards and Bank Cards for Fraudulent Use

Credit card theft occurs when a credit card is stolen, and every state has a statute directed at such theft. The Maryland statute is illustrative of these credit card theft statutes. Section 8-204 of the Maryland Code (2002) makes it a crime to either (1) take a credit card from another without the owner's consent or (2) receive a credit card knowing it was stolen and with the intent to use the card.

The methods of obtaining credit cards for fraudulent use are many and varied. They can be stolen by burglars, pickpockets, or robbers. They can be retained by workers in gas stations or restaurants or stolen from the mail. They can be counterfeited or altered. In the 2009 case of *Gheorghiu v. Commonwealth*,[38] the Virginia Court of Appeals upheld the conviction under the credit card theft statute of a defendant who produced fake credit cards using a laptop computer and a "remagger" device. The device enabled the defendant to place stolen credit card numbers on a fake card, and encode the number onto the magnetic bar used when a credit card is swiped.

The credit card itself need not be stolen; if a thief uses the card number unlawfully, it is credit card theft.[39] Many states have credit card abuse laws that make it a crime to use a revoked or canceled credit card to fraudulently obtain property.[40]

Thieves obtain credit cards to commit crimes in the following ways:

- Counterfeiting cards (29 percent)
- Stealing credit cards (22.4 percent)
- Obtaining lost or mislaid credit cards (16.4 percent)
- Theft from the mail (13.7 percent)
- Making fraudulent applications for credit cards (3.2 percent)
- Placing telephone and mail orders with false cards (9.3 percent)[41]

It is generally held that a defendant can be convicted under a credit card fraud statute even without possession of the credit card. In *Robinson v. State*,[42] the defendant handed an invalid credit card to a merchant to swipe in the card reader. When the card would not register, the defendant took the card back and "read" the numbers to the merchant. In fact, the defendant was reading numbers from credit cards the defendant had seen being used by their owners. The court held that the defendant could be convicted under the credit card statute even though he never had the credit card in his possession.

It is also generally held that possession alone of a stolen credit card constitutes credit card theft, even if the card had not been used. In the 2009 case of *State v. Jernigan*,[43] the court upheld a credit card theft conviction even though the prosecution offered no proof the defendant used or intended to use the cards. The defendant knowingly had lost or stolen cards in his possession for over two weeks, which the court said satisfied the "appropriating" requirement of the statute, ARS § 13-1802, since the defendant was both depriving the true owner of possession, and was holding the credit cards for his own use, whatever use that was.

Criminal Use of Bank Cards and Credit Cards

Fraudulent charges using stolen, counterfeit, and lost credit cards are made more frequently during the Christmas season than at any other time of the year. Merchants and salesclerks are busy and probably do not take the precautions they would at other times of the year.

Purchasing goods and services is the principal type of credit card and bank card fraud in the United States. Automated teller machines (ATMs) present another means of theft and fraud.

A large ATM fraud occurred with one bank card in 1995. The machines are supposed to give no more than $200 per day to any single card. However, because of a program changeover, thieves were able to obtain $346,770 from a single card by making 724 withdrawals from many different machines.[44]

Check Violations

Most checks that bounce are the result of negligence, mistakes, or bad bookkeeping. Persons writing NSF (nonsufficient funds) or ISF (insufficient funds) checks generally make the checks good within the period provided by the statutes of that state. For example, Florida Statutes, Section 832.07, require that a bad check be made good within seven days or a criminal prosecution may be commenced, and further makes the writer of the check liable in a civil action for triple the amount of the check.

Bad checks are a constant problem for retail businesses and banks, as the crime is easy to commit and the money losses are huge.[45] Not only are the money losses growing every year, but an *FBI Law Enforcement Bulletin* article of 1996 pointed out that half of all check fraud in the United States is committed by professional and organized groups.[46] The article pointed out that even street gangs are using sophisticated means to commit check fraud.

The problem of bad checks overwhelms most local law enforcement agencies. The sheer volume of bad checks limits the number that can be investigated and prosecuted.

Debit cards, which are used to take funds directly out of the card owner's bank account, are similar to both checks and credit cards. Theft and use of a debit card can be prosecuted under many states' credit card theft statutes, though in some states existing credit card theft statutes had to be amended to cover debit cards. For example, the Arkansas "theft by receiving" statute, ARS §5-36-106, was amended in 2011 to add "debit cards" to the kinds of stolen property covered by the statute. Earlier, in *Withers v. State,*[47] the Arkansas Court of Appeals held the defendant could not be convicted of theft of a debit card under the existing credit card statute.

The Crime of Uttering

forgery Wrongfully signing a writing or instrument in the name of the person who issued the writing or instrument, or to whom it was payable.

uttering Putting into circulation a check known to be worthless.

When a person signs a false name in the presence of a bank clerk to a check that does not belong to him or her, the felony crime of **forgery** has been committed. The bank clerk can then testify in court that he or she witnessed the forgery. When a forged check is presented for payment, the felony of **uttering** has been committed. The Supreme Court of Virginia defined the crime of uttering:

> Under our bad-check statute, the gravamen of the offense is the intent to defraud, and the offense is complete when, with the requisite intent, a person utters a check he knows to be worthless. . . . A check is uttered when it is put into circulation; for example, when it is presented for payment. . . . The presentment is more than a request for payment; it constitutes an implied representation that the check is good. The statute itself dispenses with proof of an extrinsic representation.
>
> * * *
>
> It need not be shown that the implied representation was relied upon or that anything was received in return for the check; indeed, the discovery by a payee that a check is worthless before a purchase transaction is completed does not preclude a conviction under the statute. . . . And, while we have stated that the statute is "specifically aimed to discourage the giving of bad checks for what purports to be a cash purchase," . . . such a purchase is not the only transaction proscribed; the statute clearly encompasses a worthless check given to obtain cash.[48]

The crime of uttering a forged instrument is most often committed when a person presents a forged instrument for payment. In the case of *England v. State,* the defendant handed a forged check to a bank teller without saying anything.[49] In affirming the defendant's conviction for uttering a forged instrument, the Supreme Court of Indiana held: "We conclude the offering of the check to the teller with no instructions, when this act is generally construed in the banking industry as a request to exchange said check for cash, is sufficient conduct to warrant the jury to believe that the appellant intended to cash a forged instrument." In the case of *State v. Tolliver,*[50] the defendant deposited a forged check into his own checking account through the use of an ATM. A Wisconsin Court of Appeals affirmed his conviction for uttering, holding that the defendant's act introduced the forged check "into the stream of financial commerce." The crime of uttering can be committed with a forged check or with a bad check that is not forged but is known to be worthless.

The crime of uttering can also be committed with counterfeit money or "raised" bills. In the case of *United States v. Brown,*[51] the defendant was convicted of connecting parts of different denominations of bills and uttering the altered bills. (Defendant "raised" $1 bills to $20 bills and then uttered them.)

The Crime of Forgery

Documents and writing are important in the functioning of a modern society. The crimes of forgery and uttering are offenses created primarily to safeguard confidence in the genuineness of documents and writing. Forgery is committed when a person with an intent to defraud falsely makes or alters a writing or document. Forgery may be committed by

- Creating a wholly new false writing or document
- Altering an existing document (raising the amount of a check, for example)
- Endorsing a check or other instrument with another person's name (example: X steals Y's check and cashes the check by endorsing Y's name on the back of the check)
- Filling in blanks over a signature of another, either without authority or with unauthorized terms

When a check is presented either for cash or in payment for goods, there is an implied representation that the check is good. A common business practice is to request people presenting a check to either endorse or sign the check in the presence of the person who is about to honor the document. If the presenters of the check (the bearers) know that the check is forged, they have committed the crime of uttering in presenting the forged document. If they sign a false name to the check, they have then committed the crime of forgery in the presence of the person who is about to honor the check.

The many types of forged documents include driver's licenses, identification cards, credit cards, passports, and residency cards for people illegally in the United States.

With checks, the forgery could be done by hand. However, the many desktop computers have created a new industry. Forgery and counterfeiting of documents, including checks, is a fast-growing problem throughout the United States. The American Bankers Association states that desktop counterfeiting is the number-one crime problem facing banks.[52]

Operations of Check-Forging Rings

Check forging rings operate in all large cities in the United States. Some of their blank checks are obtained as the result of burglaries or thefts from business firms.

SAFEGUARDS IN HANDLING CHECKS

- Do not endorse checks in blank (with just your name), as the check then becomes a bearer instrument that can be cashed by any person obtaining possession.
- Do not sign blank checks, as any person obtaining possession of the checks could fill in the amount and cash the checks.
- In sending checks through the mail, make the checks payable to a specific person or corporation. Make bank deposits payable to "deposit only" or "for deposit to account number."

© Cengage Learning

Other checks are the product of a computer, which is a new tool for making false copies of checks and other documents.

Checks are often forged by using names found on stolen identification cards and papers. Such identification can be obtained by purse snatching and pickpocketing. The thief looks for a victim with the same general appearance as the person who will utter (pass) the check. With a good set of identification cards and with checks that have all the appearance of payroll checks, the check-forging ring goes to work.

To minimize the possibilities of being apprehended, professional criminals often recruit other people to commit the actual uttering and passing of the checks. This can be done by selling the checks, made out in whatever amount and name the person wishes, or by making an agreement with the recruited people to share the criminal loot.

If a criminal is apprehended while attempting to pass a forged check, he or she is likely to attempt to eliminate the evidence of the crime by eating the check or destroying it in some other way. Should the offender be successful, he or she can then be charged with the offense of destroying (or attempting to destroy) evidence of a crime.

Passing Forged Checks and Other Counterfeit Securities in Interstate Commerce

In the 1930s, the U.S. Congress became concerned about the use of fraudulent securities in interstate commerce. The Congress amended the National Stolen Property Act (58 Statute 1178) by also forbidding "falsely made, forged, altered or counterfeit securities" to be used and passed in interstate commerce. The U.S. Supreme Court recognized that the "general intent" and "broad purpose" of Congress was to "curb the type of trafficking in fraudulent securities that often depends for its success on the exploitation of interstate commerce."[53]

The National Stolen Property Act, therefore, makes it unlawful to transport not only stolen property in interstate commerce but also fraudulent securities, which include forged or "falsely made" checks. The following U.S. Supreme Court cases illustrate the enforcement of the law:

United States v. Sheridan

Supreme Court of the United States (1946), 329 U.S. 379, 67 S. Ct. 332

The defendant was convicted under the National Stolen Property Act for cashing checks at a Michigan bank, drawn on a Missouri account, with a forged signature. The Supreme Court held:

> Drawing the [forged] check upon an out-of-state bank, knowing it must be sent there for presentation, is an obviously facile way to delay and often defeat apprehension, conviction, and restoration of the ill-gotten gain. There are sound reasons therefore why Congress would wish not to exclude such persons (from the statute's reach), among them the very case with which they may escape the state's grasp.

> ### McElroy v. United States
>
> Supreme Court of the United States (1982), 455 U.S. 642, 102 S. Ct. 1332
>
> The defendant used blank checks that had been stolen in Ohio to buy a car and a boat in Pennsylvania. The Supreme Court held that the defendant circulated fraudulent securities in violation of the National Stolen Property Act and that Congress's general purpose was "to combat interstate fraud."

Check Kiting

check kiting Creating multiple checking accounts at multiple banks for the purpose of writing fraudulent checks from one account and depositing them in another, and then withdrawing funds from the deposit bank.

Check kiting can be compared with a shell game at a carnival, in that manipulations are used in both to deceive. The most common reason for the deception in check kiting is to create a false bank balance from which to draw and run off with money that does not belong to oneself. The U.S. Supreme Court used the following example to explain a check-kiting scheme in the case of *Williams v. United States:*

> The check kiter opens an account at Bank A with a nominal deposit. He then writes a check on that account for a large sum, such as $50,000. The check kiter then opens an account at Bank B and deposits the $50,000 check from Bank A in that account. At the time of deposit, the check is not supported by sufficient funds in the account at Bank A. However, Bank B, unaware of this fact, gives the check kiter immediate credit on his account at Bank B. During the several-day period that the check on Bank A is being processed for collection . . . the check kiter writes a $50,000 check on his account at Bank B and deposits it into his account at Bank A. At the time of the deposit of that check, Bank A gives the check kiter immediate credit on his account there, and on the basis of that grant of credit pays the original $50,000 check when it is presented for collection.

> By repeating this scheme, or some variation of it, the check kiter can use the $50,000 credit originally given by Bank B as an interest-free loan for an extended period of time. In effect, the check kiter can take advantage of the several-day period required for the transmittal, processing, and payment of checks from accounts in different banks.[54]

A check kiter can build up a big "float" by using many accounts in different banks and then running off with all the money. In *United States v. Payne,*[55] used car dealers exchanged checks for the sale of automobiles between themselves and used the immediate credit to operate their businesses. One nonexistent car was sold seven or eight times a week for a four-month period. The Court concluded:

> Payne and Fountain successfully managed a kite for four months with a float that rose to $178,000. They obtained that credit, advance, and loan only by

falsely representing the worthless checks as worth their face value. 18 U.S.C. § 1014 makes their misrepresentation a federal offense when the injured bank is insured by the FDIC.

The banking system in the United States has begun the process of electronically debiting checks, rather than sending the paper through the banking system. This results in an immediate debit on the account on which a check is drawn, rather than the three- to seven-day wait to send a check through the system. "Floats" are likely to become a thing of the past when full electronic debiting comes into existence, and crimes such as check kiting may also decrease.

Summary

- The owners of property hold both the right to title and possession of the property. Therefore, when a thief takes possession of the property the owner's rights have been violated. Because one cannot acquire rights in property except through consent of the owner, a thief generally acquires no rights in stolen property, and cannot transfer rights in that property.
- The "money" rule, which permits good-faith purchasers for value of money or certain negotiable securities to obtain title unless they knew or should have known the money was stolen, is necessary to make sure money is freely negotiable.
- Taking can occur by direct acts, by appropriating lost or mislaid goods, by deception, or by embezzlement.
- A joint owner "takes" the property of the other joint owner if the taker had no right to use or keep the property and doing so infringes on the rights of the joint owner.
- Hiding retail goods on one's person, taking the goods out of the store, or otherwise exercising control over the goods inconsistent with the right of a shopper to possess goods prior to sale can constitute taking in a shoplifting crime.

- A suspected shoplifter in the store may be stopped and questioned, and a shoplifter outside the store may be followed to discover the person's identity. In some states, a merchant or security officer with probable cause can detain a suspected shoplifter and search for stolen goods.
- Credit card theft can be proved by showing the defendant was in actual possession of a stolen card, or by showing the defendant caused purchases to be made with the number taken from another person's credit card.
- Forgery occurs when, with the intent to defraud another, a person creates or alters an instrument or document by signing with a fictitious name or another person's name. Uttering occurs when a forged instrument is presented for payment.
- A check-kiting scheme works by establishing an account at one bank, and then writing a large check on that account, which is deposited in a second account at another bank. While the check is going through the clearing process, which can take days, money is fraudulently withdrawn from the second account.

Key Terms

theft or larceny, p. 362
taking, p. 362
fraud, p. 364
embezzlement, p. 365

shoplifting, p. 372
probable cause, p. 374
defamation, p. 375
forgery, p. 380

uttering, p. 380
check kiting, p. 383

Case Analysis and Writing Exercises

1. Simple theft (called "larceny" in many state codes) requires proof of the defendant's intent to steal. Most states have degrees of theft, often tied to the value of the goods taken, or the intent of the defendant to sell the stolen goods. What intent must the state prove in a statute that makes it a more serious offense to commit "larceny with the intent to sell or distribute" property "with a value of $200 or more"? Does the state have to prove the defendant knew the property was worth more than $200? *See Bunch v. Com.*, 2010 WL 5071183 (Va. App. 2010). Why was one conviction upheld and the other reversed?

2. A foreign exchange student lost a billfold in the gym at school. It had $200 in Japanese yen inside. The school made an announcement over the school intercom informing students about the lost wallet. One boy, A, found the wallet, and gave it to another boy, B, who arranged with an adult to take the yen to a bank to be exchanged for U.S. dollars. What crimes have the boys committed? What must the prosecution prove? *See In re B.C.*, 947 N.E.2d 724 (Ohio App. 2010).

3. In *Boyd v. Commonwealth*, 357 S.W.3d 216 (Ky. App. 2011) the defendant was convicted of possession of counterfeit currency under Kentucky law. (The federal crime of counterfeiting is discussed in Chapter 15.) The elements of that crime include proof that the bills possessed were counterfeit, and that the defendant possessed the bills with the intent to pass the bills and defraud another person. Defendant had two counterfeit hundred-dollar bills in her purse. How did the state prove the required "intent to pass" element? If you were the judge, would you have reached the same result as did the court?

4. Degrees of theft often depend on the value of the stolen items. The higher the value, the greater the offense and punishment. How is value to be determined? It is the state's burden to prove value, and a failure to do so will normally result in a not guilty verdict. If the owner of the stolen goods must establish the value (as is often the case), how does he or she do that? Consider the failure of proof of value of the prosecution in *State v. Sanchez*, 101 So.3d 1283 (Fla. App. 2012). What should it have done?

Endnotes

1. A 22A *Corpus Juris Secundum* (Criminal Law), Section 597.
2. For cases in which the owners of cars were convicted of theft when they took their car from a person with a superior right of possession, see *State v. Pike*, 826 P.2d 152 (Wash.1992) (car taken from mechanic without paying for repairs, but the conviction was reversed when it was shown that a written repair estimate was not provided as required by state law); see also *Courtney v. Rice*, 546 N.E.2d 461 (Ohio App. 1989) (car towed to police lot after a parking violation; defendant was convicted of theft and the parking violation, but both convictions were reversed on appeal).
3. 739 P.2d 1041 (1987).
4. *Theft* and *larceny* are interchangeable terms for the crime of stealing. Some states use the term *theft*; other states use *larceny*. The Model Penal Code uses *theft* (Article 223).
5. Nebraska Revised Statutes Section 28-510.
6. "Working Papers of the National Commission on Reform of Federal Criminal Laws," 2: 913.
7. See *State v. Johnson*, 432 So. 2d 758 (Fla. App. 1983), where forcing the store clerk to put money in paper bag and place it on the store counter satisfied the carry-away requirement.
8. *People v. Schlicht*, 709 P.2d 94 (Colo. App. 1985).
9. See the *Chicago Tribune* article, "$836,000 Check for GI Triggers Row," October 23, 1993. For criminal cases on the taking of mislaid or lost property, see *State v. Evans*, 807 P.2d (Idaho App. 1991) and *State v. Getz*, 830 P.2d 5 (Kan. 1992).
10. See LaFave, *Criminal Law*, 4th ed., pp. 930–931 (Belmont, Calif: West, 2003).
11. 107 Cal. Rptr. 3d 608 (Cal. App. 2010).

12. 96 Cal. Rptr. 651 (Cal. App. 1971).

13. LaFave and Scott, in *Criminal Law,* 2nd ed. (Belmont, Calif: West/Wadsworth, 1986), discuss the following on pp. 729–739: (a) Embezzlement by a person in lawful possession of money or property (an employee; a person who found the money or property; or a person who obtained it by mistake), (b) what is called fraudulent embezzlement, and (c) embezzlement by public officials.

The crime of "breaking bulk" is sometimes classified as an embezzlement crime. It is committed when a person takes a portion of goods that have been temporarily placed in his or her custody by the owner. This could be done by a warehouse employee or a common carrier in charge of transporting a shipment of goods. (For example, dockworkers loading cases of beer into a railroad car remove many bottles from cases for their own consumption.) Some states have statutorized the common law crime of breaking bulk (or breaking bale). Other states have made the offense that of larceny or embezzlement; still others include it as larceny by bailee.

14. Illinois Revised Statutes, Chapter 38, Section 15-1.

15. Minnesota Statutes Annotated Section 609.25.

16. *People v. Sanders,* 79 Cal. Rptr. 2d 806 (1998).

17. See *U.S. v. Riggs,* 739 R Supp. 414 (N.D. 111. 1990).

18. *State v. Howard,* 760 N.W.2d 183 (Wis. App. 2008), *review denied,* 775 N.W.2d 100 (2009).

19. 2009 WL 1478000 (Ark. App. 2009).

20. 22 N.Y.2d 443, 293 N.Y.S.2d 96, 239 N.E.2d 727 (1968).

21. See *People v. Schmidt* (1996 WL 350878), in which the Colorado Court of Appeals pointed out that Colorado has a statute that makes price tags attached to a stolen item prima facie evidence of the item's value in a theft prosecution, unless the price is commonly subject to negotiation, as a motor vehicle would be.

22. 823 P.2d 848 (1991). Also, in the case *of People v. Wallace,* 434 N.W.2d 423 (Mich. 1989), a Michigan Court of Appeals held that a chain given to a wife during the marriage was her property and not the jointly owned property of the husband and wife.

23. 699 S.E.2d 765 (Ga. App. 2010).

24. 43 P.3d 38 (Wash. App. 2002).

25. 269 P.3d 740 (Hawai'i 2011).

26. 342 U.S. 246, 72 S. Ct. 240 (1952). This case is also discussed in Chapter 7.

27. 2009 WL 1655486 (Ohio App. 2009).

28. The preliminary results from the survey may be viewed online at www.ncf.com/lpl0.

29. 420 N.E.2d 40 (1981).

30. In affirming the convictions of three different defendants in the *Olivo* case, the New York court held:

> In *People v. Olivo,* defendant not only concealed goods in his clothing, but he did so in a particularly suspicious manner. And, when defendant was stopped, he was moving towards the door, just three feet short of exiting the store. It cannot be said as a matter of law that these circumstances failed to establish a taking.
>
> In *People v. Gasparik,* defendant removed the price tag and sensor device from a jacket, abandoned his own garment, put the jacket on, and ultimately headed for the main floor of the store. Removal of the price tag and sensor device, and careful concealment of those items, is highly unusual and suspicious conduct for a shopper. Coupled with defendant's abandonment of his own coat and his attempt to leave the floor, those factors were sufficient to make out a prima facie case of a taking.
>
> In *People v. Spatzier,* defendant concealed a book in an attaché case. Unaware that he was being observed in an overhead mirror, defendant looked furtively up and down an aisle before secreting the book. In these circumstances, given the manner in which defendant concealed the book and his suspicious behavior, the evidence was not insufficient as a matter of law.

31. 93 Misc. 2d 151, 402 N.Y.S.2d 546 (1978).

32. 438 N.Y.S. at 246 (1981).

33. 59 Md. App. 28, 474 A.2d 537 (1984).

34. 402 N.Y.S.2d at 548 (1978).

35. *Carroll v. United States,* 267 U.S. 132, 45 S. Ct. 280 (1925).

36. *Coblyn v. Kennedy's, Inc.,* 359 Mass. 319, 268 N.E.2d 860 (1971).

37. 2012 WL 589527 (Ohio App. 2012).

38. 682 S.E.2d 50 (Va. App. 2009).

39. In *State v. Morgan,* 985 P.2d 1022 (Alaska App. 1999), a man gave his former girlfriend's credit card number to the defendant, who used it to place $3,669 worth of long-distance calls. The court held his use of the card number was obtaining a credit card by fraudulent means.

40. See *Nolan v. State,* 629 S.W.2d 940 (Tex. App. 1982).

41. MasterCard International and the *New York Times* article, "Guarding Credit Cards from the Latest Scams," July 2, 1994.

42. 780 N.E.2d 849 (Ind. App. 2002).

43. 209 P.3d 153 (Ariz. App. 2009).

44. See the *New York Times* article, "Missing Bank Card Brings Overwithdrawal of $346,770," February 12, 1995.

45. Even the Congress of the United States had a "bad check" scandal in 1992. More than 100 members of the House of Representatives had written bad checks in a year's time on the House bank. One member of Congress wrote 996 bad checks in a three-year period. See the *New York Times* articles, "Adding Up the Casualties in the House Bank Scandal" and "The House Is Getting Jittery over Bad-Check Disclosures," March 12, 1992. All the bad checks were made good, but at the time they were written there were insufficient funds to cover the checks.

46. See the *FBI Law Enforcement Bulletin* article, "Check Fraud: A Sophisticated Criminal Enterprise," August 1996.

47. 218 S.W.3d 386 (Ark. App. 2005).

48. *Warren v. Commonwealth,* 219 Va. 416, 247 S.E.2d 692 (1978).

49. 249 Ind. 446, 233 N.E.2d 168 (1968).

50. 149 Wis. 2d 166, 440 N.W.2d 571 (Wis. App. 1989).

51. 938 F.2d 1482.

52. See the *New York Times* article, "New Breed of Check Forgers Exploit Desktop Publishing," August 15, 1994.

53. See *Moskal v. United States,* 111 S. Ct. at 466 (1990).

54. 458 U.S. 279, 102 S. Ct. 3088 (1982).

55. 602 F.2d 1215 (5th Cir. 1979), *review denied,* 445 U.S. 903, 100 S. Ct. 1079 (1980).

Robbery, Burglary, and Related Crimes

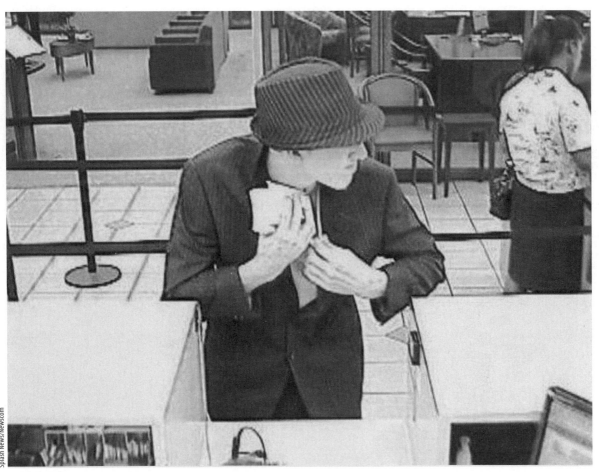

Bank robbers come in all sizes, and disguises, it appears. This man, wearing a pin-stripe suit and jaunty fedora hat and caught on a surveillance tape robbing a Florida bank, couldn't keep his identity a secret from his father, who saw the tape and recognized his son. Dad convinced son to turn himself in to the police. In 2011, Andrew Wright was convicted of bank robbery and sentenced to 76 months in prison.

OUTLINE

LEARNING OBJECTIVES

In this chapter we discuss the theft crimes of robbery and burglary, as well as the related crimes of extortion and trespass. The learning objectives for Chapter 14 are

- Describe what facts separate robbery from common theft.
- State when robbery becomes armed or aggravated robbery.
- List the requirements for home invasion robbery.
- State when purse snatching or pickpocketing can become robbery.
- Distinguish robbery from extortion.
- List the elements of the general burglary offense.
- Describe ways current state criminal codes modified the common law burglary offense.
- Distinguish criminal trespass from defiant trespass.

A t 3:20 A.M. a Burlington City, New Jersey police officer observed David Gibson leaning against the porch of a community center building owned by a private group, the "Omega" fraternity. Clearly posted in the front window of the building was a sign that stated "No Loitering." The officer approached Gibson and asked for identification. The officer then arrested Gibson for trespassing on the Omega property. In a search made after the arrest the officer found thirteen small bags of crack cocaine. Gibson was then charged with possession of illegal drugs with intent to distribute. He pled guilty, preserving the right to appeal based on his claim that the search that yielded the crack cocaine was unlawful, because the officer had no probable cause to arrest him for defiant trespass.

On appeal in 2012, the court of appeals stated the issue as "Did the facts show Gibson had committed the crime of defiant trespass"? If so, the officer was justified in arresting Gibson, and the resulting search was lawful. The court concluded Gibson did violate the New Jersey defiant trespass law, which makes it a crime to enter or remain in any place where a notice against trespass has been given by posting in a manner likely to come to the attention of intruders. The court concluded the posted "no loitering" sign conveyed the same meaning as "no trespassing." It therefore affirmed Gibson's conviction on the

drug charges. In November of 2012 the New Jersey Supreme Court granted Gibson's petition to review the judgment of the court of appeals. *State v. Gibson*, 56 A.3d 395 (N.J. 2012).

In this chapter we learn the elements of many of the crimes involving theft or other taking of property. Crimes against property occur in a variety of ways, with or without the presence of violence. The manner in which the crime occurs can change the name of the crime or the punishment for it.

For example, the value of the property taken is often important in determining if the crime is a felony or misdemeanor. In the case of burglary, the time when the crime occurs (night or day), or the manner of gaining entry to the premises where the burglary occurs (breaking a door or window or walking through an unlocked door) can aggravate the crime and resulting punishment.

We will study many of these different elements in this chapter.

Robbery

robbery Forcible stealing.

Robbery is forcible stealing. It is one of the most frequent crimes of violence in the United States. The common law crime of robbery was defined before the early English courts had defined larceny. The Model Penal Code, § 222.1, defines robbery as follows:

(1) <u>Robbery Defined</u>. A person is guilty of robbery if, in the course of committing a theft, he:

(a) inflicts serious bodily harm upon another; or
(b) threatens another with or purposely puts him in fear of immediate serious bodily injury; or
(c) commits or threatens immediately to commit any felony of the first or second degree.

An act shall be deemed "in the course of committing a theft" if it occurs in an attempt to commit theft or in flight after the attempt or commission.

The usual elements incorporated into robbery statutes by the states include

- A taking and carrying away (only a slight movement of the property is needed)[1]
- of the property of another
- with intent to steal

- from the person or from the presence of the victim
- by the use of force against the person, or
- with the threat of the use of imminent force, to compel the victim to acquiesce in the taking and carrying away of the property.

armed or aggravated robbery Forcible stealing combined with the use of a deadly or dangerous weapon, or which results in serious bodily injury to another.

Simple robbery, also called strong-arm robbery or mugging, is distinguished in most state statutes from the aggravated form of robbery, commonly called *armed robbery*. Armed robbery carries penalties that are more severe than those for simple robbery. Some of the statutory distinctions various states use in distinguishing between armed robbery and simple robbery are the following:

- That the perpetrator was armed with a "dangerous" or "deadly" weapon
- That the perpetrator intended to kill or wound if the victim resisted
- That the perpetrator did actually inflict a bodily injury[2]

State statutes differ on what is required for a conviction of armed robbery or aggravated robbery, where the presence or use of a "weapon" or "deadly weapon" is the basis for increasing the crime from simple robbery to armed robbery. The issue arises when a robber either (1) brandishes a toy or simulated weapon, like a starter pistol, or (2) states that he has a weapon, but does not actually show the weapon, and it later turns out the robber did not have a weapon.

One approach, called the objective approach, requires that the defendant actually possessed a deadly weapon during the robbery. An example of that approach is the definition *of weapon* for purposes of the Montana armed robbery statute, MCA § 45-2-101(76). That section has been interpreted as requiring proof that the defendant actually possessed a weapon, something "readily capable of producing death or serious bodily injury." See *In re L. S.*[3] A similar result was reached by the New York Court of Appeals in the 2011 case of *People v. Grant*,[4] where the court held that simply saying, "I have a gun. Fill the bag. Don't say anything or I'll shoot" did not satisfy the New York first degree (armed) robbery statute. Such a threat would satisfy the requirements for a third-degree (simple) robbery conviction, but not a first-degree conviction, the court held.

More commonly, states have adopted the subjective approach, which requires proof only that the defendant appeared to have a deadly weapon, such as a firearm. The Georgia armed robbery statute, Ga. Code Ann. § 16-8-41(a), states that the crime occurs if the defendant has a weapon, or "any replica...or device having the appearance of such a weapon." In *Kirk v. State,* 610 S.E.2d 604 (Ga. App. 2005), the court held that the defendant must give some physical manifestation of a weapon, but it was the reasonable apprehension by the victim that determined if it appeared a weapon was being used. In *State v. Wren,* 32 P.3d 717 (Kan. App. 2001), the Court interpreted the Kansas armed robbery statute, KSA § 21-3427, as requiring that the victim reasonably believed the robber had a firearm or dangerous weapon.

It is generally held that some indication or representation of a weapon is needed to make a crime armed robbery. In *State v. Muldrow,* 559 S.E.2d 847 (S.C. 2002), the defendant walked into a convenience store and handed the clerk a note that said "give me all your cash or I'll shoot you." He did not show a gun. The court reversed his conviction under the South Carolina armed robbery statute, which defined armed robbery as "alleging . . .he was armed while using a representation of a deadly weapon." The court said, "[w]ords alone are not sufficient" to support a conviction for armed robbery.

The Illinois legislature resolved the "actual" weapon problem by enacting both an armed robbery statute, 720 ILCS 5/18-2(a), which requires carrying an actual weapon, and an aggravated robbery statute, 720 ILCS 5/18-5(a), which only requires that the robber "indicate" he has a weapon, whether or not he actually does. See *People v. Gray,* 806 N.E.2d 753 (Ill. App. 2004), *appeal denied,* 823 N.E.2d 694 (Ill. 2004).

Finally, it is clear that the fact that a firearm used by a robber is unloaded is not relevant to a conviction for armed robbery. In *McLaughlin v. United States,*[5] the U.S. Supreme Court held that the "dangerous weapon" requirement in the federal bank robbery statute, 18 U.S.C. § 2113(d), was satisfied by an unloaded gun.

Changes in Bank Robbery

In 2011, 5,014 bank robberies occurred in the United States, which was about a 10% decrease from 2010. About $38 million in cash was taken in those robberies, and $8 million was recovered. The great majority of the 6,088 persons participating in the bank robberies were male; only 409 were female. The predominant method was presentation of a demand note (2,958), accompanied by the threat of the use of a weapon (2,331). However, in only 1,242 cases was a weapon actually brandished by a robber. There were eighty-eight people injured in bank robberies, and thirteen people died. Ten of those deaths were perpetrators, two were police officers, and one was a bank guard. See *Crime In America, FBI Bank Crime Statistics for 2011,* June 21, 2012. FBI statistics for 2012 are not yet available, but the *Wall Street Journal* reported on February 5, 2013, that bank robberies were down to 3,870 in 2012.

The image of the gun-wielding, masked bank robber forcing all the bank employees to lie on the floor while the bank vault is opened is one of the most common images of the crime of robbery. In fact, as a method of bank robbery, that image has changed, as the statistics stated above show. Most bank robberies are "note" jobs, where the robber presents a note to a bank employee demanding money under a threat of violence.

The identity of the robber also has changed from the classic image of a violent, career criminal. Perpetrators of note jobs have included a New York housewife, a 91-year-old man in Texas, a Florida golf pro, and a former college basketball player and his pre-med student girlfriend. Law enforcement officers have speculated that these "amateurs" have turned to bank robbery as a way to solve financial problems because they know bank tellers have been told to surrender money from their cash drawers on demand. The average take in a bank robbery is between $5,000 and $7,000; banks lose about $30–40 million a year to bank robbers. By contrast, banks lose about $700 million each year to check fraud schemes.

More than half of all bank robbers are apprehended each year. Better bank surveillance cameras, more undercover guards, and dye packs that explode and color stolen money have all contributed to the increased number of bank robbers captured. The most recent advance has been the implantation of global positioning devices in the money given to robbers, which enables investigators to follow the money with their laptops. These devices were used in only 558 of the 2011 robberies.

PROVING A BANK ROBBERY

If bank employees or video surveillance cameras are unable to provide information that leads to the identification of a bank robber, finding a suspect and proving the suspect committed the robbery can be difficult. That was the case in a bank robbery that occurred on December 17, 2010. There, the suspect entered a bank and asked to see a bank manager to open an account. The suspect was a man about 5'1" tall, wore a long-sleeve shirt and tie, a baseball cap, and had a medical patch over his left eye. After going to the manager's office, the suspect showed the manager a shoebox containing what he said was a bomb, which he would detonate unless he was given money. The manager collected $42,000 from tellers, and gave it to the suspect. The suspect left the bank, leaving the "bomb," which he said he would detonate by remote control if the bank called the police before he got away. When police arrived, bomb experts believed the bomb was real because of its detailed design and construction. In fact, after it was disabled with a robot bomb device, the bomb turned out to be a fake.

The FBI was unable to identify a suspect in the robbery after months of investigation. However, on May 11, 2011, a similar bank robbery occurred in which the suspect was dressed the same, was the same height, wore a long-sleeve shirt and baseball cap, and had a medical patch over his left eye. In this robbery a bank employee was able to identify the robber, who was arrested and confessed to the robbery. However, he denied committing the earlier robbery.

At his trial of the first robbery, the FBI agent testified that in his investigation of over seventy bank robberies, he had never seen a robbery using a customer service office, and only in the two robberies the suspect was charged with committing did the robber wear a medical patch over his left eye. This testimony, coupled with identification by the defendant's employer of the defendant on the bank surveillance tapes, was sufficient to support the jury's guilty verdict, an appeals court held. The court also noted that the failure of the government to offer evidence that the suspect possessed the ability to make a sophisticated bomb replica was not fatal to the government's case. *United States v. Cruz*, 2013 WL 627249 (11th Cir. 2013).

The *Chicago Police Department Training Bulletin* lists the following factors that favor a robber:

- He or she can carry out the crime swiftly.
- He or she will usually leave few clues that would lead to his or her arrest.
- The robbery is committed in such a short period that the victim and witnesses sometimes do not have sufficient time and composure to view the offender so as to furnish an accurate description to the police.
- The probability of interruption is limited because of the short time.[6]

Distinguishing Robbery from Theft or Larceny

Under the common law, robbery was distinguished from theft or larceny by reference to the use of force, or the threat of force, in the "taking" of the property. Thus, in charging the crime of robbery, under the common law it must be shown that (1) property was taken from the victim or taken from the presence of the victim, and (2) the use of force or the threat of force was used in the taking.

In the 2011 case of *Spencer v. State*[7] the Maryland Supreme Court held that under the common law definition of robbery, still used in Maryland, a defendant did not use the "threat of force" when he said to a Jiffy Lube cashier, "Don't say nothing." In response to this statement the cashier handed the defendant the cash drawer and the defendant left the premises. The court said that if this statement, without any other expressed or implied threat of force, satisfied the robbery definition, the distinction between theft and robbery would virtually be eliminated. The court reversed the defendant's conviction for robbery.

The common law "taking" requirement for a robbery conviction has been changed by many state statutes. A 2012 Michigan case illustrates what is called the "course of conduct" definition of robbery. The defendant entered a tobacco store with his hand in his pocket and told the clerk "You know what this is, just give me what I want." The clerk refused to give the defendant any money, and the defendant fled the store without taking anything. The defendant was convicted of armed robbery.

On appeal the Michigan Supreme Court affirmed the conviction, stating that while the common law required a completed theft, the Michigan robbery and armed robbery statutes defined robbery to include use of force or threat of force "during the course of committing" a larceny. Under this statute, it is not a requirement that the robbery be successful, the court held. The court stated that the legislature clearly recognized that the use or threat of force during a larceny were harms independent of the larceny, and thus treated it as severely as a completed larceny. The court noted twenty-three states have similar provisions, as does the Model Penal Code in § 222.[8]

The timing of the "force" used in a theft remains an issue. In some states, the required force must be part of the "taking," that is, the force must occur during the period the property is taken from the victim. For example, in the 2010 case of *Hobson v. Commonwealth,*[9] the Kentucky Supreme Court reversed a robbery conviction where the only force used by the defendant was in an attempt to escape from the robbery scene. The court held that under the Kentucky statute the force must be part of the "taking."

Many states and the MPC follow the "transactional" theory of robbery. Under this theory, the "force" needed to make a theft crime robbery could be present during any part of the "transaction," and would include force used to either retain the property or to escape after the "taking" had occurred. In the 2011 case of *Commonwealth v. Rogers,* the Massachusetts Supreme Judicial Court held that force used in escaping from a robbery scene satisfied the force requirement for robbery.[10]

Carjacking: A New Name for an Old Crime

carjacking Forcibly taking possession of a motor vehicle in the possession of another against his or her will with intent either to permanently or temporarily deprive the person of possession.

Thieves have been stealing cars from their owners or occupants by force or fear of force for years. These cases did not fit easily into theft or robbery criminal statutes because the thief often did not intend to keep the car permanently. (Figure 14.1 describes the various types of car and vehicle theft.) It is generally true that in most years more than 90 percent of the vehicles taken in carjackings were returned.

To remedy the limited applicability of standard theft statutes, most states and the federal government passed statutes making **carjacking** a separate offense. Congress

FIGURE 14.1 Car and Vehicle Theft in the United States

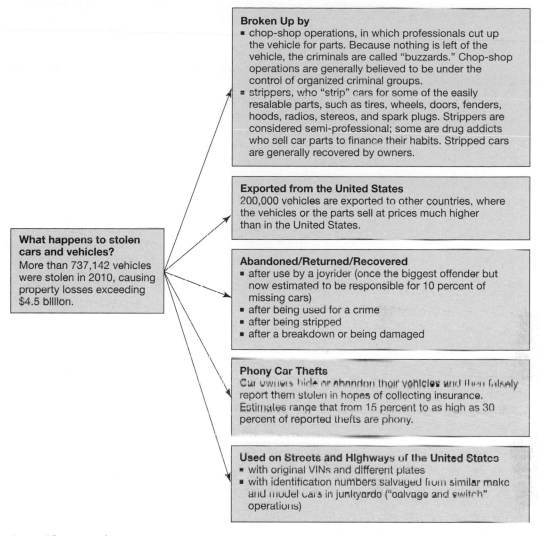

Broken Up by
- chop-shop operations, in which professionals cut up the vehicle for parts. Because nothing is left of the vehicle, the criminals are called "buzzards." Chop-shop operations are generally believed to be under the control of organized criminal groups.
- strippers, who "strip" cars for some of the easily resalable parts, such as tires, wheels, doors, fenders, hoods, radios, stereos, and spark plugs. Strippers are considered semi-professional; some are drug addicts who sell car parts to finance their habits. Stripped cars are generally recovered by owners.

Exported from the United States
200,000 vehicles are exported to other countries, where the vehicles or the parts sell at prices much higher than in the United States.

What happens to stolen cars and vehicles?
More than 737,142 vehicles were stolen in 2010, causing property losses exceeding $4.5 billion.

Abandoned/Returned/Recovered
- after use by a joyrider (once the biggest offender but now estimated to be responsible for 10 percent of missing cars)
- after being used for a crime
- after being stripped
- after a breakdown or being damaged

Phony Car Thefts
Car owners hide or abandon their vehicles and then falsely report them stolen in hopes of collecting insurance. Estimates range that from 15 percent to as high as 30 percent of reported thefts are phony.

Used on Streets and Highways of the United States
- with original VINs and different plates
- with identification numbers salvaged from similar make and model cars in junkyards ("salvage and switch" operations)

Source: The National Insurance Crime Bureau, 2011.

passed the Anti-Car Theft Act of 1992, 18 U.S.C. 2119, in response to the more than 35,000 carjackings completed or attempted each year in the United States. An example of a carjacking statute is the following California law:

> Carjacking is the felonious taking of a motor vehicle in the possession of another, from his or her person or in the immediate presence . . . against his or her will and with the intent to either permanently or temporarily deprive the person . . . of his or her possession, accomplished by force or fear.[11]

Carjacking statutes raise several problems not found in standard theft statutes concerning the requisite elements of the offense. Some of these are the following:

- A taking occurs even if the true owner of the car remains in the car during the carjacking.
- The true owner is in "possession" of the car even if he is alighting from the car when the carjacking occurs or outside the car. In the 2009 case of *People v. Magallanes*[12] the owner was standing outside her car attempting to put her child in a car seat when the defendant stole her car. The court affirmed his conviction for carjacking.
- In *People v. Lopez*, 79 P.3d 548 (Cal. 2003), the California Supreme Court reversed earlier decisions under the carjacking statute and held that movement of the car, however slight, was an element of the crime. Florida's statute, FSA § 812.133, has been interpreted as not requiring movement of the car. See *Price v. State*, 816 So. 2d 738 (Fla. App. 2002).[13]
- A carjacker may also be convicted of kidnapping, if the owner of the car is purposely kept in the car and the car is moved a substantial distance from the vicinity of the carjacking. In the 2012 case of *People v. Ortiz*[14] the court affirmed a kidnapping conviction because the purpose of the carjacking and kidnapping was to use both crimes to force payment of an illegal drug sale debt. However, movement of the car owner merely as "incidental" to the carjacking is not kidnapping. See *People v. Medina*, 161 P.3d 186 (Cal. 2007).

Home Invasion Robberies

home invasion robbery Robbery of persons inhabiting a dwelling.

Home invasion robbery differs from similar crimes, such as burglary or breaking and entering, in how the crime is defined. For example, the Illinois Criminal Code defines home invasion as an unlawful entering of a dwelling by a person who knows someone was present therein, and armed with a dangerous weapon either uses or threatens use of force or injures someone inside the home.[15]

In some states, this difference means that a defendant can be convicted of both home invasion and another crime, such as armed violence during residential burglary, based on one unlawful entry. See *People v. Cunningham*, 851 N.E.2d 653 (Ill. App. 2006). Other states hold that conviction of home invasion bars conviction of related crimes such as residential burglary based on one unlawful entry. See *Coleman v. State*, 956 So. 2d 1254 (Fla. App. 2007). Florida courts also hold that only one conviction on a count of home invasion may be obtained, even if more than one person is in the home. See *Schulterbrandt v. State*, 984 So. 2d 542 (Fla. App. 2008). Other courts have reached the opposite result. See, for example, *Commonwealth. v. Antonmarch*, 874 N.E.2d 665 (Mass. App. 2007), which upheld convictions on two counts of home invasion based on the presence of two people in the home.

Purse Snatching, Pickpocketing, and Other Thefts from a Person

The crimes of robbery and theft have many common elements, such as the requirement that there be a "taking" with intent to deprive the owner of the property stolen. One principal difference between the crimes is, of course, the use of force to accomplish the "taking." Force is not part of theft, but it is part of robbery. Another difference is the penalty that results from the crime. Robbery is typically a felony, while theft can be a misdemeanor, depending on the value of the property. Those distinctions are important in crimes where some force must be used to take property from another person, but the force does not go beyond that needed to accomplish the taking. Purse snatching and similar crimes are examples of this distinction.

The majority rule in the United States is that crimes like purse snatching are not robberies unless some force is used that is greater than that needed to take the purse is used. In the case of *State v. Sein*,[16] the Supreme Court of New Jersey stated the majority rule as follows:

> [A] simple snatching or sudden taking of property from the person of another does not of itself involve sufficient force to constitute robbery, though the act may be robbery where a struggle ensues, the victim is injured in the taking, or the property is so attached to the victim's person or clothing as to create resistance to the taking.

An example of force in a purse snatching sufficient to satisfy a robbery conviction is *Jones v. Commonwealth*.[17] There, the court held that grabbing a woman's shoulder to jerk her around so that the defendant could snatch her purse was enough force to constitute robbery.

A few courts have adopted the rule that the snatching of a purse without the use of any other force is sufficient to permit a jury verdict on the charge of robbery. The Supreme Judicial Court of Massachusetts adopted this rule in the case of *Commonwealth v. Jones*.[18] In affirming the defendant's conviction of unarmed robbery for a purse snatching, the court stated:

> The question whether the snatching or sudden taking of property constitutes robbery has arisen in other jurisdictions although not in Massachusetts. In Kentucky, the rule is that snatching, without more, involves the requisite element of force to permit a jury verdict on a charge of robbery. (Citations omitted). According to the rule prevailing in most jurisdictions, however, snatching does not involve sufficient force to constitute robbery, unless the victim resists the taking or sustains physical injury, or unless the article taken is so attached to the victim's clothing as to afford resistance. . . .
>
> We prefer the Kentucky rule on purse snatching. The majority jurisdiction rule, in looking to whether or not the victim resists, we think, wrongly emphasizes the victim's opportunity to defend himself over the willingness of the purse snatcher to use violence if necessary.

In some states this issue is resolved by adding **"sudden snatching"** to the general robbery statute. Georgia's robbery statute, Ga. Code Ann. § 16-8-40, defines robbery in the usual manner as taking by use of force, but includes a taking "by sudden snatching." Florida addressed the force issue by passing a "robbery by sudden snatching" statute, FSA § 812.131, which explicitly does not require any use of force beyond that needed to take the property, and does not need any showing the victim resisted the taking. It is a third-degree felony, unless the perpetrator

sudden snatching
A form of robbery where force is not used beyond that needed to take property from another person.

carried a firearm, in which case it is a second-degree felony. In *Walker v. State,* 933 So. 2d 1236 (Fla. App. 2006), the court reversed a conviction under the robbery by sudden snatching statute, holding that a conviction under the statute required that the victim knew her purse was being snatched.

Even if not treated as a robbery, theft from the person is punished more severely than ordinary theft, and it is a felony in most states, whether the amount taken is very small or very large. State legislative bodies and courts are well aware that injury can easily occur to a victim who is often startled by the theft and may seek to protect his or her property.

Common forms of theft from a person are pickpocketing and purse snatching. However, theft of a purse from a shopping cart was also held to be theft from the person when the victim's hand was on the cart.[19]

Extortion

extortion Obtaining property by threats of future harm. It differs from robbery in that robbery requires threat of immediate harm.

Extortion is a crime of threatened force, fear, or violence. The name comes from the Latin *torquere,* which means "to wrench or twist." The term *torture* also can be traced to this Latin root. State statutes have different definitions of extortion, but they all make it a crime to obtain "property" (usually money) of another by causing that person to consent to transfer the property because of fear or threats that the extortionist will take some action in the future. The nature of the threat varies from state to state. New York's extortion statute, McKinney's Penal Law § 155(e), lists nine kinds of threats used in "instilling a fear" of extortionate acts. The most common kinds of threats listed in state statutes are bodily injury or death, damage to property, false criminal accusations, exposure of a secret that would subject the victim to contempt or ridicule, or economic harm.

Robbery and extortion are similar in that they are both methods used to obtain money or property illegally. Extortion differs from robbery in these ways:

- There is a threat to inflict a future harm (extortion) rather than an immediate harm (robbery).
- In robbery, the victim must immediately comply with the criminal demand, or violence will immediately occur. In extortion, future compliance is demanded to avoid future harm to a third party or to the victim.
- Robbery must be committed in the presence of the victim, whereas extortion can be committed over the telephone or by mail (such conduct, however, immediately makes the offense also a federal violation).

The harm that is threatened differs also. In robbery, immediate force is threatened or used against the owner or victim to compel the victim to acquiesce in the taking of the property. In extortion, the victim must pay the amount demanded to avoid or prevent

- Destruction of property. (Bombing a restaurant or business place is a standard practice of organized crime, which could result in a serious loss of life and injuries if the restaurant or business place were open for business.)
- Kidnapping or injuries to the victim or the victim's family or friends.

- Accusations of crime, and so forth.
- Damage to the good name or business reputation of the victim or the victim's family.
- Exposure of a secret or failing of the victim or family.[20]

The U.S. Congress has passed a federal extortion act. The Hobbs Act (18 U.S.C.A. 1951(b)(2)) defines extortion as "the obtaining of property of another, with his consent, induced by wrongful use of actual or threatened force, violence, or fear." When Congress enacted the Hobbs Act, the statute was aimed primarily at gangsters who were extorting protection money from businesses. That is, the business would not be bombed or receive other violence if the protection money was paid.

The Hobbs Act also covers other kinds of threatened violence. For example, in the 2010 case of *United States v. Markle*[21] a federal court of appeals upheld the conviction under the Hobbs Act of a member of a labor union who threatened members of a rival union in order to keep the other union off a job site the defendant's union wanted to work on exclusively. While the court recognized the Supreme Court had carved out an exception to the Hobbs Act for union violence used to obtain legitimate labor objectives, the court held that the exception did not apply to illegitimate objectives.[22]

Extortion by Intimidation

Extortion is often accomplished by threats of violence, but other kinds of threats or coercive tactics can constitute extortion. For example, in *State v. Gant,*[23] a defendant was charged with extortion under the Iowa extortion statute, Iowa Code Section 711.4(6). That section states that a person commits the crime of extortion if the person takes certain actions for the purpose of obtaining anything of value from another person. Among the prohibited actions is "threaten[ing] to testify or provide information or to withhold testimony or information with respect to another's legal claim or defense." In *Gant*, a garage owner had tools and equipment stolen. Gant told the owner he could provide information concerning the location of the stolen goods but would do so only if the owner paid him $200. The court found this to be a threat to withhold information about the owner's claim to the stolen goods and affirmed the defendant's conviction for extortion.

The threat must be wrongful; that is, it must threaten some action that is not legally protected. It would not be extortion, for example, to threaten to sue a debtor if the debtor did not pay a debt on time. However, if the person making the threat is not privileged to do so, it can be extortion. In *State v. Pauling,*[24] the court held that a man who threatened to publish nude photographs of his former girlfriend if she did not repay a debt could be charged with extortion. Publishing the photographs was not protected as free speech, because its only purpose was to threaten the girlfriend.

The crime of extortion does require a threat, and the receipt of property from another without a threat is not extortion. For example, in *People v. Hesslink*[25] the court reversed the conviction of a defendant who, posing as a police officer, forced a prostitute to perform oral sex on him. The prostitute also gave the defendant money in the hope he would not arrest her, and based on that payment he was charged with extortion. The court held that because the defendant did not demand money under threat of "arrest," the money paid by the prostitute was not the result of a threat and could not sustain a conviction for extortion.

In some states extortion can be charged based on threats of future economic harm. In the 2009 case of *State v. Hynes*[26] the New Hampshire Supreme Court upheld the extortion conviction of a lawyer who threatened to bring a civil action based on a "gender discrimination" claim against a beauty salon. The New Hampshire extortion statute, like the New York statute discussed earlier, contained a listing of eight specific kinds of extortionate acts, plus a "catch-all" provision based on threatened acts that would not benefit the person making the threats but would harm the person threatened. The lawyer demanded $1,000 to avoid filing the action. The court said that the lawyer's threatened claim was groundless, because the lawyer had not himself used the salon, and he didn't have a client who had been discriminated against by the salon. As a result, the defendant would not benefit from the threatened action, and the salon would be harmed. This made the lawyer's actions extortion, the court held.

Other courts have reached a different conclusion. In the 2008 case of *Rendelman v. State,*[27] the Maryland Supreme Court held that under the Maryland extortion statute, CL § 3-701(a), threatening to file a lawsuit unless a "settlement" payment was made on a "claim" was not extortion, even if the claim was made in bad faith. The court reasoned that while a threat to file a meritless lawsuit is a threat to inflict economic harm, the extortion statute states that the threat must be "wrongful." Because it is not illegal to file a lawsuit, even in bad faith, the court concluded that the threat to do so cannot be a "wrongful threat of economic injury." The court noted that this is also the result reached by federal courts in prosecutions under the Hobbs Act based on filing frivolous civil lawsuits, citing *United States v. Pendergraft,*[28] 297 F.3d 1198 (11th Cir. 2002).

Burglary

burglary Unlawful entry into the premises of another with intent to steal or commit a felony. Two hundred years ago in England, an illegal entry into the home of another by force and at night was punishable by death if the entry was done to steal or commit a felony.

Burglary is among the most frequently committed major crimes in the United States, with more than 3.5 million burglaries committed every year. Because burglary is a crime of stealth and opportunity, the national clearance rate, as reported by the Uniform Crime Report, is low, at approximately 15 percent. (That is, arrests are made in only approximately 15 percent of the burglaries reported.)

Burglary is a crime committed by both amateurs and professionals. It is committed against residences (homes and apartments) and commercial premises (offices, business places, and so on). It is committed not only at night but also during the day.

Under the old common law, burglary was punished by death. Because of the severe penalty, burglary required a breaking under the common law. It was also limited to the dwelling house of another, at night, and with intent to commit a felony.

All states have modified and changed the definition of burglary in their jurisdictions, resulting in differences in the definitions of burglary in the United States.[29] The Uniform Crime Reporting Program defines burglary as "the unlawful entry of a structure to commit a felony or theft. The use of force to gain entry is not required to classify an offense as burglary."

Breaking

Under common law, a "breaking" or a "breach" was required to constitute the crime of burglary. An entry through an open door or window without the consent of the person living in or controlling the building was not a breaking. All states have abolished the requirement of breaking in their general burglary statutes. For example, the Texas burglary statute, VTCA Penal Code § 30.02, defines burglary as "entry" into a residence or building that is not open to the public without consent and with intent to commit a felony, theft, or assault. In *Clark v. State*,[30] the court held that entry through an open door can be burglary, if not open to the public and occurs without the owner's consent. In the 2010 case of *Martinez v. State*,[31] the court said the "entry" occurs as soon as some part of the burglar's body, such as a hand or a foot, crosses the home's threshold.

Some states, however, continue to use an act of "breaking" to gain entry as an aggravated form of burglary in addition to their regular or simple burglary statutes.

Unlawful Entry into Premises

Because burglary is a form of trespass, an unlawful entry into the premises must take place. An entry could be made by inserting a hand or arm (or even the tip of a screwdriver) into the premises. For example, suppose X threw a brick through a jewelry store window and then inserted his hand and arm through the broken window to obtain watches and rings from the window display. This would be an unlawful entry that would justify a conviction of X for burglary of the jewelry store.

Suppose that instead of using his arm, X inserted a cane and began removing watches and rings by hooking them with the cane. Would this be an entry that justifies a conviction of burglary? Most courts would hold that this was an entry, because the cane was an extension of X's body inserted into the store to carry out a criminal purpose.[32]

Any element of a crime may be proved by circumstantial evidence. In the U.S. Supreme Court case of *United States v. Edwards*, someone burglarized a U.S. post office using a pry bar on a window.[33] The defendant had in his possession property stolen from the post office. Direct evidence of the break-in could not be shown, because no witnesses were available. However, crime lab tests showed paint and wood fragments on the defendant's clothing similar to the paint and wood on the post office window. A jury held that this evidence proved unlawful entry, and the defendant's conviction was affirmed.

In the case of *State v. Tixier*, police officers responded to a triggered burglar alarm within a minute.[34] They found a small hole near the door-opening mechanism of a garage. The defendant was found hiding among tires stacked near the door. The piece of the door that had been removed was found near the defendant. It was concluded that the defendant had used an instrument to penetrate the building. In affirming the defendant's burglary conviction, the court held:

> Evidence of a break-in by use of an instrument which penetrates into the building is, in our opinion, evidence of entry into the building. The sufficiency of this evidence is not destroyed by a failure to prove that the instrument was used to steal something from the building or to commit another felony. Such proof is

EXAMPLES OF DIFFERENT THEFT CRIMES

- Theft: A man lays his ring on the edge of a sink while washing his hands. Another man takes the ring and runs off while the owner is not looking (felony if ring's value is more than the amount determined by state statute).
- Theft from Person: A ring is taken from a pocket by a pickpocket or taken in a purse by a purse-snatcher (felony in most or all states, regardless of value of ring).
- Simple Robbery (Mugging): A woman is accosted in an alley by a menacing robber who threatens to beat her if she does not give the thief the ring on her finger (felony regardless of value of ring if she gave up the ring out of fear).
- Armed Robbery: A woman is held at gunpoint by a robber who demands that she give him the ring on her finger (higher-degree felony than mugging).

© Cengage Learning

unnecessary because burglary does not depend upon actions after the entry; the crime is complete when there is an unauthorized entry with the requisite intent.

In the case of *Champlin v. State,* the defendant entered a hotel lobby open to the general public 24 hours a day and removed a television set and a cash register.[35] Instead of charging the defendant with theft, a prosecutor charged the defendant with burglary. In reversing the conviction for burglary, the court pointed out that the defendant's conduct, although illegal, was not burglary, because the premises were open to the general public.

The Dwelling House of Another

A "dwelling house" is a place where people live and sleep. Under the common law, unlawful entry into and theft from a business place would not be a burglary, because a business place is not a dwelling house. Hotel rooms and apartments are dwelling houses, because people live and sleep in such places. A new building into which no one has yet moved has been held not to be a dwelling house.[36]

All the states and the federal government have changed the common law restricting burglary to only dwelling houses. Today, virtually all buildings are contained within the scope of the crime of burglary (and some states, such as California, also include vehicles). Under Model Penal Code § 221.1 it is a felony of the third degree if one unlawfully enters any building with the intent to commit a crime. It is felony of the second degree if the unlawful entry occurs "in the dwelling of another at night."

Many states also punish the burglary of an inhabited building more severely than that of an uninhabited building. In the case of *People v. Lewis,* the court held that the question of "inhabited" or "uninhabited" turns not on the immediate presence or absence of people in the building but rather on the character of the use of the building.[37] In the 2010 case of *State v. Jackson*[38] the court reversed a burglary conviction under the Ohio burglary statute, which applied to a break-in of a building where inhabitants are "present or likely to be present." In that case, the defendant broke into a mobile home, but the owner had not regularly used the mobile home as a residence for several weeks, because he was away caring for his ailing parents. The court stated that just because a building is a "residence" does not mean persons are "likely to be present" in the building.

Nighttime

The common law required that burglary be committed at night, which was defined as the time between sunset and sunrise. An entry into a dwelling house with an accompanying theft during the day could not be charged as a burglary under this definition. The defendant, however, could be charged with the separate crimes of trespass, stealing, and, depending on the circumstances, criminal damage to property. Today, about half the burglaries in the United States are committed during the day, and all jurisdictions recognize daylight burglaries. Some states impose more severe penalties for nighttime burglaries.

Intent to Commit a Felony

Common law burglary required proof of intent to commit a felony. Most states and the federal government have broadened this element of burglary. Some states now require that the state prove intent to steal or commit a felony. Others provide that the intent must be to commit a crime (misdemeanor or felony). Other state statutes specify crimes, whereas still others require that intent to commit a larceny, theft, or other felony be shown.

Courts have held that whether the state must prove intent to commit a specific crime depends on the language of the statute. For example, in the 2009 case of *State v. Chatelain*,[39] the Oregon Supreme Court held that the Oregon burglary statute, which requires a showing that the defendant entered with "the intent to commit a crime therein," meant that the state must prove what specific crime a defendant was intending to commit. The court said that proof of the unlawful entry by itself does not satisfy the elements of the burglary statute.

INTENT TO STEAL IN A BURGLARY CHARGE

The general rule of law is that intent to steal cannot be inferred from the single fact of an unlawful entry into a building. Additional circumstances must be considered, such as these:

- Type of Entry: Was it forcible?
- Manner of Entry: Was there a breaking or splintering?
- Place of Entry: Was it the rear or side of the building?
- Type of Building: Did the building contain items that a thief would be interested in stealing?
- Time of Entry: Was it the middle of the night or the middle of the day?
- Conduct of the Defendant When Interrupted: Did he or she attempt to hide or escape?

Source: This material is adapted from a chart originated by the Supreme Court of Wisconsin in the case of *State v. Barclay*.[40]

WHAT IS THE STATE OBLIGATED TO PROVE?

In addition to the intent or mental element of each crime . . .

In order to charge	That there was a stealing (taking and carrying away)?	The value of the property taken?	Elements other than the crime of stealing?
Theft/Larceny	Yes	Yes	No
Robbery	Yes	Not necessary as long as the property was something of value	Yes, (1) that the taking was by force or threat of force and (2) that the taking was from the victim's person or presence
Burglary	No, only an intent to steal or to commit a felony as required by the statutes of that state	Not necessary as long as the property was something of value (or there was an intent to steal)	Yes, requires a showing of an unlawful entry into a dwelling or building (or an unlawful remaining after closing)

© Cengage Learning

On the other hand, because a New Jersey burglary statute required only that the defendant have entered with a "purpose to commit an offense," the court in *State v. Robinson*[41] held that the state need not prove that any specific crime was intended. General intent can be inferred from the circumstances of the break-in itself. For example, a defendant who is apprehended in a warehouse in the middle of the night with an armful of merchandise leaves little question concerning intent in that particular situation.

The intent to steal is not always presumed. In the Pennsylvania case of *Commonwealth v. Muniem,* the defendant, who had been found in an empty warehouse about noon, was convicted of burglary.[42] The door was half open and the defendant was walking out when the police arrived. He was cooperative, did not run, and had nothing in his possession. The owner testified that nothing was missing. The defendant stated that he had to go to the toilet and had looked for a lavatory in the empty building. The defendant was thirty-three years old, employed, and married, and he had no prior record. In reversing the conviction and ordering the defendant discharged, the court stated:

> In the instant case, the only evidence produced against the appellant is his presence, perhaps as a trespasser, in a vacant building in daylight at about noontime. When found by the police, he was walking to the open door by which he testified he entered the building. The owner of the building testified that nothing was missing and there was no evidence of a forcible entry, or possession of any burglary tools, other tools or anything else.

Each case must stand on its own facts in determining whether the Commonwealth has sustained its burden of proof. At best, the evidence of the

FORMS OF THEFT

Theft/larceny	Theft from the person	Robbery[a] (theft[b] by force or threat of force)	Burglary (trespass with intent to steal or to commit a felony)
■ Ordinary theft (usually done secretly)	■ Purse snatching	■ Mugging or yoking (strong-arm robbery)	■ Ordinary burglary (some states punish burglary committed at night more severely)
■ "Snatch and run" theft	■ Pickpocketing	■ Armed robbery (weapon shown or not shown)	■ Armed burglary
■ Shoplifting	■ "Rolling a drunk" (taking valuables from an intoxicated person or person in a stupor)	■ Carjacking	■ Burglary in which an occupant of the building is injured
■ Theft from autos		■ Burglaries that turn into robberies	
■ Theft from buildings		■ Purse snatching and pickpocketing in which such force is used against the person that it constitutes strong-arm robbery	■ "Break and run" burglary (breaking store window and running off with property)
■ Theft by fraud (con game)	■ Taking valuables from injured, dead, or disabled people		
■ Embezzlement			
■ Theft by bailee		■ Home invasion robbery	■ Newspapers use the term car burglary. Some states do have this crime. For example, N.J.S.A. 2C:18-1 includes "car" in the burglary statute, as does the Idaho burglary statute, I.C. § 18-1401.
■ Fraud on innkeeper, restaurant			
■ Looting—taking property from building that has been destroyed by disaster, riot, bombing, fire, tornado, and so on			

[a]Depending on the laws of the state, sentences could be enhanced (increased) when there is concealment of identity (mask), a bulletproof garment is used, or a police scanner radio is used during the commission of the crime.
[b]In robberies of banks and stores, the terms *counter jumpers* and *take-over robberies* (as distinguished from "single-teller" or "single-clerk" robberies) are sometimes used to describe the methods used by the robbers.

© Cengage Learning

Commonwealth may give rise to suspicion and conjecture of guilt but most certainly does not have such volume and quality capable of reasonably and naturally justifying an inference of a willful and malicious entry into a building with the intent to commit a felony so as to overcome the presumption of innocence and establish guilt beyond a reasonable doubt of the crime of burglary.

Proof of Burglary When Other Crimes Are Committed

As a trespass offense, burglary is most often committed by a defendant who steals or who has an intent to steal. Criminals, however, enter private premises for criminal purposes other than to steal. Offenders have entered the premises of others with intent to commit rape, arson, or other serious felonies. In the 2008 case of *State v. Jacobs*,[43] the court affirmed a conviction of burglary, holding that evidence showed the defendant entered the victim's hotel room with the intent to assault her and steal her purse.

The charge of burglary is sometimes one of multiple serious charges against a defendant who went on a criminal rampage in a private home or business place. In the *Jacobs* case discussed above prosecutors charged the defendant with both forcible rape and aggravated burglary, based on the unlawful entry and resulting battery of the victim, which increased simple burglary to aggravated burglary under the Louisiana statute. The court held that while the defendant could be convicted of both forcible rape and simple burglary, the forcible rape could not be used as the basis for a conviction of aggravated burglary under the Double Jeopardy Clause.

The charge of burglary also offers prosecutors an alternative charge when doubt exists as to whether the state can prove attempted rape, murder, arson, or another crime. If X broke into W's apartment with the intent to rape her but found that she was not home, X could be charged with burglary if the state could prove his intent to commit a felony.

The Crime of Trafficking in Stolen Goods

The crimes of trafficking in stolen goods are defined by the statutes of each state and ordinarily include (1) receiving (a single act), (2) concealing and possessing (continuing acts), and, in some states, (3) buying and transferring. In determining the statute of limitations for these offenses, the Supreme Court of Minnesota held in the 1981 case of *State v. Lawrence*, 312 N.W.2d 251:

> The crime commonly known as "receiving stolen property," when used in a shorthand sense, is a misnomer, since it includes a number of different legal concepts in addition to and separate from receiving. The offense includes not only receiving, but concealing; . . . it includes buying; and . . . it also includes possessing and transferring.

> The issue here is whether any of these terms may be deemed continuing in nature. The two most likely descriptions of defendant's conduct are possession and concealment. Does either, or both, apply? In answering this question we should keep in mind that a crime is not continuing in nature if not clearly so indicated by the legislature. . . .

> Both possessing and concealing are distinguishable from receiving in that the latter connotes a single act. Behind possessing and concealing, however, is the notion that property is being kept from someone in violation of a duty to return and this duty to return continues. One of the reasons for including possessing and concealing as crimes is to be able to prosecute even though the time has run out on receiving. Surely this serves the purpose of the statute, which is to deter trafficking in stolen goods.

> * * *

We hold, therefore, that either concealing or possessing stolen goods is a continuing offense for the purpose of the statute of limitations. We hold this defendant may not assert the statute of limitations as a bar where he kept the goods he stole in his house and garage, thereby not only possessing the goods but making their discovery more difficult for the owner.

To convict a defendant of trafficking in stolen goods, the state is ordinarily required to prove

- That the property involved was stolen property
- That the defendant received, concealed, possessed, purchased, or transferred the property as forbidden by the statutes of that state
- That the defendant knew the property was stolen. "Stolen" means that the property was obtained as a result of a theft, burglary, robbery, or any other form of theft crime, such as shoplifting or obtaining property by deception.

The Fence and Fencing Stolen Property

fence A person who traffics in stolen property (receiving, concealing, possessing, buying, transferring, and so on).

A **fence** is a person who traffics in stolen property (receiving, concealing, possessing, buying, transferring, and so on). A fence acts as a middleperson and pays the thief for stolen property, which the fence in turn attempts to merchandise at a profit. The compensation paid by the fence to the thief is usually a small fraction of the value of the goods. The report of the President's Commission on Law Enforcement and Administration of Justice makes the following observations regarding fencing in the United States:

> Nearly all professional theft is undertaken with the aim of selling the goods thereafter. Although the thief himself may retail his stolen merchandise, he probably will prefer to sell to a fence. He thereby increases his safety by reducing the risk that he will be arrested with the goods in his possession, or that they will be stolen in turn from him. He also avoids the dangers associated with the disposal process itself. In addition, large quantities of goods which may be perishable or otherwise quickly lose their value, or for which there is a specialized demand, will require a division of labor and level of organization beyond the capacity of an individual thief operating as his own retailer. The professional thief thus needs a "middleman" in the same way and for some of the same reasons as the farmer, manufacturer, or other producer.

> * * *

> Some fences engage in fencing as a supplement to their legitimate businesses, often on a more or less regular basis. The consultants learned of clothing and appliance dealers who regularly serve as outlets for stolen goods. The major outlets for stolen jewels in one of the cities studied were reported to be legitimate jewelry merchants. Other fences deal primarily or wholly in stolen goods and are therefore professional criminals themselves.

> Some narcotics pushers act as fences, taking stolen goods instead of cash for narcotics. While dealing with addicts is generally regarded as more dangerous than

dealing with nonaddicts, it is also more profitable. The addict in need of a "fix" does not bargain well.

When Property Loses Its Character as Stolen Goods

United States v. Monasterski

United States Court of Appeals for the Sixth Circuit (1977), 567 F.2d 677

Three juveniles were caught attempting to steal tires from a railroad boxcar. The juveniles cooperated with FBI agents and delivered some of the tires to the defendant, whom they identified as their prospective fence. The defendant was convicted of receiving stolen property (the tires). In reversing the defendant's conviction, the Sixth Circuit Court held that once the thieves were caught, the tires lost their character as stolen goods and could no longer support the defendant's conviction. The court further held:

> In accord with the common law rule, one cannot be convicted of receiving stolen goods when actual physical possession of the stolen goods has been recovered by their owner or his agent before delivery to the intended receiver. We further hold, also in accord with the common law rule, that the term "agent" means any person with a right to possession or control over the goods.

The Alabama Supreme Court followed the common law rule that goods that had never been stolen or goods that had lost their stolen character could not support a conviction of the crime of receiving stolen property.

Florida, however, changed the common law and enacted a law taking away this defense from a person charged with the crime of dealing in stolen property. Florida Statutes (1995), § 812.028(3), permits criminal convictions in Florida for endeavoring to traffic in stolen property without proof by the state of Florida that the property was actually stolen.

Possession of Criminal or Burglary Tools

Most states have statutes making the possession of criminal or burglary tools a criminal offense. The usual elements of this crime are as follows:

- The defendant had a device or implement in his or her possession.
- This device or implement was suitable for or was capable of being used in committing burglary.
- The defendant intended to use this device or implement to break into a building, dwelling, or depository with the intent to steal.

Like the crime of receiving stolen property, possession of burglary tools is difficult to prove. The difficult element to prove in receiving stolen property is knowledge by the defendant that the property was stolen. In possession of burglary tools, the difficult element is intent by the defendant to use the tool for purposes of burglary. Possession of ordinary work tools is not ordinarily sufficient to justify a conviction for possession of burglary tools; there must be additional evidence of intent to use them to commit burglary.

Cases in which most convictions have been obtained can be divided into the following categories:

- The defendant was apprehended while committing or attempting to commit a burglary with the tool or had the tool in his or her actual or constructive possession.
- The defendant was in the possession of a specifically designed or adapted tool under circumstances in which a judge or jury could infer the tool's use for an illegal purpose of entry.

Destroying or Damaging the Property of Another

No U.S. city, town, or village escapes the physical and psychological disfigurement vandalism brings to public and private property. Vandalism is a serious problem in most public transport systems, and it costs millions of dollars in large cities. Schools are often hit hard, with broken windows, break-ins, damaged property, and spray-painted walls.

Veteran law enforcement officers observe that vandalism (criminal damage to property) occurs in cycles. In the summertime, public parks are hit. Benches are piled up, debris is thrown into lagoons, and beaches are littered. If buildings are left vacant, they sometimes are vandalized to the point where they must be razed. Criminal damage to private property varies considerably and is a constant source of citizen complaints to law enforcement agencies.

Many states and cities have passed laws making parents of minors responsible for damage their child causes. Kansas imposes liability on the homeowner's insurance company, which gives the owner of damaged property the right to collect damages from the insurance company.

In 1990, one 18-year-old did more than $500,000 in damage by graffiti vandalism in Los Angeles. The Los Angeles city attorney said that it was "the worst case of graffiti vandalism we have seen in Los Angeles... or anywhere else in the nation [by a single individual]." Near Tampa, Florida, three teenagers pulled down more than a dozen traffic stop signs for kicks one night. Other teenagers driving home after bowling were killed when their car drove into an intersection and was hit broadside, killing the occupants. The teenagers who took down the stop sign were convicted of three counts of manslaughter.

Trespass

In its broad sense, the word *trespass* means an unlawful act against a person, property, or right of another. For example, court decisions today continue to speak of the trespassory taking of property, meaning that the property was wrongfully taken. Murder, assault, and battery are trespassory acts because they are wrongful and unlawful acts that violate the rights of other people.

trespass A wrongful intrusion on the land or into the premises of another person.

However, in its usual and more common use, **trespass** refers to a wrongful intrusion on the land or into the premises of another person. All states have statutes that reflect this usual and common concept of the offense, and when newspapers use the word, they usually mean it in this limited sense. The Washington statute, RCWA

9A.52.070, defines criminal trespass as follows: "a person is guilty of criminal trespass in the first degree if he knowingly enters or remains unlawfully in a building."

A variety of trespass statutes can be found in criminal codes and municipal ordinances. The trespass to land statutes make the unlawful entry on land (when the land has been posted or the person notified to stay off) a criminal offense if the entry or the remaining on the land is without the consent of the owner or the person in lawful possession. Trespass to dwelling statutes and ordinances forbid entry into homes and residences without the consent of an occupant.

Other trespass statutes and ordinances forbid entry into specific places, such as schools with classes in session, unless the person has legitimate business or is a parent. Trespass statutes generally have a section dealing with entry and also a section pertaining to "failure to depart."

The Crime of Defiant Trespass

defiant trespass
Remaining in a place where one is not privileged to be even after notice of trespass is given.

The crime of **defiant trespass** occurs when a person remains in a place where he is not privileged to remain after notice of trespass is given. In most states, the offense is defined by statute similar to the following definition:

(b) Defiant trespasser.—(1) A person commits an offense if, knowing that he is not licensed or privileged to do so, he enters or remains in any place as to which notice against trespass is given by: (i) actual communication to the actor; or (ii) posting in a manner prescribed by law or reasonably likely to come to the attention of intruders; or (iii) fencing or other enclosure manifestly designed to exclude intruders.

In the 2004 case of *State v. Hamilton,*[44] a New Jersey appeals court upheld the conviction for defiant trespass of a protester who trespassed on a county roadway providing access to a municipal plant. A police officer told the protesters not to stand on the roadway to block entrance to the plant, but the defendant entered nonetheless. The court said that the defiant trespass statute applied when a person entered premises as to which notice against trespass was given by "actual communication" of such notice. It didn't matter under the statute, the court held, that the premises were on public land.

Summary

- Robbery differs from common theft in that force or threat of force must be used to take property from the victim. Theft can occur without force and outside the victim's presence.
- Armed or aggravated robbery occurs when a deadly weapon is used in a robbery, or when a victim suffers serious bodily injury. In most states, the threat of the presence of a deadly weapon satisfies the statute, though in many the weapon must in some manner be shown.
- Home invasion requires unlawful entry of the dwelling of another with intent to commit a crime, with persons present in the home, and the use of force or threat of force to commit a crime. In most states, a home invasion while armed with a dangerous weapon carries an increased penalty.

- Purse snatching becomes robbery when force more than that needed to take the property is used in the crime. Grabbing the victim and turning her around to get at the purse is sufficient to make the crime robbery.
- Robbery involves a taking of property by the present threat of use of force; extortion is the unlawful taking of property by threat of force or other harm in the future, if the victim does not comply with the demand.
- Under the common law, burglary was defined as breaking into a residence of another at night with the intent to commit a felony.

- Under modern statutes, burglary is usually defined as the unlawful entry, with or without a breaking, of a residence or building, either during the day or at night, with the intent to commit a crime therein. In some states the statute requires the intent to commit a felony; in others, specific crimes are listed.
- Criminal trespass occurs when a person unlawfully and knowingly enters the land or building of another. Defiant trespass occurs when the person unlawfully entering is given notice of the trespass, but refuses to leave the premises.

Key Terms

robbery, p. 390
armed or aggravated robbery,
  p. 391
carjacking, p. 394

home invasion robbery, p. 396
sudden snatching, p. 397
extortion, p. 398
burglary, p. 400

fence, p. 407
trespass, p. 409
defiant trespass, p. 410

Case Analysis and Writing Exercises

1. The bank robber's note "Give me the money" usually satisfies the requirement under the federal bank robbery statute that the robbery be done by "force and violence, or by intimidation," because the situation instills fear in a reasonable person that force or violence might accompany a refusal to give up the money. What if the teller to whom the note was given were part of the robbery scheme? If she goes to other tellers and gets them to give her money based on the note, is the requisite "intimidation" present? See *United States v. Gordon*, 642 F.3d 596 (7th Cir. 2011).
2. We discuss the *State v. Jackson* case in the text, where an Ohio appeals court said the fact that the owner of a mobile home was not regularly living in the home meant a burglary charge could not be proved. What if an owner, who regularly comes home each night from work, decides to stay at a friend's house on the day a burglary occurs? Can the burglar be convicted?

How is the case different from *Jackson? See State v. James*, 2012 WL 762167 (Ohio App. 2012).

Exercises 3 and 4: The federal extortion act, the Hobbs Act, has been applied to situations beyond the classic "give me some money or I will burn down your house." One area where application of the Hobbs Act is difficult is determining if "property of another" has been extorted from a victim. In *Scheidler v. National Organization for Women Inc.*, 537 U.S. 393 (2003), the U.S. Supreme Court held that a violation of the Hobbs Act requires more than a showing a property right of another was prejudiced. It must be shown that the defendant actually appropriated some property of the victim. The *Scheidler* court held that protests against an abortion clinic that damaged the clinic's business did not constitute "taking property of another" under the Hobbs Act. In Case Analysis and Writing Exercises 3 and 4 similar issues were presented to federal courts of appeal. The U.S. Supreme Court has granted certiorari in the case in Exercise 4.

3. The Hobbs Act applies not only to extortion of property based on threats or fear, but also "under color of official right." In *United States v. Thompson*, 647 F.3d 180 (5th Cir. 2011) a state officer used his influence to coerce a contractor to do work on the state officer's private residence, and then arranged to have state funds used to pay the contractor. Assuming the "another" was the contractor, what "property" was taken from him, if he received full payment for his labor? Do you agree with how the court distinguishes *Scheidler*?

4. In *United States v. Sekhar*, 683 F.3d 436 (2nd Cir. 2012), a defendant was convicted under the Hobbs Act when he e-mailed the New York Comptroller's office's general counsel and threatened to disclose that person's extramarital affair if the counsel didn't recommend that the Comptroller invest state funds with the defendant's firm. What "property of another" was extorted by the defendant? Is this case more like *Scheidler*, or more like the *Thompson* case discussed in Exercise 3? The U.S. Supreme Court has agreed to hear this case, 133 S. Ct. 928 (2013), perhaps to clear up questions that linger from the *Scheidler* opinion.

Endnotes

1. The asportation or carrying away requirement in robbery is usually easily met. For example, in *State v. Johnson*, 432 So. 2d 758 (Fla. App. 1983), the court found asportation complete when the defendant forced a store clerk to put money in a paper bag and set it on the counter near the defendant, even if the defendant never touched the bag. In *Lattimore v. U.S.*, 684 A2d 357 (D.C. 1996), asportation was found when the defendant took a wallet from the victim, saw only a payroll check in the wallet, and threw the wallet back at the victim.

2. Many states also make concealing identity while committing a crime such as robbery conduct for which the degree of the crime and the penalty may be increased. The Supreme Court of Wisconsin has held that if one robber concealed his identity and the other did not, the second robber could be a party to the crime of concealing identity: *Vogel v. State*, 96 Wis. 2d 372, 291 N.W.2d 838 (1980).

3. 977 P.2d 967 (Mont. 1999).

4. 959 N.E.2d 479 (N.Y. 2011).

5. 476 U.S. 16 (1986).

6. Volume IX, No. 27, July 1, 1968.

7. 30 A.3d 891 (Md. 2011).

8. *People v. Williams*, 814 N.W.2d 270 (Mich. 2012).

9. 306 S.W.3d 478 (Ky. 2010).

10. 945 N.E.2d 295 (Mass. 2011).

11. West's Annotated Penal Code, § 215.

12. 92 Cal. Rptr. 3d 751 (Cal. App. 2009).

13. Courts facing the movement or asportation question under the general robbery statute have reached a different answer. In *State v. Johnson*, 558 N.W.2d 375 (Wis. 1996), the Wisconsin Supreme Court held that the robber must move the car to be guilty.

14. 145 Cal. Rptr. 3d 907 (Cal. App. 2012).

15. Illinois Revised Statutes 1983, Chapter 38, paragraphs 12-11.

16. 590 A.2d 665 (1991).

17. 496 S.E.2d 668 (Va. App. 1998).

18. 362 Mass. 83, 283 N.E.2d 840 (1972).

19. See *Alfred v. State*, 659 S.W.2d 97 (Tex. App. 1983).

20. In 1997 Autumn Jackson attempted to extort $40 million from actor Bill Cosby. Jackson alleged she was Cosby's illegitimate daughter, and she threatened to make her claim public if he did not pay her the $40 million. After she began writing letters to companies whose products Cosby endorsed, he went to the FBI and then began tape recording conversations between himself and Jackson. Jackson was subsequently found guilty of extortion. See the *New York Times* articles, "Cosby Describes Requests for Money from 2 Women," July 16, 1997, and "To Ask Is Not Always to Extort: In the Case Involving Bill Cosby, a Troubling Legal Issue," July 18, 1997.

21. 628 F.3d 58 (2nd Cir. 2010).

22. *United States v. Enmons*, 410 U.S. 396 (1973).

23. 597 N.W.2d 501 (Iowa 1999).

24. 69 P.3d 331 (Wash. 2003).

25. 213 Cal. Rptr. 465 (Cal. App. 1985).

26. 978 A.2d 264 (N.H. 2009), *cert denied* 130 S. Ct. 1083 (2010).

27. 947 A.2d 546 (Md. 2008).

28. 297 F.3d 1198 (11th Cir. 2002).

29. Florida's burglary statutes, adopted in 1975, provide that "burglary means entering or remaining in a structure or conveyance with the intent to commit an offense therein, unless the premises are at the time open to the public or the defendant is licensed or invited to enter or remain."

30. 667 S.W.2d 906 (Tex. App. 1984).

31. 304 S.W.3d 642 (Tex. App. 2010).

32. The New Mexico Court of Appeals held in the 1976 case of *State v. Tixier*, 89 N.M. 297, 551 P.2d 987, that "A one-half inch penetration into the building is sufficient. Any penetration, however slight, of the interior space is sufficient. The fact that the penetration is by an instrument is also sufficient. 2 *Wharton's Criminal Law and Procedure* (1957) § 421; Clark and Marshall, *Crimes*, 6th ed., § 13.04."

33. 415 U.S. 800, 94 S. Ct. 1234 (1974).

34. See note 15.

35. 84 Wis. 2d 621, 267 N.W.2d 295 (1978).

36. *Woods v. State*, 186 Miss. 463, 191 So. 283 (1939).

37. 274 Cal. App. 2d 912, 79 Cal. Rptr. 650 (1969).

38. 937 N.E.2d 120 (Ohio App. 2010).

39. 220 P.3d 41 (Ore. 2009).

40. 196 N.W.2d 745 (Wis. 1972).

41. 673 A.2d 1372 (1996).

42. 225 Pa. Super. 311, 303 A.2d 528 (1973).

43. 987 So.2d 208 (La. App. 2008), *writ denied*, 6 So.3d 769 (La. 2009).

44. 845 A.2d 669 (N.J. Super. 2004).

White-Collar Crime, Cybercrime, and Commercial Crime

Kristin Callahan/Everett Collection/Alamy

Bernard Madoff, shown leaving a federal courthouse, pled guilty in 2009 to eleven counts of violation of federal fraud laws, and was sentenced to 150 years in prison. It is estimated his Ponzi scheme cost investors more than $65 billion.

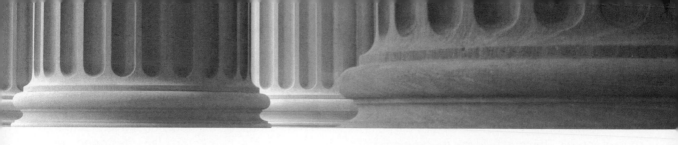

OUTLINE

White-Collar Crime

Fraud and Fraudulent Practices

Bank Fraud

Health Care Fraud

Intellectual Property Fraud

Fraud and Corruption in Government

Stock Market and Financial Market Frauds

Other Fraud Statutes in the Federal Criminal Code

The Crime of Identity Theft and False Identification Documents

Counterfeiting of Money and Commercial Products

Counterfeiting of Currency

Other Counterfeiting Problems

Computer Crime or Cybercrime

Arson

Essential Elements of Arson

Product Tampering

LEARNING OBJECTIVES

In this chapter we discuss nonviolent, mainly economic theft or harm crimes. The learning objectives for Chapter 15 are

- Define white-collar crime.
- Explain why fraud convictions require action done knowingly.
- Describe the elements of a "scheme or artifice" under federal criminal statutes.
- Explain how bribery and extortion are similar under the federal bribery and extortion statutes.
- List the laws protecting intellectual property.
- Name two federal criminal statutes frequently used to convict white-collar criminals.
- Identify one element making wire fraud different from bank fraud, and state why the element exists.
- Define insider trading.
- State the elements of identity theft crimes.

The common image of bribery as a crime involves someone saying to a public official, such as a city council member preparing to vote on a zoning law, "I will give you $10,000 if you vote no on the zoning issue." It looks like a contract: the $10,000 is given in exchange for the favorable vote. The essence of the crime is that the $10,000 is given with a *quid pro quo* expected. It is that expectation of a *quid pro quo* that makes bribery a crime, from the perspective of the person giving the $10,000.

Kevin Ring was a Washington, D.C. lobbyist with the lobbying team headed by the well-known lobbyist Jack Abramoff. (Abramoff served 43 months in federal prison on corruption charges and was released in December 2010.) Ring's duties with Abramoff's firm included giving congressional and executive officials gifts of dinners, travel, drinks, concert tickets, and sporting event tickets. These same officials often took actions that were favorable to Ring's clients.

Ring was indicted for "honest services bribery" under federal law, and convicted on three counts. On appeal, Ring contended the government failed to prove the "gifts" he made to officials were given with an explicit *quid pro quo* requested from the official, and also that the government didn't prove the official accepting the gifts agreed to that *quid pro quo*.

In 2013 his conviction was affirmed by a federal court of appeals. The court held that the government need not prove an express agreement that gifts were given in exchange for official acts; the jury could find that intent implied in Ring's actions. The court also held that it did not matter if the officials agreed

to the *quid pro quo*. The crime was committed by offering the gifts with the intent to influence the officials, whether or not the intent was successful.

In this chapter we will learn about many crimes that focus on schemes or plans designed to fraudulently deprive another person of money or other property, as well as crimes like arson and trespass that directly injure another person's property.

White-Collar Crime

white-collar crime A class or type of criminal conduct whose only goal is the criminal's economic gain.

The term **white-collar crime** is generally understood to refer to a class or type of criminal conduct whose only goal is the criminal's economic gain. While the "white-collar" language suggests the status of the wrongdoer, most definitions of the term focus on the kind of behavior made criminal, not the identity of the criminal. The U.S. Department of Justice, in its 1989 FBI report entitled *White-Collar Crime: A Report to the Public*,[1] defined white-collar crime as "those illegal acts which are characterized by deceit, concealment or violation of trust and which are not dependent upon the application or threat of physical force or violence."

The economic cost of white-collar crimes and the other commercial crimes discussed in this chapter is enormous and greatly outstrips the cost of many other crimes. For example, in the 2012 FBI report *Crime in the United States: 2011*,[2] it was estimated that the total economic cost of all robbery, burglary, theft, and car theft crimes in 2011 was $15.6 billion. By contrast, the estimated loss in 2009 suffered by investors in the Bernard Madoff Ponzi scheme was $65 billion.

In this chapter we focus on the many forms of commercial, business, financial, and fraudulent conduct that are made criminal under state and federal laws.

Fraud and Fraudulent Practices

fraud Deceitful means or acts used to cheat a person, corporation, or governmental agency.

Fraud consists of deceitful means or acts used to cheat a person, corporation, or governmental agency. Theft by fraud or larceny by fraud is often the criminal charge used, as fraud can be a form of theft and larceny. Fraud convictions require some form of specific intent, such as acting knowingly or willfully, as distinguished from negligent conduct. In the following materials this chapter examines some of the key criminal laws that target white-collar crimes of fraud.

Bank Fraud

The federal government has an important interest in fraud aimed at banks and other financial institutions. Most of these institutions are federally insured, so that losses suffered by them caused by fraud can end up being paid for by the federal government. Because of this, Congress passed the bank fraud statute, 18 U.S.C. § 1344, which makes it a federal crime to defraud a financial institution that is federally insured. Examples of **bank fraud** that would fall under this statute are check kiting (discussed in Chapter 13), check forgery, false statements on loan applications, unauthorized use of ATM machines, credit card fraud, and student loan fraud. These crimes all require proof that the defendant knowingly executed or attempted to execute a "scheme or artifice" to defraud, or, through false statements, obtained money or property from a federally insured financial institution.

bank fraud Fraud aimed at banks and other financial institutions.

The statute does not define "scheme or artifice," but 18 U.S.C. § 1346 states that a "scheme or artifice" includes a scheme to deprive another of the intangible right to honest services (discussed later in this chapter). The federal fraud statutes otherwise leave it to courts to determine whether "a scheme or artifice" exists. A definition that is too specific makes it possible for criminals to manipulate their scheme so that it falls outside the definition. The U.S. Supreme Court has held that any such scheme must include a "material falsehood," that is, one that a person would understand to be important and relied on by another. See *Neder v. United States,*[3] where the holding was made applicable to mail fraud and wire fraud statutes as well. These statutes also require proof of a "scheme or artifice."

An example of a bank fraud scheme can be seen in *United States v. Jenkins.*[4] Jenkins started a computer sales business, and he entered into an agreement with his bank that permitted him to withdraw funds from his account based on credit card receipts of computer sales. Jenkins, using his own and other people's credit cards, created receipts showing sales that had actually not occurred. He then presented these receipts to the bank as evidence that payments would be made by the credit card companies. The credit card companies refused to pay, because the sales did not occur. Jenkins was convicted under the bank fraud act.

Health Care Fraud

Health care costs in the United States in 2012 reached nearly $2.4 trillion, or about 14 percent of the gross domestic product of the United States. The federal government has many health care programs, most notably Medicare and Medicaid. These programs rely on statements, claims, and bills sent to program administrators by health care professionals, as well as persons served in the programs. False claims under these programs cost the federal government huge amounts each year. The 2012 FBI *Health Care Fraud Report* estimates that the yearly cost of health care fraud is more than $80 billion.

Congress has passed various statutes that address this problem, among them the Medicaid False Claims Statute, 42 U.S.C. § 1320a-7b(a), and the Medicaid Anti-Kickback Statute, 42 U.S.C. § 1320a-7b(b). The false claims statute makes it a crime for any person to knowingly and willfully make a false statement in any application for a federal health care benefit. An example of a crime falling within this statute includes submitting a bill for services or tests that were not performed. The anti-kickback statute is aimed at those who promise or receive payments based on referrals of patients for services paid under federal health care programs. An example of a crime coming under this statute includes accepting a fee for sending a patient to a physician or other provider for medical services. It also includes sending a patient to a health care provider with whom the referring physician has a financial relationship. Violation of these laws can lead to massive fines. In 2001 TAP Pharmaceutical Products, Inc. was fined $875 million, the largest fine ever for health care fraud.

The federal government also has a general health care fraud statute, 18 U.S.C. § 1347, which makes it a crime to willfully execute a "scheme or artifice" intended to defraud a "health care benefit" program. One typical prosecution under this statute is found in the 2009 case of *United States v. Franklin-El.*[5] The defendants ran an alcohol and drug addiction counseling clinic, which received reimbursement payments under Medicaid for qualified patients. Only diagnosed addicts were qualified patients. The defendants filed 1,331 false claims for reimbursement from Medicaid that totaled over $1.2 million, listing as "addicts" persons who were not addicts, were not enrolled in the defendant's program, or in some cases were children only a few weeks old. The court affirmed their convictions on fifty-two counts of health care fraud.

Convictions under the health care fraud statute carry both a prison sentence and a fine. In extreme cases, the prison sentence can be for life. In *United States v. Martinez,*[6] a physician operated a "pain management clinic." Some of the medical services he provided were paid for under Medicaid, Medicare, and the Ohio Bureau of Workers Compensation, each of which qualifies as a "health care benefit" program. Martinez gave his patients "nerve-block" injections, for which he billed these programs. The average number of "nerve-block" injections patients usually received was 2.5 per year; Martinez gave his patients an average of 64 injections per year, with the result that many became addicted to the medication and incurred serious bodily injury. Two patients died as a result of Martinez's treatments. He was convicted of health care fraud for claiming reimbursements of more than $14 million for improperly administered treatments and improper medical services. Because his actions resulted in the deaths of two patients, he was sentenced to life in prison under § 1347(2). In 2010 the U.S. Supreme Court denied certiorari.[7]

Intellectual Property Fraud

Intellectual property generally means property rights in ideas; inventions; artistic works such as books, movies, and songs; and the like. The theft, piracy, or counterfeiting of intellectual property costs its owners billions of dollars each year and has become even more damaging with the rise of Internet theft. The primary criminal laws aimed at **intellectual property fraud** are the federal copyright and patent acts and federal and state trade secret acts.

intellectual property fraud Theft, piracy, or counterfeiting of ideas, inventions, artistic works, and the like.

Copyright   The copyright act, 17 U.S.C. § 506, protects books, movies, and songs once they have been published. Any person who willfully infringes a valid copyright for economic gain violates the statute, and can be sentenced to up to 5 years in prison. "Infringing" means reproducing or distributing the work without permission. Thus, while it is permitted to use a copyrighted song in a free school production, it is not permitted to use the same song in a production that charges admission. Questions about the permissible use of copyrighted material are decided under the "fair use" doctrine, 17 U.S.C. § 107. "Fair use" includes classroom use, scholarship use, research, teaching, and related uses of the copyrighted materials.

The Internet has presented a great challenge to the "fair use" doctrine. Many software programs available on the Internet enable users to "share" files with other users on a "peer-to-peer" basis, meaning that the users' computers communicate directly with one another without using an Internet server. If these files contain copyrighted works, such as songs downloaded from a CD to the user's computer, the songs are being distributed and such distribution may be a violation of the copyright law. Individual criminal prosecutions for copyright infringement have not been found. However, courts have found Internet servers to be in civil violation of the copyright laws, based on the actual "sharing" done by its Internet customers.

In *M.G.M. Studios v. Grokster, LLC,* 545 U.S. 913 (2005), the Supreme Court held that two Internet companies that distributed software to its customers that enabled the customers to share copyrighted works could be found to be in violation of the copyright laws. The software created a network that allowed users to access other computers using the same software program, find designated files, and download them. Since about 90 percent of the files included copyrighted songs, the Court held that the Internet companies could be found in violation of the copyright owners' exclusive distribution and reproduction rights.

The Internet sharing of copyright materials also makes application of the "first sale" defense questionable. It has long been recognized that one who purchases a copyrighted work is entitled to sell that very work without violating the copyright act. That is because after this "first sale," the seller no longer has the work to sell and cannot use it for the kind of economic gain the copyright laws are intended to punish. However, if a computer file is "sold" or traded, the seller/trader keeps the file and can do it again. The "first sale" defense does not seem appropriate in that case.

In a 2013 decision, the U.S. Supreme Court held that the "first sale" exception to the copyright acts applied to the sale in the United States of books published in Europe or Asia. In *Kirtsaeng v. John Wiley & Sons, Inc.*[8] a student from Thailand studying in the United States had his family buy used books in Thailand and send them to him in the United States, where he sold them at a profit. The court held the first sale doctrine applied to the sales by the student because the books had been "lawfully" published outside the United States.

Trade Secrets The federal government and every state have trade secret laws that make it a crime to steal a trade secret. Generally, trade secrets are property characteristics that have been kept a secret by the owner of the property, which property is made valuable because of the trade secret. The best example of a trade secret is the recipe for Coca-Cola, which is aggressively kept secret by the Coca-Cola Company. The federal government makes it a crime under the Economic Espionage Act, 18 U.S.C. § 1831–1839, to convert a trade secret for economic gain.

Fraud and Corruption in Government

Fraud against government is as old as government itself. Reports of fraud and corruption date back to biblical times and early civilizations. The U.S. government today is spending over $3.5 trillion per year in its total budget, so it is not surprising that it has serious fraud and corruption problems.

Losses through fraud and corruption occur in many ways. Fraud can be charged criminally in federal courts as mail fraud (when the U.S. mails are used); wire fraud (when interstate or international communications are used); racketeering, bribery and theft of public funds; fraud and conspiracy to commit fraud; false entries or false statements; fraud in connection with government contracting; equity skimming; false statements and misappropriation of funds; conspiracy to defraud the United States; and interstate transportation of funds obtained by fraud.

The following areas account for many of the fraud losses in the federal government.

Contract Fraud and the False Claims Act   In the procurement of arms and military supplies, the federal government spends more than $600 billion yearly. Fraud in military procurement contracts has been discovered in the selling of inside information on contract bids, bid rigging, bribes and kickbacks, double billing, falsifying test results or failure to conduct tests, and overcharging for materials and services. The False Claims Act, 18 U.S.C. § 287, makes it a crime to present a claim to the U.S. government that is false or fraudulent and known to be false or fraudulent. The statute was first passed during the Civil War, because of the rampant fraud practiced by contractors providing goods and services to the Union Army.

The False Claims Act applies to any kind of false claim, if its purpose is to obtain payment from the government. For example, in the 2009 case of *United States v. Saybolt*,[9] defendants were convicted under § 287 for filing false income tax returns with the IRS and seeking refunds. They were also convicted under 18 U.S.C. § 286, which punishes conspiracies to defraud the government by false claims.

Program Frauds   Billions of dollars are dispersed every year through programs such as Medicaid, Medicare,[10] the Supplemental Nutrition Assistance Program (food stamps),[11] small business loans, subsidy programs, HUD (U.S. Department of Housing and Urban Development), Social Security, and various aid programs. Persons who make false claims for benefits under these programs can be prosecuted under the False Claims Act or, in some cases, under statutes directed at specific programs such as Medicaid, discussed earlier.

In many federal programs, funds are disbursed by city or state granting agencies to be used for appropriate purposes under the federal funding legislation. The federal program theft statute, 18 U.S.C. § 666, applies to theft or bribery by persons who are agents for organizations that receive in one year more than $10,000 of federal funds. A conviction under this statute requires (1) that the defendant be an agent of the organization and (2) that the theft involve property of the organization. For example, an independent contractor providing services to a regional airport that received federal funds was convicted under § 666 for overbilling the airport for services allegedly provided to the airport. The court held the contractor was an "agent" of the airport and thus was guilty of theft from the organization that received the federal funds. *United States v. Vitillo*.[12] However, not every theft of federal program funds is covered by § 666. In *United States v. Abu-Shawish*,[13] the court held that a defendant who was given a "block" grant of HUD funds by a Milwaukee city agency for development of a community organization could not be convicted for theft of property under § 666. It was not enough that the defendant defrauded the Milwaukee "organization" that disbursed the federal funds; the court said the defendant must be an agent of that organization as well, which the defendant was not. The court stated that the defendant should have been prosecuted under the federal mail or wire fraud acts.

bribery Offering a gift or payment to another with the specific intent to obtain some unlawful particular *quid pro quo* for the gift or payment.

Bribery of agents of an organization that receives federal funds is also covered by § 666. In *United States v. Caro-Muniz,*[14] the mayor of Rincon, Puerto Rico, was convicted for taking bribes to award contracts that were funded by federal grants.

In *United States v. Ganim,*[15] the mayor of Bridgeport, Connecticut, was convicted of accepting illegal "gifts" from persons who received city contracts. Often, as was the case in *Ganim,* defendants convicted under § 666 are also charged under the RICO statutes, discussed in Chapter 18. Moreover, public officials like the defendant in *Ganim* could also be prosecuted under state bribery laws such as § 53(a)-148 of the Connecticut General Statutes.

Bribery   Bribery of federal officials is covered by 18 U.S.C. § 201(b). Federal officials include everyone from members of Congress to food inspectors. In *United States v. Alfisi,*[16] produce inspectors for the U.S. Department of Agriculture were convicted for taking bribes from wholesale produce sellers in exchange for higher quality produce-inspection receipts.

Bribery prosecutions under 18 U.S.C. § 201(b) often are coupled with extortion charges under 18 U.S.C. § 872. A federal officer that "solicits" a bribe in exchange for some official act may also threaten to use his official position to prevent the official act from occurring. The former is a "bribe" under § 201, and the latter is "extortion" under § 872. Moreover, there are similarities between extortion and bribery offenses, as the Supreme Court noted in *Evans v. United States,* 504 U.S. 255 (1992). The Court said in *Evans* that while conviction of an official for extortion "under color of law" under the Hobbs Act, 19 U.S.C. § 1951, requires proof of an exchange of payment for an agreement to perform an official act, it does not require proof that the official took affirmative steps to "induce" the payment. And even if the official did solicit the payment, the Court stated that it is no defense to an extortion charge that the facts would also support a bribery conviction.

A case illustrating bribery and extortion charges under the federal statutes discussed above is *United States v. Valle.*[17] In that case, an Immigration and Customs agent approached a Mexican national being held in a detention facility pending deportation. The agent told the detainee that there were pending criminal charges against the detainee but that the agent would remove them for a payment of $20,000. The detainee told other federal officers about the conversation, and ultimately an undercover FBI officer gave the agent the $20,000 and then arrested the agent. The court affirmed his convictions under both the bribery statute and the extortion statute. It rejected the agent's defense that he never intended to remove any criminal charges because they didn't exist, stating that all either statute required was that the official enter into a "corrupt" agreement to use his official position.

quid pro quo Giving something of value ("quid") for something else.

Bribery and, to some degree, extortion crimes usually involve a **quid pro quo,** that is, an exchange of some official act for some promised payment. (See the

SCAMS, FRAUDS, AND OFFSHORE BANK ACCOUNTS

White-collar crime can take many forms. The following accounts illustrate some of the ways fraudulent schemes have been uncovered and prosecuted.

Troubled Times and Ponzi Schemes

Troubled times are said to bring more frauds to light. As Warren Buffett, the financial wizard from Omaha, put it, ". . . when the tide goes out, we can see who is swimming naked." New records for fraudulent schemes were set after the financial meltdown of 2008–2009. They include the following massive Ponzi schemes. (Ponzi schemes and their origination are described later in this chapter.)

For almost 40 years Bernard Madoff was regarded by almost everyone as a brilliant investor and a pillar of the New York and international community. Investors flocked to invest their money with him, and asked few questions about his operations. Madoff paid high dividends, and his monthly statements showed impressive paper profits to his investors, who numbered in the thousands. However, when financial markets collapsed in 2008, it was discovered that in fact Madoff had made virtually no investments with his clients' money but instead had simply used new investors' deposits to pay "investment gains" to existing investors, the classic Ponzi scheme. Madoff, age 70, was convicted in 2008 of criminal charges such as mail and security fraud, money laundering, and perjury, and in 2009 was sentenced to 150 years in prison.

Losses from this gigantic fraud totaled more than $64.8 billion. Thousands of people lost their life savings, and schools and charitable institutions that invested with Madoff took huge financial hits.

In Europe, thousands of investors who were directed to Madoff through European banks and investment houses also lost billions. However, these overseas investors were able to collect about $15.5 billion from these institutions through civil lawsuits. (See *New York Times*, May 25, 2010: "$15.5 Billion for Victims of Madoff Overseas.")

Other Ponzi schemes uncovered in 2013 include the following:

- A Colorado county deputy sheriff pled guilty in 2013 to fraud and money laundering charges. The deputy took classes in foreign currency exchanges, and solicited $1.3 million from others in law enforcement to invest in trading foreign exchange funds. In fact, he used the money for his private lifestyle, and to pay investors who wanted to withdraw their funds from the investment. The deputy faces up to 20 years in prison.

discussion of *quid pro quo* for Hobbs Act [extortion] violations in Chapter 14.) The nature of the *quid pro quo* requirement in the federal bribery statutes was described in the U.S. Supreme Court case of *United States v. Sun-Diamond Growers of California*, 526 U.S. 398 (1999). In that case the defendant was prosecuted under 18 U.S.C. § 201 (c), the crime of giving an official an illegal gratuity. The trial court had instructed the jury that the crime included giving an official a gift "simply because of his position," without tying the gift to any particular official act. The Supreme Court reversed the conviction, holding that § 201(c) required proof of a link between the gratuity and some official act.

- In March of 2013 Steven Palladino was indicted for fraud in Boston, Massachusetts. Palladino's company, Viking Financial Group, raised millions of dollars he claimed would be used to make high-interest loans to borrowers. Instead Palladino used these funds for a lavish personal lifestyle, including gambling debts and paying his mistress's rent.

Secret Offshore Tax Havens and Accounts

The U.S. Treasury Department estimates that the United States loses $100 billion per year because of offshore tax havens, bank accounts, and credit cards. Wealthy Americans can use these offshore bank accounts to hide income and other funds from authorities and thereby avoid paying taxes on those hidden funds. In 2009 Bradley Birkenfeld, an American banker who worked for UBS, the largest bank in Switzerland, was sentenced to 40 months in prison for helping American citizens use UBS to hide funds. Birkenfeld provided the Internal Revenue Service with detailed information on how UBS solicited wealthy Americans to use the bank to hide funds and avoid payment of taxes.

The U.S. Justice Department filed civil charges against UBS in 2008, which resulted in UBS paying penalties of $780 million to the United States. UBS also agreed to furnish names and account information on about 4,500 Americans who had accounts of over $1 million with UBS. In 2010 the Swiss Parliament ratified an agreement between Switzerland and the United States that opens the door for the disclosure of information about Americans with accounts in Swiss banks.

In 2009 the IRS offered an amnesty program to taxpayers with offshore bank accounts, which excused them from criminal charges if they paid back taxes and penalties. About 14,700 persons accepted the amnesty offer (*New York Times*, November 18, 2009).

The U.S. Justice Department and the IRS state there is increased scrutiny of questionable offshore accounts in many countries in addition to Switzerland, such as Liechtenstein and Hong Kong. In an unusual turn of events, Birkenfeld, after serving two and a half years in prison in Pennsylvania, was awarded $104 million dollars by the IRS in September 2012 under the American "whistle blower" law. Under that law, a person who gives information leading to the recovery of unpaid taxes is given a reward of between 15 and 30 percent of the taxes collected.

© Cengage Learning

In the course of its decision in *Sun-Diamond,* the Supreme Court made this statement about the federal bribery statute, § 201(b): "[b]ribery requires intent to 'influence' an official act (the bribe-giver) or to be 'influenced' in an official act (the public official bribe receiver). . . . In other words, for bribery there must be a *quid pro quo*—a specific intent to give or receive something of value in exchange for an official act." 526 U.S. at 404–405.

Bribery convictions under § 201(b) thus have as an element of the offense a showing that the bribe was given or solicited as part of an agreement to exchange some official action for the bribe. Courts addressing the *quid pro quo* issue in prosecutions under 18 U.S.C. § 666, the federal program bribery statute, have reached a different conclusion. Those courts hold that there need be no showing of payment for a particular official act, but only that the payment was made to influence the official "in connection" with transactions under the federal programs. *United States v. McNair*, 605 F.3d 1152 (11th Cir. 2010). The U.S. Supreme Court denied review in the *McNair* case: 131 S. Ct. 1600 (2011).

Bribery was traditionally a crime committed by or with officials, and as a result many state bribery statutes are specifically addressed to official misconduct. The Georgia bribery statute, OCGA § 16-10-2, makes it a crime to (1) offer to give an official anything of value in order to influence the official in performance of official acts and (2) solicit anything of value from another by "inducing the reasonable belief" that giving the thing of value will result in influencing the performance of official actions. Most states also have bribery statutes that are directed at persons other than public officials. One example is in sports bribery cases. As a result of famous "point-shaving" basketball scandals and other sports bribery incidents, many states have passed bribery statutes aimed directly at sports participants. Louisiana's statute, LSA-RS 14-118.1, and North Carolina's NC GSA § 14-373 are examples of these statutes.

Stock Market and Financial Market Frauds

The stock markets and financial markets of the United States and other industrial countries are important to their economic development in creating jobs and providing for economic security. Among the crimes that infect this field is insider trading. People who obtain inside information on the plans of large corporations can often make huge profits by insider trading or by selling the information illegally.

The federal criminal securities laws applicable to crimes like insider trading are generally contained in regulations promulgated in Section 10(b) of the Securities Exchange Act of 1934, 15 U.S.C. § 78j. Section 78j makes it a crime for any person to use a "manipulative or deceptive device or contrivance" in connection with the purchase or sale of a security, such as a share of stock. This includes insider trading.

Insider trading often involves a person with some fiduciary responsibility, such as a corporate officer, using information known only to corporate "insiders" to profit from the information by buying or selling corporate stock in advance of public acquisition of the information. Insider trading also includes the so-called tippee situation, where an "outsider" acquires information from an insider and uses it to his advantage. If the tippee knew the information came from an insider in breach of a fiduciary duty, the tippee can be convicted under § 78j. See *United States v. Evans*.[18]

Determining exactly what constitutes a "manipulative" device under the securities laws can be difficult. In *United States v. Finnerty*,[19] the court held that the so-called inter-positioning practice used by a trader on the New York Stock Exchange did not violate the securities laws. "Inter-positioning" refers to the practice of a trader taking a position in a stock transaction between two customers, one wishing to buy a stock and one wishing to sell. Stock Exchange rules state that in such a

In 2010 Angelo Mozilo, the former CEO of Countrywide Financial Company, was fined $22 million by the Securities and Exchange Commission based on insider trading violations committed by Mozilo. In addition, Mozilo was ordered to disgorge $45 million received by him as a result of the illegal insider trades. Mozilo sold about $140 million in Countrywide stock when the company was trading at its peak price, even though Mozilo knew the company was in fact in financial difficulty because of the number of undervalued subprime mortgage securities the company owned. In 2008 Countrywide, near bankruptcy, was purchased by the Bank of America Company for $2.2 billion. Mozilo is famous for having made favorable loans to many public figures, including members of Congress, known as "Friends of Angelo."

case, the trader is required to "match" the buyer with the seller. In inter-positioning, the trader trades separately with each customer, thereby taking advantage of any gap that existed between the two orders. The court said that while the trader was acting wrongly for his own gain, he did not deceive or manipulate his customers.

Stock market and corporate fraud reached unprecedented heights during the period 1990–2004. Although there have been previous instances of scandal and greed in American economic markets, nothing comes close to those in recent years. The bankruptcy of the energy giant Enron Corporation alone cost investors and employees billions of dollars. In February 2001, Enron stock sold for $90 per share; when it filed for bankruptcy 10 months later, those same shares were selling for pennies. Many of Enron's executives made millions of dollars selling their shares at a time when the company's employees were unable to sell their shares. In 2006 Jeffrey Skilling and Kenneth Lay, chief executive officers of Enron during the period Enron misrepresented its financial condition to investors and banks, were convicted of fraud and conspiracy. Skilling was sentenced to 24 years in prison; Lay died before he could be sentenced. Skilling appealed his conviction on various grounds; the court of appeals affirmed his convictions in 2009, but the U.S. Supreme Court reversed and remanded the case in a 2010 decision.

Skilling was charged with violations of federal fraud statutes, including "honest services" fraud under the mail and wire fraud acts. The term "honest services" was derived from federal court cases where courts interpreted the "scheme or artifice" language of the mail and wire fraud statutes as including actions that didn't directly deprive a victim of money or property, but were nonetheless fraudulent. An example would be a mayor who takes a bribe or kickback to give a city contract to a friend. Even if the contract price were fair, so that no money was fraudulently "taken" from the city, the city would have been deprived of the "honest services" of the mayor. Federal courts were frequently affirming convictions under the mail and wire fraud statutes for bribery and kickback schemes.

In 1987 the U.S. Supreme Court held in *McNally v. United States,* 483 U.S. 350, that the "scheme or artifice" language of the wire and mail fraud acts applied only to direct frauds, where victims were deprived of money or other property by the fraudulent actions. "Honest services" fraud was not covered by the statutes, the Court held. The next year Congress passed 18 U.S.C. § 1346, which stated that for the mail and other fraud statutes a "scheme or artifice" included depriving another of the "intangible right of honest services."

Courts began applying § 1346 to various kinds of fraudulent actions, if, as the result of these actions, a defendant acted dishonestly. For example, making false representations about a company's financial situation, as in the Enron case, or acting with a conflict of interest were actions treated by federal prosecutors and courts as covered by the mail and wire fraud statutes.

In *Skilling v. United States,* 130 S. Ct. 2896 (2010), the Supreme Court held that Section 1346 didn't include under the language "honest services" fraudulent actions that didn't directly deprive a victim of money or property, except for bribery or kickback schemes. Since Skilling had been convicted of "honest services" fraud without any evidence he took a bribe or received a kickback, the Court reversed and remanded his case for consideration of whether he should receive a new trial on all of the counts of his indictment. On remand, the court of appeals held in 2011 that ample evidence supported the other convictions, and affirmed those convictions. In 2012, the U.S. Supreme Court denied review of that decision.[20]

Other Fraud Statutes in the Federal Criminal Code

Each state has fraud statutes in its criminal code to punish fraudulent conduct that takes place within that state. Because most large fraud schemes involve criminal conduct that crosses state lines, Congress has power to punish these crimes under the Commerce Clause. Also, because many fraud schemes use the banking system,

NATIONAL FRAUD FACTS

Which fraud case is the largest on record?	The 2009 conviction of Bernie Madoff marked the end of a $64.8 billion Ponzi scheme that defrauded hundreds of investors. Madoff maintained elaborate books that showed investment returns on his clients' money, when in fact those investments did not exist. The 1998 accounting fraud on the Cendant Corporation, by Walter Forbes, is believed to be the next largest fraud on record, at $19 billion. After lengthy litigation, Forbes was convicted of securities fraud in 2007. See *United States v. Forbes*, 2007 WL 141952. It is likely the Enron collapse cost shareholders and other investors more than that amount. The WorldCom accounting fraud in 2004, in which the CEO, Bernard Ebbers, received a 25-year prison sentence, cost investors $11 billion.
Which fraud case led to the most criminal convictions?	The Enron case resulted in the convictions of ten executives and guilty pleas from sixteen others. Only one executive was acquitted, and one trial resulted in a hung jury.
What were the most common charges in the largest fraud cases?	Securities fraud, wire fraud, conspiracy, false statements, mail fraud, bank fraud, insider trading, and theft were the criminal charges in these frauds.
How often are government employees convicted of corruption charges?	While most government employees are honest, the FBI reports that about 500 city, state, or federal employees each year are convicted of corrupt practices. Former Illinois Governor George Ryan, former Congressman Randall Cunningham, and mega-lobbyist Jack Abramoff were among those convicted. See the *New York Times*, "FBI Focus on Public Corruption Includes 2000 Investigations," May 11, 2006.
Which computer-related crimes are prosecuted in state courts?	The type of crimes prosecuted, from the highest number to the lowest, are credit card fraud; bank card fraud, identity theft, child pornography; computer forgery (altering documents); cyberstalking (sending threatening or harassing e-mails); hacking (unauthorized access); computer sabotage (placing worms, viruses, or logic bombs—hidden programs "detonated" by a specific date or event); and theft of computer data (copyright infringement).

the stock market, or other large financial institutions regulated by federal law, Congress has passed several federal fraud crime laws, and violators are frequently charged under these laws.

Many federal crimes have a broad scope and are used in prosecutions for violations of the particular statute and also in both fraud and RICO violations (see Chapter 18). They include the following:

Mail Fraud Act

18 U.S.C. § 1341. This act has been amended to include all interstate carriers, such as FedEx and UPS.

"To prove mail fraud, the government must show that the defendant (1) intentionally participated in a scheme to defraud, and (2) used the mails to execute the fraudulent scheme; . . . conviction for mail fraud need not rest on the success of the fraudulent scheme." *United States v. Bailey*, 123 F.3d 1381 (11th Cir. 1997). The scheme need not such as to deceive a reasonable person; even one directed at the naive or ignorant is a violation. *United States v. Svete*, 556 F.3d 1157 (11th Cir. 2009).

Wire Fraud Act

18 U.S.C. § 1343

The same elements as mail fraud, plus the wire communication must cross state lines. The Commerce Clause gives the federal government jurisdiction over wire communications, whereas the mail fraud statute stems from the Constitution's grant of power to Congress over the postal service.

Travel Act

18 U.S.C.A. § 1952

To prove a violation of the Travel Act, the government must show "(1) travel in interstate or foreign commerce, or use of telephone, mail, or other facility in interstate or foreign commerce; (2) with intent to facilitate the promotion, management, establishment, or carrying on of any unlawful activity, and (3) thereafter performs an additional act in furtherance of the specified unlawful activity." *United States v. Long*, 949 F.2d 1370 (5th Cir. 1991). In 2007 the football player Michael Vick was charged with violation of the Travel Act, as well as other crimes.

Major Fraud Act

18 U.S.C. § 1031

Any person who executes a scheme or artifice to defraud the United States or obtain property under false pretenses based on a contract or grant from the United States in excess of $1,000,000 is guilty of major fraud.

Fraudulent Schemes Under State Law   Every state has enacted statutes that make fraud a crime under certain circumstances. In many states, the general fraud statute follows the language of the federal acts, such as mail or wire fraud. Arizona's statute, ARS § 13-2310, makes it a crime to execute a "scheme or artifice" intended to deprive another person of property fraudulently. Some states also have specific statutes aimed at "confidence games" or related trickery. New York's statute, titled "Fraudulent accosting," Penal Law § 165.30, is an example of such a statute. It makes it a crime to obtain property of another by trick, deception, or confidence game. Finally, many states have statutes aimed at schemes to obtain money by false pretenses. See, e.g., W. Va. Code § 61-3-24.

The Crime of Identity Theft and False Identification Documents

In a report issued November 30, 2011, the Department of Justice Bureau of Justice Statistics stated that in 2010, 8.6 million households were victims of some form of identity theft, causing direct losses of $13.3 billion. Total costs of identity theft are likely greater than $50 billion.

identity theft Theft based on stealing a real person's identification information (true name) or theft based on creating a fictitious person's identification (synthetic identity).

Identity theft can be both "true name" and "synthetic identity" theft. In true name theft, an actual person's identity—his or her name, address, Social Security number, or credit card number—is stolen. In synthetic identity theft, a fictitious person's name or Social Security number are used to commit the theft. It is reported that the number of synthetic identity thefts exceeds the number of true name thefts.

Because it is common to use stolen identity documents or numbers in computers, the mail system, or over telephone lines, many identity theft prosecutions are under federal laws. The principal federal statutes are 18 U.S.C. § 1028, identity theft; and 18 U.S.C. § 1028(A), aggravated identity theft. Section 1028 makes it a crime to "knowingly" possess, transfer, use, or produce a false identification document or authentication feature of a document, or use, possess, or transfer an identification document of another person. Section 1028(A) makes it an aggravated offense punishable by an additional 2-year prison term to use or possess the identification document of another person as part of any of the crimes listed in § 1028(a).

Prosecutions under § 1028 include production of false identification documents, as well as theft of identification documents. The statute prohibits production of identification documents that appear to be issued by an agency of the United States. However, it is not necessary for the prosecution to prove that a false document makes reference to an actual U.S. agency, like the FBI or the U.S. Marshal's Office. In *United States v. Fuller*,[21] the court upheld the conviction of a defendant who produced an identification allegedly issued by the "United States Special Response Department Anti Terrorism Unit." The court stated that the statute is violated when a false identification appeared to be issued by an agency of the United States, whether or not such an agency actually exists.

Prosecutions for theft of an identification document or number, at least under § 1028(A) for aggravated identity theft, require the prosecution to prove the defendant knew that the document or number used belonged to an actual person. In *United States v. Flores Figueroa*, 129 S. Ct. 1886 (2009), discussed in Chapter 3, the U.S. Supreme Court held that a conviction for use of the identification document of another required proof the defendant knew the identity card belonged to another person. This may also be the case for a conviction under § 1028, which employs the same "knowingly" language, though the Court did not expressly consider the requirements under that statute.

The prosecution may prove the knowledge requirement under § 1028(A) by inference. In *United States v. Holmes*, 595 F.3d 1255 (11th Cir. 2010), the court held that the fact the defendant had previously successfully used another person's name to obtain a driver's license and passport was sufficient evidence for a jury to infer she knew the name belonged to an actual person. Nor does the name have to belong to a living person. In the 2012 case of *United States v. Zuniga-Artaga*,[22] the court held that the prosecution need not prove that "another person" under § 1028(A) was living at the time the defendant used that person's identification documents.

In the 2012 case of *United States v. Hilton*[23] a federal court of appeals held that corporations are not "persons" under the federal aggravated identity theft statute. Though the term "person" usually includes corporations, the court held the identity theft statutes were vague on this issue, since those statutes also referred to means of identification of "a specific individual." It therefore held the statute should not be read to include theft of a corporation's identity.

In the 2013 case of *United States v. Lombard*,[24] the court held that identity theft included use of information about "another person" to obtain false identification documents, even though the "other person" sold that information to the defendant. There, the defendant paid another person to use his birth date and social security number to get a false driver's license and U.S. passport. He then left a fake suicide note by a bridge in Illinois, and left a voice mail at the local sheriff's office stating they would find his body and could then "kiss my cold, white, wet a***". The defendant left the country, and was arrested in Burma in 2011. He was returned to the United States and convicted of identity theft. The court of appeals affirmed his conviction, holding the federal identity theft statutes applied whenever a person used another person's identity to obtain false identification documents, since those documents were obtained "without lawful authority" under the statute.

Finally, in *United States v. Reynolds*, 710 F.3d 434 (D.C. Cir. 2013) the court held that improper use of a person's signature, even if some use was authorized, violated the aggravated identity theft statute. There, a church financial officer, who had access to the digital signatures of other church officers, used the signatures to swindle the church out of $850,000. The court also rejected the defendant's argument that under the identity theft statute the government must prove the individual whose signature was improperly used suffered economic harm. The court said all the government had to prove was the unlawful use of the signatures.

Most states have identity theft statutes similar to the federal statutes, though often with broader definitions of the crime. The Wisconsin identity theft statute, Wis. Stat. § 943.201(2)(c), includes using another person's identification information to cause harm to that person's reputation. In *State v. Baron*,[25] the court held the statute applied to a defendant who gained access to his employer's e-mail account and learned the employer was having an extramarital affair. The defendant sent out an e-mail to several persons, purporting to come from the employer, which made the affair public. The next day, the employer committed suicide. The court rejected the defendant's argument that the statute violated his First Amendment rights.

In *State v. Hardesty*,[26] the Kansas Court of Appeals held that "another person" in the Kansas identity theft statute, KSA 21-4018, includes a deceased person. Perhaps in response to that decision and the U.S. Supreme Court's decision in *Flores-Figueroa*, the Kansas legislature amended the identity theft statute in 2010 to state expressly that (1) theft of a deceased person's identification is covered by the statute, and (2) it is not a defense that the thief did not know the identification belonged to an actual person.

IDENTITY THEFT

Identity theft has grown rapidly to the point where, according to the U.S. Federal Trade Commission, over 15 million people were victims of identity theft in 2010. These thefts cost the victims and businesses an estimated $50 billion.

To commit the crime a thief needs	Your name, date of birth, Social Security number, and an estimate of your annual income.
How would a thief obtain this information?	Steal (or find) a purse or wallet, steal your mail, or go through your trash looking for credit or bank card statements. Old or recent tax returns also have this information. It can be obtained from the databases of some businesses.
A thief can then	Open a new credit card account or bank account in your name. Use the credit card (or cards) to obtain goods. Write bad checks on your bank account. Open charge accounts with retail stores. Establish telephone or wireless service in your name. Use your identity and credit to obtain many items of value.
To avoid immediate detection, the thief can	Use a change-of-address form and divert your mail and the bills to another address.

To protect your family and yourself, take the following precautions: (1) Keep an eye open for missing mail, as a change of address filed by a clever thief will send bills and credit card statements to another address; (2) reveal only such personal information as is necessary; and (3) check your credit file every year or two to make sure a thief is not borrowing money in your name.

In theft of identity, thieves seek to profit in the following ways:

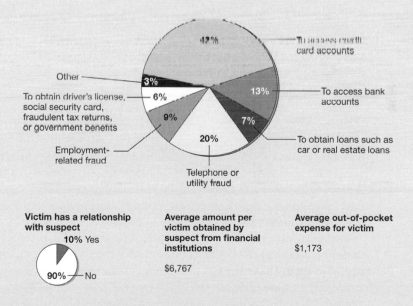

Source: Federal Trade Commission, Identity Theft Clearinghouse.

Counterfeiting of Money and Commercial Products

Counterfeiting of Currency

Counterfeiting of currency is a serious federal offense that could have a severe economic impact on society. The history of counterfeiting in the United States can be summarized as follows:

- Until and during the Civil War, counterfeiting was a serious problem. Thousands of various legitimate bills were being printed by more than 1,500 state banks. Therefore, counterfeiting was easy during that period. An estimated one-third of the currency used during the Civil War was counterfeit.
- Establishment of a single national currency in 1863 and the creation of the U.S. Secret Service immediately made counterfeiting harder. Counterfeiting the new currency required skilled people with sophisticated equipment. The diligent efforts of the Secret Service made the pooling of the necessary material and equipment plus the necessary highly trained skills difficult. Counterfeiting and alteration of currency were kept at a minimum over the following years.
- Today, sophisticated color copiers allow what law enforcement officers call "casual counterfeiters" to print thousands of crude bills. However, the principal problem is professional craftspeople, many of whom live in foreign countries and are producing counterfeit money that is difficult to detect.

In response to the growing problem of counterfeiting, the United States began issuing new folding money that is much harder to counterfeit. The introduction of new $100 bills began in 1996 and that of $50 bills began in 1997. The $20 bill, which most Americans use in their daily lives, began to be replaced in 1998. The $10 and $5 bills also have been replaced, and a "more modestly redesigned" $1 bill is to follow. Amateur counterfeiters such as high school students using school computers and color printers continue to be a problem to merchants and other people who do not look closely at the paper money they receive.[27]

Other Counterfeiting Problems

Counterfeited designer jeans, compact discs, recordings of movies, electronic components, computers, books, circuit relays, and drugs are sold extensively in the United States. Many of the counterfeited products are manufactured in foreign countries, and also sold there. Usually, the counterfeit product is a cheap or inferior copy of the real thing. However, the phony label deceives many dealers and consumers, who believe that they are buying the name-brand product.

Importation, manufacture, or sale of a counterfeit product in the United States could result in (1) prosecution under the criminal code of a state, which would probably treat the offense as a misdemeanor; (2) civil suit and sanctions in federal or state civil courts; or (3) federal prosecution under the mail fraud statute (18 U.S.C.A. § 1341), the wire fraud statute (18 U.S.C.A. § 1343), the Food, Drug and Cosmetic Act (21 U.S.C.A. §§ 301, 321, and so on), or other federal statutes.

Counterfeiting of driver's licenses and other documents has become a serious problem in the United States. This crime is committed not only by private individuals, both within and outside of the United States, but sometimes also by state employees, who have access to the necessary forms for counterfeiting official documents. The state of New York announced in March 2013 that in July 2013 it would begin issuing driver's licenses made of rigid polycarbonate, with identification information imprinted on the card with laser technology, and a black-and-white photograph of the license holder. State officials believe such a card would make counterfeiting of driver's licenses impossible.[28]

Computer Crime or Cybercrime

The rise of computer use and ownership has seen a corresponding rise in the use of computers in criminal activity. Using computers as tools in crime makes many aspects of criminal behavior easier and more efficient. Even an illegal drug gang must keep records of sales and purchases, and computers make that task easier.

Computers can also be the object of criminal activity, such as where computer hardware or software is stolen. Finally, computers can be the subject of a crime, such as where information on a computer file is stolen or damaged. The phrase **cybercrime** generally refers to the last two kinds of crimes involving computers, where computers are used to access, or are accessed through, the Internet.

cybercrime Criminal acts implemented through use of a computer or other form of electronic communication.

The earliest forms of Internet attacks on computers involved amateur hackers who invaded a computer just to prove they could. Most states have "unauthorized access" statutes that make it a crime to "knowingly" access another person's computer or computer accounts. In the 2011 case of *Muhammed v. State*[29] the court held that the Texas computer access statute requires that the prosecution prove the defendant accessed another person's computer knowing that he was doing so, and that he did so knowing he did not have that person's permission. This appears to be the majority view on the *mens rea* for unlawful computer access.

As use of the Internet exploded, computers began being used in a wide variety of crimes, including fraud, money laundering, extortion, software theft, corporate espionage, and child pornography (discussed in Chapter 12).

Most states have modified their criminal codes to account for the rise in computer use in criminal behavior. Many states have, for example, made it a crime to use computers for online harassment; see Texas Penal Code § 42.07(a)(2) (Vernon 2003). Some states have passed specific statutes making it a crime to use a computer to obtain money or property unlawfully. For example, in *Damaio v. Commonwealth*,[30] a defendant was convicted under the Virginia computer theft statute, § 18.2-152.3. The defendant quit his job as human resources director and transferred over 829 employee files to a third-party server only he could access. He told his employer he would return the files only if a debt he owed the employer were canceled. He was convicted of computer theft under the statute.

computer trespass Unlawful access to a computer or computer system with intent to commit a crime, or unlawful access to a computer or computer system maintained by a government unit.

California has passed a law, California Penal Code § 502(c)(1), directed at unlawful access to a computer system for altering or using data on the system for the purpose of advancing a scheme to fraud or extort money or property.

Most states have a statute similar to § 9A.52.110 of the Washington Criminal Code, which prohibits computer trespass. **Computer trespass** is defined as unlawful access

WHITE-COLLAR CRIMES IN THE NEWS

For a variety of reasons, white-collar crimes are frequently reported in the national press. This may be because of the identity of the criminals or because of the nature of a fraudulent scheme. The following is a list of some of the crimes that received national attention.

- *Price Fixing:* Federal law, in the form of the Sherman Antitrust Act, prohibits price fixing. In 2006, South Korean suppliers of computer memory chips were found guilty of conspiring with others to fix prices on computer chips. Several individual defendants received fines and jail sentences; one company agreed to pay a fine of $160 million.[a]

- *Insider Trading:* It is a crime to use inside information acquired in one's position at a company or investment firm to profit from stock trades. In the *New York Times* article "Insider Trading Case with a B-Movie Plot" (April 30, 2006), David Pajcin, a 29-year-old employee of an investment firm, used inside information on the sale of Reebok International to Adidas to make more than $6 million for himself and his family. He set up accounts in family member names, including that of his aunt, a seamstress in Croatia, and bought stock futures in Reebok before the sale became public. Investigators caught on when they discovered that 80 percent of the futures trades made in Reebok just prior to the announcement of the sale were by Pajcin. Pajcin cooperated with the government, and his guilty plea was sealed. Others involved received prison terms of up to four years.[b]

- *Industrial Espionage:* Stealing a company's ideas or trade secrets is a crime, and it can be done by competitors, foreign companies or governments, or trusted employees. In 2006 the Hewlett-Packard Company was experiencing leaks of corporate information. The CEO, in an effort to discover the source of the leaks, unlawfully monitored employees' personal telephones, e-mail, and Internet activities. When her actions were uncovered, she lost her position as CEO.[c]

- *Eavesdropping:* This old English crime takes its name from trespassing on another's property and listening to conversations under the eaves of a house. In 2007 seven Wall Street brokers were charged with eavesdropping when they secretly listened in on conversations of others on "squawk boxes" (intercoms) in their offices. After a seven-week trial, they were acquitted of the eavesdropping and other securities charges, but because the jury deadlocked on a conspiracy charge, the brokers will be retried.[d]

- *Mortgage Fraud:* Mortgage fraud is one of this country's fastest-growing fraud crimes. The FBI estimates it cost lenders over a billion dollars in 2005. Mortgage fraud often involves borrowers who greatly overstate the value of mortgaged property or their ability to repay loans. During the housing boom of 2001 to 2006, the rise of "no document" mortgage loans contributed to the problem. In these loans, the borrower was not required to produce documents to prove statements made on loan applications. These loans were often "subprime" loans, which in 2007 began to experience high default rates.

- *Movie and Television Show Piracy:* Wrongful sale of bootlegged copies of copyrighted movies and television shows violate the copyright and trade secrets laws. In the *New York Times* article "Hollywood Gets Tough on Movie Copying in Canada" (February 19, 2007), it was reported that 30 to 40 percent of the bootlegged DVDs sold in the United States were made in Canada.

- *Theft of Trade Secrets:* A secretary who worked for the Coca-Cola Company attempted to sell the secret recipe for Coke to the Pepsi-Cola Company for $1.5 million. Pepsi officials notified Coca-Cola, and the secretary was convicted of stealing trade secrets and sentenced to up to 10 years in prison.[e]

- *Check Kiting:* A New York University student was sentenced to over 3 years in prison for bank and wire fraud in 2006. In an elaborate check-kiting scheme, the student deposited millions of dollars in a New York bank using fake checks, transferred funds to a hedge fund he controlled, and ultimately withdrew money from the fund. The student's mother was sentenced to two years in jail for her role in the scheme.[f]

- *Payola:* Under federal law, and in many states, it is a crime to pay broadcasters to play specific songs on the radio unless the payment is disclosed to listeners. These laws stemmed from the 1950s and 1960s, when rock-and-roll radio DJs had enormous influence on the popularity of a given song or artist. In 2006, EMI Recording Company agreed to pay a fine of $3.75 million to settle payola charges brought against it and four other corporations.[g]

- *Misbranding:* It is a federal crime to place false or misleading information on a drug, or in ads used to sell a drug, or to promote it for unapproved use. The corporate producer of the drug OxyContin in 2007 pleaded guilty to misbranding and paid fines totaling $600,000. Individual defendants pleaded guilty to misdemeanors and were also fined. The company failed to disclose the addictive nature of the drug to physicians prescribing the drug and users of it.

- *Kickback Schemes:* It is a crime under every state's law for employees of a government unit like a state or city, or employees of a corporation, to accept kickbacks for making contracts with persons providing goods or services to the government unit or corporation. In an unusual case, New York authorities indicted the former mayor of Sao Paulo, Brazil, charging him with receiving kickbacks in excess of $11 million from a highway project in Brazil. The kickback money was transferred through a New York bank, giving New York jurisdiction over the crime. The New York attorney general stated that New York would not become the "Cayman Islands" of the United States.[h]

- *Bid Rigging:* This crime occurs when persons with power to award bids—frequently state, city, or federal employees—direct bids to persons or companies with whom they are in a fraudulent partnership. In 2007 Army Reserve officers were charged with receiving more than $1 million in cash and gifts as payment for giving bids on reconstruction work in Iraq.[i]

- *Con Games:* One of the oldest forms of theft or fraud is the confidence game, so named because it requires gaining the confidence of the intended victim. One famous con game, the Ponzi[j] or pyramid scheme, operates by enticing participants to pay money to the scheme's organizers, with the promise of enormous payouts if they in turn sell the scheme to more participants. The Federal Trade Commission monitors businesses closely if their marketing resembles a pyramid scheme. In the last 10 years the FTC has shut down seventeen national pyramid schemes and returned over $90 million to victims of these frauds. The FTC recently filed a complaint against a business in California that was selling rights to operate an online digital music store, a scheme that in fact paid off only if participants could entice others to buy such rights.[k]

- In March 2010 a group of computer experts was indicted under federal wire fraud and computer statutes for using computer programs to buy concert and sports event tickets and reselling them at a huge profit. The group, calling itself "Wiseguys Tickets Inc.," resold over 1.5 million tickets before being arrested and charged. The indictment states they acted fraudulently by using a computer program to circumvent rules limiting how many tickets a corporate entity could buy.[l]

[a]See the *New York Times* article "4 to Plead Guilty to Chip Pricing," March 2, 2006.

[b]*Fortune*, October 2, 2006.

[c]See the *Chicago Tribune* article "Boss, Infighter, Leakbuster, Spy," September 13, 2006.

[d]See the *New York Times* article "Ex-Brokers Face Retrial in Eavesdropping Case," May 5, 2007.

[e]See the *Wall Street Journal* article "Former Coke Secretary Sentenced in Trade-Secret Case," May 24, 2007.

[f]See the *New York Times* article "Ex-N.Y.U. Student Pleads Guilty to Fraud in Hedge Fund Scheme," June 7, 2006.

[g]See the *New York Times* article "EMI Agrees to Fine to Resolve Payola Case," June 16, 2006.

[h]See the *New York Times* article "Brazilian Politician Indicted in New York in Kickback Scheme," March 9, 2007.

[i]See the *New York Times* article "State Reservist Among Four Charged in Bid-Rigging Scheme," February 8, 2007.

[j]The pyramid scheme, also known as the Ponzi swindle, has a long history in the United States. Immigrants are particularly vulnerable to the swindle because crooks within their own group gain their confidence and cheat them. Carlo Ponzi engineered one of the first great frauds in the early 1920s in Boston. Ponzi took advantage of his fellow Italians, including family members and his parish priest. He then reached beyond Italian immigrants to defraud more than 20,000 people of more than $10 million before his scheme collapsed. Ponzi fled to Brazil, where he died a pauper. See the *New York Times* article "Immigrants Swindle Their Own, Preying on Trust" (August 25, 1992), telling of the problems of modern immigrants who are cheated by people within their own groups.

[k]See FTC Report, June 12, 2007.

[l]See March 3, 2010 article in the *Wall Street Journal*, "Four Charged in Bid to Buy, Resell Tickets."

EMPLOYEES AND UNAUTHORIZED COMPUTER ACCESS

Employees use their employer's computers at work, and are often privileged, by use of a password, to access employer or client records. Is it a violation of an applicable federal or state unlawful computer access statute for an employee to access an employer's computer for purposes other than work? That is, does "unauthorized access" include unauthorized "use" of an employer's computer or accounts? That was the issue in the following state and federal cases:

- In *Willoughby v. State*, 84 So.3d 1210 (Fla. App. 2012) an employee was convicted of violations of the Florida unlawful computer access statute and the improper acquisition of confidential information statute. The employee accessed her employer's computer at home using her laptop, and downloaded confidential information. The appeals court reversed the conviction under the "unlawful access" statute, stating the employer had given permission to the employee to use her laptop at work because it was faster than the employer's computer. However, it affirmed the conviction for improper acquisition of confidential information.

- In *United States v. Teague*, 646 F.3d 1119 (8th Cir. 2011) an employee of a company working under contract with the U.S. Department of Education was convicted of violating the CFAA. The employee had access to the National Student Loan Data System records as part of her position as an advisor on student loan debt collection. She improperly used her access privilege to acquire information on President Obama's student loan history. The court of appeals affirmed her conviction, stating the CFAA applied to computer access that exceeded lawful permission to access a computer.

- In *United States v. John*, 597 F.3d 263 (5th Cir. 2010), the court considered another violation of the CFAA. In *John* an employee of Citigroup Company accessed computer accounts of customers of Citigroup. She then gave the information gained from that access to confederates, who made fraudulent charges against those accounts. She was arrested and charged with violating CFAA, convicted on several counts, and sentenced to 108 months in prison. On appeal she contended she could not be convicted of unauthorized access under § 1030, because in her position at Citigroup she was authorized to access the accounts and view the information in the accounts. As a result, she argued, her access was not "unauthorized." The court disagreed, and it affirmed her conviction. It stated that "unauthorized access" includes accessing a computer with the fraudulent intent to take information from the computer and use it in a scheme to defraud the computer account holders.

- In *United States v. Nosal*, 676 F.3d 854 (9th Cir. 2012) the court sitting *en banc* disagreed with the Fifth Circuit's interpretation of the CFAA in *John*, discussed above. In *Nosal* employees with authorized access to an employer's computer and client files did so in order to acquire information to give to Nosal, a former employee. Nosal was charged, among other crimes, with aiding and abetting those employees in violations of the CFAA. The trial court dismissed those charges, holding the CFAA did not apply to unauthorized use of information contained on an employer's computer, but only to unauthorized access.

to a computer or computer system with intent to commit a crime or unlawful access to a computer or computer system maintained by a government unit. Most states also have a statute similar to the Maryland Code, Criminal Law, § 7-302, the "anti-hacking" statute. This law makes it a crime to enter a computer system without permission with intent to alter or damage the system or data stored in the system.

The federal government uses the Computer Fraud and Abuse Act, 18 U.S.C. § 1030 (CFAA), to target computer crime. Under this statute, a wide variety of cybercrimes are prohibited, from unlawfully accessing computers (the anti-hacking law) to unlawfully obtaining information from a financial institution, as the following cases illustrate.

In *United States v. Phillips*, 477 F3d 215 (5th Cir. 2007), the court affirmed a conviction of a University of Texas student under the CFAA. The student was granted access to the UT computer system when he enrolled as a freshman. He then used a technique called "port scanning" to find other computers on the network that could easily be accessed. The student gained access to many computers this way, and he stole information. He also found a secure UT web server called "TXClass" and, by using a "brute force" attack (a program that sends multiple possible passwords to enter a computer), was able to make multiple entries into the TXClass server. Once there, he collected sensitive data such as Social Security numbers of students and faculty. The Secret Service investigated the intrusions into the UT system, which were damaging the system and making it crash repeatedly. The student was arrested and charged with a violation of the CFAA. He was convicted, sentenced to 5 years' probation and 500 hours of community service, and ordered to pay $170,000 in restitution to UT.

The student appealed, contending the prosecution had not proven "unauthorized access" under § 1030. The court of appeals rejected his contention, stating that, under § 1030, "unauthorized access" included accessing a computer without authorization, such as hacking, and also exceeding authorized use. While the student did have authority to access the UT computer system, the court held he clearly did not have authority to use a brute force attack to gain entry to a secure server, and the court affirmed his conviction.

Arson

One of the first concerns of a fire investigator is the fire's origin. Fires can be classified by their causes as accidental fires, natural fires (caused without human intervention), **arson** (fires of incendiary origin), and fires of unknown origin.

arson A person's deliberate, willful, and malicious burning of a building or personal property.

Many fires are started accidentally, when children play with matches or people are careless with cigarettes, cigars, or pipe ashes. Some fires are of natural origin and occur without human intervention because of spontaneous combustion, defective heating units, faulty electrical appliances or wiring, and the like.

Arson is a person's deliberate, willful, and malicious burning of a building or personal property. Arson is the easiest of the major crimes to commit, the most difficult to detect, and the hardest to prove in court.

In most states, arson has several degrees or grades of commission, with gradations depending on whether the property destroyed is a residence or other kind of structure. An example of a common form of arson statute is Idaho Code § 18-802-805. First-degree arson under § 802 includes unlawfully and willfully damaging by fire or explosives a dwelling or a structure where people are commonly present or any structure in which the arsonist has reasonable grounds to believe a person might be present. Second-degree arson under § 803 is damaging any structure not covered in § 802. Third-degree arson under § 804 is damage to any other real or personal property. Finally, Idaho, like most states, has an "aggravated arson" statute, § 18-805, under which the penalty for arson is greatly increased if a person, including a firefighter, is killed or suffers serious bodily injury as a result of the fire.

The United States has an arson statute, 18 U.S.C. § 844(f), that applies to any malicious damage by fire or explosives to any property owned by or leased to the United States, an agency of the United States, or any organization receiving financial assistance from the United States. In the 2009 case of *United States v. Hersom,*[31] the court held that the federal arson statute applied to arson of four buildings owned by a private company that were undergoing renovations with financial assistance provided by block grants from HUD.

Essential Elements of Arson

All states have enacted statutes that define arson. In general, most statutes require that the state prove the following elements:

- That there was a fire and that some part of the building or personal property was damaged. Some courts require an actual burning of part of the property. In the case of *State v. Williams,* the Indiana Court of Appeals held that soot and smoke constituted "damage" within the meaning of the Indiana arson statute. Attempted arson or conspiracy to commit arson may also be possible criminal charges.[32]
- That the fire was of incendiary origin and was willfully and intentionally set. This is the required proof of corpus delicti (that a crime was in fact committed). For a fire inspector to testify in court that he or she "suspected" arson or that the fire was of "unknown origin" is insufficient to prove corpus delicti.[33] An expert witness is usually required to testify that arson did occur and support the statement with specific evidence.
- That the accused committed or was party to the crime of arson charged. Like all other crimes, the evidence required to convict a person of arson is proof beyond a reasonable doubt.

Product Tampering

Since 1982, product tampering has cost the lives of at least twelve people in the United States. The offense of poisoning over-the-counter drugs and food products was described by a high-ranking federal official as "an insidious and terrible crime. It is a form of terrorism not unlike planting a bomb in some public place to gain media attention, notoriety, or some sick sense of control over human life."

Although it is rare that a product is actually contaminated or poisoned, crimes related to product tampering include the following:

- *Extortion:* After seven people died in the Chicago area in 1982 from cyanide-laced Extra-Strength Tylenol, James Lewis tried to use the killings in attempting to extort $1 million from the manufacturer of Tylenol. Lewis was convicted in a federal court in 1983. The FBI continues to investigate the Tylenol killings, but as of 2013 the perpetrator had not been found. The Tylenol killings led to Congress enacting the federal Anti-Tampering Act discussed below.

- *Threats to Tamper and/or Threats to Allege Tampering:* Another form of extortion attempts to obtain money from manufacturers, who incur huge costs and loss of market and sales in tampering cases. In March of 2013 the makers of Red Bull announced a threat to place fecal matter in cans of the popular drink if the company did not pay a money demand.
- *Attempts to Create the Basis of a Civil Lawsuit:* A person fakes a tampering case to make it appear that a person in a family has been the victim of random tampering.

The Federal Consumer Tampering Act, 18 U.S.C.A. § 1365, forbids tampering with consumer products "with reckless disregard" that another person will be placed in danger of death or serious injury. In the 2011 case of *United States v. Wilson*[34] an ambulance paramedic developed a morphine addiction when he began using morphine stored in a safe at the premises of his employer, the rescue company. Initially he took only morphine vials marked "expired," since those would not be missed and were routinely destroyed. At some point, he began emptying unexpired vials of morphine and replacing the morphine with saline solution. He also took steps designed to limit the risk that the tampered vials would be used by other paramedics when helping injured persons. He argued he should not be convicted under the federal consumer tampering statute because he lacked the required *mens rea*: "reckless disregard." The court rejected that argument, noting that the defendant knew he did not eliminate altogether the risk of exposure of the tampered vials to injured persons, and that was enough to prove reckless disregard. He was convicted under the statute.

The federal statute also includes as product tampering actions that reduce the efficacy of a drug designed to save a life or alleviate bodily injury, as well as tampering that turns a drug into a poison. In the 2012 case of *United States v. Lyle*,[35] the defendant opened boxes stored in a secure narcotics safe that contained fentanyl patches, a narcotic much more potent than morphine. He took out the patches, and then re-secured the box. He was charged with violation of the federal anti-tampering statute, but contended the statute did not apply to his actions because he didn't substitute another substance for the drug that was stolen. The court rejected that argument, noting the § 1365 applied to tampering with the container in which drugs are stored. The defendant clearly did that, because he removed the drug listed on the container as being inside.

The crime of consumer product tampering receives a great deal of attention and concern because all societies are vulnerable to such acts. Millions of dollars have been invested in tamper-proof packaging. Most consumers are well aware of the remote possibility that the product they purchase may have been tampered with in a way that could seriously hurt them or someone in their family.

Federal statutes and the laws of most (if not all) states also make the following conduct criminal:

- Tampering with (altering) or destroying evidence of a crime
- Tampering with (altering) a financial document such as a check or another document such as a will or a mortgage
- Tampering with (altering) an odometer of a motor vehicle that is to be sold to another person
- Tampering with a witness or potential witness by telling the witness what to say or what not to say

ENVIRONMENTAL CRIMES AND CORPORATE RESPONSIBILITY

On April 20, 2010, a massive explosion struck the *Deepwater Horizon* oil rig, which was drilling for oil 70 miles off the Louisiana coast. Eleven workers were killed in the blast, which resulted in the release of over 4.9 million barrels of oil into the Gulf of Mexico. The Macondo well site where the blowout explosion occurred was finally capped in July 2010, after causing enormous damage to the ocean, ocean floor, migratory birds, ocean mammals, and the economic vitality of the Gulf Coast. BP Company was the company responsible for the well site, and Transocean owned the oil rig that exploded.

BP faced massive civil responsibility for the damages to the workers, their families, and the environment. It immediately set up a $20 billion dollar fund to address civil claims, and reached an agreement with the Justice Department to administer those funds under the Deepwater Horizon Court-Supervised Settlement Program. As of the end of 2012, over $8.2 billion had been paid under that settlement.

BP also faced criminal prosecution for violating the criminal provisions of several federal statutes passed to protect the environment. The Clean Water Act, the Migratory Bird Act, the Marine Mammal Protection Act, the Endangered Species Act, and the Outer Continental Shelf Lands Act all have criminal penalties for harm caused to the environment by the oil spill. In addition, BP could also have been prosecuted under the Seaman's Manslaughter Statute for the death of the eleven workers. The environmental crimes acts generally apply to any knowing violation of the statute, though some federal courts have applied the criminal provisions to negligent acts. See e.g., *United States v. Ortiz*, 427 F.3d 1278 (10th Cir. 2005). The Migratory Bird Act is a strict liability crime.

In December of 2012 BP agreed to plead guilty to eleven felony charges, including violations of the Clean Water Act and obstruction of justice, and manslaughter charges for the deaths of the oil workers. A federal judge approved a fine of $4.5 billion, and 5 years of probation in oil exploration ventures, where BP's actions will be monitored. Transocean, which owned the oil rig, agreed to pay criminal fines of $1.4 billion.

In the Gulf oil spill, the corporation incurred criminal liability. In environmental crimes, many federal statutes such as the Clean Water Act (CWA); the Clean Air Act (CAA); the Reserve Conservation and Recovery Act (RCHA); and the Comprehensive Environmental Response, Compliance, and Liability Act (CERCLA) also provide for criminal liability of corporate officers.

Beginning with the case of *United States v. Dotterwich*[36] the U.S. Supreme Court has held that "responsible" corporate officers may be criminally liable for actions taken by the corporation. Subsequently, Congress amended the CWA and CAA to specifically provide for "responsible corporate officer" (RCO) criminal liability for violations of those statutes. Courts have incorporated RCO criminal liability for violations of other environmental criminal provisions in a similar manner.

Virtually all the environmental criminal statutes require a showing of a "knowing" violation of the statute. Thus, in criminal suits against a corporate officer the prosecution cannot simply prove the officer is an RCO. It must also show the officer knew the corporation was taking actions that created the risk of harm addressed by the statute. In a leading case, *United States v. Hansen*,[37] corporate officers were convicted of violations of the CWA, RCRA, and CERCLA. They argued they could not be convicted because they did not personally oversee the actions of the company that violated the statutes. The court of appeals affirmed the convictions, stating that all the prosecution need prove is that the officers were aware violations were occurring, based on their knowledge of plant operations.

Finally, both the CWA and the CAA acts provide that "knowingly" can be proved by evidence a RCO took affirmative steps to shield himself from knowledge of actions that violated the statutes.

Summary

- White-collar crime refers to criminal offenses in which the criminal's only goal is economic gain.
- Fraud is in essence a crime of deceit, and therefore it must be shown that the defendant's actions were intended to be deceitful. One cannot normally be negligently deceitful.
- A "scheme or artifice" in federal criminal statutes is an intentional act that has as a goal fraudulent and unlawful gain, and includes a material falsehood one would understand to be important and would be relied on by others. It specifically includes depriving another of the intangible right to honest services.
- Bribery under the federal statute is similar to extortion because it is not necessary in an extortion prosecution to prove an official threatened to use his official authority if the extortion amount was not paid. Thus, the official's receipt of unlawful may constitute extortion and also could constitute bribery.
- The principal laws protecting intellectual property are the federal copyright, patent, and trademark laws, as well as state trade secret laws.

- The federal bank fraud act and the wire fraud act are frequently used to convict white-collar criminals.
- A communication under the wire fraud act must cross state lines. This is necessary to give Congress jurisdiction over the crime under the Commerce Clause. By definition, use of the U.S. mails involves interstate commerce.
- Insider trading includes using information acquired by an insider and not available to the public to profit in a sale of securities. It also includes use of such information by a person not an insider, if the person acquired the information knowing it came from an insider and was not available to the public.
- A conviction under the federal identity theft statute requires proof that a person produced a false identification document or possessed or used an identification document that belonged to another person. The federal statute requires that the defendant know the identification document belongs to another person, though some state statutes do not have this requirement.

Key Terms

white-collar crime, p. 416
fraud, p. 416
bank fraud, p. 417
intellectual property fraud, p. 418

bribery, p. 421
quid pro quo, p. 421
identity theft, p. 429
cybercrime, p. 433

computer trespass, p. 433
arson, p. 437

Case Analysis and Writing Exercises

1. In the *Nosal* case discussed in this chapter, a federal court of appeals held that "unauthorized access" under the CFAA did not include unauthorized use. It therefore reversed the convictions of Nosal on some of the counts against him, and remanded the case to the district court. The district court refused to dismiss the remaining CFAA counts against Nosal, stating those counts did allege "unauthorized access" to the employer's computer. How did those counts differ from the ones dismissed by the appeals court? What does the district court mean when it said if the employee (J.F.) entered a password and logged on, and then gave the computer terminal over to the defendant (M.J.), it is the functional

equivalent of the defendant using the password to log on by himself? *See United States v. Nosal*, 2013 WL 978226 (N.D. Cal. 2013).

2. The federal mail and wire fraud statutes both require proof that a defendant entered into a scheme to defraud another of money or property based on fraudulent misrepresentations. In *United States v. Wynn*, 684 F.3d 473 (4th Cir. 2012), an engineer doctored construction plans to make it appear a state environmental regulatory agency had approved the plans to expand a county's airport runway. How was this a scheme to take money or other property from the county?

3. As we saw in the text, "agents" of state entities that receive federal funds who commit fraud or bribery violate the federal program fraud statute, 18 U.S.C.A. § 666. Exactly who qualifies as an agent for purposes of the act? Must a person in some fashion be responsible for the funds granted to the state entity? Consider two cases: (1) State judges accept bribes from lawyers arguing cases before the judges. The judges are officers of the courts, and the state courts have received federal funds. However, the judges have nothing to do with control or disbursement of those funds. Can they be convicted under § 666? No; *See United States v. Whitfield*, 590 F.3d 325 (5th Cir. 2009), *cert. denied*, 131 S. Ct. 136 (2010). (2) A county zoning official falsified documents that he used to obtain a low-income housing grant. The county had received federal funds under a federal assistance program. The defendant was a county official, but had nothing to do with disbursement of the county funds. Can he be convicted under § 666? Yes; *see United States v. Keen*, 676 F.3d 981 (11th Cir. 2012), *cert. denied*, 133 S. Ct. 573 (2012). There is now a split among the federal circuit courts of appeal. Do you think the Supreme Court should resolve that split?

4. Federal sentencing rules provide for enhanced sentences for defendants who use a "computer" to entice a minor into engaging in sexual acts. The meaning of "computer" for sentencing purposes is taken from the Computer Fraud and Abuse Act, discussed in this chapter. If a defendant uses his cell phone to call and text the minor who he entices to engage in prohibited sex acts, should he receive the enhanced sentence for use of a "computer"? Is your cell phone a computer? *See United States v. Kramer*, 631 F.3d 900 (8th Cir. 2011), *cert. denied*, 131 S. Ct. 2977 (2011).

Endnotes

1. U.S. Department of Justice, 1989, p. 3.
2. U.S. Department of Justice, "Crime in the United States: 2011."
3. 527 U.S. 1 (1999).
4. 210 F.3d 884 (8th Cir. 2000).
5. 554 F.3d 903 (10th Cir. 2009).
6. 588 F.3d 301 (6th Cir. 2009).
7. 131 S. Ct. 538 (2010).
8. 2013 WL 1104736 (2013).
9. 577 F.3d 195 (3rd Cir. 2009).
10. Investigating fraud in Medicaid and Medicare programs is discussed in two *FBI Law Enforcement Bulletins:* "Medicaid Fraud Control" (October 1992) and "Health Care Fraud" (October 1992).

    See the *New York Times* editorial, "Fraud and Waste in Medicare" (August 1, 1997), and other news articles reporting that federal auditors estimate $23 billion in fraud and mistake loss in Medicare payments in 1996. These losses fell into the following categories: (1) "raw fraud," which for the most part was services not provided; (2) a gray area requiring the exercise of judgment; and (3) violations of the anti-kickback provision, which forbids payment for referrals.

11. See the *New York Times* article "Agents Uncover Rampant Food Stamp Fraud," September 11, 1994, which estimates that in a $24 billion program, $2 billion is used for fraudulent purposes.
12. 490 F.3d 314 (3rd Cir. 2007).
13. 507 F.3d 550 (7th Cir. 2007).
14. 406 F.3d 22 (1st Cir. 2005).
15. 510 F.3d 134 (2nd Cir. 2007).
16. 308 F.3d 144 (2nd Cir. 2002).
17. 538 F.3d 341 (5th Cir. 2008).
18. 486 F.3d 315 (7th Cir. 2007).
19. 533 F.3d 143 (2nd Cir. 2008).
20. *United States v. Skilling*, 638 F.3d 480 (5th Cir. 2011), *cert. denied*, 132 S. Ct. 1905 (2012).
21. 531 F.3d 1020 (9th Cir. 2008).

22. 681 F.3d 1220 (11th Cir. 2012).

23. 701 F.3d 959 (4th Cir. 2012), *cert. denied*, 133 S. Ct. 1839 (2013). State identity theft statutes may have different interpretations. In *State v. Evans*, 298 P.3d 724 (Wash. 2013) the court held theft of a corporation's identity violated the Washington identity theft statute.

24. 706 F.3d 716 (6th Cir. 2013).

25. 769 N.W.2d 34 (Wis. 2009).

26. 213 P.3d 745 (Kans. App. 2009).

27. See the *New York Times* article "Teens Accused of Using Computers to Counterfeit," February 17, 1997.

28. *New York Times*, March 16, 2013: "Black and White, Wallet Size, Unfit for Faking."

29. 331 S.W.3d 187 (Tex. App. 2011).

30. 621 S.E.2d 696 (Va. App. 2005).

31. 588 F.3d 60 (1st Cir. 2009).

32. 600 N.E.2d 962 (Ind. App. 1992). If the completed crime of arson cannot be proved beyond a reasonable doubt, the state may then consider charging attempt to commit arson (or in an appropriate situation, conspiracy to commit arson).

33. See *Hughes v. State*, 6 Md. App. 389, 251 A2d 373 (1969), in which the court pointed out that mere presence of the accused at the scene of a fire is not proof beyond reasonable doubt that the fire was willfully and maliciously set. In *Hughes v. State*, a fire chief testified that he could not determine the cause of the fire. The court reversed the defendant's conviction, holding that the evidence was legally insufficient to establish the corpus delicti of the crime of arson.

34. 2011 WL 3876949 (C.D. Cal. 2011).

35. 2012 WL 3067424 (E.D. Wa. 2011).

36. 320 U.S. 277 (1943).

37. 262 F.3d 1217 (11th Cir. 2001), *cert. denied*, 535 U.S. 1111 (2002).

Drug Abuse and Alcohol-Related Crimes

Kevork Djansezian/Getty Images News/Getty Images

These two women are getting their prescriptions filled at a medical marijuana dispensary in Los Angeles, California. In many states, medical use of marijuana is legal if recommended by a physician. A small number of states have made the recreational use of marijuana legal without the need for a medical prescription. It remains unclear what, if anything, federal authorities will do to enforce federal drug laws under which possession of marijuana is still illegal.

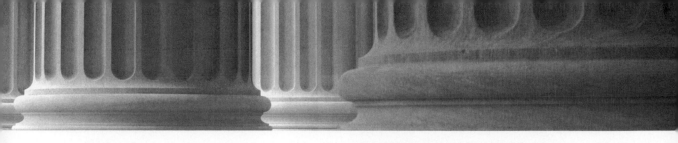

OUTLINE

Drug Abuse

The Frightening Drug Problem

Illegal Drug Users

Drug Laws in the United States

The Uniform Controlled Substances Act

Types of Possession of Controlled Substances

To Convict of Possession of an Illegal Drug, Must the State Present a "Usable Amount" as Evidence?

Delivery of Controlled Substances

State–Federal Clash Over the Medical Use of Marijuana

Controlled Substances Used in Religious Ceremonies

Drug Rip-Off Cases and Simulated Drugs

Criminal Liability for Drug-Induced Deaths

Possession or Sale of Drug Paraphernalia

Alcohol-Related Crimes

Alcohol's Relation to Crimes and Deaths

Drunk Driving: The Criminal Homicide Causing the Most Deaths

Elements and Defenses in Drunk-Driving Prosecutions

"Booze It and Lose It" Laws

When Is a Person Driving, Operating, or "In Physical Control" of a Vehicle?

LEARNING OBJECTIVES

In this chapter we discuss crimes related to drugs, drug abuse, and alcohol abuse. The learning objectives for Chapter 16 are

- List the ways a person can violate the Uniform Controlled Substances Act.
- Identify the elements of the crime of possession of an illegal drug with intent to deliver.
- State the current status of state medical-use-of-marijuana statutes.
- Explain the rationale of the Supreme Court's holding in *Gonzales v. Raich.*
- Identify the elements that must be proved for a conviction under a state drug-induced death statute.
- Learn the statistics for alcohol-related deaths among college students.
- Learn the statistics for alcohol-related motor vehicle deaths.
- Identify what must be shown to prove a person was operating a motor vehicle.

S ince California voters approved the medical use of marijuana in 1996, nineteen other states and the District of Columbia have done the same. In those states, possession and limited cultivation or distribution of marijuana is no longer a crime. As of March 2013, bills to legalize medical use of marijuana were near approval in the Maryland, Illinois, and Florida legislatures. Under most of these laws, a resident of the state (in most of the states, non-residents may not obtain the required medical use ID) may obtain a medical use identification card (ID) if a physician approves or recommends the use of marijuana for a medical condition. Acceptable medical conditions in most states include cancer, epilepsy, HIV or AIDS, multiple sclerosis, and "chronic pain." Montana requires a second physician's recommendation for "chronic pain" as the basis for obtaining the ID.

Fifteen states permit the medical user or caregiver to cultivate marijuana plants, but in a limited amount. All states that permit medical use have set up supervised distribution centers for distributing marijuana to persons with the necessary documents. Most states do not honor a medical use ID obtained from another state, though that may change. The bill proposed in Florida appears to do so, though it also requires that any marijuana possessed by a person with a medical use ID be grown in Florida.

In 2012, voters in the states of Colorado and Washington legalized the recreational use of marijuana. However, many questions, such as how to regulate the growth and sale of the drug, how to prevent exportation to surrounding states, and how to tax the sale and use of the drug, remain uncertain. Most importantly, what will the U.S. Justice Department do? Marijuana sale and possession are still crimes under the federal Controlled Substances Act, and the prospect of massive federal prosecutions remains a distinct possibility.

In this chapter we will study the many ways the criminal laws are used to combat the illegal drug problem in the United States. We will also study the relationship of the abuse of alcohol to criminal behavior and government's attempts to control that behavior.

Drug Abuse

The Frightening Drug Problem

The possession, sale, and use of illegal drugs is a problem of epic proportion in the United States. Illegal drugs have shattered many lives, led to suicides and murders, and caused serious health problems in many people. Sections of many American cities where illegal drugs are readily available have become seriously disrupted; where drugs are available, other crimes follow.

Drug lords all over the world have become rich and powerful. Gangs and organized criminals in the United States find selling drugs to be an easy way to make money and gain power, which in turn leads to even greater lawlessness. For example, where criminals have huge amounts of cash available, the crime of bribery becomes more common. A 2011 report by the Homeland Security Studies and Analysis Institute disclosed extensive corruption in the U.S. Customs & Border Protection Agency. The Border Agency has over 60,000 employees. Since October 1, 2004, 147 Agency officers and agents have been charged with corruption, including bribery and allowing illegal drugs to be brought into the United States. The report identifies at least fifteen attempts by drug cartels to infiltrate the Border Protection Agency. Since 2010, when the Agency began giving polygraph tests to all applicants, 75 percent of the applicants have been rejected because they either failed the polygraph or did not show up to take the test.

The FBI has thirteen task forces operating along the United States' southwest border with Mexico, investigating corruption and other problems in the Border Protection Agency.

Illegal smuggling goes both ways on the United States-Mexico border. Going north is the largest constant flow of illegal drugs in the world. Illegal immigrants seeking work in the United States are also a steady flow across the border, along with smuggled counterfeit goods, money, prescription drugs, and electronic products.

Going south are smuggled American dollars for the purchase of illegal drugs. The Drug Enforcement Agency (DEA) estimates that $18 billion to $39 billion crosses the border each year. In 2008 alone the DEA seized $138 million of illegally smuggled money (*New York Times*, December 26, 2009: "Torrent of Illegal Cash Flows Where the U.S. and Mexico Meet"). More than 16,000 vehicles cross the border each day in Laredo, Texas, alone, making policing the border almost impossible.

Also going south are smuggled firearms. Mexican drug gangs are a fertile market for sales of illegal weapons. There reportedly are about 6,600 American gun dealers along the Mexican border, and these dealers sell high-powered pistols and military rifles to the drug gangs. Data released by the Bureau of Alcohol, Tobacco and Firearms (ATF) on April 26, 2012, show that from 2007 to 2011 96,691 firearms seized in Mexico crime scenes were traced back to their manufacturer. Of those, 66,161 came from a source in the United States. In the failed "Fast and Furious" campaign conducted between 2008 and 2009, federal officials allowed over 2,000 automatic weapons to "walk" in to Mexico so that U.S. agents could follow the weapons to their purchasers. However, most of the guns were "lost," and the plan was scrapped. The "lost" guns later turned up at several crime scenes, including the murder in December 2010 of Border Patrol agent Brian Terry.

The year 2006 marked renewed efforts in the "war on drugs." In the United States, billions of dollars were allocated to increasing border security and hiring more border and customs agents. In Mexico, then-President Felipe Caldron launched a "federal assault" on drug cartels, using federal police to attack drug cartels in areas of Mexico where they operated.

The results on illegal drug smuggling and production since 2006 are mixed. While marijuana is harder to smuggle across the border with Mexico, the increase in production in the United States is dramatic. The Drug Enforcement Agency (DEA) reports that Mexican drug cartels are now sending members to the parks and forests of the United States to plant and harvest the drug. The DEA also reports that 80 percent of the marijuana grown in the United States is grown on state or federal land.

The production and import of methamphetamine has also increased over 2006 levels, according to the Justice Department's National Drug Intelligence Center. The Center's 2010 Methamphetamine Threat Assessment report stated that the supply of methamphetamine was the highest since 2005, the quality was the best, and the price was the lowest. Domestic manufacture in small "one-pot" operations is also at a high level. In 2009 drug enforcement agencies seized 5,308 of these small operations, up from 3,096 in 2007. As an additional problem, Mexican drug cartels are frequently producing methamphetamine using non–ephedrine-based methods. Both the United States and Mexico have passed laws making it harder to obtain ephedrine and pseudoephedrine, the preferred base chemicals used in the manufacture of methamphetamine. This method produces drugs with the highest potency. Mexican drug cartels are now producing the drug by the "P2P" method, which produces drugs with lower potency, and then using other chemicals, such as tartaric acid, to increase the potency.

National or international figures on methamphetamine production are not known. However, based on the number of lab seizures made by Mexican and U.S. authorities in 2009, and the quantity of the drug seized by border officials, 5,187 kilograms in 2009, the report concluded that traffic in and use of methamphetamine would increase in 2010 and beyond.

The "war on drugs" has had tragic consequences for Mexican border towns. Since the crackdown efforts commenced in late 2006, more than 25,000 people have been killed by drug cartel gunmen, or in gunfights between federal police and drug cartels. One border city, Ciudad Juarez, which shares a border with El Paso, Texas, has been especially hard hit by the killings. On July 17, 2010, the Mexican drug gang La Linea exploded a car bomb in a trap set for federal police, killing three officers. In the weeks preceding the car bomb attack, fourteen police officers were killed by drug gunmen. In Juarez alone, 4,000 people have been killed since 2006 in drug cartel-related killings.

Heroin production and use has increased since 2005. Opium, a product derived from certain kinds of poppy plants, was produced in amounts significantly greater than previous years starting in 2006. Afghanistan, which produces about 90 percent of the world's opium, produced about 6,100 metric tons of opium in 2006, a 49 percent increase over the previous year. The 2007 crop was about 8,300 metric tons. The volume dropped in 2008, when opium having a value of about $3.4 billion was exported from Afghanistan. In 2009 exported opium dropped again, when $2.8 billion worth was exported. Based on crops planted in 2010, the United Nations believed opium production would drop again in 2010, which would mean a one-third drop since the highs of 2007.[1] Of the opium grown in Afghanistan, 80 percent comes from villages controlled by Taliban forces, according to the United Nations. The proceeds from the sale of the illegal opium is believed to be a source of money to fund the insurgents and terrorists fighting the UN forces, who are seeking to establish a stable, democratic government in Afghanistan.

With virtually unlimited sources, illegal drugs have become readily available to anyone seeking them. Not only are the drugs available, but they are cheaper and of a better quality, making them attractive to the poor and the young. The Partnership for a Drug-Free America points out that

- Americans spend billions of dollars yearly for the purchase of illegal drugs.
- Many organized criminal groups, gangs, and terrorists depend on drug money. Police surveys show that there are now more than 30,000 gangs in the United States, with more than 800,000 members. (See Chapter 18.)
- Each year, more than 25 million Americans use illegal drugs.

Illegal Drug Users

The war against illegal drugs is being fought on both the supply side and on the demand side. Most cocaine, heroin, crack, and marijuana are produced outside the

METH: A CHEMICAL TIME BOMB, AND THE MOST HIGHLY ABUSED DRUG IN THE WORLD

In 2006 the United Nations reported that methamphetamine ("meth"), also known as "crank," "ice," or "poor man's cocaine," was the most highly abused hard drug in the world, with almost as many addicts as cocaine and heroin combined. Huge quantities of meth are smuggled into the United States each year by gangs and organized criminals. Increasingly, meth is also being produced in the United States by small "one-pot" or "shake-and-bake" operations.

Meth labs have always presented risks for both producers and law enforcement officers. An article in the April 2000 *FBI Law Enforcement Bulletin* stated that raiding a meth lab ". . . has become one of the most dangerous operations a law enforcement officer can undertake." The labs also present a danger to third parties who encounter waste or trash from the site of a meth lab.

A meth lab contains highly volatile chemicals used in the manufacture of the drug. These can include battery acid, drain cleaner, Coleman fuel, kerosene, lacquer thinner, mineral spirits, Heet®, denatured alcohol, and Epsom salts. The key ingredient in meth operations is pseudoephedrine, which can be found in over-the-counter drugs such as Sudafed and Contac. In 2005 Congress passed the Combat Methamphetamine Epidemic Act, 21 U.S.C. § 830, which requires retail sellers of ephedrine or pseudoephedrine products to keep them "behind the counter," demand identification from purchasers, and report sales figures to the government. Most states have similar laws regulating sales of products that contain pseudoephedrine. Two states, Oregon and Mississippi, require a prescription for the purchase of such products. In a letter to the *New York Times*, published April 23, 2010, Ron Wyden, a U.S. senator from Oregon, stated that the results of requiring a prescription appear to be good. Prior to the law, police in Oregon raided over 500 meth labs per year. In 2009, after the law was passed, they raided only ten labs.

Despite the intense efforts by state and federal legislatures and law enforcement agencies, home-based meth labs continue to flourish. The demand for meth is huge, the production easy, and the profits immense. Recently, new methods of producing meth have surfaced. In an April 15, 2010 article in the *New York Times* titled "With Cars as Meth Labs, Evidence Litters Roads," law enforcement officers report that the "mobile method has grown in popularity because it is easier, cheaper, and harder to get caught than making (meth) indoors. . . . most of the cooks are addicts themselves, not dealers or distributors." It is reported that for every pound of meth produced in these small labs, five or six pounds of toxic, flammable, corrosive waste are generated, and left as litter on back roads and highways

United States. Great efforts are being made to prevent illegal drugs from entering the United States. Efforts to win the supply-side war have been going on since the 1950s, but an estimated 90 percent of these illegal drugs get into the United States.

The demand-side problem is that millions of Americans are willing to pay billions of dollars yearly for illegal drugs. More money is spent annually in the United States on illegal drugs and legal alcohol than is spent for clothing.[2] The United States is the biggest market in the world for illegal drugs and the profits are huge;

therefore, criminals take great risks to bring the illegal drugs into the country. The users of illegal drugs can be classified as follows:

- *The "Situational" Drug Abuser:* A person who uses illegal drugs for a specific or "situational" purpose, such as to accomplish some other objective. A person who is under a great deal of stress or tension might use a drug such as marijuana to relax. A performer or a truck driver might use a stimulant, or an upper, to stay awake.
- *The "Party" or "Weekend" User:* A drug abuser who might use drugs for kicks or just for the experience. These users are great sources of profits for drug pushers.
- *The Drug Addict:* A person who is physically and/or psychologically dependent on drugs. He or she cannot perform daily without drug support. Addicts have a "monkey on their back," which can be very expensive to support. To raise the money for their daily supply of drugs ($50, $100, or even $150 per day), addicts steal, break into cars, commit burglaries, rob, snatch purses, or push drugs. Women and men who trade sex for drugs are among those most susceptible to disease, including AIDS.

Today, common forms of drug abuse include so-called street drugs, such as marijuana, cocaine or crack, methamphetamine, heroin, and other drugs; prescription drugs, whether obtained legally through a prescription or by theft of either the drugs or a prescription slip to obtain the drugs; and over-the-counter substances that produce a "high," such as cold medicines and inhalants. Combining any of these drugs with each other, or with alcohol, creates the risk of stroke, seizure, coma, or even death. Accidental drug overdoses doubled in the period from 1999 to 2004 and in 2007 became the nation's second leading cause of accidental deaths, behind only automobile accidents. The National Center for Health Statistics reported 38,329 deaths from drug overdose in 2010. Prescription drug overdose accounted for much of the increase in fatalities, causing 16,651 unintentional deaths, more than cocaine or heroin.

Prescription Drugs   Abuse of prescription drugs, mainly painkillers, has also risen markedly over the past few years. A July 15, 2010, report by the Substance Abuse and Mental Health Services Administration concluded that prescription painkiller abuse increased by 400 percent in the 10 years prior to the report. The percentage of hospital admissions for substance abuse of painkiller medications increased from 2.8 percent in 1998 to 9.8 percent in 2008. Admissions for cocaine and alcohol abuse during the same period went down, the report stated.

In a June 3, 2010, report the Centers for Disease Control stated that in 2009 it conducted its National Youth Risk Behavior Survey, and for the first time it obtained data on high school students' use of prescription drugs without a prescription. It found that one in five high school students has used prescription drugs like OxyContin, Percocet, Vicodin, or Adderall.

Adderall is a prescription psychostimulant that is commonly prescribed for persons with attention deficit hyperactivity disorder. It has become popular on college campuses as a stimulant used during exam and "cramming" periods. While college students generally regard the drug as harmless, it is a Schedule II drug under the Controlled Substances Act, which means that while it has accepted medical usages it carries a high potential for addiction.

Drug Laws in the United States

The first law enacted in the United States was an anti-opium smoking ordinance passed in San Francisco in 1875 because of the opium problem there.[3] This was one of the few restrictions on drugs in the United States at that time.

In the 1880s and 1890s, people in the United States could still concoct and sell to the American public practically any drug or drug compound they wished. Drugs were available in stores, through mail-order catalogs, and from traveling vendors and peddlers. Little was known at that time about the effects of drugs on human beings. Drug promoters claimed their drugs cured sickness and other human problems.

A German firm, for example, marketed a newly discovered drug in the 1890s as a cough suppressant. The name the firm gave the drug is well known today—heroin.

Heroin did a wonderful job of suppressing coughs, but years passed before people realized the terrible problems of addiction to heroin. Other drugs and compounds, which often contained either cocaine or heroin, were advertised and promoted as cures for everything from ingrown toenails to cancer. Medications were sold that guaranteed sex rejuvenation, new hair for bald people, breast enlargement, a cure for arthritis, and more.

Cocaine was used in Coca-Cola[®], a very popular soft drink even in those days. Cocaine was not replaced by the drug caffeine in Coca-Cola until 1906.

Responding to the use of cocaine and heroin in some everyday products, U.S. President William Howard Taft stated in 1910 that "the misuse of cocaine is undoubtedly an American habit, the most threatening of the drug habits that has ever appeared in this country." In 1906, the federal Pure Food and Drug Act was enacted because of the concern over heroin addiction. In 1914 the federal Harrison Narcotics Act was passed.

The Food and Drug Administration (FDA) now requires a firm or person who wishes to market and sell a drug in the United States to show that

- The drug or medication is not harmful to humans.
- The drug or medication will do what it is advertised to do.

The Uniform Controlled Substances Act

uniform controlled substances act Model act identifying illegal drug crimes, drafted by a national conference of uniform law commissioners and adopted by the states and the federal government.

Today, the federal government and all of the states have enacted the **Uniform Controlled Substances Act**, which was approved by the National Conference of Commissioners on Uniform State Laws in 1970.[4] The purposes of this act have been stated as follows:

This Uniform Act was drafted to achieve uniformity between the laws of the several States and those of the Federal government. It has been designed to complement the new Federal narcotic and dangerous drug legislation and provide an interlocking trellis of Federal and State law to enable government at all levels to control more effectively the drug abuse problem. (Uniform Controlled Substances Act, 9 U.L.A., Commissioners' Prefatory Note, 1979, p. 188)

controlled substance
A drug that may be possessed or sold only as permitted by state or federal law.

In their **controlled substance** acts, most states forbid and make it criminal conduct to

- Manufacture[5] or deliver a controlled (forbidden) substance.
- Possess with intent to manufacture or deliver a controlled substance.
- Create, deliver, or possess with intent to deliver a counterfeit substance.
- Offer or agree to deliver a controlled substance and then deliver or dispense a substance that is not a controlled substance.
- Possess a controlled substance.
- Knowingly keep or maintain a store, dwelling, building, vehicle, boat, or aircraft, or other place resorted to by persons illegally using controlled substances.
- Acquire or obtain possession of a controlled substance by misrepresentation, fraud, forgery, deception, or subterfuge.

FIVE SCHEDULES OF CONTROLLED SUBSTANCES

Schedule	Abuse Potential	Examples of Drugs Covered	Some of the Effects	Medical Use
I	Highest	Heroin, LSD, hashish, marijuana, methaqualone (Quaalude), "designer drugs"	Unpredictable effects, severe psychological or physical dependence, or death	No accepted use; some are legal for limited research use only
II	High	Morphine, PCP, codeine, cocaine, methadone, Demerol, Benzedrine, Dexedrine	May lead to severe psychological or physical dependence	Accepted use with restrictions
III	Medium	Codeine with aspirin or Tylenol, some amphetamines, anabolic steroids	May lead to moderate or low physical dependence or high psychological dependence	Accepted use
IV	Low	Darvon, Talwin, phenobarbital, Equanil, Miltown, Librium, diazepam (Valium)	May lead to limited physical or psychological dependence	Accepted use
V	Lowest	Over-the-counter or prescription compounds with codeine, Lomotil, Robitussin A-C	May lead to limited physical or psychological dependence	Accepted use

© Cengage Learning

The Uniform Controlled Substances Act has five schedules of controlled substances according to their potential for abuse, degree of accepted medical use, and relative physical danger to the abuser. These schedules were summarized by the U.S. Bureau of Justice Statistics in its 1992 *Report on Drugs, Crime and the Justice System* (see box).

Types of Possession of Controlled Substances

The most common criminal (or ordinance) illegal drug charge is that of possession of a controlled substance.[6] Possession must be proved to sustain an arrest and conviction. The federal Controlled Substances Act (21 U.S.C. § 841(a)(1)) defines the possession offenses to include a *mens rea* requirement: that the person knowingly or intentionally possessed the controlled substance. See *United States v. Abdulle,* 564 F.3d 119 (2d Cir. 2009). As a result, when states adopted their own controlled substances acts, they usually included the requirement that the possession be done "knowingly." For example, the Texas statute, VTCA § 481.115, states, "Except as authorized by this Chapter, a person commits an offense if the person knowingly or intentionally possesses a controlled substance listed in Penalty Group I...."

Some states make the simple fact of possession a crime. The Washington Supreme Court held in *State v. Bradshaw,*[7] that because the Washington state legislature omitted the "knowingly" language when it adopted its controlled substances act, mere possession of a controlled substance is a criminal offense. The *Bradshaw* court stated that there is "no *mens rea*" in RCWA 69.50.4013, the Washington illegal possession statute.

It is uniformly held in both state and federal courts that as long as a defendant knew he possessed *some* kind of controlled substance, the prosecution need not prove he knew the exact nature and kind of drug possessed. For example, in the 2010 case of *United States v. De La Torre,*[8] the court held that a defendant carrying a backpack that he knew contained marijuana could be convicted of possession of methamphetamine that was also in the backpack, whether or not the defendant knew that fact.

For some kinds of controlled substances, which are not as well known as marijuana or cocaine, proof of knowledge of possession can be more difficult. Khat is the name of an African plant commonly chewed in African countries as a stimulant. Khat is not a controlled substance. After harvest, khat contains a chemical called catherinone, a Schedule I controlled substance. However, over a short time, the plant decays and the catherinone is replaced by a different substance, cathine, a Schedule IV controlled substance. A person in possession of khat may thus be in possession of either catherinone or cathine, depending on how much the plant has decayed. In *United States v. Hassan,*[9] the court reversed a conviction of a defendant charged with conspiracy to possess catherinone with intent to distribute. The court said that it was not enough to prove the defendant intended to import khat. The government needed to prove the defendant knew khat contained catherinone, and that he intended to import khat that had catherinone.

Proof of possession may be satisfied by either of the following:

- *Actual possession,* which is possession on the person of the defendant, or within an area of his or her immediate control and reach. Actual possession may be within a container (e.g., purse, package, or suitcase) that the defendant may be carrying or has within reach. Actual possession may also occur in a vehicle when the controlled substance is under the seat of the person or in the glove compartment of the vehicle owned or driven by the defendant.

- *Constructive possession* of a controlled substance, which occurs when illegal drugs are in a place immediately accessible to the accused and subject to his or her domination and control. Examples of constructive possession would be drugs found in the trunk of a car the defendant owned or was the driver of, or in a home or business place controlled and dominated by a defendant, to such an extent that a strong inference of possession could be drawn by a judge or jury.

To Convict of Possession of an Illegal Drug, Must the State Present a "Usable Amount" as Evidence?

State courts differ on the question as to whether a "trace" amount of an illegal drug (that is, an amount so small that it is unusable) will sustain a conviction for possession of that drug.

In the case of *People v. Mizell*,[10] the highest court in the state of New York followed the majority of the states and held that "any amount of an (illegal drug) is sufficient to sustain a conviction for possession." In the *Mizell* case, cocaine residue found on the sides of vials was used to support the criminal charge and conviction for possession. The conviction was affirmed, with the court holding that "cocaine residue—though unusable—is nevertheless a controlled substance" under the criminal code of the state of New York.[11]

In *Beeler v. State*,[12] the court found that possession of an electronic scale with minute quantities of cocaine residue satisfied the requirements for illegal "possession" of a controlled substance. The defendant contended that he could not "knowingly" possess a miniscule amount of a drug and thus could not be convicted under the Indiana statute, Ind. Code § 35-48-4-6. That statute, like other possession statutes in most states, prohibits one from "knowingly or intentionally" possessing a controlled substance. The court said that circumstantial evidence, such as the admitted use the defendant planned for the scale, was sufficient to prove he "knew" the residue was a controlled substance.

However, other courts follow the "usable quantity" rule and hold that a blackened residue or a useless trace amount is not a **usable amount** and will not sustain a criminal conviction for possession of an illegal drug. Courts holding that a usable quantity of drugs must be presented include California[13] and Florida, at least where the trace amount of the substance is found on a commonly exchanged object, such as a dollar bill.[14]

The "knowing" element of the federal Controlled Substances Act may also be satisfied by "deliberate ignorance" on the part of the person in possession of illegal drugs. The 2012 case of *United States v. Vasquez*[15] illustrates this rule. The defendant worked in Laredo, Texas, but walked across the border to Nuevo Laredo, Mexico on a regular basis. His employer stated that the defendant did not drive a car, and was not believed to own a car. The defendant was stopped at a border patrol inspection station in the United States. He was driving a Chevrolet Suburban. Officers searched the vehicle, and under

usable amount In contrast to a useless trace amount, a quantity of an illegal drug sufficient to be used.

POSSESSION OF A SMALL AMOUNT OF MARIJUANA

The offense of possession of a small amount of marijuana is charged in different ways throughout the United States.

Criminal Offense

If the person is charged and convicted under a statute and could receive a jail sentence, the conviction is a criminal conviction and the person has been convicted of a crime.

Civil Offense

If the only penalty that can be imposed after conviction is a monetary fine, the conviction is for a civil offense and is similar to a speeding ticket or a parking ticket. Under these circumstances, the offense of possession of a small amount of marijuana has been "decriminalized," as it is no longer charged as a crime.

Legalized Conduct

If neither criminal nor civil punishment is imposed for possession of a small amount of marijuana, the conduct has then been legalized and is no longer a crime or a civil offense. The Alaska Supreme Court has held that under the Alaska Constitution's right of privacy, adults may possess up to four grams of marijuana in their homes. See *State v. Crocker*, 97 P.3d 93 (Alaska App. 2004).

© Cengage Learning

the hood found two car batteries. Since vehicles usually have only one battery, officers dismantled the batteries. Inside they found small motorcycle batteries used to start the car, and 5 kilograms of cocaine in each battery. The defendant admitted he owned the car, but stated that another unidentified man bought the car for him, placing defendant's name on the title. The defendant stated he did not know the batteries had cocaine inside. The court of appeals upheld his conviction, stating that the circumstances of the purchase of the car, the presence of the two batteries, and the request to disassemble the batteries under the front seat put the defendant on notice something was wrong. His refusal to discover what was actually in the batteries was an example of "deliberate ignorance," the court held.

Delivery of Controlled Substances

The acts that are prohibited under the Uniform Controlled Substances Act, as illustrated in Florida's Criminal Code Section 893.13, include the following:

> [I]t is unlawful for any person to sell, purchase, manufacture, or deliver, or possess with intent to sell . . . a controlled substance.

Delivery of an illegal drug can be either an actual delivery, or it could be the crime of possession of a controlled substance with intent to deliver (sell or transfer).

In most of the actual delivery cases that come into criminal courts throughout the United States, the government presents evidence showing that the accused sold (delivered) illegal drugs to an undercover law enforcement officer. In other actual delivery cases, the state proves its case by producing a witness to the illegal drug transaction (either the receiver of the drugs or an observer of the delivery). Videotapes or a film of the delivery can also be used as evidence.

possession with intent to deliver A criminal case in which the state presents evidence showing that the accused had possession of a large amount of an illegal drug, meaning more than the accused would personally use.

In the typical criminal case of **possession with intent to deliver** (sell), the state presents evidence showing that the accused had possession of a large amount of an illegal drug (more than he or she would personally use). A combination of the following evidence is also generally presented: that the accused also possessed scales and/or small plastic bags with evenly weighed-out illegal drugs, a large amount of money, a pager, or a cellular phone. Evidence that the accused did not have a job but lived very well and drove an expensive car could also be presented.

The evidence presented by the government must be sufficient to justify a conclusion by the fact finder (jury or judge) that the accused possessed the illegal drug with intent to deliver (sell or transfer) it to another person. To do this, the U.S. Supreme Court requires that there must be a "rational connection"[16] between the facts presented and the conclusion drawn by the fact finder.

State–Federal Clash over the Medical Use of Marijuana

As of 2013, eighteen states and the District of Columbia had adopted some type of "Compassionate Use Medical Marijuana" statute. Under these statutes, doctors may prescribe the personal use of marijuana for pain management for people with serious illnesses who do not respond to other treatments. These laws, such as the California Compassionate Use Act of 1996 (California Health & Safety Code, Section 11362.5), created what is termed a "medical use" exception to the state's drug laws.

The federal government did not initially challenge these laws, but beginning with President George W. Bush's first administration, the attorney general began directing federal prosecutors to prosecute, under the federal Controlled Substances Act (CSA), persons distributing prescribed marijuana. In *United States v. Oakland Cannabis Buyers' Cooperative*,[17] the Supreme Court held that the CSA had no "medical use" exception and that as a result manufacturers and providers, such as the cooperative, of marijuana for medical use could be prosecuted under the CSA. The Court did not specifically hold that *users* of marijuana for medical purposes could be prosecuted under the CSA, but it did suggest as much in a footnote: "nothing in our analysis, or the statute, suggests that a distinction should be drawn between the prohibition on manufacturing and distributing and the other prohibitions in the Controlled Substances Act" (532 U.S. at 495).

After *Oakland*, several seriously ill persons using marijuana brought an action to declare the CSA unconstitutional, alleging that prosecutions of *users* of marijuana was not permitted because their use did not affect interstate commerce. That being so, they alleged, Congress had no constitutional authority to prohibit the medical use of marijuana.

In *Raich v. Ashcroft*,[18] the Ninth Circuit Court of Appeals agreed, holding that medical use of marijuana "does not have any direct or obvious effect on interstate commerce." (See Chapter 2 for a discussion of the Commerce Clause as authority for federal laws.) In 2005 the U.S. Supreme Court reversed the Ninth Circuit Court, holding that because the in-state use of marijuana might have an effect on the inter-state market for marijuana, the federal government had the power under the Commerce Clause to prohibit the use of marijuana for medical purposes. See *Gonzales v. Raich.*[19]

In the years immediately following the decision in *Raich* federal law enforcement agencies conducted many "raids" on medical-use marijuana suppliers and users. On October 19, 2009, U.S. Attorney General Eric Holder announced that prosecutions of medical-use marijuana suppliers and users would be relaxed, with law enforcement focusing on large-scale marijuana operations. However, in an announcement made October 15, 2010, Holder stated that if California voters voted to approve a measure making possession of marijuana legal, the federal government would act to enforce provisions of the federal Controlled Substances Act that make such possession illegal under federal law. That measure did not pass in California in 2010. In 2011, federal drug agents conducted raids on medical dispensaries in several states, raising questions about the continued force of the 2009 Holder statement. Since Washington and Colorado legalized the recreational use of marijuana in 2012, state governors and some members of Congress have pushed the Justice Department for a determination of how marijuana users in states that permit marijuana use will be treated. In August 2013, the Justice Department advised all 94 U.S. Attorney offices that states will be permitted to pass recreational-use of marijuana laws, so long as they have strict regulatory policies to protect public health and safety.

In July 2010 the House of Representatives passed a bill that changes the sentencing structure for "crack" cocaine convictions. Under the present law, possession of 5 grams of crack triggers the mandatory 5-year prison sentence rule, while for powder cocaine the triggering amount is possession of 500 grams. Because crack convictions overwhelmingly involve black defendants, many persons and organizations objected to the sentence disparity on grounds that it led to racial distinctions in sentencing decisions. Under the new law, which the Senate passed earlier in 2010, the amount of crack needed to trigger the 5-year mandatory sentence has been raised to 28 grams. The powder cocaine amounts remain the same.

Controlled Substances Used in Religious Ceremonies

When Congress adopted the Controlled Substances Act, the issue of religious use of substances included in the schedules of controlled substances arose. An immediate exception to the Act's prohibitions was made for the use of peyote by members of the Native American Church. In 1994, Congress passed 42 U.S.C. § 1996a(b)(l), which made this exception applicable to all Indian tribes.

Other religious groups had no specific exception to the Controlled Substances Act's prohibitions. Moreover, the Supreme Court had held that the Free Exercise Clause of the Constitution did not require judges to consider the burden placed on religious exercise by facially constitutional laws, such as the Controlled Substances Act. See *Employment Div. Dept. of Human Resources of Ore. v. Smith,* 494 U.S. 872 (1990). However, in 1993 Congress passed the Religious Freedom

Information Act, 42 U.S.C. § 2000bb. Section 2000bb-l(a) of the Act prohibits the government from placing a "substantial burden" on the exercise of religion, even if the "burden results from a rule of general applicability" (such as the drug laws), unless the government can show a compelling interest in doing so. This section has been used by religious groups to resist federal prosecutions under the Controlled Substances Act.

The U.S. Supreme Court considered the application of the Religious Freedom Restoration Act in *Gonzales v. O Centra Espirita*.[20] In that case the government sought to use the Controlled Substances Act to prohibit a practice followed by a religious sect located in the United States but with ties to a Christian Spiritist sect in Brazil, with origins in the Amazon rainforest. That sect uses a ceremonial drink called *hoasca*, made from plants that contain a Schedule I controlled substance called DMT. The Supreme Court said that since the government agreed the group using the *hoasca* was sincere in its religious significance, it could prohibit that use only if it could show some "compelling interest" for doing so. The Court rejected the government's argument that the fact DMT was a controlled substance by itself justified the prohibition. Because the government made no other showing of a compelling interest, the Court said it was barred from prosecuting the religious sect.

The original Religious Freedom Restoration Act applied to the states as well as the federal government, but in *Boerne v. Flores*,[21] the Supreme Court held that Congress lacked the power to make the law effective against the states. As a result, state prosecutions for use of a controlled substance in a religious ceremony are possible, unless the state has made its own exception to state controlled substances laws. Some have: Arizona has a statute, ARS § 541-1493.01, that is similar to the federal Religious Freedom Restoration Act. Other states have specific exceptions for the Native American Church for use of peyote; Wis. Code § 161.115 is such a statute. The Utah Supreme Court has held that the federal exception for the Native American Church was incorporated into the Utah Controlled Substances Act. See *State v. Mooney*.[22]

Drug Rip-Off Cases and Simulated Drugs

In *State v. Glover*,[23] the defendant planned to "rip off" a buyer of illegal drugs. Instead of cocaine, the defendant delivered two bags of baking soda to the buyer, at $50 a bag. His conviction for attempted trafficking in cocaine was affirmed. Glover's buyer was an undercover police officer.

Other states, among them Iowa, have statutes that make the delivery or possession of a "simulated controlled substance" a crime. A simulated controlled substance is a substance "represented to be [an illegal drug]… [that] because of its nature, packaging, or appearance would lead a reasonable person to believe it to be a controlled substance" (Iowa Statute 204.401(1)).

Georgia has a similar statute, which makes it a crime to sell an uncontrolled substance that the seller has represented to be a controlled substance. (See Georgia Code Annotated § 16-13-30.1.) In *Brown v. State*,[24] the court held that a defendant who sold a fake "rock" of crack cocaine to an undercover agent could be convicted under the statute.

Criminal Liability for Drug-Induced Deaths

Drug overdose cases occur regularly in every city in the United States, as drugs have become purer, cheaper, and easier to obtain. Cocaine is particularly dangerous because it is an unpredictable killer that can cause life-threatening complications that are not related to the dose taken, the length of use, or the manner in which the drug is taken. Swallowing an "eight-ball" of cocaine (one-eighth of an ounce) can easily cause acute cocaine intoxication and death.[25]

A number of states have enacted laws that make people who illegally manufacture, distribute, or dispense illegal drugs strictly liable for a death that results from the injection, inhalation, or ingestion of such a drug.[26] Such laws are often called *Len Bias laws.* Len Bias was a basketball star at the University of Maryland. Shortly after being drafted by an NBA team, he died as the result of using cocaine. The following cases illustrate prosecutions under these laws.

People v. Moore

Court of Appeals of Illinois (2013), 2013 WL 1190833

The defendant was taking prescription medicine containing morphine for pain relief. Her daughter invited two teenagers to their home, where they smoked marijuana and drank alcohol. At some point in the evening a 14-year-old boy obtained two of defendant's morphine pills from defendant. He swallowed the pills, and died during the night. The defendant was convicted of first-degree murder and drug-induced homicide under the Illinois "drug induced homicide statute," 720 ILCS 5/9-3.3. On appeal the court reversed the murder conviction, stating there was no evidence the defendant either intended to cause the victim's death or had reason to know that death was "practically certain" to follow ingestion of the morphine. However, the court affirmed the drug-induced death conviction, because no *mens rea* is required for violation of the statute.

State v. Hladun

Superior Court of New Jersey (2013), 2013 WL 216142

Defendant and the victim of a heroin overdose were both addicts who bought heroin together and for each other. Both were trying to escape the addiction. The defendant gave the victim two small bags of heroin at 9:00 one night, which the victim ingested that evening. He died of an overdose early the next morning. The appeals court affirmed the conviction, holding that the evidence was sufficient to show the defendant "distributed" the heroin to the victim on the night he died, and that is all that is needed for a conviction under NJSA 2C: 35-19, the new drug-induced death law. *cert. denied* N.J. July 19 2013.

Possession or Sale of Drug Paraphernalia

drug paraphernalia
Objects that are primarily intended or designed for use with illegal drugs.

State criminal codes and the federal government make the possession or sale of **drug paraphernalia** a crime. The Federal Criminal Code defines *drug paraphernalia* as "any equipment, product or material of any kind which is primarily intended or designed for use" with illegal drugs.[27]

Some products have only one use, and that is as drug paraphernalia. For example, bongs, which are water pipes used for the smoking of marijuana, were called "hardcore paraphernalia by virtue of (their) physical features… (because bongs have) no alternative uses."[28]

An example of an item that has more than one use is inositol, an optically inactive alcohol. Inositol is a common cocaine-cutting ingredient. Because inositol has dual purposes, the government must establish that the inositol was "primarily intended" as drug paraphernalia in order to convict a defendant under the statute.[29]

Drug paraphernalia charges and convictions are most often obtained when the item or paraphernalia is seized along with drugs such as marijuana and cocaine. In the 1994 case of *People v. Veld* (641 N.E.2d 924), an Illinois appellate court held that the state failed to establish that boxes and small wooden pipes were drug paraphernalia. The defendant, a manufacturer, was not apprehended using the boxes and wooden pipes for illegal drug use.

The federal Mail Order Drug Paraphernalia Control Act (21 U.S.C.A. § 857) was upheld in *Posters V Things Ltd. v. United States,* 969 F.2d 652 (1992), *affirmed,* 511 U.S. 513 (1994). The defendant in the *Posters* case sold scales and substances commonly used by cocaine dealers to dilute cocaine. The defendant advertised the products for such use, and purchases were made in such large quantities that it showed that dealers rather than other users were buying the items.

SNIFFING, BAGGING, AND HUFFING INHALANTS

Inhalants are chemicals that give off fumes or vapors that slow the body's reactions and cloud thinking when breathed in. Many common household products are inhalants. Common products available to children that will produce a high include glue, gasoline, correction fluid, and felt-tipped markers. The Partnership for a Drug-Free America estimates that more than 1,200 products available to kids are capable of producing highs, and states that the use of inhalants has become an "epidemic."

Inhalants can be "sniffed" (inhaling the substance into the nose directly from the container); "bagged" (dumping the substance into a bag and inhaling the fumes); or "huffed" (soaking a rag with a mixture, putting the rag to the mouth, and inhaling the fumes).

Inhalants can cause suffocation, heart attack, or even death. Common symptoms in a child (or an adult) of inhalant use are staggering gait and uncoordinated walk and movement; delirium; slurred speech; chemical odor on breath, body, or clothes; loss of appetite; intoxication; nausea or vomiting; belligerence; and impaired hearing.

© Cengage Learning

The Washington Times/ZUMAPRESS/Newscom

Some of the items used to manufacture methamphetamine in so-called "mom and pop" meth labs that have sprung up in many parts of the U.S

Alcohol-Related Crimes

Alcohol is a drug used by an estimated 95 million Americans in some form and in varying amounts. It is a mood-altering drug that many people use as a tranquilizer. It has been observed that if alcohol were discovered today for the first time, the FDA would be obligated by law to forbid its over-the-counter sale without prescription. Alcohol is an addictive drug, and it is toxic—it is a poison. However, alcohol has, for a long time, been part of our economic, social, and cultural environment. Because of the beverage's long history of social acceptance and our society's economic dependence on it, it continues to be sold openly on the market.

Alcohol's Relation to Crimes and Deaths

British and U.S. studies of accidental deaths in the 1980s and a National Institutes of Health study in 2002 showed that alcohol has a high relationship to deaths caused by drowning, choking, burns and fires, and falls.[30] A pedestrian who is intoxicated was reported 3.5 times more likely to be killed or injured in a traffic accident.

OTHER STATUTES AND LAWS USED IN THE WAR ON DRUGS

Subject Matter of Law	Problem Addressed by Law
"Drug kingpin" statutes	The federal government and many states have created a separate crime of being the leader of a narcotics trafficking network. Many criminal codes punish this offense with life imprisonment. New Jersey is one of the states that does, and defines the leader's role as follows in New Jersey Statute 2C-35-3: A person is a leader of a narcotics trafficking network if he conspires with others as an organizer, supervisor, financier or manager, to engage for profit in a scheme or course of conduct to unlawfully manufacture, distribute, dispense, bring into or transport in this State any substance classified in Schedule I or II, or any controlled substance analog thereof.
Additional imprisonment for using or carrying a firearm during and in relation to a drug-trafficking crime	The Federal Criminal Code (18 U.S.C.A. § 924(c)) and the statutes of most (if not all) states provide for additional punishment for a person using or carrying a firearm during and in relation to a drug-trafficking crime.[a]
Nuisance laws and drug house abatement statutes and ordinances	Landlords are often warned that if they allow tenants to sell drugs from the landlord's property, an abatement or nuisance proceeding could be started against the property. Drug houses could also be taken over by a state or local government because of failure to pay taxes, or they could be condemned because of fire or code violations.
Forfeiture of property	Under the Controlled Substances Act and other forfeiture statutes, the following may be seized under court order: (1) instruments of the crime (such as vehicles or watercraft used to commit the crime); (2) profits of the crime (money from drug dealing, stolen goods, and so on); and (3) proceeds of the illegal act (houses, condos, yachts, farms, or other luxury goods purchased from profits of the crime). If the offender did not pay taxes on the profits of drug dealing, the Internal Revenue Service may take action against drug traffickers.

Alcohol is the most widely abused and misused drug in America and in many other countries. Alcoholism is one of the biggest health problems in the United States, just behind heart disease and cancer. Excessive use of alcohol is also a factor causing heart disease and cancer.

When public drunkenness was prosecuted as a crime throughout the United States, it was always high on the yearly list of crimes.[31] Alcohol continues to be an important factor in many disorderly conduct, battery, assault, rape, child abuse, domestic relations disputes, and criminal damage to property cases in the United States every year. The movement from other drugs to alcohol is sometimes condoned by parents who, in their relief that their children are not involved in the use of other forms of drugs, do not recognize the dangers of alcohol.

Use of communications facility to further a drug violation	The use of a communications facility to commit or facilitate a drug violation is a crime under federal law if the defendant has a prior conviction for a felony drug violation.
Possession of wiretapping devices, illegal bugs, and eavesdropping equipment	Title 18, Chapter 119 of the Omnibus Crime and Safe Streets Act makes it illegal to own, manufacture, or sell eavesdropping and wiretapping equipment specifically designed for "the surreptitious interception of wire, oral or electronic communications." Only law enforcement agencies are permitted to buy or use such devices and then only with a court order. Some drug dealers and other criminals illegally possess and use these devices.
"Schoolyard" or "Schoolhouse" laws	In an attempt to keep drugs from schoolyards and neighborhoods, "schoolyard" laws were passed that increase jail time for dealing drugs within 1,000 feet of an elementary or secondary school.
Loss of financial aid and student loans for a year for students who are found guilty of simple possession of an illegal drug such as marijuana	Under federal law, 20 U.S.C.A. § 1091(r)(1), a student convicted of sale or possession of illegal drugs while receiving federal student aid funds is ineligible for financial aid for either one year (possession) or two years (sale).
Laws punishing the sale of counterfeit medical drugs	Medical personnel report an increase in counterfeit drugs for the treatment of diseases such as tuberculosis, AIDS, and malaria as well as antibiotics. The World Health Organization has reported that labs in China produce most of these counterfeit drugs, which cause thousands of unnecessary deaths each year.[b]
"Doctor shopping" as violation of Controlled Substances Act	Doctor shopping is obtaining multiple prescriptions from different doctors for the same drug. Police affidavits state that Rush Limbaugh, the radio commentator, received 2,000 painkillers from four different doctors in a 6-month period.

[a]In 1998 Congress amended § 924(c) to add "possession" to "uses or carries" a weapon under the statute. This was done to change the Supreme Court's decision in 1995 that "use" did not include mere possession. Now, simple possession of a firearm during a drug trafficking crime violates the statute. See *United States v. O'Brien*, 130 S. Ct. 2169 (2010).

[b]See *The New York Times*, "In the World of Life-Saving Drugs: A Growing Epidemic of Deadly Fakes," March 15, 2007.

A 2002 National Institutes of Health study surveyed drinking among the 8 million college and university students in the United States. The study showed that most students drink moderately or not at all, but 44 percent of students drink in binges.

Alcohol-related student deaths numbered 1,445 a year—4 per day. An additional 1,370 students suffered injuries (some very serious) tied to drinking, and an estimated 192 students each day are raped or sexually assaulted after drinking, the study stated.

Drunk Driving: The Criminal Homicide Causing the Most Deaths

About twenty-seven people are killed every day in the United States because of driving under the influence of drugs or alcohol, the Centers for Disease Control and Prevention reported in 2012. In 2011, 9,878 people died in alcohol-related motor vehicle traffic accidents, accounting for about 31 percent of all traffic deaths. This number is down from 10,228 in 2010, and reflects a steady decrease in alcohol-related traffic deaths. In 1982, by comparison, 26,173 people died in alcohol-related motor vehicle traffic accidents. About 18 percent of all motor vehicle traffic deaths involved drug use. In addition, about 1 million people are injured annually. The National Highway Traffic Safety Administration estimates the yearly costs of drunk driving to be $51 billion. In 2011, 1.4 million people were arrested for driving under the influence of alcohol or drugs. It is estimated that each year there are as many as 112 million episodes of drunk driving.

Tougher laws and enforcement, taking more blood alcohol tests of suspected drunk and drugged drivers, and increased efforts to educate students and the public on the dangers of drunk and drugged driving are being used to decrease the dangers

DRIVING AND ALCOHOL

Does Your State Regulate the Following Conduct or Have the Following Laws?

Conduct	Statute
Driving a vehicle while under the influence of alcohol or drugs. (Does "vehicle" include watercraft, aircraft, moped, etc.?)	
First offense	_____
Second offense	_____
Third offense	_____
The legal drinking limit is	_____
Drinking and driving age is	_____
"Booze it and lose it" statute (administrative license revocation laws that give police the right to seize licenses of drivers who fail or refuse sobriety tests)	_____
Punish refusal of driver to take Breathalyzer or other test when lawfully requested	_____
Ban open containers of alcoholic beverages in motor vehicles	_____
While driving under the influence:	
▪ causes property damage	_____
▪ causes serious injury to another person	_____
▪ causes the death of another person	_____
Leaving scene of accident (failing to stop and report):	
▪ property damage	_____
▪ injury to person	_____
▪ fatal accident	_____
Can law enforcement agencies in your state set up sobriety checkpoints?	_____

on our streets and highways. The punishment for drunk driving has been increased, and some states have enacted laws forbidding or curbing happy hours by taverns and clubs. Victims of drunk driving are reminded that they may commence lawsuits in most states under "dram shop"[32] laws (a dram being a small drink of liquor) that permit civil lawsuits under some circumstances against bars and individuals who furnish or sell the alcoholic drinks.

All fifty states have now set the blood-alcohol content (BAC) limit for operating a motor vehicle at .08 percent. That limit is still higher than in most European countries and Japan. Insurance companies and the American Medical Association join in noting that alcohol can unravel driving skills subtly and insidiously, long before people look and act drunk.

Experts now point out that it is the driver with a drinking or drug problem who is the problem. Too many people with severe alcohol and/or drug problems continue to drive while impaired and under the influence. Problem drinkers continue to drink and drive even after their licenses have been revoked. They are generally the danger on the highway.

Elements and Defenses in Drunk-Driving Prosecutions

Drunk driving statutes differ from state to state, but most follow a format similar to the following statute, Neb. Rev. Stat. § 60-6,196:

> It shall be unlawful for any person to operate or be in the actual physical control of any motor vehicle:

(a) While under the influence of alcoholic liquor or of any drug;
(b) When such person has a concentration of eight-hundredths of one gram or more by weight of alcohol per one hundred ten liters of his or her blood; or
(c) When such person has a concentration of eight hundredths of one gram or more by weight of alcohol per two hundred ten liters of his or her breath.

Most states also increase the penalty for a conviction based on a blood-alcohol count appreciably higher than the statutory limit, and for subsequent convictions. See, e.g., NJSA § 39:4-50(a)(1), (2), and (3). At some point, repeated violations can be treated as felonies.

Under the most common type of statute, the prosecution can prove the violation either by evidence the driver was under the influence of alcohol or drugs, or by use of a blood or breath test. Blood tests are more reliable, but they are more expensive, time-consuming, and not always available. As a result, breath tests on a Breathalyzer° or similar machine are often used to prove the violation.

A prosecution based on evidence of impairment due to drugs or alcohol, where no results from breath or blood tests are available, usually includes police evidence from **field sobriety tests**. These tests, done according to guidelines established by the National Highway Traffic Safety Administration (NHTSA), are given by officers in the field who suspect a motorist they have stopped is impaired by alcohol or drugs. Because alcohol can cause **nystagmus**, a condition in which the eye demonstrates abnormal and involuntary movement, horizontal gaze nystagmus (HGN) testing can be used as evidence of alcohol impairment. While there has been some controversy about the reliability of HGN testing, most courts conclude the results

field sobriety tests Field tests used to evaluate a motorist's alcohol or drug impairment. They include HGN testing, the walk-and-turn test, and the one-leg stand test.

nystagmus A persistent, rapid, involuntary, side-to-side eye movement.

CASE CLOSE-UP

People v. Martin
Supreme Court of Illinois,
955 N.E.2d 1058 (2011)

Around 10:00 p.m. the defendant left a bar to drive home on a two-lane state highway. His car suddenly veered across the center lane and struck another car head-on, killing the driver and the passenger. The defendant was taken to a hospital, where the sheriff's deputy investigating the accident requested blood and urine tests, and defendant consented to the tests. The blood tests showed no presence of alcohol or controlled substances, but the urine test showed trace amounts of methamphetamine. The defendant was indicted on one count of aggravated DUI.

The defendant admitted he had used "crystal meth" before, but not on the night of the accident. The jury convicted the defendant of aggravated DUI, which applies when a person guilty of ordinary DUI is involved in an accident that kills another person, and he was sentenced to 6 years in prison. The court of appeals reversed the conviction, holding the state failed to show the unlawful methamphetamine in the defendant's body was the proximate cause of the victim's deaths. The state appealed, and the Illinois Supreme Court reversed and reinstated the conviction and sentence.

Under subsection (a) of the Illinois DUI statute, a person commits a violation by driving a motor vehicle while "under the influence" of alcohol or drugs, or by driving with "any amount" of a controlled substance such as methamphetamine. Any violation is "aggravated" if the defendant is involved in a motor vehicle accident " . . . that resulted in the death of another person, when the violation of subsection (a) was a proximate cause of the death." 625 ILCS 5/11-501.

The court of appeals concluded that the defendant violated subsection (a), the ordinary DUI crime, because even a trace amount of methamphetamine satisfied the statute, and the state need not show the defendant was "impaired" by the unlawful use of the drug. However, the court held the state needed to make a causal link between the use of the drug and the death of the victims in order to prove aggravated DUI.

The Illinois Supreme Court disagreed with the court of appeals. It held that while some parts of the DUI statute require proof of "impairment," the use of unlawful drugs section does not: "A driver with controlled substances in his body violates section 11-501(a)(6) simply by driving." Such a driver is "presumed impaired" under the statute, the court stated. Therefore, the court concluded the causal link between the "violation" and the deaths required by the aggravated DUI statute requires only that the state prove the driving caused the death, not any impairment caused by the use of the illegal drug. Since it was uncontroverted that the defendant's driving was the proximate cause of the victims' deaths, the state proved the necessary elements of aggravated DUI.

In a related case, the Michigan Supreme Court held in 2013 that a patient permitted to use marijuana under the Michigan Medical Marihuana Act (MMMA) could not be convicted of driving while impaired unless the use of the drug caused actual impairment. Like Illinois, Michigan has a "zero tolerance" law that prohibits driving with any amount of a controlled substance, which still includes marijuana, in the bloodstream. The Michigan court said that the MMMA statute superseded the zero tolerance law. *People v. Koon*, 2013 WL 2221602 (Mich. 2013).

are admissible. See, e.g., the 2010 case of *People v. McKown*.[33] Observation of the other two field tests can be combined with results from the HGN testing and can be used as evidence of impairment, if the tests are conducted according to NHTSA guidelines. Most states require that the NHTSA guidelines be strictly or substantially followed for the test results to be admitted. See, e.g., *State v. Boczur*.[34] Prosecutors will usually have additional observed evidence of impairment, such as the suspect's physical condition, the smell of alcohol on the breath, slurring of words, and so forth. This evidence can be sufficient to convict a defendant of driving while intoxicated, or driving while impaired as it is called in some states.

Breath testing results are also generally admissible, so long as the person administering the test follows proper procedures. Currently, two machines, the Datamaster and the Intoxilizer, are commonly used by law enforcement agencies. The sophistication of breath testing machines has increased over the years. In 2003 New Jersey began using a new computer-operated machine called the Alcotest. In a 2008 decision, *State v. Chun*,[35] the New Jersey Supreme Court upheld the reliability of the machine and stated that results from the machine could be used to prove a drunk driving charge, if the machine's procedures were followed.

With all breath testing machines, defenses in DUI cases can turn on the operation of the machine and how the machine has been maintained. Procedures for routinely checking the machine for reliability are required to guarantee its accuracy, and law enforcement agencies must keep detailed records of maintenance checks. Many DUI defense arguments are based on the absence of such records or checks. See, e.g., *Blazier v. Vincent*.[36]

"Booze It and Lose It" Laws

"booze it and lose it" laws Laws, enacted in more than thirty states, that give the police the authority to immediately seize the driver's licenses of people who fail or refuse sobriety tests.

More than thirty states have passed **"booze it and lose it" laws**, which give the police the authority to immediately seize the driver's licenses of people who fail or refuse sobriety tests. After these new laws became known to the drinking public, nighttime fatal crashes dropped dramatically. The National Safety Board estimated that if all fifty states adopted such laws, 2,000 lives could be saved in the United States each year.

Many states have laws that take away the driver's licenses of motorists under age 21 who drive after drinking even a small amount of alcohol.

When Is a Person Driving, Operating, or "In Physical Control" of a Vehicle?

States forbid operating motor vehicles, watercraft, snowmobiles, and aircraft while under the influence of alcohol or of a controlled substance. In most drunk driving cases, either a police officer or a witness testifies to seeing the defendant drive a vehicle while intoxicated. However, when no witnesses are available to testify about the driving, courts must decide when a person is driving, operating, or "in physical control" of a vehicle.

It is not a crime to be intoxicated inside a motor vehicle. Leaving a party or bar and deciding to "sleep it off" in one's car by itself is not a violation of the law. However, though these laws are referred to as "drunk driving" laws, in fact courts find violations whenever an intoxicated person "operates" a motor vehicle. One can be "operating" a motor vehicle without actually driving the motor vehicle. As a result, courts have generally rejected the defense of defendants who admitted being in their cars with the motor running, but who claimed they were not driving the car. Sitting intoxicated behind the wheel of a running car with the key in the ignition, with the potential to drive it, is exactly the harm the statutes are designed to avoid, courts uniformly hold.

What actions, short of placing the key in the ignition and turning on the car's engine, constitute "operating"? For most courts, the question is whether some action has been taken to initiate the sequence of acts that activate the motor vehicle. The following cases are examples of courts considering when a person has begun that sequence. In each example the defendant was intoxicated:

- *State v. Fitzgerald*, 63 So.3d 75 (Fla. App. 2011): Defendant was behind the wheel of the parked car at intersection. Motor was not running, and keys were in defendant's right hand. Court held this constituted "physical control" under the Florida statute.
- *State v. Haight*, 903 A.2d 217 (Conn. 2007): Key was in the ignition with the defendant sitting in the driver's seat. The court held this constituted "operating" whether or not the key was turned to the "on" position.
- *Nelson v. Commonwealth*, 707 S.E.2d 815 (Va. 2011): The court held the ignition key must be turned to the "on" or "accessory" position, but need not be turned to the position that starts the engine.
- *State v. Cyr*, 967 A.2d 32 (Conn. 2009): Defendant started car's engine by remote device, but had not placed key in ignition, which was required to move car. The court held starting the car began the sequence leading to activate the motor vehicle.
- *State v. Rogers*, 224 S.W.3d 564 (Mo. App. 2007) (contrasting result): Operating is not begun until keys are in the engine, even though engine has been started by remote control device.

Summary

- All states and the federal government have enacted the Uniform Controlled Substances Act of 1970. Under this law, which is part of the criminal code of your state, the following are crimes:
1. Manufacture or delivery of an illegal drug
2. Possession with intent to deliver an illegal drug
3. Delivery or possession with intent to deliver a counterfeit substance
4. Offering or agreeing to deliver an illegal drug and then delivering a substance that is not a controlled substance
5. Possession of an illegal drug
6. Knowingly allowing a store, dwelling, building, vehicle, boat, aircraft, or other place to be used by people using illegal drugs

7. Obtaining possession of an illegal drug by misrepresentation, fraud, forgery, deception, or subterfuge
- Intent to deliver illegal drugs can be proved by showing a "rational connection" between the facts of possession, such as the large quantity of the drug, and an intent to sell the drugs.
- Medical use of marijuana is permitted in eighteen states, if done as prescribed treatment for listed illness or conditions. While medical users can be prosecuted under federal laws, in 2010 the Justice Department stated it would not do so. It is not clear if that remains the position of the federal government now that Colorado and Washington have legalized the recreational use of marijuana.

- In *Gonzales v. Raich* the court reasoned that private use of marijuana might have an adverse impact on federal drug laws, and thus Congress had the power under the Commerce Clause to regulate even purely intrastate use of marijuana.
- The state must show only that the defendant provided the drugs to the victim, and that the victim died as a proximate result of the defendant's actions. That means no other intervening event must have caused the death.
- An intoxicated suspect can be found to have been operating a motor vehicle by being behind the wheel of a car with the keys in the ignition, though in some states the key must be turned to the "on" position.

Key Terms

Uniform Controlled Substances Act, p. 451
controlled substance, p. 452
usable amount, p. 454

possession with intent to deliver, p. 456
drug paraphernalia, p. 460
field sobriety tests, p. 465

nystagmus, p. 465
"booze it and lose it" laws, p. 467

Case Analysis and Writing Exercises

1. 21 U.S.C.A. § 841(c)(2) makes it a crime to possess chemicals while "knowing or having reasonable cause to believe" the chemicals would be used to produce a controlled substance. Pseudoephedrine, found in over-the-counter cold medicines, is the main ingredient of methamphetamine. Retailers are limited in how much pseudoephedrine they can sell to a given customer, either in one purchase or over a period of time. Possession of large amounts of pseudoephedrine suggests a purpose to make meth. How does the government prove the required "knowing or reasonable cause to believe" requirement in the statute? Should a defendant who bought pseudoephedrine be allowed to argue she was unusually naïve and didn't have the same knowledge a reasonable person would have about the use others had for the pseudoephedrine she obtained? *See United States v. Munguia*, 704 F.3d 596 (9th Cir. 2012).

2. Sleeping while intoxicated behind the wheel of a car, with the motor running, is usually enough for a conviction under a DUI statute. Why wasn't it enough in *Village of Cross Plains v. Haanstad*, 709 N.W.2d 447 (Wis. 2006)?

3. New York courts have developed the "agency defense" for defendants who act solely as intermediaries for buyers of controlled substances. Under that defense, the intermediary who directs a prospective buyer of illegal drugs to a seller is not guilty of the sale or possession of the drugs sold to the buyer. Is he guilty of any other offense? Or does the agency defense apply to other charges? *See People v. Watson*, 981 N.E.2d 265 (N.Y. 2012).

4. As we saw in the text, simple possession of a firearm during commission of a drug trafficking crime results in an enhanced penalty, in addition to the penalty for the drug trafficking crime, of 5 years in prison under the applicable federal statute. The enhanced penalty is 10 years if the firearm is discharged during commission of the crime. What happens if the defendant carries a firearm while attempting to regain possession of illegal drugs stolen from him, and the intended victim gains possession of the firearm and fires it? *See United States v. Echeverry*, 649 F.3d 159 (2nd Cir. 2011).

Endnotes

1. See the February 10, 2010, report of the United Nations Office of Drug Control.

2. A UN report in 1997 estimated that the illegal drug trade makes up 8 percent of world trade. This illegal industry is estimated at between $400 billion and $1 trillion worldwide. It is as large as the worldwide trade in textiles and bigger than the sales of iron or steel. See the *Pensacola News Journal* article "UN Report: Social Costs of Drug Abuse About $120 Billion," November 16, 1997.

3. The "Opium War," which Great Britain waged against China from 1839 to 1842, was conducted to force China to permit the importing of opium into China. China had silk and many other goods to sell to the world but would not buy goods from Britain and other nations. As a result, the British ran up a huge trade deficit. To pay off this deficit, the British commenced selling opium to the Chinese and established a British colony at Hong Kong. When the Chinese government tried to stop the sale of opium, the Opium War began.

   To supply the opium trade, opium was grown in the British colony of India and shipped to China to be traded for Chinese exports. By 1850, India's largest export was opium, exceeding the export of Indian cotton textiles.

   American shippers also brought opium into China to sell in exchange for goods from China. The biggest American trader was Warren Delano (the grandfather of President Franklin Delano Roosevelt). Delano became a very wealthy man in the trade with China. But this trade created thousands of opium addicts and was denounced in churches and in newspapers throughout the United States. After trading in opium was forbidden, illegal shipping and trading in opium continued to supply this deadly drug. See the *New York Times* articles "The Opium War's Secret History" and "Hong Kong's Colonial Ghosts," June 22, 1997. Also see Martin Booth, *Opium: A History* (New York: St. Martin's Press, 1998).

4. This act replaced the 1933 Uniform Narcotic Drug Act and the 1966 Model State Drug Abuse Control Act.

5. A designer drug is a drug that is cheaply made from chemicals and is sometimes similar to a commonly known illegal drug. New designer drugs come on the market regularly. To prevent the invention, manufacturing, and distribution of designer drugs before they are permanently scheduled in the Uniform Controlled Substances Act, the U.S. Congress enacted a law permitting the quick and temporary placement of a new designer drug in the federal Controlled Substances Act. If this law had not been passed, a new designer drug could be sold throughout the United States for up to a year before it was permanently made a part of the Uniform Controlled Substances Act. The U.S. Supreme Court unanimously upheld the quick scheduling of new designer drugs in the 1991 case of *Touby v. U.S.* (111 S. Ct. 1752).

6. Many courts hold that a person cannot be convicted of possession of a drug solely because the drug is in the person's body. See *State v. Thronsen,* 809 P.2d 941 (Alaska App. 1991) and *State v. Vorm,* 570 N.E.2d 109 (Ind. App. 1991). However, people with an illegal drug in their bodies may be charged with the crime of "being under the influence of a controlled substance." See *Junior v. State,* 807 P.2d 205 (Nev. 1991).

7. 98 P.3d 1190 (Wash. 2004), *cert. denied,* 544 U.S. 922 (2005).

8. 599 F.3d 1198 (10th Cir. 2010).

9. 542 F.3d 968 (2nd Cir. 2008).

10. 532 NE.2d 1249 (N.Y. 1988). Surprisingly, tests done by the Argonne National Laboratory in 1997 showed that many $1 and $2 bills circulated in Chicago, Miami, and Houston were tainted with microscopic traces of cocaine. The chemists conducting the tests stated that $1 and $2 bills are used to wrap "rocks" (chunks of solid cocaine chipped off a cocaine brick). The rock is then sold. Paper money is used instead of newspaper because the money does not transfer ink to the cocaine as newspaper does. Dollar bills are also rolled into tubes and used to snort cocaine powder.

    Defense lawyers have used these findings in cocaine possession cases. The report also states that people who handle cocaine-tainted money do not show traces of cocaine on their person except when money comes into contact with large amounts of cocaine immediately before a person handled it. See the *New York Times* article "Cocaine Turns Up in Many $1 and $2 Bills," September 23, 1997.

11. The Court of Appeals of South Carolina held that ordinarily a measurable quantity is necessary, but when the cocaine was the "remnant of a larger amount previously possessed in the past," the conviction was affirmed. The cocaine residue was in a crack pipe; *State v. Robinson,* 411 S.E.2d 678 (1991). In *State v. Wood,* 1994 WL 250015 (N.M. App. 1994), the cocaine residue was in syringes (conviction sustained).

12. 807 N.E.2d 789 (Ind. App. 2004).

13. *People v. Rubacalba,* 859 P.2d 708 (Calif. 1993).

14. *Lord v. State,* 616 So. 2d 1065 (Fla. App. 1993). In *Gilchrist v. State,* 784 So. 2d 624 (Fla. App. 2001), the court suggested that the holding in *Lord* applied only to common objects like dollar bills. Where the trace amounts are on a device used to ingest the drug, as was the case in *Gilchrist,* the usable quantity rule does not apply.

15. 677 F.3d 685 (5th Cir. 2012).

16. See *County Court of Ulster County v. Allen,* 442 U.S. 140, 99 S. Ct. 2213 (1979).

17. 532 U.S. 483 (2001).

18. 352 F.3d 122 (9th Cir. 2003).

19. 545 U.S. 1 (2005). A spokesperson for the California attorney general's office stated in 2005 that there was now "a sort of detente" between federal and state law enforcement agencies over medical use of marijuana. He stated that federal law enforcement agencies for the most part are targeting

individuals who seem clearly to be using marijuana for purposes other than medical treatment, something the state of California was doing also. As of July 2013, eighteen other states and the District of Columbia had passed laws permitting the medical use of marijuana.

20. 546 U.S. 418 (2006).
21. 521 U.S. 507 (1997).
22. 96 P.3d 420 (Utah 2004).
23. 594 A.2d 1086 (Me. 1991).
24. 581 S.E.2d 35 (Ga. 2003).
25. See the *Harvard Medical School Heart Letter* article "Cocaine: An Unpredictable Killer" (April 1992). The article points out that until 1914, cocaine was an ingredient in many cough syrups and home remedy medications sold in the United States. The article also notes that cocaine was used in Coca-Cola until it was replaced by caffeine in 1906. The Harrison Narcotics Act of 1914 classified cocaine as a narcotic in 1914 and limited its use to prescription medical purposes. The article states that cocaine "then went underground, where it remains (today)."
26. If a person was committing a felony in supplying an illegal drug that directly caused a drug-induced death, a prosecutor could issue a criminal charge of felony murder in addition to other criminal charges if the case met the requirements of the felony murder law of that state. (See Chapter 10 of this text for a discussion of the crime of felony murder.)
27. 21 U.S.C.A. § 863(d).
28. *U.S. v. Dyer*, 750 F. Supp. 1275 (E.D. Va. 1990).
29. *United States v. Mishra*, 979 F.2d 301 (3d Cir. 1992).
30. *Harvard Medical School Health Letter* (September 1993) citing *British Medical Journal* and *Southern Medical Journal*. The April 2002 report is entitled *A Call to Action: Changing the Culture of Drinking at U.S. Colleges*. The study was done by the National Institute of Alcohol Abuse and Alcoholism, which is a branch of the National Institutes of Health. (See the *New York Times* article, "Study Calculates the Effects of College Drinking in U.S.," April 10, 2002.)
31. Although many states have decriminalized public drunkenness, other states continue to make public drunkenness a crime. In cities and states where public drunkenness is not a crime, a person who is intoxicated in a public place is often ignored if not getting into trouble or endangered. If such people are a problem, they could be taken to a detoxification center (if available) or a homeless shelter. Such people could also be arrested for disorderly conduct or another offense.
32. Most states have dram shop liability laws under which taverns and bars can be liable to innocent victims of alcohol-related accidents and crimes. Social hosts who provide alcohol can also be liable under the laws of some states. Providing alcohol to an intoxicated minor creates the greatest dram shop liability.
33. 924 N.E.2d 155 (Ill. 2010).
34. 863 N.E.2d 155 (Ohio 2007).
35. 943 A.2d 114 (N.J. 2008).
36. 204 S.W.3rd 658 (Mo. App. 2006).

Terrorism

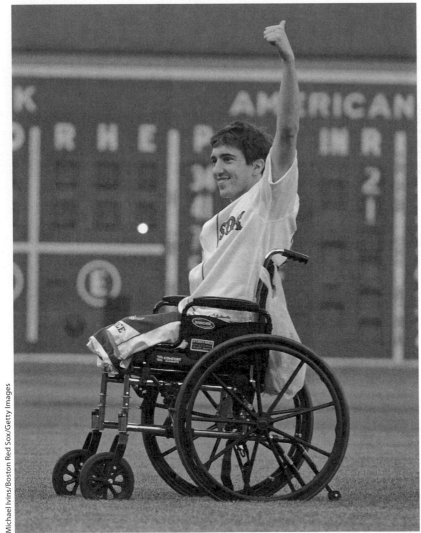

Boston Marathon bombing victim Jeff Baumann gestures to the crowd before throwing out a ceremonial first pitch during a game between the Boston Red Sox and the Philadelphia Philles on May 28, 2013, at Fenway Park in Boston, Massachusetts.

LEARNING OBJECTIVES

In this chapter we discuss criminal statutes aimed at punishing and preventing terrorism. The learning objectives for Chapter 17 are as follows:

- Attempt to write a working definition of terrorism.
- Explain why federal criminal statutes must define terrorism.
- Explain one method by which a group can be identified as a terrorist group.
- List the elements of the crime of terrorism under most state laws.
- Define a terrorist threat under state criminal laws.
- Explain the concept of the rules of war.
- List ways terrorists obtain financial support for their terrorist actions.
- List ways money is sent into and out of the United States by terrorist supporters.
- Identify when a seizure is an extraordinary rendition.

Terrorism is not limited to suicide bombers blowing up buildings, airplanes, or passenger buses. It also includes words and actions designed to threaten victims and put them in fear of injury or death. "Terrorist threats" are made a crime in every state, and in the federal criminal code. Moreover, state terrorist threat statutes have been amended to reflect the many ways a threat can be made, as the following episode shows.

The defendant, John Holcomb, and his former girlfriend, Miranda Rollman, were involved in a bitter custody battle over their young daughter. Both Holcomb and Rollman maintained accounts on MySpace, where they could enter posts on their profile webpages that could be accessed by other MySpace users. Holcomb entered numerous incendiary posts on his webpage, in the form of lyrics to songs in which he explicitly and graphically threatened to kidnap the daughter and slit Rollman's throat. Rollman was told by others about these posts, and accessed Holcomb's webpage to read them. Frightened, she moved out of her home to live with her parents.

Holcomb was charged and convicted under the Virginia written threat statute, which had been amended in 1998 to include threats in "electronically transmitted communications." On appeal, he contended the statute didn't apply to his MySpace posts, because they were not directed at Rollman, and were viewable by anyone. The court rejected that argument, holding that Holcomb knew Rollman used MySpace, and could easily access his webpage and see the threats. The court said all the statute requires is that the defendant intended to communicate the threat, and the threat was communicated. The court also rejected Holcomb's argument that a reasonable person would have understood the posts were just lyrics to a song, because Holcomb said he was known to be a musician. The court said the posts clearly were intended to strike fear in Rollman, and she was in fact fearful because of the posts. That is all that is required under the statute. The court affirmed the conviction.[1]

In this chapter we will study the many forms terrorism takes and the criminal laws passed by governments to punish terrorism. We will learn the criminal laws enacted to address both terrorist acts committed by U.S. citizens and those committed by citizens of other countries.

Terrorism

Terrorists are criminals who use force and violence in the pursuit of extreme political, ideological, or religious goals. They are willing to take innocent lives to make their statements. Terrorists may be domestic or international. They may be stateless (acting on their own), or they may be domestic (homegrown) acting against their own people and government. They might be acting for a nation, backed by a nation, or supported by people within a nation.

terrorism The use of force and violence in the pursuit of extreme political, ideological, or religious goals, without regard to the innocent lives that may be lost.

Terrorism can be cheap and relatively easy. Terrorists use surprise and vulnerability to their advantage. A handful of dedicated individuals can cause great harm. Timothy McVeigh and Terry Nichols killed 168 people in seconds by blowing up the Alfred P. Murrah Federal Building in Oklahoma City. Fewer than 100 foreign terrorists killed thousands on September 11, 2001.

Terrorism has existed for ages. The term *terrorism* comes from the Latin word *terere*, which means "to frighten." The word *zealot* originated as a term for militant Jews who used terrorism to fight the Roman occupation of Israel in the first century. The word *assassin* comes from the name of a group of Shiite Muslims who used terrorism against Persia in the twelfth century. In 1901 an American president, William McKinley, was killed by an American terrorist. Four European heads of state were assassinated by terrorists between the years 1894 and 1900.

Terrorists can be religious or ethnic zealots. They might be people seeking to avenge a perceived wrong or maniacs who get their kicks out of violence. They are sometimes oppressed people angry or desperate enough to use bombs and guns.

Terrorism is a tactic—a means of striking out suddenly, using surprise. The goal is to intimidate and coerce a civilian population, or influence or punish a government. It has put governments around the world on the defensive, forcing them to spend billions of dollars to protect their civilian populations.

While terrorism has existed for centuries, the international community has yet to agree on a definition of the term. The term first appeared during the French Revolution in 1789 and was used to describe the actions of the republican government, mainly Prime Minister Robespierre, in executing more than 17,000 people. In subsequent years the term came to be applied to specific kinds of crimes in which the criminal had a political motivation.

The United Nations has never defined international terrorism. Rather, it has adopted several international agreements, called "conventions," which member nations must follow. For example, after the bombings of civilian aircraft in the 1960s and 1970s, the UN adopted the Tokyo and Montreal Conventions against attacks on civilian aircraft. As part of these Conventions, every member nation was required to make the specified acts criminal under their domestic law.

Similar conventions have been adopted to deal with nuclear terror, financing terrorists, holding hostages, and bombing. These conventions are aimed at individual terrorists, not at member nations. Their goal is not to identify international terrorism as a specific offense, but rather to identify various kinds of conduct used by terrorists or that supports terrorists and to require member nations to make such conduct criminal.

The United States has a definition of international terrorism in 18 U.S.C. § 2331(1). International terrorism is defined as violent acts that would be crimes in the United States, and are intended to

1. Intimidate or coerce a civilian population,
2. Influence government by intimidation or coercion, or
3. Affect government by mass destruction, assassination, or kidnapping.

Because of the constitutional prohibition against vagueness (see Chapter 1), terrorism as an offense must be clearly defined under U.S. law.

Terrorists differ from other criminals because they commit their crimes to send a political or ideological message or to retaliate for a wrong that they believe has occurred. They may seek a change, such as people who wanted to stop abortions by burning down clinics and shooting doctors.

Terrorism is also a form of warfare that has existed since wars have been waged and conducted. Northern Ireland witnessed terrorism for more than a half century. To people who are believers in the cause of the terrorist, the terrorist may be viewed as a hero. However, to the great majority of the civilized world, terrorists are criminals.

Early Terrorist Acts

Anarchists (people who oppose organized government) historically have used terrorism to convey their political message. In May 1886, after local anarchists printed and distributed fliers calling for workers to arm themselves, a bomb exploded at a Haymarket Square rally in Chicago. It killed a policeman and wounded several other people. Two editors of an anarchist newspaper and six other men were convicted of conspiracy in the bombing; four were hanged.

In the years between 1894 and 1900, four European heads of state (the president of France, the prime minister of Spain, the empress of Austria, and the king of Italy) were assassinated by anarchists. President McKinley's assassin, an anarchist, stated in 1901 before his execution, "I don't believe we should have any rulers. It is right to kill them."[2]

World War I was started, in part, by the assassination in Sarajevo (now part of Bosnia) of Archduke Franz Ferdinand, the heir to the Austrian throne, by a terrorist in 1914. That war, which lasted for four years, caused the deaths of more than 20 million people.

International and Domestic Terrorism in Recent Years

Terrorism has become a global problem, and all nations have become vulnerable to terrorist attacks. In September 2004, more than 300 people, mostly children, were killed by terrorists in Beslan, Russia, in a protest against Russian policy in Chechnya. In Madrid, Spain, in March 2004, more than 200 people were killed when terrorists exploded bombs on crowded city commuter trains.

Because of these and other terrorist attacks, police all over the world are on almost constant alert for suspected terrorist activities. The United States in particular is a stated target of the terrorist group al-Qaeda, a radical Islamic fundamentalist group.

In 2004 the U.S. government created the National Counterterrorism Center (NCTC) to act as a clearinghouse on international terrorism intelligence and information. In a report published in July 2012, the NCTC gave these statistics on international terrorism:

- In 2011 there were 10,283 terrorist attacks worldwide.
- 12,533 people were killed in these attacks.
- Afghanistan, Iraq, and Pakistan accounted for 64 percent of attacks worldwide.
- Sunni Muslim extremists accounted for 56 percent of all attacks, and 70 percent of all fatalities.
- Al-Qaeda and its affiliates caused almost 2,000 deaths in 688 attacks, while the Taliban caused about 1,900 deaths in over 800 attacks.
- The Nigeria-based Boko Haram increased its attacks in 2011 to 136, up from 31 in 2010.
- More than one-half of the victims killed were civilians, and 755 were children. However, the percentage of governmental employees and contractors killed in 2011 marked an increase over previous years.

Recent domestic terrorist acts include these:

- During the 1980s and 1990s antiabortion extremists bombed, shot at, and torched abortion clinics in the United States and Canada, killing six people.
- The Unabomber (Theodore Kaczynski), during a 17-year period, killed three people and injured twenty-eight others by sending letter bombs through the mail.
- Deadly anthrax spores were sent through the mail in many eastern U.S. cities in 2001, killing five people.
- In 1995, the Federal Building in Oklahoma City was destroyed by a massive bomb, killing 168 people and injuring more than 500 others. Timothy McVeigh received the death sentence for this crime and was executed in 2001. Terry Nichols was sentenced to life in prison for his role in the bombings.[3]
- In 2007, six Muslim men were arrested and charged with planning an attack on Fort Dix, a federal military base in New Jersey. Using automatic weapons and hand grenades, they planned "to kill as many soldiers as possible." Authorities also thwarted a 2003 plot to blow up the Brooklyn Bridge.[4]
- In January 2011 a lone gunman killed six people in a Tucson, Arizona shopping mall.
- In a September 29, 2012, report to Congress, the FBI stated that the number of sole "lone wolf" terrorist acts has increased. The 2012 attacks at the movie theatre in Aurora, Colorado, at a Sikh temple in Wisconsin, and at the Family Research Council in Washington, D.C. killed a total of eighteen people and injured over fifty others.

The Council on Foreign Relations reported on February 7, 2011, on trends in domestic terrorism in the United States. It stated in part:

- *Leftist Groups:* Weather Underground, Black Liberation Army, and Black Panther Party terrorist acts peaked in the 1980s, and have declined dramatically since.
- *Antigovernment and White Supremacist Groups:* Terrorist acts by white supremacist groups and conservative militia groups have increased in recent years.
- *Single-Issue Groups:* Terrorist acts by groups of extremists tied to a single issue, such as the environment or abortion rights, peaked in 2004, when the FBI named them the number-one threat of domestic terrorism.
- *"Lone Wolf" Terrorists:* By far the greatest increase in terrorist acts was by individual, "lone wolf" terrorists, who are not affiliated with any group. Before the Oklahoma City bombing in 1995, only about 6 percent of domestic terrorist acts were committed by a sole terrorist. Since 1995, more than 30 percent of domestic terrorist acts have been committed by a "lone wolf."

The Antiterrorism and Effective Death Penalty Act (AEDPA), 18 U.S.C. § 1332, and the USA Patriot Act, 18 U.S.C. § 2239, make it a federal crime to provide "material support or resources" to an organization that has been designated and named as a foreign terrorist organization in the United States by the State Department. The penalty for violation of these statutes is imprisonment for up to 15 years or, if a death occurs, for life. In addition, triple civil damages may be recovered from any organization that provides support to a terrorist organization that injures or kills a U.S. citizen.[5]

As the statistics above state, Muslim extremists were responsible for the majority of terrorist attacks worldwide. The following are some of the terrorist acts that were committed by Muslim extremists against the United States:

- Pan Am World Airways Flight 103 was blown out of the sky over Lockerbie, Scotland, killing all 259 on board the aircraft and 11 people on the ground.
- Seven U.S. overseas buildings were bombed between 1985 and 1998. More than 150 people were killed and more than 2,000 injured. Many of the dead and injured were foreign nationals working for the United States. The locations were U.S. Air Force bases in Spain and Germany, a military training center and barracks in Saudi Arabia, and the U.S. embassies in Kenya, Tanzania, and Peru.
- A truck bomb damaged the New York World Trade Center in 1993, killing 6 people and injuring more than 1,000. Sheik Omar Rahman and nine other militant Muslims were convicted of this attack and of a conspiracy which, if carried out, would have destroyed the United Nations building and many other New York City landmarks.
- The U.S. naval ship *U.S.S. Cole* was seriously damaged in a suicide bombing in the Middle Eastern country of Yemen, killing seventeen sailors and injuring thirty-nine.
- On September 11, 2001, four U.S. commercial aircraft were hijacked by nineteen terrorists. Two planes loaded with jet fuel were deliberately flown into the 110-story twin towers of the New York World Trade Center, causing the towers

THE TORTURE ACT

In 1988 President Reagan signed the United Nations Convention against Torture (CAT). This international agreement was aimed at persons who, under color of law, torture individuals for political or other reasons. Nations who sign the convention agree to prosecute persons who violate international law by torturing others. In 1994 Congress passed the Torture Act, 18 U.S.C. § 2340–2340A, which punishes any person who subjects another person to torture, defined as the intention, under color of law, to inflict severe pain or suffering. Federal courts are given jurisdiction to try persons charged under this statute for torture that occurred outside the United States if they are U.S. nationals, or were arrested within the United States.

The first person charged under the Torture Act was Charles Arthur Emmanuel, a/k/a Charles Taylor, Jr. Emmanuel was the son of Charles Taylor, a Liberian citizen living in the United States, where Emmanuel was born. In the 1990s Taylor led a revolt that ended with his election to the Liberian presidency in 1997. From 1999 to 2003, when Taylor was forced out of Liberia, Emmanuel was his father's security chief. In that position he tortured and killed Liberian citizens, and he was known as "the demon." After his father left Liberia, Emmanuel returned to the United States in 2006, where he had lived with his mother under the name of Belfast. He was arrested in Florida that year and charged under the Torture Act. He was convicted and sentenced to 97 years in prison. His conviction and sentence were affirmed in *United States v. Belfast,* 611 F.3d 783. *(*11th Cir. 2010).

Emmanuel's father, Charles Taylor, was extradited to The Hague, Netherlands, where in April 2012 he was convicted of multiple war crimes for aiding and inciting the rape and murder of thousands of civilians. He was sentenced on May 30, 2012, to 50 years in prison. Taylor's conviction is the first conviction of a former head of state for international war crimes since the Nazi trials after World War II.

to collapse. One aircraft was flown into a section of the Pentagon in Washington, D.C., while passengers in the fourth aircraft fought with the hijackers, causing the plane to crash in Pennsylvania. More than 2,800 people died in these attacks. In 2006, Habib Zacarias Moussaoui was convicted in federal court of conspiring with and aiding the 9/11 attackers and was sentenced to life in prison without parole. He is currently incarcerated at the Federal ADX Supermax prison in Florence, Colorado. Khalid Sheikh Mohammed, believed to be the ringleader of the 9/11 terrorists, is being detained at the U.S. detention center in Guantanamo Bay, Cuba, awaiting trial on terrorist charges.

Criminal Charges Against Terrorists

After the 1995 terrorist attack that destroyed the Oklahoma City Federal Building, Congress enacted the Federal Antiterrorism Law, 18 U.S.C.A. § 1331, which gives the federal government jurisdiction to act against terrorism toward the United States, whether it occurs in the United States or elsewhere in the world.

Because the federal government lists thousands of crimes in the Federal Criminal Code, terrorists have been and will generally be charged under existing federal or state criminal law.

Terrorism and Support of Terrorism Under State Laws

Over the years, states have enacted many of their own antiterrorism laws, and other laws protecting the state and the state government. At least twenty-four states have adopted antiterrorism statutes. An example of a state statute is Florida Statutes Annotated, § 775.30. Many states have adopted a definition of the crime of terrorism closely modeled after the federal definition. For example, the Alabama Criminal Code, § 13-A-10-151, defines the crime of terrorism as an act or acts intended to

a. Intimidate or coerce a civilian population.
b. Influence the policy of a unit of government by intimidation or coercion.
c. Affect the conduct of a unit of government by murder, assassination, or kidnapping.

Many states have passed statutes similar to the Alabama statute, punishing terrorist threats that are directed at civilian populations or governments. Michigan's terrorist threat statute, MCL 750.543m, makes it a crime to threaten to perform a "terrorist act." A terrorist act is defined as a (1) violent felony, that (2) is dangerous to human life, and (3) is intended to intimidate or coerce a civilian population or influence a government by coercion or intimidation. In *People v. Osantowski*,[6] the Michigan Supreme Court upheld the conviction under § 750.543m of a high school student who sent e-mails to his 16-year-old girlfriend threatening to commit "mass murder" at his high school with guns and explosives.

States also have enacted statutes making it a crime to make a false report of a bomb or explosive threat with the purpose of either frightening a group of people, or causing the evacuation of a building. In *State v. Tanis*,[7] the court upheld a conviction under the Missouri terrorist threat act, V.A.M.S. 574.115, of a man who falsely told police he had

CASE CLOSE-UP

Hamdan v. United States
U.S. Court of Appeals for the District of Columbia,
696 F.3d 1238 (2012)

Salim Hamdan, a native of Yemen, was an al-Qaeda member who worked for Osama bin Laden as his personal driver and bodyguard. He was captured in Afghanistan in 2001, and transferred to the detention center at the U.S. Naval base in Guantanamo Bay, Cuba. Since the United States is in ongoing hostilities with al-Qaeda, under applicable laws captured enemy combatants may be detained until the end of hostilities between the United States and al-Qaeda. Enemy combatants who act unlawfully, by violating domestic or international law, can also be tried by a military commission.

Hamdan was charged with "material support of terrorism," a war crime specified in the Military Commissions Act (MCA) of 2006, based on actions Hamdan took from 1996 to 2001 to support al-Qaeda. He was tried and convicted by a military commission, and sentenced to 66 months in prison. When he completed his sentence he was transferred to Yemen and released. However, he continued to prosecute the appeal of his conviction, which is permitted under federal law.

On appeal, Hamdan contended the 2006 MCA did not apply retroactively to actions taken before the act became effective, which included all the actions Hamdan was charged with as "material support of terrorism." The Court of Appeals agreed, and stated that Handan's conviction could stand only if existing federal or international law made "material support of terrorism" a crime.

The court first found that federal law prior to 2006 did not make "material support of terrorism" a war crime triable by a military commission. The relevant statute in place before the 2006 MCA limited military commissions to trying violations of the "law of war," which was understood to mean the international law of war.

The court then found that international law did not include "support of terrorism" under the list of war crimes or crimes against humanities. It concluded that while support of terrorism has always been condemned, international law has left the criminal prosecution of such actions to individual nations. While there might have been existing international law crimes such as "aiding and abetting" terrorism, the court said, that was not the charge filed against Hamdan.

The court reversed his conviction, noting that its decision did not rule out charging Hamdan with a crime that was covered by international law when he acted, or charging him with violations of the "material support for terrorism" based on actions taken after 2006, when the MCA became effective. The U.S. government has not sought review by the Supreme Court in the *Hamdan* case, but it is possible that review will be requested in a similar case decided in 2013, *Al Bahlul v. United States*, 2013 WL 297726 (D.C. Circuit 2013), where the circuit court granted review *en banc* by the full court.

explosives in his truck and would use it to blow up a college building. The police evacuated the building, but a search of the truck revealed no explosives. The court affirmed his conviction, stating that the statute is aimed at actions that are intended to cause fear, and the evidence showed that was the intent of the defendant in making the false report.

Most state statutes also make it a crime for a person to support a terrorist act or organization. Actions that could constitute support include providing financial support, lodging, training, safe houses, false documents, communications equipment, weapons, lethal substances, explosives, personnel transportation, and other physical assets, except religious or medical material.

Other Possible Criminal Charges Against Terrorists

treason Acting to overthrow one's government, or in violation of allegiance to one's country.

Treason   **Treason** is the only crime defined in the U.S. Constitution. Article III, Section 3, provides:

> Treason against the United States, shall consist only in levying War against them, or in adhering to their Enemies, giving them Aid and Comfort. No Person shall be convicted of Treason unless on the Testimony of two Witnesses to the same overt Act, or on Confession in open Court.

Treason is a difficult crime to prove. In the history of the United States, treason has been charged only some thirty times. Aaron Burr was charged with treason in

Anwar al-Awlaki, a suspected terrorist, killed by a U.S. drone aircraft in 2011.

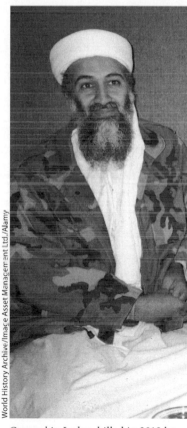

Osama bin Laden, killed in 2012 by U. S. Navy Seals.

Samir Khan, a U.S. citizen who produced an English-language magazine that listed ways to carry out terrorist attacks in the U.S., was killed in Yemen in the same drone attack that killed Anwar al-Awlaki.

1807 and, after a trial, was acquitted on a technicality. After World War II, Tokyo Rose, among others, was convicted of treason and served 7 years in prison for urging American military personnel to desert during World War II.

Sedition   All democratic countries have had to pass laws to protect their governments from overthrow by the use of force and violence. The **sedition** law now in effect in the United States is the Smith Act of 1940, 18 U.S.C. § 2385. It forbids advocating the forceful overthrow of the U.S. government, distributing with disloyal intent materials teaching and advising the overthrow of the government by violence, and organizing or helping to organize any group having such purpose.

The seditious conspiracy statute, 18 U.S.C. § 2384, makes it a crime to conspire with another person to destroy by force the government of the United States. In

sedition The crime of advocating the forceful overthrow of the established government. In this country, the Smith Act makes such advocacy a crime.

ANTITERRORISM LAWS ENACTED BY U.S. CONGRESS

Year	Popular Name/Citation	Purpose of Law
1903 and 1918	Immigration Act of 1903 and Act of 1918	Permitted exclusion of aliens advocating overthrow of government or affiliated with organizations who did so.
1940	Alien Registration Act and Smith Act of 1940	Requires deportation of aliens violating Act of 1918. Forbids advocating the forceful overthrow of the U.S. government, distributing with disloyal intent materials teaching and advising the overthrow of government by violence, and organizing any group having such purpose.
1950	Internal Security Act of 1950, 50 U.S.C.A. § 402	Further regulated actions of resident aliens.
1976	Foreign Sovereign Immunities Act, 28 U.S.C.A. § 1602	Permits civil lawsuits by persons injured by terrorists against nations supporting those terrorists.
1978 and 2000	Foreign Intelligence and Surveillance Act of 1978 as amended by the Act of 2000	Gives government broad power to conduct electronic and other surveillance of suspected terrorists.
1984	Hostage Taking, 18 U.S.C.A. § 1203	Makes it a federal crime to take an American citizen hostage anywhere in the world if purpose is to coerce person or government.
1996	Antiterrorism Act of 1996, 18 U.S.C.A. § 2332(d)	Makes it a crime for U.S. citizens to support any group listed as a foreign terrorist organization by either money or with other meaningful assistance. Also makes it a crime to enter into a financial transaction with a nation designated as a supporter of terrorism.
1996	Iran and Libya Sanctions Act of 1996, 50 U.S.C. § 1701	Places sanctions on persons or nations that engage in trade with Iran or Libya.

United States v. Rodriguez,[8] the court upheld the conviction under the seditious conspiracy statute of a member of FALN, a terrorist group seeking the independence of Puerto Rico. The court rejected the defendant's argument that the statute violated the Treason Clause of the U.S. Constitution, which is Article III, Section 3. That clause limits convictions for treason by requiring proof of overt acts and corroboration by two witnesses in open court. The defendant contended the seditious conspiracy act was "constructive treason," but the court disagreed, finding it served a different interest than the Treason Clause. The purpose of the conspiracy statute, the court said, was to combat "urban terrorism" and make government property and officials safe. It was not simply directed at those making war on the United States.

The U.S. Supreme Court affirmed the conviction of an officer in the American Communist Party in the case of *Dennis v. United States*.[9] At that time, Communist

Year	Popular Name/Citation	Purpose of Law
2001	USA Patriot Act of 2001, 18 U.S.C. § 1993	
	Title III	Criminal penalties and forfeiture rules for money laundering by or for terrorist organizations.
	Title IV	Establishes new rules for protecting U.S. borders.
	Title V	Removes obstacles to investigating terrorism; pays rewards and uses DNA to identify terrorists.
	Title VI	Payments to victims of terrorism.
	Title VIII	Strengthens criminal laws against terrorism. New crimes governing attacks against mass transportation systems, harboring terrorists, or providing support to terrorists.
2006	18 U.S.C. § 2709 (as amended in 18 U.S.C. § 3511)	Requires communication systems, such as Internet servers, to give FBI access to records of communications by suspected terrorists.
2006	Animal Enterprise	Prohibits acts of violence against animal enterprises and person associated with such enterprises.
2011	Terrorism Act, 18 U.S.C. § 43 National Defense Authority Act of 2012, 125 Stat. 1298	Permits federal government to detain indefinitely enemy combatants who have given material aid to al-Qaeda or the Taliban. In a 2013 decision, *Hedges v. Obama*, 2013 WL 3717774 (2nd Cir. 2013), the court held the Act did not apply to U.S. citizens or individuals arrested in the United States, and thus did not change the existing law on detention of citizens or others arrested in the United States, which generally does not permit such detention.

literature distributed in the United States urged the violent overthrow of the U.S. government. Following the conviction of defendant Dennis, the Communist Party stopped urging the violent overthrow of the U.S. government and now advocates change through peaceful and lawful means.

sabotage The crime of damaging or injuring national defense material or utilities with the intention of interfering with national defense.

Sabotage   Sabotage is made a crime by 18 U.S.C.A. § 2155. The offense forbids damaging or injuring national defense material or national defense utilities "with intent to injure, interfere with, or obstruct the national defense."

A person can be convicted under 18 U.S.C. § 2155 for any acts that obstruct or interfere with any national defense installation or material. In *United States v. Platte,*[10]

THE CONTINUING BATTLE AGAINST TERRORISM

The many national and international incidents of terrorism, both attempted and successful, force authorities all over the world to maintain a constant state of vigilance against these attacks. The following reports show some of the incidents that received national and international coverage, the ways terrorists can be prosecuted, and international concerns about future terrorist attacks:

Failed Attempts to Ignite Explosives

In 2010 a terrorist parked a van loaded with explosives in New York's Times Square, and triggered the device. The explosives smoldered, but did not ignite. Nearby vendors noticed the van and informed police, who broke into the van and disarmed the explosives. The driver of the van was quickly apprehended, and after talking freely to the police about his terrorist goals, pled guilty to criminal charges.

In 2009 a passenger on a commercial airplane attempted to ignite explosives he had concealed in his clothing. Although other passengers heard a series of loud pops, the explosives did not ignite.

In 2008 a passenger traveling by airplane from Europe to New York attempted to trigger explosives concealed in his shoes. There was smoke but no explosion.

Incidents of International Terrorism

Nations all over the world have been the victims of attacks by terrorist groups. In one of the most deadly since 9/11, in 2008 ten Pakistani terrorists attacked India's largest city, Mumbai (formerly called Bombay), illustrating the brazen and deadly tactics terrorists employ. Armed with assault rifles and grenades, the terrorists entered the city on small boats, and for 3 days launched attacks against hotels and other targets in the city, killing as many as 164 people, including 6 Americans, before 9 of the terrorists were killed by police. A Chicago man, David Headley, pled guilty in March 2010 to providing surveillance support to the terrorists. In exchange for an agreement not to seek the death penalty or extradite Headley to India, prosecutors obtained his cooperation in investigations of other terrorist actions.

In one of the longest, costliest, and most serious trials in English history, in 2008 a London jury convicted three terrorists of plotting to use liquid explosives to bring down in one day at least seven airliners traveling from England to the United States or Canada. Other members of the conspiracy were convicted in 2010. The suicide bombers planned to carry "liquid bombs" made by injecting liquid explosives into soft drink containers to be carried unto the airplanes. London police discovered the plot only days before the men planned the attacks. Worldwide airport security was changed to adjust to this new threat.

three Sisters of the Dominican Order were convicted under the statute for breaking into a Minuteman III missile site in Colorado. The defendants cut through a chain fence surrounding the property, and using ball-peen hammers they pounded on the rails that held the blast doors on nuclear missile silos. The court rejected their contentions that they did nothing that would have prevented the missiles from launching, stating that the statute required only that their actions interfere with or obstruct the national defense. Because the national defense includes training, the fact that the defendants' actions forced the virtual shutdown of the missile base for a period meant that their actions violated the statute.

Prosecuting Terrorists

Both federal and state courts could have jurisdiction to try a terrorist, if the terrorist's conduct were a violation of their respective criminal codes. Most terrorist crimes are tried in federal courts, since federal procedures offer more flexibility in determining venue and bringing in witnesses. Moreover, because federal courts have a long and successful history of trying difficult and complex cases such as espionage or those involving highly classified information, federal officials believe federal courts to be a "good fit" for these cases.

Military courts may also be used to try these cases when they involve a member of the military. Nidal Hasan, the army major charged with killing thirteen people at Fort Hood in 2009, will be tried in military courts. That trial is scheduled to begin in August 2013. Prosecutors have indicated they will seek the death penalty. Military commissions created to try "enemy combatants" may also try these kind of cases, but not if the defendant is a citizen of the United States.

Placing Terrorists on the "Kill List"

The Central Intelligence Agency is permitted under federal law to maintain a list (called the "kill list") of enemy targets, and is authorized to mount attacks against those targets. This list includes names of persons found to be enemies of the United States. If the person placed on the list is a U.S. citizen, the CIA must get approval from the White House. Anwar al-Awlaki, an American-born cleric hiding in Yemen, was placed on this list, based in part on his statement that "it is a religious duty to attack the United States." Anwar al-Awlaki was believed to have actively plotted and supported violence against the United States, and has been involved in more than a dozen terrorist plots, including the recent failed Times Square bombing plot. He is known to have had contact with Nidal Hasan, the army major discussed above, and in a statement posted on the Internet he praised Hasan's actions. In September 2011 a CIA drone fired a rocket into vehicles holding al-Awlaki and Samir Khan, an American living in Yemen who founded the militant, anti-American Internet magazine "Inspired," killing them both. In 2012, a U.S. Navy Seal team found and killed Osama bin Laden.

Concern over Future Terrorist Attacks

The National Intelligence has stated that the United States, and other democracies, face an enemy that has "no scruples about employing any weapon or tactic." This could include nuclear weapons. At a 2010 nuclear summit meeting President Obama and other world leaders voiced great concern about the prospect of terrorists using stolen or homemade nuclear devices to kill thousands of civilians in major cities.

The Crime of Terrorizing (Terrorism by Threats)

crime of terrorizing A crime that creates a state of extreme fear, dread, or fright.

The term *terror* means a state of extreme fear, dread, or fright. Crimes that create such a condition are sometimes labeled "terrorist" crimes or the **crime of terrorizing** in state criminal codes. (See discussion of assault crimes in Chapter 11.)

Prosecutions for making terrorist threats under state criminal codes generally require proof that the defendant threatened violence against another person, with the purpose of terrorizing that person. An example of the application of a terrorist threat statute in a terrorist threat prosecution is *Cobble v. State*.[11] The defendant stood outside his former girlfriend's house and shouted obscenities at her, in violation of a protective order obtained by the woman. Police were called and arrested the defendant. The defendant struggled with the arresting officers and was subdued by pepper spray, which required his hospitalization. While he was in the hospital, in the presence of officers, the defendant stated that when he was released he "would kill" the woman. He was then charged with making terrorist threats and was convicted. On appeal the defendant argued that he could not be convicted under the Georgia terrorist threat statute for two reasons: first, because the threat was never communicated to the victim, and second, because the statute specifically stated a

RULES OF WAR

Rules of war are a body of customs, practices, treaties, and agreements that most nations subscribe to for the conduct of wars openly declared against sovereign nations. President Abraham Lincoln began the codification of these rules in 1864, and since that time most nations have signed the international conventions adopting these rules. Under these rules, combatants in a war are liable for violation of ordinary criminal laws, such as rape or theft, even if carried out pursuant to orders from a superior. Such combatants can be charged with violation of their own nation's laws or the laws of the nation where the crimes took place. Saddam Hussein, the former president of Iraq, was tried and convicted in an Iraqi court of murder (under Iraqi law) and crimes against humanity (under international law).

The rules of war create three categories of crimes:

- *Crimes Against Peace:* These laws forbid the planning, commencement, and conduct of an aggressive war. The United Nations recognizes only wars fought in self-defense as lawful wars. Hermann Goering and other Nazi leaders were convicted at the Nuremberg war crimes trials of violation of this law.
- *Crimes Against Humanity:* These laws forbid deportation, enslavement, persecution, and extermination of groups of people based on their race, religion, or ethnic origin. These laws were the result of the concentration camps and slave labor camps used by the Nazis during World War II.
- *Traditional War Crimes:* These are traditional laws concerning rules of conduct of the combatants toward prisoners of war and toward civilians living in the war zone. After World War II, Japanese General Yamashita was convicted and executed for "failing to provide effective control" over Japanese troops who raped and killed Philippine civilians.

conviction could not be based solely on the uncorroborated testimony of the person to whom the threat was communicated.

The Georgia Court of Appeals disagreed. It held that it did not matter if the victim did not actually hear the threat; it was enough if the defendant made the threat under circumstances where he intended or knew the threat would be communicated to the victim. It also held that the defendant's actions in violation of the protective order were sufficient corroboration of his intent to carry out his threat.

The 804 Terrorism Prosecutions from 2001 to 2009

In 2010 the Center on Law and Security at New York University School of Law published an excellent study entitled "The Terrorist Trial Report Card, 2001–2009." The study analyzed the public records of 804 terrorist prosecutions conducted during that 8-year period, and reached conclusions from those records. Some of the findings of the study, used with the kind permission of the Center on Law and Security, appear here. A copy of the full study may be obtained by contacting the Center at http://www.lawandsecurity.org.

Where Did the 804 Persons Charged Come from and What Was the Conviction Rate?

The persons charged came from at least forty-seven different countries (there was no information on the home countries of about 20 percent of the defendants). The largest group indicted (273) comprised persons with U.S. citizenship. Next were Colombia, South America (98), Pakistan (60), the Palestinian Territories (22), Jordan (18), Iraq (14), Egypt (13), and the United Kingdom (12). The remainder came from a group of thirty-nine countries.

What Were the Most Common Categories of Criminal Charges Brought by the Prosecutors?

The crime of terrorism was charged in 244 of the cases, followed by racketeering (127), national security or hostage taking (102), fraud and false statements (77), drug charges (60), commercial fraud, embezzlement, and theft (54), immigration violations (43), obstruction charges (9), and violent crimes (4).

What Conduct Constituted a Violation of a "Terrorist Statute"?

Two hundred forty-four of the defendants were convicted under terrorism statutes that required proof of involvement with terrorism, which included terrorist conduct, knowingly or intentionally aiding a "terrorist organization," or acting in furtherance of a terrorist objective.

What Conduct Constituted Violation of "National Security Statutes"?

One hundred two prosecutions were brought under statutes forbidding hostage taking; sabotage (including destruction of national defense material, premises, or utilities); or possession or use of chemical weapons.

488 PART 4: Other Criminal Conduct

Were Terrorism Actions Used for Sentence Enhancement Purposes?

Terrorism was also used for sentence enhancement in convictions under the following principal crimes: immigration violations (1), obstruction of an investigation (1), and crimes of terrorism or against national security (20).

What Conduct Did the Study Include Under "Domestic Terrorism"?

In this study "domestic terrorism" focused on white supremacy advocates, anti-abortion activists, animal liberation groups, and environmental terrorism.

How Many Prosecutions Involved Weapons of Mass Destruction?

One hundred sixty-one prosecutions alleged weapons of mass destruction (WMD) charges. Pursuant to 18 U.S.C. § 2332a, a federal statute, WMD include a broad list of weapons, such as "destructive devices" like explosives, grenades, or other explosives and poison gases. This list is larger than what the general public considers WMD to include, which is probably limited to nuclear, chemical, radioactive, and biological weapons. Many of the violations occurred overseas against American military targets. Groups behind these violations were al-Qaeda (22), FARC (71), Cambodian Freedom Fighters (1), the Free Papua (New Guinea) Movement (1), Ku Klux Klan (1), and Tamil Tigers (5). In fifty-seven of the cases no affiliation was found. Narco-terrorists, covered by 21 U.S.C. § 960, were briefly mentioned in the study, in connection with four persons in Afghanistan charged with narco-terrorism.

Financing Terrorism: Where Does the Money Come From?

Terrorists need money to operate. INTERPOL (the International Criminal Police Organization, located in Lyon, France) has said: "The frequency and seriousness of international terrorist acts are often proportionate to the financing that terrorist groups might get."

The 9/11 Commission report[12] issued in 2004 found no evidence of any foreign government knowingly helping to finance the 9/11 attack. The 9/11 Commission found that most of the $400,000 to $500,000 used to finance that operation came from donations to "charitable organizations," which then funneled the necessary funds to the terrorists.[13] At least nineteen terrorists lived and trained in the United States for a period of 18 months to 2 years before the 9/11 attack. Organizations that knowingly provide aid to terrorists violate the Anti-Terrorism Act,[14] 18 U.S.C. § 2339B, and also can be sued for civil damages under 18 U.S.C. § 2333(a).

The shortage of financial support can affect the scope of a terrorist attack. In the February 2007 issue of the *FBI Law Enforcement Bulletin,* the 1993 attack on the World Trade Center is used to illustrate this fact. The terrorists in that first attack on the World Trade Center had plans to use larger bombs as well as chemical and biological weapons that would have hampered rescue efforts and increased fatalities. Because of a shortage of funds, they were unable to execute the attack as planned, which greatly limited the harm caused and casualties inflicted.

Terrorists frequently use other criminal activity to finance their terrorism, the FBI article states. So-called low-risk, high-reward crimes are favored by terrorists. These include drug trafficking ("if we can't kill them with guns, we kill them with drugs"); theft; and fraud crimes, such as identity theft, credit card, Social Security, welfare, and insurance fraud. In one instance, the theft of baby formula netted a terrorist ring $18 million during an 18-month period. Intellectual property crimes were also committed by terrorists, such as counterfeiting watches, selling fake driver's licenses, and pirating software. One terrorist group made $750,000 in one year smuggling cigarettes.

Stopping the flow of funds to terrorists is an extraordinarily difficult task. One major obstacle is the international source of funds. The 9/11 Commission stated that Saudi Arabian charities alone funneled hundreds of millions of dollars to jihad groups and al-Qaeda cells over the last few years. There is little the United States can do to prevent such transfers.

For groups with assets within the United States, the Trading With the Enemy Act, 50 U.S.C. § 1702(a)(1)(b), permits the president to establish a "Specially Designated Terrorist List" and freeze assets of those groups or those who contribute financial support to the groups. The USA Patriot Act, passed after 9/11, includes a provision permitting the president to block assets held by any group or person being investigated for involvement with terrorist attacks.

Moving Money into and out of the United States

Moving funds into and out of the United States happens on a massive scale each business day and can be part of a lawful banking or business activity. However, it can also be illegal money laundering, movement of funds in illegal operations, or transfer of funds to terrorist groups for future operations.

Funds can be transferred by human couriers, a time-honored custom in many parts of the world, or could be moved through high-tech electronic wire transfers. Web pages on the Internet can be used to solicit funds, which can then be sent to terrorist groups. One large fund, the Benevolence International Foundation, used a website that appealed to Muslim donors to send money to the foundation. The director of the foundation, Enaam Arnaout, pleaded guilty to a count of racketeering in 2003, admitting he sent money from the foundation to support Muslim "fighters" in Bosnia and Chechnya. He was sentenced to 10 years in prison, and the foundation has been banned everywhere in the world.

Funds can also be transferred through the use of so-called informal value transfer systems (IVTS). An example of an IVTS is the ancient system known as Hawala, which originated in India. In a Hawala transaction a person in one location gives money to a representative of the network. The money is not physically or electronically transferred. Instead, a representative of the system in the location where the sender wants the money to go gives funds to the intended recipient. The advantages of the Hawala system are that the cost of the transaction can be lower than more traditional transfer methods, and there is virtually no paper trail for the transaction. The 9/11 Commission Report stated that al-Qaeda cells used the Hawala system for moving funds in and out of Afghanistan, the headquarters of al-Qaeda.

Illegal use of the Hawala system violates many federal money-laundering laws and could also violate provisions of antiterrorism laws. The case of *United States v. Anvari-Hamedani,* 378 F. Supp. 2d 821 (N.D. Ohio 2005), illustrates use of the Hawala system in violation of these laws. An Iranian doctor living in Ohio was indicted for money laundering and violating the federal International Emergency Economic Powers Act (IEEPA) based on transfers of money and goods to Iran. In Executive Order 13059, the president had placed Iran on the list of designated countries that support terrorism and made any investment in business in Iran or commitment of funds to groups in Iran a violation. The defendant instructed Merrill Lynch to send funds from an account he had with that brokerage firm to persons in Iran. Merrill Lynch filed a Suspicious Financial Activity Report, as required under federal law, detailing the transaction. The FBI investigated and found that the defendant also sent funds to Iran through a Halawa system.

However, in the 2012 case of *United States v. Banki*[15] a federal court of appeals held that noncommercial intrafamily transfers of money to and from Iran through the Hawala system did not violate the U.S. Treasury Department's Iranian Transactions Regulations. It reversed a conviction of an Iranian national living in New York who arranged the transfer of over $3.4 million from his family in Iran to him in New York.

International Criticism of Aspects of the U.S. War Against Terrorism

The war against terrorism has been in some ways an international effort. The United Nations has adopted a number of conventions aimed at specific kinds of terrorist acts, such as attacks on civilian aircraft or kidnapping of government officers. Member nations are expected to pass local laws to implement these conventions. Prior to 9/11 the United States was mainly content to participate in these internationally sponsored efforts.

But after 9/11, the United States, together with some of its allies, began fighting terrorism without the formal cooperation of the United Nations. Some of the actions taken by the U.S. government have received criticism from other nations and their governments; chief of these is the war in Iraq. Other actions have also engendered controversy. They include these:

- Kidnapping and Abductions: In 2007 both Italy and Germany issued criminal complaints and warrants against thirty-nine Americans working in a U.S. program called "extraordinary rendition." Under this program, first used pursuant to a presidential directive by President Clinton in 1995, suspected terrorists are seized by U.S. agents and are transported to another country for interrogation. Many of the pre-9/11 "ghost detainees" were suspected al-Qaeda operatives, and they were sent to Egypt for interrogation. Since 9/11, persons detained under this program have been sent to several countries for interrogation, including Jordan, Syria, Morocco, and Uzbekistan. Critics of the program say it permits the United States to indirectly use torture to interrogate detainees, something forbidden under U.S. law and the United Nations Convention Against Torture. Supporters of the program contend it makes sense to send detainees to countries that know the detainees' language and cultural background.[16]
- Secret Over-Flights of European Countries: A European Union Parliament committee has objected to flights by U.S. military and civilian government

aircraft over European airspace without prior approval from the countries affected. The committee stated that at least 1,245 secret CIA flights were made over Europe from 2003 to 2007.

- Canadian Citizen's Treatment: Canada, historically a U.S. ally, in 2003 participated with American agents in the seizure of a Canadian citizen in New York by American agents and transferred to Syrian authorities. The man was held for more than 10 months in Syria, where he stated he was subjected to torture. Though Canadian authorities denied any knowledge that the United States was planning to send the man to Syria, Canadian intelligence officials acknowledged they sent a list of questions for the man to American agents. The man ultimately was returned to Canada, where he was awarded $9.75 million in damages for his wrongful detention.[17]

LAW ENFORCEMENT NEEDS CITIZENS' HELP TO DETER HOMEGROWN TERRORISTS

Timothy McVeigh, the man who masterminded the bombing of the Federal Building in Oklahoma City in 1995, appeared to be a "regular guy." He was a U.S. Army veteran who served with great distinction. He held a regular job after leaving the service and seemed like a man who believed in the ideals upon which the United States was founded. In fact, McVeigh had become deeply bitter about the role of federal agents in the Waco, Texas, action against the Branch Davidians, a religious sect, in which several members died, and the Ruby Ridge action against a separatist group, which caused the death of a woman and a 14-year-old girl.

In 1995, McVeigh, with the help of Terry Nichols, constructed a massive fertilizer bomb and blew up the Federal Building in Oklahoma City. The attack killed 168 innocent people and injured more than 500 others. During the Vietnam War, radical students had used a similar device to blow up buildings on the campus of the University of Wisconsin.

Constructing these bombs required the purchase of large amounts of materials that were known to be capable of destructive power. Nonetheless, no one reported anything unusual to the authorities until after the bombs were detonated.

In 2006, a Circuit City employee in New Jersey became concerned about a video he saw that showed men apparently training for combat. He called the police, and the FBI were able to place an informant with the group, which was, in fact, planning a terrorist attack on the soldiers at Fort Dix. After 16 months of investigation, in 2007 the FBI arrested the men and stopped the terrorist plan before it could be executed.

Also in 2006, the FBI received a tip on its website that led it to place two New Jersey men under surveillance for suspected terrorist plans for a "jihad" against the United States. The men were arrested in 2010. Both tips were essential to the success of the investigations and demonstrate that help from the public in spotting "homegrown" terrorists is an ongoing need for law enforcement officers.

Because extremists like McVeigh can come from a large and varied pool of disaffected people, the help of the public in identifying potential terrorist threats is vital to the success of law enforcement efforts to curb "homegrown" terrorists.[a]

[a]See the *Chicago Tribune* article, "FBI Says Domestic Extremists Big Threat," May 13, 2007.

Summary

- Terrorism is the use of unlawful force to coerce or intimidate persons or governments in the pursuit of political, social, or religious goals.
- International law does not clearly define terrorism. When the United States became a signatory to international conventions that addressed specific terrorist acts, Congress passed laws to implement those conventions. Because of the vagueness limitation on statutes, Congress was required to clearly define the acts that constituted terrorism and were condemned under the conventions.
- The State Department is authorized to identify groups or organizations as terrorist organizations.
- The crime of terrorism under most state laws requires proof that a defendant took acts intended to
  (1) intimidate or coerce a civilian population, or
  (2) influence a government by intimidation or coercion, or
  (3) affect the conduct of government by intimidation or coercion.
- A terrorist threat is a threat to (1) commit a violent felony that (2) is a danger to human life, and is made to (3) intimidate or coerce a civilian group or a government.

- Rules of war are customs and practices followed by most nations in wartime, and now are the subject of international conventions. They create three classes of crimes: crimes against peace, crimes against humanity, and traditional war crimes.
- Terrorists raise money for their actions both directly and indirectly. Some countries contribute directly to terrorist organizations. The U.S. president has the power to identify such countries and place them on a list of countries that support terrorism. Individuals contribute indirectly to terrorist organizations by giving money and support to phony charitable groups that support terrorists.
- Money can be sent out of the United States through normal banking channels, or by funneling the cash through international business organizations. It can also be sent by human carrier, such as is done in the Hawala system used for centuries in the Middle East.
- An extraordinary rendition occurs when a person is seized in one country and then transported to another country for interrogation. The country to which the person is transported often has a relationship with the person, or the country permits interrogation procedures not permitted by the country where the seizure occurred.

Key Terms

terrorism, p. 474
treason, p. 481

sedition, p. 482
sabotage, p. 484

crime of terrorizing, p. 486

Case Analysis and Writing Exercises

1. A member of a New York Mexican-American street gang murdered a suspected member of a rival gang. It was his stated purpose to intimidate other Mexican-American gang members and make them afraid to enter the gang's "territory." After 911, New York passed a terrorism law directed at, among other conduct, acts designed to "intimidate a civilian population." Can the street gang member be convicted for violating this statute based on his murder of the rival gang member? If not, why not? *See People v. Morales*, 982 N.E.2d 580 (N.Y. 2012).

2. Threats to bomb a school or public building are damaging, even if a threat is a hoax. As a

result, most states make it a crime to make a bomb threat against a public place or building, even if the person making the threat does not intend to carry out the threat. The *mens rea* requirement under these statutes is typically "knowingly" making the threat with the intent to cause alarm. Does a call from an inmate at a mental institution to a 911 operator, stating bombs have been hidden at an airport, violate this statute? *See State v. Ballew*, 272 P.3d 925 (Wash. App. 2012). *Review denied* 290 P.3d 994 (Wash. 2012).

3. The United States is a party to a global chemical weapons treaty. To implement that treaty, Congress passed 18 U.S.C. § 229, which makes it a crime to use "for non-peaceful purposes" any chemical that can cause death or permanent harm to humans. Does a wife who tries to kill her husband's mistress by smearing deadly chemicals on the victim's car door handles and front doorknob violate this statute? If so, does that mean any criminal use of a household chemical will qualify as an offense under the statute? *See United States v. Bond*, 681 F.3d 149 (3d Cir. 2012). The U.S. Supreme Court has agreed to review that decision, 133 S. Ct. 978 (2013). What do you think the court should do?

4. Many state "terroristic threat" statutes require a threat of "imminent" violence or harm against a person. A threat to do something in the future would not violate this kind of statute. Assume a defendant called a 911 operator in San Antonio, Texas, and demanded an officer be sent to his home "to verify he was denied visitation rights" with his children. When he was told this was a civil matter, he became angry, and in subsequent calls renewed the demand for an officer to come to his house, but said "don't send Officer Steve Christian because I will blow his brains out." The defendant was convicted of violating V.T.C.A. Penal Code § 22.07, the Texas terroristic threat statute. Is this a threat of "imminent" harm or violence? If not, how did the court justify the conviction under the Texas law? *Phillips v. State*, 2013 401 S.W.3d 282 (Tex. App. 2013).

Endnotes

1. *Holcomb v. State*, 709 S.E.2d 711 (Va. App. 2011).

2. After McKinley's death, President Theodore Roosevelt stated that anarchism was "a crime against the whole human race." The United States passed immigration laws that excluded anarchists from entry into the country.

3. A jury found McVeigh guilty of all charges against him, which were the federal crimes of (1) conspiracy to use a weapon of mass destruction, (2) use of a weapon of mass destruction, (3) destruction by an explosive, and (4–11) the eight counts of the murders of the eight federal law enforcement officers killed in the blast. All three men were charged in federal courts for federal crimes.

   The third man, Michael J. Fortier, pleaded guilty to four federal charges and was sentenced to 12 years in prison. Because of his cooperation, this sentence was a reduction of the longer sentence he would have received. One of the federal criminal charges was "misprision of a felony." Fortier had known of the planned bombing but had not warned anyone. See Chapter 19 on the federal crime of misprision of a felony.

4. See the *New York Times* article, "Men Arrested in a Terror Plot Against Ft. Dix," May 9, 2007.

5. See *Boim v. Quranic Literacy Inst. & Holy Land Foundation*, 291 F.3d 1000 (7th Cir. 2002).

6. 748 N.W.2d 799 (Mich. 2008).

7. 247 S.W.3d 610 (Mo. App. 2008).

8. 803 F.2d 318 (7th Cir. 1986), *cert. denied*, 480 U.S. 908 (1987).

9. 341 U.S. 494, 71 S. Ct. 857 (1951).

10. 401 F.3d 1176 (10th Cir. 2005).

11. 603 S.E.2d 86 (Ga. App. 2004).

12. *The 9/11 Commission Report: Final Report of the National Commission of Terrorist Attacks Upon the United States* (Washington, D.C., 2004).

13. See the article "Dealing with Hawala" in the February 2007 issue of the *FBI Bulletin* and the 9/11 Report.

14. See *Weiss v. Westminster Bank PLC*, 453 F. Supp. 2d 609 (E.D.N.Y. 2006).

15. 685 F.3d 99 (2nd Cir. 2012).

16. See the *New York Times* article, "Italy Indicts 26, Many From C.I.A. in '03 Abductions," February 17, 2007.

17. See the *New York Times* article, "Canadian Court Limits Detention in Terror Cases," February 24, 2007.

Organized Crime and Gangs

Neil Marriott/Digital Vision/Getty Images

Portrait of four members of a Hispanic gang.

OUTLINE

Organized Crime and Criminal Gangs

Federal and State Laws Passed After 1970 to Fight Organized Crime

Limits on Federal Jurisdiction and RICO Prosecutions

The Federal Witness Protection Program and the Crime of Witness Tampering

The Crime of Money Laundering

Transactions Covered by the Federal Money Laundering Statutes

Currency Transaction Reports and the Crime of Smurfing

Other Criminal Laws Used to Fight Gangs and Organized Crime

The Travel Act

Extortion

Bribery

Kickbacks

Mail Fraud

Honest Services Fraud

LEARNING OBJECTIVES

In this chapter we discuss organized crime and gangs and the various ways the federal and state governments combat this criminal activity. The learning objectives for Chapter 18 are the following:

- List the requirements for a RICO conviction.
- Identify the jurisdictional requirements for a federal RICO charge.
- List three ways money can be laundered.
- List four federal statutes used to combat interstate crime.
- State the knowledge needed for a conviction under the federal money laundering statute, specifically the section on transportation of illegal proceeds.
- Define proceeds under the money laundering statutes.
- Explain why federal and state prosecutions of organized crime figures before 1970 were generally unsuccessful.
- Describe the advantages statutes passed after 1970 gave to the prosecution.

The federal Racketeer Influenced and Corrupt Organizations Act (RICO) has been a valuable weapon in the fight against organized crime. It is directed at "criminal enterprises" that commit crimes in the United States as part of the criminal goals of the enterprise.

What happens if the "criminal enterprise" is located entirely in a foreign country, but some actions taken by the members of the criminal enterprise occur in the United States, and are illegal under U.S. law? Can those people be prosecuted for RICO violations? That was the issue in a 2013 case decided by the Ninth Circuit Court of Appeals.[1]

Four Chinese nationals, employees of the Bank of China, embezzled or misdirected over $482 million of Bank of China funds before they were discovered by Chinese bank audits. Millions of those dollars were deposited in casinos in Las Vegas, where the four defendants traveled to gamble. They traveled in the United States by using false U.S. visas obtained by entering into fraudulent marriages with U.S. citizens. When the Bank of China discovered the thefts, all four escaped to the United States, where they were arrested. However, they weren't returned to China, because the United States does not have an extradition treaty with China. Instead, the four were charged with violations of federal law, including the RICO act.

The defendants contended they could not be tried for violations of RICO, because the "criminal enterprise" was located entirely in China. The trial court disagreed, and they were convicted of the RICO violation, as well as violations of other criminal laws. The court of appeals agreed with the trial judge. It held that while RICO has no foreign application, and thus could not use the "criminal enterprise" located in China as a basis for jurisdiction, it did apply when criminal actions were taken in the United States in furtherance of the criminal enterprise. Since the four defendants all committed multiple violations of U.S. immigration laws in order to transfer money and hide it in the United States, those crimes made RICO applicable. The court affirmed the RICO conviction in 2013.

In this chapter we will study the state and federal criminal laws enacted to give prosecutors the tools to go after criminals who engage in criminal acts but who are protected by the nature of an organization engaged in a criminal enterprise. We will also see how those laws can be used to prosecute individuals like criminal gang members who commit criminal acts as part of a plan to further a criminal enterprise. Finally, we will study the limitations the Constitution places on those uses.

Organized Crime and Criminal Gangs

Gangs of organized criminals have operated in the United States for over 200 years, and in Europe for much longer. Bands of criminals soon realized that working together greatly increased their chances of success.

In most periods of American history, the character of gangs was dictated by the environment. In the Wild West of the late nineteenth century, outlaw gangs traveling around on horseback specialized in cattle rustling or stagecoach robbery. At the same time, in the infamous Five Points section of New York (what is now Lower Manhattan's Chinatown), various gangs of Irish, Italian, and German immigrants practiced murder, prostitution, theft, and extortion. With the rise of the automobile in the 1920s and 1930s, gangs became mobile and could travel about the country, robbing small-town banks. Indeed, it was the inability of the local police to coordinate efforts to apprehend gangs like the Dillinger gang that played a significant role in the creation of the FBI as a national crime-fighting agency.

The Prohibition period helped the spread of the most notorious gang in the twentieth century, the mafia. While the mafia had its roots in a much earlier period in Italy and Sicily, controlling the market in illegal alcohol sales during Prohibition made it possible for the mafia to branch out and control many other criminal endeavors.

In 2002, the U.S. Department of Justice, with the participation of about 2,000 law enforcement agencies, published a study of gangs in the United States.[2] The study, which was prompted by a 1996 report that identified more than 30,000 gangs with more than 800,000 members, focused on the nature and growth of violent gangs in the past 20 years.

The study concluded that most law enforcement agencies distinguished between "gangs" and "organized crime" associations by the nature of their organizations.

ATTEMPTS BY CITIES AND STATES TO REGULATE GANG ACTIVITY

Cities and states have used a variety of laws in attempts to curb gang violence:

- Nuisance laws, both civil and criminal, are used to seize and tear down crack houses and other drug houses and to prosecute landlords who permit drug use by gangs in rented premises.

- Laws against the crimes of unlawful assembly, rioting, stalking, and curfew violation (see discussion in Chapter 9) are used to curb gang activity.

- Injunction laws are used to deter gang action. Because of its serious gang problems, the city of Los Angeles is seeking injunctions (court orders) against gang members that forbid a specific gang to gather, even in groups as small as two, in specified public places. In defending these injunctions, a Los Angeles city attorney states: "People deserve protection. . . . Gang members are terrorizing our communities." Penalties for violating the injunction include up to a year in jail.[a]

- Graffiti laws, cruising laws, and laws making membership in a gang a crime (found in a few states) are used.

- If the offense was committed by gang members, laws to increase criminal penalties can be used.

- Laws punishing parents for the gang behavior of their children.

- Laws making parents civilly liable for the criminal behavior of their children may be applied.

- Laws forbidding intimidation and threats (discussed in Chapter 9).

- Forfeiture laws such as those found in the Uniform Controlled Substances Act permit the government to seize the proceeds and profits of a crime, as well as cars, boats, airplanes, or real estate used in the commission of crimes. In Los Angeles prosecutors have seized homes and businesses owned by members of the 18th Street gang which were shown to be the proceeds of or instrumentalities used in drug crimes, extortion, money laundering, and related crimes.

- Deportation of those who enter the United States illegally, or commit crimes while in the United States.

- Street gang terrorism and drug conspiracy laws may be used, such as Illinois Comp. Stat. Ch. 720, Section 5/12-6 (1998).

Many state and city loitering laws and ordinances criminalize specific acts, such as "overt acts or evidence of criminal intent" or "loitering for the purpose to engage in drug-related activities," which have been upheld in state courts. However, in *City of Chicago v. Morales*, 527 U.S. 41 (1999), the U.S. Supreme Court struck down the Chicago gang congregation ordinance as unconstitutional because it was too vague and did not give citizens fair notice of what was required of them to comply with the law. (See Chapter 1 on the "void for vagueness" doctrine.)

[a]See the *New York Times* article "Gangs Without Borders, Fierce and Resilient, Are Confronting the Law," September 26, 2004.

Organized crime generally involved a highly structured leadership arrangement, designed in part to insulate those at the top from criminal accountability. These organizations generally have a chief or "don" who makes policy and issues orders, which are carried out by captains, lieutenants, and soldiers, all of whom are sworn career criminals.

Laura Duffy, the United States Attorney in San Diego, California, appears at a news conference on July 23, 2010, to announce the indictment on conspiracy charges of forty-three defendants for violation of federal RICO laws. The indictment that U.S. Attorney Duffy holds in her hand represents the results of an extensive investigation into the defendants' alleged criminal activities, involving border violence on the American-Mexican border and illegal drug trafficking.

Gangs, the study found, tended to be a far looser affiliation of criminals:

Most gangs are loosely knit coalitions of small, autonomous cliques. Apart from a general commitment to their "hood" and the gang lifestyle, the only unifying force is combat with outsiders. Gang leadership is usually decentralized, nonhierarchical, even situational; it is more a function of individual prowess and reputation than a formalized structure for making collective decisions. Leadership changes rapidly and may vary by activity. . . . The type of gang leadership varies from gang to gang and by geographical area.

Some gangs, and most groups of organized criminals, have long histories of criminal activities as groups. Others are recent entries into organized crime. The Russian mafia is an example of the latter group; the FBI in 2004 identified it as the fastest-growing criminal organization in the United States. Terrorist groups would probably be classified as criminal organizations because they generally have more structured leadership organizations.

Law enforcement agencies participating in the study reported that

> the delinquent gang was the most typical gang in their jurisdiction . . . consisting primarily of juveniles who engaged in vandalism and other delinquent behavior.... Yet police reported that most gangs, regardless of type, participated in many different types of crimes.

The membership and location of gangs varied greatly, the report found. Street gangs made up of delinquents were found in inner cities, suburbs, rural areas, and small towns. Gangs organized along ethnic or racial lines included Asian, Hispanic, Jewish, Russian, African American, and Irish. The nature of the activity, such as drug dealing, sometimes served as the identifying feature of a gang. Shoplifting, purse snatching, check forging, insurance fraud, and identity theft are examples of these kinds of gangs.

The report found that most gangs began as local groups that, if successful, expanded to nearby cities and states. If a gang was involved with illegal drugs or weapons, expansion included violence to achieve dominance. Criminal networks crossing state lines can be formed, which the report stated could use "modern

WILL THE MOB EVER GET OUT OF THE CRIME BUSINESS?

The criminal organization known as "the mob" in most parts of this country has many different names. In Chicago, it is called the outfit. In New York it is called the family; in Italy and Sicily it is known as *la cosa nostra* ("our thing"). In other areas, organized crime is referred to as "bent noses," or simply "thugs." "The mob" is perhaps a suitable generic name for this band of criminals.

Over the years, large American cities such as New York and Chicago have experienced hundreds of mob-related killings, most of them unsolved. In 2005, indictments were handed down against top Chicago mobsters, charging them with eighteen Chicago area murders. In June 2007, five of these mobsters went to trial for these murders; of the others indicted, six pleaded guilty, one died, and one was too ill to be tried.

The trial received national attention, as hit men, bookies, career burglars, gamblers, pornographers, and other street associates of the defendants testified about their dealings with the outfit. A key witness was Nick Calabrese, a "made" member of the outfit. He confessed to participating in fourteen of the murders, and he testified against his brother, Frank Calabrese, and other defendants. For this reason, the press labeled the trial as "The Family Secrets Case."

It took years and millions of federal and state dollars to put this case together. In September 2007, a jury convicted Frank Calabrese, Joseph "Joey the Clown" Lombardo, and James Marcello of ten murders on behalf of "the Outfit." In December 2012, Calabrese died in a federal prison in North Carolina.

Will this be the end of the Chicago mob? Law enforcement experts say no. Younger up-and-coming members of the outfit will quickly replace the older members who disappear. An FBI spokesman stated that the outfit continues to have influence in vice rackets, labor unions, and political corruption and will continue to function in Chicago, though perhaps in a smaller capacity.

weapons, communication technology, and transportation in their operations to control and expand their operations more effectively."

The waves of immigrants coming to the United States since the 1970s, especially from Asian, Latin American, and eastern European nations, have changed the membership of old gangs and caused the creation of many new gangs.

The youth gang known as the Bloods has demonstrated that recruiting new members is possible, including from the populations in prisons and jails. The name Bloods reflects the fact that blood must be spilled for one to become a new member, and blood will be spilled if a member tries to leave the gang. The blood spilled is frequently that of an innocent passerby, slashed by a gang member in a random act of violence.

Some gangs are extremely large. The Black Gangster Disciples (BGD) gang, for example, is reported to have as many as 30,000 members heavily involved in drug trafficking. The Latin Kings have an estimated membership of 5,000 to 15,000. Gangs continue to grow despite the criminal convictions or deaths of key leaders.

In the 2011 National Gang Threat Assessment, the Justice Department released information on gang membership and crimes, based on statistics gained from law enforcement jurisdictions from all fifty states. Based on those reports, the Threat Assessment concluded:

- There are about 1.4 million gang members nationwide. Of those, about 150,000 are in prison.
- In the years since the last report (2009), gang activity increased the most in the Northeast and Southeast regions of the United States.
- Gang members are moving to other crimes, including prostitution, alien smuggling, and human trafficking.
- Gangs account for 48 percent of all violent crimes nationally, and as much as 90 percent in some cities.
- Outlaw Motorcycle Gangs (OMG) have increased dramatically since 2009. There are presently 3,000 OMGs, with more than 44,000 members.

In 2008 the city of Chicago launched a concentrated attack on gangs and gang-related crime, including the hiring of 400 officers to form a special unit to work with communities to reduce violence. While these efforts resulted in the arrest and conviction of many gang leaders, the approximately seventy gangs located in Chicago still have an estimated 100,000 members. In 2011, 435 homicides occurred in Chicago, up to 80 percent of them gang-related. While final statistics for 2012 are not available, as of December 29, 2012, the number of homicides was 500. Thus, even though violent crimes have dropped nationwide since their peak in the 1990s, gang-related murders have increased in Chicago. Gang members also now tend to be younger (most under 20 years of age) and more violent.

The Police Department of the city of Los Angeles reported that from 2007 to 2009 (the last date for which statistics were available) there were 16,398 gang-related crimes committed in Los Angeles; 491 of those crimes were homicides, 98 were rapes, and 5,518 were robberies. Recruiting younger members from schools and illegal immigration has helped make the Mara Salvatruchas and the 18th Street Gang two of the fastest-growing gangs in the United States, with branches and operations as far east as Washington, D.C., New York, and North Carolina. Former Los Angeles Police Chief William J. Bratton refers to gangs as "domestic terrorists" and urges that gang problems receive top priority from state and federal authorities.[3]

Federal and State Laws Passed After 1970 to Fight Organized Crime

Prior to 1970, federal and state criminal codes did not have effective laws to penetrate the code of silence that insulated organized crime leaders from prosecution. Because lower-ranking gang members actually committed most crimes under orders from above, the lack of success in linking crimes to the leaders meant that they were rarely prosecuted. Indeed, the long-time director of the FBI, J. Edgar Hoover, went so far as to deny the existence of the mafia, a denial that mystified much of the population that saw and read reports of horror stories of mafia crime.

A well-known mafia leader, Al Capone, enjoyed a reputation as a vicious killer, yet he was ultimately convicted not of murder but of income tax evasion, and was sentenced to 11 years in prison.[4] Other crime leaders then saw the danger presented by prosecutions for tax evasion, and instituted what we now call money laundering (which was made a separate crime in 1986) to obscure or eliminate any paper trail linking illegal gains to the crime bosses who reaped those gains.

In the federal and state fight against organized crime, 1970 marked the beginning of a concentrated effort against criminal organizations like the mafia. Two important federal statutes were the Racketeer Influenced and Corrupt Organizations Act (**RICO**) and the **Continuing Criminal Enterprise Statute (CCE)**. The state laws often had similar titles, such as Organized Crime Control Act or Offenses Concerning Racketeering.

The RICO laws, and the similar state laws commonly known as "little RICO" laws, were drafted to enable prosecutors to focus on the conspiratorial nature of organized crime. That is, the statutes made individuals, groups, and organizations criminally liable for multiple criminal acts that established a pattern of criminal activity.

The federal and state RICO laws generally require the government to prove that the defendants committed or conspired to commit acts of racketeering, called "predicate acts." The list of criminal acts that qualify as predicate acts is very long in both federal and state RICO statutes, including drug trafficking, violent crimes, witness tampering, mail or wire fraud, and illegal gambling. To obtain a RICO or "little RICO" conviction, the prosecution must prove:

- That the enterprise existed and was engaged in racketeering activity
- Two or more incidents of racketeering conduct "that have the same or similar intents, results, victims, or methods of commission" (Fla. Stat. § 895.02)
- That the defendants in the criminal action were members of the racketeering enterprise

RICO The Racketeer Influenced and Corrupt Organizations Act. Passed by Congress to enable prosecutors to charge all people engaged in unlawful activity who own or invest in an enterprise that affects interstate commerce.

Continuing Criminal Enterprise Statute (CCE) Federal law making prosecution possible for those whose actions enable a criminal enterprise to function, whether or not those same people can be proved to have performed specific criminal acts.

- That the racketeering conduct by the defendants was committed for the purpose of maintaining or advancing their positions in the racketeering enterprise

The RICO and CCE laws, both federal and state, are written very broadly and permit convictions for more than a half dozen separate and distinct racketeering crimes.[5] Each year hundreds of criminal and civil prosecutions under the RICO laws are brought in the United States, for a wide variety of criminal violations. RICO has been successfully used to stop illegal activities by anti-abortion groups, violations by brokers and traders on stock exchanges, Taft-Hartley violations, porn shop violations, Medicare and public assistance frauds, and many other illegal acts.

MAKING GANG MEMBERS PAY

Crime, it is said, doesn't pay. Most states have statutes that try to do the same for gang membership by increasing the penalty for crimes that are committed by gang members. The following cases are illustrative of these statutes:

- New York has a "gang assault" statute that elevates an assault into a class B felony if the assault is "aided by two or more persons actually present" and causes serious physical injury. In *People v. Sanchez,*[6] the court upheld a conviction under the gang assault statute even though the prosecution did not prove the persons aiding the defendant intended to cause serious bodily injury.
- Most states have statutes that elevate the seriousness of an offense if the defendant is a member of a "criminal street gang." The Texas statute, VTCA Penal Code § 71.02, elevates the offense to the next level if it is proved the defendant was a member of a criminal street gang. See the 2010 case of *Coleman v. State.*[7] California's statute, Cal. Penal Code § 186.22, provides for sentence enhancements of 1 to 10 years, depending on the nature of the underlying offense, if the defendant is a member of a criminal street gang, or acts to further the interests of a criminal street gang. Both state statutes define "criminal street gang" in a similar manner: a criminal street gang is a group of three or more persons who have a common name or symbol, have as a primary purpose the commission of crimes, and have a pattern of criminal activity. In *People v. Bragg,*[8] the court upheld sentence enhancements under the statute for a defendant who attempted to murder a rival gang member. The court said the prosecution need not prove the defendant was a current member of the gang, but only that his actions were taken to further the interests of the gang.
- Minnesota § 609.229 provides for sentence enhancements of up to 10 years if the underlying offense is a felony and was committed "for the benefit of a gang," with a definition of gang similar to the definition of a criminal street gang in the Texas and California statutes.
- Street gang membership is also relevant in juvenile courts. Under Florida law, F.S.A. § 985.433, a court making a disposition order for a juvenile adjudicated a delinquent must take into consideration the fact that the juvenile is a member of a street gang.

RICO laws target membership in a "criminal enterprise." In the 2009 case of *Boyle v. United States*,[9] the U.S. Supreme Court considered the meaning of "enterprise" for a conviction under the federal RICO law, 18 U.S.C. § 1962. The defendant was one of a group of criminals who robbed bank night deposit boxes. They did this over a period of several years. However, the group had no leader, no hierarchy, no long-term plan, and no formal structure. The defendant appealed his conviction under § 1962, claiming he did not belong to a "criminal enterprise."

The Supreme Court concluded he did. While the Court agreed an "enterprise" under the RICO act must have an ascertainable structure, it need not have a formal or business structure. It was enough that a group was an "association in fact" with a common purpose, and with some longevity. The Court rejected the defendant's claim that to be an "enterprise" the group must have a leader or a manager. It compared the RICO act to the illegal gambling act, 18 U.S.C. § 1955(b) and the Continuing Criminal Enterprise act, 21 U.S.C. § 848(c), which each have a requirement that the enterprise have an owner, supervisor, or other manager. Because the RICO act says nothing about owners or organizers, the Court concluded a "criminal enterprise" includes an informal group with a common purpose, even if no structural hierarchy exists within the group.

As we saw in Chapter 4, RICO conspiracy violations do not require an "overt act" for conviction; all that is required is that the defendant agreed to participate in the "criminal enterprise." In the 2012 case of *United States v. Harris*[10] the court held that a conspiracy to violate RICO did not require proof that a "criminal enterprise" in fact existed; it was enough that the defendant agreed to participate in such an enterprise.

Limits on Federal Jurisdiction and RICO Prosecutions

The federal RICO statute permits federal prosecutions based on criminal acts that would normally fall under state criminal jurisdiction. (See Chapter 2 of this text.)

Federal jurisdiction is possible under RICO if the underlying acts affect interstate commerce, because Congress has the authority to pass laws, including criminal laws, to regulate interstate commerce. However, if the underlying predicate acts do not affect interstate commerce, the federal government has no jurisdiction over those crimes and cannot charge defendants under the RICO law. *Waucaush v. United States*[11] is an example of a case where a federal court of appeals held the predicate acts did not affect interstate commerce.

The defendant Waucaush was a member of a Detroit, Michigan street gang called the Cash Flow Posse (CFP). In CFP's effort to control its turf from encroachment by rival gangs, the government alleged that members of the CFP murdered members of those other gangs. Waucaush and other gang members were charged with violation of the RICO laws. The indictment identified the gang as the criminal enterprise but included only the murders and other acts of violence as the predicate acts.

Waucaush initially pleaded guilty to the RICO charges, but after his conviction, two U.S. Supreme Court decisions were announced that potentially placed restrictions on the ability of Congress under the Commerce Clause to make the RICO laws applicable to criminal acts. In *United States v. Morrison*,[12] the Court held that Congress could pass a law regulating conduct that did not have a direct interstate element only if the conduct had an economic effect on interstate commerce. In *Jones v. United States,*[13] the Court held that the arson of a private residence did not affect interstate commerce, even though it was insured by an out-of-state entity. Based on these decisions, Waucaush sought to retract his guilty plea and have the charges against him dismissed. Charges against other defendants, who had not been sentenced when these decisions came down, had already been dismissed.

The court of appeals held that the murders and other violent acts were not by themselves sufficient to sustain federal jurisdiction under the Commerce Clause. Where a gang is not involved in economic activity, RICO requires a criminal enterprise that substantially affects interstate commerce, the court held.

MEXICAN DRUG CARTELS AND THEIR AFFILIATES

Since 2006, when the president of Mexico announced increased efforts to stamp out drug cartels, Mexican drug cartels have waged violent battles with one another and the Mexican government to determine who will control the lucrative drug and contraband smuggling market into the United States. The U.S. Department of Justice stated in 2009 that the Mexican drug cartels "represent the greatest organized crime threat to the United States." The Justice Department also identified 230 cities in the United States and Canada (up from 100 cities in 2006) where the Mexican drug cartels and their affiliates "maintain drug distribution networks or supply (illegal) drugs to their distributors."

The Mexican government stated in 2010 that over 28,000 people have been killed since the drug crackdown was started by the government in 2006. Of those killed, 2,076 were Mexican local, state, or federal police officers. The Mexican government has offered rewards of up to $2 million for information leading to the arrest of any of the known top drug kingpins, and up to $1 million for similar information on any of thirteen named lieutenants.

Violence has spread north over the borders. Officials in Vancouver, Canada, believe that drug traffickers are responsible for the increased shootings in that city. There have also been increased kidnappings and home invasions in border states like Arizona, as well as increased violence in other American cities, such as Birmingham, Alabama, where several murders have been linked to drug cartels. In 2010 three American diplomats were murdered by drug terrorists in Ciudad Juarez, which is "ground zero" in the battle against drug cartels. See the *New York Times*, March 15, 2010.

While it is difficult to document Mexican cartels' movements, many law enforcement officials believe the cartels are sending agents into the United States to establish the cartels in American cities. Statistics from the DEA show that in 2008 about 230 cities reported the presence of a believed cartel member; in 2011 that number increased to 1,200. Once established, the cartels, like other criminal organizations, may expand operations to include other criminal activity, such as human trafficking, prostitution, and money laundering.

The Mexican government has thousands of federal troops, in addition to the other law enforcement officers, fighting the drug cartels in northern Mexico. On the American side of the border, thousands of Border Patrol officers, state and local police officers, and National Guard troops seek to enforce laws and maintain public order. States from Texas to California are affected by the turmoil, with Arizona suffering the most violence. Truly, as the *New York Times* opined in a May 28, 2010 editorial, "Mexico is in a vicious fight to the death with drug cartels."

Violent crimes can be prosecuted under RICO only if they are done for the purpose of furthering the criminal enterprise. Because the CFP was engaged in no proven economic activity, such as drug dealing, gambling, or credit card fraud, the murders were not undertaken to further an enterprise that affects interstate commerce.

The court agreed that every person's death has an effect in some way on interstate commerce—"a corpse cannot shop"—but "we may not 'follow the but-for causal chain from the initial occurrence of violent crime (the suppression of which has always been the prime object of the States' police power) to every attenuated effect upon interstate commerce.'"

After *Waucaush* was decided, the Supreme Court issued its opinion in *Gonzales v. Raich*[14] (discussed in Chapter 2). In this decision the Court suggested that the Commerce Clause should be read broadly to give Congress power to pass laws regulating interstate commerce. That decision has persuaded at least one federal circuit court to reject the reasoning of the *Waucaush* court. In *United States v. Nasceminto,*[15] the court upheld a RICO conviction of gang members who, like the gang members in *Waucaush,* were not engaged in economic activity but merely focused on violence against other gangs. The court held that the activities of the gang had a *de minimis* effect on interstate commerce, in part because one of the gang members bought a gun in another state and brought it into his home state, and that a *de minimis* effect was sufficient to satisfy the interstate commerce requirement. The court accordingly rejected the requirement of "substantial effect" applied by the *Waucaush* court.

The Federal Witness Protection Program and the Crime of Witness Tampering

Organized crime leaders were often insulated from the violent crimes they ordered committed. As a result, prosecutors needed the testimony of witnesses familiar with the leaders' role in the organization to charge and convict those leaders. Moreover, the Sixth Amendment's Confrontation Clause required that a defendant be permitted to be "confronted with the witnesses against him."

Obtaining witnesses to testify against gang and organized crime figures has always been a problem, both because in many cases the witnesses were themselves gang or organized crime members who had sworn a blood oath of silence and because of real fears of reprisal against the witness or his or her family. Threats of violence, bribery of witnesses, and extortion of witnesses and their family members were common methods criminals used to prevent witnesses from testifying.

witness protection program Established as part of the Organized Crime Control Act of 1970, this program provides new identities and relocation for witnesses and their families in both state and federal criminal prosecutions of organized crime.

In an effort to break these barriers to prosecution, Congress passed significant legislation in 1970 and 1982. As part of the Organized Crime Control Act of 1970,[16] Congress established the **witness protection program**. This program provides new identities and relocation for witnesses and their families in both state and federal criminal prosecutions of organized crime. Since its creation, this program has protected more than 7,500 witnesses and 9,500 family members from fear of reprisals, enabling them to safely testify against gang and organized crime figures.

witness tampering
Criminal interference with someone who plans to testify in either a criminal or a civil trial.

In 1982, Congress passed the Federal Victim and Witness Protection Act of 1982. This statute created the crime of **witness tampering** and punishes any person who by any means tampers with a witness, victim, or informant.[17] Tampering is a crime, whether the witness plans to testify in a criminal trial or a civil trial. The U.S. Supreme Court has held that the duty to testify and give information in both civil and criminal cases is inherent in being a citizen of the United States, even when witnesses fear for their lives because of such testimony.[18] These and other federal laws are designed to make it possible for witnesses to perform their duties and to convict gang and organized crime members.

In October 2004, Dustin Honken, a methamphetamine dealer, was convicted in the U.S. District Court for Iowa of murdering five people. Two were witnesses the government planned to have testify against him in a drug charge, one was the girlfriend of one of the witnesses, and two were the girlfriend's small children. He was charged with the murders as furtherance of a continuing criminal enterprise and witness tampering, both federal laws that permit imposition of the death penalty. Even though Iowa is one of twelve states that do not have the death penalty, under the federal murder statute the jury sentenced Honken to life imprisonment for the murders of the adults and sentenced him to death for the murders of the children. The Eighth Circuit Court of Appeals upheld his sentence, and the U.S. Supreme Court denied certiorari in December 2009.[19]

The Crime of Money Laundering

money laundering The crime of disguising money obtained illegally by channeling it through legitimate commercial and financial transactions.

Money laundering is defined by the U.S. Department of the Treasury as "the process by which criminals or criminal organizations seek to disguise the illicit nature of their proceeds by introducing them into the stream of legitimate commerce and finance."[20] The Bank Secrecy Act of 1970[21] was the first attempt by Congress to prevent criminals from concealing or laundering money through banks or other financial institutions. The Money Laundering Control Act of 1986 created the crimes of money laundering and knowingly helping with money laundering of the proceeds of criminal activities.[22] Because terrorists must conceal and launder money to achieve their criminal purposes, the USA Patriot Act of 2001[23] toughened laws prohibiting the concealment or laundering of money for criminal purposes. Under this statute, U.S. banks dealing with foreign customers are held accountable, sentences for cash smuggling are increased, and both civil and criminal penalties for violation of the law are enlarged.

Money laundering has been called the world's third largest business. Drug dealers, terrorists, and organized crime figures need to have money move undetected through the world's financial systems. "Following the money" is one effective way for investigators to find the criminals who made the money. The International Monetary Fund estimates that money laundering activities account for between 2 and 5 percent of the world's gross domestic product, or about $600 billion annually.[24]

In addition to laundering money through legitimate businesses owned or controlled by them, criminals use several other methods. In the July 2006 issue of the *FBI Law Enforcement Bulletin,* the article "Breaking the Bank" listed the following methods of money laundering and transfer used by drug dealers:

. . . some of the more common laundering methods include . . . the Black Market Peso Exchange, cash smuggling (courier or bulk cash shipments), gold purchases, structured deposits to or withdrawals from bank accounts, purchases of monetary instruments (e.g., cashier's checks, money orders, traveler's checks), wire transfers, and forms of underground banking, particularly the Hawala system.

The article points out that while drug money is the leading source of money laundering, persons laundering money gained from other criminal activity can also be prosecuted under federal law.

Transactions Covered by the Federal Money Laundering Statutes

Title 18 of the United States Code prohibits the following money laundering activities, among others:

- Section 1956: "intending to transport or transfer monetary funds knowing that the property represents the proceeds of unlawful activity"
- Section 1957: "knowingly engaging in a monetary transaction involving criminally derived property valued at more than $10,000"

Prosecutions under 18 U.S.C. § 1957 require only that the defendant engage in a transaction where he knew the money being transferred was over $10,000 and came from criminal activities. In *United States v. Johnson*,[25] the court affirmed the conviction of a defendant who accepted over $10,000 from a person to use as a down payment on a house, knowing the money came from illegal drug transactions.

Recent court decisions by the U.S. Supreme Court and Courts of Appeals have addressed some of the issues raised in prosecutions under 18 U.S.C. § 1956, the principal money laundering statute. In *Whitfield v. United States*,[26] the U.S. Supreme Court held that convictions for conspiracy to violate the money laundering statute did not require proof of an overt act. While the general federal conspiracy statute, 18 U.S.C. § 371, does require proof of the commission of an overt act in furtherance of the conspiracy, the Court held that when Congress leaves out that specific requirement, as it did in the money laundering statutes, it intended to exclude the necessity of proof of that element.

Prior to 2008, the federal courts of appeals were split on the elements the prosecution must prove for a conviction under the transportation part of the money laundering statute. Section 1956(a)(2)(B)(i) states that it is a crime to transport certain funds into or out of the United States with a design "to conceal or disguise the nature, the location, the source, the ownership, or the control of the proceeds of specified unlawful activity." Some courts interpreted this provision as requiring proof that the defendant intended to give the transported funds "the appearance of legitimacy." See *United States v. Morales-Rodriguez*.[27] These courts reasoned that the "classic" example of money laundering was schemes designed to make illegal money look legal, using a "disguise" of some sort.

Other federal courts disagreed. In *United States v. Ness*,[28] the court of appeals held that conviction under the "transportation" money laundering statute did not require proof that the defendant intended to give the transported funds the appearance of legitimate wealth. The defendant, who operated an armored car company, transported proceeds from illegal drug sales to persons outside the country. He contended that he made no effort to pass the money as legal wealth and thus could not be guilty of "concealing" under the statute. The court disagreed, finding that the concealment element was satisfied because the defendant used "elaborate" methods attended by a high degree of secrecy in transporting the money.

The U.S. Supreme Court settled the split in the circuits in the 2008 case of *Cuellar v. United States*.[29] There, the defendant was caught in Texas on his way to Mexico carrying $81,000 of illegal drug money in a concealed compartment of his car. He was convicted under the transportation part of § 1956. On appeal, the Fifth Circuit affirmed his conviction, concluding that evidence the defendant made an elaborate attempt to conceal the money satisfied the money laundering requirements of a "design" to transfer funds to conceal their unlawful source. The defendant appealed to the Supreme Court, contending the prosecution did not prove he made any attempt to give the money the "appearance of legitimate wealth."

The Supreme Court held the prosecution was not required to prove the defendant tried to give the money the appearance of legitimate wealth. However, it also held that the prosecution under § 1956 had to prove that the defendant knew the purpose of the transportation of the money to Mexico was to conceal its unlawful origin. Simply proving the defendant concealed the money did not suffice to prove he knew the purpose of the transportation to Mexico was to conceal its source. "There is a difference between concealing something to transport it, and transporting something to conceal it."[30] Because the prosecution offered no evidence on the defendant's knowledge of the purpose of the transportation, all the elements of § 1956 were not proved, the Court said, and reversed the conviction.

The Supreme Court also remanded the *Ness* case back to the Second Circuit Court, and in 2009 that court reversed the convictions under the money laundering statute.[31] In the later case of *United States v. Garcia*,[32] the court held that the financial transaction part of the money laundering statute, § 1956(a)(1), also required proof that the defendant knew the purpose of the transaction was to conceal the unlawful origin of the money transferred.

18 U.S.C. § 1956 expressly prohibits using the "proceeds of specified unlawful activity" in financial transactions or transportation transactions. For example, if a thief used stolen money as a down payment when buying a house, the use of the money in a "financial transaction" would be a separate crime from the theft of the money. However, in *United States v. Santos*,[33] the U.S. Supreme Court held that the term *proceeds* in the money laundering statutes covers "profits" from unlawful activity, not "gross receipts." In *Santos* a defendant ran an illegal lottery in Indiana. He used money paid by lottery players for their tickets to pay expenses of running the illegal lottery, such as making payouts on winning tickets. He kept the profits after paying all expenses. He was convicted under the federal money laundering statute based on transactions where he "used" receipts from the unlawful activity to pay expenses. The government contended these transactions qualified as money laundering because the funds transferred were "proceeds" of the illegal lottery, and thus were "proceeds" under § 1956. The Supreme Court rejected the government's position, and reversed the conviction under the money laundering statute. Congress did not define "proceeds" in the money laundering statute, and

the Court concluded either "receipts" or "profits" would fit within the meaning of "proceeds" as used in the statute. That being so, "Under a long line of our decisions, the tie must go to the defendant. The rule of lenity requires ambiguous criminal laws to be interpreted in favor of the defendants subjected to them."[34] The Court also reasoned that because there were 250 "predicate" offenses that could produce unlawful proceeds, every time a criminal paid the costs of committing one of those crimes (such as thief renting a car to move his stolen property) a money laundering violation would occur. The Court did not think that was the intended result of the money laundering legislation.

In 2009 Congress amended the money laundering statute to make it clear proceeds means either profits of illegal activities, or "gross receipts of such activity." In addition, courts after the decision in *Santos* continued to hold that in illegal drug transactions, any money obtained from the sale of illegal drugs constitutes "proceeds" for purpose of the money laundering statutes. Thus, in the 2011 case of *United States v. Richardson*[35] a defendant who used illegal drug money to make the down payment on a house purchase was convicted of violating the money-laundering act.

Currency Transaction Reports and the Crime of Smurfing

With drug-trafficking revenues as high as $300 billion a year, many drug dealers and other criminals reap huge profits. A large amount of such criminal profits is spent purchasing expensive cars, houses, condos, jewelry, furs, clothing, and other luxuries.

Businesses and financial institutions in the United States are required to report cash transactions of $10,000 or more under the Currency Transaction Reporting Act (31 U.S.C.A. § 5311). The **CTRs (currency transaction reports)** filed by businesses, banks, and other financial institutions are used to determine whether tax fraud or money laundering is occurring. Further investigation could then uncover illegal drug dealings and racketeering.

Unfortunately, businesspeople who want to make profits sometimes cooperate with drug dealers and other criminals seeking to hide cash transactions. Car dealers, real estate agents, and jewelers sometimes illegally agree to structure a transaction. In a structured transaction, the buyer makes a series of payments in cash or cashier's checks of under $10,000 each over a period of weeks. When the sales price is reached, the dealer or real estate agent turns the car or condo over to the buyer. For a $50,000 car, six or seven payments under $10,000 would be the structured transaction. This illegal practice is sometimes called "smurfing" and is made a crime by the Federal Money Laundering Control Act of 1986 (31 U.S.C. § 5324).

Section 5324(a)(3) prohibits "structured transactions" involving financial institutions. It states, "No person shall, for the purpose of evading the reporting requirements of section 5313(a) … structure or assist in structuring … any transaction with one or more domestic financial institutions." The U.S. Supreme Court defined "structuring" in *Ratzlaf v. United States*[36] as any plan "to break up a single transaction above the reporting threshold into two or more separate transactions for the purpose of evading a financial institution's reporting requirement." In *United States v. Morales-Rodriguez,*[37] the court affirmed the conviction under § 5324(a)

CTRs (currency transaction reports)
Reports that businesses, banks, and financial institutions are required to file for cash transactions of more than $10,000. CTRs can help determine whether tax fraud or money laundering is occurring.

CASE CLOSE-UP

United States v. Haddad
U.S. Court of Appeals for the 7th Circuit,
462 F.3d 783 (2006)

Defendant Haddad operated a "mom-and-pop" grocery store in Chicago, R&F Grocery. Pursuant to an agreement with the U.S. Department of Agriculture (USDA), R&F participated in the USDA food stamp program. Under this program, eligible recipients exchanged food stamps for specified groceries. Recipients were issued a "LINK" card that operated as a debit card. At the first of each month a recipient's account with the USDA was credited with the amount of food stamps for which that person qualified. This LINK card could be presented to a participating grocery store, where a special point-of-sale machine would debit the recipient's account for the amount of groceries purchased. The USDA would then credit a designated account maintained by the store accepting the food stamps. Participating stores agreed not to exchange food stamps for cash.

After investigation by Chicago police, R&F was discovered to be exchanging food stamps for cash. Police observed long lines of customers standing at the entrance to R&F on midnight of the first day of the month, the time when their LINK cards were credited with the food stamp amounts. These customers entered the store and emerged later without groceries, but with cash.

Subsequent investigation of the bank account used by R&F showed that during a 30-month period more than $1,117,000 was deposited in that account. Expert analysis by a federal officer determined that all but $345 of the deposits were from the USDA, and that during the period of the deposits R&F sold only $45,000 worth of groceries

to food stamp recipients. Thus, over a million dollars in the account came from illegal exchanges of food stamps for cash, the expert concluded. Haddad wrote checks to himself from that account in excess of $708,000.

Haddad was charged with money laundering under 18 U.S.C. § 1957, which makes it a crime to knowingly engage in a monetary transaction in criminally derived property over the value of $10,000, derived from certain specified unlawful activity, which included misappropriating money under the food stamp program. To satisfy § 1957, the prosecution introduced two checks in the amounts of $15,000 and $16,000 drawn on the R&F account and payable to Haddad. He was convicted, and he appealed, contending the prosecution failed to prove the money laundering charge because it failed to prove the two checks contained only funds from the unlawful activity.

The court of appeals affirmed the conviction. It noted that based on the evidence, it was clear that virtually all the funds in the R&F account on the dates the two checks were written came from unlawful cash exchanges. Moreover, the court held, even if other funds were commingled in that account with funds from illegal transactions, the government did not have to prove the actual source of each dollar taken from the account and transferred to Haddad. It was clear from the evidence that some part of the two checks constituted funds from unlawful exchanges, and that was sufficient to satisfy the requirements of § 1957.

(3) of a vice president of a non-profit organization that provided benefits to police officers and fire fighters. The defendant received monthly checks from the organization's 18,000 members and deposited them in bank accounts. He then had the banks issue him hundreds of checks made out to cash for just under $10,000. Over a two-year period he received about $1.2 million dollars in this manner, none of which was reported anywhere.

Title 31 of the United States Code, which contains rules for monetary recording and reporting, requires in § 5316 that a CMIR (currency or other monetary instruments report) be filed when more than $10,000 is taken out of or brought into the United States. Because illegal drugs are a major source of profit for many criminals and criminal organizations, law enforcement officers look not only for importation of illegal drugs but also for the money making the narcotics deals possible. These statutes enable law enforcement officers to "follow the money," if it is laundered in legal entities, and prosecute those engaged in the laundering activities.

Failing to file a report, or filing a false report, is a violation of § 5316, and under § 5317 the funds taken out of the country can be confiscated.[38]

Other Criminal Laws Used to Fight Gangs and Organized Crime

The Travel Act

Travel Act Legislation that can be used to prosecute those involved in criminal activities that cross state borders or involve foreign commerce.

Title 18 of the United States Code, § 1951, titled the **Travel Act**, can be used to prosecute those involved in criminal activities that cross state borders or involve foreign commerce. That act prohibits traveling in interstate or foreign commerce or use of the mail or any facility in interstate or foreign commerce with intent to:

1. Distribute the proceeds of any unlawful activity; or
2. Commit any crime of violence to further any unlawful activity; or
3. Otherwise promote, manage, establish, carry on, or facilitate the promotion, management, establishment or carrying on of any unlawful activity

Felony convictions for violations of the Travel Act have been obtained for interstate travel as part of a scheme to

* Bomb a homosexual bar.[39]
* Travel with the intent to violate state law.[40]
* Place illegal gambling wagers using telephones, which are included in the meaning of a "facility" under the act.[41]
* Use a telephone to demand the payment of a ransom for the release of a person held unlawfully.[42]
* Travel to facilitate an illegal narcotics transaction.[43]

Extortion

Both the federal government and the state governments have statutes making extortion criminal. The federal statute, known as the Hobbs Act (discussed in Chapter 14), permits prosecution under that act if the extortion can be shown to interfere with interstate commerce. The Hobbs Act defines *extortion* as "obtaining of property of another, with his consent, induced by wrongful use of actual or threatened force, violence, or fear, or under the color of official right" (18 U.S.C. § 1951). In a 2013 case, *Sekhar v. United States,* 133 S. Ct. 2720, the U.S. Supreme Court held that attempts to bully a government lawyer to give his employer favorable legal advice about the defendant so he could obtain a government contract did not constitute extortion under the Hobbs Act. The court held that a lawyer's opinion did not constitute "property" under the Hobbs Act; "property," the court held, must be something that can be transferred from one person to another.

A common example of extortion used by gangs or organized crime members is the threat of violence against a business that does not pay "protection" money. Often, a business owner is forced to pay one gang extortion money to protect the business from another gang. An example of the use of the "color of official right" is the city health inspector who threatens to charge a business with serious sanitation violations unless the official is paid off.

ILLEGAL GAMBLING IN THE UNITED STATES

During Prohibition in the United States (1919–1933), organized crime made huge profits selling illegal beer and alcohol to the many people who wanted to drink.

With the legalization of alcoholic drinks, organized crime turned to other illegal activities. It is widely believed that until the 1970s, illegal gambling was the greatest moneymaker for organized crime.

With the legalization of many forms of gambling in the United States and with the effective use of RICO, profits from gambling dropped rapidly, while the risks in illegal gambling went up. Illegal gambling is no longer as attractive to criminals as it previously was. However, some forms of gambling continue to be illegal.

Distinguishing Illegal Gambling from Friendly Gambling

For a game of chance or a lottery to be illegal, it must violate a specific law or ordinance. Illegal gambling is often distinguished from legitimate commercial promotions by the fact that illegal gambling or lotteries have (1) a prize, (2) consideration, and (3) chance elements.

Therefore, a company that wishes to run a promotion can offer a prize if the customer does not have to buy anything or pay anything (no consideration). Or the contest can be legal if, instead of a chance element, there is a skill element (writing an essay or naming a new product, for example).[a]

The Federal Crime of Gambling: 18 U.S.C.A. § 1955

(b) *As used in this section—*

   (1) "illegal gambling business" means a gambling business which—
      (i) is a violation of the law of a State or political subdivision in which it is conducted;
      (ii) involves five or more persons who conduct, finance, manage, supervise, direct, or own all or part of such business; and
      (iii) has been or remains in substantially continuous operation for a period in excess of thirty days or has a gross revenue of $2,000 in any single day.

The Federal Professional and Amateur Sports Protection Act (Public Law 102-559) Prohibiting Sports Gambling

Section 3702 makes it unlawful for states or individuals to sponsor, operate, advertise, promote, or license a lottery, sweepstakes, or betting on one or more competitive games in which amateur or professional athletes participate.

Bribery

Bribery has always been a problem for society. Using money, property, or "favors" to influence a public or private official to act in some agreed manner is a crime in all the states and under federal statutes. The problem has been acute in recent years because of the huge amounts of money controlled by criminal organizations. The presence of this money not only encourages criminals to approach officials to attempt to buy their actions but also serves as an illegal incentive for corrupt officials to solicit such payments.

Several exemptions are provided, including betting on parimutuel animal racing and jai alai, and some casino betting.[b]

Sports Betting and States' Rights

The PASPA, discussed above, contains exceptions for four states (Nevada, Delaware, Oregon, and Montana), where sports betting is permitted. In Nevada in 2012, over $288 million was bet on sorting contests, mainly college games. The "March Madness" in 2013 is expected to produce over $200 million in legal sports bets in Nevada.

Other states want in. In 2012 New Jersey voters passed a resolution permitting sports betting in the state's twelve casinos and four horse racing tracks. The legislature passed a bill doing so, and Governor Christie signed the bill into law. The NCAA, the NBA, NFL, and other sports institutions, and the U.S. Justice department, immediately brought a suit in federal district court challenging the law. In March 2013 a federal district judge held the law violated federal gambling laws. The state is appealing the decision.

[a]When is gambling a "social game" between friends, between neighbors, or in an office or factory pool? The court in the 1991 case of *State v. Hansen*, 816 P.2d 706 (Or. App.), cited Oregon Statute 167.117(4)(c):

"Social game" means:

  (a) A game, other than a lottery, between players in a private home where no house player, house bank or house odds exist and there is no house income from the operation of the social game; and

  (b) If authorized pursuant to ORS 167.121, a game, other than a lottery, between players in a private business, private club or place of public accommodation where no house player, house bank or house odds exist and there is no house income from *the operation of the social game* ORS 167.117(13). [Emphasis added.]

Friendly gambling (office or factory football pool, neighborhood poker game, and so on) can be distinguished from commercial gambling by some or all of the following factors:

- Where the game is played and who the players are
- Size of the pot
- Whether the house takes a percentage of each pot
- Whether the players bet against the house and the house acts as the banker, and whether the house acts as the dealer in such games as blackjack and craps
- Other factors such as the type of game played

[b]Sports betting is a big business in the United States, with billions of dollars, most of it illegally, wagered each year.

An example of a state bribery law is Chapter 838 of the Florida Criminal Code, which makes it a crime to offer a bribe to any state, county, or city employee or official, or any employee or official of any political subdivision in the state. Both the person offering the bribe and the person taking the bribe can be charged under the statute. It is also the crime of bribery to offer money to "fix" an athletic contest (§ 838.12). The crime of "commercial bribery" (§ 838.15) is committed when a bribe is offered to any employee or agent of a business or another person; a trustee, guardian, or other fiduciary; a lawyer, physician, accountant, appraiser, or other professional advisor; an officer, director, or manager of an organization; or an arbitrator, adjudicator, or referee.

Bribery is a specific intent crime, and to obtain a conviction the prosecution must prove the bribe was offered with "corrupt intent," that is, with intent to influence the actions of the person to whom the bribe was paid. It is not necessary that the bribe be offered to influence a specific official act, but only that its purpose is to cause favorable results in the future.

In some states the prosecution must prove the bribed official was actually influenced by the bribe. See, for instance, Nebraska Revised Statutes § 28-917 (Reissue of 1995), though even there the defendant can be convicted of attempted bribery if the official action is not in fact influenced by the bribe; see *State v. Kao*.[44] Attempted bribery is often the charge, because in many cases of bribery of officials the official is a law enforcement officer posing as the official, or the actual official is cooperating with the police.

The Federal Foreign Corrupt Practices Act of 1977, 15 U.S.C. § 78, prohibits U.S. companies and individuals from making payments to win contracts from foreign governments. This law was enacted after it was disclosed that the Lockheed Corporation had paid Japan's prime minister more than $1.9 million so that Japan would purchase Lockheed jet aircraft.

Kickbacks

It is not uncommon for parties in a sales transaction to agree that some part of the purchase price paid by the buyer will be returned to the buyer. In new car sales, for example, this practice goes under the name of a "factory rebate" or "dealer participation" bonus. A bank may agree with a car dealer that if the car dealer sends credit customers to the bank for new car loans, part of the interest charged to the customer will be returned to the car dealer. These agreements, commonly called kickbacks, are not all illegal, but many of them are.

In one famous case, Spiro T. Agnew, then vice president of the United States, was forced to resign the vice presidency because of kickback schemes he was involved in as governor of Maryland. Agnew forced engineering firms seeking government contracts to kick back a percentage of the contract amount to various people, including him. He also required every vendor selling cigarettes in the state capitol building to kick back five cents on every pack sold. In addition to being forced to resign, Agnew pleaded guilty to income tax evasion because of his failure to report the kickbacks as income.

Kickbacks can be charged under a state bribery law because the person receiving the kickback is soliciting payment to influence her or his actions. Kickbacks are

THE ADVANTAGES OF FEDERAL PROSECUTION

A December 2003 publication of the U.S. Department of Justice titled "Fighting Urban Crime: The Evolution of Federal-State Collaboration" (NCJ #197040) discussed the following advantages of federal over state prosecution of criminals:

- *Federal Grand Jury:* This body can be called at any time, can be kept in action for as long as three years, can hear hearsay evidence, and is armed with national subpoena power. State grand juries have a shorter duration, "no hearsay" rules, and limited subpoena power.
- *Immunity:* Limited immunity for a grand jury witness conferred by federal prosecutors does not impede later prosecution of the witness for perjury, obstruction of justice, or contempt. Most states have only blanket transactional immunity, which provides less flexibility and leverage against potential witnesses.
- *Search Warrants:* Federal standards for obtaining a search warrant are generally lower than those of most states.
- *Preventive Detention:* The federal bail statute provides for preventive detention in a range of circumstances. State laws do not have such provisions.
- *Electronic Surveillance:* Most states require a higher burden of proof for wiretaps than the federal government.
- *Witness Protection:* In contrast to the well-developed federal witness protection program, most states do not have such a program.
- *Accomplice Testimony:* Federal rules permit conviction on the basis of an accomplice's uncorroborated testimony. State rules generally do not.
- *Discovery:* Federal rules provide that a statement by a government witness need not be made available to the defense until the witness has testified at trial. Also, the defense has no entitlement to a witness list before trial or to interview government witnesses prior to trial. Most state rules provide otherwise.

It should also be recognized that federal prosecutors generally have much more money than state prosecutors to spend on investigations and trials.

also covered under the Foreign Corrupt Practices Act of 1977, discussed previously, and kickback agreements between a contractor and a federal procurement officer or other employee are prohibited under the federal bribery and anti-gratuity statute, 18 U.S.C. § 201. However, any payment received by the official must be made "for an official act." In *United States v. Valdes*,[45] the court held that a gratuity is an unlawful payment "for an official act" only if it was paid in order to influence some pending public question. In *Valdes* an FBI agent posing as a judge paid a District of Columbia police inspector $50 to run the names of four fictitious people through a law enforcement database to see if they had any outstanding warrants. The court held that the inspector's use of the government database was not an "official act" under Section 201(c)(1)(B), because it was not intended to have any effect on any pending charge or issue.

Mail Fraud

People who commit crimes involving fraud on another person can usually be prosecuted under state criminal fraud laws. However, when they use the U.S. mail or any other interstate delivery system such as Federal Express or United Parcel Service to defraud a victim, they can be prosecuted under the federal mail fraud statute (18 U.S.C. § 1341–1346). In 1994, Congress expanded the **mail fraud** crime to include "any matter or thing whatever to be sent or delivered by private or commercial interstate carrier." Any fraudulent scheme, whatever its purpose or method, that uses any of these delivery services can be prosecuted as a felony under the mail fraud statute.

mail fraud A fraudulent scheme, no matter its purpose or method, that uses either private or public delivery service.

Incidental use of the mail or other interstate carrier does not violate the mail fraud statute. For example, in *United States v. Maze*,[46] the U.S. Supreme Court held the mail fraud act was not applicable to a defendant who stole his roommate's credit card and made local purchases. The merchants who sold the goods sent their invoices through the mail for payment from the credit card company, and based on this use of the mails, the federal prosecutor charged the defendant under the mail fraud statute. The Supreme Court said the merchants' use of the mail did not trigger the mail fraud statute because the mails were not used to perpetrate the theft or fraud, but were only incidental to the crime.

Honest Services Fraud

The wire fraud act (discussed in Chapter 15) prohibits any scheme to defraud another by use of wire services. A **wire fraud** scheme is defined to include a scheme to deprive another of the "intangible right of honest services." This definition was added to the wire and mail fraud acts because of the Supreme Court's holding in *McNally v. United States*,[47] which limited the scope of the fraud statutes to deprivations of money or property. The fraud statutes can thus be used to prosecute persons whose scheme is designed not to take money from another, but to deprive him or her of the right to the "honest services" of some person.

wire fraud A fraudulent scheme that uses interstate or international wire or other electronic communications.

The U.S. Supreme Court limited the scope of honest services fraud in the 2010 case of *Skilling v. United States*,[48] discussed more fully in Chapter 15. As a result, prosecutions under the federal mail and wire fraud acts based on deprivations of the right to honest services will be limited to classic property crimes, where the defendant defrauds another out of money or property, and bribery or kickback schemes. Prosecutions for breach only of a fiduciary duty, as was the case in *Skilling*, can no longer be brought under honest services fraud.

Summary

- A RICO conviction requires proof that an enterprise existed that engaged in racketeering activity, that the defendants were members of the enterprise and participated in the activity, and that the enterprise had a pattern of racketeering activity.

- The federal RICO adds the jurisdictional requirement that the racketeering activities affected interstate commerce. Most courts now hold that any effect on interstate commerce satisfies the jurisdictional requirement.

- Money can be laundered by transporting it to another country, buying cash or bearer instruments, passing it through a legitimate business, or using underground banking like the Hawala system.
- The mail fraud act, wire fraud act, money laundering act, and the RICO act are principal federal laws that are used to combat organized crime.
- Money laundering by transporting the proceeds of unlawful activity requires knowledge that the purpose of the transportation is to conceal the origin of the money.

- Proceeds for purpose of the money laundering statutes means profits gained from unlawful activities.
- Because lower-ranking members of crime families were the ones usually arrested with specific crimes such as murder or extortion, heads of organizations could not be prosecuted without testimony from those arrested. Such testimony was rarely given.
- The grand jury system, witness protection program, immunity doctrines, and federal court discovery rules all make prosecution in federal courts advantageous.

Key Terms

Racketeer Influenced and Corrupt Organizations Act (RICO), p. 501

Continuing Criminal Enterprise Statute (CCE), p. 501

witness protection program, p. 505
witness tampering, p. 506
money laundering, p. 506
CTRs (currency transaction reports), p. 509

Travel Act, p. 511
mail fraud, p. 516
wire fraud, p. 516

Case Analysis and Writing Exercises

1. The Chicago "Outfit" is undoubtedly a "criminal enterprise" under the RICO laws. But the Outfit operates through "street crews," run by a member of the Outfit, but under that person's power and control. For some kinds of crimes, like murder, only the Outfit may authorize commission of the crime by a street crew. The Chicago defendants in the "Family Secrets Case," discussed in this chapter, were convicted of violating RICO to advance the interests of the "criminal enterprise" of the "street crews." Can they also be convicted of RICO violations for advancing the interests of the Outfit, even if crimes committed in furtherance of the "criminal enterprise" were many of the same crimes committed in furtherance of the "street crews" criminal

enterprise? *See United States v. Schiro*, 679 F.3d 521 (7th Cir. 2012), *cert. denied*, 133 S. Ct. 363 (2012).

2. Prosecutors like charging conspiracy crimes, in part because they can charge a defendant with both the underlying crime and the conspiracy (see Chapter 4), and if convicted, get tougher sentences. California makes it a crime to participate in a criminal street gang, which is defined to mean any group having a common name and a pattern of criminal gang activity. Can a gang member be convicted of conspiracy to commit the crime of criminal street gang participation? The court in *People v. Johnson*, 140 Cal. Rptr. 3d 711 (Cal. App. 2012) said no. Why not? The California Supreme Court accepted review of the decision, 282 P.3d

1216 (2012). What do you think should be the result? See 2013 WL 3746124 for the California Supreme Court's decision.

3. Most states have a sentence enhancement for committing a crime if the intent in doing so is "for the benefit of a criminal street gang." Assume a defendant, a known criminal street gang member, is convicted of sexual assault on a female victim. When would that crime be "for the benefit" of the street gang? *See People v. Kidd*, 2012 WL 243250 (Cal. App. 2012).

4. Is playing "Texas Hold'em" gambling under federal Law? Surprisingly (perhaps), one federal district court judge held it was not in a 2012 case,

United States v. Dicristina, 886 F. Supp.2d 164 (E.D. N.Y. 2012). There, the defendant operated an establishment where poker, mainly Texas Hold'em, was played. Federal investigators charged him with violation of 18 U.S.C. § 1955, the Illegal Gambling Business Act. A jury convicted the defendant under the Act, but on motions to dismiss the indictment made after the verdict, the court held the Act did not cover Texas Hold'em games. Why did the court reach that conclusion? Do you agree? The case was appealed to the Circuit Court of Appeals. What do you think that court decided? For the opinion, go to 2013 WL 3984970 (2nd Cir. 2013).

Endnotes

1. *United States v. Chao Fan Xu*, 706 F.3d 965 (9th Cir. 2013).
2. See the 2002 U.S. Department of Justice publication NCJ 190351, "Responding to Gangs: Evaluation and Research."
3. See the *New York Times*, "Gangs Without Borders, Fierce and Resilient, Confront the Law," September 26, 2004.
4. See Chapter 19 of this book for materials on tax evasion.
5. Most, if not all, state RICO statutes create three distinct crimes: (1) using or investing the proceeds of racketeering activity, (2) acquiring an interest in property or an enterprise engaged in racketeering activity, and (3) conducting or participating in the enterprise. Each of these crimes requires proof of a fact the others do not and can therefore result in multiple convictions without violating the Double Jeopardy Clause. (See Chapter 7 of this book for additional material on the Double Jeopardy Clause.)

   Courts have uniformly held not only that the substantive violations may be charged but also that the corresponding conspiracy violations may be charged. In addition, the underlying predicate offenses may also be charged. See *Iannelli v. United States,* 420 U.S. 770 (1975).
6. 921 N.E.2d 570 (NY 2009).
7. 2010 WL 2741534 (Tex. App. 2010).
8. 75 Cal. Rptr. 3d 200 (Cal. App. 2008).
9. 129 S. Ct. 2237 (2009).
10. 695 F.3d 1125 (10th Cir. 2012).
11. 380 F.3d 251 (6th Cir. 2004).
12. 529 U.S. 598 (2000).
13. 529 U.S. 848 (2000).
14. 545 U.S. 1 (2005).
15. 491 F.3d 25 (1st Cir. 2007), *cert. denied,* 552 U.S. 1297 (2008).
16. Public Law No. 91-452, 84 Stat. 938.
17. 18 U.S.C. § 1512.
18. For additional material on witnesses, see Thomas Gardner and Terry Anderson, *Criminal Evidence, Principles and Cases,* 8th ed., Chapter 5 (Belmont, CA: Wadsworth, 2013). The May 2004 *FBI Law Enforcement Bulletin* article "Hiding in Plain Sight: A Peek into the Witness Protection Program," is an excellent description of the witness protection program.
19. 130 S. Ct. 1011 (2009).
20. *U.S. Department of the Treasury,* "2000–2005 Strategic Plan," p. 1.
21. 11 U.S.C. § 5311–5332.
22. 18 U.S.C. § 1956.
23. 18 U.S.C. § 5332.
24. In what has been called the biggest drug bust in history, the United States invaded Panama in 1989 to stop the use of Panama as a money-laundering center.
25. 450 F.3d 366 (8th Cir. 2006).
26. 543 U.S. 209 (2005).
27. 467 F.3d 1 (1st Cir. 2006).
28. 466 F.3d 79 (2nd Cir. 2006).
29. 128 S. Ct. 1994 (2008).
30. 128 S. Ct., at 2005.
31. 565 F.3d 73 (2nd Cir. 2009).
32. 587 F.3d 509 (2nd Cir. 2009).
33. 128 S. Ct. 2020 (2008).

34. 128 S. Ct. at 2024.

35. 658 F.3d 333 (3rd Cir. 2011).

36. 510 U.S. 135, 136 (1994).

37. 467 F.3d 1 (6th Cir. 2006).

38. See *United States v. United States Currency in Amount of Two Hundred Forty-Eight Thousand Dollars,* 2004 WL 958010 (E.D.N.Y. 2004).

39. *United States v. Winslow,* 962 R2d 1488 (9th Cir. 1992).

40. *United States v. Briggs,* 700 F.2d 408 (7th Cir. 1983), *cert. denied,* 103 S. Ct. 2463 (1983).

41. *United States v. Hanon,* 428 F.2d 101 (8th Cir. 1970).

42. *Mcintosh v. United States,* 385 F.2d 274 (8th Cir. 1967).

43. *United States v. Bernaugh,* 969 F.2d 858 (10th Cir. 1992).

44. 531 N.W.2de 555 (Neb. App. 1995).

45. 475 F.3d 1319 (D.C. Cir. 2007).

46. 94 S. Ct. 603 (1974).

47. 483 U.S. 350 (1987).

48. 130 S. Ct. 2896 (2010).

Immigration Crimes, Contempt, and Other Crimes Against Government

Norma Jean Gargasz/Alamy

The border wall divides Nogales, Arizona (left), and Nogales, Sonora, Mexico. At one time, the area was referred to as Ambos Nogales.

OUTLINE

Immigration Crimes

Criminal Charges for Illegal Immigration Offenses

Contempt

Civil Contempt

Criminal Contempt

Contempt Is a Specific Intent Crime That Requires Proof of Intentional Wrongdoing

Language by a Witness or Attorney That Would Justify a Contempt Finding

Contempt and the Crime of Failure to Appear (Bail Jumping)

Crimes by Public Officials

Some Crimes Committed by Public Officials and Others

Crimes Against Government

Espionage

Obstruction of Justice

Tax Evasion

Other Criminal Violations

LEARNING OBJECTIVES

In this chapter we discuss various crimes in which a government body or court is the complaining party. The learning objectives for Chapter 19 are the following:

- List the various kinds of conduct made criminal under the immigration laws.
- Distinguish civil contempt from criminal contempt.
- Make the connection between a gift and an official act required for conviction under the bribery laws.
- State the reason the U.S. Supreme Court declared invalid some provisions in the Arizona laws directed at illegal aliens.
- State the limits on summary contempt convictions.

oreigners who wish to immigrate to the United States must apply for and receive permission, in the form of various kinds of visas issued by U.S. consulates in the applicant's home country. Once a person comes to the United States as a lawful alien and has been granted permanent resident status, the steps toward becoming a naturalized citizen may begin.

Not every request for a visa is granted, and as a result many people resort to other means of entering the United States. The immigration laws discussed in this chapter highlight some of the many criminal laws that are tied to illegal attempts to enter or remain in this country.

One method for obtaining lawful alien presence in the United States is marriage to a U.S. citizen. If a foreign national and a U.S. citizen decide to marry, the foreign national or the U.S. citizen may either apply for a "fiancé" visa or, if the couple marry abroad, an "alien spouse" visa. If the decision to marry occurs while the alien is lawfully in the United States, the alien can apply for a change of status to a permanent resident.

The marriage exception can be abused by fraudulent marriages, and such marriages are made a criminal violation under federal immigration laws. Entering into a fraudulent marriage with a U.S. citizen is a crime for both parties to the fraudulent marriage, as well as for any "brokers" who facilitate the false marriage. An example is the 2012 case of *United States v. Adriatico-Fernandez.*[1] The defendant in that case arranged several "marriages" between U.S. citizens and foreign nationals, in which the U.S. citizen received a substantial "down payment" when the marriage occurred, plus monthly payments until the "spouse" obtained permanent resident status. Upon conviction under the immigration laws the U.S. citizens faced fines and imprisonment, and the foreign "spouses" were deported.

Many illegal aliens, such as those who enter the United States illegally across our borders, have been in this country for many years, and have entered into legitimate marriages with U.S. citizens. In the past, the only way illegal aliens could use marriage as a way to change their status to legal resident was to leave the United States, and apply for an alien spouse visa. However, once the illegal alien left the United States, immigration laws banned that person from re-entry for 10 years. In 2012 President Obama approved changes to the 10-year ban policy, effective March 4, 2013, which will permit an illegal alien in the United States to seek a waiver of the ban based on "extreme hardship" suffered by family members if the alien is forced to stay out of the country for the 10-year period. In that case, the illegal alien may seek permanent resident status without the 10-year delay.

In this chapter we will study immigration crimes, because these crimes are essentially crimes against government. We will study civil and criminal contempt and how those charges are used by government. We will also learn about other crimes directed against government, such as perjury, espionage, and tax evasion, where the criminal laws are used to protect the integrity or financial security of governments.

Immigration Crimes

In 1997, the Center for Immigration Studies estimated that there were more than 5 million illegal immigrants in the United States. Ten years later, in 2007, the U.S. government estimated that the number of illegal immigrants living and working in the United States was over 12 million. Despite efforts to secure the borders of the United States, the wave of illegal immigrants was increasing. Most experts believed at least 500,000 and perhaps as many as 1,000,000 illegal immigrants crossed the borders each year. The U.S. Congress passed bills starting in 2006 designed to construct both actual and "virtual" barriers on the 2,000-mile U.S.-Mexico border. Actual walls, varying from chain-link fence to concrete and steel, have been constructed at key points along the border, covering perhaps one-third of the border. Virtual borders, consisting of cameras and other electronic monitoring devices, have also been put in place, though not in the quantity anticipated by sponsors of that barrier.

Comprehensive immigration reform has been debated by Congress, but no legislation has been passed. In 2010, Arizona passed a state statute aimed at illegal immigrants, which permitted police to detain persons suspected of being in this country illegally and also required aliens to carry valid immigration registration documents; failure to carry valid alien registration documents thus became a crime under Arizona law. States that pass laws aimed at immigration problems may run afoul of the Supremacy Clause of the U.S. Constitution. Under that clause, if the

Constitution has expressly given Congress the power to regulate a field, such as immigration and naturalization of aliens, the power of the states to pass laws in that area is preempted by any congressional acts. In the 2012 case of *Arizona v. United States*[2] the U.S. Supreme Court held that some of the provisions in the Arizona law conflicted with federal immigration laws, and were thus preempted by federal law. It struck down the state requirement that aliens carry and produce valid alien registration papers, as well as the provision permitting law enforcement officers to make warrantless arrests of suspected illegal aliens who might be removable under federal law. The Supreme Court did uphold one provision in the Arizona law, which requires state police officers to check with Immigration and Customs Enforcement ("ICE") to determine the immigration status of persons lawfully detained. That provision does not violate federal immigration law, the Court held, since it applies only to persons lawfully stopped or detained by state police officers where the state officers have "reasonable suspicion" that the person is an illegal alien. The Court noted that under the Arizona law, "reasonable suspicion" cannot be based on the detained person's race, color, or national origin, and that the presentation of a valid Arizona driver's license creates a presumption of legality.

Illegal immigrants enter this country through many methods. The United States has thousands of miles of borders with Mexico and Canada, and many illegal immigrants simple walk across the border into the United States. Others are smuggled in ships docking at any of the many ports on the Atlantic and Pacific oceans. Still others arrive under student, visitor, work, or business visas and remain after their visas have expired. It is estimated that 30 percent of all illegal immigrants in this country arrived here legally but then overstayed their visas. Because some of the 9/11 terrorists were in the United States under expired visas, efforts were made by the government to develop a system to monitor persons here under a visa. However, because of the prohibitive cost of such a system, and the lengthy lead time for it to become effective, there is not presently in place a reliable method to track those in the United States under an expired visa.

Illegal aliens generally come to the United States for work. Many "melt" into society and stay in the country for years. Forged green cards and other documents necessary to remain in this country are often used by illegal aliens to secure employment and housing. While many illegal aliens remain in the United States without attempting to change their illegal status, some attempt to obtain legal alien status.

The U.S. Congress has in the past granted limited amnesty to some illegal aliens. In 1986 it passed a law granting amnesty and legal resident status to persons who illegally entered the United States prior to 1982. In 2000 the INS released a report that while about 2.7 million aliens were given legal status under that law, the number of illegal aliens in the United States actually increased. This was in part because family members of those granted legal status entered the country illegally to join their relatives.

In 2013 eight members of Congress, called the "gang of eight," proposed immigration reform laws that would make it possible for many of the estimated 11.5 million illegal aliens in the United States to obtain lawful status. Under the proposals, any alien in the United States as of December 3, 2011, may apply for Registered Provisional Immigrant status, including the applicant's spouse and children. After

APPREHENDING THE "WORST OF THE WORST" OF ILLEGAL IMMIGRANTS: THE "SECURE COMMUNITIES" PROGRAM

The "Secure Communities" program was begun under the Bush administration, and continued under the Obama administration. The purpose of the program is to help law enforcement officers identify the "worst of the worst" of violent criminals, drug traffickers, gang members, and other dangerous aliens by checking the immigration history of a person arrested. Law enforcement officers holding a person may either contact the Immigration and Customs Enforcement Department (ICE), or have the person's fingerprints run through an immigration database under the "Secure Communities" program. The latter process is much faster, and costs nothing.

As of July 31, 2012, the Immigration and Customs Enforcement Department reported that 97 percent of the 3,181 law enforcement jurisdictions in the United States have activated the information sharing system of the Secure Communities program. ICE also reported that 159,409 convicted criminal aliens have been removed from the United States under the program.

6 years, the application can be renewed, and after 10 years the applicant can apply for permanent resident status. Then, after 3 more years, the applicant may seek to become a naturalized citizen. To qualify for this program the alien must have committed no serious crimes, and must show proof of income of at least 125 percent of poverty level. In June of 2013 the Senate passed an immigration reform bill based on the above model. It also contained an expedited process for the "dreamers," children brought illegally into the United States who graduated from high school or college, or served in the U.S. armed forces. The House of Representatives must also approve the bill for it to be sent to the President for his signature.

Illegal aliens can place significant economic pressure on state social service programs. In response to this, a few states have passed laws limiting the availability of social services to illegal aliens. Most recently, in 2006 and 2011 Georgia passed laws that declared illegal aliens ineligible for such services, required employers to verify the legal status of workers before hiring them, and required police to inform the INS when illegal aliens were arrested for crimes. It is unclear what effect the Supreme Court's decision in *Arizona v. United States* will have on these state laws, though in 2013 the Supreme Court denied review of a federal court's opinion declaring many sections of the Alabama immigration law invalid.[3]

Criminal Charges for Illegal Immigration Offenses

There are many criminal laws aimed at illegal immigration. Violators of these laws can be charged in criminal courts, or they can be deported after a hearing in an immigration court. In some cases, immigration officials may simply transport the illegal alien to a border and release that person without formal prosecution. The chart shows some of the various crimes that can be charged for immigration offenses, and the maximum punishments possible if convicted (see 8 U.S.C. § 1301 and the following).

Felonies

- Failure of alien to deport after order to do so (10 years)
- Counterfeiting alien papers or application to enter (5 years)
- Bringing in or harboring illegal aliens (5 years)
- Illegal entry, second offense (2 years)
- Reentry of deported alien (2 years)
- Aiding subversive alien to enter (5 years)
- Importing alien for immoral purposes (10 years)

Misdemeanors

- Failure to register (6 months)
- Failure to notify of change of address (30 days)
- Making false statements (6 months)
- First illegal entry (6 months)
- Knowingly hiring an illegal alien (6 months)

Deportation laws, now called removal laws, provide for removal of a person from the United States for a variety of reasons. Most directly, 8 U.S.C. § 1225 states that an immigration officer who inspects an immigrant at the place of entry may order the removal of the person if the person is inadmissible for any of the reasons set forth in 8 U.S.C. § 1182. In some situations an immigration judge may hold a hearing on inadmissibility, though in others the decision that a person is inadmissible is not reviewable.

A person within the United States and who is not a citizen or legal resident may be removed for any of the many reasons set forth in 8 U.S.C. § 1227. These include violation of entry conditions, overstaying a visa, helping smuggle in other illegal immigrants, commission of crimes of "moral turpitude," which carry a sentence of one year or more in prison, multiple convictions, or conviction of an aggravated or violent felony. Failing to register as a sex offender, using false documents, trafficking in controlled substances, or committing crimes of domestic violence are also reasons for removal of an illegal immigrant. During the removal process the alien may be detained pending removal, and removal is to occur within 90 days of the removal order.

Many persons removed from the United States subsequently reenter this country, usually illegally. Because of this, a federal statute, 8 U.S.C. § 1231(a)(5), permits immigration officials to reinstate former removal orders where any person reenters illegally. Such reinstatement orders are not subject to review.

Reports show that more than a million people are detained annually for violations of the immigration laws; most of these people are removed to their home countries. In some cases, the illegal alien's home country does not want and will not consent to the return of the alien. Federal Statute 8 U.S.C. § 1231(a)(6) permits immigration authorities to detain an alien after a removal order has been entered. In *Zadvydas v. Davis*,[4] the U.S. Supreme Court held that such a detention could not extend beyond the "reasonable time" necessary to remove the alien. In *Tuan Thai v. Ashcroft*,[5] the court found that a detention for more than 16 months, with no prospect of removal, was unreasonable, and ordered the government to release the alien. In *Suarez-Martinez v. Rozos*,[6] the U.S. Supreme Court held that the reasoning of *Zadvydas* applied also to aliens detained after having been convicted of a crime that would result in deportation, even though the homeland of the detainee would not accept the detainee's return. The Court reasoned that notwithstanding the above, a person cannot constitutionally be detained indefinitely and that a reasonable time to detain an alien while deportation is pending should not exceed six months.

Illegal entry or reentry into the United States accounts for about 40 percent of immigration investigations. Harboring or bringing in foreign citizens with forged or inadequate documents accounts for about 38 percent of the criminal offenses investigated. Misusing visas or permits accounts for approximately 8 percent of the offenses, and fraud and forgery involving passports and other documents comprise another 8 percent, according to the INS.

INTENT UNDER IMMIGRATION LAW VIOLATIONS

Many immigration crimes require the government to prove some mental state of the defendant, such as "knowingly," "deliberately," or "intentionally." Where that is the case, federal courts have sometimes reached different results on how the required mental state must be proved. The following federal statutes and decisions illustrate this problem.

Marriage Fraud

8 U.S.C. § 1325(c) makes it is a criminal violation for any person who "knowingly enters into a marriage for the purpose of evading any provision of the immigration laws." What does "knowingly" require the government to prove? Some federal courts have held that the government must prove the alien defendant had no intent to "establish a life" with the U.S. citizen. Under that reading of the statute, even if the purpose of the marriage was to obtain resident status in the United States, the intent to "establish a lifetime relationship" would save the marriage from being fraudulent. *See United States v. Gonzales*, 404 F.3d 96 (1st Cir. 2005), and *United States v. Yang*, 603 F.3d 1024 (8th Cir. 2010). More recent cases have held that the government need only prove that the marriage was entered with the purpose to obtain lawful resident status. The "intent to establish a life" would only be a factor in determining the "purpose" of the marriage. *See United States v. Ortiz-Mendez*, 634 F.3d 837 (5th Cir. 2011).

Harboring Illegal Aliens

8 U.S.C. § 1324 makes it a crime for any person "knowing or in reckless disregard" of the fact a person is an illegal alien to "harbor or shield from detection" the illegal alien. Some courts have held that the statute is violated if a person takes "any means" to shield the alien from discovery by the government. *See United States v. Ye,* 588 F.3d 411 (7th Cir. 2009). Other courts have held that the government must show the defendant intended to give the illegal alien "refuge" or "safe haven" from the government. Thus, in *United States v. Costello*, 666 F.3d 1040 (7th Cir. 2012), the court reversed a conviction for harboring an illegal alien when all the defendant did was permit the alien, her boyfriend, to live with her in her home.

Contempt

Contempt is the willful disregard of the authority of a court of law or of a legislative body. Acts that delay, impede, or frustrate the functioning or the dignity of a court or legislative body may be held to be in contempt of that body. The deliberate, willful, and contumacious (obstinate) disobedience of a lawful order is a common reason for finding a person in contempt. Contempt that occurs in the presence of the court, often called "direct" contempt, can be punished summarily, that is, by an immediate finding of contempt and appropriate sentence. However, courts commonly require that the contempt occur completely in the court's presence for this summary action to be upheld. That is because actions taken outside the presence of the court are not personally observed by the judge, and thus must be proved in the usual manner. In that case, the usual procedures for proving facts must be followed. An example of this principle is the 2010 case of *Scialdone v. Commonwealth.*[7] In that case two attorneys introduced into evidence documents that appeared to have been altered. The trial judge conducted an investigation of how the documents were altered, which included questioning witnesses who may have been involved in the alteration. The judge concluded the attorneys altered the document, and that offering the altered document was criminal contempt. It summarily sentenced the attorneys to short jail terms. On appeal, the Virginia Supreme Court reversed the contempt convictions, holding that because some of the facts needed for the contempt charge did not occur in the presence of the court, the summary finding of contempt was improper.

Civil Contempt

Contempt is classified as either civil or criminal. **Civil contempt** is used to compel people to do something they are obligated to do. **Criminal contempt** can be used to punish people for what they have done. Civil or criminal contempt is sometimes used in divorce cases, child custody cases, and other matters to compel people to comply with court orders.

A contempt order is treated as a civil contempt if the purpose of the contempt is to compel compliance with a court order. In such a case, confinement is permitted until the person confined complies with the order. However, where it becomes clear compliance will not or cannot occur, a civil contempt order of confinement is normally lifted. An example of this kind of contempt is the 2011 case of *Warmkessel v. Heffnee.*[8] There, the defendant failed to pay child support, and was sentenced to three months in jail. Pennsylvania law provides that imprisonment for civil contempt is permitted, but requires the sentencing judge to set a "purge" amount, the payment of which will obtain release of the defendant from prison.

In the 2011 case of *Turner v. Rogers,*[9] the U.S. Supreme Court for the first time considered the question of the right to appointed counsel in civil contempt cases, where the failure of a defendant to comply with a civil order resulted in imprisonment. In *Turner* a defendant owed $5,728.76 in back child support to the mother of his child. He was brought before a judge, and because he did not pay the amount owed, was sentenced to 12 months in jail, which sentence he could "purge" only by paying the full amount due. The defendant contended his imprisonment violated the Constitution, because he was not represented by counsel at the contempt hearing. State courts disagreed, and the U.S. Supreme Court granted review.

The Court held that the Sixth Amendment, which requires appointment of counsel for indigent defendants in criminal cases, did not apply to civil contempt cases. However, under the Due Process Clause, because of the prospect of incarceration, an attorney must be provided for an indigent defendant unless certain procedural protections were provided to the defendant. Those include (1) informing the defendant his ability to comply with the court order was a "critical issue" in the contempt proceeding, (2) use of a form to determine the defendant's financial ability to comply with the order, (3) an opportunity at the hearing for the defendant to respond to questions about his financial ability, and (4) an express finding by the court that the defendant possessed the financial ability to comply with the order. Since that did not happen in this case, the Court held, the defendant's incarceration violated the Due Process Clause.

Criminal Contempt

Criminal contempt is designed to protect the public interest by ensuring the effective functioning of the judicial and legislative systems. In 1968, the U.S. Supreme Court stated in *Bloom v. Illinois* that "criminal contempt is a crime in the ordinary sense; it is a violation of the law, a public wrong which is punishable by fine or imprisonment or both."[10] The Court quoted Justice Oliver Wendell Holmes in stating that "these contempts are infractions of the law, visited with punishment as such. If such acts are not criminal, we are in error as to the most fundamental characteristic of crimes as that word has been understood in English speech."

The defendant in the *Bloom* case was sentenced to 24 months in prison for submitting a falsely prepared will for probate. His demand for a jury trial was denied. In holding that in serious contempt cases the defendant had a right to a jury, the Court stated:

> Prosecution for contempt plays a significant role in the proper functioning of our judicial system; but despite the important values which the contempt power protects, courts and legislatures have gradually eroded the power of judges to try contempts of their own authority. In modern times, procedures in criminal contempt cases have come to mirror those used in ordinary criminal cases.[11]

Criminal contempt is treated as a crime, as stated above, which includes application of the Double Jeopardy Clause. In *United States v. Dixon*,[12] the U.S. Supreme Court held that a prior conviction of a defendant on a criminal contempt charge for violation of a protection order barred subsequent prosecution by the government for the crime that constituted the violation of the order. However, in a 2010 case the U.S. Supreme Court reversed its decision to grant a petition for certiorari on the question of whether a subsequent criminal contempt charge brought by a woman who obtained a protective order violated the Double Jeopardy Clause. In *In re Robertson*,[13] a federal court of appeals upheld a criminal contempt order based on the defendant's assault on the woman who filed the action. In an earlier proceeding the woman had obtained a civil protection order against the defendant, who subsequently violated the order on more than one occasion. The defendant and the government had entered into a plea agreement on criminal charges related to those violations, and the defendant served time in prison. The defendant thus argued that under *Dixon* the criminal contempt prosecution brought by the woman was barred by the Double Jeopardy Clause. The Supreme Court initially granted certiorari on that question, 130 S. Ct. 1011, but subsequently voted to deny certiorari as "improvidently granted," 130 S. Ct. 2184 (2010). Four Justices dissented, believing the subsequent criminal contempt conviction violated the Double Jeopardy Clause.[14]

Contempt Is a Specific Intent Crime That Requires Proof of Intentional Wrongdoing

In the 1976 case of *Commonwealth v. Washington,* the Supreme Court of Pennsylvania quoted other courts, holding,

> There is no contempt unless there is some sort of wrongful intent. *Offutt v. United States,* 98 U.S. App. D.C. 69, 232 F.2d 69, 72 (1956), *cert, denied* 351 U.S. 988, 76 S. Ct. 1049, 100 L. Ed. 1501 (1956). "[A] degree of intentional wrongdoing is an ingredient of the offense of criminal contempt." *In re Brown,* 147 U.S. App. D.C. 156, 454 F.2d 999, 1006 (1971). "Willfulness is, of course, an element of criminal contempt and must be proved beyond a reasonable doubt." *United States v. Greyhound Corporation,* 508 F.2d 529, 531 (7th Cir. 1974).[15]

In the *Washington* case, the defendant overslept and failed to appear on time at his trial. In reversing his contempt conviction, the Pennsylvania Supreme Court held,

> Were we to accept the prosecution's argument, any person, judge, attorney, witness, or party, who comes into the courtroom late can be held guilty of contempt of court, regardless of the reason for the lateness. We cannot accept such a conclusion. Unless the evidence establishes an intentional disobedience or an intentional neglect of the lawful process of the court, no contempt has been proven. Such is the case here. Judgment of sentence reversed.

> In the 1976 case of *People v. Harris,* the defendant failed to pay a fine imposed for a prior criminal conviction.[16] Although the defendant showed that he had no money and was unemployed, he was found in contempt for failure to pay the fine. The Illinois Court of Appeals reversed the contempt finding, holding that there was no showing that the defendant willfully placed himself in a position to be unable to pay the fine.

Language by a Witness or Attorney That Would Justify a Contempt Finding

While answering a question on cross-examination, a witness used the expression *chicken shit.* As a result, the witness was found to be in direct contempt for the use of this term in a courtroom. The U.S. Supreme Court reversed the defendant's conviction in the case of *Eaton v. City of Tulsa,* holding,

> This single isolated usage of street vernacular, not directed at the judge or any officer of the court, cannot constitutionally support the conviction of criminal contempt. "The vehemence of language used is not alone the measure of the power to punish for contempt. The fires which it kindles must constitute an imminent, not merely a likely,

threat to the administration of justice." *Craig v. Harney,* 331 U.S. 367, 376 (1947). In using the expletive in answering the question on cross-examination "it is not charged that [petitioner] here disobeyed any valid court order, talked loudly, acted boisterously, or attempted to prevent the judge or any other officer of the court from carrying on his court duties." *Holt v. Virginia,* 381 U.S. 131, 136 (1965); see also *In re Little,* 404 U.S. 553 (1972). In the circumstances, the use of the expletive thus cannot be held to "constitute an imminent … threat to the administration of justice."[17]

Contempt and the Crime of Failure to Appear (Bail Jumping)

In all states and in the federal court system, a criminal defendant free on bail may be charged with criminal contempt if he or she intentionally fails to appear at a scheduled hearing in his or her criminal case. The penalty for bail jumping is generally determined by the severity of the underlying crime charged. For example, in *Curley v. Commonwealth,*[18] the court reversed a conviction of first-degree bail jumping because the underlying criminal charge had been reduced from a felony to a misdemeanor before the bail jumping occurred. Under most state bail jumping statutes, the crime is committed if the defendant is free on bail as a result of being charged with a crime. If the defendant does not appear at a scheduled hearing on

CONTEMPT

Classification	Type	Procedure Used to Punish
Civil contempt is remedial and is used to force people to do what they are lawfully required to do (answer questions, identify themselves, pay support money as ordered by a divorce court, and so on).	Direct contempt is committed in the immediate presence and view or hearing of the court or legislative body.	Summary process: Only direct contempt may be punished summarily. If the court or legislative body does not act at the time the contempt is committed, notice and an opportunity for a hearing must be given to the person.
"Criminal contempt is a crime in the ordinary sense; it is a violation of the law, a public wrong which is punishable by fine or imprisonment or both." U.S. Supreme Court in *Bloom v. Illinois,* 391 U.S. 194, 88 S. Ct. 1477 (1968).	Constructive, or indirect, contempt is committed out of the presence or hearing of the court or legislative body. Although the matter or incident does not occur in or near the presence of a court or legislative body, it obstructs or delays the functioning of the court or the legislative body.[a]	Contempt hearings: Notice and an opportunity for a hearing (plus other due process rights) must be given for constructive (indirect contempt) and for direct contempt when the court or legislative body does not act immediately.

[a]State legislatures and the U.S. Congress have the constitutional power to hold persons in contempt, as well as the authority to issue subpoenas, grant immunity from prosecution, and demand within the law that persons appearing before them answer questions.

the criminal charge, he or she can be convicted of bail jumping, even if the criminal charge is subsequently dismissed.[19]

Most states provide an affirmative defense to bail jumping if the defendant can show that his or her failure to appear at a scheduled hearing was the result of "uncontrollable circumstances" not created by the defendant. Hospitalization for a serious illness would be an example of this defense.

Crimes by Public Officials

If all people were angels who lived in peace and harmony with one another, then, as James Madison observed in *The Federalist Papers* of the 1780s, there would be no need for governments. But people are not angels, nor are they governed by angels (as Madison also pointed out more than 200 years ago).

The U.S. Supreme Court observed that "nothing can destroy a government more quickly than its failure to observe its own laws, or worse, its disregard of the charter of its own existence."[20] In 1928, Justice Louis D. Brandeis stated in his dissenting opinion in *Olmstead v. United States:* "Our Government is the potent, the omnipresent teacher. For good or ill, it teaches the whole people by its example. . . . If the Government becomes a lawbreaker, it breeds contempt for law; it invites every man to become a law unto himself; it invites anarchy."[21]

Cicero wrote long ago in *Pro Cluentio 53* that "we are in bondage to the law in order that we may be free." While president of the United States, Calvin Coolidge observed:

> Wherever the law goes, there civilization goes and stays. When the law fails, barbarism flourishes. Whoever scorns the law, whoever brings it into disrespect, whoever connives at its evasion, is an enemy of civilization. Change it if you will . . . but observe it always. That is government.

Some Crimes Committed by Public Officials and Others

Some of the many offenses committed by public officials and private individuals are as follows:

- Unauthorized (or excessive) use of force (assault and battery)
- False imprisonment
- Unauthorized wiretapping (federal felony) or bugging (state offense)
- **Perjury[22] or subornation of perjury** (the crime of perjury consists of knowingly and materially testifying falsely while under oath; the crime of subornation of perjury is inducing or knowingly permitting another person to testify falsely). The federal perjury statute, 18 U.S.C. § 1623, makes it perjury to "knowingly" make a "false material declaration" to a court or grand jury. In *Bronston v. United States,*[23] the U.S. Supreme Court held that an answer that is literally true, but either unresponsive to a question or that creates a false impression, cannot be perjury. For example, if the president of a corporation is asked "Have you ever had a Swiss bank account," and he answered "The company has never had a Swiss bank account," his answer cannot be perjury even though it created the

perjury The crime of knowingly and materially testifying falsely while under oath.

subornation of perjury The crime of inducing or knowingly permitting another person to testify falsely while under oath.

false impression the president did not personally have such an account. In *United States v. Thomas*,[24] the court held the "literal truth" defense was not available to a professional cyclist who gave false answers to a grand jury investigating a company called BALCO about the distribution and use of steroids by athletes. Called before a grand jury, the defendant was asked if she had ever been "given" steroids by a BALCO representative. She testified "no." She was subsequently indicted for perjury under § 1623, and she raised the literal truth defense. She claimed her answer was literally true, because she paid for the steroids, and thus they were not "given" to her. The court said the defense is not available when the witness understands the meaning of the question in the context it was asked, and the answer is false as to that meaning.

- Official misconduct and misconduct in public office (using the powers of one's office to obtain a dishonest advantage for oneself, or falsifying an entry in a record or report)
- Aiding, assisting, or permitting the escape of a prisoner
- Intimidating witnesses, prisoners, or others
- **Tampering with evidence** or falsifying evidence
- **Misprision of felony.** Some states and the federal government have codified this old common law crime. In 1998, Michael Fortier pleaded guilty to misprision of a felony (and other crimes) because he failed to warn officials of the plot to blow up the Alfred P. Murrah Federal Building in Oklahoma City.[25] Federal courts define the crime of misprision of a felony as follows:

> [T]o sustain a conviction . . . for misprision of felony it was incumbent upon the government to prove beyond a reasonable doubt (1) that . . . the principal had committed and completed the felony alleged; . . . (2) that the defendant had full knowledge of that fact; (3) that he failed to notify the authorities; and (4) that he took . . . affirmative steps to conceal the crime of the principal.[26]

- Bribery. The U.S. Supreme Court held that to prove a violation of the federal gratuity statute (18 U.S.C.A. § 201(c)(1)(A)), the government must prove a link between the thing of value given to a public official and a specific "official act" for which it was given.[27]

The federal court in the case of *United States v. Arthur* described the crime of bribery as follows:

> Not every gift, favor or contribution to a government or political official constitutes bribery. It is universally recognized that bribery occurs only if the gift is coupled with a particular criminal intent. . . . That intent is not supplied merely by the fact that the gift was motivated by some generalized hope or expectation of ultimate benefit on the part of the donor. . . . "Bribery" imports the notion of some more or less specific quid pro quo for which the gift or contribution is offered or accepted.[28]

- Extortion by a public official or employee in violation of the Hobbs Act, 18 U.S.C.A. § 1951. The public official or employee obtains payment because of his or her office and by use of "force, violence or fear." In *United States v. Swift*, the defendant was a city sewer director who received payments from a contractor

tampering with evidence Knowingly altering or damaging evidence intended to be used in a court proceeding.

misprision of felony Failing to report knowledge of a felony to the appropriate authorities.

in return for approval of payments made for work done on sewage pumping stations.[29] Another example of extortion under the Hobbs Act is as follows:

EXAMPLE

A bail bond agent who was also an alderman in a small town conspired with members of the police department to extort money from travelers passing through town in exchange for dismissal or reduction of drunk driving charges against the travelers.[30]

* Fraud and corruption.

Crimes Against Government

Espionage

espionage Giving or selling national military or defense secrets to a foreign nation.

Spying and being a party to **espionage** are forbidden by all democratic countries. Giving or selling national military or defense secrets to a foreign nation is a serious felony. A shocking number of Americans have been charged with or convicted of spying. Most spies today sell secrets for money.

The Federal Espionage Act forbids disclosing, transmitting, stealing, or receiving information that has been classified. Experience has shown that most of the violators of this act either work for the U.S. government and have security clearances or are part of a foreign government's spy operation. Espionage cases receiving national attention include the following:

* *Aldrich Ames* was an alcoholic for years, yet he worked for the Central Intelligence Agency and received regular promotions within the organization. On a civil servant's pay, he bought an expensive home in Washington, D.C., for cash, and he drove a Jaguar. To obtain the money to live a luxurious life, Ames delivered vast amounts of highly secret documents and information to the Soviet Union, which paid Ames millions of dollars. Ames betrayed at least a dozen of the United States' best spies working within Russia. All were jailed, and most were executed. Ames and his wife were taken into custody in 1994 after nine years of espionage.
* *Robert P. Hanssen* was convicted in May 2001 of selling highly sensitive national secrets to Russia for 15 years. Hanssen was a high-ranking FBI counterintelligence agent. It is believed that Hanssen also corroborated information that Aldrich Ames provided to the Russians.
* *John A. Walker, Jr.,* headed a spy ring of family members and friends. Officials called it the most damaging espionage conspiracy in decades. Walker received life imprisonment and said the Soviet Union paid $1 million for his information on military communication codes.
* *Jonathan Jay Pollard* provided secret information to Israel that was available to him as a U.S. Navy intelligence analyst. He received a long prison sentence.[31]
* The highest-ranking military officer to be convicted of spying was German-born George Trofimoff, a retired Army Reserve colonel. He was convicted in September 2001 of selling military secrets to Russia for more than 20 years.
* *Ronald A. Pelton* was convicted of selling military secrets from the National Security Agency to Russia.

Former Alabama Governor Don Siegelman, convicted in 2007 on federal bribery and obstruction of justice charges, was sentenced to six-and-one-half years in prison in 2012. Siegelman was free for most of the seven years after his conviction while has case was on appeal. He began serving his sentence in September 2012.

- *Richard W. Miller,* a former FBI agent, became involved with a Russian woman and provided national secrets to Russia.
- In 2010 ten people who had lived in the United States for more than 10 years as ordinary citizens working ordinary jobs were arrested as "deep-cover" Russian spies. After revealing their true identities they all pled guilty to conspiracy to commit espionage. They were then returned to Russia in a "swap" for the release of four Russian citizens who had been jailed in Russia, accused of spying for England or the United States. Two of the four Russians released under this swap were high-ranking Russian military officers. See the *New York Times*, June 29, 2010 and July 9, 2010.

obstruction of justice
Intentional acts that hinder, corrupt, or impede the functioning of the judicial system.

Obstruction of Justice

The offense of **obstruction of justice** was a common-law misdemeanor and is now part of the criminal code of the federal government and states. The offense seeks to protect the judicial system, both civil and criminal, from intentional acts that would hinder, corrupt, or impede the functioning of the system. Attempting to influence a juror, destroying or suppressing evidence, and seeking to prevent a witness from testifying or from attending a trial are some of the acts that have justified charging the offense of obstruction of justice.

CRIMES UNCOVERED BY THE WATERGATE AND WHITEWATER INVESTIGATIONS

Watergate

This burglary led to a White House cover-up that resulted in a presidential resignation. After the botched break-in at the National Democratic Headquarters at the Watergate apartment building, the White House became involved in a cover-up that then led to

- The resignation of President Richard Nixon
- Eighteen months in prison for former Attorney General John Mitchell for perjury and cover-up conspiracy
- Seven months in prison for Jeb Magruder for perjury and conspiracy to obstruct justice
- Thirty-three months in prison for E. Howard Hunt for burglary, conspiracy, and wiretapping
- A prison term for James McCord, Jr., for burglary
- Eighteen months in prison for H. R. Haldeman for perjury, conspiracy, and obstruction of justice
- Prison terms also for John Ehrlichman (18 months), John Dean (4 months), and Chuck Colson (18 months)

Whitewater

This was a six-year investigation of the Arkansas business dealings of President Bill Clinton and Hillary Clinton. Neither President nor Mrs. Clinton was accused or found guilty of any wrongdoings, but fourteen other people were convicted:

- A former law partner of Mrs. Clinton, Webster Hubbell, pleaded guilty to felonies of tax evasion, mail fraud, and concealment by scheme.
- Former Arkansas Governor Jim Guy Tucker was found guilty by a jury of conspiracy and mail fraud. He pleaded guilty to conspiracy to defraud the IRS.
- Jim McDougal, Whitewater land development partner of the Clintons, was convicted by a jury of eighteen felonies in the collapse of his savings and loan, which cost taxpayers $73 million.
- Susan McDougal was convicted of four felonies by a jury, and then served 18 months for failure to answer grand jury questions about Whitewater.
- Former judge David Hale pleaded guilty to two felonies.
- Little Rock appraiser Robert Palmer pleaded guilty to conspiracy.
- Also convicted of felonies: William Marks (one) and Christopher Wade (two).
- Convicted of misdemeanors: Stephen Smith (one), Larry Kuca (one), attorney John Haley (one), banker Neal Ainley (two), Charles Matthews (two), and Eugene Fitzhugh (one).
- White House advisor Bruce Lindsey was named an unindicted co-conspirator in a case that ended in mistrial.

In the early days of the law, resisting, hindering, or obstructing a law enforcement officer was a common form of obstruction of justice. Many states, however, have made this offense a separate offense from obstruction of justice.[32] For example, Chapter 843 of the Florida Criminal Code is entitled "Obstructing Justice." Within Florida Chapter 843 are 18 separate offenses, two of which forbid "resisting an officer." Tampering with evidence (destroying, concealing, or altering) is found in Florida Chapter 918.

Police officers can also be guilty of obstructing justice. In the 2013 case of *United States v. Moore*[33] a rookie police officer was convicted of obstruction of justice when he filled out an incident report that backed up the false incident report filed by his training officer. The training officer had beaten a suspect, who subsequently died from his injuries. The training officer reported the incident as a "medical incident," and did not mention the use of force.

It is a crime under federal and state statutes to escape from lawful custody. This includes not only the classic "jailbreak" scenario, but also many other kinds of "custody." For example, in the 2010 case of *United States v. Gowdy*[34] a defendant convicted in federal court was transferred to a state prison to serve a pending state sentence. After doing so he was to be transferred back to serve the federal sentence. By mistake, the defendant was released after serving the state sentence. Federal marshals discovered the mistake, and contacted the man, who agreed to turn himself in to the U.S. Marshal's office. When he didn't show up, the marshals tracked him down, and he was charged with escape under federal law. The defendant argued he was not in custody, and thus could not illegally escape. The court disagreed, saying "custody" required only that there exist a lawful judgment of conviction and sentence ordering the defendant confined to a federal prison.

Tax Evasion

To operate and provide services, government needs money. Former U.S. Supreme Court Justice Oliver Wendell Holmes pointed out that taxes are the price we pay for civilization. Much of the money needed to fund government services and activities is obtained through taxes. Deliberate tax evasion and tax fraud are generally punished as crimes. Tax evasion cases that have received national attention include the following:

- In 1973, the vice president of the United States, Spiro T. Agnew, resigned after pleading no contest to tax evasion charges.
- Socially prominent hotel owner Leona Helmsley was convicted of failure to report and pay taxes on $1.8 million in 1990. She was sentenced to four years in prison and fined $7.1 million.
- Former baseball player and manager Pete Rose spent five months in prison in 1990 for tax charges related to gambling and other income earned but not reported. In 2003, it was reported that Rose still owed about $1 million, on which he is making monthly payments.
- In the 1920s, gangster Al Capone and his gang had an extraordinary grip on Chicago. Law enforcement officials were unable to convict Capone of any of the many felonies they believed he had committed, but they were able to convict him of income tax fraud and send him to prison. Capone was one of the first

people to be convicted with the use of the "net worth" method (circumstantial evidence). The U.S. Supreme Court affirmed the use of the net worth method in the case of *Holland v. United States*.[35]

- In a 2012 case, *Kawashima v. Holder*,[36] the U.S. Supreme Court held that a conviction for tax evasion qualified as an "aggravated felony" for purpose of immigration laws, and affirmed a decision ordering deportation of two Japanese citizens lawfully.

Other Criminal Violations

The President's Commission on Law Enforcement reported that the federal government alone has more than 2,800 crimes in the Federal Criminal Code. The President's Commission also pointed out that each state has the same number or more crimes in their state statutes. The following are a very few of the many crimes reported in daily newspapers:

- States often make the failure of an employer to withhold income taxes on employees' wages and salaries a crime. Under California law, employers who fail to withhold can be charged with a felony. (See the May 3, 2001, *New York Times* article, "California Raids a Business that Refuses to Withhold Taxes.")
- State election laws sometimes make it a felony to induce a person to vote if the inducement is worth one dollar or more. A New York woman came to Wisconsin and passed out packages of cigarettes to homeless men as an inducement to vote in the presidential election of 2000. She was fined $5,000. (See *Milwaukee Journal Sentinel*, "$5,000 Settles Election Case," May 4, 2001.)
- States often make failure to report for jury duty when summoned a crime. In Wisconsin, the misdemeanor is punished by a $40 fine, and ignorance of the law is not a defense. (*Milwaukee Journal Sentinel*, "County Prosecuting Jury Service No-Shows," October 31, 2000).
- Bootlegging whiskey has made millionaires of some families in the Appalachian hills of Virginia and West Virginia. Cigarette smuggling is a problem in the Detroit area. Both crimes cause federal and state government to lose tax revenue. The federal government claimed a loss of $2.9 million in unpaid federal taxes for one moonshiner alone. (See the September 9, 2001, *New York Times* article, "Alleged Bootleggers Face Sobering Case," and the May 20, 1997, *Detroit Free Press* article, "Cigarette Smugglers Busted.")
- Criminal nonpayment of child support is a crime in all states, and is frequently charged. The federal government also makes such nonpayment a crime, primarily as a way to assist states in their efforts to apprehend nonpaying defendants who flee a state to avoid prosecution.
- Criminal antitrust laws, such as the Sherman Antitrust Act (1890), the Clayton Act (1914), and the Robinson-Patman Act (1936). These laws prohibit individuals and corporations from taking actions to create monopolies or engaging in unreasonable restraints of trade, such as discriminatory pricing schemes, market allocation agreements, or agreements to restrict production, output, or competition. These laws have successfully protected consumers from many predatory practices of persons and businesses in the United States.

Summary

- The immigration laws make it a crime to make a false entry into this country, either by illegal crossing or by using false documents, to assist others to make an illegal entry into or stay in this country, to reenter after being removed, or to harbor or hire an illegal alien.
- Civil contempt is punishment used to coerce a defendant into obeying a lawful court order; criminal contempt is punishment for actions that constitute a "public wrong," just like ordinary criminal laws.
- All that is required for a gift to be an illegal gratuity is that the gift was given or received with the

specific intent to obtain some favorable treatment for the giver in the future, although the exact nature of the return need not be expressed.
- In *Arizona v. United States* the Supreme Court held that provisions of the Arizona law directed at alien registration and control interfered with federal laws on those subjects, and thus were preempted by the federal laws.
- Summary contempt is proper only where all the actions making up the contempt occurred in the presence of the judge.

Key Terms

contempt, p. 527
civil contempt, p. 527
criminal contempt, p. 527

perjury, p. 531
subornation of perjury, p. 531
tampering with evidence, p. 532

misprision of felony, p. 532
espionage, p. 533
obstruction of justice, p. 534

Case Analysis and Writing Exercises

1. What must a defendant do to constitute illegally "bringing" an alien into the United States? Is it enough to give the illegal alien fraudulent documents that are used to get through passport checks? What did the court in *United States v. Garcia-Paulin* say was required? (627 F.3d 127 (5th Cir. 2010))

2. Attorneys who fail to obey court orders can be charged with criminal contempt. Do you agree with the Kentucky Supreme Court's affirmation of a criminal contempt conviction of the attorney in the case of *Poindexter v. Commonwealth*, 389 S.W.3d 112 (Ky. 2012)? What did the attorney do that was "bad"? What would you have done differently?

3. States have their own "tampering with evidence" statutes, and they no doubt vary from state to state. Like all criminal laws, a tampering statute has an *actus reus* and a *mens rea*. Assume a person on probation is required to submit a urine sample on a regular basis as a condition of probation. On one occasion he is caught submitting a "fake"

sample obtained from another person. Is he guilty of tampering with evidence? The New Mexico Court of Appeals and Supreme Court disagreed on this question in *State v. Jackson*, 237 P.3d 754 (N.M. 2010). Did they disagree about the *actus reus* or the *mens rea* required under the New Mexico tampering statute?

4. People who make false statements to law enforcement officers conducting an investigation can be guilty of obstruction of justice. The same is true for giving false statements to Congress during that body's investigation of suspected criminal activity. Is a political candidate guilty of obstruction of justice if he filed required financial statements with a state election board, but knowingly failed to identify all campaign contributions made to his campaign? Do you agree with his contention that because he filed these reports before any investigation of his actions had begun, there could not have been an obstruction of justice? What did the court say to this argument? *See State v. Wright*, 696 S.E.2d 832 (N.C. App. 2010).

Endnotes

1. 2012 WL 6200276 (7th Cir. 2012).
2. 132 S. Ct. 2492 (2012).
3. *United States v. Alabama*, 691 F.3d 1269 (11th Cir. 2012), *cert. denied*, 2013 WL 210698 (2013).
4. 533 U.S. 678 (2001).
5. 366 F.3d 790 (9th Cir. 2004).
6. 125 S. Ct. 716 (2005).
7. 689 S.E.2d 716 (Va. 2010).
8. 17 A.3d 408 (Pa. Super. 2011), review denied, 34 A.3d 833 (Pa. 2011).
9. 131 S. Ct. 2507 (2011).
10. 391 U.S. 194, 88 S. Ct. 1477 (1968).
11. *Bloom v. Illinois,* 391 U.S. 194, 206 (1968). New Jersey courts have held that "before a judge makes a contempt determination the accused should be permitted to speak," 357 A.2d at 276 (1976). In the case of *In re Logan Jr.,* 52 N.J. 475, 246 A.2d 441 (1968), the court held: "The pronouncement of guilt before according that opportunity places the defendant at the disadvantage of trying to persuade a mind apparently already made up, and also puts the judge in the possibly embarrassing position of reversing himself if such persuasion results."
12. 509 U.S. 688 (1993).
13. 940 A.2d 1050 (D.C. Cir. 2008).
14. After remand, the U.S. Court of Appeals for the D.C. Circuit held that the contempt prosecution was brought by the government, but that the contempt prosecution did not violate the earlier plea agreement.
15. 466 Pa. 506, 353 A.2d 806 (1976).
16. 41 Ill. App. 3d 690, 354 N.E.2d 648 (1976).
17. 415 U.S. 697, 94 S. Ct. 1228 (1974). In a dissenting opinion, Justice William H. Rehnquist suggests "a flat rule, analogous to the hoary doctrine of the law of torts that every dog is entitled to one bite, to the effect that every witness is entitled to one free contumacious or other impermissible remark."
18. 895 S.W.2d 10 (Ky. App. 1995).
19. See *State v. Downing,* 93 P.3d 900 (Wash. App. 2004).
20. *Mapp v. Ohio,* 367 U.S. 643, 81 S. Ct. 1684 (1961).
21. 277 U.S. 438, 48 S. Ct. 564 (1928).
22. In 1968, the President's Commission on Crime noted that perjury has always been widespread and that there must be more effective deterrents against perjury to ensure the integrity of trials. Another writer commented that few crimes "except fornication are more prevalent or carried off with greater impunity." See "Perjury: The Forgotten Offense," *Journal of Criminal Law & Criminology* 65 (1974).
23. 409 U.S. 352 (1973).
24. 612 F.3d 1107 (9th Cir. 2010), *cert. denied,* 131 S. Ct. 1836 (2011).
25. See the *New York Times* article, "Sentencing the Man Who Failed to Warn of a Fatal Conspiracy," May 13, 1998.
26. Court in *U.S. v. Stuard,* 556 F.2d 1, 22 CrL 2337 (6th Cir. 1977), quoting *Neal v. U.S.,* 102 R2d 643 (8th Cir. 1939). See also *Pope v. State,* 284 Md. 309, 396 A.2d 1054 (1979).
27. *U.S. v. Sun-Diamond Growers of California,* 119 S. Ct. 1402 (1999). In other criminal cases concerning the biggest sting operation conducted by the FBI, more than sixty lawyers, bailiffs, judges, and other people in the Chicago court system were indicted for bribery. Operation Greylord was conducted because money was used to buy and fix criminal and civil Chicago court cases. Other criminal charges resulting from Operation Grey-lord included mail fraud, racketeering, and obstruction of justice.
28. 544 F.2d 730 (4th Cir.). The decision of the court continues as follows:

    This requirement of criminal intent would, of course, be satisfied if the jury were to find a "course of conduct of favors and gifts flowing" to a public official in exchange for a pattern of official actions favorable to the donor even though no particular gift or favor is directly connected to any particular official act. *U.S. v. Baggett* (4th Cir. 1973) 481 F.2d 114, *cert. denied,* 414 U.S. 1116 (1973) (Travel Act prosecution involving alleged bribery of Maryland County Commissioner). Moreover, as the Seventh Circuit has held, it is sufficient that the gift is made on the condition "that the offeree act favorably to the offer or when necessary." *U.S. v. Isaacs* (7th Cir. 1974) 493 F.2d 1124, 1145, *cert. denied,* 417 U.S. 976 (1974) (construing Illinois statute in a Travel Act prosecution). It does not follow, however, that the traditional business practice of promoting a favorable business climate by entertaining and doing favors for potential customers becomes bribery merely because the potential customer is the government. Such expenditures, although inspired by the hope of greater government business, are not intended as a quid pro quo for that business; they are in no way conditioned upon the performance of an official act or pattern of acts or upon the recipient's express or implied agreement to act favorably to the donor when necessary.
29. 732 F2d 878 (11th Cir. 1984). In the 1992 case of *Evans v. U.S.* (504 U.S. 255, 112 S. Ct. 1881), the U.S. Supreme Court held that a demand or other act of inducement by the public official was not necessary to convict of extortion under the Hobbs Act.
30. See *United States v. Stephens,* 964 F.2d 424 (5th Cir. 1992).
31. See *United States v. Pollard,* 959 F.2d 1011, *review denied,* U.S. Supreme Court, 52 CrL 3033 (1992).
32. An example of "resisting law enforcement" is *Jackson v. State,* 576 N.E.2d 607 (Ind. App. 1991), in which the defendant refused to provide identification under circumstances that obligated him to do so. An example of "interfering with an officer" is *State v. Peruta,* 591 A.2d 140 (Conn. App. 1991), in which a jury found that the defendant, a news cameraman, interfered with law enforcement officers at the scene of a fatal automobile accident.
33. 708 F.3d 639 (5th Cir. 2013).
34. 628 F.3d 1265 (11th Cir. 2010).
35. 348 U.S. 121 (1954).
36. 132 S. Ct. 1166 (2012).

Appendix

Sections of the U.S. Constitution Related to Criminal Law

(Ratified in 1788)

Preamble
We the People of the United States, in Order to form a more perfect union, establish Justice, insure domestic Tranquility, provide for the common defense, promote the general Welfare, and secure the Blessings of Liberty to ourselves and our Posterity, do ordain and establish this Constitution for the United States of America.

Article I
Section 1   All legislative Powers herein granted shall be vested in a Congress of the United States, which shall consist of a Senate and House of Representatives. . . .

Article II
Section 1   The executive Power shall be vested in a President of the United States of America. . . .

Article III
Section 1   The judicial Power of the United States, shall be vested in one supreme Court, and in such inferior Courts as the Congress may from time to time ordain and establish. . . .

Article IV
Section 4   The United States shall guarantee to every State in this Union a Republican Form of Government, and shall protect each of them against Invasion; and on Application of the Legislature, or of the Executive [when the Legislature cannot be convened] against domestic Violence. . . .

Article VI
This constitution, and the Laws of the United States which shall be made in Pursuance thereof; and all Treaties made, or which shall be made, under the Authority of the United States, shall be the supreme Law of the Land; and the Judges in every State shall be bound thereby, any Thing in the Constitution or Laws of any State to the Contrary notwithstanding. . . .

American Bill of Rights (Ratified in 1791)

Amendment 1
Congress shall make no law respecting an establishment of religion, or prohibiting the free exercise thereof; or abridging the freedom of speech, or of the press; or the right of the people peaceably to assemble, and to petition the Government for a redress of grievances.

Amendment II
A well regulated Militia, being necessary to the security of a free State, the right of the people to keep and bear Arms, shall not be infringed.

Amendment III

No Soldier shall, in time of peace be quartered in any house, without the consent of the Owner, nor in time of war, but in a manner to be prescribed by law.

Amendment IV

The right of the people to be secure in their persons, houses, papers, and effects, against unreasonable searches and seizures, shall not be violated, and no Warrants shall issue, but upon probable cause, supported by Oath affirmation, and particularly describing the place to be searched, and the persons or things to be seized.

Amendment V

No person shall be held to answer for a capital, or otherwise infamous crime, unless on a presentment or indictment of a Grand Jury, except in cases arising in the land or naval forces, or in the Militia, when in actual service in time of War or public danger, nor shall any person be subject for the same offence to be twice put in jeopardy of life or limb; nor shall be compelled in any criminal case to be a witness against himself, nor be deprived of life, liberty, or property, without due process of law; nor shall private property be taken for public use, without just compensation.

Amendment VI

In all criminal prosecutions, the accused shall enjoy the right to a speedy and public trial, by an impartial jury of the State and district wherein the crime shall have been committed, which district shall have been previously ascertained by law, and to be informed of the nature and cause of the accusation; to be confronted with the witnesses against him; to have compulsory process for obtaining witnesses in his favor, and to have the Assistance of Counsel for his defence.

Amendment VII

In suits at common law, where the value in controversy shall exceed twenty dollars, the right of trial by jury shall be preserved, and no fact tried by a jury, shall be otherwise reexamined in any Court of the United States, than according to the rules of the common law.

Amendment VIII

Excessive bail shall not be required, nor excessive fines imposed, nor cruel and unusual punishments inflicted.

Amendment IX

The enumeration in the Constitution, of certain rights, shall not be construed to deny or disparage others retained by the people.

Amendment X

The powers not delegated to the United States by the Constitution, nor prohibited by it to the States, are reserved to the States respectively, or to the people....

14th Amendment, Ratified 1868

Amendment XIV

Section 1   All persons born or naturalized in the United States, and subject to the jurisdiction thereof, are citizens of the United States and of the State wherein they reside. No State shall make or enforce any law which shall abridge the privileges or immunities of citizens of the United States; nor shall any State deprive any person of life, liberty, or property, without due process of law; nor deny to any person within its jurisdiction the equal protection of the laws....

Glossary

accomplice   One who aids another in the commission of a crime. An accomplice is generally treated the same as a principal.

actus reus   The criminal act.

administrative crime   Crime created by government administrative agencies under specific authority and guidelines granted to the regulatory or administrative agency by law of that state or the federal government.

affirmative defense   A defense to a criminal charge in which the defendant generally admits doing the criminal act but claims an affirmative defense such as duress (he or she was forced) or entrapment.

aggravated assault   Assault made more serious by presence of a firearm or as part of intent to commit a felony

aggravated battery   Battery that causes serious bodily injury or is committed with a deadly weapon.

aggravating circumstances   A consideration in imposing the death penalty that judges and juries must make a finding of statutory aggravating circumstances to justify the penalty.

aider and abettor   One who provides help to the person who commits a crime, either before or after the crime is committed.

alibi   A defense to criminal prosecution on the grounds that the defendant physically could not have committed the crime because at the time the crime was committed, he or she was at another place.

armed or aggravated robbery   Forcible stealing combined with the use of a deadly or dangerous weapon, or which results in serious bodily injury to another.

arson   A person's deliberate, willful, and malicious burning of a building or personal property.

assault   In many instances, an assault is an attempt to commit a battery, but many states also make other conduct an assault. Could be combined with a charge of battery to constitute the crime of "assault and battery."

assisting suicide   The act of furnishing the means of a suicide, pursuant to a statute that permits such assistance.

attempt crimes   Acts that are a substantial step toward the commission of a crime that is not yet completed.

bank fraud   Fraud aimed at banks and other financial institutions.

battered woman defense   Evidence of past abuse offered by women charged with violence against their abusers to show its psychological effects as part of their claim of self-defense.

battery   A successful assault, in which the victim is actually and intentionally (or knowingly) struck by the defendant.

benefit of clergy   A medieval limit on capital punishment. People convicted of a capital crime entitled to claim the benefit of clergy (by the fifteenth century, anyone who could read) could not be executed for their offense. By the end of the eighteenth century, the privilege had been eliminated for most crimes.

bill of attainder   Legislative act that inflicts punishment without trial; prohibited by Article I, Sections 9 and 10, of the Constitution.

"booze it and lose it" laws   In more than thirty states, laws that give the police the authority to immediately seize the driver's license of people who fail or refuse sobriety tests.

"born alive" requirement   To be able to charge homicide of a newborn baby, the prosecution must be able to prove that the child was living at the time it was killed.

bribery   Offering a gift or payment to another with the specific intent to obtain some unlawful particular quid pro quo for the gift or payment.

burglary   Unlawful entry into the premises of another with intent to steal or commit a felony. Two hundred years ago in England, an illegal entry into the home of another by force and at night was punishable by death if the entry was done to steal or commit a felony.

capital punishment   Inflicting deadly injury as punishment for criminal conduct.

carjacking   Forcibly taking possession of a motor vehicle in the possession of another against his or her will with intent either to permanently or temporarily deprive the person of possession.

"castle" doctrine   The doctrine permitting people who have been assaulted in their homes by a trespasser to stand their ground and use such force as is necessary and reasonable to defend themselves.

certiorari   A form of review of lower court decisions by the Supreme Court. Certiorari is discretionary with the Court, and most petitions requesting it are denied. Traditional legal doctrine is that no conclusion can be drawn from a denial of certiorari.

check kiting   Creating multiple checking accounts at multiple banks for the purpose of writing fraudulent checks from one account and depositing them in another, and then withdrawing funds from the deposit bank.

child pornography   Movies, pictures, or drawings that depict children in explicit sexual relations. Unlike adult pornography, child pornography need not be obscene to be criminal.

civil contempt   This is a remedial form of contempt order used to force people to do what they are lawfully required to do (answer questions, identify themselves, pay support money as ordered by a divorce court, and so on).

"clear and present danger" test   One of the tests used to judge government restrictions on speech.

coercion   A person who forces (coerces) another to commit a crime can be charged and convicted of the crime committed in addition to other offenses.

common design or plan   Scope of liability of persons who are party to a conspiracy or other agreement to do an unlawful act.

common law   The earliest type of law. Common law was created by judges based on custom, usages, and moral concepts of the people. Most law today is statutory law enacted by legislative bodies.

common law crime   Crime created by judges.

competency to stand trial   Defendants must have the ability to cooperate with their attorneys and the ability to understand the charges and proceedings against them.

computer trespass   Unlawful access to a computer or computer system with intent to commit a crime, or unlawful access to a computer or computer system maintained by a government unit.

concurrence   The requirement in crimes requiring proof of mental intent that the forbidden act and guilty mind must occur at the same time or otherwise be linked. For example, trustees, guardians, and lawyers might have possession of another person's money (physical act). For the crime of embezzlement to occur they must intentionally and wrongfully misappropriate this money (forbidden act and guilty mind).

conspiracy crimes   An agreement between two or more persons to engage in unlawful acts.

conspirator   A person who is a party to an agreement to commit an unlawful act.

contempt   Failure or refusal to obey a court order (civil contempt), or interfering with the functioning of a court or legislative body (criminal contempt). Criminal contempt that occurs in the presence of the court can be punished summarily; other criminal contempts require the normal prosecution procedures.

Continuing Criminal Enterprise Statute (CCE) Federal law making prosecution possible for those whose actions enable a criminal enterprise to function, whether or not those same people can be proved to have performed specific criminal acts.

controlled substance A drug that may be possessed or sold only as permitted by state or federal law.

corporal punishment Inflicting nondeadly physical injury as punishment for criminal conduct.

corpus delicti In all criminal cases, the government must prove that the crime charged was committed (corpus delicti) and that the defendant was party to the crime (committed the crime or was an accomplice).

corroborative evidence Physical evidence or witness testimony, other than from the victim which supports the claim that a crime occurred.

crime of terrorizing A crime that creates a state of extreme fear, dread, or fright.

criminal contempt A criminal charge based on a person's actions in a court case or legislative proceeding and used to punish people by a fine or imprisonment for what they have done.

criminal liability of corporations The rules for making corporations liable for actions taken by officers, directors, or employees. Corporations can be vicariously criminally liable for actions of their agents if the offense is minor, a duty is specifically assigned to a corporation, a statute explicitly creates vicarious criminal liability, or the person committing the crime is acting in the interest of the corporation and is a high managerial agent.

criminology The sociological and psychological study of the causes, development, and control of crime, as well as the conditions under which criminal law developed.

cruel and unusual punishment Under the Eighth Amendment, a limitation on punishment for criminal conduct.

CTRs (currency transaction reports) Reports that businesses, banks, and financial institutions are required to file for cash transactions of more than $10,000. CTRs can help determine whether tax fraud or money laundering is occurring.

cybercrime Criminal acts implemented through use of a computer or other form of electronic communication.

deadly force Force that is likely to cause or is capable of causing death or serious bodily injury.

defamation The offense of injuring the character or reputation of another by oral or written communication of false statements. Defamation consists of libel (written offense) or slander (oral offense).

defamation Wrongful injury to another's reputation.

defense of another The elements to evaluate whether an act of force for defense of another is justified include the unlawfulness of the action toward the other, the necessity to defend the other immediately, and the reasonableness of the act of defense under the circumstances.

defiant trespass Crime charged when a person remains in a place where he or she is not privileged to remain even after notice of trespass is given.

diminished capacity defense A defense for criminal responsibility based on the fact that because of mental or emotional conditions, the defendant did not possess the required *mens rea* for conviction of the crime charged.

disorderly conduct Loud, obnoxious, or other offensive conduct in a public place.

double jeopardy A defense, stated in the Fifth Amendment, to prosecution on the grounds that the defendant has been tried before on the same charge, and acquitted.

drug paraphernalia Objects that are primarily intended or designed for use with illegal drugs.

"dual sovereignty" doctrine A doctrine that different governments may each file separate criminal actions for the same criminal act.

due process The constitutional guarantee that criminal arrests and trials must meet certain minimum standards of fairness (procedural due process) and that laws not violate constitutional rights (substantive due process).

duress A defense to criminal prosecution on the grounds that the defendant was forced to commit the criminal act.

embezzlement Wrongfully appropriating money or property entrusted to one for one's own use.

entrapment The defense that a law enforcement officer used excessive temptation or urging to wrongfully induce the defendants to commit a crime they would not have ordinarily committed.

espionage Giving or selling national military or defense secrets to a foreign nation.

euthanasia A killing of a terminally sick or injured individual with only a short time to live. Also called mercy killing.

ex post facto Criminal law made retroactive to punish prior conduct not criminal when done. Prohibited by Article I, Sections 9 and 10, of the Constitution.

extortion Obtaining property by threats of future harm. Differs from robbery in that robbery requires threat of immediate harm.

extradition The surrender of an accused criminal under the provisions of a treaty or statute by one authority to another having jurisdiction.

false imprisonment Unlawful restraint or detention of a person.

federal enclaves Federally owned and controlled lands.

felony The most serious grade of crime; usually includes possibility of prison sentence.

felony murder All states and the federal government have felony murder statutes that punish as murder the causing of death of another while the defendant is committing a felony of violence. A felony murder conviction does not require a showing of malice or deliberate intent to kill.

fence A person who traffics in stolen property (receiving, concealing, possessing, buying, transferring, and so on).

feticide Murder of an unborn child.

field sobriety tests Field tests used to evaluate a motorist's alcohol or drug impairment. They include HGN testing, the walk-and-turn test, and the one-leg stand test.

fighting words Speech which, because it will likely incite immediate violence, is not protected by the First Amendment.

forfeiture Going back to early English law, the concept and use of seizing the property that was used to commit a crime.

forgery Wrongfully signing a writing or instrument in the name of the person who issued the writing or instrument, or to whom it was payable.

fraud Deceitful means or acts used to cheat a person, corporation, or governmental agency.

fraud Use of deceit or trickery to obtain profit or advantage.

Good Samaritan laws Laws that encourage people to come to the aid of another or to defend another against unlawful force or interference.

guilty but mentally ill A defendant may be found guilty but mentally ill if all the following are found beyond a reasonable doubt: (1) defendant is guilty of the offense; (2) defendant was mentally ill at the time the offense was committed; (3) defendant was not legally insane at the time the offense was committed.

habeas corpus A writ that compels the authority holding a person in confinement to explain the basis for that confinement. Used frequently as a method for state and federal prisoners to attack the constitutionality of their imprisonment. Both the federal government and states have some form of habeas corpus laws, often called *post-conviction relief* laws.

home invasion robbery Robbery of persons inhabiting a dwelling.

homicide The killing of one human being by another. There are three types of homicide: justifiable, excusable, and felonious.

honest services fraud   Unlawful actions that cause another person to lose the honest services of a person obligated to perform such honest services.

hostage taking   The use or threat of use of force to restrain or confine a person with the intent to use the person as a hostage to compel another person to perform some act.

identity theft   Theft based on stealing a real person's identification information (true name) or theft based on creating a fictitious person's identification (synthetic identity).

immunity   An exemption from criminal prosecution based on the U.S. Constitution, statutes, or international agreements.

imperfect self-defense   A homicide in which the killer subjectively, but unreasonably, believes that his or her conduct was necessary. It may be unlawful if the killing was done with excessive or unnecessary force. An unnecessary killing in self-defense, in defense of another, or to prevent or terminate a felony of violence could be imperfect self-defense.

***in loco parentis* (Latin; "in place of the parents")**   Any person taking the place of the parents has the duties and responsibilities of the parents and may reasonably discipline a child in his or her care. This category includes legal guardians, foster parents, and public school teachers.

incest   Sexual relations between persons closely related.

inciting   The offense of urging another to commit an unlawful act.

infant (child)   Under the civil law, a person who has not yet reached the age of majority, whether that age is 18, 19, 20, or 21, as determined by the law of each jurisdiction.

inference   A conclusion or deduction that a jury or judge *may* draw from a fact or a group of facts presented.

insanity tests   Tests to determine legal and moral liability.

intellectual property fraud   Theft, piracy, or counterfeiting of ideas, inventions, artistic works, and the like.

intent   The mental purpose or design to commit a specific act (or omission).

jurisdiction   Subject-matter jurisdiction is the authority to regulate conduct. Personal jurisdiction is the authority to prosecute and punish an offender.

kidnapping   False imprisonment coupled with movement of the victim.

Magna Carta   The document signed by King John in 1215 giving certain rights to his nobles. Successive English kings affirmed this charter before Parliament.

mail fraud   A fraudulent scheme, no matter its purpose or method, that uses either private or public delivery service.

"make my day" rules   Rules adopted by some states that put no limits on the use of deadly force by the occupant of a dwelling in response to a trespasser.

manslaughter   Criminal homicides other than murder. Most states provide for two degrees of manslaughter, voluntary and involuntary.

maritime jurisdiction   Jurisdiction of the United States over actions within territorial waters of the United States on U.S. ships, or stateless vessels on the high seas.

martial law   A state of military control over civilian populations as declared by state or federal government.

mayhem and malicious disfigurement   Willfully inflicting an injury on another so as to cripple or mutilate the person.

Megan's laws   Laws passed in many states requiring convicted sex offenders to register with a state or local registration office. Named after a young girl killed by a convicted sex offender.

menacing   Intentionally placing or attempting to place another in fear of immediate serious physical injury.

mens rea   The criminal intent or state of mind.

misdemeanor   Offenses that carry punishment of a degree less than felonies. Usually misdemeanor crimes do not involve prison sentences.

misprision of felony   Failing to report knowledge of a felony to the appropriate authorities.

mistake of law   A claim by a defendant that the defendant did not know the action taken violated the criminal law.

mitigating circumstances   A consideration in imposing the death penalty that judges and juries must make findings of the mitigating circumstances that would weigh against the imposition of the death penalty.

M'Naghten rule   The insanity defense rule requiring proof that because of mental disease or defect defendants did not know the scope or character of their actions.

Model Penal Code (MPC)   Proposed criminal law developed by the American Law Institute, a group of lawyers, judges, and teachers. Many states have modeled their criminal codes on the Model Penal Code.

money laundering   The crime of disguising money obtained illegally by channeling it through legitimate commercial and financial transactions.

motive   The cause, inducement, or reason why an act is committed.

murder   Unlawful homicide with malice aforethought.

necessity   A defense to criminal prosecution on the grounds that the harm to be avoided outweighed the harm caused by the crime committed. Necessity will not justify taking another person's life.

nulla poena sine lege   The principle of legality; no act should be made criminal or punished without advance warning in the form of legislative act.

nystagmus   A persistent, rapid, involuntary, side-to-side eye movement.

obscenity   Communication that the average person, using contemporary community standards, would find appeals to the prurient interests or depicts sexual conduct in a patently offensive manner and, taken as a whole, lacks serious artistic, literary, political, or scientific value.

obstruction of justice   Intentional acts that hinder, corrupt, or impede the functioning of the judicial system.

offensive touching   Unpermitted physical contact with another person, usually limited to "private" or genital parts.

"overbreadth" doctrine   The constitutional law doctrine that invalidates laws that regulate conduct so broadly as to interfere with individual freedoms.

parties to the principal crime   Under common law, persons who either committed the crime, or aided or abetted the commission of the crime or the persons who committed the crime.

perfect self-defense   A homicide in which the killer not only subjectively believes that his or her conduct was necessary and reasonable, but that, by objective standards, a reasonable person would believe it was lawful and complied with the requirements of the law. The homicide is either justifiable or excusable, and it carries no criminal liability.

perjury   The crime of knowingly and materially testifying falsely while under oath.

Pinkerton **rule**   The rule followed in federal courts that one conspirator is liable for crimes committed by another conspirator, if foreseeable and done in furtherance of the conspiracy.

police power   The inherent power of every state and local government, subject to constitutional limits, to enact criminal laws.

pornography   Movies, pictures, writings, and other expressions that are intended to arouse sexual incitement and have no artistic merit or redeeming social value.

possession with intent to deliver   A criminal case in which the state presents evidence showing that the accused had possession of a large amount of an illegal drug, meaning more than the accused would personally use.

posse comitatus Latin, meaning "power of the country." In the United States it generally refers to the military forces.

post-crime offenses Actions taken after a crime has been committed with knowledge that it had been committed that provide aid to the person who committed the crime.

preliminary, anticipatory, or inchoate crimes Criminal acts that lead to or are attempts to commit other crimes.

premeditation Mental determination to unlawfully kill another person after planning or reflection on actions causing death.

preponderance of the evidence The greater weight of the evidence, though not necessarily the amount needed to remove every reasonable doubt. It is proof sufficient to incline a reasonable person toward one side of an issue rather than the other.

presumption A rule of law that the trier of fact shall assume the existence of a state of facts without evidence being produced. Presumptions are rebuttable or irrebuttable.

probable cause Reasonable grounds to believe.

procedural due process A claim under the Fourteenth Amendment that there is an absence of fair procedures regulating state conduct.

procuring, promoting, and pimping Actions taken to provide services of a prostitute.

proportionality An objective evaluation of the appropriateness of a punishment for a particular crime.

prostitution Providing sex for money or other value.

proximate cause The ordinary and probable cause of a result.

public law Criminal law in England and the United States.

quid pro quo Giving something of value ("quid") for something else.

rape Anal, vaginal, or oral penetration by force or threat of force.

rape shield laws Laws passed by many states to limit the extent to which defense attorneys in a rape case can inquire into the victim's past sexual life.

reasonable doubt Proof beyond a reasonable doubt means that it is not enough to prove it was more likely than not that an element of the crime was true. The proof must be such that a reasonable person could not conclude the element was not true.

recidivist One who is a habitual criminal.

res judicata Doctrine that states once an issue has been judicially determined in a case involving the same parties, it cannot be relitigated by those parties.

RICO The Racketeer Influenced and Corrupt Organizations Act. Passed by Congress to enable prosecutors to charge all people engaged in unlawful activity who own or invest in an enterprise that affects interstate commerce.

"right and wrong" test An insanity test that claims that defendants are not legally responsible for their acts if, due to a defect of the mind, at the time of the crime they were unable to understand the difference between right and wrong.

riot Under the common law, a tumultuous disturbance of the peace by three or more people assembled with a common purpose to do an unlawful act.

robbery Forcible stealing.

sabotage The crime of damaging or injuring national defense material or utilities with the intention of interfering with national defense.

sanctuary In the Middle Ages in England, a sanctuary was a religious place where criminals could take refuge. The concept of sanctuary later broadened to include asylum for refugees.

scienter A form of specific intent requiring a showing that the actor knew of the existence of certain facts. For example, one cannot be guilty of possession of stolen property if one does not know property is stolen.

sedition   The crime of advocating the forceful overthrow of the established government. In this country, the Smith Act makes such advocacy a crime.

self-defense   The elements to evaluate whether an act of force for self-defense is justified include the unlawfulness of the other's action, the necessity to defend oneself immediately, and the reasonableness of the act of self-defense under the circumstances.

sexual assault   The crime in most states that includes the crime of rape, as well as other lesser degrees of assault.

shoplifting   Stealing goods from retail stores by concealment, generally on the person of the defendant. Commission does not require removal of the goods from the store.

solicitation or incitement crimes   Attempting to get another to commit a crime.

specific intent   The intent necessary for one or more elements of an offense. Murder, for example, requires the specific intent that the act be done intentionally or purposely.

stalking   A crime involving activities such as spying on the victim, following the victim, or attempting to communicate with the victim through the telephone or mail. Cyberstalking through the Internet is also a crime.

"stand your ground" laws   Recent laws passed in many states that permit using deadly force in response to an unlawful attack rather than the traditional "duty to retreat" policy.

status crime   Criminal laws that punish a status, such as drug addiction, with no act requirement.

statute of limitations   A defense to a criminal prosecution based on a statute that sets the maximum time the government has to prosecute a violation of a criminal law.

statutory rape   Sexual intercourse with a minor under a certain age, usually 16–18. Consent and, generally, mistake as to age are not defenses to this crime.

strict liability crime   Crime that does not require proof of the mental element essential to true crimes.

subornation of perjury   The crime of inducing or knowingly permitting another person to testify falsely while under oath.

"substantial capacity" test   A test to determine criminal responsibility based on whether the defendant could (1) distinguish between right and wrong or (2) conform his or her conduct to the requirements of law.

substantive due process   A claim under the Fourteenth Amendment that state conduct is so brutal, demeaning, and harmful as to shock the conscience.

sudden snatching   A form of robbery where force is not used beyond that needed to take property from another person.

symbolic speech   Nonverbal expressions that convey a belief or idea.

taking   The act of obtaining physical possession or control of another's property. The key to taking is that the thief exercises unauthorized dominion over the property.

tampering with evidence   Knowingly altering or damaging evidence intended to be used in a court proceeding.

terrorism   The use of force and violence in the pursuit of extreme political, ideological, or religious goals, without regard to the innocent lives that may be lost.

theft or larceny   Stealing property of another with the intent to deprive the owner of possession.

threats of violence   Statements or actions that unequivocally convey the message that violent actions will be taken.

"three strikes" laws   Laws that impose increased penalties for multiple felony convictions.

tort   A noncontractual civil wrong.

transactional immunity   Total or full immunity for the criminal offense to which compelled testimony relates.

transferred intent   A doctrine used when the intention to harm one individual inadvertently causes a second person to be hurt instead. The individual causing the harm will be seen as having "intended" the act by means of the "transferred intent" doctrine.

Travel Act   Legislation that can be used to prosecute those involved in criminal activities that cross state borders or involve foreign commerce.

treason   Acting to overthrow one's government, or in violation of allegiance to one's country.

trespass   A wrongful intrusion on the land or into the premises of another person.

trial by ordeal   A test used to determine criminal responsibility in ancient England involving subjecting the individual to a torturous ordeal. These ordeals were essentially appeals to God; surviving the ordeal was viewed as God's judgment of innocence.

true threat   A serious expression of an intent to inflict bodily harm.

Uniform Controlled Substances Act   A model act identifying illegal drug crimes, drafted by a national conference of uniform law commissioners and adopted by the states and the federal government.

United Nations Conventions   An agreement between nations on a specific subject, such as piracy at sea.

unlawful assembly   Under the common law, a gathering of three or more people for any unlawful purpose or under such circumstances as to endanger the public peace or cause alarm and apprehension.

unreasonable seizure   A seizure made by a government officer that is unreasonable under the circumstances and thus violates the Fourth Amendment.

usable amount   In contrast to a useless trace amount, a quantity of an illegal drug sufficient to be used.

use immunity   Prohibits prosecutorial authorities from using the compelled testimony in a criminal prosecution, but does not make the witness totally immune from prosecution based on evidence other than the witness's testimony and not derived from that testimony.

uttering   Putting into circulation a check known to be worthless.

"void for vagueness" doctrine   The constitutional law doctrine that invalidates criminal laws written in such a manner as to make it unreasonably difficult for a defendant to know whether or not conduct is prohibited by the law.

Wharton rule   The requirement that crimes needing more than one person for commission, such as bigamy, require three or more people for a conspiracy conviction.

"what one did, they all did"   The rule that all parties to a conspiracy or other agreement to perform an unlawful act are liable for every action taken by any party in furtherance of the conspiracy or agreement.

white-collar crime   A class or type of criminal conduct whose only goal is the criminal's economic gain.

wire fraud   A fraudulent scheme that uses interstate or international wire or other electronic communications.

witness protection program   Established as part of the Organized Crime Control Act of 1970, this program provides new identities and relocation for witnesses and their families in both state and federal criminal prosecutions of organized crime.

witness tampering   Criminal interference with someone who plans to testify in either a criminal or a civil trial.

Case Index

Subject Index